INSURANCE LAW

TEXT AND MATERIALS

Second Edition

Cavendish
Publishing
Limited

London • Sydney • Portland, Oregon

INSURANCE LAW

TEXT AND MATERIALS

Second Edition

Ray Hodgin, LLB, LLM
School of Law
University of Birmingham

Cavendish
Publishing
Limited

London • Sydney • Portland, Oregon

Second edition first published in Great Britain 2002 by
Cavendish Publishing Limited, The Glass House,
Wharton Street, London WC1X 9PX, United Kingdom
Telephone: + 44 (0)20 7278 8000 Facsimile: + 44 (0)20 7278 8080
Email: info@cavendishpublishing.com
Website: www.cavendishpublishing.com

Published in the United States by Cavendish Publishing
c/o International Specialized Book Services,
5804 NE Hassalo Street, Portland,
Oregon 97213-3644, USA

Published in Australia by Cavendish Publishing (Australia) Pty Ltd
3/303 Barrenjoey Road, Newport, NSW 2106, Australia

First edition 1998
Second edition 2002

British Library Cataloguing in Publication Data
Hodgin, RW
Insurance law: text & materials – 2nd ed
1 Insurance law – Great Britain
I Title

Library of Congress Cataloguing in Publication Data
Data available

ISBN 1-85941-724-8

1 3 5 7 9 10 8 6 4 2

Printed and bound in Great Britain

PREFACE TO THE SECOND EDITION

The aims of this new edition remain the same as the first edition (see Preface to the First Edition, below).

In this edition, new cases, Codes of Conduct, alterations to legislation, both in the UK and Australia, new directives and extracts from recent articles, have been added to the Appendices while the text has been amended to reflect these changes.

Chapter 1. The effect of the Financial Services and Markets Act 2000 (FSMA) impacts on several chapters. In Chapter 1 the Financial Compensation Scheme has taken over the role of the Policyholders Protection Board and the text and Appendices reflect this. Certain additions to reflect the continued importance of European Directives are made. Facts and figures have been updated.

Chapter 2. *Lambert* (1999) and *Deepack* (1999) have been added to the text and changes to the Australian Insurance Contracts Act 1984 have been made in the Appendices.

Chapter 3. Changes at Lloyd's are noted in the text and also the jurisdiction of the FSMA over unauthorised insurers.

Chapter 4. The House of Lords' interpretation of s 17 of the Marine Insurance Act in *The Star Sea* (2001) is discussed in the text and extracted in the Appendices. Also referred to in the text are *Merc-Skandia* (2001); *Sirius International* (1999); *HIH Casualty* (2001). Several new articles are referred to in the text and extracts from two articles are added to the Appendices.

Chapter 5. The following cases are worked into the text: *Printpak* (1999); *Kler* (2000); *Virk* (2000); *Alfred McAlpine* (2000); *Jacobs* (2000); *Kazakstan* (2000); and *HIH v Axa Corporate* (2001) which has also been added to the Appendices.

Chapter 6. Reference is made to the newly created General Insurance Standards Council and its two Codes which are added to the Appendices. The following cases have been added to the text: *O and R Jewellers* (1999); *Bollom* (1999) and added to the Appendices together with the House of Lords decision in *Aneco* (2002). Changes in Lloyd's supervisory regime are noted. The recent draft Directive on Insurance Mediation (intermediaries) is outlined in the text. Changes to the Australian Insurance (Agents and Brokers) Act 1984 are included.

Chapter 7. Lord Hoffmann's views in *ICI v West Bromwich BS* (1998) are added to the text together with the decisions in *Kumar* (1998); *Sargent* (2000); and *Rohan* (1999) which is also extracted in the Appendices. The 1999 Unfair Terms in Consumer Contracts Regulations replace the 1994 version in the Appendices.

Chapter 8. The Association of British Insurers' (ABI) Claims Code is added to the Appendices. The House of Lords judgment in *The Star Sea* (2001) is referred to in the text and extracted in the Appendices together with *Merc-Skandia* (2001); *Sprung* (1999); and *Pride Valley* (1999). Changes to the Australian Insurance Contracts Act are noted.

Chapter 9. *Co-operative Retail Services* (2001) is discussed in the text.

Chapter 10. The Final Report of the Law Commission (No 272) 2001 is interwoven at various points in the chapter.

Chapter 11. The text has been largely rewritten to reflect the new basis on which the former Insurance Ombudsman now operates as part of the Financial Ombudsman Service. Parts of its Rulebook are added to the Appendices. A comparison with other EU Members and their approach to insurance dispute resolution is added to the text. New examples of the Ombudsman decisions have been added to the Appendices.

Ray Hodgin
University of Birmingham
July 2002

PREFACE TO THE FIRST EDITION

Insurance underpins many branches of law. The most obvious example is the law of torts and, in particular, the tort of negligence. Hopefully, tort teachers start with a brief explanation of the role of insurance in modern tort law.

Although insurance law, as an optional subject, does appear on the curricula of some institutions, such courses are, sadly, all too few. One problem may be that the sources of insurance law are not always sufficiently accessible in law libraries to support such courses. The historical foundation cases of the subject are to be found in the *English Reports*; modern cases are found largely in *Lloyd's Law Reports, Insurance and Reinsurance*, while many aspects of modern consumer insurance law are to be found in self-regulatory Codes. Students taking the professional examinations of the Chartered Insurance Institute who may also suffer limited access to law libraries will find this book useful.

It is hoped that this book will make available to students of insurance law a range of essential materials. In various chapters, there is also an emphasis on law reform, much mooted by some critics in this country, but with little visible success. Thus, there are numerous references to English suggestions for reform and many extracts taken from Australian statutory reform literature. Australian insurance law was based exclusively on the English common law and it is, therefore, instructive to see how those English rules have fared under the legislature's reforming zeal.

The format of this book is different from most 'materials' books. I have prefaced each chapter with a textual introduction, explaining the topic under discussion. The materials referred to in the text then appear as appendices to each chapter. The hope is that the reader can gain an overview of the topic in question and then build on that by reference to the materials. It should also provide a useful tool for final revision.

Needless to say (but I will!), a materials book is but a halfway house to achieving your aims – students should look to read the materials referred to in their entirety wherever possible. There are several excellent texts on insurance law and these should obviously be used in conjunction with this book.

Chapter 1 is a general introduction to the subject. It contains extracts from two excellent essays on aspects of the historical background to insurance law and its development. It looks also at the meaning of insurance, the different types of insurance, the size of the United Kingdom and world markets. It also summarises the important contribution that Brussels has made to the development of the subject.

Chapter 2, on insurable interests, illustrates how English law has narrowly defined what can and cannot be insured. The appendices here contain extracts from articles which criticise this narrow approach and, in particular, include the very important American article by Harnett and Thornton. The Australian reforms appear here, as well.

Chapter 3 is concerned with the formation of the insurance contract – premiums, cover notes, terms. This chapter covers the problem area of illegality in insurance law.

Chapter 4 is a long chapter, reflecting the vast importance of the duty of good faith in insurance law. It traces the cases from 1766 to the 1990s, when the House of Lords had their most recent say on the matter. There are numerous references to law reform suggested in England, but not implemented, and reform carried out in Australia.

Conditions and warranties in insurance law, and the difficulties posed by the terminology are reviewed in Chapter 5. The effect of the breach of such terms has had dire results for the insured and criticisms of the rules are included.

In Chapter 6, the important role played by insurance intermediaries in insurance law is discussed. At the time of completing this book, the Government announced its intention to repeal the Insurance Brokers (Registration) Act 1977, which had been used as a model for other countries to follow. All is in a state of uncertainty at the moment – a very unimpressive way to set about reform, if it *is* reform at all! The basic rules relating to the liability of intermediaries are, however, based on the common law, and these rules obviously still remain in place, despite the Government upturning certain aspects of the administrative details of supervision and accountability.

In Chapter 7, the problems of policy construction are considered: just what do certain policies mean? The chapter could easily have been the longest in the book by simply taking case after case and illustrating the difficulties. An attempt has been made, however, to follow certain rules used in aiding construction. There are no references to reform, other than the Unfair Terms in Consumer Contracts Regulations 1994, which have only limited applicability to insurance contracts. The reason for this is that only the insurer can put his own house in order by concentrating on the language used and seeking constantly to improve it.

Chapter 8 covers the claims process in the event of a loss. This involves deciding whether the loss has been caused by an insured peril; whether the claim is fraudulent and, if it is a legitimate loss, how the loss should be quantified.

Chapter 9 is concerned with the somewhat technical, but highly important, questions of subrogation and contribution. These topics reflect, in different ways, how insurers deal with one another when a claim is made which involves more than one insurer.

Technical problems are also dealt with in Chapter 10, in particular, those problems that arise when an insurance company faces financial ruin and the effect that this has on the insured and those who have claims on the insured. Reform is mooted in this area.

Finally, in Chapter 11, the pioneering work of the Insurance Ombudsman Bureau in the area of consumer complaints is examined. The success of the Bureau has been looked at closely and used as a guide for many other countries. In 1998, the Government announced its intention to bring together all the disparate dispute resolution mechanisms affecting the financial service providers under one umbrella. Hopefully, this will not adversely affect the contribution that the Insurance Ombudsman Bureau has and will make in the area of consumer complaints.

Publishers, like universities, are now into the numbers game and therefore my thanks go to Cavendish Publishing for agreeing to publish this book, the first under such a title.

The numbers game, in universities, usually means doing more with less. I am most grateful, therefore, to Denise Lees, who undertook the word processing of this book. I did not tell her how long the book would be when I first asked for her help – but that was an innocent non-disclosure, rather than fraudulent!

Ray Hodgin
University of Birmingham
October 1998

ACKNOWLEDGMENTS

The publishers and author wish to thank the following for permission to reprint certain selected materials. Full citations to the materials appear in the appendices.

Columbia University Press

University of North Carolina Press

Harvard Law Review

Blackwell Publishers

Cambridge Law Journal

Tolley Publishing

Sweet & Maxwell

Informa Professional (These articles were originally published in *Lloyd's Maritime and Commercial Law Quarterly* and are reproduced with the permission of the editor and the publishers, Informa Professional Publishing, Informa House, 30–32 Mortimer Street, London W1W 7RE Tel: 020 7017 5198, fax: 020 7017 5221, website: www.informalaw.com.)

Crown Copyright is reproduced with the permission of the Controller of Her Majesty's Stationery Office.

Please note that all footnotes in the extracted publications have been omitted.

Every effort has been made to trace copyright holders but if any have been inadvertently overlooked the publishers will be pleased to make the necessary arrangements.

We are also gratefully acknowledge the important sources of information gained from various websites including:

Financial Services Authority: www.fsa.gov.uk

Financial Ombudsman Scheme: www.fos.gov.uk

also www.theiob.org.uk

Financial Compensation Scheme: www.fscs.org.uk

Court service: www.courtservice.gov.uk

Law Commission: www.lawcom.gov.uk

General Insurance Standards Council: www.gisc.co.uk

Association of British Insurers: www.abi.org.uk

Lloyd's of London: www.lloydsoflondon.com

Australia (but much more!): www.austlii.edu.au

New Zealand: www.lawcom.govt.nz

USA: www.law uconn.edu

CONTENTS

TABLE OF CASES

TABLE OF STATUTES

TABLE OF STATUTORY INSTRUMENTS

TABLE OF EUROPEAN LEGISLATION

DIRECTIVES

RECOMMENDATIONS

TREATIES

COMMONWEALTH AND OTHER LEGISLATION

A GENERAL INTRODUCTION

INTRODUCTION

This chapter is something of a mixed bag of disparate subjects, important nonetheless, for setting the scene for what will follow in later chapters. Reference is made in this chapter to the historical foundations of insurance law; a definition of insurance is formulated and some of the statutory background, mainly procedural, affecting insurance, is described. Some facts and figures about insurance law are provided and European issues affecting insurance are also considered.

Historical background

According to Holdsworth (Appendix 1.1), the earliest remaining example of an insurance policy (*polizza*) is to be found in Genoa, dating from 1347. The Greeks, however, were no strangers to agreements which had the appearance of insurances (on marine adventures). An insurance court was set up in Bruges in 1310. The first English policy appears to date from 1547 (a marine policy). The development of English insurance law was largely due to the judgments of Lord Mansfield, in the second half of the 18th century, wherein he tackled many of the subjects which form the basis of later chapters of this book. (See Oldham, Appendix 1.2.) By 1688, Edward Lloyd's coffee house had become a venue for the transaction of insurance business and, in 1696, he published a newssheet entitled *Lloyd's News*, in which movements of ships were entered. (See Clayton, *British Insurance*, 1971, London: Elek.) The article and book referred to above provide a wealth of historical detail.

What is insurance?

A definition of the subject matter of a book on a specialist area of law seems a sensible requirement. Most law books, however, irrespective of the branch of law with which they are concerned, are usually forced to admit that there is no single accepted definition of their subject area. Insurance law is no different, despite the fact that there are numerous statutes regulating this area. Writing in 1753, Nicolas Magens, in 'An essay on insurance', described the situation thus:

> The contracting parties are: the insured, who pays a consideration, which is called a premium; and the insurer, who receives it. For the premium the insurer engages to satisfy, and make good to the insured, unless a fraud appears, any loss, damage, or accident that may happen; according to the terms of the contract or policy.

In *Prudential Insurance Co v IRC* [1904] 2 KB 658, Channell J stated that there were three requirements for a valid contract of insurance. First, it should provide some benefit for the policy holder on the occurrence of some event; secondly the occurrence should involve some element of uncertainty; and thirdly the uncertain event should be one which is *prima facie* adverse to the interest of the assured. The judge then added that this was not an exhaustive definition!

Why is it important to struggle to find a definition? (See Appendices 1.3, 1.4, and 1.5.) One of the main reasons is that there are a number of statutes that dictate certain consequences for the parties affected by the contract of insurance. For instance, as will be seen below, an insurer needs to be authorised to carry on insurance business in the European Union and where an insurance company is wound up certain consequences follow to aid the policy holder. Certain classes of insurance are subject to particular statutory requirements such as the Life Assurance Act 1774 (Appendix 2.2) and the Marine Insurance Act 1906 (Appendix 4.3). In 1994, the Finance Act introduced an insurance premium tax in relation to an insurance contract.

The controlling legislation for authorisation is the Insurance Companies Act 1982. From 1871 until 1998, the Department of Trade and Industry was the Government department charged with responsibility for overseeing the regulatory powers. However, in 1998, these responsibilities were switched to the Treasury.

The key players in the insurance market are the insurance/reinsurance companies; Lloyd's of London and insurance intermediaries.

What is the legal standing of an insurance contract issued by a company that is not authorised? In the 1980s, there were conflicting court decisions as to the answer. The Financial Services Act 1986 presented the opportunity, in s 132, to resolve the problem. The solution has been retained in the Financial Services and Markets Act 2000, see below. The answer is that a contract issued in contravention of the Insurance Companies Act 1982 (s 2) shall be unenforceable against the other party, but that that party shall be entitled to recover any money or other property paid or transferred by him under that contract, together with any loss sustained by that party. However, the Act gives the court the discretion to enforce the contract on behalf of the unauthorised insurer – if the company can show that it reasonably believed that it was not in contravention of the authorisation requirements and if it is just and equitable for the contract to be enforced.

Insurance companies

There are approximately 800 companies authorised to conduct insurance business in the United Kingdom, and 4,000 in the European Union. They range from the mega companies, which are household names, to small companies that are in very specialised areas of insurance. A company may seek authorisation for any of the following individual classes of business (Insurance Companies Act 1982; Insurance Companies Regulations 1994; and Insurance Companies (Third Insurance Directives) Regulations 1994).

Long term business and reinsurance

Long term business and reinsurance covers:

(a) life and annuity;

(b) marriage and birth;

(c) linked long term;

(d) permanent health;

(e) tontines;

(f) capital redemption;

(g) pension fund management;

(h) collective insurance;

(i) social insurance.

General business and reinsurance

General business and reinsurance includes cover for:

(a) accident;

(b) sickness;

(c) land vehicles;

(d) railway rolling stock;

(e) aircraft;

(f) ships;

(g) goods in transit;

(h) fire and natural forces;

(i) damage to property;

(j) motor vehicle liability;

(k) aircraft liability;

(l) liability for ships;

(m) general liability;
(n) credit;
(o) suretyship;
(p) miscellaneous financial loss;
(q) legal expense;
(r) assistance.

Financial Services and Markets Act 2000

The Financial Services Act 1986 was a massive and ambitious piece of legislation aimed at supervising all forms of financial services, of which insurance, but not all types of insurance, is one. Its replacement, the Financial Services and Markets Act 2000 (FSMA), is even more comprehensive in its coverage. Despite its intimidating length, 433 sections and 22 Schedules, it is only the tip of the iceberg. In its wake will come handbooks covering all aspects of the Act, in similar fashion to the 1986 Act. Only parts of the FSMA concern insurance. The key body in the superstructure of the FSMA is the Financial Services Authority (FSA):

- The Insurance Brokers (Registration) Act 1977 is repealed by the FSMA but no statutory replacement was envisaged. However problems with the newly created self-regulatory system (GISC) that was intended to replace the 1977 Act has caused the FSA to say that by 2004 the work of the GISC will be absorbed into the FSA (See Chapter 6, below for more detail).
- The Insurance Ombudsman Scheme, created in 1981, together with other voluntary schemes in other areas of financial undertakings, have been brought together in one Financial Ombudsman Service (FOS) (see Chapter 11 for more detail).
- The Policyholders Protection Act 1997 whereby the victims of insolvent insurance companies could seek compensation from a central fund is also recast under the FSMA (see below).
- Lloyd's was always self-governing but has now been brought within the jurisdiction of the FSA. However the Council of Lloyd's will maintain supervisory control as in the past but with the FSA having the ability to intervene if deemed necessary.

Lloyd's of London

(Some of the figures below are changing rapidly, reflecting the recent traumas at Lloyd's.)

A few facts to set the background to Lloyd's:

- a little over 300 years old (founded in 1688);
- a market place of underwriters not an insurance company;

- financed for over 300 years only by individuals, called Names. But with the Lloyd's litigation problems of the 1990s (where Names sued managing agents for negligence) the number of Names has dropped from over 32,000 to less than 2,500 within 10 years;
- in place of Names, since 1994, the concept of limited liability companies providing the financial basis has been allowed. That base (2002) exceeds £12 billion in capacity.

In 2001 the corporate capacity was over £9 billion and there were 894 corporate members.

In 2001 individual Names capacity was almost £2 billion and there were 2852 individual Names:

- Names and corporate members join syndicates which tend to specialise in certain areas of insurance. The number of syndicates has also decreased in recent years and in 2001 there were 108. The active underwriter of each syndicate has the responsibility for making the day to day insurance decisions;
- the Corporation of Lloyd's is the administrative base of Lloyd's, supplying the support infrastructure, for example: Lloyd's Policy Signing Office, claims service, membership vetting, liaison with Lloyd's brokers, public relations, complaints procedures (although, as a last resort, Lloyd's is a member of the Ombudsman service);
- Lloyd's is only to be found in Lime Street in London, there are no branch offices, but Lloyd's has representatives in other countries to look after their and their clients' interests.

Insurance intermediaries

The importance of the intermediary to the British insurance market can not be over-estimated. Highly skilled intermediaries not only provide a valuable professional service to insureds in this country but they play an invaluable part in advising overseas clients and thus play a major part in making insurance the important invisible export earner that it is today.

Intermediary covers a range of people. Classification is important in order to determine the legal responsibilities of intermediaries and to whose self-governing rules they are subject. In simple terms we can talk of employees or agents of a particular insurer on the one hand and the truly independent broker or insurance consultant on the other. The subject is dealt with in Chapter 6.

THE SINGLE EUROPEAN MARKET IN INSURANCE

Supervision of insurance companies dates back to 1870. United Kingdom membership of the European Union in 1973 and the declared aim of producing a single market in insurance within the European Community, required the United Kingdom Government to introduce numerous changes (for greater detail, see Merkin and Rodgers, *EC Insurance Law*, 1997, London: Longman).

When faced with the difficult task of dismantling barriers to a single market in insurance, it was inevitable that the easiest barriers were dealt with first and then slowly (and in the case of insurance, very slowly) the more difficult obstacles were tackled.

The declared aim of the Treaty of Rome is to 'ensure the economic and social progress' of their countries by common action to eliminate the barriers which divide Europe. Of course to eliminate barriers, which must mean protective barriers, will have the inevitable effect of exposing the weak markets to the strong markets. In insurance, it is assumed, at least by the United Kingdom, that a long and influential history in insurance, the major invisible export earner, must put the United Kingdom in the 'strong' camp. It may well be that the international flavour of the United Kingdom industry, together with mega firms of insurance brokers, and Lloyd's in particular, is seen by outsiders as a major strength.

Many of the articles of the Treaty inevitably concern insurance, which, of course, is only one segment of financial services. Of particular importance are Arts 52–58, which are concerned with the right to establishment, and Arts 59–66, which are concerned with freedom to provide services.

Freedom of establishment is the right to set up in business and to carry on that business in any Member State; freedom to provide services means the facility to provide a service in one country without having any business location in that country. Various court decisions have dealt with the meaning of these articles, but none of the cases, prior to 1986, had been specifically concerned with insurance (see *Reyners v The Belgium State* [1974] CMLR 305; *Patrick v Minister for Cultural Affairs* [1977] 2 CMLR 523; *Van Binsbergen v Board of Trade Association of the Engineering Industry* [1975] 1 CMLR 298).

In 1986, important decisions were handed down by the European Court of Justice (see [1986] ECR 3755; Edwards (1987) EL Rev 231; Hodgin (1987) CML Rev 273) specifically concerning insurance and the above mentioned articles of the Treaty of Rome. The case was brought by the Commission and two Member States with liberal insurance rules (the United Kingdom and the Netherlands), under Art 169, against Member States who had conservative and self-protective insurance regimes (that is, the Federal Republic of Germany, France, Italy, Ireland, Belgium, Denmark). Article 169 allows the

Commission to deliver a reasoned opinion for the consideration of any Member State whom it feels has failed to fulfil an obligation under the Treaty. If there is no compliance by the Member State, the Commission can take the matter to the European Court of Justice.

The outcome of the case was, unfortunately, somewhat ambiguous, although there was a distinct moral victory for the liberal approach. The court held that a Member State could not insist that in order to carry on insurance business in one Member State an insurer from another Member State must set up an establishment in that Member State. Thus, there was a victory for providing services on a transnational basis. But, the effect of this pronouncement was somewhat tempered by the court's acceptance of the defendants' argument that, as insurance was a sensitive area, in the sense that the protection of the policyholder was paramount, certain limited and more protective supervisory laws of a particular Member State should be followed by any insurer wishing to do business in that Member State. In particular, what the court had in mind as being in need of special protection, was the solvency of insurance companies and the contractual conditions of the policy. The real difficulty with the court's decision was in identifying when a Member State was entitled to demand strict observance of its own national rules. What is clear, however, is that a Member State must not require observance of conditions which exceed what is necessary for the protection of policy holders and insured persons. It is also obvious that with so many different types of insurance in the market, the concept of consumer protection, while applicable to some (that is, mass risks) would be inapplicable to others (for example, large risks). These two types of risks are explained below. There is little doubt that the judgment had a very important effect on the wording of later Directives.

A brief summary of some but not all of the insurance Directives and how UK law implemented them

Reinsurance Directive 1964 (64/225/EEC)

The declared aim of this Directive was to abolish restrictions on freedom of establishment and freedom to provide services in the very specialist area of reinsurance. It was obviously passed before the United Kingdom's accession, and it caused no real problems to United Kingdom practices when the United Kingdom finally joined in 1973. This was because United Kingdom domestic law had no barriers to competition in this area of insurance law, operating, as it does, an open door policy.

Motor Insurance Directives (72/166/EEC; 72/430/EEC; 84/5/EC; 90/232/EC; 90/618/EC; 2000/26/EC)

The 1972 Directive, as amended, obliged Member States to introduce compulsory motor insurance for vehicles normally based in its territory. It also required the Member States to see that the insurance covered any loss or injury caused in other Member States in accordance with the laws in force in those other Member States. The Directive eliminated green card checks at frontiers.

The 1983 Directive extended compulsory third party motor insurance to cover damage to property, to a minimum guaranteed level. This was a new requirement for United Kingdom insurers. The Directive also further enhanced the protection of the victims of uninsured drivers.

The 1990 Directive filled gaps left by the above two Directives. It extended cover to all passengers (other than those who enter a vehicle knowing it to be stolen). It also required insurers to provide compulsory third party cover throughout the European Union at the level required by the Member State where the accident occurs or of the Member State where the vehicle is normally based, if that cover is higher. This means that the victim of a United Kingdom policyholder injured outside the United Kingdom will benefit from the unlimited liability of United Kingdom motor policies.

The above requirements are to be found in the Road Traffic Act (RTA) 1988 and the Motor Vehicles (Compulsory Insurance) Regulations 1992 (SI 1992/3036).

The importance to the citizen of Directives can also be seen in Motor Vehicles (Compulsory Insurance) Regulations 2000 (SI 2000/726). The House of Lords had interpreted the compulsory insurance provisions of the RTA 1988 as being inapplicable to accidents occuring in a car park (*Cutter v Eagle Star Insurance* [1998] 4 All ER 417). The cumulative effect of the above Directives is to see that all civil liability arising out of the use of a motor vehicle is covered by insurance. This SI therefore amends the RTA 1988 to include public places other than roads. The latest Directive (2000/26/EEC) requires that victims of negligently inflicted road traffic injuries, where liability is not contested, should have a direct right of action against the insurer on risk. Insurers will be expected to establish a claims representative in every Member State to deal with such claims. The emphasis is on speeding up settlements.

The first two key Directives on non-life and life assurance

Non-Life Directive 1973 (73/239/EEC)

This Directive was of major importance and required the United Kingdom to introduce important changes to its domestic law. These were implemented, and have been consolidated, in the Insurance Companies Regulations 1994 (SI

1994/1516). The Directive's aim was to achieve one set of regulatory rules applicable to all Member States governing the supervision of insurance companies, other than life companies and pure reinsurance. To do this Member States had to dismantle their own supervisory systems, some of which had been very protective of their own industries, to the disadvantage of insurance companies in other Member States. There is little doubt however that the Directive called for controls stricter than had ever existed previously in the United Kingdom. The new, more onerous, requirements should produce a more secure financial regime for policyholders.

Reference should also be made to the Directive (84/641/EC) amending, particularly as regards tourist assistance, the first Directive on direct insurance other than life.

The various insurance Directives omit any definition of an insurance contract. Thus Directives are no more helpful than United Kingdom domestic legislation has been over the years (see above). The 1973 non-life Directive classified insurance contracts into 17 categories. Doubt persisted as to whether a contract which provided specified services or assistance, rather than money indemnity, were to be regarded as insurance contracts and thus subject to the new regulations. The doubt had been answered in the affirmative in the United Kingdom by the court in *Department of Trade and Industry v St Christopher Motorists' Association* (see Appendix 1.3).

This Directive similarly treats such 'assistance' contracts as insurance contracts and therefore subjects them to the supervisory regime of the 1973 First Directive, thus creating an 18th class of non-life business. This requirement required only textual changes to the United Kingdom's insurance companies legislation.

First Council Directive relating to Life Assurance (77/92/EEC)

This Directive (77/92/EEC) was introduced in 1979. This followed the same basic procedures as the non-life Directive. The main aims, therefore, were to introduce a State system of authorisation and to require a solvency margin, although calculated by a different formula. The Directive also attempted to deal with a major conflict between Member States concerning 'composite' insurance companies. 'Composites' are companies which transact both life and non-life business. The United Kingdom, Belgium and Luxembourg recognise composites while other Member States do not. The argument levelled against composites was that life assurance, which is seen, by many policyholders, as a means of saving and providing security for the family, would be in the same financial grouping as non-life business, which is more volatile. On this assumption, there was potential financial danger for the life policyholder. Germany was the main opponent of composites. A compromise is found in Art 13 which banned the formation of any new composites, or any new branch of an existing composite, but recognised that existing composites could continue. However, things have moved on and composites are now fully recognised in the Third Generation Directives (see below).

The 1979 Directive did not require changes to United Kingdom law.

The Insurance Intermediaries Directive 1977 (77/92/EEC); the Commission Recommendation on Insurance Intermediaries 1991 (92/48/EC) and a new Proposal for a Directive of insurance mediation 2001

These are discussed in Chapter 6.

Community Co-insurance Directive 1978 (78/473/EEC)

Co-insurance describes the situation where two or more insurers join together to cover a risk, usually because of the financial implications of that risk. The Directive was necessary because some Member States had legislation, which prevented an insurer who was not established in that Member State from participating in the cover. The United Kingdom had no such barriers and, therefore, the Directive presented no problems of implementation. The method of implementation caused a serious disagreement between Member States and was one of the major points of contention in the December 1986 decisions of the European Court of Justice (referred to above).

This Directive was implemented by various measures now consolidated in the Insurance Companies Regulations 1994 (SI 1994/1516) and Insurance Companies (Accounts and Statements) Regulations 1996 (SI 1996/943).

Directive (87/343/EC)

Amending, as regards credit insurance and suretyship insurance, the First Directive on non-life business. Certain types of insurance were not affected by the First Directive on non-life insurance in 1973, mainly because of their specialised nature (this was particularly so in the Federal Republic of Germany). This 1987 Directive called for harmonisation of this class of insurance by requiring Germany to fall into line.

Directive relating to legal expense insurance 1987 (87/354/EC)

This Directive seeks to harmonise the law relating to legal expense insurance, by allowing freedom of establishment and it also seeks to stamp out any conflict of interest problems. Such problems can be illustrated by the example where X has a claim on his policy with insurer A and his legal expense insurer is also insurer A. The Directive requires that those who handle legal expense claims must not handle other types of claims. It also attempts to resolve the possible conflict where the same legal expense insurer represents both parties to the dispute. This is achieved by giving the insured complete freedom to choose his own lawyer to represent his interests.

The Directive allows exemption from the requirement of choosing one's own lawyer in certain conditions. The conditions appear to apply, as far as the

United Kingdom is concerned, to the legal expense support offered by membership of the AA and the RAC. Thus, in such situations, those associations will be able to choose the lawyer to represent their members. Naturally, when both parties to the dispute are members of that organisation, different firms of lawyers would have to be instructed.

The second two key Directives on non-life and life assurance (1988)

Second Non-Life Directive (88/357/EC)

This was a most important Directive, crucial for the completion of the internal market in insurance services. The aim was to allow an insurer who is established in one Member State to offer services in another Member State. As we saw above, that objective was not fully achieved by the important ruling of the European Court of Justice in 1986. The Court accepted the argument of the Federal Republic of Germany that consumer protection was of paramount importance and therefore it was permissible for a Member State to insist on authorisation in that State, before certain types of insurance was sold. The problem, however, remained as to what types of insurance qualified for the special, restrictive, treatment. This Directive attempted an answer. It did so by introducing the concept of 'large risks', or commercial risks, and 'mass' or consumer risks. The mass risk policyholder required some protection while the former did not.

The Second Life Assurance Services Directive 1990 (90/619/EC)

This built on the 1979 Life Establishment Directive and laid down specific provisions, which would allow limited freedom of life assurance services. The two major areas thus freed related to life assurance and annuities; a notable exclusion was that of pension fund management.

The 1992 third generation Directives for non-life (92/49/EC) and life assurance (92/96/EC)

These two Directives complete the single European market for insurance by introducing the 'single passport'. This means that once an insurer has been authorised in the Member State (the Home State) in which it has its head office, that insurer is then free to sell its products in any other Member State (the Host State). There is one major exception to complete freedom, and this exception was created by the 1986 European Court of Justice decision, with the protection of the consumer in mind. Thus, the Host State can prevent persons entering into insurance contracts and prevent insurance advertising if it is considered by the regulatory authority to be in the 'general good'. Unfortunately, the phrase was not defined by the European Court of Justice.

The Court, however, determined that:

> ... any measure imposed in the interest of the general good must:
>
> - be objectively necessary;
> - be in proportion to the objective;
> - not duplicate a restriction with which the insurer must comply in its Home State;
> - not discriminate between insurance companies operating in a Member State.

What specific points can be found in the two Directives that can be said to be tailored to the private consumers' needs?

There existed, in some Member States, the necessity to obtain prior approval from the regulatory authority of premiums and of policy conditions. Such approval, which did not exist in the United Kingdom, is now abolished. In its place, however, is a list of points in the Life Directive, that must be disclosed to the policyholder, most of which are concerned with describing the assurance undertaking and describing the product (see Appendix 1.6).

Insurance contract law

Now we come to the one great failing in European Union insurance harmonisation. The Draft Insurance Contracts Directive (1979), as amended (Com (79) 355 and Com (80) 854), was referred to by the Law Commission, *Insurance Law, Non-Disclosure and Breach of Warranty*, in some detail (see Appendix 4.8). The report described the draft Directive as one which 'would necessitate far reaching changes in our law of insurance'. The key provisions, Arts 3–6, relating to consumer protection were seen to be modelled on French law. In particular, they introduced the concept, unknown to English law, of proportionality (this concept is discussed in Chapter 4). The report described this principle as having inherent limitations and practical drawbacks which would render its introduction into English law undesirable. That, together with other objections, caused the report to state that the draft Directive did not achieve a fair balance between the interests of the insurer and the insured.

In the face of such opposition, it is not surprising that the draft was doomed to failure, 'its basic features ... are likely to be non-negotiable'. In its place, the report advocated legislative reform of United Kingdom law, which has not been forthcoming. What we do have are the Association of British Insurers' self-regulatory Statements of Insurance and Codes of Practice, which were also criticised by the Law Commission report (see Appendix 4.10).

Where does that leave the consumer? The answer seems to be that he is faced with a complex choice of law framework (Appendix 1.6). What then if a consumer chooses to insure with a United Kingdom authorised insurer? To adopt MacNeil's classification ('The legal framework in the United Kingdom for insurance policies' (1995) 44 ICLQ 19) after explaining that the common law does not restrict choice of law in the field of insurance:

(1) an express choice of law determines the applicable law;

(2) where there is no express choice, the intention of the parties is to be inferred from the terms and nature of the contract and from the general circumstances of the case;

(3) where there is no express choice and no inference is possible from the circumstances, the contract is governed by the system of law with which it has its closest and most real connection; this test will normally result in the contract being governed by the law of the country in which the insurer carries on its business, and if it carries on business in more than one country, by the law of the country in which the head office is located.

The possibility must surely be that for private consumers buying from United Kingdom companies, the applicable law will be the English law of insurance contracts and that will be chosen by both parties because these are the legal rules best known to them. If that is so, it will be necessary for the insured to look at those areas of difficulty that beset English insurance law, and these problem areas could be detrimental to the interests of consumers in other Member States, if they agree to be bound by contracts which are subject to English law.

The draft insurance contract law proposal was formally abandoned in 1994.

Conclusions

Insurance, perhaps more than other areas of commercial activity, has illustrated strongly held beliefs from different Member States. Large sums are involved and nearly the whole adult population of the European Union has an interest in insurance.

The Directives outlined above have been concerned mainly with the administrative framework of setting up a single market in insurance. Occasionally, a Directive has been concerned with the direct and immediate interests of the private consumer; the motor Directives present the best examples.

Harmonisation of insurance contract law has been the great failure. Instead, complicated choice of law rules have been introduced (Appendix 1.6). Insurers, presumably, will prefer to follow their own national rules. The history of their own national development in this area over many decades must surely be reflected in their products and in their approach to the insured risk.

It is unlikely that the private consumer will be convinced to deal with 'foreign' insurers on their terms. Not only will there be language and cultural barriers but also doubts as to whether the legal rules applicable in the various Member States are necessarily to the consumers' advantage. The criticisms that appear in later chapters of English insurance contract rules, and the apparent inapplicability of the self-regulatory rules to those buying abroad, will present a barrier to expansion in the private consumer area. If this somewhat pessimistic view is correct, then the single market in insurance will perhaps have little impact on the private citizen in the immediate future. What is perhaps more important to United Kingdom insurers, is whether a single market will lead to greater penetration of the European Union market in the area of commercial insurance.

POLICYHOLDER PROTECTION

The above overview of the Directives shows that the aim has been largely to create an open single market for the selling and buying of both commercial and consumer insurance products. Many of these developments have had the consumers' interests at heart but harmonisation of contract law was not achieved. In terms of domestic reform, the Law Commission Recommendations of 1980 were not enacted (Appendix 4.8). What the consumer has instead is the Association of British Insurers self-regulatory statements (Appendix 4.10) and Code of Practice (Appendix 6.5). To this should be added the Unfair Terms in Consumer Contracts Regulations 1994 (now 1999) (Appendix 7.1) which originated from a Directive.

In addition to the above, the influence of the Insurance Ombudsman (see Chapter 11) should not be under estimated.

Finally, reference should be made to the Policyholders Protection Acts of 1975 and 1997 and to Part XV of the FSMA (Appendix 1.7).

Introduction

The greatest calamity that can face the insured is to find that his policy is worthless. The most dramatic way in which this can happen is for his insurance company to go into liquidation and be wound up.

Where the policy affected is annual indemnity cover, such as car insurance, house buildings or contents, the insured may suffer financial loss if he needs to make a claim. But where the policy is a long term policy such as life assurance or a pension arrangement a much greater catastrophe ensues. Every policyholder is affected and long term savings plans will be ruined. When compulsory insurance is concerned then the victims' compensation may be at risk.

The history of insurance company supervision in this country showed, until relatively recently, a kid-glove approach. The battle cry of the industry was 'freedom with publicity'. The 'freedom' related to freedom from too much government control. In recent years, things have changed, for three main reasons.

First, a number of insurance company crashes in the 1960s and 1970s highlighted the problem, exposing thousands of policyholders, and sometimes their victims, to great financial losses. The Government was forced to act. This took the form of increased government inspection of insurance companies, as referred to in this Chapter, and of the intermediary market as seen in Chapter 6 (although the changes were subsequently rejected in favour of further self-regulation). Secondly, membership of the European Community resulted in the application of Directives, some of which were concerned with the solvency of insurance companies. Thirdly, the growing wave of consumer protectionism demanded that some safety provisions exist, to cover situations where, despite the growing stringency of supervision, an insurance company failed its policyholders. This resulted in the Policyholders Protection Act 1975, amended by the 1997 Act.

The desire to protect the insured by means of statutory intervention outweighed the hostile opposition of many companies who, at the most, wanted to arrange non-statutory protection. Reputable insurers were particularly incensed by the fact that they would need to bail out the disreputable or incompetent insurer.

The legislation

The Policyholders Protection Act was passed in 1975 and changes to it brought about by the Act of 1997, although much of the later Act was never brought into force. The reason for that was that the Financial Services and Markets Act 2000 was intended to make further changes to the way that consumers were protected when companies or institutions failed. Protection existed in areas other than insurance and the intention was to bring all of the different regimes under one roof. The statutory outline of how that is to be accomplished is set out in Part XV of the FSMA (Appendix 1.7). As the new body, the Financial Services Compensation Scheme (FSCS), was only up and running from 1 December 2001 it is too early to comment in detail on how things have progressed. (For the latest developments, see www. fscs.org.uk.)

We are here concerned only with insurance aspects of the new scheme. The general principles to be found in the Policyholders Protection Acts will still provide the main emphasis of how the newly created FSCS will operate.

Compensation is available at two levels depending on the type of policy that is threatened by the financial difficulties faced by the insurer. Where it is a compulsory policy (thus one covering motor insurance, employers' liability insurance, Riding Establishment Act 1964 requirements or those of the

Nuclear Installations Act 1965) then there is 100% cover. For any other type of insurance (including life cover) it will be 100% of the first £2000 and thereafter 90% of the remainder. There is no maximum sum that is claimable which therefore distinguishes the treatment of insurance from other investment business which tends to have a maximum level of compensation. Lloyd's policies are not covered by the scheme because it has its own central fund to provide compensation. Certain specialist categories of insurance are also not covered by the scheme: marine, aviation, transport business, and credit insurance. These areas of cover are not considered to be areas where the consumer would normally be involved.

Wherever possible the aim is for the FSCS to try to arrange for another insurer to take over the failed insurer's policy thus safeguarding the policyholder's interests.

Those eligible for compensation are individual policyholders and small businesses, defined as a business with a turnover of £1 million or less. This is a change from the 'old' law which gave compensation to partnerships but made no mention of small businesses. Out go the former and in come the latter.

What are the territorial limits of the insurance policies that are covered by the new scheme? Under the original Policyholders Protections Act (PPAct) 1975 all policies issued by UK insurers were covered and this led on one occasion to a massive claim from North American insureds (*Scher and Akerman v Policyholders Protection Board* [1993] 4 All ER 840). The 1997 PPAct changed the law to limit compensation to those policyholders who are insured with companies authorised to carry out business in the UK, EEA, Channel Islands and Isle of Man and where the policy coverage is similarly confined. The new scheme follows these jurisdictional limits.

Who pays? Under the original scheme all insurers paid by means of a levy based on their turnover. This approach will be followed under the new scheme, thus insurers will pay for insolvent insurers and other groups, such as banks or building societies, will pay for their insolvent competitors.

Between 1975 and 2000 the Policyholders Protection Board paid out, and thus levied from insurers, £348 million. In January 2002 the new FSCS levied £150 million. This would seem to indicate that despite the increased solvency margins required under European directives and the increased regulatory supervision under the Financial Services Act 1986 things have got worse rather than better!

Some facts and figures about the insurance market

It is not easy to be precise or absolutely up to date about insurance facts and figures because the accounting periods usually stretch over several years and some institutions such as Lloyd's of London have their own way of doing things.

The following figures are taken from the Association of British Insurance and from Sigma publications:

United Kingdom Insurance Figures.

- The UK insurance industry is the largest in Europe.
- It employs over 300,000 people, a third of all financial services jobs.
- It contributes about £8 billion to UK overseas earnings.
- It pays out £225 million a day in pensions and life insurance benefits and £41 million a day in general insurance claims.
- Just over 800 insurers are authorised to carry on insurance business in the UK.
- The largest 10 insurers handle 85% of that business.
- The largest 10 property insurers handle 80% of that market.
- The net premium income in general insurance business (see above for how insurers are classified) is £20.6 billion and for long term business it is £116 billion.
- In 1999/2000 those who buy insurance spent on average (figures in brackets represent the percentage of households which purchase that class of insurance):

Home contents	£132	(75%)
Motor	£370	(67%)
Home buildings	£158	(61%)
Life insurance	£911	(55%)
Mortgage protection	£278	(17%)
Personal pension	£1707	(16%)
Medical	£608	(9%)
Income protection	£380	(2%)

UK in the insurance international markets

Biggest insurance markets as a percentage of the global market 2000

USA	35%
Japan	20%

UK	10% (including being the largest life market in Europe and third largest in the world: the non-life market is the second largest in Europe and fourth in the world)
Germany	5%
France	5%

A GENERAL INTRODUCTION

APPENDIX 1.1

Holdsworth, W, 'The early history of the contract of insurance' (1917) 17 Col LR 85

In this paper, I propose to deal with the origins of the contract of marine insurance; with the beginnings of the development of this form of insurance in English law; and with the origins of other forms of insurance.

(1) THE ORIGIN OF THE CONTRACT OF MARINE INSURANCE

Insurance has been defined as a contract by which one party (the insurer) in consideration of a premium, undertakes to indemnify another (the insured) against loss. The researches of M Bensa have proved that the earliest variety of this contract was the contract of marine insurance; that as a separate and independent contract it dates back to the early years of the 14th century; and that it evolved, like so many other modern mercantile institutions, in the commercial cities of Italy. As M Lefort has said, this contract was not devised by a legislator. It was the last term in the evolution of various legal devices invented to provide against the risks of the sea; and though there is no evidence of the existence of an independent contract of insurance before the beginning of the 14th century, we can see in these various devices the germs from which this contract evolved. And, even when in practice it had come to be recognised as a distinct species of contract, it still continued to be disguised under the forms of a sale, an exchange, or a maritime loan, in order to prevent any question that it could be illegal on the grounds that it infringed the laws against usury.

Among both the Greeks and Romans we meet with stipulations, accessory to the contract of carriage, which settled the incidence of the risk of loss of, or damage to the goods carried. For instance, either the carrier or the consignee might guarantee the safe arrival of the goods carried; and the maritime loan – *trajectitia pecunia* – can be analysed into a contract of *mutuum* with a contract of insurance added to it. The higher interest paid by the borrower represented a premium, in consideration of which he was not liable to pay if the ship were lost. Then again we meet, in the earlier medieval period, mutual associations formed to guard against certain risks of the sea, as for insurance against the risks which arose from the issue of letters of *marque*, or from the practice of reprisals; and at Genoa there was established an institution – the *Officium Robarie* – to give redress against Genoese citizens who had committed acts of piracy against any trader, which really gave a sort of state insurance against this particular risk.

More immediately connected with the development of the contract of insurance were the stipulations as to risk introduced into the ordinary commercial contracts of the 13th century. Indeed, M Valery thinks that, in the 13th century, some of these contracts, for example, contracts of sale or loan, were never intended to be sales or loans, but insurances. Thus in the contract of 'commenda', under which A advances money or other property to B to trade with, there is usually a stipulation as to the party on whom the risk of accidental loss is to fall. In the contract of *mutuum* it is probable that, though it evaded the canonical prohibition of usury by calling itself *mutuum 'gratis et amore'*, the lender often paid over the money advanced with a deduction, in consideration that nothing should be payable if the money were lost by accident, and such a deduction is, as M Bensa has said, a true premium of insurance. Similarly, contracts of sale or exchange (*cambium*) were used to disguise transactions intended to operate as loans at sufficient interest to compensate the lender, both for the use of his money, and for the provision that nothing was to be payable if the money were accidentally lost. The form of a contract of sale was adapted to this purpose as follows: instead of B buying goods with money lent by A, A buys the goods himself and sells them to B, and the price which B agrees to pay will be: (a) payable at a future date; (b) contingent upon the safe arrival at the place of payment, either of the original goods or the goods into which they have been converted; and (c) sufficient to meet the sum paid by A with maritime interest. Similarly, in the case of exchange, B received coins from A on the terms of paying different coins (which would be of a different value) at another time or place; and accordingly, as the coins were at the risk of the borrower or lender, the value of the coins to be returned would differ. The difference between the rates of exchange, depending on whether the money was repayable in any event, or only on the prosperous termination of the voyage, represents again a premium of insurance. As M Bensa has said, it is only necessary to split up such arrangements into their component parts in order to arrive at the idea of an independent contract of insurance:

> It would only be necessary for a third person to intervene between a purchaser who intended to purchase goods arrived safely, and a vendor who wished to throw on the purchaser the risks of the sea, and to offer to take these risks for the sum, which the course of trade and the rate of exchange had fixed as the difference in the price, depending whether one or other party took these risks.

In 1347, we have, in the archives of Genoa, what is perhaps the oldest contract of insurance; and the archives of Florence show that, in the first 20 years of this century, it was an ordinary commercial transaction in the principal commercial towns of Italy. But, as we have seen, the contracts in which the market value of the element of risk had been thus worked out were chiefly contracts of maritime loan, and all were concerned with the risks incurred in transport – generally by sea. It is not surprising, therefore, to find that when the contract of insurance first appears as an independent contract it is modelled on the maritime loan, which developed into the contract of bottomry. No very large modification was needed. In the maritime loan, the debtor, who has borrowed the money, declares that he has received the sum advanced, and promises to restore an equivalent sum on the safe arrival of the ship or goods: in the insurance, the assurer plays the part of the debtor, states that he has received the amount for which the ship or goods are insured, and promises to repay it in the event of the ship or goods not arriving safely. It was only natural that the earliest insurers should be shipowners – they could charge a smaller premium because they could more easily guarantee a safe arrival; and it was inevitable that those who drew up the earliest contract of insurance should be the same persons as those who were in the habit of drawing up contracts of loan on bottomry. Hence, it was from the latter contract that some of the most important of the technical terms applicable to insurance at the present day (such, for instance as 'policy' and 'premium'), were originally taken.

But, later in the century, the form changed. It came to be modelled on a sale; and the analogy of a sale was used to explain its incidents. The contract of sale was adapted to the purposes of an insurance by regarding the property insured as sold to the insurer, subject to a resolutive condition in the event of its safe arrival. It was for this reason that the goods were at the insurer's risk during the whole of the voyage, and that he could sue for their recovery during this period. Two important principles of insurance law flowed from this conception. In the first place, the insured must be the owner, or at least have some interest in the property insured. A man cannot transfer to another what he does not own. Therefore, from the first, the contract was a true contract of indemnity, and not a mere wager on the safe arrival of ship or merchandise. In the second place, if the ship or goods did not arrive safely, and the resolutive condition failed to operate, the insurers were entitled to so much of the property insured as could be recovered.

During the 14th century, the business of insurance grew and flourished. In the first half of the 14th century Florentine and Genoese merchants treated the cost of insurance as a regular part of the cost of transport. Genoa seems to have been the centre of the insurance business. Societies of insurance brokers, employed solely in this business, were known there, and that their business flourished can be seen from the fact that on a single day in 1393, a single Genoese notary made more than 80 insurance contracts ...

In these early days, there was no rule as to the form in which the contract must be drawn up. There is reason indeed to think that, in the earlier part of the 14th century, contracts of insurance were sometimes made verbally. But the procedural advantages obtained by getting the contract drawn up in writing by a notary or a sworn broker led the parties in almost all cases to adopt this method of contracting. In the first instance, these contracts were sometimes very informally drawn. Mere notes of the necessary clauses to be inserted in the agreement were taken. Probably, the instrument was embodied in complete form only if it was necessary to take legal proceedings upon it. But it is clear that the practice of employing sworn brokers will lead to the evolution of a stereotyped form. The form which the brokers of Genoa, Florence and Pisa evolved in this century has in substance shaped the policies of our modern law ...

This growth of the practice of insurance caused, in the first place, the ascertainment and elaboration of the rules of law governing the contract and, in the second place, its regulation by statutes which were passed, either in the interests of the state, or in the interests of the parties to the contract. Since these rules and statutes are the basis of the insurance law observed in Europe and in England at the present day, we must glance briefly at them:

(a) we have seen that, from the first, the contract of insurance was a contract of indemnity, and that therefore the person insured must have some interest in the subject matter of the insurance. This requirement sometimes gave insurers the opportunity of evading their obligations, and led to the insertion of clauses, which bound the insurers to pay whether or not the insured had any interest. But the prevalence of these clauses soon gave rise to the serious evil of facilitating, by means of insurance, mere wagering contracts on the safety of ships or other property insured ...;

(b) the earliest legislation on the subject of insurances comes from Genoa and Florence. The earliest enactment is a Genoese statute which comes from the last quarter of the 14th century ...

(2) THE INTRODUCTION AND DEVELOPMENT OF THE CONTRACT OF MARINE INSURANCE IN ENGLAND

As we might expect, the earliest mention of a policy of insurance in England is to be found among the records of the court of Admiralty. Insurance, as was pointed out in a 16th century petition to the Council, 'is not grounded upon the laws of the realm, but rather a civil and maritime cause, to be determined and decided by civilians, or else in the high court of the Admiralty'. This earliest policy is to be found in the record of the case of *Broke v Maynard* (1547), in which an action was brought by the insured on a policy written in Italian, and subscribed by two underwriters ...

If we compare the state of the law of insurance at the end of the 17th century with its state at the end of the 16th century, we can see that it has made no appreciable progress. In neither period has there been any legislation, comparable to that of continental states, directed against obvious abuses, such as the practice of cloaking mere wagers under policies of insurance. In neither period has much progress been made in the work of converting those mercantile customs and that continental jurisprudence which Malynes describes, into ascertained rule of English law. In one respect indeed there has been a retrogression. The business of underwriting was subject to some sort of control in the 16th century; but, in the 17th century, that control ceased with the disappearance of the Office of Assurances. It was not till the early part of the following century that the legislature attempted to repress some of the abuses which were disfiguring the law; and it was not till later in that century that Lord Mansfield developed from mercantile custom and foreign precedents the principles of our modern law. Similarly we must look to the same period for the humble beginnings, at Lloyd's coffee house, of the voluntary association which has supplied, far more efficiently than any governmental institution, that measure of control over the business of underwriting which had been attempted by the Council in the 16th century.

(3) THE ORIGINS OF OTHER FORMS OF INSURANCE

I have dealt so far only with marine insurance. During the whole of this period it was by far the most important branch of insurance law. It was the only branch which the legislature noticed.

Analogous to insurances against the risks of transport by sea are insurances against the risks of transport by land. We have seen that this species of insurance was known abroad; and perhaps it was known in England, though there is not much evidence of this. Gradually, in addition to these insurances of property against the risks of transport, insurances against other dangers to property developed. But, during the 16th and 17th centuries the only other danger to property which could be insured against was danger by fire; and as yet it was only houses that could be insured. As early as 1591, a system of fire insurance was in operation in Hamburg; and proposals to establish this kind of insurance in England had been made in 1635 and 1638. But it was not till after the Great Fire that it was actually established. In 1667, Barbon established an office which, in 1680, was transferred to a company. In 1682, the City of London started a rival undertaking. About the same time two partners established a mutual society known as the Friendly Society; and, in 1696, another mutual society, known as the Hand in Hand, was started.

But, before fire insurance had developed, insurances against risks, not to property, but to the person were known both on the continent and in England. Of the early history of this form of insurance I must say a few words.

In modern times the contract of insurance against risks to the person takes the form either of life or accident insurance; and both are very different in character to the insurances against risks to property. Life insurance is a contract of indemnity, in so far as it enables the insured to make provisions against death or the incapacities of old age. But it is also, both in England and elsewhere, a method of investment; and it is this aspect of the contract which is the most important, and causes it to differ essentially from insurances against risks to property. The latter class of insurances are, as we have seen, simply contracts of indemnity. The result is that, if the loss occurring from the happening of the risk is otherwise made good, the insurer is not liable because the loss has not been incurred. On the other hand, the contract of life insurance is not simply a contract of indemnity. It is an absolute promise to pay at the death of the insured a fixed sum of money, in consideration for the payment of certain premiums during life, the amount of which is calculated by reference to the probable duration of the life insured. The amount insured is payable whether or not any loss is incurred as a result of the death; and in this important respect the contract of accident insurance resembles the contract of life insurance.

During this period we can see nothing resembling the modern contracts of life or accident insurance. The statistical knowledge, which has rendered those contracts possible in modern times was wholly wanting; and even if it had been available, it is probable that the dangers and uncertainties of life in a comparatively turbulent age would have made these contracts commercial impossible. But we do see in Italy, in the Middle Ages, and in England, during the 16th and 17th centuries a few insurances against certain risks to the person, which we can regard as the germs from which our modern life and accident insurances have grown up ...

There is some evidence that contracts of this kind were known in England during this period. In the only two cases on the subject which have got into the books we have an insurance upon the life of one who was going abroad, and an insurance upon the life of a certain person for one year ...

It is not until the 18th and 19th centuries that the legal incidents and consequences of these new forms of insurances, whether against personal risks or against risks to property other than risks of transport, begin to be defined.

APPENDIX 1.2

Oldham, J, *The Mansfield Manuscripts and the Growth of English Law in the 18th Century*, 1992, North Carolina: North Carolina Press, Vol 1

As in the cases of usury and negotiable instruments, the English law of insurance developed in order to facilitate international trade. Just as the legal acceptance of the international negotiable instrument (the foreign bill of exchange) preceded and shaped the elaboration of domestic variants, so the articulation of a legal doctrine governing the insurance of international trade (marine insurance) invited the development of domestic life and fire insurance. Foreshadowed by Chief Justice Holt at the turn of the 18th century, it fell to Lord Mansfield to rationalise and elucidate the legal principles of insurance. The coherence of his efforts was one of his greatest achievements.

Guided by the convictions informing all of his decisions in commercial law (that the mercantile law is 'the same all over the world'); that to be functional, the mercantile law must be within the apprehension of those who must obey it; and, as a consequence, that 'the great object in every branch of the law, but especially in mercantile law, is certainty', Lord Mansfield established the principle that an insurance contract is an agreement requiring the utmost fidelity between parties. Fraud, concealment of a material fact that would alter the risk, breach of implied or express warranties, or deviation from the route implied by the terms of the contract would invalidate the contract. Furthermore, by consistently characterising the contract as one of indemnification, Lord Mansfield applied the principle that the risk insured against must be commensurate with the risk actually run. This was related to the broader principle that the insured must have an 'insurable interest' in the thing or person insured. Necessarily, one cannot be indemnified, held harmless, if one cannot be harmed. The requirement of an insurable interest became the validating test. Life and fire insurance were developed by analogy to the principles of marine insurance; cases in which the insured lacked an insurable interest were deemed wagering and fell under statutory proscription ...

MANSFIELD'S CONTRIBUTION

Procedurally, Lord Mansfield moved to eliminate the necessity that the insured bring separate actions against each underwriter, emphasizing the advantages of a proposal that the court 'stay the proceedings in all the actions but one', with the understanding that the underwriters would pay 'the amount of their subscriptions with costs, if the plaintiff should succeed in the cause which was tried' ...

Lord Mansfield derived his principles of marine insurance from his knowledge of continental practice and custom, refined by consultation with merchants and underwriters. In *Lewis v Rucker* (1761) 2 Burr 1167, he determined the proper amount payable upon a partial loss 'by conversing with some gentlemen of experience in adjustments', while underwriters were consulted in *Glover v Black* (1763) 3 Burr 1394, as to the practice of drafting policies. Lord Mansfield's knowledge of general civil maritime law led him to see that 'the mercantile law ... is the same all over the world. For, from the same premises, the sound conclusions of reason and justice must universally be the same'. At the same time, his familiarity with mercantile practices led him to realise that:

> ... the daily negotiations and property of merchants ought not to depend upon subtleties and niceties; but upon rules, easily learned and easily retained, because they are the dictates of common sense, drawn from the truth of the case ...

By 1765, just nine years after Lord Mansfield became Chief Justice, Blackstone was able to report that 'the learning relating to marine insurances hath of late years been greatly improved by a series of judicial decisions, which have now established the law'; but he noted that 'it is not easy to reduce them to any general heads in mere elementary institutes'. The cases can nonetheless be separated for discussion purposes into four categories, grouped around the principle of good faith. The first three categories involve the asserted absence of good faith due to fraud or material misrepresentation, breach of warranty, and deviation from implied contract terms. The fourth category consists of cases assessing the implications of the *presence* of good faith by determining the consequences of indemnification upon loss.

FRAUD OR MATERIAL MISREPRESENTATION

A series of Mansfield cases fixed the contours of the doctrine that fraud or misrepresentation voids *ab initio* an insurance contract ...

Carter v Boehm (1766) 3 Burr 1905 was considered a seminal case, for, as Park noted, 'from it may be collected all the general principles upon which the doctrine of concealments, in matters of insurance, is founded, as well as all the exceptions'.

As Park reported, Lord Mansfield first reviewed the difference between a warranty and a representation. To the subsequent underwriters, who argued that the specifications were part of their agreement, Lord Mansfield stated, 'The answer to this is, read your agreement: read your policy. There is no such thing to be found there'. As to the first underwriter, who saw the representation, Mansfield argued that if the specifications had induced him to underwrite, 'he would have said, put them into the policy; warrant that the ship shall depart with 12 guns and 20 men'. Since the specifications were not a warranty, Lord Mansfield then determined whether they amounted to a material misrepresentation:

> The representation amounts to no more than this; I tell you what the force will be, because it is so much the better for you. There is no fraud in it, because it is a representation only of what, in the then state of the ship, they thought would be the truth. And in real truth the ship sailed with a larger force ...; the underwriters therefore had the advantage by the difference.

BREACH OF WARRANTY

Park defined a warranty in a policy of insurance as 'a condition or a contingency, that a certain thing shall be done or happen, and unless that is performed, there is no valid contract'. While a representation might underlie a contract or shape the parties' agreement, a warranty was regarded as an essential element of that agreement; thus:

> A warranty must be strictly and *literally* performed; and therefore whether the thing, warranted to be done, be or be not essential to the security of the ship; or whether the loss do or do not happen, on account of the breach of the warranty, still the insured has no remedy ... And though the condition broken be not, perhaps, a material one, yet the justice of the law is evident from this consideration: that it is absolutely necessary to have one rule of decision, and that it is much better to say, that warranties shall in all cases be strictly complied with, than to leave it in the breast of a judge or jury to say, that, in one case it shall, and another it shall not.

Here, the requirement of good faith and the need for certainty were seen to be mutually reinforcing, while representations, because external to the agreement, required an inquiry into materiality. 'A representation may be *equitably* and *substantially* answered', Lord Mansfield stated in *De Hahn v Hartley* (1786) 1 Term Rep 343, 'but a warranty must be *strictly* complied with'.

The difficulty, of course, came in deciding whether a statement constituted a warranty or a representation ...

THE CONSEQUENCE OF INDEMNITY

A fundamental implication of the principle of indemnity was articulated by Lord Mansfield in *Stevenson v Snow* (1761) 3 Burr 1237. There, a ship insured 'at and from' London to Halifax was warranted to sail with convoy from Portsmouth, but she was unable to do so because the convoy had already left when she reached Portsmouth from London. Lord Mansfield required a return of the premium for the voyage from Portsmouth to Halifax, stating:

> Equity implies a condition that the insurer shall not receive the price of running a risque, if he runs none. This is contract without any consideration, as to the voyage from Portsmouth to Halifax: for he intended to insure that part of the voyage ... and has not ... If the risque is not run, though it is by the neglect or even the fault of the party insuring, yet the insurer shall not retain the premium ...

A second implication of indemnification, that the amount recovered be commensurate with the amount lost, emerged in cases like *Goss v Withers* (1758) 2 Burr 683, where Lord Mansfield stated, 'The insurer runs the risk of the insured, and undertakes to indemnify: he must therefore bear the loss actually sustained; and can be liable for no more' ...

An insurer could not, because of the nature of indemnification, pay less in damage than the damage suffered (up to the policy amount), but neither could the insured recover more than the value of his loss, even if he had effected double insurance. In *Newby v Reed* (1763) 1 Wm Bl 416, Lord Mansfield affirmed 'that upon a double insurance, though the insured is not entitled to two satisfactions; yet, upon the first action, he may recover the whole sum insured, and may leave the defendant ... to recover ... from the other insurers'. 'It is a principle of natural justice', Park concluded, 'that the several insurers should all ... contribute in their several proportions, to satisfy that loss, against which they have all insured'.

The ultimate implication of indemnity was the reality of the loss being risked, for one could not be held harmless if one could not be harmed. In other words, there must have been an insurance interest at risk. The centrality of this requirement to insurance law becomes even more apparent upon consideration of another form of contract involving risk assessment – the wager.

INSURANCE VERSUS WAGERING

As Lord Mansfield stated in *Da Costa v Jones* (1778) Cowp 729, 'Indifferent wagers upon indifferent matters, without interest to either of the parties, are certainly allowed by the law of this country, in so far as they have not been restrained by particular acts of Parliament'. The piecemeal statutory pattern then in place attempted to regulate professional gambling and other wagering or gaming contracts deemed immoral.

The issue of whether an insurance contract is valid even when the insured lacks an interest in the object of the contract is as old as the English legal records of insurance cases. The pleading in the *Ridolphye* case (1562), after citing that the practice of insuring was within the custom of merchants 'time out of mind', alleged that merchants commonly carried goods in which they had 'no interest or property' to be insured from port to port. In the years prior to Mansfield, courts of law and equity differed on the question of validity. In *Goddart v Garrett* (1692) 2 Vern 269, the Court of Chancery took it 'that the law is settled, that if a man has no interest, and insures, the insurance is void, though it be expressed in the policy, *interested or not interested*', because 'insurances were made for the benefit of trade, and not that persons unconcerned therein, and who were not interested in the ship, should profit thereby'. As Holdsworth pointed out, however, the law courts had taken the opposite view. In *Sadlers Co v Babcock* (1743) 2 Atk 554, Lord Hardwicke observed that 'the common law leant strongly against the policies (interest or no interest) for some time, but being found beneficial to merchants, they winked at it' ...

The issue was brought to a head by a dramatic increase in the practice of insuring upon interest or no interest in the early 18th century. Park observed:

> The security given to the insured was very considerably increased by the erection of two assurance companies ... incorporated by royal charter in the year 1720 ... But this additional security for the insured soon produced many dangerous and alarming consequences, which, if they had not been checked, would have proved very detrimental to ... trade ... For instead of confining the business of insurances to real risks, and considering them merely as an indemnity to the fair dealer against any loss which he might sustain in the course of a trading voyage, which ... was the original design of them; that practice, which only prevailed since the revolution, of insuring ideal risks, under the names of *interest or no interest, or without further proof of interest than the policy, or without benefit of salvage to the underwriters*, was increasing to an alarming degree, and by such rapid strides as to threaten the speedy annihilation of that lucrative and most beneficial branch of trade.

Accordingly, the legislature passed the statute of 19 Geo 2, c 37 (1746) 'to regulate insurance on ships belonging to Great Britain, and on merchandises or effects laden thereon'. All insurance contracts upon 'interest or no interest, or without further proof of interest than the policy, or by way of gaming, or wagering, or without benefit of salvage to the assurer' were – with exceptions for 'private ships of war' and for goods leaving English or American ports in the possession of Spain or Portugal – declared 'null and void to all intents and purposes'. A similar statute was enacted in 1774, which invalidated 'all insurances upon lives, or any other event or events, without interest in the parties'.

These statutes proved useful to Lord Mansfield, although their scope was not immediately realised. Without the statutes, the possibility of a valid wagering policy threatened to undermine the principle of indemnification. As Park noted:

> There was one very remarkable difference between policies upon interest, and such as were not ... namely, that in policies upon interest, you recover for the loss actually sustained, whether it be total or partial: but, upon a wager-policy, you can never recover but for a total loss.

Indemnity became the key to the differentiation between valid insurance and invalid wagering ...

OTHER CONTEXTS: LIFE AND FIRE INSURANCE

Although the underwriting of non-marine insurance, principally upon lives and buildings, antedated Lord Mansfield, its doctrinal structure did not take shape until the system of marine insurance was virtually complete. In Cunningham, T, *The Law of Bills of Exchange, Promissory Notes, Banknotes and Insurances*, 1766, only 16 of the 230 pages on insurance were devoted to life and fire insurance combined. Even in Park's insurance treatise, written after and in response to Lord Mansfield, only 33 of the 600 plus pages were given to life and fire insurance, and most of the cases cited (at least by the sixth edition) were post-Mansfield. Both types of insurance are, however, well represented in Lord Mansfield's trial notes.

Life insurance

Insurance upon a life was defined by both M Postlethwayt and Park as a contract:

> ... by which the underwriter for a certain sum, proportioned to the age, health, profession, and other circumstances of that person, whose life is the object of insurance, engages that the person shall not die within the time limited in the policy: or, if he do, that he will pay a sum of money to him in whose favour the policy was granted.

The right to insure upon a life was granted by Royal Charter in 1706 to 'The Amicable Society for a Perpetual Assurance Office', and the practice grew throughout the 18th century, with more charters granted to accommodate increasing demand.

As with marine insurance, however, life insurance:

> ... became so much a mode of gambling (for people took the liberty of insuring anyone's life, without hesitation, whether connected with him, or not; the

> insurers seldom asked any question about the reasons for which such insurances were made) that it at last became a subject of parliamentary discussion.

The result of that discussion was the statute of 14 Geo 3, c 48 …

Fire insurance

The law of fire insurance was less developed when Lord Mansfield departed the bench than the law of life insurance. Indeed, Lord Mansfield's single important fire insurance decision (that the insured could not collect upon the burning of his house during the Gordon Riots because 'civil commotion' was excluded from the policy) did not have implications for the underlying doctrine. Nonetheless, Park anticipated the analogy to marine insurance that was to come:

> As the purest equity and good faith are essentially requisite … to render the contract effectual when it relates to marine insurances; so it need hardly be observed, that it is no less essential to the validity of the policy against fire: because in the latter, as well as in the former, the insurer, from the nature of the thing, is obliged … to rely upon the integrity and honesty of the insured, as to the representation of the value and quantity of the property, which is the object of the insurance.

CONCLUSION

As in other commercial contexts, the insurance cases exemplify the dynamic tension between the need for certainty and the desire to accomplish individual justice. One response to this tension was to create the appearance of certainty, which served almost as well as certainty itself. Strict proof was required in a life insurance case built upon a warranty, but strict proof of what? Of the insured's having been in reasonably good health.

Nevertheless, the marine insurance cases decided by Lord Mansfield established the central principle of indemnity and attached to it the implications of the requirement of good faith in the formation and coverage of the insurance policy. This structure, in turn, facilitated the coherent development of other types of insurance such as fire and life, permitting an advantageous diffusion of societal risk throughout the growth and industrialisation of the 19th century.

Lord Mansfield's trial notes display the many and varied disputes that made up the raw material out of which a coherent body of insurance principles was constructed. These principles were fully discussed by Park, drawing extensively upon trial court proceedings …

APPENDIX 1.3

Department of Trade and Industry v St Christopher Motorists' Association Ltd [1974] 1 All ER 395

Templeman J: This is a summons by which the Department of Trade and Industry seek a declaration that by undertaking to provide benefits for the members of the proprietary club known as St Christopher Motorists' Association in accordance with the rules of the association, the defendant company, St. Christopher Motorists' Association Ltd, is carrying on insurance business and is an insurance company to which the Insurance Companies Act 1958 applies, and a declaration that by accepting applicants as members of the association the company does effect contracts of insurance. That raises the question of what is insurance? The Department wish to find out whether the company is carrying on insurance business because the department is contemplating exercising powers under the Insurance Companies Amendment Act 1973 and earlier Acts, the object of which is to ensure that when companies take premiums in return for specified obligations, those companies keep in hand, in some form or another, sufficient moneys to be able to provide a margin of solvency so that, in the public interest, the chances of insurance companies falling on hard times, in a manner which has been painfully familiar in the past, will be eliminated or, at any rate, reduced …

So far this looks very much like insurance. A member pays an annual sum which looks like a premium; he pays it because he is frightened of some uncertain disaster which may fall upon him and which will have adverse consequences to him, and the company engages to see that he is indemnified or compensated if the awful even happens. But if the member qualifies for benefits he does not get a sum of cash or money from the company. He is entitled to what are called the benefits of the chauffeur service …

Prima facie that would appear to me to be coming very near what, without any guidance, I would have thought was the essence of insurance.

Mr Chadwick drew my attention to *Chitty on Contracts* … in which the editor says:

> A contract of insurance is one whereby one party (the insurer) undertakes for a consideration to pay money to or for the benefit of the other party (the assured) upon the happening of an event which is uncertain, either as to whether it has or will occur at all, or as to the time of its occurrence, where the object of the assured is to provide against loss or to compensate for prejudice caused by the event, or for his old age (where the event is the reaching of a certain age by the assured) or (where the event is the death of the assured) for the benefit of others upon his death.

That definition seems to cover the present case except for the requirement which is stated by the editor to be necessary, namely, that the insurer must undertake to pay money to the assured. Mr Chadwick, as he was bound to do appearing without opposition, drew my attention to the possible argument that in the present case it could be said that there is no policy of insurance because the company does not undertake to pay money to the member but only to provide services whatever those services may cost. True, the company must pay money to the chauffeur in order to employ him but that is not what the editor means when he says that the insurer must undertake to pay money to or for the benefit of the other party …

We have a contract not for the payment of a sum of money but for some corresponding benefit, the provision of a chauffeur or the provision of a hired car and chauffeur to become due on the happening of an event. The event is a physical accident which debars the member from driving himself or the interposition of the law which positively forbids him to drive himself. Then, the event must have some amount of uncertainty about it. Well, there is a great deal of uncertainty about it. The event must be of a character more or less adverse to the interest of the person affecting the insurance. Well, that is fulfilled here because it is adverse to the interests of the individual member that he should be immobilised either for physical reasons or because the requirements of the law.

That definition, including Channell J's careful pronouncement that there must be the payment of a sum or some corresponding benefit, seems to me to meet the present case and particularly so when, in substance there seems to me to be no difference between the defendant company paying a chauffeur on the one hand, and on the other hand agreeing to pay to the individual member a sum of money which would represent the cost to him of providing himself with a chauffeur in the event of his being disabled from driving himself. I cannot see any difference in logic between the two and, therefore, I see no reason why, in the present case, the arrangement made by the defendant company should not amount to insurance.

It does not follow that the definition given by Channell J in a case based on the facts with which he was concerned and applied by me to the case in which I am now concerned is an exhaustive definition of insurance. There may well be some contracts of guarantee, some contracts of maintenance which might at first sight appear to have some resemblance to the definition laid down by Channell J and which, on analysis, are not found to be true contracts of insurance at all. I wish to guard myself, particularly in view of the fact that, as I have said, Mr Chadwick has had no vocal opposition except mine, against deciding anything other than that the rules and trade of the company in the present case amount to insurance. Mr Chadwick himself suggested some further limitation in that the event which must happen must not be an event within the control of the insurer, but whether that, in fact, be so, I need not now decide. It is sufficient for my purposes that the narrow distinction which might have been argued to differentiate the case of the company from the normal type of insurance, that narrow distinction being the insistence that the company pays for a service instead of the paying member the amount which it will cost him to provide a service, is not one which enables the company to carry on business outside the provision of the Insurance Companies Acts …

APPENDIX 1.4

The Medical Defence Union Ltd v The Department Of Trade [1979] 1 Lloyd's Rep 499

Sir Robert Megarry VC: The major issue in resolving this question is whether the term 'contract of insurance' applies to a contract under which a member of the union against whom some claim has been made can merely require the union to consider whether to conduct the proceedings on his behalf, and whether to provide him with some indemnity, and has no right to require the union to assist him in this way. In other words, the question is whether there is a contract of insurance where the benefits are discretionary and not obligatory, and the member's contractual right is no more than a right to require the union to consider properly any request for assistance of this kind that he makes. There is a subsidiary question whether as regard the conduct of proceedings (as distinct from the grant of indemnity) the benefit is merely discretionary, or whether the member has a right to it ...

The leading authority, I think, is the judgment of Mr Justice Channell in *Prudential Insurance Company v Commissioners of Inland Revenue* [1904] 2 KB 658 ... as read in the light of *Gould v Curtis* [1913] 3 KB 84 ... From these cases it appears that a contract is a contract of insurance if three elements are present ...

The three elements in a contract of insurance may be expressed as follows: and in this I draw largely on what Mr Justice Channell said in the *Prudential* case ... First, the contract must provide that the assured will become entitled to something on the occurrence of some event. This, of course, is the disputed element, and the dispute is about what the 'something' is. For Mr Chadwick it is 'some benefit', whereas for Mr Alexander it is 'money or money's worth'. To this I shall have to return. Secondly, the event must be one which involves some element of uncertainty. Mr Chadwick would add 'outside the control of the insurer'. This may be right, but I do not have to decide the point, and like Mr Justice Templeman in *Department of Trade and Industry v St Christopher Motorists' Association Ltd* [1974] 1 All ER 395 ... I leave it undecided. Thirdly, the assured must have an insurable interest in the subject matter of the contract. On the three elements as a whole, I would also follow Mr Justice Templeman in the *St Christopher* case ... and say that I do not aspire to any exhaustive or comprehensive definition, good for all purposes and in all contexts. I only say that for the purposes of this case it seems to me that a contract which contains these three elements is likely to be a contract which contains these three elements is likely not to be a contract of insurance. I may add that Mr Justice Templeman instanced some contracts of guarantee or of maintenance which might satisfy such a test and yet be no true contracts of insurance ...

I do not know whether a satisfactory definition of 'a contract of insurance' will ever be evolved. Plainly it is a matter of considerable difficulty. It may be that it is a concept which it is better to describe than to attempt to define; and, as I have said, I do not seek to lay down an exhaustive or comprehensive definition. It is enough if I can find a principle which suffices for the decision of the case before me. Plainly, a provision for the payment of money is one of the usual elements in a contract of insurance. The main difficulty lies in formulating what extension of this concept there should be; for plainly there must be some.

If the extension is framed in terms of the equivalent of money, then this will be both limited in extent and consonant with the central concept. If on the other hand the extension is framed in terms of 'some benefit', then that seems to me to be far more than a mere extension: it is a reformulation of the concept in wider terms. In other words, 'money's worth' is merely an extension of 'money', whereas 'benefit' is no mere extension of 'money' but a wider concept which engulfs money. 'Money' would then be subsumed, under 'benefit', with many other things. Obviously, much is a 'benefit' which is not money or money's worth, ranging from matters such as peace and quiet to the pleasure of listening to the arguments of counsel in this case, and much else besides.

I am quite unable to see any justification for replacing 'money' or its equivalent by 'benefit' as a constituent part of the definition of a contract of insurance. I can see nothing in the authorities which gives any real support for so wide and extensive a generalisation, especially as the term 'money or money's worth' seems to be adequate for all normal circumstances. It may be that in view of the *St Christopher* case some further addition should be made, so as to cover explicitly the provision of services, but I shall defer the consideration of this until I turn to the services provided by the union in this case.

In rejecting the term 'benefit', I may say that I think that one is in a different world from the world of insurance when the only contractual right is a right to have a claim fairly considered. No doubt one must not attach too much importance to the basic meaning of words; but terms such as 'inure' and 'assure', like 'ensure', seem to me to convey the sense of making something certain, and not merely of giving a hope or expectation, no matter how well founded. When a person insures, I think that he is contracting for the certainty of payment in specified events, and not merely for the certainty of proper consideration being given to his claim that a discretion to make a payment in those events should be exercised in his favour. The certainty must be direct, and not at one remove ...

Looking at the case as a whole, I have no hesitation in rejecting Mr Chadwick's contention that the union is an insurance company carrying on insurance business within the meaning of the 1974 Act. I do not have to decide whether 'money or money's worth', with or without an addition relating to providing services such as I have discussed, is the right phrase to appear in the first of the three elements of a contract of insurance. I only say that I think that something of that kind is probably on the right lines. What I do decide is that 'benefit' is far too wide an expression, and I reject it. In particular, I reject the contention that the right to have an application properly considered suffices for a contract of insurance. I also consider that the general nature of the business carried on by the union is too far removed from the general nature of the businesses carried on by those who are generally accepted as being insurers for the union's business to be fairly regarded as the effecting and carrying out of contracts of insurance ...

APPENDIX 1.5

Hodgin, R, 'Problems in defining insurance contracts' [1980] LMCLQ 14

Despite the long and influential history of insurance in the United Kingdom, the basic questions of what is an insurance contract and therefore what is an insurance company still pose a difficult problem. The number of cases that the courts have had to answer are few, but it may well be that the growing governmental powers of supervision of insurance companies will generate more cases in the near future, particularly as the requirements of the EEC Directives on various aspects of insurance regulation are introduced into the domestic law of the United Kingdom.

The handful of cases that do exist divide into two groups, those where a shareholder or policy holder seeks to prove that the company is acting *ultra vires* and should cease a particular type of insurance business and those where a government agency is endeavouring to show that the company is transacting insurance business and therefore is governed by their regulatory powers. The cases are dealt with below, however, in chronological order.

In *Prudential Insurance Company v Commissioners of Inland Revenue* [1904] 2 KB 658 the company sought the opinion of the Inland Revenue as to the stamp duty payable under s 12 of the Stamp Act 1891, on a policy they had issued. The policy was entitled, 'Old age endowment with life assurance from entry to 65 years of age'. In consideration for a weekly premium of 6d the company agreed to pay a sum of £95 should the assured reach the age of 65 years and, if he died before that age, the company would pay £30 to the deceased's executors or administrators. Additionally, the policy provided for further payments if it remained in force for five years. The policy was taken out by a father for the benefit of his 13 year old son. The calculation of the sums involved were made after reference to actuarial life tables. This type of endowment had first appeared at the beginning of the 18th century, and, by 1863, had become very common, so much so that, by the turn of the century, they comprised (apart from industrial assurance), the largest part of the business transacted by life assurance companies. The Commissioners were of the opinion that the main part of the policy was not one of life assurance as defined in the Stamp Act 1891, whereby the duty payable would have been one shilling but considered it coming under the heading 'Mortgage, bond, debenture, covenant', and was thus subject to duty of 2s 6d. The court held against the Commissioners. The Stamp Act, while defining a policy of insurance, merely included within its definition the phrase 'contract of insurance' but was then silent as to the meaning of that important phrase. Counsel for the Commissioners fell back on what he considered to be the basic ingredient of an insurance contract, namely the making of some provision against a loss occurring. The company responded that while such a definition applied to other branches of insurance, a policy of life assurance was not a contract of indemnity. Channell J considered that there were three requirements for a valid contract of insurance. First, it should secure for the policy holder some benefit upon the happening of some event. That benefit would usually, but not necessarily, be the payment of money. Secondly, the event insured against should be one that involves some element of uncertainty. That uncertainty could be either as to whether it will happen or as to when it will happen. The third requirement was one that was criticised by the Court of Appeal in a later case (see below), namely, that the uncertain event should be one which is, *prima facie*, adverse to the interest of the assured. Apart from finding these three requirements present in the case, the judge also thought it proper to look at the agreement as a whole. When that was done, he found no real problem in describing it as a contract of insurance. As we will see below, later cases have also adopted this approach of looking at the overall transaction rather than trying to categorise it into pre-existing insurance groupings. Two cases in 1912, one English and one Irish, had similar fact situations both requiring the courts, at the insistence of shareholders or policy holders of the insurance companies involved, to define the meaning of life assurance.

In *Flood v Irish Assurance Co Ltd* [1912] 2 Ch 597 the plaintiff policy holders of the defendant company sought a declaration that the company was carrying on the business of life assurance and an injunction to restrain them, or in the alternative, a return of all premiums. The plaintiffs had been issued with endowment policies for fixed sums payable at fixed dates at fixed weekly premiums which provided that should the assured die before the expiration of the endowment period, the company would return to the persons legally entitled a percentage of the amount of all premiums which should have become due up to the date of death of the assured if they had been duly paid by the assured.

The main cause of concern of the plaintiffs was to show that such policies were life assurances and therefore that the company was legally obliged under the Life Assurance Act 1870 to deposit £20,000 with the authorities. The plaintiffs had become alarmed at the financial state of affairs of the company and consequently refused to pay their premiums and their policies had lapsed. They were willing to make good their lapsed premiums if the £20,000 was deposited. Part of the company memorandum of association stated that 'nothing herein contained shall authorise the company to grant annuities or assurances on human life'.

The court held that the plaintiffs' first claim could not stand on the grounds that if the policies were void as being *ultra vires* the company memorandum, then they would have no grounds on which to maintain their suit. The court did, however, allow the second claim relating to the return of premiums. To do this, Walker LC allowed the argument that the policies were void life policies and arrived at that conclusion by looking at the wording of the prospectus, renewal dates, policies, stamp duty paid and the terms of the policies issued. The defendant company argument that these were endowment policies and different in kind from life policies was thus rejected. They were, as Holmes LJ, explained, 'policies of assurances upon or in any way relating to human life'.

The English case of *Joseph v Law Integrity Insurance Co Ltd* [1912] 2 Ch 581 made reference to the Irish case and the fact were very similar, including reference in the memorandum that nothing therein empowered the company to transact the business of life assurances. No deposit had been lodged in accordance with the Assurance Companies Act 1909, as required of companies transacting life assurance. The plaintiffs were shareholders in the company and they sought a declaration that certain policies issued were *ultra vires* and void, and an injunction to restrain further issues. The Court of Appeal, overturning the lower court's decision, held that the policies were ones of life assurance within the meaning of the Act and not bond investment business as claimed by counsel for the company. Cozens-Hardy MR relied on Bunyon's definition of life assurance which states that:

> ... the contract of life assurance may be further defined to be that in which one party agrees to pay a given sum upon the happening of a particular event contingent upon the duration of human life, in consideration of the immediate payment of a smaller sum or certain equivalent periodical payments by another.

The alternative obligations under the policies in question were either to pay the sum named if the proposer was alive at a certain date or to return the premiums or a percentage of them, if the assured died before that date. Consequently, these policies appeared to correspond with Bunyon's definition of life assurance. Both Farwell LJ and Kennedy LJ agreed with the earlier decision in the *Prudential* case, explaining that although that case was concerned with a different piece of legislation from the present case, the definition could apply to both situations.

The following year the Court of Appeal were asked to define a contract of life assurance for the purposes of the Income Tax Act 1853. In *Gould v Curtis* [1913] 3 KB 84, the assured appealed against his income tax assessment arguing that certain deductions should have been made reflecting the total premiums paid under a lift policy. The policy, entitled a double endowment policy, called for an annual premium which would provide either £100 on the assured's death within 15 years, or £260 if alive at the end of that period. Such policies had been in common use since the middle of the 18th century and the tax authorities had allowed a certain deduction for tax purposes but only as a concession and without any admission of legal right except to such part of the premium as would be applicable to the sum payable at death. The assured argued that the percentage deduction was wrong and full allowance should be made. The court was faced with the problem of defining this type of policy. Cozens-Hardy MR referred to his decision in the *Law Integrity Insurance Co Ltd* case and considered that it was right to refer to the definition of the leading writers on the subject and also to ask what would be commonly understood by the business world and the insurance industry, in particular, when confronted with a policy of this kind. He was also of the opinion that Channel J's approach in the *Prudential Company* case was correct, although he did disagree that a contract of insurance had to cover an event that was in its nature adverse to the assured. Looking at the policy as a whole, it was one of life assurance and therefore the premiums were entitled to full tax allowances.

There was then a long gap until the two recent cases in 1974 and 1978. Both cases were brought by the Department of Trade in an effort to enforce their considerably enlarged supervisory powers under the Insurance Companies Acts of 1958 and 1974.

In *Department of Trade and Industry v St Christopher Motorists' Association Ltd* [1974] 1 All ER 395, the plaintiff sought a declaration that the business conducted by the defendant company was insurance business and therefore subject to certain solvency margins.

The company was incorporated with the objects of protecting the interests of motorists and with providing facilities for members who were unable to drive due to injury or disqualification. This was done by providing the member with a driver and sometimes a car and driver up to a certain number of hours a week. The company very properly took steps by way of reinsurance to meet the demands of government regulations once the issue was raised by the Department, but the action came before the court at the insistence of the Department in order to obtain guidance as to whether this type of contract was to be regarded as a contract of insurance. It should be added that the company made no appearance and the decision was given in the Department's favour after hearing evidence only from the plaintiff. Templeman J explained that after a diligent search of the various pieces of legislation no all-embracing definition of insurance had been found. The answer to the problem must therefore lie in evaluating what the company offered under its contract with its members. This, as explained above, was to provide either a driver or a car and driver in return for an annual premium. There were, however, 40 rules defining the circumstances and explaining restrictions that might apply to a member's request for assistance. This could give rise to the argument that the company was not contractually bound to meet a member's claim but that it could do so purely as a discretionary matter. Having examined the rules, Templeman J was of the opinion that the member was contractually entitled to the benefits, assuming of course that he did not fail one of the company's requirements, for instance, as to the truthfulness of his answers on the original application form.

Another problem, however, was that the benefits were not in monetary payments but in the form of services and the provision of services would compensate him for the loss or disadvantage that had befallen him. This, the court felt, was very near to the essence of insurance. However, the Department argued that because no monetary payment was made to the member himself, than an essential ingredient of a contract of insurance was missing. The Department were unable to support this argument with sufficient authority and the court was able to explain away the authorities quoted as not in point with the present set of facts.

Templeman J was also able to quote Channell J's judgment in the *Prudential* case where he said:

> It must be a contract whereby for some consideration ... you secure to yourself some benefit, usually but not necessarily the payment of money ...

In addition, the court could see no real logical difference between paying a chauffeur and paying to a member a sum of money which would represent the cost to him of providing himself with a chauffeur, which was one of the options available under the contract.

The most recent case is *The Medical Defence Union Ltd v The Department of Trade* [1979] 1 Lloyd's Rep 499, where three of the cases mentioned above were considered. The Medical Defence Union claimed that they were not conducting any class of insurance business and were thus free from any supervisory control created by the Insurance Companies Act 1974. The Medical Defence Union had been established in 1885 and among its objects was the conduct of legal proceedings on behalf of its members, who numbered some 75,000 doctors and 4,500 dentists, with a view to indemnifying them against claims for damages and costs arising from their professional work. The bulk of their work, however, was giving advice on various other problems relating to the profession. The crucial point was that the Medical Defence Union were given an absolute discretion as to whether they would grant assistance to a member. The question therefore faced by the court was whether a contract of insurance could exist where the benefits obtainable were purely discretionary. Sir Robert Megarry VC decided that an insurance contract did not exist. The court dealt with the problem in some detail as the matter was seen to be of importance for other bodies carrying on similar types of business.

The court made the point that had been made in the earlier cases that no definition of insurance business had been given in the legislation ... What was agreed to by both parties was that the term, 'insurance business', fell to be construed according to the general law. The judge then relied on the approach displayed in the *Prudential* case, with the reservations on part of the judgment as expressed in *Gould v Curtis*. The three basic requirements of a valid contract of insurance, as set out by Channell J, were correct, and what called for special consideration in the present case was whether a member of the Medical Defence Union was 'entitled to' some form of benefit on the occurrence of a particular event, and whether the benefit should be money or money's worth or something else. The Medical Defence Union argument was that they were not obliged to provide any form of benefit; it was merely at their discretion whether or not they would do so. The Department argued that even that facility should be regarded as a benefit. The court did not accept this argument, to do so would mean replacing a discretionary word like 'may' with a mandatory one like 'shall' at the beginning of some of the Union's articles. Consequently, all that a member could expect in return for his payment was to have his request fairly considered by the council or one of its committees. Even if this could be described as a 'benefit', would such a 'benefit' need to be 'money or money's worth'? Here, the court examined the previous cases and textbooks on this point. After due consideration, it was felt that the wider approach adopted in the *St Christopher* case, based, as we have seen, on Channell's judgment, was more acceptable, and decisions to the contrary were too narrow in their interpretation. At the same time, the court saw difficulties in some aspects of the views expressed in both the *Prudential* and *St Christopher* decisions. While payment of money was the normal element of a contract of insurance, an extension of that concept was clearly recognised in the cases but it was not easy to define exactly the true limitations of such an extension. Sir Robert Megarry VC felt quite unable to see any justification for replacing 'money' or its equivalent by 'benefit' as a constituent part of the definition of a contract of insurance.

Looking at the contract generally, there were other aspects that tended to show a gulf between the commonly accepted attributes of a contract of insurance and the present contract. The most obvious was the fact that the obligation on the Medical Defence Union was merely to consider the member's claim, and, as the judge remarked, 'one may speculate on the prospects of commercial success' of an insurance company that offered no contractual right to payment. Secondly, there appeared to be no real provision for increasing premiums or refusing membership to those who had a poor claims record. Thirdly, the bulk of the Medical Defence Union's work was merely advisory and if this was to amount to a contract of insurance, then the definition would go far beyond any previous case on the same point and the effect would be to bring within the supervisory control of the Department of Trade many professional and other bodies who would never have contemplated being so controlled.

CONCLUSIONS

The wording of numerous statutes gave rise to the problems set out above. In none of these pieces of legislation was a contract of insurance defined and each judgment, expressly depending as it must on the facts before the court, fails to give a comprehensive definition. Such failure is intentional. It is the realities of the companies business contract that needs to be investigated and abstract declarations of what constitutes a contract of insurance should be avoided. As Templeman J said in the *St Christopher* case:

> ... the probability is that it is undesirable that there should be (an all-embracing definition) because definitions tend sometimes to obscure and occasionally to exclude that which ought to be included.

APPENDIX 1.6

The Insurance Companies (Third Insurance Directives) Regulations 1994 (SI 1994/1696)

SCHEDULE 5

[Schedule 2E to 1982 Act]

Information for policy holders of United Kingdom insurers and European Union companies

Information before contract of long term insurance

1 (1) Subject to sub-para (2) below, this paragraph applies to a contract entered into by a United Kingdom or European Union company or a member of Lloyd's the effecting of which constitutes:

(a) the carrying on in the United Kingdom of long term business which is not reinsurance business; or

(b) the provision there of long term insurance.

(2) This paragraph does not apply to a contract entered into by an authorised person the effecting of which constitutes the carrying on in the United Kingdom of investment business; and in this sub-paragraph expressions which are also used in the Financial Services Act 1986 have the same meanings as in that Act.

(3) Before entering into a contract to which this paragraph applies, the company or member ('the insurer') shall furnish the other party to the contract in writing with the information required by sub-para (4) below and:

(a) in the case of a company, the information required by sub-para (5) below; and

(b) in the case of a member, the information required by sub-para (6) below.

(4) The information required by this sub-paragraph is:

(a) a definition of each benefit and option;

(b) the term of the contract and the means by which it may be terminated;

(c) the method of paying premiums and the duration of the payments;

(d) the method of calculating bonuses and the distribution of bonuses;

(e) an indication of surrender and paid-up values and the extent to which such values are guaranteed;

(f) an indication of the premiums for each benefit, whether a main or supplementary benefit;

(g) in the case of a contract for a unit-linked policy, a definition of the units to which benefits are linked and an indication of the nature of the underlying assets;

(h) information as to the following, namely:

(i) the arrangements with respect to the period within which the policy holder may cancel the contract;

(ii) the tax arrangements applicable to the policy to be effected by the contract;

(iii) the arrangements for handling any complaints concerning the contract, whether by the other party or any other person who is a life assured or beneficiary; and

(iv) any compensation or guarantee arrangements which will be available if the insurer is unable to meet its liabilities under the contract; and

(v) whether the parties to the contract are entitled to choose the law applicable to the contract and:

(i) if so, the law which the insurer proposes to choose; and

(ii) if not, the law which will be so applicable.

(5) The information required by this sub-paragraph is:

(a) the name and legal form of the company;

(b) the company's home State and, where appropriate, the Member State of the branch through which the contract is to be entered into; and

(c) the address of the company's head office and, where appropriate, the address of the branch through which the contract is to be entered into.

(6) The information required by this sub-paragraph is:

(a) the name or number of the syndicate which is to enter into the contract and a statement that it is a syndicate of members of Lloyd's;

(b) a statement that the syndicate's home State is the United Kingdom and, where appropriate, the Member State of the branch through which the contract is to be entered into; and

(c) the address of the syndicate in the United Kingdom and, where appropriate, the address of the branch through which the contract is to be entered into.

(7) Any information required by sub-para (4), (5) or (6) above shall be furnished in English except that, where the other party to the contract so requests, it may instead be furnished in an official language of a Member State other than the United Kingdom.

2 (1) This paragraph applies where a United Kingdom or European Union company or a number of Lloyd's has, on or after 1 July 1994, entered into a contract the effecting of which constitutes:

(a) the carrying on in the United Kingdom of long term business which is not reinsurance business; or

(b) the provision there of long term insurance.

(2) If during the term of the contract there is:

(a) any change in the information mentioned in paras (a) to (g) of sub-para (4) of para 1 above; or

(b) in the case of a company, any change in the information mentioned in sub-para (5) of that paragraph; or

(c) in the case of a member, any change in the information mentioned in sub-para (6) of that paragraph,

the company or member ('the insurer') shall inform the other party to the contract in writing of the effect of the change.

(3) If the contract provides for the payment of bonuses, the insurer shall, at least once in every calendar year except the first, inform the other party to the contract in writing of the amount of any bonus:

(a) which has become payable under the contract; and

(b) of which that party has not been previously informed under this sub-paragraph.

(4) There is a sufficient compliance with sub-para (3) above if the insurer furnishes the other party to the contract with such information as will enable him to determine the amount of any such bonus as is mentioned in that sub-paragraph, or if the insurer informs that party of:

(a) the total value of the benefits (including bonuses) which have accrued under the contract; and

(b) the rates of bonus which have been declared since that party was previously informed under this sub-paragraph.

(5) In this paragraph 'bonus' does not include a bonus the amount of which is specified in the contract.

Information before contract of general insurance

3 (1) This paragraph applies to a contract entered into by a United Kingdom or European Union company or a member of Lloyd's if:

(a) the effecting of the contract constitutes:

(i) the carrying on in the United Kingdom of general business which is not reinsurance business; or

(ii) the provision there of general insurance; and

(b) the risk covered by the contract is situated in the United Kingdom.

(2) Before entering into a contract to which this paragraph applies, the company or member ('the insurer') shall, if the other party (or one of the other parties) to the contract is an individual, inform that party in writing:

(a) of any arrangements which exist for handling complaints concerning the contract including, where appropriate, the name and address of any body which deals with complaints from any party to the contract;

(b) that the existence of a complaints body does not affect any right of action which any party to the contract may have against the insurer; and

(c) as to whether the parties to the contract are entitled to choose the law applicable to the contract and:

(i) if so, of the law which the insurer proposes to choose; and

(ii) if not, of the law which will be so applicable.

(3) If the information required by sub-para (2) above is furnished otherwise than in writing before the time when the contract is entered into, there is a sufficient compliance with that sub-paragraph if it is also furnished in writing as soon as practicable after that time.

4 (1) Subject to sub-para (2) below, this paragraph applies to a contract to which para 3 above applies.

(2) This paragraph does not apply to a contract entered into by a United Kingdom company or a member of Lloyd's unless the effecting of the contract constitutes the provision of general insurance in the United Kingdom.

(3) Before entering into a contract to which this paragraph applies, the United Kingdom or European Union company or the member of Lloyd's ('the insurer') shall, unless the contract is for the coverage of large risks only, inform the other party to the contract in writing of the Member State in which is situated the establishment which will cover the risks; and any document issued to that party by the insurer shall also contain that information.

(4) If the information required by sub-para (3) above is furnished otherwise than in writing before the time when the contract is entered into, there is a sufficient compliance with that sub-paragraph if it is also furnished in writing as soon as practicable after that time.

(5) Any relevant document issued by the insurer in relation to a contract to which this paragraph applies shall state:

(a) the address of the establishment through which the risk is to be covered; and

(b) where the contract relates to relevant motor vehicle risks and the effecting of the contract constitutes the provision of insurance in the United Kingdom, the name and address of the claims representative.

(6) In this paragraph 'relevant document', in relation to a contract to which this paragraph applies, means any proposal, policy or other document which, or statements contained in which, will or may bind the other party to the contract.

APPENDIX 1.7

Financial Services and Markets Act 2000

PART XV

THE FINANCIAL SERVICES COMPENSATION SCHEME

The scheme manager

212 The scheme manager

(1) The Authority must establish a body corporate ('the scheme manager') to exercise the functions conferred on the scheme manager by or under this Part.

(2) The Authority must take such steps as are necessary to ensure that the scheme manager is, at all times, capable of exercising those functions.

(3) The constitution of the scheme manager must provide for it to have–

(a) a chairman; and

(b) a board (which must include the chairman) whose members are the scheme manager's directors.

(4) The chairman and other members of the board must be persons appointed, and liable to removal from office, by the Authority (acting, in the case of the chairman) with the approval of the Treasury.

(5) But the terms of their appointment (and in particular those governing removal from office) must be such as to secure their independence from the Authority in the operation of the compensation scheme.

(6) The scheme manager is not to be regarded as exercising functions on behalf of the Crown.

(7) The scheme manager's board members, officers and staff are not to be regarded as Crown servants.

The scheme

213 The compensation scheme

(1) The Authority must by rules establish a scheme for compensating persons in cases where relevant persons are unable, or are likely to be unable, to satisfy claims against them.

(2) The rules are to be known as the Financial Services Compensation Scheme (but are referred to in this Act as 'the compensation scheme').

(3) The compensation scheme must, in particular, provide for the scheme manager–

(a) to assess and pay compensation, in accordance with the scheme, to claimants in respect of claims made in connection with regulated activities carried on (whether or not with permission) by relevant persons; and

(b) to have power to impose levies on authorised persons, or any class of authorised person, for the purpose of meeting its expenses (including in particular expenses incurred, or expected to be incurred, in paying compensation, borrowing or insuring risks).

(4) The compensation scheme may provide for the scheme manager to have power to impose levies on authorised persons, or any class of authorised person, for the purpose of covering the cost (whenever incurred) of establishing the scheme.

(5) In making any provision of the scheme by virtue of subsection (3)(b), the Authority must take account of the desirability of ensuring that the amount of the levies imposed on a particular class of authorised person reflects, so far as practicable, the amount of the claims made, or likely to be made, in respect of that class of person.

(6) An amount payable to the scheme manager as a result of any provision of the scheme made by virtue of subsection (3)(b) or (4) may be recovered as a debt due to the scheme manager.

(7) Sections 214–217 make further provision about the scheme but are not to be taken as limiting the power conferred on the Authority by subsection (1).

(8) In those sections 'specified' means specified in the scheme.

(9) In this Part (except in sections 219, 220 or 224) 'relevant person' means a person who was–

(a) an authorised person at the time the act or omission giving rise to the claim against him took place; or

(b) an appointed representative at that time.

(10) But a person who, at that time–

(a) qualified for authorisation under Schedule 3; and

(b) fell within a prescribed category,

is to be regarded as a relevant person in relation to any activities for which he had permission as a result of any provision of, or made under, that Schedule unless he had elected to participate in the scheme in relation to those activities at that time.

Provisions of the scheme

113 General

(1) The compensation scheme may, in particular, make provision–

(a) as to the circumstances in which a relevant person is to be taken (for the purposes of the scheme) to be unable, or likely to be unable, to satisfy claims made against him;

(b) for the establishment of different funds for meeting different kinds of claim;

(c) for the imposition of different levies in different cases;

(d) limiting the levy payable by a person in respect of a specified period;

(e) for repayment of the whole or part of a levy in specified circumstances;

(f) for a claim to be entertained only if it is made by a specified kind of claimant;

(g) for a claim to be entertained only if it falls within a specified kind of claim;

(h) as to the procedure to be followed in making a claim;

(i) for the making of interim payments before a claim is finally determined;

(j) limiting the amount payable on a claim to a specified maximum amount or a maximum amount calculated in a specified manner;

(k) for payment to be made, in specified circumstances, to a person other than the claimant.

(2) Different provision may be made with respect to different kinds of claim.

(3) The scheme may provide for the determination and regulation of matters relating to the scheme by the scheme manager.

(4) The scheme, or particular provisions of the scheme, may be made so as to apply only in relation to–

(a) activities carried on;

(b) claimants;

(c) matters arising; or

(d) events occurring,

in specified territories, areas or localities.

(5) The scheme may provide for a person who–

(a) qualifies for authorisation under Schedule 3; and

(b) falls within a prescribed category, to elect to participate in the scheme in relation to some or all of the activities for which he has permission as a result of any provision of, or made under, that Schedule.

(6) The scheme may provide for the scheme manager to have power–

(a) in specified circumstances;

(b) but only if the scheme manager is satisfied that the claimant is entitled to receive a payment in respect of his claim–

(i) under a scheme which is compatible to the compensation scheme; or

(ii) as the result of a guarantee given by a government or other authority, to make a full payment of compensation to the claimant and recover the whole or part of the amount of that payment from the other scheme or under that guarantee.

215 Rights of the scheme in relevant person's insolvency

(1) The compensation scheme may, in particular, make provision–

(a) as to the effect of a payment of compensation under the scheme in relation to rights or obligations arising out of the claim against a relevant person in respect of which the payment was made;

(b) for conferring on the scheme manager a right of recovery against that person.

(2) Such a right of recovery conferred by the scheme does not, in the event of the relevant person's insolvency, exceed such right (if any) as the claimant would have had in that event.

(3) If a person other than the scheme manager presents a petition under section 9 of the 1986 Act or Article 22 of the 1989 Order in relation to a company or partnership which is a relevant person, the scheme manager has the same rights as are conferred on the Authority by section 362.

(4) If a person other than the scheme manager presents a petition for the winding up of a body which is a relevant person, the scheme manager has the same rights as are conferred on the Authority by section 371.

(5) If a person other than the scheme manager presents a bankruptcy petition to the court relation to an individual who, or an entity which, is a relevant person, the scheme manager has the same rights as are conferred on the Authority by section 374.

(6) Insolvency rules may be made for the purpose of integrating any procedure for which provision is made as a result of subsection (1) into the general procedure on the administration of a company or partnership or on a winding-up, bankruptcy or sequestration.

(7) 'Bankruptcy petition' means a petition to the court–

(a) under section 264 of the 1986 Act or Article 238 of the 1989 Order for a bankruptcy order to be made against an individual;

(b) under section 5 of the 1985 Act for the sequestration of the estate of an individual;

or

(c) under section 6 of the 1985 Act for the sequestration of the estate belonging to or held for jointly by the members of an entity mentioned in subsection (1) of that section.

(8) 'Insolvency rules' are–

(a) for England and Wales, rules made under sections 411 and 412 of the 1986 Act;

(b) for Scotland, rules made by order by the Treasury, after consultation with the Scottish Ministers, for the purposes of this section; and

(c) for Northern Ireland, rules made under Article 359 of the 1989 Order and section 55 of the Judicature (Northern Ireland) Act 1978.

(9) 'The 1985 Act', 'the 1986 Act', 'the 1989 Order' and 'court' have the same meaning as in Part XXIV.

216 Continuity of long-term insurance policies

(1) The compensation scheme may, in particular, include provision requiring the scheme manager to make arrangements for securing continuity of insurance for policyholders, or policyholders of a specified class, of relevant long-term insurers.

(2) 'Relevant long-term insurers' means relevant persons who–

(a) have permission to effect or carry out contracts of long-term insurance; and

(b) are unable, or likely to be unable, to satisfy claims made against them.

(3) The scheme may provide for the scheme manager to take such measures as appear to him to be appropriate–

(a) for securing or facilitating the transfer of a relevant long-term insurer's business so far as it consists of the carrying out of contracts of long-term insurance, or of any part of that business, to another authorised person;

(b) for securing the issue by another authorised person to the policyholders concerned of policies in substitution for their existing policies.

(4) The scheme may also provide for the scheme manager to make payments to the policyholders concerned–

(a) during any period while he is seeking to make arrangements mentioned in subsection (1);

(b) if it appears to him that it is not reasonably practicable to make such arrangements.

(5) A provision of the scheme made by virtue of section 213(3)(b) may include power to impose levies for the purpose of meeting expenses of the scheme manager incurred in–

(a) taking measures as a result of any provision of the scheme made by virtue of subsection (3);

(b) making payments as a result of any such provision made by virtue of subsection (4).

Insurers in financial difficulties

(1) The compensation scheme may, in particular, include provision for the scheme manager to have power to take measures for safeguarding policyholders, or policyholders of a specified class, of relevant insurers.

(2) 'Relevant insurers' means relevant persons who–

(a) have permission to effect or carry out contracts of insurance; and

(b) are in financial difficulties.

(3) The measures may include such measures as the scheme manager considers appropriate for–

(a) securing or facilitating the transfer of a relevant insurer's business so far as it consists of the carrying out of contracts of insurance, or of any part of that business, to another authorised person;

(b) giving assistance to the relevant insurer to enable it to continue to effect or carry out contracts of insurance.

(4) The scheme may provide–

(a) that if measures of a kind mentioned in subsection (3)(a) are to be taken, they should be on terms appearing to the scheme manager to be appropriate, including terms reducing, or deferring payment of, any of the things to which any of those who are eligible policyholders in relation to the relevant insurer are entitled in their capacity as such;

(b) that if measures of a kind mentioned in subsection (3)(b) are to be taken, they should be conditional on the reduction of, or the deferment of the payment of, the things to which any of those who are eligible policyholders in relation to the relevant insurer are entitled in their capacity as such;

(c) for ensuring that measures of a kind mentioned in subsection (3)(b) do not benefit to any material extent persons who were members of a relevant insurer when it began to be in financial difficulties or who had any responsibility for, or who may have profited from, the circumstances giving rise to its financial difficulties, except in specified circumstances;

(d) for requiring the scheme manager to be satisfied that any measures he proposes to take are likely to cost less than it would cost to pay compensation under the scheme if the relevant insurer became unable, or likely to be unable, to satisfy claims made against him.

(5) The scheme may provide for the Authority to have power–

(a) to give such assistance to the scheme manager as it considers appropriate for assisting the scheme manager to determine what measures are practicable or desirable in the case of a particular relevant insurer;

(b) to impose constraints on the taking of measures by the scheme manager in the case of a particular relevant insurer;

(c) to require the scheme manager to provide it with information about any particular measures which the scheme manager is proposing to take.

(6) The scheme may include provision for the scheme manager to have power–

(a) to make interim payments in respect of eligible policyholders of a relevant insurer;

(b) to indemnify any person making payments to eligible policyholders of a relevant insurer.

(7) A provision of the scheme made by virtue of section 213(3)(b) may include power to impose levies for the purpose of meeting expenses of the scheme manager incurred in–

(a) taking measures as a result of any provision of the scheme made by virtue subsection (1);

(b) making payments or giving indemnities as a result of any such provision made by virtue of subsection (6).

(8) 'Financial difficulties' and 'eligible policyholders' have such meanings as may be specified.

Annual report

218 Annual report

(1) At least once a year, the scheme manager must make a report to the Authority on the discharge of its functions.

(2) The report must–

(a) include a statement setting out the value of each of the funds established by the compensation scheme; and

(b) comply with any requirements specified in rules made by the Authority.

(3) The scheme manager must publish each report in the way it considers appropriate.

Information and documents

219 Scheme manager's power to require information

(1) The scheme manager may, by notice in writing given to the relevant person in respect of whom a claim is made under the scheme or to a person otherwise involved, require that person–

(a) to provide specified information or information of a specified description; or

(b) to produce specified documents or documents of a specified description.

(2) The information or documents must be provided or produced–

(a) before the end of such reasonable period as may be specified; and

(b) in the case of information, in such manner or form as may be specified.

(3) This section applies only to information and documents the provision or production of which the scheme manager considers–

(a) to be necessary for the fair determination of the claim; or

(b) to be necessary (or likely to be necessary) for the fair determination of other claims made (or which it expects may be made) in respect of the relevant person concerned.

(4) If a document is produced in response to a requirement imposed under this section, a scheme manager may–

(a) take copies or extracts from the document; or

(b) require the person producing the document to provide an explanation of the document.

(5) If a person who is required under this section to produce a document fails to do so, the scheme manager may require the person to state, to the best of his knowledge and belief, where the document is.

(6) If the relevant person is insolvent, no requirement may be imposed under this section on a person to whom sections 220 or 224 applies.

(7) If a person claims a lien on a document, its production under this Part does not affect the lien.

(8) 'Relevant person' has the same meaning as in section 224.

(9) 'Specified' means specified in the notice given under subsection (1).

(10) A person is involved in a claim made under the scheme if he was knowingly involved in the act or omission giving rise to the claim.

220 Scheme manager's power to inspect information held by liquidator etc

(1) For the purpose of assisting the scheme manager to discharge its functions in relation to a claim made in respect of an insolvent relevant person, a person to whom this section applies must permit a person authorised by the scheme manager to inspect relevant documents.

(2) A person inspecting a document under this section may take copies of, or extracts from, the document.

(3) This section applies to–

(a) the administrative receiver, administrator, liquidator or trustee in bankruptcy of an insolvent relevant person;

(b) the permanent trustee, within the meaning of the Bankruptcy (Scotland) Act 1985 on the estate of an insolvent relevant person.

(4) This section does not apply to a liquidator, administrator or trustee in bankruptcy who is–

(a) the Official Receiver;

(b) the Official Receiver for Northern Ireland; or

(c) the Accountant in Bankruptcy.

(5) 'Relevant person' has the same meaning as in section 224.

221 Powers of court where information required

(1) If a person ('the defaulter')–

(a) fails to comply with a requirement imposed under section 219; or

(b) fails to permit documents to be inspected under section 220, the scheme manager may certify that fact in writing to the court and the court may enquire into the case.

(2) If the court is satisfied that the defaulter failed without reasonable excuse to comply with the requirement (or to permit the documents to be inspected), it may deal with the defaulter (and, in the case of a body corporate, any director or officer) as if he were in contempt.

(3) 'Court' means–

(a) the High Court;

(b) in Scotland, the Court of Session.

Miscellaneous

222 Statutory immunity

(1) Neither the scheme manager nor any person who is, or is acting as, its board member officer or member of staff is to be liable in damages for anything done or omitted in the discharge, or purported discharge, of the scheme manager's functions.

(2) Subsection (1) does not apply–

(a) if the act or omission is shown to have been in bad faith; or

(b) so as to prevent an award of damages made in respect of an act or omission on the ground that the act or omission was unlawful as a result of section 6(1) of the Human Rights Act 1998.

223 Management expenses

(1) The amount which the scheme manager may recover, from the sums levied under the scheme, as management expenses attributable to a particular period may not exceed such amount as may be fixed by the scheme as the limit applicable to that period.

(2) In calculating the amount of any levy to be imposed by the scheme manager, no amount may be included to reflect management expenses unless the limit mentioned in subsection (I) has been fixed by the scheme.

(3) 'Management expenses' means expenses incurred, or expected to be incurred, by the scheme manager in connection with its functions under this Act other than those incurred–

(a) in paying compensation;

(b) as a result of any provision of the scheme made by virtue of section 216(3) or (4) or 217(1) or (6).

224 Scheme manager's power to inspect documents held by Official Receiver etc

(1) If, as a result of the insolvency or bankruptcy of a relevant person, any documents have come into the possession of a person to whom this section applies, he must permit any person authorised by the scheme manager to inspect the documents for the purpose of establishing–

(a) the identity of persons to whom the scheme manager may be liable to make a payment in accordance with the compensation scheme; or

(b) the amount of any payment which the scheme manager may be liable to make.

(2) A person inspecting a document under this section may take copies or extracts from the document.

(3) In this section 'relevant person' means a person who was–

(a) an authorised person at the time the act or omission which may give rise to the liability mentioned in subsection (1)(a) took place; or

(b) an appointed representative at that time.

(4) But a person who, at that time–

(a) qualified for authorisation under Schedule 3; and

(b) fell within a prescribed category,

is not to be regarded as a relevant person for the purposes of this section in relation to any activities for which he had permission as a result of any provision of, or made under, that Schedule unless he had elected to participate in the scheme in relation to those activities at that time.

(5) This section applies to–

  (a) the Official Receiver;

  (b) the Official Receiver for Northern Ireland; and

  (c) the Accountant in Bankruptcy.

INSURABLE INTEREST

INTRODUCTION

Insurance is intended to provide the insured with an indemnity against loss although life assurance does not fit easily with the description. The insurance moneys should not provide a profit for the insured (see Chapter 9). If an insured was allowed to insure in situations where he stood to make a profit from the insurance, this would have the appearance of gambling and there might also be a temptation to bring about the loss. Various statutes and court decisions over the last 200 years have struggled to deal with these two problems.

In English law the result has been to create a narrow definition of what can be legally insured. So narrow is the definition that it can be argued that the results do not suit modern conditions, in either domestic or commercial settings, and it may well be that insurers do not necessarily abide by these outdated rules. That is not to say, however, that when faced with a claim which the insurer considers to be unmeritorious on the facts that it would not choose to fall back on the argument that there was no insurable interest.

DEFINITION

Section 5 of the Marine Insurance Act 1906 (which, it should be remembered throughout this book, is not restricted merely to marine insurance, many of its sections apply to all types of insurance policies) provides a definition of insurable interest, which, if one omits the specific references to marine matters, reads (s 5(2)):

> In particular a person is interested ... where he stands in any legal or equitable relation ... to any insurable property at risk ... in consequence of which he may benefit by the safety ... of insurable property, or may be prejudiced by its loss, or damage thereto ... or may incur liability in respect thereof.

Ownership of property or goods is clearly sufficient to found an insurable interest whether it be a house or a factory, personal possessions or commercial goods. Ownership is not, however, essential. A bailee may be liable for damage or loss to another's goods and thus has an interest in insuring his 'liability in respect thereof'.

Negligently inflicted harm, on the roads or in the work place, would lead to incurring legal liability and this exposure to liability thus creates an insurable interest for the potential defendant.

An early leading case illustrating the application of the definition of an insurable interest is *Lucena v Craufurd* (1806) 2 Bos & PNR 269 (Appendix 2.1). England and France were at war and Holland was neutral, but under threat from France. Legislation provided that Crown commissioners could take possession of, and manage the affairs of, ships owned by Dutch nationals, but only when such ships were brought into a British port. Ships were taken into possession by British naval vessels but losses were suffered before they reached a British port. The commissioners had insured the vessels when they were at sea. It was held that there was no insurable interest vested in the commissioners at that time. The fact that there was an expectation that ultimately they would reach the safety of a British port was not sufficient to create an insurable interest while they were still at sea.

LIFE ASSURANCE

While marine policies are governed by ss 4–16 of the Marine Insurance Act 1906, life assurance is governed by the Life Assurance Act 1774 (Appendix 2.2). The preamble to that Act helps to explain its origins:

> Whereas it hath been found by experience that the making insurances on lives or other events wherein the assured shall have no interest has introduced a mischievous kind of gaming.

The first thing to comment upon is that the phrase, 'or other events', appears to suggest that areas other than life assurance are covered by the Act. In recent times, however, the Act has been interpreted as applying only to life assurance, as one might have expected it to be from the title.

In *Mark Rowlands Ltd v Berni Inns* [1985] 3 All ER 473 (Appendix 2.3), Kerr LJ, when dealing with building insurance, stated that the words, 'or other event or events', if applied literally in non-life policies would 'create havoc in much of our insurance law' and he refused to apply the Act to such insurance.

In *Siu Yin Kwan v Eastern Insurance Co Ltd* [1994] 1 All ER 213 (Appendix 2.4), when dealing with a claim on a liability policy, the Privy Council refused to apply the Act, Lord Lloyd arguing that 'by no stretch of the imagination could indemnity insurance be described as a mischievous kind of gaming'.

Even where a policy is not subject to the 1906 or 1774 legislation, it will still need to avoid the strictures of the Gaming Act 1845 (Appendix 2.5) in order to be viewed as an enforceable insurance contract.

A review of a number of cases helps to illustrate the narrowness of the English rules in relation to life assurance. The cases indicate that, while a person has an insurable interest on his own life and a spouse has such interest in the other spouse, other family relationships are not considered sufficient.

Family relationships

In *Halford v Kymer* (1830) 10 B & C 724 (Appendix 2.6), a father attempted to insure the life of his son, naming himself as beneficiary, should the son die within two years. The court rejected the father's claim that he had a pecuniary interest in that he expected the son to reimburse him the cost of his education and maintenance at some date in the future. Such policies do, today, in fact, exist and do not appear to lead to litigation which, as suggested above, indicates that insurers are prepared to ignore the narrowness of the interest rules.

However, early attempts to avoid the 1774 Act met with no success in situations where the insurer chose to rely on the Act in his refusal to pay. In *Wainwright v Bland* (1835) 1 Mood & R 481 (Appendix 2.7), the assured appeared to have taken out life policies in her own name. It was clear that she could not have afforded to pay the premiums from her own modest income. It was assumed that the plaintiff had in reality provided the sums insured in the expectation that he would take the insurance money on her death. A later court found that the policy was void for misrepresentation and concealment of existing policies, but it is clear that the above facts, if found to be true, would have indicated no insurable interest.

On the other hand, in *Worthington v Curtis* (1875) 1 Ch D 419 (Appendix 2.8), a father took out a policy in the name and on the life of his son. He clearly had no insurable interest. The son died and the insurer, honourably, paid the money to the father's benefit. Creditors of the son objected, arguing that the money should have gone to the estate against which they could have claimed. This argument was rejected. The 1774 Act provides a defence for an insurer not to pay when there is no insurable interest. If they choose to pay then the payment must remain with the person to whom it was voluntarily paid.

It is possible under s 11 of the Married Women's Property Act 1882 for a married person to insure their own life expressly intending to benefit the survivor or children. The advantage of this is that the insurance money does not then form part of the deceased's estate and this escapes, for example, the grasp of any creditors of the deceased. However, the intention of such an arrangement was surely not to defraud any such creditors.

Creditor-debtor

A case of considerable importance is that of *Dalby v India and London Life Assurance Co* (1854) 15 CB 365 (see Appendix 2.9). It showed that a creditor can insure the life of her debtor, at least up to the limit of the debt and it also answers the question, in relation to life policies, as to when the insurable interest must be shown to exist. Two possibilities arise: either it is the date at which the policy is taken out; or at the date of the death. For life assurance, it is the former date. In the case of indemnity policies, for instance, motor insurance, it is the latter date, for if there is no loss then no indemnity is required. In *Dalby*, an insurer had insured the life of X and then reinsured that exposure with the defendant insurer. The original insurance policy was terminated, but the reinsurance was continued and was in existence at the time of X's death. The reinsurer was held liable.

The implication of the rules as pointed out by McGee, *The Law and Practice of Life Assurance Contracts*, 1995, London: Sweet & Maxwell are that:

> ... divorce has no effect on the validity of a life of another policy affected by one spouse on the life of the other during the marriage, and the ex-spouse is perfectly entitled to maintain the policy by continuing to pay the premiums ...

In a more straightforward debtor-creditor relationship protected by a life policy, it would also mean that, even though the debt was repaid, the creditor could choose to continue to pay the premiums and on the eventual death would reap a financial benefit.

The facts in *Hebdon v West* (1863) 3 B & S 579 (Appendix 2.10) raised two issues relating to insurable interest. The plaintiff worked for a bank at a salary of £600 a year and was guaranteed employment at that salary for seven years. He had also received a loan from the bank of £4,700 and the managing partner had told him that the loan would not need to be repaid during the lifetime of the partner. The plaintiff, with the partner's permission, insured the partner's life for £5,000 with insurer A and later for £2,500 with insurer B. After six years, the partner died and the employment ceased. He was paid the £5,000 and then sought to claim on the second policy. The claim was successfully rejected. It was held that the £5,000 was an enforceable policy as it protected the agreement as to the security of his employment. However, the promise not to enforce the loan repayment was a bare promise, unsupported by consideration and therefore could not form the basis of insurable interest. Insurer A did not make any objection that the £5,000 exceeded the total salary by £800, and as insurable interest dates from when the life is assured they could not object to the fact that he had received six years' salary before the death.

Key-man

Again, in a key-man policy, a policy where, usually, an employer insures the life of an important employee, whose death while in employment might have serious repercussions on the profitability of a contract in which he was involved, the policy could be continued even though the employee is no longer employed by that employer. The cases do not deal with the question of how a key-man policy is calculated. This, presumably, is a matter for negotiation and once the figure is agreed the insurer abides by its decision. For instance, how do you set about calculating the value of a leading footballer? It is not unknown for the life of a judge to be insured by the litigants in a situation where he has been assigned to a trial which is expected to last a long time (a fraud trial perhaps). If he dies part way through a trial, a new trial would be required and thus considerable legal fees would have been wasted by the litigants.

Assignment

Assignment of insurance policies has an important role in commercial life. A common example is where a mortgagee requires the mortgagor to effect a life policy to cover the extent of the loan should the mortgagor die before the loan is repaid. The policy is then assigned to the mortgagee. Assignment can be made in equity, or under s 136 of the Law of Property Act 1925, or, more commonly, under the Policies of Assurance Act 1867, which requires that notice of such assignment be given in writing to the insurer. Under the 1867 Act, the assignment may be made either by an endorsement on the policy or by a separate document using the wording set out in the Schedule to the Act.

The desire of the courts to make the policy assignable and therefore as flexible as possible is illustrated in the United States decision in *Grigsby v Russell* 222 US 149 (1911). A life policy was taken out by X on his own life. He paid two premiums and then required money for medical care. He assigned the policy to Y for value, who in turn continued to pay the premiums. X later died and the insurer wanted to know whether it should pay the proceeds to Y or to X's estate. The Supreme Court of the United States held that it should be paid to Y. The comments of Mr Justice Holmes are noteworthy:

> Of course, the ground suggested for denying the validity of an assignment for a person having no interest in the life insured is the public policy that refuses to allow insurance to be taken out by such persons in the first place ... the ground for the objection to life insurance without interest in the earlier English cases was not the temptation to murder but the fact that such wagers came to be regarded as a mischievous kind of gaming ... On the other hand, life insurance has become in our days one of the best recognised forms of investment and self-compelled savings. So far as reasonable safety permits, it is desirable to give to life policies the ordinary characteristics of property ... To deny the right to sell except to persons having such an interest is to diminish appreciably the value of the contract in the owner's hands.

Sales of life policies are now quite common and there are auctions of such policies. Pension fund managers buy such policies. They continue the payment of premiums and when the life dies the proceeds go into the fund.

Return of premiums

Section 1 of the 1774 Act states that a contract made in breach of the Act shall be null and void to all intents and purposes whatsoever. However, s 2 states that breach of that section renders the contract unlawful. The question that confronted the court in *Harse v Pearl Life Assurance Co* [1904] 1 KB 558 (Appendix 2.11) was whether premiums paid for a policy that was in breach of the Act could be reclaimed by the proposer. The insurance agent in good faith represented to the plaintiff that the plaintiff could effect a policy on his mother's life and to cover funeral expenses. (Possible actions against intermediaries are discussed in Chapter 6.) Twelve years later, the plaintiff was told that the policy was void for want of insurable interest. The Court of Appeal refused to order a return of the premiums. Only in a case where it could be shown that one party had deceived, or oppressed the other party into making the contract would a return of premiums be ordered.

Reform

The narrowness of English law's definition of insurable interest in relation to life assurance has been commented on above. Merkin (Appendix 2.12) presents an overview of the various problems and suggests reform. No reforms have been forthcoming.

Australia introduced reforms in the Insurance Contracts Act 1984 (Appendices 2.13 and 2.20). Section 16 does, however, retain the requirement for an insurable interest in life assurance and in personal accident and sickness policies, which provide health cover as part of the policy. The retention was on the basis that there should be an incentive against murder committed for financial gain. The right to assign is mentioned along the lines suggested by Holmes J in *Grigsby* and, thus, *contra* to Merkin's suggestion. It is in s 19 that the main difference (that is, a widening of the categories of those who have an interest) can be seen from English Law (although it should be said that the advances had already been made by the Life Insurance Act (Cth) in Australia as early as 1945). The Act specifically abolishes the need to name the beneficiary in the policy as required by the English Act of 1774 (Appendix 2.2).

PROPERTY INSURANCE

Property insurance, unlike life assurance, is a contract of indemnity. Unlike life assurance, the interest must exist at the time of loss and not when the contract is made. Also, unlike life assurance, the courts have often been active in interpreting interest in a way that meets commercial needs, but not always.

The narrow approach

A leading House of Lords case illustrates a narrow approach. In *Macaura v Northern Assurance* [1925] AC 619 (Appendix 2.14), the insured was the sole shareholder in a company. He was also an unsecured creditor of the company. In his own name, he insured the timber of the company, which was its only asset, against fire. A fire destroyed the timber and his claim on the policy was rejected. As every student of company law knows, a company has its own legal personality separate from that of its shareholders. The company should have insured in its own name. The plaintiff 'stood in no legal or equitable relationship to the timber' (*per* Lord Sumner).

It is possible, although the wording of the policy would need to be very carefully drawn, for a shareholder to insure his interest in the value of the shares which he holds in the company. This was achieved in *Wilson v Jones* (1867) LR 2 Ex 139 (Appendix 2.15). Here, the insured held shares in a company that was attempting to lay the first transatlantic telegraph cable on the bed of the ocean. If it was an attempt to insure the cable, the insured would fail, as he had no legal or equitable interest in the cable. It was held that he had in fact insured his interest in the shares of the expected profit on the successful completion of the venture.

More than 100 years ago, New York law considered that a factual expectancy would be sufficient to support an insurable interest. In *National Filtering Oil Co v Citizen's Insurance Co* 106 NY 535 (1887), the insured had agreed with X & Co that X & Co would use a patent owned by the insured in X & Co's factory. From this arrangement the insured would receive royalties on the production. A certain minimum royalty would remain payable even if the factory was destroyed or damaged by fire. The insurance was to cover any shortfall in royalties and it was an insurance on the factory itself. The insured successfully claimed on the policy, it being held that: '... an interest in property connected with its safety and situation as will cause the insured to sustain a direct loss from its destruction is an insurable interest.' A legal or equitable interest in the property, as would be demanded by English law, was not a necessary ingredient of insurable interest.

More recently (in 1987), the Supreme Court of Canada has rejected the narrowness of the *Macaura* approach. In *Constitution Insurance Co of Canada v Kosmopoulos* 34 DLR (4th) 208 (1997) (Appendix 2.16), the insured was the sole shareholder, director and lessee of a business. He insured in his own name and when the premises were damaged he was held to have an insurable interest as a sole shareholder. The *Macaura* rule was considered to be an 'imperfect tool to further the public policy against wagering'. Many jurisdictions in the United States have abandoned the restrictive definition of insurable interest in favour of the 'factual expectancy test'.

It is perhaps not surprising that the (Australian) Insurance Contracts Act 1984 (Cth) has taken a similar stance in s 17 (Appendix 2.13). Here, the requirement is not that there should be a legal or equitable interest but that the insured has suffered a pecuniary loss by the property damage.

Damage to goods

The owner of goods obviously has an insurable interest. But, many people may have a relationship to goods, damage to which may have an adverse pecuniary effect on them. In such a case there is an insurable interest.

A typical example would be a bailee of goods. He has a lien over such goods; he may be liable for damage to such goods. In *Waters v Monarch Fire and Life Assurance Co* (1856) 5 E & B 870 (Appendix 2.17), warehousemen took out two floating policies, policies taken out in general terms which leave the particulars to be later defined, usually because the exact details are unascertainable at the time the policy is effected. One policy was on goods on trust or held on commission and the second policy on goods which they owned or held on commission. A fire destroyed goods owned by others and the plaintiffs claimed. Some owners did not know that the plaintiffs had insured the goods and some had taken out their own policies. The insurers offered to pay only the value of the lien, for warehousing charges due to the plaintiffs, arguing that the plaintiffs had no insurable interest in the goods not owned by them. The insurer's defence was rejected. It was a valid insurance, not tainted by any illegality and it would be commercially inconvenient if such an insurance could not be taken out. Obviously, the insured can not be allowed to make a profit from such insurance. The insurer, however, is bound to pay the full value of the goods damaged or destroyed. The insured may then take out the value owed to him and he will be deemed to hold any balance as trustee for those who have suffered a loss, for example, the owners. If payment over of the balance fully compensates the owner of the goods, they would obviously have no claim on their own policies. If there was a shortfall, then only the shortfall would need to be paid by the insurers. If there was a payment made by the insurers and the original loss was due to the negligence of the warehousemen, then the insurers of the goods' owners would have subrogated rights against those insurers (see Chapter 9).

Waters was a short judgment, referring to only one earlier decision, but its commercially sensible approach was endorsed by the House of Lords in *A Tomlinson (Hauliers) Ltd v Hepburn* [1966] 1 All ER 418 (see Appendix 2.18). The plaintiff haulage company insured goods of a third party which were to be carried on the plaintiff's lorries. The goods were stolen without any negligence on the plaintiff's part. The plaintiffs were bailees of the goods and, following *Waters*, were held to have an insurable interest to the full value of the goods. They could retain a sum to cover any sums due to them and then hold the remainder of any moneys in trust for the owners of the goods.

Other situations

What follows is but a selection of certain relationships where insurable interest has been recognised. Clarke, M, *The Law of Insurance Contracts*, 1997, 3rd edn, London: LLP, sets out 14 situations: ownership; trust; receivership; sale of land; sale of goods; leases; security interests; possession; bailment; risk; liability; company shareholders; debt; and profit.

The above commercially expedient approach to the definition of insurable interest is also seen in cases other than bailment. A practical application of just what the expediency might be is provided by Lloyd J in *Petrofina (UK) Ltd v Magnaload Ltd* [1983] 2 Lloyd's Rep 91 (Appendix 2.19), relying on *Waters* and *Hepburn*.

The main contractors on a site took out contractor's all risk insurance to include damage to property. The insureds were defined as including main contractors, sub-contractors, owners and lessees of the site. Serious damage was caused by the negligence of what was really a sub-sub-contractor. The owners were compensated under the policy and the insurers sought to subrogate against the negligent party (see Chapter 9 for issues of subrogation), who in their defence argued that they were insureds within the policy definition. In answer to that, the insurers countered that, if the defendants were insured under the policy, then their interest extended only to their own property and not to the damaged property. The insurer's arguments were rejected and the subrogation claim failed. The court was prepared to extend the bailee principle found in *Waters* and *Hepburn* to cover the situation so that a head contractor could insure the entire contract works in his own name and the name of all the subcontractors. The precise wording of the policy will need to be examined and it may be that it contains words of limitation which would militate against the commercially convenience approach. In *National Oilwell (UK) Ltd v Davy Offshore Ltd* [1993] 2 Lloyd's Rep 582 (Appendix 9.9), although two parties were held to be insured under the policy, the coverage, and thus the protection, offered was not identical. One party had less cover once the wording of the policy had been construed by the court, and the insurers were able to subrogate against that party.

The entangling of insurable interest and subrogated rights is also illustrated by *Rowlands v Berni Inns Ltd* [1985] 3 All ER 472 (Appendix 2.3). A landlord under the terms of the lease agreed to insure the building and the tenant was to contribute towards the premium. The lease stated that should there be fire damage, the tenant would be relieved from any repairing obligations and the insurance moneys would be used for such repairs. Due to the tenant's negligence, there was a fire, the insurer paid the landlord and then sought to subrogate against the tenant. The insurers argued, in part, that the tenant had no insurable interest. The subrogated claim was rejected. Lord Justice Kerr was of the view that there was no legal principle, which prevented a person from agreeing that where an insurance was affected by one person, which was intended to enure for his benefit to the extent of his interest in the subject matter, that such insurance could not be for his benefit. However, as with *National Oilwell*, the precise interests covered will need to be carefully considered.

It is important however that attention is paid to the precise wording used. Thus while one party may be protected by the policy held in the name of another party the question needs to be addressed as to the breadth of the protection afforded by that policy (see the Scottish case of *Barras v Hamilton* 1994 SLT 949) An interesting legal argument was developed in *Lambert v Keymood* [1999] Lloyd's Rep IR 80. The claimant owned a number of adjoining properties and they were occupied by the defendant. The defendant's negligence caused a fire which damaged the properties. The defendant alleged that the contractual arrangements with the claimant were such that it was the claimant's responsibility to arrange insurance and that would provide for the defendant not to be liable under subrogation (see Chapter 9).

The claimant denied that this was the arrangement. He also argued that even if it was then any policy would require the defendant to act in a reasonable way towards the insured property and in the present circumstances the defendant had acted with wanton disregard to safety and would have been in breach of any reasonable precautions clause.

The court held the defendant liable. The arrangement between the parties would be read as requiring the claimant to insure the properties. But even if this was to be assumed it was not always the case that a policy is intended to exonerate the tenant. That question could only be decided by looking at the wording of the lease and/or the insurance policy. There was no intention here. If there had been a policy which covered the tenant then the reasonable precautions argument would also have worked in the claimant's favour. In the *Berni Inns* case the policy covered acts of negligence but no policy would cover the acts of recklessness that had occurred in *Lambert*.

As with the landlord and tenant comparisons, above, care must be taken to check that the wording said to cover the interests of one party do in fact cover every eventuality to which that party might be exposed. *Deepack Fertilisers etc v ICI Chemicals etc* [1999] 1 Lloyd's Rep 387 was a complicated case of a construction contract wording including who was insuring whom and for what. A completed factory in India exploded. Following an earlier line of cases the Court of Appeal held that the second defendants, who were providing technical know-how for the construction, would have an insurable interest in the plant itself while under construction on the grounds that if it was damaged they would lose the opportunity to continue the work and thus lose profits. After completion however the only losses that they could suffer would be any liability that they might face in contract or in negligence. This type of liability would be expected to be covered by liability insurance or, where relevant, professional indemnity insurance. But what the second defendants could not do, after completion of the project, was to argue that they still had an insurable interest in the property insurance.

Thus the moral of the story, as seen in earlier cases, is that the policy under which one party has been told it is insured, may not necessarily extend to the particular losses that later occur. Therefore the 'insured' and his adviser must take great care to test the wording of that particular cover against the full range of liabilities to which it might be exposed.

Reform

In the non-life section, it can be seen that the English courts have made efforts to find an insurable interest, often to avoid the need for overlapping insurance policies and to prevent subrogated insurance litigation. We have seen, however, that *Macaura* is still part of English law although it has been rejected in Canada and Australia and that the United States had taken the factual expectancy route more than 100 years ago.

More than 50 years ago, an article by Harnett and Thornton critically exposed the weakness in the perceived underlying assumptions behind the need for insurable interest (Appendix 2.21). It is worth quoting a paragraph from that article here:

> The term insurable interest is manifestly a misnomer; the proper term is insurable *relationship*. Factual expectation of damage should be the exclusive test of an insurable relationship. To those who cling to strict property delineations in fear of the process of drawing the line between a genuine factual expectation of damage and a wager, it can be said not only that judicial wisdom is equal to the task, but that a just line drawn with difficulty exceeds in value a simple line which works disproportionate injustice.

Insurers and insureds in England would benefit from legislation that reflected the advances made elsewhere in the definition of insurable interests.

INSURABLE INTEREST

APPENDIX 2.1

Lucena v Craufurd (1806) 2 Bos & PNR 269, HL

Lord Eldon: The questions now are, First, whether upon the matters disclosed on the first count the commissioners had an insurable interest in any of the ships and cargoes upon which they have recovered? Secondly, if they had an insurable interest in any, whether there are not some on which they had no such right? Whether your Lordships shall come to the conclusion that they have no right to recover upon any of these ships and cargoes, or to a more limited conclusion, and take such steps as may be in your power to collect the true result of the proceedings which have been had, it seems to me due to the importance of the subject to enter into some of the topics which have been discussed at the bar; and to determine the real character of the plaintiffs which led to the existence of their commission ...

... Since the 19 Geo 2 (Marine Insurances Act 1745–1746), it is clear that the insured must have an interest, whatever we understand by that term. In order to distinguish that intermediate thing between a strict right, or a right derived under a contract, and a mere expectation or hope, which has been termed an insurable interest, it has been said in many cases to be that which amounts to a moral certainty. I have in vain endeavoured, however, to find a fit definition of that which is between a certainty and an expectation; nor am I able to point out what is an interest unless it be a right in the property, or a right derivable out of some contract about the property, which in either case may be lost upon some contingency affecting the possession or enjoyment of the party ...

If moral certainty be a ground of insurable interest, there are hundreds, perhaps thousands, who would be entitled to insure. First, the dock company, then the dock master, then the warehouse keeper, then the porter, then every other person who to a moral certainty would have any thing to do with the property, and of course get something by it. Suppose A to be possessed of a ship limited to B in case A dies without issue; that A has 20 children, the eldest of whom is 20 years of age; and B, 90 years of age; it is a moral certainty that B will never come into possession, yet this is a clear interest. On the other hand, suppose the case of the heir at law of a man who has an estate worth £20,000 a year, who is 90 years of age; upon his deathbed intestate, and incapable from incurable lunacy of making a will, there is no man who will deny that such an heir at law has a moral certainty of succeeding to the estate; yet the law will not allow that he has any interest, or any thing more than a mere expectation ...

APPENDIX 2.2

Life Assurance Act 1774 (14 Geo 3, c 48)

ARRANGEMENT OF SECTIONS

Section

An Act for regulating insurances upon lives, and for prohibiting all such insurances except in cases where the persons insuring shall have an interest in the life or death of the persons insured.

Whereas it hath been found by experience that the making insurances on lives or other events wherein the assured shall have no interest hath introduced a mischievous kind of gaming:

(1) No insurance to be made on lives, etc, by persons having no interest, etc

From and after the passing of this Act no insurance shall be made by any person or persons, bodies politick or corporate, on the life or lives of any person or persons, or on any other event or events whatsoever, wherein the person or persons for whose use, benefit, or on whose account such policy or policies shall be made, shall have no interest, or by way of gaming or wagering; and that every assurance made contrary to the true intent and meaning hereof shall be null and void to all intents and purposes whatsoever.

(2) No policies on lives without inserting the names of persons interested, etc

And ... it shall not be lawful to make any policy or policies on the life or lives of any person or persons, or other event or events, without inserting in such policy or policies the person or persons name or names interested therein, or for whose use, benefit, or on whose account such policy is so made or underwrote.

(3) How much may be recovered where the insured hath interest in lives

And ... in all cases where the insured hath interest in such life or lives, event or events, no greater sum shall be recovered or received from the insurer or insurers than the amount of value of the interest of the insured in such life or lives, or other event or events.

(4) Not to extend to insurances on ships, goods, etc

Provided, always, that nothing herein contained shall extend or be construed to extend to insurances *bona fide* made by any person or persons on ships, goods or merchandises, but every such insurance shall be as valid and effectual in the law as if this Act had not been made.

APPENDIX 2.3

Mark Rowlands Ltd v Berni Inns Ltd [1986] QB 211; [1985] 3 All ER 473, CA

Kerr LJ: I therefore turn to the question whether there is anything in law which precludes the conclusion that the insurance effected by the plaintiffs in this case was also intended to enure for the benefit of the defendants. In my view the answer is *no*. Provided that a person with a limited interest has an insurable interest in the subject matter of the insurance, an issue to which I turn in a moment in relation to the circumstances of the present case, there is no principle of law which precludes him from asserting that an insurance effected by another person was intended to enure for his benefit to the extent of his interest in the subject matter, whether the insurable interest of the person effecting the insurance be on the whole of the subject matter or only to the extent of a limited interest in it. Illustrations of relationships which may give rise to this consequence are those of bailee and bailor and mortgagee and mortgagor. I do not see why the relationship between landlord and tenant should not be capable of giving rise to the same consequence ...

The submissions of counsel for the plaintiffs against the conclusion that the insurance in the present case should be treated as having been effected for the benefit of the defendants as well as of the plaintiffs were based on two grounds. First, he submitted, albeit faintly, and understandably without enthusiasm, that this conclusion would infringe s 2 of the Life Assurance Act 1774. This provides that:

> ... it shall not be lawful to make any policy or policies on the life or lives of any person or persons, or other event or events, without inserting in such policy or policies the person or persons name or names interested therein, or for whose use, benefit, or on whose account such policy is to be made or underwrote.

Although obviously directed primarily to life insurance, the words, 'or other event or events', admittedly widen its scope. A literal application of the language of s 2 would create havoc in much of our modern insurance law ...

In my view, counsel for the defendants was right in his submission that this ancient statute was not intended to apply, and does not apply, to indemnity insurance, but only to insurances which provide for the payment of a specified sum on the happening of an insured event ...

The second and more substantial submission of counsel for the plaintiffs in this connection was that the defendants had no insurable interest in the building as such, including, as I understood him to say, the parts of it which they themselves occupied as tenants. He pointed out that, under the provisions of the lease, the tenants were relieved from all their covenanted obligations in the event of its destruction by, *inter alia*, fire, as well as from their obligation to pay rent ...

Again, I cannot accept this submission.

To conclude that by virtue of the provisions of the lease the defendants had no interest in the continued existence of the building in which they were carrying on their business is in my view untenable, and, if one were dealing with the tenant of a flat in the upper stories of an apartment block with a similar lease, such a submission would be virtually unarguable …

In my view, without the need for further elaboration, the provisions of the lease cannot have the effect that the defendants were thereby deprived of any insurable interest in the continuing existence of the building or ceased to be exposed to any prejudice if it were destroyed.

I therefore conclude, in agreement with the judge, that the defendants are right in their submission that the insurance effected by the plaintiffs enured for their benefit as well as for that of the plaintiffs themselves. All the Canadian and American decisions to which I refer later proceeded on this basis.

However, in my view this does not decide the real issue between the parties. This is whether the terms of the lease, and the full indemnification of the plaintiffs by their receipt of the insurance moneys, preclude them from recovering damages in negligence from the defendants, or whether the plaintiffs' right to recover such damages remains unaffected. In the former case the plaintiffs' insurers would obviously be equally precluded from bringing the present action in the name of the plaintiffs by virtue of their rights of subrogation. This is the issue which has been much litigated in Canada and the United States. The judge was not referred to any of these decisions, which all went in favour of the tenants, but in most cases only by a majority, and their citation on this appeal resulted from the researchers made by senior counsel for the defendants, who had not appeared below. The only English authority cited to the judge in this connection was the decision of Lloyd J in *Petrofina (UK) Ltd v Magnaload Ltd* [1983] 3 All ER 35; [1984] QB 127. That decision is of considerable importance to insurances in the field of the construction industry, but for present purposes it is at most only of indirect relevant and distinguishable on its facts …

An essential feature of insurance against fire is that it covers fires caused by accident as well as by negligence. This was what the plaintiffs agreed to provide in consideration of, *inter alia*, the insurance rent paid by the defendants. The intention of the parties, sensibly construed, must therefore have been that in the event of damage by fire, whether due to accident or negligence, the landlords' loss was to be recouped from the insurance moneys and that in that event they were to have no further claim against the tenants for damages in negligence. Another way of reaching the same conclusion, on which counsel for the defendants also relied, is that in situations such as the present the tenant is entitled to say that the landlord has been fully indemnified in the manner envisaged by the provisions of the lease and that he cannot therefore recover damages from the tenant in addition, so as to provide himself with what would in effect be a double indemnity. Although the receipt of insurance moneys by an innocent party is of course normally no defence to a wrongdoer …

I do not think it necessary to elaborate on this line of argument in the present case save to say that I accept it and regard it as complementary to the conclusion which is to be derived from the construction and effect of the terms of the lease itself, as indicated above …

[Note: See Birks (1986) 6 OJLS 304.]

APPENDIX 2.4

Siu Yin Kwan and Another v Eastern Insurance Co Ltd [1994] 1 All ER 213, PC

Lord Lloyd: They now turn to consider the second main defence, based on s 2 of the Life Assurance Act 1774. It can be dealt with quite shortly. Mr Thomas submits, and the majority of the Court of Appeal have held, that the policy is payable on the happening of an event, within the meaning of s 2 of the Act, that event being the insured's liability to pay compensation in respect of injury to his employees. Since the name of the person interested, that is to say Axelson, was not inserted in the policy, the insurance is unlawful and void.

The meaning of s 2 of the Act was considered recently by the Court of Appeal in *Mark Rowlands Ltd v Berni Inns Ltd* [1985] 3 All ER 473; [1986] QB 211, a case of fire insurance. The plaintiff was the freeholder of premises. The defendant was tenant of the basement. The question was whether the policy taken out by the plaintiff enured for the benefit of the defendant, although his name did not appear in the policy. It was held that the policy did not infringe s 2 of the Act, since the Act was not intended to apply to indemnity insurance.

On the other hand, in *Re King, Robinson v Gray* [1963] 1 All ER 781, p 790; [1963] Ch 459, p 485, Lord Denning MR said:

> When a policy of fire insurance of a building (as distinct from goods) is taken out, the names of all the persons interested therein, or for whose use or benefit it is made must be inserted in the policy. No person can recover thereon unless he is named therein and then only to the extent of his interest. This is clear from ss 2, 3 and 4 of the Life Assurance Act 1774, which by their very terms apply to policies on 'any other event' as well as life. If, therefore, the tenant insures in his own name alone, the policy is good only to the extent of his interest.

Faced with this conflict of authority, their Lordships prefer the decision of the Court of Appeal in the former case. In *Re King*, the point was not argued. The observation of Lord Denning MR was *obiter* and is not reflected in the judgments of the other two members of the court. Some doubt as to the correctness of *Mark Rowlands Ltd v Berni Inns Ltd* is expressed in MacGillivray and Parkington, *Insurance Law*, 8th edn, 1988, London: Sweet & Maxwell, para 154. But their Lordships do not share these doubts.

There are two reasons why their Lordships prefer the decision in *Mark Rowlands Ltd v Berni Inns Ltd*. In the first place, the words 'event or events' in s 2, while apt to describe the loss of the vessel, are hardly apt to describe Axelson's liability arising under the Employees Compensation Ordinance, or at common law, as a consequence of the loss of the vessel. Secondly, s 2 must take colour from the short title and preamble to s 1. By no stretch of the imagination could indemnity insurance be described as 'a mischievous kind of gaming'. Their Lordships are entitled to give s 2 a meaning which corresponds with the obvious legislative intent.

Various other defences were pleaded in the amended points of defence. But these have all been dismissed, or fallen by the wayside. Their Lordships are glad to have reached the conclusion that the plaintiffs are entitled to succeed, because the defence of the respondents, knowing what they did, was wholly without merit ...

APPENDIX 2.5

Gaming Act 1845 (8 & 9 Vict, c 109)

AN ACT TO AMEND THE LAW CONCERNING GAMES AND WAGERS

(18) Contracts by way of gaming to be void, and wagers or sums deposited with stakeholders not to be recoverable at law; saving for subscriptions for prizes

... All contracts or agreements, whether by parole or in writing, by way of gaming or wagering, shall be null and void; and ... no suit shall be brought or maintained in any court of law and equity for recovering any sum of money or valuable thing alleged to be won upon any wager, or which shall have been deposited in the hands of any person to abide the event on which any wager shall have been made: provided always, that this enactment shall not be deemed to apply to any subscription or contribution, or agreement to subscribe or contribute, for or towards any plate, prize, or sum of money to be awarded to the winner or winners of any lawful game, sport, pastime, or exercise.

APPENDIX 2.6

Halford v Kymer and Others (1830) 10 B & C 724

Bayley J: It is enacted by the third section, 'That no greater sum shall be recovered than the amount of the value of the interest of the insured in the life or lives'. Now, what was the amount or value of the interest of the party insuring in this case? Not one farthing certainly. It has been said that there are numerous instances in which a father has effected an insurance on the life of his son. If a father, wishing to give his son some property to dispose of, makes an insurance on his son's life in his (the son's) name, not for his (the father's) own benefit, but for the benefit of his son, there is no law to prevent his doing so; but that is a transaction quite different from the present; and if a notion prevails that such an insurance as the one in question is valid, the sooner it is corrected the better.

APPENDIX 2.7

Wainwright v Bland and Others (1835) 1 Mood & R 481

Lord Abinger CB (in his address to the jury): This case presents features of novelty. In regard to the manner by which the lady whose life was insured came by her death, there is no evidence from which you ought to infer, that she died any other than a natural death; but even if such evidence had been brought before you, still, supposing the policy to have been effected *bona fide* by her, I should direct you to find your verdict for the plaintiff, unless you thought that she had wilfully destroyed herself. The greatest good faith is required at the hands of a person effecting an insurance: if that person wilfully assist in bringing about the event which is to subject the insurer to the payment of the money, he cannot enforce it; but if a third person unlawfully brings about the event, that is no reason why the innocent assured, or his representatives, should not enforce the policy.

But the question in this case is, who was the party really and truly effecting the insurance? Was it the policy of Miss Abercromby? Or was it substantially the policy of Wainwright the plaintiff, he using her name for the purposes of his own? If you think it was the policy of Miss Abercromby, effected by her for her own benefit, her representative is entitled to put it in force; and it would be no answer to say that she had no funds of her own to pay the premiums; Wainwright might lend her the money for that purpose, and the policy still continue to be her own. But, on the other hand, if, looking to all the strange facts which have been proved before you, you come to the conclusion that the policy was, in reality, effected to Wainwright; that he merely used her name, himself finding the money, and meaning (by way of assignment, or by bequest, or in some other way), to have the benefit of it himself; then I am of opinion such a transaction would be a fraudulent evasion of the statute 14 Geo III, c 48, and that your verdict should be for the defendants ...

APPENDIX 2.8

Worthington v Curtis (1875) 1 Ch D 419, CA

Mellish LJ: ... the question is, whether a policy of assurance which was effected by the father on the life of his son, and in his son's name, was the son's policy or the policy of the father, who is his administrator, and claims it, not as administrator, but on the ground that he is the person, as between himself and his son, who is entitled to the money ...

... It was, however, contended on behalf of the Appellants, that, assuming the policy to be the property of the father, it would follow that it was an illegal policy within the statute 14 Geo 3, c 48, because although it was made in the name of the son, the father, who really effected it for his own benefit, had no insurable interest in his son's life. I agree that even if the story told by the father is true as to the expense to which he had been put in his son's education, that gave him no such interest in his son's life as would support the policy; and I am therefore of opinion that the insurance company would have had a good defence under the Act if an action had been brought against them on the policy. But although the company had sufficient knowledge of the circumstances to call their attention to the question, they acted as insurance companies usually do, and never attempted to set up this defence, and when administration to the son was taken out by the father they paid the money without further dispute to him. The question, then, is, whether the money having been so paid, it is part of the intestate's assets, or belongs to the father.

Now, the creditors are claiming under the son, and they can have no greater right to the money than the son had when alive. They claim through him in the same way as executors or trustees in bankruptcy, and have no greater right than the testator or the bankrupt in ordinary cases. This case, therefore, really depends on the question whether, as between the father and the son, the policy belonged to the one or the other. I think it clearly belonged to the father. One test of this is whether, if the son had brought an action of detinue for the policy against the father, he could have recovered it on the ground that the father had no right to it be reason of the statute of Geo 3? Clearly not. It did not belong to the son but to the father, who had obtained it from the company, and had paid the premiums out of his own money. Again, if the father had wished to surrender it to the company for a valuable consideration, could the son have interfered to prevent him from carrying the surrender into effect? Could he have brought an action for money had and received to recover the amount paid by the company on such a surrender, or could he have maintained a suit in equity to restrain the transaction from being completed? Clearly not. He had nothing to do with it; both the policy and the value of it belonged to the father.

Then the son dies, and the money becomes payable on the policy. Assuming that a creditor, instead of the father, had taken out administration, could he have maintained an action of detinue against the father for the policy? Certainly not. He would have been in the same position as the son before his death, and the son having no property in the policy his administrator would have had no right to it either. Then, supposing the company chooses voluntarily, and without taking advantage of the statute, to pay the money to the father – I say voluntarily, because neither party could have maintained an action against the company – could the administrator of the son have recovered the money from the father? Clearly not.

In my opinion, therefore, there are two reasons for which the appeal must fail. First, because the statute is a defence for the insurance company only, if they choose to avail themselves of it. If they do not, the question who is entitled to the money must be determined as if the statute did not exist. The contract is only made void as between the company and the insurer. And, secondly, if that is not so, and if the effect of the statute is that the court will give no relief to any party because of the illegality of the transaction, in that case the maxim, *melior est conditio possidentis,* must prevail, and the party who has the money must keep it ...

APPENDIX 2.9

Dalby v The India and London Life Assurance Co (1854) 15 CB 365

Parke B: The contract commonly called life assurance, when properly considered, is a mere contract to pay a certain sum of money on the death of a person, in consideration of the due payment of a certain annuity for his life, the amount of the annuity being calculated, in the first instance, according to the probable duration of the life: and, when once fixed, it is constant and invariable. The stipulated amount of annuity is to be uniformly paid on one side, and the sum to be paid in the event of death is always (except when bonuses have been given by prosperous offices) the same, on the other. This species of insurance in no way resembles a contract of indemnity ...

The contract, therefore, in this case, to pay a fixed sum of £1,000 on the death of the late Duke of Cambridge, would have been unquestionably legal at common law, if the plaintiff had had an interest thereon or not: and the sole question is, whether this policy was rendered illegal and void by the provisions of the statute 14 Geo 3, c 48 (Life Assurance Act 1774). This depends upon its true construction.

The statute recites that the making insurances on lives and other events wherein the assured shall have no interest hath introduced a mischievous kind of gaming: and, for the remedy thereof, it enacts:

> ... that no insurance shall be made by any one on the life or lives of any person or persons, or on any other events whatsoever, wherein the person or persons for whose use and benefit, or on whose account, such policy shall be made, shall have no interest, or by way of gaming or wagering; and that every assurance made contrary to the true intent and meaning hereof shall be null and void to all intents and purposes whatsoever.

As the Anchor Assurance Company had unquestionably an interest in the continuance of the life of the Duke of Cambridge, and that to the amount of £1,000, because they had bound themselves to pay a sum of £1,000 to Mr Wright on that event, the policy effected by them with the defendants was certainly legal and valid, and the plaintiff, without the slightest doubt, could have recovered the full amount, if there were no other provisions in the Act.

This contract is good at common law, and certainly not avoided by the first section of the statute 14 Geo 3, c 48 this section, it is to be observed, does not provide for any particular amount of interest. According to it, if there was any interest, however small, the policy would not be avoided.

The question arises on the third clause. It is as follows:

> And be it further enacted, that, in all cases where the insured hath interest in such life of lives, event or events, no greater sum shall be recovered or received from the insurer or insurers, than the amount or value of the interest of the assured in such life or lives, or other event or events.

Now, what is the meaning of this provision?

On the part of the plaintiff, it is said it means only, that, in all cases in which the party insuring has an interest when he effects the policy, his right to recover and receive is to be limited to that amount; otherwise, under colour of a small interest, a wagering policy might be made to a large amount – as it might if the first clause stood alone. The right to recover, therefore, is limited to the amount of the interest at the time of effecting the policy. Upon that value, the assured must have the amount of premium calculated: if he states it truly, no difficulty can occur: he pays in the annuity for life the fair value of the sum payable at death. If he misrepresents, by overrating the value of the interest, it is his own fault, in paying more in the way of annuity than he ought; and he can recover only the true value of the interest in respect of which he effected the policy: but that value he can recover. Thus, the liability of the assurer becomes constant and uniform, to pay an unvarying sum on the death of the *cestui que vie*, in consideration of an unvarying and uniform premium paid by the assured. The bargain is fixed as to the amount on both sides.

This construction is effected by reading the word 'hath' as referring to the time of effecting the policy. By the first section, the assured is prohibited from effecting the policy. By the first section, the assured is prohibited from effecting an insurance on a life or on an event wherein he 'shall have' no interest – that is, at the time of assuring: and then the third section requires that he shall cover only the interest that he 'hath'. If he has an interest when the policy is made, he is not wagering or gaming, and the prohibition of the statute does not apply to his case. Had the third section provided that no more than the amount or value of the interest should be insured, a question might have been raised, whether, if the insurance had been for a larger amount, the whole would not have been void: but the prohibition to recover or receive more than that amount, obviates any difficulty on that head.

On the other hand, the defendants contend that the meaning of this clause is, that the assured shall recover no more than the value of the interest which he has at the time of the recovery, or receive more than its value at the time of the receipt.

The words must be altered materially, to limit the sum to be recovered to the value at the time of the death, or (if payable at a time after death) when the cause of action accrues.

But there is the most serious objection to any of these constructions. It is, that the written contract, which, for the reasons given before, is not a wagering contract, but a valid one, permitted by the statute, and very clear in its language, is by this mode of construction completely altered in its terms and effects. It is no longer a contract to pay a certain sum as the value of a then-existing interest, in the event of death, in consideration of a fixed annuity calculated with reference to that sum; but a contract to pay, contrary to its express words, a varying sum, according to the alteration of the value of that interest at the time of the death, or the accrual of the cause of action, or the time of the verdict, or execution; and yet the price, or the premium to be paid, is fixed, calculated on the original fixed value, and is unvarying; so that the assured is obliged to pay a certain premium every year, calculated on the value of his interest at the time of the policy, in order to have a right to recover an uncertain sum, viz, that which happens to be the value of the interest at the time of the death, or afterwards, or at the time of the verdict. He has not, therefore, a sum certain, which he stipulated for an bought with a certain annuity; but it may be a much less sum, or even none at all.

This seems to us so contrary to justice and fair dealing and common honesty, that this construction cannot, we think, be put upon this section. We should, therefore, have no hesitation, if the question were *res integra*, in putting the much more reasonable construction on the statute, that, if there is an interest at the time of the policy, it is not a wagering policy, and that the true value of that interest may be recovered, in exact conformity with the words o the contract itself.

The only effect of the statute is, to make the assured value his interest at its true amount when he makes the contract ...

APPENDIX 2.10

Hebdon v West (1863) 3 B & S 579

Wightman J: There are two questions in this case. The first is whether Hebdon had any insurable interest at all in the life of Pedder; and the second, whether, assuming that he had an insurable interest, the payment of the £5,000 by the Glasgow Life Insurance Company, as stated in the second plea, is an answer to the plaintiff's claim.

... In the present case, it was contended for the plaintiff that he had two kinds of insurance interest in the life of Pedder – one, on the ground of a promise that Pedder had made to him that he (Pedder) would not enforce the payment of any debt that the plaintiff might owe him during his (Pedder's) lifetime, and the other, on the ground that the plaintiff was in the employ of Pedder at a salary of £600 a year, under an agreement that the engagement should last for seven years. We do not think that the first kind of interest in the life of Pedder, namely that he had said that he would not enforce payment of debts due to him from the plaintiff during his (Pedder's) life, without any consideration or any circumstance to make such a promise in any way binding, can be considered as a pecuniary or indeed an appreciable interest in the life of Pedder. The other kind of interest, namely that which arises from the engagement by Pedder to employ the plaintiff for seven years at a salary of £600 a year, may, we think, be considered as a pecuniary interest in the life of Pedder, to the extent at least of as much of the period of seven years as would remain at the time the policy was effected, which appears to have been about five years. This, at the rate of £600 per annum, would give the plaintiff a pecuniary interest in the life of Pedder to the amount of £3,000 which would be sufficient to sustain the present policy, which is for £2,500 only.

We assume, then, that the plaintiff had a pecuniary interest in the life of Pedder to the extent of £2,500 at the time he effected the policy with the defendant's office. If that be so, the question then arises whether payment, after the death of Pedder, of £5,000 by another life insurance Company, with whom the plaintiff had also insured Pedder's life to that amount, is a bar to the plaintiff's claim by virtue of the third section of the 14 Geo 3, c 48, it being taken as a fact that the £5,000 included all the insurable interest that the plaintiff had at the time of making both policies ...

... Looking to the declared object of the legislature, we are of opinion that though, upon a life policy, the insurable interest at the time of the making the policy, and not the interest at the time of the death, is to be considered, it was intended by the third section of the Act that the insured should in no case recover or receive from the insurers (whether upon one policy or many) more than the insurable interest which the person making the insurance had at the time he insured the life. If for greater security he thinks fit to insure with many persons and by different contracts of insurance, and to pay the premiums upon each policy, he is at liberty to do so, but he can only recover or receive upon the whole the amount of his insurable interest, and if he has received the whole amount from one insurer he is precluded by the terms of the third section of the statute from recovering or receiving any more from the others. Any argument arising from the supposed hardship of allowing the insurers in such a case to receive and retain the premiums without being obliged to pay the consideration for which such premiums were paid, would be equally applicable to the case of marine insurances, upon which, however many policies there may be, the underwriters are only liable to the extent of the value insured …

APPENDIX 2.11

Harse v Pearl Life Assurance Co [1904] 1 KB 558, CA

Collins MR: It appears that the plaintiff effected with the defendants through their agent two insurances on the life of his mother. He continued to pay the premiums for some years till they came to more than the amount insured, and now seeks to recover them back. Dealing with the first policy in point of time, and assuming, though without deciding the matter, that the plaintiff had not a sufficient insurable interest in his mother's life to entitle him to take out a policy with regard to her funeral expenses, there remains the question of his claim to recover the premiums that he has paid. The ground on which the claim is based is that there has been a total failure of consideration, and that depends on the hypothesis that I have adopted of the illegality of the first transaction under the statute of 14 Geo 3, c 48; for if the plaintiff had been under any liability to pay the funeral expenses of his mother, the policy would be valid, and the premiums could not be recovered back. On the assumption that the policy was illegal, the plaintiff has paid money to the defendants upon an illegal bargain, and the question is whether he can recover it back. As to the other policy, the plaintiff effected it, on his own shewing, in his own interest. The jury have found as to both policies, in answer to questions (4) and (5) put to them by the county court judge, that they were taken out in consequence of the representation of an agent of the defendants that they were good policies, but that the agent was not guilty of any fraud. The county court judge held that even if both policies were void for want of insurable interest, the representations having been innocently made, the premiums could not be recovered back. It is clear law that where one of two parties to an illegal contract pays money to the other in pursuance of the contract, it cannot be recovered back ...

The statement, however, made by the agent was not a statement of fact, but one of the law, and was made innocently, as the jury have found. Unless there can be introduced the element of fraud, duress, or oppression, or difference in the position of the parties which created a fiduciary relationship to the plaintiff so as to make it inequitable for the defendants to insist on the bargain that they had made with the plaintiff, he is in the position of a person who had made an illegal contract and has sustained a loss in consequence of a misstatement of law, and must submit to that loss. Neither on the findings of the jury, nor in the evidence, can I find anything that brings the case within any of the classes that I have indicated. Under those circumstances, the plaintiff cannot recover back the premiums that he has paid ...

APPENDIX 2.12

Merkin, R, 'Gambling by insurance – a study of the Life Assurance Act 1774' (1980) 9 Anglo-Am L Rev 331

(1) THE NEED FOR INSURABLE INTEREST

(1) The reasons for requiring insurable interest

The paramount purpose of the 1774 act was to stamp out gambling hidden by a notional insurance. There were three factors behind this. In the first place, there was a growing objection in this period to gambling in all its forms because of the social consequences that it inevitably produced. Blackstone expressed his outrage thus:

> Taken in any light, it is an offence of the most alarming nature; tending by necessary consequence to promote public idleness, theft and debauchery among those of a lower class; and among persons of a superior rank, it hath been attended with the sudden ruin and desolation of ancient and opulent families, an abandoned prostitution of every principle of honour and virtue, and too often hath ended in self-murder.

Similar views in a more modern setting have been expounded by Paterson:

> ... a sense of antagonism is aroused in a community of workers against persons who obtain a means of livelihood without participating in the machinery of social or economic production or distribution – in short, against 'social slackers'. More specifically, unearned gains lead to idleness, and the wagerer becomes a social parasite. On the moral side, idleness leads to vice; and the impoverishment of the loser entails misery, and, in its consequence, crime.

Secondly, the particular practice of wagering on lives brought in its wake an unfortunate consequence:

> The duration of lives of persons believed to be on their death bed was a common hazard, and the dissolution of persons, who saw themselves insured in the public papers at 90%, was, not unlikely, hastened by such announcement.

Finally, there is a strong possibility that if the only interest of X in Y is an insurance policy there may be a temptation on the part of X to expedite Y's demise. The preamble to Marine Insurance Act 1746 expressly recognised the danger in these words:

> ... it hath been found by experience, that the making of insurances, interest or no interest, or without further proof of interest than the policy, hath been productive of many pernicious practices, whereby great numbers of ships, with their cargoes, have ... been fraudulently lost or destroyed ...

(2) The position at common law

The legality of wagers at common law did not arise for decision until the second quarter of the 18th century. Up to this period, the courts were laying down general contractual principles and it seems never to have occurred that wagers were anything other than ordinary contracts. As Professor Simpson has pointed out, important concepts have their origins in decisions on wagers. Perhaps the most common and important type of non-gaming wager, at least until 1746 (the year of the first Marine Insurance Act), was that disguised as marine insurance. Such wagers were readily enforceable and although the courts did adopt the 'unsettling tendency to impute more serious motives to the parties than they intended' by construing such policies as requiring proof of loss, policies which were expressed as mere wagers (normally, by the statement that the holder of the policy was deemed to have interest, commonly known as PPI insurances) were undoubtedly lawful. The Marine Insurance Act 1745–1746 (subsequently replaced by the Marine Insurance Act 1906) passed, as we have seen, as a reaction to the fraudulent destruction of insured property and rendered null and void all marine policies by way of gaming or wagering. Given this lead, the courts began a century of seeking ways to avoid their own basic rule as to the legality of wagers, a task in which they were more successful, and the exceptions they developed more numerous, that is commonly supposed. As it is hoped to demonstrate it is highly likely that the courts would have held life policies without interest to be illegal at common law. In addition to the early 19th century rule that mere frivolous wagers were unenforceable as being degrading to the courts, there were four grounds on which wagers were regarded as fully illegal:

(a) Public matters: it was argued in *Foster v Thackeray* (1781) 1 TR 57 that a wager on matter of public importance was *per se* unlawful, and although there is no record of any judgment ever having been delivered in that case, the dichotomy between public and private affairs was expressly adopted by Lord Mansfield in *Murray v Kelly* and Buller J in *Atherfold v Beard* (1788) 2 TR 610. Such *dicta* ran counter to actual decisions, notably that in *Andrews v Herne* (1662) 1 Lev 33, in which the validity of a wager on the possibility of Charles II being restored to the throne was not doubted, although the decision did not turn on the point. The full potential of the principle was in fact never properly investigated for most of the cases falling within it were decided on other grounds, principally the evidence rule (see, in particular, *Shirley v Sankey* (1800) 2 B & P 130) and, at a later stage, public policy.

(b) Cases in the 17th (*Allen v Rescous* (1676)) and early 18th (*Walkhouse v Derwent* (1747)) centuries established that wagers leading to physical violence, bribery and other results contrary to morality would not be enforced. In the landmark decision of Lord Mansfield, in *Jones v Randall* (1774) 1 Cowp 37, it was settled that wagers were subject to the same limitations applicable to other contracts, in particular, that a wager against sound public policy was illegal. Of the cases applying this principle, the most important, for our purposes, is *Gilbert v Sykes* (1812) 16 East 150, in which, as a consequence of a discussion as to the possibility of Napoleon being assassinated, G deposited 100 guineas with S, S repaying one guinea for every day that Napoleon lived. This wager was held to be unlawful for the reason that each party might be tempted to take steps to ensure that events turned out to his own advantage. Although the case is exceptional, in that the court was primarily concerned with the effect of Napoleon's life or death on England, it is express recognition of the danger faced by those whose death is of interest to others, and arguably supports the proposition that gambling on the lives of public personalities was banned by the common law.

(c) Wagers affecting third parties: in the notorious case of *March v Pigot* (1771) Burr 2802, two young men wagered as to which of their fathers would live the longer. Unknown to the parties (one of whom was actually a mere assignee) one of the fathers in question had died before the time of the bet. A claim of total failure of consideration was dismissed and the wager upheld by a court headed by Lord Mansfield, but it must again be noted that although the question of enforceability was peripherally discussed the court was willing – albeit reluctantly – to assume the correctness of the jury's finding that the intention of the original parties was not to wager but to protect their own future interests. Later courts, treating the case as one of wagering *simpliciter*, regularly expressed their surprise at the result reached but could do no more than lay down the necessarily limited proposition that a wager affecting a third party was illegal only if it were a threat to public peace. However, there are signs that at turn of the 19th century the courts were more willing to bypass March and to hold that when a third party was in any way affected a wager was void and illegal. Uninhibited by March, it seems fairly certain that the courts would have reached this result far sooner (Buller J in *Good v Elliott* ...).

(d) Improper evidence: using the authority of *Coxe v Phillips* (1763) Lee temp Hard 237, the courts developed the independent procedural rule whereby if it was apparent that improper evidence was to be introduced the plaintiff would be nonsuited, or if the impropriety appeared at a later stage in the proceedings the trial would be stopped. In some cases, the principle was taken further and nonsuits were granted where such evidence could potentially be introduced even though, in the circumstances, there was no factual possibility of its introduction, as in *Atherfold v Beard* (1788) 2 TR 610, where a bet on the amount of hop duty collected could not be enforced due to the confidentiality of the subject matter even though there was no question of its discussion, the loser of the bet having conceded. In other cases, actual introduction was insisted upon. Whatever the extent of the rule, its importance to us is its effect on wagers affecting third parties, notably, its use as an alternative ground for avoiding the wager in *Da Costa v Jones* (1778) 2 Cowp 729. It is evident that life assurances are likely to produce evidence equally damaging to the life in question.

Given the width of these exceptions, it is arguable that the common law would not have tolerated insurances without interest. It is, therefore, to be expected that the courts would have made optimum use of the 1774 Act to stamp out this particular form of wagering. Despite a promising start that expectation has not been fulfilled. Before the reasons are examined, it is necessary to examine the wording to the Act itself ...

THE TIMING OF INSURABLE INTEREST

(1) *Godsall v Boldero* (1807) 9 East 72

The policy underlying a decision of exactly when insurable interest should be required to exist reflects a view of the nature of life insurance. If such insurance is to be regarded as providing an indemnity interest must be fixed at time of death, for loss by death is the insured risk. If so, on the other hand, the investment element is to be regarded as paramount the need for the ultimate beneficiary to suffer and show loss diminishes. As with the nature of interest, the 1774 Act is silent on this vital issue and the matter has been one for resolution by litigation.

The question first arose squarely in *Godsall v Boldero* in which a creditor, being owed over £1,000, insured the life of his debtor for £500. The debtor died insolvent but nevertheless the debt was satisfied by his executors from funds granted by Parliament for this purpose. The creditor then brought an action on the policy. Lord Ellenborough CJ denying recovery refused to regard life assurance as *sui generis* and applied the normal indemnity principle applicable to other insurances as laid down by Lord Mansfield in the context of a marine policy: 'It is a contradiction in terms, to bring an action for an indemnity, where, after the whole event, no damage has been sustained' (*Hamilton v Mendes* (1761) 2 Burr 1198). On principle, the decision cannot be doubted – the policy was a mere security by way of guarantee, and, to have allowed recovery would have been to assert that a security is enforceable even though the debt has been paid off. *Godsall v Boldero* was followed in *Henson v Blackwell* (1845) 4 Hare 434, in which Wigram VC, using the language of guarantee, held that payment on a life policy after loss of interest was wrongful and thus could not be relied on by the debtor of the insured in reduction of the debt.

(2) *Dalby v India and London Life Assurance Co* (1854) 15 CB 365

Despite these decisions, 19th century insurers continued to pay on life policies where interest had lapsed by the time of death. Thus, in *Barber v Morris* (1831) 1 M & Rob 62, the court admitted evidence from an insurer that as a general principle payment would in practice be made interest or no interest. Finally, in the *Dalby* case, as a result of the 'chorus of disapprobation' following the decision in *Godsall*, the law was altered to coincide with commercial understanding – it was conclusively laid down that insurable interest need only exist at the time of the contract. It is more than a little curious to note that the very decision which established this crucial precedent involved not a life policy but a true indemnity. Anchor Life had insured the life of the Duke of Cambridge by four policies worth £3,000, the holder being one Wright. Anchor reinsured with the defendants for £1,000. Wright subsequently surrendered his policies, thereby terminating Anchor's insurable interest, but the reinsurance was maintained until the Duke's death. Parke B allowed Anchor's claim on the policy holding that, for two reasons, *Godsall* was incorrect in equating life with indemnity insurance.

In the first place, it was pointed out that the premium on a life policy is fixed at the time of the contract only, thereby measuring the interest of the holder at that point. It would therefore be 'contrary to justice, and fair dealing, and common honesty' (*per* Parke, B, at p 391) if the happening of an event causing loss of interest deprived the policyholder of the sum purchased by his premium. Further, closely connected with the first point, it was decided that life policies are different in nature from other insurances – the latter seek to compensate for specific loss whereas the former are simply agreements under which a specific sum is to be paid to the insured on death of the life in question. Although these arguments are superficially attractive, it is submitted that both are subject to fundamental objections.

(i) Loss of the premium

Once it is accepted that the object of the 1774 Act was to suppress wagers on lives, it seems strange that a court should be willing to place the interests of a company taking a calculated gamble on the life of the Duke above those of statutory public policy. This admits, however, that there can be a loss – on careful scrutiny of the fact of *Dalby* (or, for that matter, of any other case in which interest has lapsed), it is hard to see the injustice complained of. There was clearly no loss of the past premiums: Anchor had bargained for an indemnity on the Duke's death and, had Wright not surrendered his policies, would have obtained no more than that. A legal requirement lapsing the reinsurance on loss of interest would have left Anchor no worse off – admittedly no indemnity would have been recovered but there would have been no need for one. Nor can it be argued that the defendants would have been unjustly enriched by the *Godsall* rule, for they had provided adequate consideration by being on risk until loss of interest. In short, Anchor had received full value for its past premiums. Similarly, there was no future loss: all that Anchor would have been deprived of by a lapsing of its policy would have been the chance to gamble, the chance to assess whether the reward on death would be outweighed by the cost of premiums payable in the meantime. This is precisely what the 1774 Act was intended to prevent, yet is precisely what is granted by *Dalby*. It therefore seems clear that the only possible loss of which the law should take account on cesser of interest is represented by the unexpired portion of the last premium. Although the common law did not permit the severance of premiums (*Tyrer v Fletcher* (1777) 2 Cowp 666), it would have been far less damaging to create an exception to that rule than to authorise widespread wagering. In any event, the modern practice of assigning surrender values to life policies ensures that sum of money is available on surrender and in the vast majority of cases this would well exceed any premium loss. To summarise then, no hardship is caused by abrogating the rule in *Dalby* – indeed there will normally be a gain of the amount by which the surrender value exceeds the unexpired portion of the last premium. Further, as will be demonstrated, in most cases of lapse of interest there is a sensible alternative to allowing wagering.

(ii) Promise to pay on death, not indemnity

This was the key issue in *Dalby*. The justification for regarding life policies as non-indemnity is not apparent from *Dalby* but appears to be based on the notion that loss caused by death is incapable of measurement and thus can never be fully made good. This principle has led to two legal differences between life and other insurances which are of undoubted wisdom. First, own life insurance may be for an unlimited amount so that a man may provide for his family to the best of his financial ability. Secondly, subrogation has been disallowed. Subrogation operates on the basis that, where a man has bargained for an indemnity, he should receive no more than that, so that, on payment of the policy moneys, the insurer becomes entitled to the benefit of rights accruing to the insured in respect of his loss; see generally *Castellain v Preston* (1883) 11

QBD 380. By holding that an indemnity can never be granted, the courts have allowed the insured or his estate to retain the benefit of such rights. It is, however, open to serious doubt whether the decision in *Dalby* can be justified by the use of this principle. There are two fundamental objections:

(1) it is illogical to hold that, because loss is not always quantifiable in cases of death, there is no need to prove any loss at all. It is not the absence of loss that allows unlimited recovery under own-life policies and takes life and accident policies out of the grip of subrogation – in the former case the loss is self-evident, in the latter proof of loss is absolutely vital to the claim – but the impossibility of quantification;

(2) it is now generally accepted that certain life policies do, in fact, provide indemnities in the full sense. Reinsurance and creditor-debtor policies are in effect indistinguishable from property insurance in that they seek to provide protection against a fixed loss, and there seems to be no good reason for not requiring that loss has to be shown. This possibility has been discounted by the compounding of two fallacies: firstly by the principle that no loss need be proved on death, and secondly by its application to true indemnities which fall under the general description of 'life' policies.

What, then, of the non-indemnity forms of life insurance, the family and key-man policies? It has been suggested by Kimball and Davis that such policies, while not whole indemnities, may be equated to valued policies on property – the sum recoverable is the sum agreed by the parties, and that should be regarded as an indemnity equivalent. Provided, therefore, that some interest (albeit incapable of measurement) does exist on death the policy moneys are treated as 'liquidated damages'.

Taking a wider perspective, it is strongly arguable that all life insurance is in real terms indemnity in nature (Kimball and Davis):

> ... personal insurance is rarely designed to compensate for the loss of ... intangible things; rather it is designed to compensate for the accompanying economic loss. In this respect it indemnifies ... just as much as do fire and marine insurance. If there is a difference, it is only one of degree. No one would deny the indemnity character of a policy ... on an animal or painting. But the loss of a beloved animal or favourite painting may far transcend the economic loss. Yet it is the latter against which the insurance is taken out, and which makes it indemnity insurance. Moreover, even in personal insurance, there is an underlying assumption that ... it indemnifies for economic loss actually suffered even if there is not a precise quantitative equivalence between loss and reimbursement.

It is not necessary to adopt this view in its entirety to accept that the bland statement that a life policy can never be an indemnity is far too simplistic and superficial an analysis of the position.

(3) The legal consequences of *Dalby*

The above has been an attempt to show that the supposed non-indemnity role of life assurance is inadequate justification to support the rule in *Dalby*, for not requiring interest on death. Indeed, the law up to *Dalby*, inclined in favour of the indemnity construction and the subsequent superimposition of the *Dalby* rule has inevitably caused inconsistency and problems in application. The major inconsistency is with the definition of insurable interest itself. As already demonstrated, the law adheres to a strict financial evaluation based on principles of indemnity. It is thus strange to find that such calculations are relevant only at the date of the policy and have no bearing on the actual amount recoverable.

If further proof of inconsistency is required it is to be found in s 3 of the 1774 Act which, it will be remembered, confines recovery to the amount of the interest. *Dalby* limited s 3 to the insurable interest as valued at the time of the contract. The effect is that only in cases where the interest has remained constant throughout the currency of the policy does s 3 attain its intended purpose. If the interest lapses after the policy is issued, the result is the possibility of speculation; if it diminishes – as in debtor-creditor cases – the result is potential profit. Conversely, if the interest increases in that period it cannot be insured against. Thus, where an employer insures the life of a key employee he is confined to the value of the employee's services at the date of the policy, disregarding the likely increase in his worth. Such difficulties would have been averted by a contrary decision in *Dalby*.

(4) The operation of *Dalby*

Perhaps the most damning criticism of *Dalby* is that the decision frustrates the primary object of the 1774 Act by authorizing forms of gambling at least as repugnant as the initial procuring of a policy without interest. Such gambling can occur in four common situations.

(i) Husband and wife

In *Connecticut Mutual Life Insurance Co v Schaeffer* 94 US 457 (1877), a husband and wife took out a joint life policy, the proceeds being payable to the survivor. They were later divorced (both in fact remarried) but the policy was maintained by the ex-wife and on the death of her ex-husband she brought an action on it. The Supreme Court, holding that the combined effect of the 1774 Act and *Dalby* represented United States common law, allowed the action. Bradley J, giving judgment on behalf of the whole court, rested his decision on two grounds: that the law is concerned only to prevent gambling at the inception of the policy, and that it is unfair to deny recovery after a valid policy has existed for a considerable period (the same argument presented in *Dalby*'s case).

> ... it would be very difficult, after the policy had continued for any considerable time, for the courts, without the aid of legislation, to attempt an adjustment of equities arising from a cessation of interest in the insured life. A right to receive the equitable value of the policy would probably come as near to a proper adjustment as any that could be devised. But if the parties themselves do not provide for the contingency, the courts cannot do it for them.

The court here strongly implies that allowing recovery was a lesser evil than denying it. If there were no other alternative, the lesser evil would have been justified, but there are in fact two further possibilities. First, it is desirable on the break up of marriage for the parties to settle their affairs as justly as possible and there is no reason for insurance to be excluded from any agreement. A policy by one spouse on the other can easily be converted into an own-life policy, as can a policy of the *Schaeffer* type. If, however, agreement is impossible, the second alternative – the surrender for an 'equitable value', recognised by Bradley J – comes into play. Surrender values are today universal in life policies but are often subjected to the charge of being too low, especially in the early stages of the policy. Here it is pertinent to go no further than to point out that England is one of the few countries not to regulate surrender values. The important matter is that *Schaeffer* is a decision resting on plainly dubious assumptions – not following the decision does not result in unfairness, it merely eliminates the opportunity of the surviving spouse to gamble, or to sell the policy and thereby allow a total stranger to gamble.

(ii) Employer and employee

A similar problem arises when an employer maintains a key-man policy on the life of an employee. On principle, *Dalby* authorises this, and it has been held by the Michigan Court of Appeals that an employer is entitled to retain the proceeds of such a policy for his own benefit. Again it seems unnecessary to authorise gambling when there are better alternatives. The fairest solution is allow the employee to purchase the policy from the employer at an agreed price so that it becomes an own-life policy ... but in the absence of the employee's willingness to buy, the surrender value should be the employer's only right of recovery.

(iii) Creditor and debtor

Dalby itself illustrates that a creditor is entitled to insure for the amount of the debt owing when the policy is taken out, so that when the debt is fully paid the policy can be kept up by the creditor. Conversely, it appears that if on the debtor's death the debt is unpaid, payment on the policy by the insurer does not discharge the debt. As a result, when the debt is paid the policy becomes nothing more than an opportunity to wager but when the debt is unpaid the chances of double indemnity rest only on the solvency of the debtor's estate. These consequences are defended by MacGillivray ... on the grounds of privity of contract: in the former case the insurer has contracted to pay a fixed sum and thus cannot complain if he is forced to pay it even though the creditor has been fully reimbursed under his contract with the debtor; in the latter case there is no reason for the debtor to benefit from a personal contract made by the creditor with the insurer. It is submitted that, once the guarantee nature of this type of insurance is recognised, these results are unsupportable. Payment by the debtor ought to discharge the contract of insurance subject to the surrender value, whilst payment by the insurer ought to discharge the debtor (with no possibility of subrogation). Adopting this approach, taken by the common law in *Henson v Blackwell* (1845) 4 Hare 434, before *Dalby*, would have the additional benefit of allowing the creditor to insure for future interest and premiums. Alternatively, such policies should be banned, and wholly replaced by policies which are in essence own-life by the debtor but render the creditor beneficiary until repayment of the debt. The choice of continuing or lapsing the policy rests with the debtor and not the creditor, thereby eliminating the wager.

(iv) Assignment to a person without interest

The present law authorises a subsequent assignment of either the policy itself or of the right to recover its proceeds on death to a third party, whether or not that person has an insurable interest. There is, however, one important limitation:

... there is nothing to prevent any person from insuring his own life a hundred times ... provided it is *bona fide* an insurance on his own life, and at the time, for his benefit, and that there is nothing to prevent him from dealing with such policies by assigning them to someone else ... even though at the time he effected the policies he had the intention of so dealing with them ... But if, *ab initio*, the policy effected in the name of A is really and substantially intended for the benefit of B and B only ... that is within the evil and mischief of [the 1774 Act].

The law thus seems to be that general intent to assign on taking out the policy is outside the Act but an intent to assign to a specified person is within it, where no interest exists. Although this may be an easy proposition to state it is not so easy to apply to practical situations. Admittedly, the facts may be clear cut, where the use of an own-life policy to hide an insurance without interest is the obvious intent, but other cases involving purely innocent transactions require very fine distinctions to be drawn, of necessity without the evidence of the leading witness. Although such assignments are a regular feature of commercial life, it must seriously be questioned whether they are justifiable on principle ...

Practical justifications of *Dalby*

The true reason for the vociferous objects of the insurance world to *Godsall v Boldero* and of insurers' subsequent adherence to *Dalby* is best explained by Holmes J in *Grigsby v Russell* 222 US 149 (1911): life insurance has become in our days one of the best recognised forms of investments and self-compelled saving. So far as reasonable safety permits, it is desirable to give life policies the ordinary characteristics of property ... To deny the right to sell except to persons having an interest is to diminish the value of the contract in the owner's hands ...

Suggestions for reform

... The circumstances in which the insured will be able to recover his premium are very limited. A major criticism which can be levelled at the present effect of lack of interest is the total disinterest of the law in the relative fault of the parties. There can be no sympathy for a fraudulent assured who misrepresents his interest, but should the result be the same where the illegality is largely attributable to the insurer? This question may arise at two stages during the formation of the contract:

(a) most of the cases have involved insurance sold by unskilled commission agents, and, in some, the policies have been positively canvassed by the agents. While it seems that over enthusiasm rather than fraud has been the cause of the majority of misrepresentations it is difficult to see why the insured rather than the insurer should bear the burden of the agent's inadequate lack of training. Unskilled agents are rarer today but if an insurer considers them to be an economic advantage it is outrageous that he should be allowed to retain the premiums obtained by their deficiencies;

(b) an insurer is under no legal obligation to check the validity of the policies that he issues – on the contrary if he fails to do so he will receive the benefit of the premiums. Although the point has not been seriously argued in England it has been held in the United States that issuing a policy without interest in the absence of reasonable investigation is actionable negligence (*Liberty National Life Insurance Co v Weldon* 267 Ala 171 (1957)).

Perhaps the most important consideration in the quest for reform is to determine whether premium confiscation is an appropriate sanction, for it can do little to prevent the formation of illegal insurances. It is submitted that, in order to stop the problem at source, it is necessary to place on the insurer the major burden of ensuring that policies without interest are not issued. In order to assist in this task, it has already been suggested that a code of insurable interests should be drawn up, and it is further suggested that an insurer should incur a fine for issuing a policy in breach of that code unless he can show that he could not reasonably have discovered the lack of interest, as when the insured is himself fraudulent.

It remains to determine the fate of the premiums when no interest exists. When the insured is fraudulent and the insurer has no reasonable method of discovering the fraud, the common law produces a satisfactory result. When, however, the fraud could have been discovered, justice denies either party the benefit of the premiums. In such a case, it seems fairest to offer the opportunity to take up the policy to the life insured thereunder or, if the contingency has occurred, to pay the sum insured to his estate, unless, of course, he is a party to the fraud. It may be argued that this gives a windfall to the life assured under the policy but as against that must be weighed the importance of stamping out wagering insurances and also the fact that, while such insurance exists, his life is in potential danger. Finally, where the insured has taken out a policy without interest in good faith, the simplest and fairest solution is to allow recovery of the premiums and their proceeds.

APPENDIX 2.13

(Australian) Insurance Contracts Act 1984 (Cth) (as amended)

PART III – INSURABLE INTERESTS

Division 1 – General insurance

Insurable interest not required

16 (1) A contract of general insurance is not void by reason only that the insured did not have, at the time when the contract was entered into, an interest in the subject matter of the contract.

Legal or equitable interest not required at time of loss

17 Where the insured under a contract of general insurance has suffered a pecuniary or economic loss by reason that property the subject matter of the contract has been damaged or destroyed, the insurer is not relieved of liability under the contract by reason only that, at the time of the loss, the insured did not have an interest at law or in equity in the property.

Division 2 – Other contracts of insurance. Insurable interest not required

18 (1) This section applies to:

(a) a contract of life insurance; or

(b) a contract that provides for the payment of money on the death of a person by sickness or accident.

(2) A contract to which this section applies is not void by reason only that the insured did not have, at the time when the contract was entered into, an interest in the subject matter of the contract.

Division 3 – Naming of persons benefited

Persons benefited need not be named

20 An insurer under a contract of insurance is not relieved of liability under the contract by reason only that the names of the persons who may benefit under the contract are not specified in the policy document.

APPENDIX 2.14

Macaura v Northern Assurance Co Ltd and Others [1925] AC 619, HL

Lord Buckmaster: Now, no shareholder has any right to any item of property owned by the company, for he has no legal or equitable interest therein. He is entitled to a share in the profits while the company continues to carry on business and a share in the distribution of the surplus assets when the company is wound up. If he were at liberty to effect an insurance against loss by fire of any item of the company's property, the extent of his insurable interest could only be measured by determining the extent to which his share in the ultimate distribution would be diminished by the loss of the assets – a calculation almost impossible to make. There is no means by which such an interest can be definitely measured and no standard which can be fixed of the loss against which the contract of insurance could be regarded as an indemnity ...

Lord Sumner: This appeal relates to an insurance on goods against loss by fire. It is clear that the appellant had no insurable interest in the timber described. It was not his. It belonged to the Irish Canadian Sawmill Co Ltd of Skibbereen, County Cork. He had no lien or security over it, and, though it lay on his land by his permission, he had no responsibility to its owner for its safety, nor was it there under any contract that enabled him to hold it for his debt. He owned almost all the shares in the company, and the company owed him a good deal of money, but, neither as creditor nor as shareholder, could he insure the company's assets. The debt was not exposed to fire nor were his shares, and the fact that he was virtually the company's only creditor, while the timber was its only asset, seems to me to make no difference. He stood in no 'legal or equitable relation to' the timber at all. He had no 'concern in' the subject insured. His relation was to the company, not to its goods, and after the fire he was directly prejudiced by the paucity of the company's assets, not by the fire. No authority has been produced for the proposition that the appellant had any insurable interest in the timber in any capacity, and the books are full of decisions and *dicta* that he had none. *Paterson v Harris* (1861) 1 B & S 336 and *Wilson v Jones* (1867) LR 2 Ex 139 are very special cases, and neither is in point here. In the former, there was no plea traversing the allegation that the plaintiff had an insurable interest. The court, construing the policy as one really expressed to be on the cable, dealt with the case as one in which interest was admitted therein, but its decision of the case after this admission of interest is not a decision that a shareholder as such has an insurable interest in a company's assets themselves. In the latter, where the policy described the subject matter of the insurance in a very obscure manner, it was held that the shareholder insured had an interest that he could insure in the profits of the adventure so described, but it was expressly stated that he had no such interest in his shares in the company ...

APPENDIX 2.15

Wilson v Jones (1867) LR 2 Ex 139

Willes J: The first question, therefore, is what was the subject matter insured? Is this, as has been contended, an insurance on the cable or is it an insurance of the plaintiff's interest in a share of the profits to be derived from the cable which was to be laid down? In one sense, indeed, it is an insurance on the cable; that is, it affects the cable, as an insurance on freight affects the ship. The state of the ship and freight are so connected that it is impossible that they should be dissevered, except in cases where the loss of freight is effected by the loss of the goods only, in which case it might equally be said that the insurance on freight is an insurance on the goods. But except in that sense, it will appear, when the language of the policy is examined, that the insurance is an insurance, not on the cable, but on the interest which the plaintiff had in the success of the adventure. The words in which the object is described are as follows:

> The said ship, & c, goods and merchandise, & c, for so much as concerns the assured, by agreement between the assured and assurers in this policy are and shall be valued at 2,00 l on the Atlantic cable.

If these words stood alone, they would be obviously an insufficient description of the interest which the plaintiff possessed. But they are followed by the words 'value, say on 20 shares, valued at 10% per share', which qualify the previous words, and are themselves followed by a context, plainly shewing that the thing insured was the value of the plaintiff's shares, or rather his interest in the profits to be derived from his shares when the cable should be laid, either on that occasion or at some future time. In the margin the following words are written: 'It is hereby understood and agreed that this policy, in addition to all perils and casualties herein specified, shall cover every risk and contingency attending the conveyance and successful laying of the cable.' Looking at the subject matter and at these words, and excluding any argument as to the meaning put by judicial construction on the more general words printed at the end of the policy, 'touching the adventure and perils, & c, they are of the seas, & c, and all other perils, losses, and misfortunes, & c', it is impossible to avoid arriving at the conclusion stated by Martin B, as the opinion of the court below, that this was an insurance on the plaintiff's interest in the adventure.

The argument addressed to us in opposition to this view at one time almost took the form of saying that such a contract would be a wager. If it is meant that it would be within the [Gaming Act 1845], we must reject the argument, for that statute has no application to a contract upon a matter in which the parties have an interest. It relates to betting upon a mere future event, not to contracts of indemnity; which, though they may be properly classed with wagers in the scientific distribution of law, are differently dealt with in its practical administration. But it is said that the transaction is unusual, improbable, and out of the ordinary course, and that the court ought not to support an insurance of so speculative an interest. If, however, we start with the consideration that this policy is an insurance on profits, though we admit the danger, the only conclusion will be that we ought to make ourselves quite sure that the language used has the meaning attributed to it; but we are not to be deterred from giving it effect by reason of the alleged danger. It would, indeed, be extremely dangerous to do so, when we consider that the same argument might have been urged in *McSwiney v Royal Exchange Assurance* (1849) LR 14 QB 634 as to the insurance of profits on goods ...

The insurance, then, was on the adventure, but what was the extent and duration of that adventure? I will here refer to the language describing the duration of the risk. The policy is to cover every risk attending the laying of the cable:

> ... from and including its loading on board the Great Eastern, until 100 words be transmitted from Ireland to Newfoundland, and vice versa; and it is distinctly declared and agreed that the transmission of the said 100 words from Ireland to Newfoundland, and vice versa, shall be an essential condition of the policy.

The true conclusion to be drawn from these words, and especially from the concluding ones, is either that the insurance was on the adventure limited to the endeavour to lay the cable on the occasion; or, if not, it must at least be imputed to the parties that they supposed, unless the result were then arrived at, and there would be an end of the matter.

The second question is, whether this is a loss by the perils insured against. If the insurance were limited to the printed language in an ordinary policy, it would be necessary to do that in which we should have little authority to guide us, namely to put a construction on the words ordinarily occurring at the end of the clause enumerating the risks insured against: '... all other perils, losses, and misfortunes that have or shall come to the hurt, detriment, or damage of the said goods, and merchandises, and ship, & c, or any part thereof.' But this is unnecessary; for, on reading the marginal words, which provide that the policy 'shall cover every risk and contingency attending the conveyance and successful laying of the cable', those words being introduced by the words 'in addition to the ordinary perils', it appears that the parties have decided this question for themselves; and that this being a risk and contingency attending the successful laying of the cable, it is within the policy, unless the facts shew that the loss was caused by a peril only to be attributed to an inherent vice of the cable itself, or to some other implied exception to the perils included in the policy ...

I will therefore conclude by saying, that this was an insurance on the plaintiff's interest to the extent of £200, in an adventure, which consisted in laying down the *Electric Telegraph Cable* in such a condition as to transmit a message, either on that particular trial by the *Great Eastern*, or if not on that particular trial, then in the adventure generally. The former opinion is, I think, right; but, taking into consideration the nature of the subject matter, it was in any case totally lost by the loss of all chance of laying the cable on that voyage. The judgment must therefore be affirmed.

APPENDIX 2.16

Constitutional Insurance Co of Canada et al v Kosmopoulos 34 DLR (4th) 208 (1997)

Wilson J: The issue in this appeal is whether a sole shareholder of a corporation has an insurable interest in the assets of that corporation. The traditional view is that a sole shareholder has neither the legal nor the equitable interest in the corporate assets required for a valid insurance on those assets: *Macaura v Northern Assurance Co Ltd* [1925] AC 619, HL. In examining the issue, it will be necessary to consider first whether *Macaura* would provide the insurers with a valid defence in this case and, if so, whether *Macaura* is or should continue to be the law in Ontario ...

(A) LIFTING THE CORPORATE VEIL

... There is a persuasive argument that:

> ... those who have chosen the benefits of incorporation must bear the corresponding burdens, so that if the veil is to be lifted at all that should only be done in the interests of third parties who would otherwise suffer as a result of that choice.

Mr Kosmopoulos was advised by a competent solicitor to incorporate his business in order to protect his personal assets and there is nothing in the evidence to indicate that his decision to secure the benefits of incorporation was not a genuine one. Having chosen to receive the benefits of incorporation, he should not be allowed to escape its burdens. He should not be permitted to 'blow hot and cold' at the same time ...

I would not lift the corporate veil in this case. The company was a legal entity distinct from Mr Kosmopoulos. It, and not Mr Kosmopoulos, legally owned the assets of the business ...

I would conclude, therefore, that Mr Kosmopoulos was a sole shareholder with neither a legal nor an equitable interest in the assets of the company. If *Macaura* is presently the law in Ontario and should continue to be the law in Ontario, then the defence of lack of insurable interest must succeed. It is to that question that I now turn ...

Three policies have been cited as underlying the requirement of an insurable interest ... They are: (1) the policy against wagering under the guise of insurance; (2) the policy favouring limitation of indemnity; and (3) the policy to prevent temptation to destroy the insured property. Does the implementation of these policies require the restrictive approach to insurable interest reflected in *Macaura*?

(1) The policy against wagering

... If wagering should be a major concern in the context of insurance contracts, the current definition of insurable interest is not an ideal mechanism to combat this ill. The insurer alone can raise the defence of lack of insurable interest; no public watchdog can raise it. The insurer is free not to invoke the defence in a particular case or it can invoke it for reasons completely extraneous to and perhaps inconsistent with those underlying the definition ...

The *Macaura* principle, in my view, is an imperfect tool to further the public policy against wagering. By focusing merely on the type of interest held by an insured the current definition gives rise to the possibility that an insured with the 'correct' type of interest, but no pecuniary interest, will be able to receive a pure enrichment unrelated to any pecuniary loss whatsoever. Such an insured is, in effect, receiving a 'gambling windfall'. But this same approach excludes insureds with a pecuniary interest, but not the type of interest required by *Macaura*. Such insureds purchase insurance policies to indemnify themselves against a real possibility of pecuniary loss, not to gain the possibility of an enrichment from the occurrence of an event that is of no concern to them.

(2) Indemnification for loss

The public policy restricting the insured to full indemnity for his loss is not consistent with the restrictive definition of insurable interest set out in *Macaura*. Indeed, an extension of that definition may better implement the principles of indemnity. At present, insureds such as Mr Kosmopoulos who have suffered genuine pecuniary loss cannot obtain indemnification because of the restrictive definition. The *Macaura* case itself shows how the indemnity principle is poorly implemented by the current definition of insurable interest. Had *Macaura* named the corporation as the insured, or had he taken a lien on the timber to secure the debt, he would have been held to have had an adequate interest. But without these formal steps, Macaura's interest satisfied the principle of indemnity ...

The only effect of the *Macaura* definition of insurable interest in such a case is to 'trap the unwary person whose interest truly satisfies the principle of indemnity rather than to advance that principle': Keeton, R, *Insurance Law* [1971, Eagan: West Group Publishing].

(3) Destruction of the subject matter

It has also been said th at if the insured has no interest at all in the subject matter of the insurance, he is likely to destroy the subject matter in order to obtain the insurance moneys. Thus, the requirement of an insurable interest is said to be designed to minimise the incentive to destroy the insured property. But it is clear that the restrictive definition of insurable interest does not necessarily have this result. Frequently, an insured with a legal or equitable interest in the subject matter of the insurance has intimate access to it and is in a position to destroy it without detection. If Lawrence J's definition of insurable interest in *Lucena v Craufurd* (1806) 2 Bos & PNR 269, were adopted, this moral hazard would not be increased. Indeed, the moral hazard may well be decreased because the subject matter of the insurance is not usually in the possession or control of those included within Lawrence J's definition of insurable interest, that is, those with a pecuniary interest only. It seems to me, therefore, that the objective of minimizing the insured's incentive to destroy the insured property cannot be seriously advanced in support of the *Macaura* principle ...

In summary, it seems to me that the policies underlying the requirement of an insurable interest do not support the restrictive definition: if anything, they support a broader definition than that set out in *Macaura* ...

Many jurisdictions in the United States have abandoned the restrictive definition of insurable interest in favour of the 'factual expectancy test'...

No material has been referred to us by counsel to show that these developments in the United States have led to insoluble problems of calculation, difficulties in ascertaining insurable interests, wagering, over-insurance or wilful destruction of property. Indeed, the commentators both in the United States and Canada seem to be uniformly in favour of the adoption of the factual expectancy test for insurable interest and the rejection of the test set out by the House of Lords in *Macaura* ...

In my view, there is little to commend the restrictive definition of insurable interest. As Brett MR has noted over a century ago in *Stock v Inglis* ... it is merely 'a technical objection ... which has no real merit ... as between the assured and the insurer'. The reasons advanced in its favour are not persuasive and the policies alleged to underlie it do not appear to require it. They would be just as well served by the factual expectancy test. I think *Macaura* should no longer be followed. Instead, if an insured can demonstrate, in Lawrence J's words:

> ... some relation to, or concern in the subject of the insurance, which relation or concern by the happening of the perils insured against may be so affected as to produce a damage, detriment, or prejudice to the person insuring ...,

that insured should be held to have a sufficient interest. To 'have a moral certainty of advantage or benefit, but for those risks or dangers', or 'to be so circumstanced with respect to [the subject matter of the insurance] as to have benefit from its existence, prejudice from its destruction' is to have an insurable interest in it.

APPENDIX 2.17

Waters v Monarch Fire and Life Assurance Co (1856) 55 E & B 870

Lord Campbell CJ: It would be extremely inconvenient if such an insurance were not allowed, although the plaintiffs had no order from the owner of the goods to insure, and the plaintiffs never told the owner that they had insured. It would be extremely inconvenient if a floating policy of insurance could not be kept up, which the plaintiffs might apply to the benefit of those whose goods they were entrusted with, and which, as far as I can see, causes no injury to commerce or the interests of society.

Then the question arises, to what extent do the policies go? I am of opinion that they extend to the whole *corpus* of the goods. If it is a valid contract, the contract is to pay or make good all such damage or loss as shall happen by fire to the property mentioned in the policies – not the mere particular interest which the plaintiffs might have in the property, but the whole value of the property. The plaintiffs will be entitled to take sufficient to cover their own interest in the goods, and may be regarded as trustees of the remainder for those parties who have the ulterior interest in the property. There are authorities to show that the owners of the property although they had given no orders to insure, or had the fact of an assurance of their property communicated to them, may at any time ratify the insurance. The plaintiffs are now entitled to recover the full amount which they have claimed.

APPENDIX 2.18

A Tomlinson v Hepburn (Hauliers) Ltd [1966] AC 451; [1966] 1 All ER 418, HL

Lord Reid: The case must in my view depend on the true construction of the policy, but before considering its provisions I think it best to consider the principles of law applicable to such cases. There can be no doubt that a bailee has an insurable interest in goods entrusted to him, and it has not been denied that the respondents were bailees of the cigarettes when they were stolen. I think that the law was accurately stated by Lord Campbell CJ, in *Waters v Monarch Fire and Life Assurance Co* ...

A bailee can if he chooses merely insure to cover his own loss or personal liability to the owner of the goods either at common law or under contract, and if he does that he can recover no more under the policy than sufficient to make good his own personal loss or liability. Equally, he can, if he chooses, insure up to his full insurable interest – up to the full value of the goods entrusted to him; and if he does that he can recover the value of the goods, though he has suffered no personal loss at all. In that case, however, the law will require him to account to the owner of the goods who has suffered the loss or, as Lord Campbell said, he will be trustee for the owners. I need not consider whether this is a trust in the strict sense or precisely on what ground the owner can sue the bailee for the money which he has recovered from the insurer. A similar situation would arise if a bailee sued a wrongdoer for the full value of goods converted or destroyed by him; there is no doubt that such an action can succeed, and equally I should think that there can be no doubt that the bailee must then account to the true owner. The fact that a bailee has an insurable interest beyond his own personal loss if the goods are destroyed has never been regarded as in any way inconsistent with the overriding principle that insurance of goods is a contract of indemnity. The question is whether the bailee has insured his whole insurable interest – in effect has taken out a goods policy, or whether he has only insured against personal loss – has taken out a personal liability policy ...

This case has been complicated by the supposed existence of a rule that, if the assured has only a limited interest in the subjects insured, he cannot recover more than sufficient to indemnify him against his own personal loss, unless it is shown that he intended to insure for the benefit of the owner of those subjects. It is said that under this supposed rule that intention need not appear from the terms of the policy and need not have been communicated to the insurer, but that the intention can be proved by evidence. It is, however, a fundamental principle that the construction of a contract cannot be governed or affected by the intention or belief of one of the parties not communicated to the other: and for very good reason. It would be most unfair if one party were to find his apparent rights under the contract altered by reason of some state of mind of the other party of which he was not and could not be aware. The supposed rule appears to have been deduced by text writers from *obiter dicta* of Bowen LJ, in *Castellain v Preston* (1883) 11 QBD 380, and it appears to me to have arisen from failure to distinguish cases where the assured insures his own insurable interest from cases where, as in marine insurance policies, he is insuring on behalf of undisclosed principals. Under the ordinary law of principal and agent an undisclosed principal cannot come in to take advantage of a contract unless the agent intended to act on his behalf. The law of marine insurance may not correspond in all respects with the ordinary law of principal and agent, but I see nothing really anomalous in it. It is, however, a very different matter when the assured is insuring on his own behalf. In the present case Imperial are not coming in as undisclosed principals, and there is no room for the introduction of a requirement that the respondents must have intended to act as their agents or on their behalf. If there were any question whether the policy was a wagering policy, intentions would be relevant, but no such question arises in this case and it could hardly arise in a case of this character.

Lord Pearce: Insurance policies can be gaming transactions if they are effected on goods in which the assured has no interest. In the 18th century, such policies were common, particularly in marine insurance, and they were enforceable (but without any judicial enthusiasm) at common law. In 1745, however, an Act to regulate insurance on ships referred in its preamble to the mischievous kind of gaming or wagering under the pretence of assuring the risk on shipping, and enacted that no assurances should be made on any goods on board any British ships:

> ... interest or no interest, or without further proof of interest than the policy, or by way of gaming or wagering ... and that every such assurance shall be null and void to all intents and purposes.

Thereafter, various statutes, down to the Marine Insurance (Gambling Policies) Act 1909 dealt with this matter.

The Life Assurance Act 1774 extended similar principles to other contracts of insurance without interest, but excepted insurance on goods against land risks. These, although made without interest, were enforceable until 1845 when the Gaming Act 1845 was passed. That Act rendered void all contracts which in substance are wagers made without interest in the subject matter of the insurance. Thus, if insurance was effected by a person without an insurable interest, he could not recover ...

There have been many cases dealing with circumstances where it is doubtful whether an assured has an insurable interest, and questions have arisen when he is seeking to recover moneys where the loss falls on others. It may be that he is insuring as agent or as trustee. Even though he is not strictly the one or the other, the circumstances may be such that he has only a limited interest in the goods but that commercial convenience makes it reasonable for him to insure the whole property in the goods and to recover the whole of the moneys holding the balance in trust for those whose loss it represents. In such a case he is not gaming and there is no reason why he should not so act.

In *Robertson v Hamilton*, Lord Ellenborough CJ said:

> The plaintiffs, having an insurable interest in the whole mass of the property restored, may recover upon this policy as trustees for those who are interested with themselves in the whole; though they may be afterwards called upon to divide it amongst the several claimants in the proportions due to each; and a recovery in this action will not exclude any of the parties from unravelling the account in equity. If we were not accustomed in this place to handle questions among the *apices juris*, it would appear extraordinary that this should be considered as a gambling policy within the statute, in which the plaintiffs had no real interest, when it is stated in the case that they are the owners of one of the captured ships, and that after the mass of the captured property had been

> redeemed by the sacrifice of a part for the benefit of the whole, they expended their own money in securing the whole concern, which had been brought into hotchpot. In what sense can we consider the plaintiffs as gamblers ...?

So far as concerns an agent who has no interest and is effecting an insurance for others, however, his unilateral intention is of importance to this extent that, unless he intends to effect the insurance on behalf of his principal, he is simply wagering and there is nothing which an undisclosed principal can ratify.

The bailee of goods, however, is in a very different position. He has a right to sue for conversion, holding in trust for the owner such of the damages as represent the owner's interest. He may likewise sue in negligence for the full value of the goods, though he would have had a good answer to an action by the bailor for the loss of the goods bailed (*The Winkfield*). It would seem irrational, therefore, if he could not also insure for their full value. Both those who have the legal title and those who have a right to possession have an insurable interest in the real or personal property in question. There seems, therefore, no reason in principle why they should not be entitled to insure for the whole value and recover it. They must, however (like plaintiffs in actions of trover or negligence), hold in trust for the other parties interested so much of the moneys recovered as is attributable to the other interests. Is proof of an intention to insure for the interest of others a necessary condition precedent for a plaintiff seeking to recover on an insurance policy in such circumstances? I do not think so ...

A bailee or mortgagee, therefore (or others in analogous positions), has, by virtue of his position and his interest in the property, a right to insure for the whole of its value, holding in trust for the owner or mortgagor the amount attributable to their interest. To hold otherwise would be commercially inconvenient and would have no justification in common sense. In my opinion there is no burden on him to prove his intention to insure their interest on their behalf. If, however [the insurer] can affirmatively prove that he [the bailee or mortgagee] had an intention not to do so, his insurance *quoad* that other interest is gaming and he cannot recover. But the burden of proving that is on [the insurer] ...

APPENDIX 2.19

Petrofina (UK) Ltd and Others v Magnaload Ltd and Another [1984] QB 127; [1983] 3 All ER 35; [1983] 2 Lloyd's Rep 91

Lloyd J: That brings me to the central question in the case. In *A Tomlinson (Hauliers) Ltd v Hepburn* [1966] AC 451, p 481, it was held, indeed it was conceded, that if the policy was an insurance on goods, then the carriers could, as bailees, insure for their full value, holding the proceeds in trust for the owners. In the present case the defendants could not be regarded as being in any sense bailees of the property insured under the policy. Does that make any difference? Can the defendants recover the full value of the property insured, even though they are not bailees? It is here that one leaves the construction of the policy, and enters, hesitatingly, the realm of legal principle.

What are the reasons why it has been held ever since *Waters v Monarch Fire and Life Assurance Co* (1856) 5 E & B 870 that a bailee is entitled to insure and recover the full value of goods bailed? Do those reasons apply in the case of the sub-contractor? One reason is historical. The bailee could always sue a wrongdoer in trover. If his possessory interest in the goods was sufficient to enable him to recover the full value of the goods in trover, why should he not be able to insure that interest? Another reason was that, as bailee, he was 'responsible' for the goods. Responsibility is here used in a different sense from legal liability. A bailee might by contract exclude his legal liability for loss of or damage to the goods in particular circumstances, for example, by fire. But he would still be 'responsible' for the goods in a more general sense, sufficient, at any rate, to entitle him to insure the full value.

It is clear that neither of these reasons apply in the case of a sub-contractor. But there is a third reason which is frequently mentioned in connection with a bailee's right to insure the full value of the goods. From a commercial point of view it was always regarded as highly convenient. Thus, in *Waters v Monarch Fire and Life Assurance Co* ... itself, Lord Campbell CJ said, at p 880:

> What is meant in those policies by the words 'goods in trust'? I think that means goods with which the assured were entrusted; not goods held in trust in the strict technical sense ... but goods with which they were entrusted in the ordinary sense of the word. They were so entrusted with the goods deposited on their wharfs: I cannot doubt the policy was intended to protect such goods; and it would be very inconvenient if wharfingers could not protect such goods by a floating policy.

Similarly, Lord Pearce in *A Tomlinson (Hauliers) Ltd v Hepburn* [1966] AC 451, p 481:

> A bailee or mortgagee, therefore (or others in analogous positions), has, by virtue of his position and his interest in the property, a right to insure for the whole of its value, holding in trust for the owner of mortgagor the amount attributable to their interest. To hold otherwise would be commercially inconvenient and would have no justification in common sense.

In the case of a building or engineering contract, where numerous different sub-contractors may be engaged, there can be no doubt about the convenience from everybody's point of view, including, I would think, the insurers, of allowing the head contractor to take out a single policy covering the whole risk, that is to say covering all contractors and sub-contractors in respect of loss of or damage to the entire contract works. Otherwise, each sub-contractor would be compelled to take out his own separate policy. This would mean, at the very least, extra paperwork; at worst it could lead to overlapping claims and cross-claims in the event of an accident. Furthermore, as Mr Wignall pointed out in the course of his evidence, the cost of insuring his liability might, in the case of a small sub-contractor, be uneconomic. The premium might be out of all proportion to the value of the sub-contract. If the sub-contractor had to insure his liability in respect of the entire works, he might well have to decline the contract.

For all these reasons I would hold that a head contractor ought to be able to insure the entire contact works in his own name and the name of all his sub-contractors, just like a bailee or mortgagee, and that a sub-contractor ought to be able to recover the whole of the loss insured, holding the excess over his own interest in trust for the others.

If that is the result which convenience dictates is there anything which makes it illegal for a sub-contractor to insure the entire contract works in his own name? This was a question which was much discussed in the early cases on bailment. But it was never illegal at common law for a bailee to insure goods in excess of his interest. As for statute, the Marine Insurance Acts obviously do not apply. It is true that the Life Assurance Act 1774, by s 3, prohibited an insured from recovering more than his interest on the happening of an insured event. But policies on goods were specifically excluded by s 4 of the Act. Accordingly, it was held that neither at common law nor by statute was there anything to prevent the bailee from insuring in excess of his interest ...

APPENDIX 2.20

Tarr, AA, 'Insurable interest' (1986) 60 Aust LJ 613

Speculation in the guise of insurance was rife in England in the mid-18th century. A national addiction to gambling made it inevitable that entrepreneurial gamblers should be attracted to the insurance market. For example, it is recorded that wagers on the lives of famous people were particularly popular at this time:

> A practice ... prevailed of insuring the lives of well known personages, as soon as a paragraph appeared in the newspapers announcing them to be dangerously ill. The insurance rose in proportion as intelligence could be procured from the servants, or from any of the faculty attending, that the patient was in great danger. This inhuman sport affected the minds of men depressed by long sickness; for when such persons, casting an eye over a newspaper for amusement, saw that their lives had been insured in the Alley ... they despaired of all hopes, and thus their dissolution was hastened. [Clayton, *British Insurance*, 1971, London: ELEK.]

Similarly, 'insurance' was effected on whether there would be a war, whether a particular vessel would return from some foreign destination, and the like, regardless of whether the person effecting the insurance had any pre-existing interest in the subject matter of insurance. Not only was this perceived as increasing the risk of destruction by the insured of the subject matter of insurance, but there was a general abhorrence with this wagering within the insurance market.

These factors led to the enactment of the Marine Insurance Act 1745–1746 and the Life Assurance Act 1774 which required that a person taking out a policy of insurance must have an insurable interest in the subject matter of insurance ...

In addition to the strict requirement of insurable interest imposed by such statutes, legislation dealing generally with gaming and wagering indirectly imposed on an insured a requirement of interest in the subject matter of insurance at the time when the insurance is effected. Moreover, a quite separate requirement of interest at the time of loss came to be imposed by contract. All insurance contracts, apart from those of life, sickness and personal accident are contracts of indemnity and the principle applied to this genus of indemnity insurances is that the insurer is under an obligation to reimburse the insured in respect of his/her actual loss from the accepted risk; namely, the insured must be restored, subject to the terms and conditions of the policy, to the financial position he/she enjoyed immediately before the realisation of the peril insured against. It follows from this that the insured must have an interest in the subject matter of insurance, for without such an interest, the insured cannot suffer a loss and hence can obtain no indemnity.

To summarise, therefore, the requirement of an interest in the subject matter of insurance may derive from three sources. First, an insurable interest requirement may be imposed by certain statutes dealing directly with insurance. Secondly, gaming and wagering legislation indirectly imposes a requirement of interest in the subject matter of insurance, and third, as a matter of contract such interest may be required. Against the background of these introductory comments, attention may now be focused on the interest requirements pertaining to particular classes of insurance ...

LIFE INSURANCE

The (Australian) Insurance Contracts Act 1984 (Cth) repealed the Life Assurance Act 1774 in its application to a contract or proposed contract of insurance to which the new legislation applies. However, the (Australian) Insurance Contracts Act 1984 (Cth) preserves the requirement of insurable interest at the inception of the insurance as a condition of the validity of the insurance, for life insurance and sickness or accident insurances which include death cover.

In order to resolve any ambiguity and to avoid any difficulty the Law Reform Commission (Cth) advocated that the categories of insurable interest be re-cast in a new statutory provision. This recommendation was accepted as the categories of insurable interests are again declared in s 19 of the (Australian) Insurance Contracts Act 1984 (Cth). This section provides as follows:

(1) a person has an insurable interest in his own life and in the life of his spouse;

(2) a parent of a person who has not attained the age of 18 years, and a guardian of such a person, has an insurable interest in the life of that person;

(3) a person who is likely to suffer a pecuniary or economic loss as a result of the death of some other person has an insurable interest in the life of that other person;

(4) without limiting the generality of sub-s (3) a body corporate has an insurable interest in the life of an officer or employee of the body corporate; (b) an employer has an insurable interest in the life of his employee and an employee has an insurable interest in the life of his employer; and (c) a person has an insurable interest in the life of a person on whom he depends, either wholly or partly for maintenance and support;

(5) where a person has an insurable interest in the life of some other person, the amount of that interest is unlimited.

A number of important points should be emphasised ...

All of the insurable interests set forth in s 19 are unlimited. The retention of the concept of insurable interest reflects a continuing social concern with the temptation of an insured to murder the life insured. Making the insurable interest unlimited seems to involve some resiling from this purpose, leaving the control to the good sense of the life insurance industry in refusing unrealistic covers even if the premium may be attractive to the insurer. Third, the general category of insurable interest declared in s 19(3) extends the test of interest to reasonably apprehended economic loss that may result from the death of the life insured. Thus, a person has an insurable interest in the life of another whenever he stands to suffer economic loss on the death of that other, and a pecuniary interest based on strict legal duties need not be shown. Doubts as to the validity, and the extent of cover, of insurances by creditor of debtor, employer of employee, and by business and *de facto* domestic partners of each other are removed.

GENERAL INSURANCE

The general principle at common law, as far as general insurance is concerned, is that the insured must stand in some legally recognised relationship to the subject matter of insurance, in consequence of which he may benefit by its safety or be prejudiced by its loss. In 1925, the House of Lords dealt with the concept of insurable interest in *Macaura v Northern Assurance Co Ltd* [1925] AC 619.

The comment by the Law Reform Commission (Cth) on the *Macaura* case was that the strict proprietary interest test be abandoned in favour of one based on economic loss; that is, that legislation should provide that where an insured is economically disadvantaged by damage to or destruction of the insured property, the insurer should not be relieved of liability by reason only that the insured did not have a legal or equitable interest in the property. This, in their opinion, would allow more flexibility to the insuring public and insurers alike without in any way promoting gaming and wagering in the form of insurance or adding to the risk of destruction of the property insured.

The (Australian) Insurance Contracts Act 1984 (Cth) gives the Law Reform Commission's recommendations the statutory stamp of approval ...

The *Macaura* ... case is overturned; all that is required is that the insured suffers a pecuniary or economic loss through the damage or destruction of the thing insured. It is, of course, vital to appreciate that s 17, while it has changed the nature of the interest required to validate a contract of general insurance, has not relieved the insured from possessing *any interest at the time of the loss*.

As far as indemnity insurance is concerned, the insurer is under an obligation to reimburse the insured for his actual loss from the accepted risk; that is, the insured must be restored, subject to the terms and conditions of the policy to the financial position that he enjoyed immediately before the realisation of the peril insured against. The measure of indemnity is the loss suffered by the insured and not necessarily the value of the subject matter of insurance which is destroyed or damaged. Consequently, the insured under an indemnity policy must have an interest in the subject matter of the insurance at the time of the loss, for without such an interest, he will be unable to prove a loss and will be disentitled from recovery under the policy. Therefore, notwithstanding that by virtue of s 17 the insurer is not relieved of liability under the contract by reason only that, at the time of the loss, the insured did not have an interest at law or in equity in the property, the very nature of an indemnity policy dictates that an interest in the subject matter of insurance must be present at the time of the loss before compensation is payable. However, the way is now clear to move away from the narrow confines of cases such as *Macaura* ... towards a test of economic loss; that is, satisfaction of the indemnity principle simply demands that the insured show that he has suffered a pecuniary or economic loss through the occurrence of a defined event, and he does not have to go further and satisfy a strict proprietary test of insurable interest. The legislative intent of s 17 is quite clear and may be confirmed by reference to a wide range of seminal materials.

It is submitted that the approach adopted in ss 16 and 17 is to be welcomed. The courts are invited to return to the underlying rationale behind the concept of insurable interest, namely, the desire to avoid the evil inherent in wagering contracts of insurance or adding to the risk of the destruction of the property insured, and to ask whether or not the particular contract of insurance constitutes a wager or promotes the destruction of the property insured. Where the insured suffers a pecuniary or economic loss be reason of the damage to or destruction of insured property, and where the measure of indemnity is the loss suffered by the insured, there can be no justification for barring recovery on the ground of technical rules pertaining to strict proprietary interests.

APPENDIX 2.21

Harnett, B and Thornton, JV, 'Insurable interest in property: a socio-economic re-evaluation of a legal concept' (1948) 48 Col LR 1162

The requirement of insurable interest in property insurance, like most legal abstractions, has developed over the centuries primarily through judicial resolution of relatively isolated problems. Seldom have the courts examined the entire picture in terms of meaningful underlying policies, and the myopic views of older cases, canonised by precedent, often reflect themselves too brightly in later years to the detriment of sound modern analysis. Since the insurable interest question is a phase of the insurance problem which intimately concerns the buyer, the trade, the home office counsel, the specialist, and the general legal practitioner, it is the very warp and woof of the enforceability of insurance contracts. Without the prerequisite of insurable interest, the contract is unequivocally unenforceable. No conduct on the part of the insurer, verbal or non-verbal, can be relied upon to constitute a waiver or an estoppel to assert the defect. To further illustrate the strong public policy enunciated in this requirement, it is only necessary to realise that the incontestability clause typically found in life insurance contracts does not operate as a bar to a defence rooted in the lack of insurable interest. The defence is similarly available, notwithstanding the fact that the policy sued on is in a valued form. Because the business of insurance is at the very nucleus of the modern commercial economy, and because the general public is a gigantic daily consumer of the insurance product, a legal requirement which permits the insurer's escape from contractual liability in such sweeping terms must be constantly re-evaluated for utility and correspondence to social and economic practices and expectations.

In defining insurance interest, it is most helpful to define the words individually, and then taken together. Insurance properly viewed is a contract:

> ... whereby one party ... is obligated to confer benefits of pecuniary value upon another party ... dependent upon the happening of a fortuitous event in which the insured or beneficiary has, or is expected to have at the time of such happening, a material interest which will be adversely affected by the happening of such event.

Interest is traditionally defined in terms of rights in the insured property, but it may also be characterised as such a relationship to property as makes a happening adversely affecting the insured property economically disadvantageous to the interest-holder. Insurance interest, then, is that kind of relationship to an occurrence, or, traditionally viewed, that kind of interest in the property insured, which a claimant must show in order to have a legally enforceable claim to recovery. As to when insurable interest must exist, there is a sharp conflict of authority. Some jurisdictions require the insurable interest to exist both at the inception of the policy and at the time of the loss. Many others hold the presence of the insurable interest at the time of loss sufficient, merely demanding entire good faith in the insured at the inception.

The objective of this study is to restate generally the types of insurable interests which have merited judicial recognition, followed by a critical analysis of the three policies supposedly underlying this *sui generis* requirement. These three policies are the policy against wagering, the policy against rewarding and thereby tempting the destruction of property, and the policy of confining insurance contracts to indemnity. Upon the report of observed judicial conduct, and the analysis of the purposes of the requirement, a re-evaluation of the entire concept will be set forth ...

(II) THEORY VERSUS PRACTICE: THE INSURABLE INTEREST CONCEPT AS A WORKING TOOL

(A) Generic regrouping of conventional insurable interest categorisations

As seen through the eyes of modern courts, the insurable interest concept possesses four main heads. The first and broadest heading embraces property rights, whether legal or equitable. The second and closely allied category includes those types of interests which are reflected in contract rights. The possibility of legal liability as a result of the insured event is the third division while the fourth is the controversial residuum category of 'factual expectation of damage'.

(1) Property right

In the law of insurable interest, an interest, operationally considered, is such a relation to property that an adverse occurrence may result in economic disadvantage upon the happening. In the usual course of events, the absolute owner of a unit of property is the individual most likely to suffer economically from its destruction ...

Thus it is that to courts, thinking in terms of property interests, insurable interest contains a distinct in *rem* connotation in the sense that the insured is required to have an enforceable interest in the *res*, the destruction of which constitutes the insured event. A very common formulation of the property right grouping is in the terms, 'an interest that would be recognised and protected by the courts'. This in essence is the conception of a property interest in the thing insured; the test seemingly is whether a court would enforce the interest in the property if the question should arise in an ownership controversy ...

The ownership concept, for classification purposes, serves well to categorise those insurable interests which are estates in land and personality. While holders of these estates are the persons most likely to seek property insurance, it must always be borne in mind that property interests such as theirs are not the only ones acceptable to the courts. Qualified property interests such as those of life tenants, remaindermen, reversioners, lessors, and lessees are sufficient to be insurable interests ...

Equitable interests in property which will be protected or enforced by the courts are widely held to be insurable interests. These include the interest of a vendee under an executory contract to sell land, a mortgagor holding an equity of redemption, and a beneficiary of a trust. It is also held that one of multiple owners of property possesses an insurable interest in his own right, as in such relationships as partners, shareholders or corporations, joint tenants, tenants in common, and spouses in community property jurisdictions. Homestead rights likewise give rise to insurable interest.

Pressing further on into the field of more shadowy property interests, it is discovered that generally a holder of the property itself or of legal title in representative, trust, or bailment relationship is held to have an insurable interest. Of course, the insurance proceeds paid on the destruction of the *res* inure to others where the policyholder himself has no beneficial interest in the property. This classification encompasses executors and administrators, trustees, and bailees. In the same way, receivers and trustees in bankruptcy probably have insurable interests for the benefit of creditors.

Broadly summarised, then, ownership of all or part of a property unit, whether it be traditionally denominated legal or equitable, is regarded as sufficient to constitute an insurable interest. However, ownership of a physical allocation of property is not strictly necessary to come within the property right conception. As indicated above, the main factor in the property right category is the essentially in *rem* theme of enforceable rights in a specific *res*. In the nature of the modern commercial economy the security device occupies a prominent niche, and these security devices typically do provide the creditor with enforceable rights in a specific *res*. Therefore, the courts have recognised the insurability of the interest of lienors and secured creditors, as well as that of their debtors. Thus, it is that mortgagor and mortgagee, pledgor and pledgee, conditional vendor and conditional vendee, all have insurable interests. Similarly, lienors holding mechanics' liens or artisans' liens, and judgment creditors with statutory liens have insurable interests. A vendor who has contracted to sell realty also has an insurable interest so long as he retains legal title or a lien on the property ...

(2) Contract rights

... There are few cases allowing an insurable interest based on contract right without property right. Generalisation is difficult, but a rule may be stated in these terms: a contracting party whose contractual rights are directly contingent on the continued existence of a property unit has sufficient insurable interest to recover on a policy of insurance, the insured event of which is damage to, or destruction of, that property unit. This rule covers a contract situation in which the contractual rights are conditioned on the continued existence of the property, either expressly or by implication. In the case of the unsecured simple contract creditor, generally the contract does not depend on the existence of any particular piece of the debtor's property, and evidently this distinction, while questionable on closer analysis, is relied upon by the courts in denying insurable interest in that situation.

In one case, the insured held a royalty contract under which payment to him was based upon a percentage of the monetary value of the total output of an oil refinery. He was adjudged to have an insurable interest in the oil refinery premises, and was allowed to recover on a policy of fire insurance which insured him against diminution of royalties. In another action, an insured who entered into a long term contract to operate a factory was held to have an insurable interest in the equipment of that factory. In still a third case, a buyer insured a cargo of sugar being shipped to him in the United States from the Phillipines Islands. The contract specified 'no arrival, no sale', and although title did not pass from the seller, the court allowed the buyer an insurable interest in the sugar while in transit.

In a sense, the contract right classification might well be included in the property right concept, for it represents a category of rights which the courts will enforce. However, it seems to belong in a distinct analytical grouping inasmuch as judicial concern here is not so much with an ownership or security interest in a *res* as it is with a relationship of economic disadvantage flowing from the insured event, with such relationship originating *ex contractu*.

(3) Legal liability

Often times, fortuitous damage to a property unit will result in some form of legal liability on the part of one individual to another. If the occurrence of an insured event will cause an individual economic disadvantage in the form of legal liability, courts have tended to find an insurable interest in that happening. The policy of liability insurance itself is to be distinguished, however, from legal liability as an insurable interest in property. In liability insurance, the coverage does not attach to the destruction of an insured physical property unit, but rather the policy amounts to an assurance that the insurance carrier will provide financial protection from personal liability which might accrue to the insured. Thus, in liability insurance, an individual has unlimited interest in his own personal liability.

The majority of the cases in which a potential legal liability engendered by destruction of the insured subject matter is held sufficient to establish an insurable interest has involved a liability accruing primarily through contract. It is familiar law that, in the absence of contractual stipulation, a builder stands the loss arising from fortuitous destruction of a building in the course of construction. Since the builder is legally liable to the owner for the completion of the contract, he has an insurable interest which is sufficient to support a 'builder's risk' policy covering the premises while under construction. Similarly, a bailee who agrees contractually to insure the bailor's interest in the bailed property has an insurable interest, and he may insure the property in his own name. A guarantor of a secured obligation, if held liable, would be subrogated to the lien against the secured property, and so he has been held to have an insurable interest in that property. The possibilities, however, are not limited to contract situations. An innocent convertor, under some circumstances, may be liable to a rightful owner, and his insurable interest in the converted chattel has been recognised.

(4) Factual expectation of damage

This fourth conception, the so called factual expectation of damage, is broad enough to occupy the entire field of juridical inquiry into the existence of insurable interest. However, despite early entry into the common law of insurance, this concept has enjoyed but uncertain recognition by the courts even to this modern day. The factual expectation is the simplest expressed, yet most all inclusive of the insurable interest concepts; it is the expectation of economic advantage if the insured property continued to exist, or, stated negatively, the expectation of economic disadvantage accruing upon damage to the insured property.

The origin of the factual expectation concept may perhaps be traced to Lord Mansfield's equivocal opinion in *Le Cras v Hughes* (1782) 3 Doug KB 81. However, it is first clearly set forth by Lawrence J in *Lucena v Craufurd* (1806) 2 Bos & PNR 269: '... it is applicable to protect men against uncertain events which may in any wise be of disadvantage to them.' In that case, Lord Eldon, writing another opinion laying down the requirement of legally enforceable interest in the property, said: 'That expectation though founded on the highest probability, was not interest ...' As indicated previously, Lord Eldon's strict formulation has become classical in the law, and the result has been an undue emphasis on property interests in the thing insured. In the overwhelming majority of the cases, judicial reasoning proceeds on the premise that a legally enforceable right is the measure of insurable interest. Nevertheless, factual expectation, a divergent concept, has had some judicial currency.

A complicating factor is the wide circulation given factual expectation language through the media of several widely cited treatises and encyclopaedias. Many courts adopt these quotations *in toto* and give the impression that factual expectation as an insurable interest is settled law. Actually, most of the cases with liberal sprinklings of factual expectation language involve situations where actual property rights exist in the insured. Actions often belie words, for while a court may speak benevolently of the factual expectation in a case where there is already a property interest, later the same court will deny recovery to another claimant without property interest but with a factual expectation of damage.

In the limited area in which factual expectations have gained recognition, there have been a few recurrent situations where more realistic courts have allowed the interest. A favourite situation involves a possessor or operator of real property who has no judicially enforceable property right. In *Liverpool and London and Globe Insurance Co v Bolling* 176 Va 182 (1940), a land and building owner allowed his former daughter-in-law to occupy the property rent free and to operate it as a business. There was some showing of intention on the part of the owner to convey a fee simple to the woman later, but no promise enforceable in equity appears. On destruction of the property by fire, the court allowed her a fee simple measure of recovery. Citing many of the widely circulated factual expectation quotations, the court clearly puts the interest in terms of deriving economic support from the productivity of the premises ...

(III) POLICY CONSIDERATIONS UNDERLYING THE INSURABLE INTEREST CONCEPT

(A) The policy against wagering under the guise of insurance

(1) Analysis of the policy

The policy against enforcement of wagering contracts was developed in England primarily through the legislative rather than the judicial process. The common law courts tolerated wagers, and it was only by a series of statutes culminating in the Gaming Act of 1845 that all wagering contracts came to be considered anathema. With the English experience as a background, it was not unusual that, in the main, American jurisdictions early condemned wagering agreements as contrary to their common law policy ...

(2) Wagering and insurance differentiated

It is not the purpose of this article to take a stand in the controversy as to the validity of the policy against wagering. Assuming the validity of that policy, it is, however, pertinent to inquire as to the relationship between wagering and insurance, in order that evaluation may be made of the extent to which the policy against wagering should be carried over into insurance law.

While a perfectly fair wager is demonstrably unsound from the purely economic viewpoint, the insurance contract is not unsound, and in fact produces a net gain to society. Assume that X procures a $5,000 policy of fire insurance for a premium of $50. Further assume ideally fair conditions such that the chance of the destruction by fire of the $5,000 worth of property is one in one hundred. The bargain is then sound, because the $5,000 X may lose by fire represents a greater loss in terms of sacrifice in marginal utilitarian terms than one hundred times the loss of the $50 required to pay the premium.

It is also clear that the sociological arguments against gambling have in general little bearing on insurance. There is no anti-social aspect to insurance, for it is not a matter of one losing and the other gaining; rather do both gain. The insured is fortified by the knowledge of the security of his economic expectations, enjoying quiet reliance, and the successful insurer reaps a profit which, unlike that of the typical gambler, is invested for socially beneficial purposes. The criminal and domestically disruptive aspects of gambling are not at all in evidence in insurance contracts. Property insurance is not commonly contemplated as a wagering transaction; if a wager is desired, far more usual and convenient devices are available with far greater chance of fortuitous success.

It should not be supposed, however, that there is no gambling aspect to insurance. Where the insured has no valuable relationship to the property or where the insurance is in excess of the insured's interest, that is, 'whenever there is no genuine risk to be hedged', the evils of wagering in part reappear. Thus, while the requirement of an insurable interest in the form of some valuable relationship to the occurrence insured against does have validity, the prime danger to be avoided policywise is the equating of the economically necessary 'insurable interest' with the legal categories customarily embraced within that term. While some form of valuable relationship to the occurrence is necessary to avoid the wagering aspect, the policy against wagering is satisfied by any valuable relationship which equals the pecuniary value of the insurance, regardless of the legal nature of that relationship.

(B) The policy to prevent temptation to destroy the insured property

The theory behind this policy is simple: if the insured has no 'interest' in the subject matter of the insurance, he is likely to destroy the subject matter in order to gain the benefit of the insurance. It is believed that closer analysis of this policy will reveal that the dangers envisioned by it are more fanciful than real.

An important consideration striking at the validity of the temptation argument is the fact that in numerous instances the presence of an insurable interest not only does not minimise the alleged temptation but actually increases it. What if the impecunious fee simple owner the market value of whose property has in an economic depression declined beneath the level of his insurance coverage? Knowing his recovery will be the replacement value or perhaps a fixed valuation, will not this owner, although he has the greatest possible insurable interest – the fee simple, yet be tempted? What of the life tenant whose recovery is measured by the value of the fee simple interest? Will not he, despite his universally approved 'insurable interest', be tempted to destroy the property?

Furthermore, it is believed that the minimisation of temptation allegedly produced by the requirement of insurable interest is completely neutralised by the fact that the presence of an insurable interest ordinarily gives the greatest assurance that destruction of the subject matter can be effectuated without detection. Assume that X, an individual of criminal mind, seeks to defraud an insurance company. Assume further that the requirement of insurable interest does not exist in his state. Can anyone reasonably suppose that X will insure Building A, in which he has no property interest, burn it down, and then seek to collect the insurance? This is unlikely because his collection of proceeds on the loss would be probative of his criminal guilt, and the criminal law serves as a deterrent force against such conduct. Likewise, the watchfulness of the insurer who stands to lose by destruction of the property serves as an assurance that policies will not be recklessly issued to throngs of wrongdoers. Typically, X, as a reasonably prudent criminal, will burn down his own property which he has over-insured. Since the property is his own, he can systematically plan the fraud and carry it out, undisturbed by prying eyes, and leaving a minimum of evidence – things he could do only with great difficulty were the property in the control of another. Therefore, it is unrealistic to assume that the requirement of insurable interest minimises temptation; it may well in fact increase it. The requirement is based on theoretical considerations viewed *in vacuo* rather than in terms of social facts.

(C) The policy favouring limitation of indemnity

The traditional view of the insurance contract is that it is one of indemnity against loss. This view is in accord with the layman's notion of insurance. Typically, the layman takes out insurance not for any wagering purpose but to assure himself of financial protection in the event of the subject matter of the insurance is destroyed.

But what is behind the policy of insurable interest as a limitation on indemnity? Is it a separate and independent policy consideration in addition to those policies against wagering and against the promotion of temptation to destruction? It is submitted that it is not in any sense an independent policy, but merely another head of the hydra that is the policy against wagering. To the extent that a possible insurance recovery is in excess of the insured's interest, it is a wager, and limiting indemnity to the extent of the interest is simply the way in which an insurance contract is removed from the wager category. The traditionally distinct purpose of insurable interest as a limitation on indemnity is, then, merely the wagering policy accoutered in different verbal cloth.

(IV) RE-EVALUATION: SOCIO-ECONOMIC UTILITY AND THE LEGAL CONCEPT

A realistic analysis of the purposes of the requirement of insurable interest yields the conclusion that the strong public policy against the enforceability of wagering contracts is at the base of the concept. While the general policy to discourage destruction of property has moral soundness and laudable social purpose, it is improperly associated with insurable interest. The historic notion that insurance is a contract of indemnity is doubtless true both in the contemplation of society and in the typical motivation for procuring an insurance policy, but as related to insurable interest it is merely another manifestation of the antagonism to the wager.

Procurement of a policy of insurance is an investment prompted by commercial foresight. This foresight involves a recognition of a desirable economic relationship to a thing capable of destruction or damage, and the prudence of allocating certain monetary sums to insure financial protection in the event of a catastrophic occurrence. While in a broad semantic sense all insurance contracts are wagers, the notion has developed in the law that if there is an interest in the subject matter of the insurance, independent of the occurrence of the insured event, then there is no wager. The qualification of interest independent of the happening of the occurrence is necessary because any wagerer has an economic interest in the happening of the wagered occurrence, that is, either winning or losing the stakes …

If a policyholder has absolutely no relation to the property insured in any conceivable way, except that its destruction will inure to his benefit because he has staked money on that contingency, it is clearly a wager and not a *bona fide* commercial risk to be shifted. If the policyholder is the sole and unconditional owner of unencumbered property, his insurance policy is patently a legitimate exercise of economic foresight, a shifting of a risk which will be regarded as an investment, not as a wager. But between the wagerer and the absolute owner is situated a vast assortment of persons, standing in various relationships to the property insured. Through this mass, the men of the law have drawn a line, and those who find themselves in the company of the wagerer on his side of the line are damned as wagerers themselves and denied the right to enter into an enforceable contract of insurance. The distressing factor in this picture is that the assemblage on the wagering side of the line contains relatively few sinister individuals of the popular gambler stereotype, for most are productive law abiding citizens who have freely paid insurance premiums in prosecution of the traditional freedom of contract. These latter 'wagerers' are drawn from diffused economic segments; they are unsecured creditors, occupiers of land, spouses and others anticipating a factual expectation of damage from the insured event.

Based on economic analysis it is submitted that there is only one true concept of insurable interest, and that is the factual expectation of damage …

(V) CONCLUSION

The law of insurable interest in property is entangled in considerations of the general policy against wagering. While the early English underwriters, particularly of life and marine risks, presented the courts with many invidious wagering transactions, the wager is clearly exaggerated in modern property insurance contemplation. Property insurance is procured almost universally by those seeking indemnification; the wagerer finds the cold precision of the calculated premium and the actuarial computation less attractive a gaming board than more conventional gambling devices. The question of an intended wager rarely arises; typically, the insured thinks he is exercising legitimate commercial foresight, only to discover upon later judicial analysis that he is a wagerer.

Since men unlearned in the law regard their insurance policies as instruments of security and assurance, it is a grievous sociological error on the part of the judicial fraternity to allow insurance policy obligations to flake away mysteriously, and to prevent the procurement of insurance policies by interested parties who do not own traditional property rights. There must be a true perception of property right concepts in insurable interests, and a thorough recognition that 'insurable interest' implies merely a relationship to a property unit that will lead to economic disadvantage if the property unit is impaired. The insurance carrier serves a valuable function in society, that of shifting economic risks. His service as indemnitor should not be limited to a judicially approved panel, but should extend to all the members of society who possess economic relationships confronted with loss by potential fortuitous events.

The term insurable interest is manifestly a misnomer; the proper term is insurable *relationship*. Factual expectation of damage should be the exclusive test of an insurable relationship. To those who cling to strict property delineations in fear of the process of drawing the line between a genuine factual expectation of damage and a wager, it can be said not only that judicial wisdom is equal to the task, but that a just line drawn with difficulty exceeds in value a simple line which works disproportionate injustice.

CHAPTER 3

MAKING AND BREAKING THE INSURANCE CONTRACT

INTRODUCTION

All of the normal rules relating to the formation of a valid contract apply equally to an insurance contract: offer, acceptance, consideration and an intention to form legal relations. However, there are several 'special' topics relating to insurance contracts not normally found in other commercial contracts, for example, cover notes (or interim insurance) and renewals. All of the normal contract pitfalls that may hinder the enforcement of a contract also apply to insurance contracts. Thus, mistake, illegality, misrepresentation and non-disclosure require comment. Mistake, as a topic, requires only the briefest mention, while illegality has a special importance in insurance contract law. Misrepresentation and non-disclosure play such a vastly important role that the discussion necessitates its own chapter (Chapter 4).

Formation

Offer and acceptance

As with other contracts, the insurance contract need not be in writing. But, as with other contracts, there are exceptions: s 22 of the Marine Insurance Act 1906 states that a contract of marine insurance is inadmissible in evidence unless it is embodied in a marine policy.

It will be rare for an insurance contract not to be in writing and both parties will find greater certainty in having the agreement reduced to writing. Contracts made with a Lloyd's syndicate require a special note (see below). The vast majority of consumer insurance contracts and the vast majority of commercial insurance contracts will start out with a proposal form drawn up by the insurer. However, such proposal forms do not necessarily contain standard forms of wording. The competitive nature of insurance selling leads to companies competing in trying to convince applicants that their form is more user friendly than their competitors. Common sense should dictate that, in order to elicit full information from the applicant, and, in order that the insurer can make a sound underwriting decision, the questions should be detailed. However, that clashes with the desire to make things simple and user friendly. The battle has been won by the short, simple proposal form. It will be seen in Chapter 4, however, that the form may become a trap for the applicant. In addition, the huge growth in direct insurance selling, usually by means of the telephone and presumably, before long, the internet, may pose additional problems for the courts to resolve just as did the telephone and telex contracts of yesteryear. Normally, it can be said that the proposal form is a document, the completion of which becomes an offer by the applicant to the insurer. Any questions from the insurer arising from the completed application would probably amount to 'negotiations' or possibly a counter-offer if the language was sufficiently certain.

If the application is accepted unconditionally, then a contract is formed – at least that appears to be the conventionally held view. The problem with that view is that the price/premium has yet to be relayed to the applicant. Obviously, it will be relayed at the time of the 'acceptance'. But what if the premium is higher than the applicant anticipated? If it is a valid acceptance by the insurer, it would be too late for the insured to complain. In consumer insurance, it is not unknown for the applicant wishing to compare premiums to complete several application forms simultaneously, particularly when several appear, unsolicited, through the post. It cannot be that the applicant must pay several premiums. The applicant intends to select that which is most suitable to his needs. The concept of a fixed tariff for certain types of risk is alien to British insurance practice. Each insurer prides himself on being able to compete with many competitors. The sensible way out of the conundrum is that the applicant should be in the position of accepting one policy and rejecting the others. Life insurers generally avoid the problem by making the cover dependant on receiving the first premium. Even in commercial insurance, the applicant will want to test the water by receiving at least an indication of the premium before he commits himself.

Section 31 of the Marine Insurance Act 1906 provides its own answer to the problem by stating that, if the insurance is effected at a premium to be arranged and this is not done, then a reasonable premium becomes payable. The courts will have to determine what is reasonable, if the parties fail to do so, by looking at all the circumstances of the case and market practice at that date. It seems, then, that the offer-acceptance formula applicable to non-insurance situations does not readily and easily translate to the insurance contract.

These problems are well illustrated by the decision in *Canning v Farquahar* (1886) 16 QBD 727 (Appendix 3.1). C completed a proposal form for life insurance which contained questions as to his state of health. The form contained a declaration that the answers were true and that they were to form the basis of the contract (see further Chapter 5). The proposal was accepted, but stated that no insurance was to take effect until the first premium was paid. Before that premium was paid, C fell from a cliff and was seriously injured. The premium was then tendered but the insurers refused to accept it. C later died and a claim was unsuccessfully made by the administrators. While the court was unanimous in its decision, the different analyses illustrate how difficult this area of insurance law can be. Lord Esher MR was of the view that all that transpired between C and the insurer were negotiations lacking contractual force, while the majority of the court was of the view that the insurer had made a counter-offer and, if C had remained healthy, he could have paid the premium and the contract would then have been activated.

Another example is given in *Looker and Another v Law Union and Rock Insurance Co* [1928] 1 KB 554 (Appendix 3.2). This was also an application for a life policy, wherein the applicant stated that he was free from disease or ailment and the answers were to form the basis of the contract. The insurers accepted the proposal, adding that the risk would not commence until the first premium was paid. Illness was diagnosed seven days after the letter of acceptance was received and he died four days later. The day before his death, the insurers received the first payment and, unaware of the illness, they sent him the certificate of insurance. The insurers were held not liable on the policy. The decision illustrates a general point of insurance law; that known changes in the factual situation, prior to the inception of the policy, need to be communicated to the insurer, thus allowing him the opportunity not to continue. Failure to do so infringes the good faith requirement discussed in Chapter 4.

Consideration

The premium is normally the consideration which cements the contract. Obviously, it is not the actual payment that is required, except in situations as in *Canning*, but the obligation to pay the premium. If the obligation to pay arises, then the contract does not date from when payment is made. This is important should there be a change of circumstance before payment. Unless there are delaying words, as used in *Canning* and *Looker*, then there would be no requirement to inform the insurer of the change because the contract is already in being.

Life insurance is usually paid by instalment, although it is possible to have a single premium policy. A growing trend is to allow motor insurance to be paid by instalments as a method of alleviating the financial burden on the insured to pay a large sum annually. Instalment payments will only really work where the insured is able to utilise one of the banking transactions now available. Failure by the bank to pay one of the instalments would allow the customer (the insured) to sue his bank for failure to carry out his instruction. Some insurers will allow a late payment by virtue of any 'days of grace' provisions.

Most insurance policies in Britain, other than life insurance, are annual contracts and thus need to be renewed. In some other Member States of the EU, insurance contracts are often for more than 12 months.

There is no legal requirement for an insurer to notify the insured of the need to renew although this will normally be done in order to maintain the business connection. However, if this is not done, perhaps due to an administrative mistake at the insurer's end or due to the postal system, the insured is in the precarious situation of being unknowingly uninsured.

Although there would appear to be no common law rule requiring notification it is interesting to note that the General Insurance Standards Council (GISC, see Chapter 6, below, and Appendix 6.1) in both its General Insurance Code for private customers and in its Commercial Code requires its members, which include both insurers and intermediaries, to give the customer notice of renewal in time for the customer to consider and arrange any necessary continuation of cover. Of course the Code is self-regulatory and in that sense not legally binding but it could be used by a court to find that a necessary duty of care is owed.

The (Australian) Insurance Contracts Act 1984 (Cth) (Appendix 3.3) deals with the problem of renewal in a way beneficial to the insured. Section 58 requires the insurer to provide notice no later than 14 days before expiration of the policy and if this is not done the policy will be automatically renewed. Section 58(4) is truly remarkable, in that the renewal contract is free of charge unless a claim is made, in which case a formula is set out whereby the insured will have to pay a renewal premium, but only one which is financially related to the previous year's premium.

Cover notes – interim insurance

In many instances speed in completing the insurance cover is essential to the insured – or so he believes. Motor insurance is a good example, as explained by Pearson J in *Julien Praet et Cie v Poland* [1960] 1 Lloyd's Rep 416 (Appendix 3.4):

> The typical motorist is an impatient person ... having bought a car he wishes to take delivery and drive off in it at once and he would not be willing to wait for the traditional steps to be taken ...

The insurance industry responded to such urgent needs by means of interim insurance, more commonly known as a cover note. This will provide the applicant with immediate cover, typically for 14 or 28 days, and it will also provide the insurer with the time to consider the application in more detail. At the end of the time period, the policy will either be confirmed by both parties, or it will allow one of them to decide not to enter into an annual contract.

If the contract matures into a full term policy, it may be on different terms to that found in the cover note, for this may reflect the insurer's assessment that different terms are required as a result of his underwriting practices.

The greatest danger that faces an insured when applying for a cover note is that the full duty of disclosure, discussed in Chapter 4, is required. It may well be that only a limited number of questions are asked of him at this stage, but the rules relating to non-disclosure (as set out in the next chapter) still apply.

There appears to be no English case directly on this point, but, if the interim cover is to be classified as a distinct insurance, then the preceding view is probably correct. The leading case is an Australian decision: *Mayne Nickless Ltd v Pegler* [1974] 1 NSWLR 228. This also illustrates the added problems that may arise when dealing with an intermediary at this stage. (For insurance intermediaries generally, see Chapter 6.) In this case, it was a garage that had been given authority, by the insurer, to grant cover notes and it is unlikely that the applicant would have received detailed advice as to the pitfalls of the law of misrepresentation and non-disclosure. The wording of the cover note stated that the cover was subject to 'a satisfactory proposal for your insurance'. The insured did not divulge at the garage that he had been involved in an accident a few months previously. Two days after the cover note was issued, he was involved in a collision with the plaintiff's vehicle and the insured later died. His wife completed the proposal form and she failed to answer correctly a question seeking information about earlier accidents. The insurers were able to avoid their liability under the cover note. The decision was approved by the Privy Council in *Marene Knitting Mills Ltd v General Pacific Insurance* [1976] 2 Lloyd's Rep 631. For criticisms of *Mayne Nickless*, see Birds, J (1977) 40 MLR 79.

The heavy burden placed on an insured by the decision has, at least in Australia, been mitigated by s 38 of the (Australian) Insurance Contracts Act 1984 (Cth) (Appendix 3.3), which renders void any provision in an interim contract of insurance whereby the liability of the insurer is dependent on the acceptance by him of a proposal which is intended to replace the interim cover.

Insurers' usual terms

One of the basic rules of contract law is that there must be 'certainty of terms'. Without certainty there can not be a true agreement because there will be vagueness preventing a meeting of the minds.

Insurers however sometimes refer to the acceptance being made on their 'usual terms', which may or may not be known to the proposer. If such terms are known, and constructive knowledge will be sufficient, for instance when the parties have had previous dealings, then there is deemed to be sufficient certainty for a valid contract.

In consumer contracts, reference should be made to the Unfair Terms in Consumer Contracts Regulations 1994 (now 1999) (Appendix 7.1 and Clarke, M, *The Law of Insurance Contracts*, 3rd edn, London: LLP, pp 19–5A, 19–5A5). One of the illustrations in the regulations of an unfair term in a consumer (insurance) contract is where the consumer is bound by terms with which he had had no real opportunity of becoming acquainted before the conclusion of the contract. This would appear to strike at the very core of the way insurers presently transact business. The policy wording is rarely transmitted to the proposer until some time after the contract has been concluded. The

Association of British Insurers, in commenting on the original Regulations in 1995, appeared, however, to be unconcerned. Their view was:

> The Association of British Insurers' Statement of General Insurance Practice [Appendix 4.10] already provides that unless the prospectus or the proposal form contains full details of the standard cover offered, and whether or not it contains an outline of that cover, the proposal form shall include a prominent statement that a specimen copy of the policy form is available on request. The regulations, therefore, do not impose any additional requirements in this regard.
>
> In addition, when the product is sold by an intermediary other than a registered broker, Association of British Insurers member companies are required to use their best endeavours to ensure that those selling their policies observe the provisions of the Association of British Insurers' General Insurance Business Code of Selling Practice [see Appendix 6.5].

The Office of Fair Trading's Unfair Contract Terms Bulletin No 1 of 1996, without specifically singling out any particular type of supplier, stated that one of the categories of unfair terms most commonly encountered in consumer contracts was one where consumers were bound by terms they could not get to know before signing the contract. It remains to be seen whether the Association of British Insurers' views prove to be correct. One answer may be to provide a 'cooling-off' period in situations where the proposer receives the policy at a later stage, similar to that which applies to investment contracts under the Financial Services and Markets Act 2000 (FSMA).

An early case which helps to illustrate the problem of knowledge of terms is *Re Coleman's Depositaries Ltd v Life and Health Assurance Association* [1907] 2 KB 798 (Appendix 3.5).

The plaintiff, on 28 December, applied for insurance to cover his liability as an employer under the Workmen's Compensation Act. He received a cover note from the insurer's agent and later, on 10 January, he received the policy. The note contained no reference to any conditions. On 2 January, a workman was injured and at that time the injuries were not considered to be serious and no notice was given to the insurer until 14 March. On 15 March, the workman died. On 27 March, the employer received notice of a claim from the deceased's widow. This information was sent on to the insurer on 29 March and they refused the claim on the grounds that clause 2 of the policy, which required 'immediate notice of any accident', had been breached by the employer. The Court of Appeal, by a majority, found against the insurers. You may feel, however, that Fletcher-Moulton LJ's dissent is more compelling.

Formation of contract at Lloyd's

Insurance business placed at Lloyd's has its own unique procedures. Historically, it was only possible to place business at Lloyd's by using an accredited Lloyd's broker. However during the 1990s there was an easing of this requirement as a reflection of Lloyd's desire to open its doors to a wider class of business and as a reflection of modernising the way insurance business is transacted in general. The controlling byelaw is the Lloyd's Brokers Byelaw 2000 (see Chapter 6 for more detail).

The method of obtaining cover is for the Lloyd's broker to prepare a slip, which is a document which sets out the main essentials of the cover required. The language on the slip is heavily abbreviated which makes it incomprehensible to those who do not have a working knowledge of Lloyd's, for example: AOL (any one loss); AP (additional premium); fc & s (free of capture and seizure); LPSO (Lloyd's Policy Signing Office); NCAD (notice of cancellation at anniversary date); wtd (warranted). The Lloyd's broker approaches an underwriter of a syndicate who he knows specialises in the type of cover required. The underwriter will usually become the lead underwriter and he will initial the slip for the percentage of the risk that he is prepared to cover. The Lloyd's broker will then trawl the rest of the market in an effort to place the whole business, or he may combine this with percentages obtained from other non-Lloyd's insurers. Each party completes a binding contract for the percentage of any loss that becomes payable. Often no policy is issued and then the slip remains the most important document.

For detailed accounts of the way business is placed at Lloyd's, see *Rozanes v Bowen* (1928) 32 Ll L Rep 98; *American Airlines Inc v Hope* [1974] 2 Lloyd's Rep 301; *Fennia Patria* [1983] 2 Lloyd's Rep 287; *The Zephyr* [1984] 1 Lloyd's Rep 58.

Vitiating factors

Mistake

Insurance cases affected by mistake rarely come before the courts. This is fortunate, as mistake is a notoriously difficult area of the law of contract, with the common law and equity dealing with the problem in different ways. The leading texts on insurance law afford the topic little room. Standard contract textbooks tend to divide the discussion of mistake into common mistake, mutual mistake and unilateral mistake.

Common mistake is said to apply where the parties to the contract share a common misunderstanding material to the foundation of the agreement. So, in *Strickland v Turner* (1852) 7 Exch 208, the plaintiff appeared to purchase by way of agreement an annuity on the life of X. Unknown to the purchaser and seller, X had died three weeks earlier. The plaintiff was entitled to a return of his money on the grounds that he had received no consideration for the price paid.

Mutual mistake arises when the parties are at cross-purposes to a sufficient degree to prevent a true agreement. There must, however, be a genuine mistake and not merely a situation where only one party alleges a mistake. Thus, in *Zurich General Accident Insurance Co v Rowberry* [1954] 2 Lloyd's Rep 55, brokers acting on behalf of the insured, for travel insurance, wrongly stated the destination as Paris whereas it was Nice. The Court of Appeal held that there was no genuine mutual mistake as the brokers had the authority to nominate the destination, which they had done. The insured was required to pay the premium.

Unilateral mistake applies where one party has made a mistake and the other party knows of the mistake.

It is possible for either party to ask the court to rectify a mistake, but the burden on the applicant is heavy, because the court works from the assumption that the parties intended what they said, and to which they appeared to agree. Rectification was refused in *Mint Security Ltd v Blair* [1982] 2 Lloyd's Rep 188.

Illegality

Illegality in general contract law also poses real problems of classification, leading the major texts to subdivide their discussion into many parts.

One of the reasons for this difficulty is the problem of isolating the fundamental cause when describing a contract as illegal. One of the trickiest areas is where the courts have decided that the transaction is against public policy. Public policy is notoriously difficult to define and, as society changes, so, too, have the courts' views. In insurance law, the problem is increased because in some contracts, while the behaviour of the insured can be described as being against public policy, the ultimate purpose of the insurance is to provide compensation for an innocent third party. The most obvious example is where there is compulsory insurance, for example, under the Road Traffic legislation.

You should first start by reading 'Illegal insurance' (Appendix 3.6) and 'Unblinkering the unruly horse: public policy in the law of contract' (Appendix 3.7), wherein many of the following cases are discussed.

Illegal under statute

The Life Assurance Act 1774 (Appendix 2.2) does not contain the word 'illegal', but merely declares that the contract without an insurable interest is *void*. Case law, however, has described such contracts as illegal, as in *Harse v Peal Life Assurance Co* [1904] 1 KB 558 (Appendix 2.11). Similar language in s 4 of the Marine Insurance Act 1906 has, by contrast, been held not to make a contract lacking an insurable interest illegal. Whereas s 41 of the Marine Insurance Act 1906 declares that there is to be an implied warranty that the (marine) adventure insured is a lawful one.

It has been explained, in Chapter 1, that an insurance company must be authorised to carry on a business. What then of insurance contracts issued by an unauthorised insurer? There were conflicting decisions in the 1980s as to the answer. The opportunity was first taken in s 132 of the Financial Services Act 1986 to settle the matter.

The same approach is to be seen in ss 26–28 of the FSMA. Where a policy has been issued by a person who is unauthorised to carry out that activity then it is not enforceable by the party in breach, the insurer. It is enforceable by the innocent party. The Act goes on however to allow the court a discretion to permit the unauthorised party to enforce the contract if the court believes that it would be just and equitable to do so in the circumstances. The usual reason to exercise the discretion would be where the offending party reasonably believed that it had authorisation to carry on that class of business. This could arise where there has been an administrative slip-up in seeking authorisation.

Life insurance and public policy

As a general principle of insurance law, the insured must not voluntarily bring about the insured event. That then raises the question of suicide and payment under a life policy. Until the Suicide Act 1961, it was illegal to attempt or to commit suicide. The leading case on the pre-1961 situation is *Beresford v Royal Insurance Co Ltd* [1937] 2 KB 197 (Appendix 3.8). The House of Lords refused to order the payment on a life policy where the insured had committed suicide, on the grounds that it would be against public policy, even though the policy provided for payment in the case of a sane suicide committed more than one year after the inception of the policy. After the abolition of suicide as a crime in 1961, the question must still be answered as to whether payment in such situation is still contrary to public policy. Society's attitude to suicide has changed and, in the intervening years, cases, particularly in the law of negligence, have allowed claims for damages where a person has been negligently allowed to commit suicide while in the care of others, for example, in police or prison custody or in hospital. Presumably, courts today will allow a claim on a life policy unless, of course, the claim was expressly excluded in the policy. To avoid the possibility of a person who is contemplating suicide taking out a policy just prior to the suicide, it is normal practice to agree to pay only if the suicide occurs more than one year after the policy is taken out.

Aiding and abetting a suicide remains a crime. In *Dunbar v Plant* [1997] 4 All ER 289 (Appendix 3.9), a man and a woman agreed on a suicide pact largely at the instigation of the woman. The attempt resulted in the death of the man but the woman survived. The man held a life policy with the woman as beneficiary. Despite the fact that the woman was guilty of the crime of aiding and abetting, the Court of Appeal held that her claim to the insurance moneys should be allowed. To arrive at the decision, the court (by a 2:1 majority) exercised its discretion to modify the forfeiture rule under the Forfeiture Act 1982 which is defined, in s 1(1), as meaning the rule of public policy which, in certain circumstances, precludes a person who has unlawfully killed another from acquiring a benefit in consequence of the killing. This result may surprise some people, but it goes to illustrate how the public policy decisions of the court can be finely balanced.

The *Beresford* decision was referred to in *Davitt and Another v Titcumb* [1989] 3 All ER 417 (Appendix 3.10). In *Davitt*, two parties had bought a house which was part financed and supported by an endowment policy. One murdered the other (an example of the fears that lay behind the Life Assurance Act 1774?) and, once the mortgage lender had been repaid, a surplus sum of money remained. The personal representatives of the deceased successfully argued that the murderer should not be entitled to take his share. To allow the claim would: 'run counter to the reasoning that underlies the rule of public policy ...' These three cases illustrate the range of issues that the death of one party can have on the courts' interpretation and application of public policy in relation to an insurance claim.

It is convenient here to discuss the decision in *Gray and Another v Barr* [1971] 2 Lloyd's Rep 1 (Appendix 3.11), which involved accident insurance rather than life insurance. B's wife was having an affair with G. B believed that his wife was at G's house. He entered with a shotgun, intending to scare him rather than harm him. A scuffle broke out, the gun was discharged and G was killed. B was acquitted of murder and manslaughter, but was successfully sued under the Fatal Accident Acts and the dependents were awarded £6,000. B had a domestic policy that would pay out should B become legally liable to pay damages in respect of bodily injury caused by accidents. Two questions arose. Was the death caused by an accident? And, if so, would public policy (that is, indemnifying B against his liability to pay the damages) be invoked to prevent such indemnification? The answer was that it was *not* an accident, because B had entered the house with a loaded gun with the intention of frightening G and had fired the first shot into the ceiling. However, we are here concerned with the courts' attitude to public policy *if* it had been classed as an accidental death. The court also held that it would be against public policy to require the insurers to indemnify B against his liability to G's dependants. Some commentators have criticised the decision and it will be difficult to distinguish it from the motor cases below. The purpose of that part of the domestic policy was to provide compensation for liability for causing bodily injury to others. One could be forgiven for thinking that the dominant public policy issue should be that victims receive their damages, rather than that wrongdoers must not be indemnified against the liability to pay those damages. What effect, if any, do you think the opening sentence of Lord Denning's judgment had on the final outcome? 'Mr and Mrs Barr have a prosperous business at Tooting in ladies blouses ...'

The motor cases and public policy

Accidents caused by drivers which result in personal injury to others will usually lead to the prosecution of that driver. The seriousness of the charge will reflect the seriousness of the driving offence. If the injured party makes a claim in negligence for damages against that driver should the public policy reasons referred to in *Gray v Barr*, above, apply also to road traffic situations? In other words, should a grossly negligent drunk driver be indemnified against the successful claim made by the injured party? Should there be a sliding scale of seriousness, at some point on which, indemnification of the driver is appropriate? The answer is that, in road accidents caused by the criminal behaviour of the insured, no matter how grave may be the seriousness of the offence, it will result in the innocent victim receiving compensation from the insurer, or the Motor Insurers' Bureau when the motorist is uninsured. Thus, the interpretation of public policy requirements are different in motor cases than in other situations. It probably is the case, however, that the victim's procedural right to claim directly against the insurer under the Road Traffic Acts is the major reason for the victim's successful claim (see *Hardy*, below).

The following three cases help to illustrate the courts' approach to the situation.

In the early case of *Tinline v White Cross Insurance Association Ltd* [1921] 3 KB 327 (Appendix 3.12), the motorist had insurance, even though at that date it was not a compulsory requirement. He drove at an excessive speed, killing one person and injuring two others. He was convicted of manslaughter. The victims commenced proceeding against the driver and he sought a declaration that the insurers would be liable to indemnify him. It was held not to be against public policy to grant the declaration. So here we have the personal indemnification of the wrongdoers and it was therefore necessary in *Gray v Barr*, above, for Lord Denning to distinguish *Tinline*. Lord Denning added that if the driver's behaviour could be categorised as wilful and culpable then the insured was not himself entitled to be indemnified. This leads us to the next major case in this area.

In *Hardy v Motor Insurers' Bureau* [1964] 2 QB 745 (Appendix 3.13), the plaintiff security officer was injured by the driver of a stolen van when, having stopped to question him, the driver drove off at speed. The driver was convicted of various offences, including driving while uninsured and causing grievous bodily harm. The plaintiff obtained judgment and damages against the driver, which were not paid, and he therefore commenced the present action against the Motor Insurers' Bureau. The Motor Insurers' Bureau defended the action on the grounds that the driver intended to cause harm to the plaintiff and such behaviour was not covered by third party compulsory insurance. The Court of Appeal found for the plaintiff. Lord Denning explained that the wrongdoer himself could not recover on the policy, but where he refused to pay the damages the wording or the Road Traffic Act allowed the victim a direct right to recover against the insurer. Where, as here, there was no insurer, then the role of the Motor Insurers' Bureau came into play. Lord Justice Pearson, quoting from an earlier case, explained that 'the rule of public policy should be applied so as to exclude from benefit the criminal and all claiming under him, but not so as to exclude alternative or independent rights'. If the driver had honoured the judgment he would not then have been able to recover from his insurers if he had been insured. At that point the rule of public policy would be invoked whereby a wrongdoer may not benefit from his wrongdoing.

It was perhaps inevitable that the House of Lords would eventually be called upon to decide if *Hardy*'s case was correctly decided. The question was dealt with in *Gardner v Moore* [1984] 1 All ER 1100 (Appendix 3.14). D1 intentionally drove his car at the plaintiff. He was convicted of causing grievous bodily harm. He was not insured. The plaintiff sued D1 and joined the Motor Insurers' Bureau as D2. The House of Lords found for the plaintiff, upholding the decision in *Gardner*. Lord Hailsham LC said:

> To invoke, as the Motor Insurers' Bureau now do, the well known doctrine of public policy, that a man may not profit by the consequences of his own wrongdoing, seems to me to stand the principle of public policy on its head.

One final case can be referred to in an effort to find a dividing line in public policy attitudes to the motor cases. In *Marcel Beller Ltd v Hayden* [1978] 1 QB 694 (Appendix 3.15), the plaintiff took out a key-man policy on an employee which covered the employee's death. An exclusion operated if the death was due to a deliberate exposure, by the employee, to exceptional danger or if the death was a result of the employee's own criminal act. The employee died in a motor accident when his blood alcohol level was in excess of the legally prescribed limit. The court held that the employee had not deliberately exposed himself to danger; however, the claim failed on the grounds that he had committed the criminal offence of drink driving.

In terms of public policy, the major difference between this case and the cases of *Hardy* and *Gardner* is that there was no innocent, physically injured, third party victim for the court to worry about. In *Pitts v Hunt* [1990] 3 All ER 344, a motorcycle passenger was held to have no claim for his injuries caused by the drunken driver because he had aided and abetted the criminal act; Lord Justice Beldam said:

> The policy underlying the provisions for compulsory insurance for passengers and others injured in a road accident is clearly one intended for their benefit ... If, however, the offence ... is so serious that it preclude the driver on grounds of public policy from claiming indemnity under a policy ... that public policy would ... also preclude the passenger jointly guilty of that offence from claiming compensation.

Do you agree that that is the appropriate 'public policy'? Why did the Road Traffic Act 1972 abolish the defence of *volenti*? The present decision allows the defence of *ex turpi causa* to replace the abandoned *volenti* defence.

Miscellaneous cases and public policy

Two cases can here be compared in an effort to find the dividing line between what is, and is not, regarded as against public policy in an insurance setting.

In *Geismar v Sun Alliance and London Insurance Ltd and Another* [1978] QB 383 (Appendix 3.16), the plaintiff imported jewellery without declaring the items to customs. Such items were liable to forfeiture at any time under the relevant legislation. These items, together with other possessions, were insured by the plaintiff under his home and contents policy. Numerous items were stolen and the plaintiff claimed. The insurers rejected the claim for the undeclared items partly on the grounds of public policy. The court found for the insurers on the grounds that the plaintiff was seeking an indemnity against the loss of items, which he had deliberately imported into the country in breach of the Customs and Excise Act 1952. This was a deliberate breach of the law from which the plaintiff should not be permitted to derive a profit. Losses untainted by the breach were however claimable.

In *Euro-Diam Ltd v Bathurst* [1988] 2 All ER 23 (Appendix 3.17), the plaintiffs were wholesale diamond merchants who supplied diamonds to German customers on a sale or return basis. At the request of the customer, the invoice stated the value as half of the true value, so that if the customer purchased the diamonds he would only pay half of the German customs duty. The plaintiffs insured the diamonds for approximately half the true value. The diamonds were stolen and the plaintiffs claimed the declared, lesser, value. The Court of Appeal allowed the plaintiffs' claim deciding that the insurance contract was not tainted by illegality. The insurers had relied on s 41 of the Marine Insurance Act 1906, referred to above – an implied warranty that the insured venture was a lawful one – and it was thus against public policy to enforce the contract. Section 41 was held not to apply, as it was said to have no application to non-marine policies. Why was the insurance contract not tainted by illegality? The reason was that the understated value has no connection with the policy, there was no deception of the insurers and the plaintiffs did not stand to gain financially from this behaviour. This last point was sufficient to distinguish the present case from *Geismar* where the insured did stand to gain from his illegal importation.

Confused?

The combination of the above cases merely goes to show that public policy really is an 'unruly horse'. When faced with an examination question asking for a discussion of the role played by public policy in insurance law, you could try repeating paras 14–49 of MacGillivray, *Insurance Law*, 9th edn, 1998, London: Sweet & Maxwell:

> We do not believe it is now possible to state a simple distinction between loss intentionally caused by a criminal act, in respect of which no indemnity is permitted, and a loss caused by a negligent act of the assured, also criminal, in respect of which a claim is maintainable. The distinction should be sought in terms of the requirements of public policy …

But I wouldn't!

MAKING AND BREAKING THE INSURANCE CONTRACT

APPENDIX 3.1

Canning v Farquahar (1886) 16 QBD 727, HL

Lord Esher MR: This seems to me to be a very important case in insurance law, and at the beginning of it I was much taken with the ordinary proposition that a proposal and an acceptance of that proposal make a contract. Whether that is so or not depends on whether the one was meant to be a proposal, and the other an acceptance by way of contract, and we are bound to look further and see what was the subject matter. What is the contract of life assurance? It is this, 'Taking the life to be good at the commencement of the risk I insure that life for a year at a certain premium'. From this, it is apparent that the material moment for the agreement as to the state of health is when the risk commences, that is, at the beginning of the year, for it is not denied that the agreement is only for a year. Now, it is said that before that year commenced there was a binding agreement to insure. But is it possible to say that when parties are discussing beforehand the conditions of the risk they mean to treat what they then say are the existing facts as binding them when the moment to make the contract arrives? No one can bind himself as to the state of his health a short time hence, and a man who makes a statement as to his state of health cannot mean to be bound as to what it will be a month hence, neither can the person to whom the statement is made be taken to rely on it further than as it may guide him in accepting the insurance or not. These considerations show that all these statements which are made preliminary to the moment of insurance are not considered by either party as contractual statements, but as expressions of intention on the one side to insure, on the other to accept the risk. That seems to me to be the view at which we must arrive looking at this as a business transaction. Now, there is no case that supports affirmatively this view, but it is supported negatively by the fact that during all the years that life insurance has been known and practised, there is no case in the books or known to any one in which an action such as this has been maintained. These considerations are conclusive to my mind that what was said was preliminary to the contract of insurance, and was never intended by either party to be a contract in itself.

From this it follows that after the insurance company have said that they accept the proposal, and that if the premium is paid they will issue a policy, although there is no change in the circumstances, and all that has happened is that they alter their mind, yet they are not bound to accept the premium. I do not shrink from saying that in my view of insurance law there is no contract in such a case binding them to accept the premium. If so this action fails, because tender is only equivalent to payment if the person to whom the money is offered is bound to accept it. If the premium is offered and accepted there is at once an insurance, and the year for which the insurance runs commences then, and if the policy is drawn up properly that will appear in it …

... If there has been a material change there ought to be an alteration of the representation, and the ground for entering into the contract is altered. In this case, the ground of the contract to give an insurance being changed, it was not binding on the society at the time of the tender of the premium, and they had a right to say 'the circumstances are altered, therefore we will not insure', even though, if the circumstances had not been altered, they would have been bound by their contract. It seems to me, therefore, that the appeal fails. In my opinion, however, the real ground for our decision is that the negotiations before the time when the policy is effected are mere statements of intention, and that till the insurance company accept the premium they have a right to decline to accept the risk.

Lindley LJ: It was urged on the part of the plaintiff that there was then a complete contract binding the office on payment or tender of the premium to issue a policy of insurance. It is true that there had been an acceptance of Canning's offer, but he had not at this time assented to the company's terms; and until he assented to them there was no contract binding the company. The company's acceptance of Canning's offer was not a contract but a counter offer. Subsequently, the premium was tendered, and I think there would be considerable difficulty, if there had been no change in the risk, in saying that the company, under such circumstances might decline to accept the premium and issue the policy. In the case supposed the counter offer would be a continuing offer, the tender would be an acceptance of it, and the company would be bound to issue the policy. But the case supposed is not the case we have to deal with here, because another element is introduced by reason of the material change in the risk in the interval between what I have called the counter offer and the tender of the premium. If Canning had tendered the money and had not informed the office of the alteration in the character of the risk, he would have been attempting to take advantage of an offer intended to cover one risk in order to make it cover another risk not known to the office. In other words, if he had paid the money without disclosing to the office the fact that his statements, which were true when he made them, were so no longer, he would have done that which would have been plainly dishonest. But that was not done – the alteration was disclosed, and the company refused to take the risk. I think they were perfectly justified in so refusing. It comes to this: there was no contract before the tender; and the risk being changed the company's offer could not fairly be regarded as a continuing offer which Canning was entitled to accept. His tender was, in truth, a new offer for a new risk which the company were at liberty to decline. It appears to me, therefore, that this action fails, and the appeal ought to be dismissed.

APPENDIX 3.2

Looker and Another v Law Union and Rock Insurance Co Ltd [1928] 1 KB 554

Acton J: It is said, in the first instance, for the insurance company that the rule applicable in circumstances such as these is that the acceptance is made in reliance upon the continued truth of the representations made in the proposal which it was agreed should form the basis of the contract of insurance, in the belief that there has been no material change in the risk offered, and therefore, that if anything has happened materially to increase the risk between the proposal and the acceptance the insurance company are not bound, because that which they had made a condition of the contract going to the root of it has not been fulfilled. The authority for this statement is to be found in *Canning v Farquahar* and *Harrington v Pearl Life Assurance Co* [(1914) 30 TLR 613]. It is also said materially to strengthen the position of the insurance company that, in this case, their notice of 15 July 1926, in terms intimated to the proposer, that any subsequent acceptance by them of premium and risk would be subject to the condition that the health of the life proposed should remain meanwhile unaffected. That it had not remained unaffected cannot be disputed. It is not indeed putting it too high to say that when the insurance company accepted the premium and the risk on 26 July the deceased was dying, and if the insurance company had known the facts they would never have entertained the notion of accepting the risk for a moment. I think there is no answer in this case to these contentions ...

APPENDIX 3.3

(Australian) Insurance Contracts Act 1984 (Cth) (as amended)

DIVISION 2 – GENERAL PROVISIONS RELATING TO INSURANCE CONTRACTS

Interim contracts of insurance

38 (1) Where, under a provision included in an interim contract of insurance that is, liability of the insurer is dependent upon the submission to, or the acceptance by, the insurer of a proposal for a contract of insurance intended to replace the interim contract of insurance, the provision is void.

(2) Where:

(a) an insurer has entered into an interim contract of insurance; and

(b) before the insurance cover provided by the contract has expired, the insured has submitted a proposal to the insurer for a contract of insurance intended to replace the interim contract of insurance,

the insurer remains liable in accordance with the interim contract of insurance until the earliest of the following times:

(c) the time when insurance cover commences under another contract of insurance (whether or not it is an interim contract of insurance) between the insured and the insurer or some other insurer, being insurance cover that is intended to replace the insurance cover provided by the interim contract of insurance;

(d) the time when the interim contract of insurance is cancelled;

(e) if the insured withdraws the proposal – the time of withdrawal …

PART VII – EXPIRATION, RENEWAL AND CANCELLATION

Insurer to notify of expiration of contracts of general insurance

58 (1) In this section, 'renewable insurance cover' means insurance cover that:

(a) is provided for a particular period of time; and

(b) is of a kind that it is usual to renew or for the renewal of which it is usual to negotiate.

(2) No later than 14 days before the day on which renewable insurance cover provided under a contract of general insurance (in this section called the 'original contract') expires, the insurer shall give to the insured a notice in writing informing him of the day on which and the time at which the cover will expire and whether the insurer is prepared to negotiate to renew or extend the cover.

(3) Where:

(a) an insurer has failed to comply with subsection (2); and

(b) before the original contract expired, the insured had not obtained from some or other insurer insurance cover to replace that provided by the original contract,

then, by force of this section, there exists between the parties to the original contract a contract of insurance that provides insurance cover as provided by the original contract, except that the cover provided is in respect of the period that:

(c) commences immediately after the insurance cover provided by the original contract expires; and

(d) expires, unless the contract is sooner cancelled, at:

(i) the expiration of a period equal to the period during which insurance cover was provided by the original contract; or

(ii) the time when the insured obtains from some other insurer insurance cover to replace that provided by the original contract,

whichever is the earlier.

(4) Where a contract of insurance is in force by virtue of subsection (3):

(a) except in a case to which para (b) applies, no premium is payable in respect of the contract; but

(b) if a claim is made under the contract, there is payable by the insured to the insurer, as a premium in respect of the contract, an amount ascertained in accordance with the formula, where:

'A' is the number of days in the period that commenced on the day on which the contract came into force and ended on the day on which the claim was made;

'B' is the amount that, if the original contract had been renewed for the same period and on the same terms and conditions (including the same contract matter and risk) would have been payable by the insured in respect of the renewal; and

'C' is the number of days in the period of the original contract.

APPENDIX 3.4

Julien Praet et Cie v Poland [1960] 1 Lloyd's Rep 416

Pearson J: Traditionally, the underwriter of a syndicate sits in his box in the underwriting room at Lloyd's, and a Lloyd's broker who has prepared the proposed policy presents a slip giving details of the proposed risk to the underwriter, and the underwriter, if he finds the risk acceptable, insures it by initialling the slip. The policy is then prepared and issued. The Lloyd's broker is the agent of the assured. The underwriter deals only with the Lloyd's broker and not with any outside broker, nor with the assured. This procedure, if it had to be maintained in its full rigour without relaxation or modification, would impede foreign insurance business and would make motor insurance business impossible.

The typical motorist is an impatient person in the sense that, having bought a car, he wishes to take delivery and drive off in it at once, and he would not be willing to wait for the traditional steps to be taken at Lloyd's before he could obtain cover. Therefore, even in the United Kingdom, there has to be the familiar system of the cover note, which is issued at once on receipt of a proposal, and covers the assured and puts the underwriters on risk for the period while the proposal is being considered and until a policy is either granted or refused.

There are hundreds of motor distributors and dealers and other persons in the United Kingdom who are authorised to issue cover notes on behalf of Mr Poland's syndicate when proposals for 'HP' policies are made. Great care is taken, however, to comply with the requirements of Lloyd's. The authority to issue cover notes is applied for and granted through a Lloyd's broker, and the proposals are sent to him and presented by him to the underwriter, and he receives the policy from the underwriter and sends it to the assured as his agent. The underwriter looks to the Lloyd's broker for the premium, and has his account with the Lloyd's broker. The main insurance is duly granted at Lloyd's, and the preliminary cover note, which is inevitably granted outside Lloyd's by a person acting as agent for the underwriter, is regarded as merely an incidental or ancillary matter.

In the case of foreign motor insurance business, the practice is similar in principle, but the 'coverholder', as he is called, has to have a more extensive range of duties and therefore a wider authority from the underwriters to act on their behalf. The coverholder is the person authorised to grant temporary cover so as to bind the underwriters, and the agreement by which he is so authorised is sometimes called a 'binder'. The coverholder has to do the 'servicing' of the policies, and that includes collecting premiums, adjusting premiums, issuing indorsements, receiving claims, settling the smaller claims and referring larger claims to assessors. In the present case, the Praet Company were coverholders for Mr Poland's syndicate, and were acting under an agreement which could be called a binder, and were servicing the policies which had been issued to the Belgian assured ...

APPENDIX 3.5

Re Coleman's Depositories Ltd v Life and Health Assurance Association [1907] 2 KB 798

Vaughan Williams LJ: I hold that, on the face of the award, there is no evidence that the employer knew, or had the opportunity of knowing, the conditions of the policy, and that the onus is on the association; and, in my opinion, the risk undertaken by the association for the period prior to the delivery of the policy did not impose upon the employer the obligation to give immediate notice of the accident to Corrin on 2 January 1905, prior to the receipt by the employer of the policy or of information of its containing such a condition or obligation. The only question in this case is the obligation of this condition as to immediate notice. As to the condition as to forwarding notice of claim received by the employer within three days of the receipt of such notice, I agree with Bray J, that there was no obligation to forward such notice after the association had repudiated. The result is that, in my opinion, this appeal should be dismissed.

Fletcher Moulton LJ (dissenting): The facts of the case are as follows: An accident occurred on 2 January 1905, on the premises of the employer used by him for storing, he being a furniture remover and warehouseman. The injuries to the workman were not in the first instance supposed to be serious, but they showed themselves to be so later. No notice of the accident was, however, given by the employer to the association until 14 March, which was the day before the workman died from the consequences of the accident. No reason was assigned for the omission on the part of the employer to give notice of the accident to the association, and it must be taken to have been deliberate and intentional on his part. Under these circumstances, I confess that I am unable to come to any other conclusion that the employer has wholly failed to fulfil the obligation to be performed by him which was of the essence of the contract. If the default had been a trifling one – that is to say, if some slight delay had taken place in giving the notice stipulated in the policy, different considerations might have arisen. The courts have not always considered that they are bound to interpret provisions of this kind with unreasonable strictness, and although the word 'immediate' is no doubt a strong epithet, I think it might be fairly construed as meaning with all reasonable speed considering the circumstances of the case. But we have here a substantial and persistent breach of a provision obviously of great importance to the association, and which is by the terms of the policy itself declared to be of the essence of the contract – that is to say, to go to the root of it. Moreover, the condition interpreted in this way is a most reasonable one, and I can see nothing which ought to render the court unwilling to enforce the full consequence of the breach. The association, who have to bear the pecuniary consequences of the accident, and who have stipulated that they should at once be informed of it, are entitled to have this obligation performed by the assured in order that they may be able to inquire in to the circumstances of the accident while the matter is still fresh. In my opinion, both from the nature of the condition and from the express stipulation of the policy, the prompt giving of this notice is a fundamental condition of recovery under the policy, and if it be not given, the employer is disentitled to claim the benefit of the indemnity in respect of the accident as to which he has failed to give notice ...

APPENDIX 3.6

Clarke, M, 'Illegal insurance' [1987] LMCLQ 201

...

(D) INSURANCE AND PUBLIC POLICY

Unlicensed insurers

In *Phoenix* [1986] 2 Lloyd's Rep 552, Hobhouse J, raised the question whether, as a matter of public policy, unlicensed insurance should be enforced. As regards the primary assured, there has been general agreement that public policy requires that he should be able to enforce the insurance against an unlicensed insurer. Leggatt J, in *Stewart* [1984] 2 Lloyd's Rep 109, noted that while:

> ... it might be argued that rendering contracts of insurance illegal would or might help the conduct of insurance business in the long term, the more immediate effect would be the wholly undesirable one of allowing offending insurers to keep premiums paid whilst releasing them from their obligations to pay claims.

He did not think this result was intended by Parliament in order to increase the chances that the licence requirement would be observed. In the Financial Services Act 1986, Parliament has indicated that he was right.

The importance of parliamentary purpose to protect the assured is less evident in the case of reinsurance, when the assured is himself an insurer, in a better position than laymen to know whether he is dealing with someone licensed to write the business concerned. As regards reinsurance, it was argued in *Phoenix* that, if the unlicensed insurer could not enforce his reinsurance, this might adversely affect his ability to pay the prime assured, for whose protection the licensing was required by Parliament. The argument was rejected by Hobhouse J, as 'too subtle' and because:

> ... it could be said with equal logic that the [unlicensed insurers] should be allowed to enforce the original contracts against the original assureds as collecting the premiums might turn out to provide the funds necessary to pay other original assureds.

But, we are not concerned here with logic, but with public policy. The effect on the solvency of the insurer of an unenforceable premium, on the one hand, and the effect of an unenforceable reinsurance contract, on the other hand are of a different order of magnitude. In the current climate the unlicensed insurer is more likely to face the plea of illegality from a reinsurer, who does not want to pay reinsurance money, than from an assured, who does not want to pay premium. Whether the difference is sufficient to justify the enforcement of reinsurance contracts at the request of the unlicensed insurer is a question which the writer is not competent to answer. However, sight should not be lost of broader policy considerations. First, courts should be slow to apply punishment in addition to that stipulated by Parliament. Secondly, as recently reaffirmed by the Court of Appeal, it is in the interests of society that contracts should be enforced.

Liability insurance: serious crime

It was argued in *Phoenix* that, if public policy required that a person guilty of causing death by dangerous driving might enforce his motor insurance, why not also a person 'guilty' of contracting with an unlicensed insurer? Against this, it was said that liability for some crimes could be insured, but not others. This can be explained, if at all, only by seeking the public policy affecting liability insurance.

Deterrence

In 1971, in *Gray v Barr* [1971] 2 Lloyd's Rep 1, the assured, carrying a gun, tried to push past his wife's lover, to see if his wife was there, and the lover was shot dead. Having been acquitted of manslaughter, the assured was held liable in a civil action by the deceased's wife. The Court of Appeal further held that his liability insurance did not cover the event. Motor insurance was distinguished. Salmon LJ said: 'Crimes of violence, particularly when committed with loaded guns, are amongst the worst curses of that age. It is very much in the public interest that they be deterred.' One may wonder whether a husband, inflamed by jealousy, is likely to be deterred from attacking his wife's lover by thoughts of insurance? Has there been any significant drop in the number of spouses shot since 1971? It is submitted that deterrence is neither a sufficient reason for not enforcing insurance contracts nor an indicator of the boundaries of such a rule.

Thou shalt not profit from thy wrong

It has been often said that a man should not profit, whether by insurance money or in other ways, from his own wrong. This maxim is appealing in relation to property insurance ... It was raised but rejected in a case of liability insurance in the House of Lords in 1984, in *Gardner v Moore* [1984] All ER 1100. One night, D opened his door to find G on the ground with a gaping hole in his stomach. G had kicked M's dog. M had driven his van at G. G went to hospital. M went to prison. G recovered, but he found that M lacked both money and motor insurance. The question for the House of Lords was whether the Motor Insurers' Bureau was liable to pay G's claim. The House held the Motor Insurers' Bureau liable because: (a) this was a claim in respect of which persons were required to insure; and (b) there being no such insurance, the Motor Insurers' Bureau was bound to pay the uninsured claim.

It had been argued for the defendant 'that a person (or those who claim through such a person) may not stand to gain an advantage from the consequences of his own iniquity'. From this principle it was argued that any insurance that appeared to cover what happened in this case, whether actually taken out by the driver, or notionally so on the hypothesis of liability of the Motor Insurers' Bureau should not be enforced. But Lord Hailsham, with whom the other members of the House agreed, thought that the principle 'ought not to be stretched beyond what is necessary for the protection of the public'. The House approved both the decision and reasoning of the Court of Appeal in *Hardy v Motor Insurers' Bureau* [1964] 2 QB 745, with the following results:

(a) the offending motorist in a case such as *Gardner* could not enforce his insurance for damage to the van;

(b) the court has to weigh the gravity of the anti-social act (running people down) and the extent to which such acts might be encouraged by enforcing the insurance, against the social harm caused, if the insurance is not enforced (no damages for the victim). This is perhaps the key point;

(c) it appears that it was significant in the motor cases that the action against the insurer was brought by an innocent third party in pursuance of a right given by statute. Yet a wife, who drives negligently and whose husband is killed in the accident, may still be able to enforce his life insurance in her favour.

The balance of public policy

If there are conflicting factors of public policy, the court will weigh them and follow the most important, enforcing the contract or not, as the case may be. It is submitted that this is the 'rule' that emerges from *Gardner v Moore*, but that the result in the cases may give pause for thought. Official statistics do not show figures for spouses shot; but they do show that in 1971, the year of *Gray v Barr*, there were 30 known cases of homicide by firearms, but 685 cases of causing death by reckless or dangerous driving. One may wonder whether, as affirmed by Salmon LJ, in *Gray v Barr*, shootings are so much greater a social evil than death by Datsun or slaughter by Sierra.

In the BBC Reith Lectures for 1986, Lord McCluskey, a Scottish judge, argued that it is not the function of a judge to advance social or moral aims, except when they have been clearly made part of the law. The judge should be 'not an architect but a bricklayer'. He lacks the 'Brandeis brief' – evidence on which to predict the social consequences of his decision. Public response was sure and swift. Adjudication, it was said, can never be a mechanical process. Legislation can never cover every case, so the function of statute, such as one regulating insurers, is to state the aims of Parliament, leaving it to the judges to find the means, and hence to decide when means end and ends begin. Every decision of the court involves an element of public policy and it is better not to pretend otherwise. This is one reason why the recognition, in cases like *Gardner v Moore*, of the policy function of the courts is welcome.

In balancing the factors of public policy, how will the court proceed?:

(a) the court will consider the gravity of the illegal conduct. Intentional illegality is worse than negligent illegality. There is some suggestion that, while murder is obviously bad, whether committed here or abroad, the infringement of foreign trade laws is not, or at least not bad enough for related contracts, such as insurance contracts, to be refused enforcement;

(b) the court will ask whether enforcing insurance contracts of that kind will encourage the illegal conduct;

(c) the court will consider the effect of non-enforcement on third parties, not only victims, but also society as a whole. In a case of motor insurance an American court said:

> The primary purpose of compulsory motor vehicle liability insurance is to compensate innocent victims who have been injured by ... motorists. Its purpose is not, like that of ordinary insurance, to save harmless the tortfeasor himself. Therefore, there is no reason why the victim's right to recover from the [insurer] should depend on whether the conduct of the insured was intentional or negligent. In order to accomplish the objective of the law, the perspective here must be that of the victim and not that of the aggressor for whom the law provides criminal penalties calculated to minimise any profit he might derive from the insurance.

Property insurance

Property insurance may be affected by illegality, if the insurer is unlicensed ... but, more often, the insurance contract is lawful as formed and as performed, but performance of the insurance contract may promote an ulterior illegal purpose. So, for example, transit insurance on heroin, or burglary insurance of illegal gambling machines will not be enforced.

The mixed bag

If under the same insurance there are both goods that are lawful and goods that are not, the insurance may be enforced for loss of the first but not of the second. In *Geismar v Sun Alliance and London Insurance Co Ltd* [1978] QB 383, household goods stolen included goods that were lawful and goods which were not. The claim failed in respect of the latter, but not, apparently, in respect of the former. However, in that case the goods were unlawful because they were smuggled. A more serious view might be taken of heroin, with the result that the unlawful infects the lawful and the court will not enforce the contract of insurance at all.

Tainted goods

If jewellery alone has been insured, and imported illegally, for example, without payment of duty, the insurance will not be enforced: *Geismar* ... The reason is that to enforce the insurance would be to allow the assured to recover the value of goods which, as undeclared goods but not as insurance money, might have been confiscated. If substitute goods were available to the assured, he would be better off with the insurance money than with the jewellery; public policy requires that the court should not assist the assured to profit from his illegal act, even though the profit is sought indirectly through insurance. The same follows if the insurance covers goods that the assured has stolen. In *Thackwell v Barclays Bank plc* [1986] 1 All ER 676, an action for conversion of a cheque representing part of the proceeds of a fraudulent transaction failed, for to allow it would affront conscience: the court would be indirectly assisting the commission of a crime.

If, however, the assured deals with the goods in breach of a (fiscal) provision that does not give rise to confiscation, loss of the goods may be compensated by insurance. This was the decision in *Euro-Diam Ltd v Bathurst* [1988] 2 All ER 23, which concerned insurance on diamonds being sent by the assured to V in Germany for sale or return, together with an invoice requested by V stating a price substantially lower than the price the assured would receive, if the diamonds were sold. The assured must have known that the purpose of the invoice was to deceive the German customs, although there was no direct evidence that V did deceive them. Staughton J considered German law and concluded that neither the actions of V in Germany nor of Euro-Diam in England would have led to confiscation of the diamonds by a German court. He went on to decide that, if the case had concerned only English customs law, the contract of insurance would have been enforced. Staughton J distinguished *Geismar*, where the jewellery insured was liable to confiscation, from the case before him, where the diamonds were not.

In *Euro-Diam* the contract of insurance (and by implication the diamonds) were not 'tainted with illegality', that is, not so connected with some other illegal activity as to render the contract too obnoxious for the court to enforce. At what point does the property lose its taint? That, said Staughton J, in *Euro-Diam*, was a question of proximity between the plaintiff's insurance claim and the criminal behaviour, the answer to which will vary with the circumstances of the case. It seems that some temporal proximity is required between the illegality and the insurance: in *Geismar* this was found in the continuing liability to confiscation. In other cases the taint of illegality wears off with time. Conversely, property intended for but yet to be used for an illegal purpose may be validly insured, unless the court considers that to enforce the insurance will encourage the illegality.

In *Geismar*, the jewellery was liable to confiscation (called 'forfeiture') under customs legislation. Further, s 43 of the Powers of the Criminal Courts Act 1973 and s 27 of the Misuse of Drugs Act 1971 permit confiscation of tangible assets directly related to an offence, such as equipment used to promote illegal activity, but not assets representing the profits of the activity. A new power of confiscation has been created by s 2 of the Drug Trafficking Offences Act 1986. It relates to property held by a person convicted of a drug trafficking offence, and who has benefited from such trafficking. Relevant property is property held by him either since his conviction or for six years up to the time proceedings for such an offence were commenced against him. The confiscation order does not specify property to be forfeited, but takes the form of an order to pay a sum, being the court's estimate of his proceeds from trafficking, and which is determined having regard to relevant property. The court, when making an order, will take into account insured property, and if such property has been destroyed, will take into account the person's right under an insurance contract. So, payment of insurance money to that person will not leave him better off than if the insured event had not occurred or than if the policy had not been enforced. Hence, in such cases, the *Geismar* rule does not require non-enforcement of the policy.

The Criminal Justice Bill [ss 69 and 71 of the Criminal Justice Act 1988] empowers the court to make a confiscation order against a person who has been convicted of an offence and whom the court considers to have benefited from the offence. However, although this power is broadly like that under the Drug Trafficking Offences Act, the amount of the order cannot be less than £10,000, that is, it does not apply to benefit below that figure or to prodigal offenders whose realizable assets are below that amount. When an order can be made, it seems that insurance on the offender's property will be enforceable, as it is in cases subject to the Drug Trafficking Offences Act ... When an order cannot be made, for example, against the prodigal offender, his property is not therefore liable to a confiscation order, and the *Geismar* rule against enforcing the insurance does not apply.

Transmutation: laundered assets

If, after it was tainted by illegality, there is a change in the form in which the property is held, it may be cleansed of illegality by transmutation. In *Euro-Diam*, Staughton J concurred with the decision in *Bird v Appleton* that neither cargo nor its insurance was illegal because the goods had been bought with the proceeds of an earlier cargo which was illegal. Lord Kenyon CJ rejected the contrary argument, that the court must scrutinise the past of the assured and of his funds, as impractical, and so it is, but his conclusion that the court must confine itself to the immediate transaction does not necessarily follow. It was, however, accepted by Staughton J, who observed that it 'may be that money in the shape of coins and notes, being negotiable, has a tendency to become cleansed of illegality more swiftly than other property'. But a simple change from goods to money may not be enough, for another factor is the degree of outrage felt by the court. If the assured sold property in breach of trust, and then invested the proceeds in a house in the Home Counties, the court would trace the money in the exercise of its equitable jurisdiction. It is hard to believe that, if the assured bought the house with money from selling heroin, he could purge his property of taint by a good blaze and a claim under his fire insurance. Undeclared jewellery is one thing, heroin is another.

Illegality by foreign law

Although it was not necessary to his decision, the judge in *Euro-Diam* considered whether the rules of the conflict of laws justified reference to German law, under which the assured had committed an offence. He found that an English court would not enforce a contract, if it was void for illegality under: (a) the proper law of the contract; (b) the law of the place of performance; and (c) the law of the forum. In this case, the forum was England and he had already decided that the contract of insurance could be enforced. As to the proper law and the law of the place of performance, these too were English and, therefore, the contract was enforceable ...

It followed that, whereas a contract to smuggle diamonds into Germany would be unenforceable in England, a contract of insurance on those diamonds which, as in the *Euro-Diam* case, was not performed in Germany nor governed by German law, would not be tainted by illegality and could be enforced in the English courts.

APPENDIX 3.7

Shand, J, 'Unblinkering the unruly horse: public policy in the law of contract' (1972) 30 CLJ 144

... A good illustration of the rigid application of public policy is to be found in the rule that no man shall be allowed to benefit from his criminal acts. Conceding, for the purpose of argument, that 'no one would cavil at the proposition', how have the courts set about the task of deciding if indeed the criminal is the person who would benefit? This decision is vital to the sensible application of the doctrine, for if the criminal is not the person to benefit the justifications of deterrence, inducement, punishment and purity of the jurisdiction all fall to the ground.

The problem was before the House of Lords in *Beresford v Royal Insurance Co Ltd* [1937] 2 KB 197, a claim by the executors of the estate of Major Rowlandson under a policy of insurance on his life. The defendants took the point that the claim was barred by public policy because the deceased had committed suicide, a crime at common law. In what way could it be said that the deceased would derive benefit from his crime if the right under the policy was upheld? It was plain that the benefit could never be enjoyed by the assured himself, but their Lordships found no difficulty in thinking that 'the principle of public policy was not so narrow' as to exclude 'the increase of the criminal's estate' from the benefits considered to arise from his crime.

Stranger still is the courts' totally unrealistic attitude to insurance indemnity as being a benefit to the insured. In most cases of insurance – whether compulsory road traffic or industrial accident insurance or policies taken out purely voluntarily by the insured – the people most likely to be harmed by withholding indemnity are the innocent victims of the fault insured against, who more likely than not will be left with an empty judgment against a man of straw. This is the basis of cogent criticism of the decision in *Gray v Barr*, and it is all the more surprising that Lord Denning, whose robust appreciation of the importance of road traffic insurance has not been fettered by orthodox convention, should have been a party to the decision.

Thus, one of the most rigid and unsatisfactory modern applications of the principles of public policy is in the area of insurance indemnity were third party interests are prejudiced by a refusal of relief. Of course, it can be argued that the same result would be achieved independently of public policy because of the 'ordinary principles of insurance law [whereby] an assured cannot by his own deliberate act cause the event upon which the insurance money is payable'. These principles arise from 'the correct construction of the contract'; in other words, they are yet another example of a judicially implied term. The point did not avail the insurers in *Beresford*'s case, because a proper construction of the policy provided for cover in the event of suicide one year or more after the taking out of the policy; but the 'implied term' doctrine as traditionally applied could, in the case of a differently drafted policy, mean that the estate of an insured who had committed suicide could not recover even today irrespective of the Suicide Act or any change (as envisaged by Salmon LJ) in modern moral reactions to self-killing.

It is submitted that public policy should be recognised as the dominant factor, not only in deciding whether to give relief under a policy of insurance, but also in the proper construction of its terms. As Lord Simonds has openly conceded:

> The real question becomes not what terms can be implied in a contract between two individuals who are assumed to be making a bargain ... We have to take a wider view for we are concerned with a general question which, if not correctly described as a question of status, yet can only be answered by considering the relations in which (on the facts of that case) drivers of motor vehicles and their employers generally stand in relation to each other.

It is submitted that such policy considerations are relevant to an even greater extent in the context of insurance indemnity where third parties also stand in relation to the status created.

HARDY v MOTOR INSURERS' BUREAU – A FRESH APPROACH

In order to bring coherence to this area of the law, it is necessary to decide first whether any justification can be made out for the operation of public policy and, if so, what that justification is.

Public policy applies *ex post facto* and the judge thereby invalidates or refuses to uphold rights which would otherwise have been enjoyed by the parties. Such rights may have been created by the freely negotiated contract of the parties, and the issue surely becomes whether the court should uphold a reasonable expectation that the bargain will be kept, and, if so, what is a reasonable expectation. This test of reasonableness opens up a whole range of relevant and maybe conflicting claims which, under their conventional formulation, the principles of public policy have not even considered, far less attempted to balance. One can agree that:

> ... the conventional emphasis of stating the various social and economic interests which are protected by this branch of the law has obscured the fact that even when it is agreed on all hands that those interests should be protected, their protection may not necessarily demand the invalidation of a given contract.

Thus, the only rational basis for the operation of public policy is to determine the interests at stake in a given case and to weigh the consequences of enforcing the contract against the consequences of refusing to do so.

Any starting point for such an approach must be the recognition that 'because a contract is part of an illegal transaction is no reason for disregarding its existence or declining to weigh the consequences of holding it to be void'. This is not to say that the English courts have been oblivious of this fact, but the means they have adopted for avoiding the nullification of the bargain have, in nearly every case, been the evasion of the issue by such fictions as the device of statutory interpretation. A useful indication of how a fresh start might be achieved is, however, to be found in the important but generally neglected judgment of Diplock LJ (as he then was) in *Hardy v Motor Insurers' Bureau* [1964] 2 QB 745 ...

... It is also interesting to observe how Diplock LJ went on to consider the factors relevant to the case before him. Having recognised that the whole purpose of road traffic insurance was the protection of persons who sustain injury by the wrongful acts of the insured, he went on:

> The liabilities of the assured, and thus the rights of third parties against the insurers, can only arise out of some wrongful (tortious) act of the assured. I can see no reason in public policy for drawing a distinction between one kind of wrongful act, of which a third party is the innocent victim, and another kind of wrongful act; between wrongful acts which are not crimes; or between wrongful acts which are crimes of carelessness and wrongful acts which are intentional crimes.

Thus, in one sentence, his Lordship swept aside the factors which traditionally have governed the operation of the principles of public policy. One must ask what would be the consequences of applying his new criteria.

Let us take *Gray v Barr* [1971] 2 Lloyd's Rep 1. Applying the Diplock test, the gravity of Mr Barr's anti-social act was certainly considerable; but there the weighting of the insurers' side of the scales ends. The encouragement of similar anti-social acts, despite the frequent references to deterrence, would in reality be non-existent. Nor, would considerations of punishing Mr Barr or abating public outrage be relevant, for in all probability, it would not be he would benefit from the indemnity, but the plaintiffs. On the other side of the scale, the social harm which would be caused by refusal of indemnity, both in the specific case and generally, would be enormous; for not only would the innocent dependants of the deceased be deprived of redress, but the business efficacy of indemnity insurance in cases of this kind, would be undermined. Having received Mr Barr's premiums over the years, all that remained to the insurers was to cover the loss arising from the accident. It is submitted with some confidence that if such broader considerations of public policy were admitted, the result in *Gray v Barr* would be reversed.

THE CASE FOR REFORM

Thus, the modern law of contract has provided its own pointers to reform; but it is submitted that, in the light of such House of Lords decisions as *Beresford v Royal Insurance Co Ltd* [1937] 2 KB 197, it is impossible for the common law to put its own house in order and to formulate coherent and rational principles of public policy. Accordingly, legislation is the only way out of the dilemma ...

... It is argued that the judge should retain a discretion, albeit within the limits of recognised criteria, to refuse to enforce rights which would otherwise have existed and been enforceable. The mere fact that a claim is based on a criminal act should not in itself be a bar to its success. It should, however, open the door to the judge's scrutiny, and, if balancing the criminality against other considerations, the judge concludes that to enforce the contract would be overwhelmingly socially harmful, the plea of illegality should succeed. The juridical status of such a balancing process has already been discussed and it is true that, under the present law, the problem does not often arise, for the judges have themselves reacted from the broad and vaporous concept of public policy and reduced it to a set of rules whose operation is predictable and whose application is obligatory and not a matter of discretion. Even under the present law, however, there remains the troublesome survival of general principles of public policy which may be called in aid where authority does not cover the precise case. Here again it can be argued that they are no more or less than any other rule of law, for the judges 'have to apply the recognised principles to the new conditions along the lines of logic and convenience, just as they do when dealing with any other rule of the common law or equity'; and when they apply these general principles to new situations they do so with the rigidity and inflexibility that they would have done in more readily recognised traditional categories. In any event, this problem may be academic today when, having extended the ambit of the maxims as far as they have, the courts may be hard pushed to extend them any further. If in the case of the criminal contract the categories are now closed, the principles of public policy may properly be regarded as rules of law ...

APPENDIX 3.8

Beresford v Royal Insurance Co Ltd [1937] 2 KB 197, HL; [1937] 2 All ER 243; [1938] 2 All ER 602

Lord Atkin: In discussing the important subject of the effect of suicide on policies of life insurance, it is necessary to distinguish between two different questions that are apt to be confused: (1) What was the contract made by the parties? (2) How is that contract affected by public policy?

(1) On the first question, if there is no express reference to suicide in the policy, two results follow. In the first place, intentional suicide by a man of sound mind, which I will call sane suicide, ignoring the important question of the test of sanity, will prevent the representatives of the assured from recovering. On ordinary principles of insurance law, an assured cannot by his own deliberate act cause the event upon which the insurance money is payable. The insurers have not agreed to pay on that happening. The fire assured cannot recover if he intentionally burns down his house, nor the marine assured if he scuttles his ship, nor the life assured if he deliberately ends his own life. This is not the result of public policy, but of the correct construction of the contract. In the second place, this doctrine obviously does not apply to insane suicide, if one premises that the insanity in question prevents the act from being in law the act of the assured.

On the other hand, the contract may and often does expressly deal with the event of suicide: and that whether sane or insane. It may provide that death arising at any time from suicide of either class is not covered by the policy. It may make the same stipulation in respect of suicide of either or both classes happening within a limited time from the inception of the policy. The rights given to the parties by the contract must be ascertained according to the ordinary rules of construction: and it is only after such ascertainment that the question of public policy arises. In the present case, the contract contained in the policy provided that the company would pay the sum assured to the person or persons to whom the same is payable upon proof of the happening of the event on which the sum assured was to become payable. It further provided that the policy was subject to the conditions and privileges endorsed so far as applicable. It contained the further stipulation that unless it was otherwise provided in the schedule the policy, subject to the endorsed conditions, was indisputable ...

... The only relevant condition is condition 4, which reads as follows:

> If the life or any one of the lives assured (being also the assured or one of them) shall die by his own hand, whether sane or insane, within one year from the commencement of the assurance, the policy shall be void as against any person claiming the amount hereby assured or any part thereof, except that it shall remain in force to the extent to which a *bona fide* interest for pecuniary consideration, or as a security for money, possessed or acquired by a third party before the date of such death, shall be established to the satisfaction of the directors.

My Lords, I entertain no doubt that on the true construction of this contract the insurance company have agreed with the assured to pay to his executors or assigns on his death the sum assured if he dies by his own hand whether sane or insane after the expiration of one year from the commencement of the assurance. The express protection limited to one year, and the clause as to the policy being indisputable subject to that limited exception seem to make this conclusion inevitable. The respondents' counsel appeared shocked that it should be considered that a reputable company could have intended to make such a contract: but the meaning is clear: and one may assume from what one knows of tariff conditions that it is a usual clause. There is no doubt therefore that on the proper construction of this contract the insurance company promised Major Rowlandson that if he in full possession of his senses intentionally killed himself they would pay his executors or assigns the sum assured.

(2) The contract between the parties has thus been ascertained. There now arises the question whether such a contract is enforceable in a court of law. In my opinion, it is not enforceable ...

... I think that the principle is that a man is not to be allowed to have recourse to a court of justice to claim a benefit from his crime whether under a contract or a gift. No doubt the rule pays regard to the fact that to hold otherwise would in some cases offer an inducement to crime or remove a restraint to crime, and that its effect is to act as a deterrent to crime. But, apart from these considerations, the absolute rule is that the courts will not recognise a benefit accruing to a criminal from his crime.

The application of this principle to the present case is not difficult. Deliberate suicide, *felo de se*, is and always has been regarded in English law as a crime, though by the very nature of it the offender escapes personal punishment ...

The remaining question is whether the principle applies where the criminal is dead and his personal representative is seeking to recover a benefit which only takes shape after his death. It must be remembered that the money becomes due, if at all, under an agreement made by the deceased during his life for the express purpose of benefiting his estate after his death. During his life, he had power of complete testamentary disposition over it. I cannot think the principle of public policy to be so narrow as not to include the increase of the criminal's estate amongst the benefits which he is deprived of by his crime. His executor or administrator claims as his representative, and, as his representative, falls under the same ban.

Anxiety is naturally aroused by the thought that this principle may be invoked so as to destroy the security given to lenders and others by policies of life insurance which are in daily issue for that purpose. The question does not directly arise, and I do not think that anything said in this case can be authoritative. But I consider myself free to say that I cannot see that there is any objection to an assignee for value before the suicide enforcing a policy which contains an express promise to pay upon sane suicide, at any rate so far as the payment is to extend to the actual interest of the assignee. It is plain that a lender may himself insure the life of the borrower against sane suicide; and the assignee of the policy is in a similar position so far as public policy is concerned. I have little doubt that after this decision the life companies will frame a clause which is unobjectionable ...

APPENDIX 3.9

Dunbar (Administrator of Dunbar) v Plant [1997] 4 All ER 289, CA

Phillips LJ:

THE FORFEITURE RULE

The forfeiture rule is defined by s 1(1) of the 1982 Act as meaning:

> … the rule of public policy which in certain circumstances precludes a person who has unlawfully killed another from acquiring a benefit in consequence of the killing.

The rule as so formulated is an example of a wider principle that a person cannot benefit from his own criminal act. As Evans P said in *Re Crippen (Decd)* [1911] P 108 …:

> It is clear that the law is, that no person can obtain, or enforce, any rights resulting to him from his own crime; neither can his representative, claiming under him, obtain or enforce any such rights. The human mind revolts at the very idea that any other doctrine could be possible in our system of jurisprudence.

There is a difference between obtaining rights and enforcing them, and there is scope for debate as to the extent to which the forfeiture rule differs from the similar principle that a litigant cannot base a cause of action on his own wrong. The two principles are frequently confused, and I do not find it necessary in this judgment to explore the differences between them. The difficulty of so doing is exemplified by the following passage in the judgment of Fry LJ in *Cleaver v Mutual Reserve Fund Life Association* [1892] 1 QB 147 …:

> It appears to me that no system of jurisprudence can with reason include amongst the rights which it enforces rights directly resulting to the person asserting them from the crime of that person. If no action can arise from fraud, it seems impossible to suppose that it can arise from felony or misdemeanour.

What is important is that neither principle is absolute. It is not every criminal offence which will bring the principle into play. The issue raised on this appeal is whether aiding and abetting the suicide of another necessarily brings the forfeiture rule into operation. That question can be considered in the context of the rule as formulated in the Forfeiture Act, that is, in the context of crimes which consist of unlawfully killing another.

Unlawful killing

When the forfeiture rule was first applied by the courts, any unlawful killing consisted of one or other of two crimes – murder or manslaughter, and the ambit of the crime of murder was much wider than it is today. The forfeiture rule was always applied in a case of murder and in *Beresford v Royal Insurance Co Ltd* [1938] 2 All ER 602 … it was applied in a case of suicide …

Since the cases to which I have referred were decided, there have been significant changes in the law in relation to unlawful killing which reflect the public appreciation of the different degrees of culpability that attend conduct that used to be designated as murder. In particular: (1) the Homicide Act 1957 abolished constructive malice; (2) the same Act provided for a conviction of manslaughter rather than murder in the case of diminished responsibility; (3) the same Act provided for a conviction of manslaughter rather than murder in the case of provocation; (4) the same Act, by s 4, made special provision in relation to suicide pacts. Under this section, the survivor of a suicide pact, who would previously have been guilty of murder, whether he killed the other party to the pact or merely aided, abetted, counselled or procured his suicide, became guilty of manslaughter; (5) the 1961 Act abrogated the rule of law whereby it was a crime to commit suicide and provided that a person who aids, abets, counsels or procures the suicide of another commits, not manslaughter, but an indictable offence subject to a maximum of imprisonment of 14 years ...

A desire on the part of the courts to avoid the rigour of the forfeiture rule was first manifest in *Tinline v White Cross Insurance Association Ltd* [1921] 3 KB 327. The issue in that case was whether a plaintiff, who had been convicted of manslaughter by reckless driving, was debarred by public policy from obtaining an indemnity under his insurance policy in respect of his civil liability. Bailhache J held that he was not. He observed ...:

> If the law is not logical, public policy is even less logical, for, by common consent, these third party indemnity insurances have been treated as valid and effective.

Nonetheless, it has proved possible to justify this and other similar decisions in relation to unlawful killing by the manner of driving a motor vehicle on the ground that an overriding public policy requires the existence of valid insurance in such circumstances for the benefit of the family of the victim (see the comment of Greer LJ in *Haseldine v Hosken* [1933] 1 KB 822) ...

It is time to pause to take stock. Thus far, apart from the motor cases, there has been no instance of the court failing to apply the forfeiture rule to a case of unlawful killing. So far as the rule is concerned, it is hard to see any logical basis for not applying it to all cases of manslaughter. Lord Denning MR himself remarked in *Gray v Barr* [1971] 2 Lloyd's Rep 1 ... in manslaughter of every kind there must be a guilty mind. Without it, the accused must be acquitted ...

In the crime of manslaughter, the *actus reus* is causing the death of another. That *actus reus* is rendered criminal if it occurs in one of the various circumstances that are prescribed by law. Anyone guilty of manslaughter has, *ex hypothesi*, caused the death of another by criminal conduct. It is in such circumstances that the rule against forfeiture applies.

However, the harshness of applying the forfeiture rule inflexibly to all classes of manslaughter in all circumstances is such that I do not consider that, absent the statutory intervention which occurred, the rule could have survived unvaried to the present day. The *obiter dicta* of Salmon and Phillimore LJJ in *Gray v Barr* and Lord Lane CJ in *Ex p Connor* [1981] 1 All ER 769 were straws in the wind. The rule is a judge made rule to give effect to what was perceived as public policy at the time of its formulation. I believe that, but for the intervention of the legislature, the judges would themselves have modified the rule. Furthermore, it seems to me that the only logical way of modifying the rule would have been to have declined to apply it where the facts of the crime involved such a low degree of culpability, or such a high degree of mitigation, that the sanction of forfeiture, far from giving effect to the public interest, would have been contrary to it. Alternative suggestions that the rule should be restricted to cases of deliberate killing, or deliberate violence leading to death, do not cater for cases of diminished responsibility or provocation, where the mitigating features may be such as to render it particularly harsh to apply the forfeiture rule.

The pressure for judicial intervention of the type contemplated was removed by the Forfeiture Act ...

Aiding and abetting suicide

Thus far, I have been considering the application of the forfeiture rule in cases of manslaughter. My reasoning leads, however, to the conclusion that the rule applies equally to the offence of aiding and abetting suicide contrary to s 2(1) of the Suicide Act. This conclusion seems to have been shared by those who drafted the Forfeiture Act. Section 1(2) of the Act provides:

> References in this Act to a person who has unlawfully killed another include a reference to a person who has unlawfully aided, abetted, counselled or procured the death of that other person ...

As the Act does not apply to the crime of murder, these words can only have been intended to apply to the crime of aiding, abetting, counselling or procuring the suicide of another, contrary to the 1961 Act. That offence can be very serious, as the maximum sentence of 14 years' imprisonment indicates. When the Act is considered, however, it gives clear indication that the circumstances in which the offence is committed may be such that the public interest does not require the imposition of any penal sanction. This, in my judgment, is the logical conclusion to be drawn from the provision in s 2(4) of the Act that 'no proceedings shall be instituted for an offence under this section except by or with the consent of the Director of Public Prosecutions'.

Where the public interest requires no penal sanction, it seems to me that strong grounds are likely to exist for relieving the person who has committed the offence from all effect of the forfeiture rule.

Suicide pacts

If, as I believe, the forfeiture rule applies to offences under the Suicide Act and the application of the rule is not dependent upon the degree of culpability attaching to the crime, it must follow that the rule applies to aiding and abetting the suicide of another in pursuance of a suicide pact. Such an offence is likely, however, to fall into the category of those in respect of which the public interest does not require the imposition of a penal sanction. In 1957, the Homicide Act recognised that aiding and abetting the suicide of another pursuant to a suicide pact called for a degree of leniency. Where two people are driven to attempt together, to take their lives and one survives, the survivor will normally attract sympathy rather than prosecution. A suicide pact may be rational, as where an elderly couple who are both suffering from incurable diseases decide to end their lives together, or it may be the product of irrational depression or desperation. In neither case does it seem to me that the public interest will normally call for either prosecution or forfeiture should one party to the pact survive. In such circumstances, the appropriate approach under the Forfeiture Act is likely to be to give total relief against forfeiture. Of course, this will not always be the case. One can think of instances of suicide pacts where one would not acquit the instigator of serious culpability.

Discretion under the Forfeiture Act

It is common ground that it was appropriate for the judge to make an order under the Act modifying the effect of the forfeiture rule, if it applied. The issue that arises is whether he exercised his discretion according to the correct principles. As to these, the judge had little guidance, either from the Act or from previous authority as to the relevant factors to be taken into account. Nor did he explain in any detail how he arrived at his decision. He indicated that his approach was to attempt 'to do justice between the parties'. I agree with Mummery LJ that this is not the appropriate approach to the exercise of the discretion given by the Act. The discretion is a broad one, and it is legitimate to have regard to all the consequences of the order, but it is not right to approach the exercise of the discretion as if dealing simply with an inter parties dispute. In these circumstances it is for this court to exercise afresh the discretion given by the Forfeiture Act.

The first, and paramount consideration, must be whether the culpability attending the beneficiary's criminal conduct was such as to justify the application of the forfeiture rule at all. The question of the extent to which the criminal should be blamed for committing the crime is a familiar one for the sentencing judge in the criminal jurisdiction, but not one that the judge exercising a civil law jurisdiction welcomes as the test for determining entitlement to property. I have already given my reasons for suggesting that it is likely to be appropriate to relieve the unsuccessful party to a suicide pact of all effect of the forfeiture rule. Each case must be assessed on its own facts.

Had Miss Plant's decision to take her own life been an understandable reaction to the pending consequences of her theft, a case could well have been made out for saying that this gave to her participation in the suicide pact a culpability that should properly be reflected by the application, at least to a degree, of the forfeiture rule. I do not, however, see this case in that light. The desperation that led Miss Plant to decide to kill herself, and which led to the suicide pact, was an irrational and tragic reaction to her predicament. I do not consider that the nature of Miss Plant's conduct alters what I have indicated should be the normal approach when dealing with a suicide pact – that there should be full relief against forfeiture. The assets with which this case is concerned were in no way derived from Mr Dunbar's family. They are the fruits of insurance taken out by Mr Dunbar for the benefit of Miss Plant. So far as his family is concerned, the judge rightly described the consequence of the forfeiture rule to be the conferring on them of an unwelcome windfall. While I can appreciate, and sympathise with, the emotions which I suspect underlie this litigation, I have reached the conclusion that there should be full relief against the forfeiture rule, and I would allow this appeal so as to grant that relief ...

APPENDIX 3.10

Davitt and Another v Titcumb [1989] 3 All ER 417

Scott J: On 25 January 1986, Julie Gilford was stabbed to death by the defendant. He was subsequently convicted of murder, his appeal against conviction was dismissed and he is currently serving a life sentence of imprisonment.

The building society, as legal assignee of the policy, applied to Commercial Union for payment of the sum assured. The defendant could not himself have claimed under the policy. This has for a long time been the law ...

This action is concerned with the entitlement of the defendant to the remaining £7,011.83, representing his 19/34ths of the net proceeds of sale. If he is entitled to claim this sum, then he will have benefited by his own criminal act, without which the proceeds of the endowment policy would not have become payable, and the £14,950 would not have been available to be applied in reduction of the indebtedness secured on 38 Salisbury Road.

I have already referred to *Re Crippen (Decd)* and to Evans P's reference to the rule of public policy that bars a criminal from claiming or enforcing rights resulting to him from his own crime. I should refer also to *Cleaver v Mutual Reserve Fund Life Association* [1892] 1 QB 147; [1891–94] All ER 335. This case too resulted from a notorious murder. James Maybrick was murdered by his wife Florence. He had effected a Married Women's Property Act policy on his life with the defendant association. At his death, the policy became vested in his executors. The trust of the policy required the executors to hold the policy money in trust for Florence. The association resisted payment of the proceeds to the executors on the ground that since the assured had been murdered by Florence it would be contrary to public policy to allow a claim under the policy to be enforced. The Court of Appeal rejected this defence. It agreed that Florence was barred from benefiting under the policy, but held that the proceeds were none the less payable to the deceased's executors who, instead of holding on trust for Florence, would hold on a resulting trust for the deceased's estate and the beneficiaries therein, excluding Florence ...

Counsel for the defendant submitted that no public policy point arose in this case. The defendant had not claimed under the policy: the claim had been made by the building society. It was therefore irrelevant that public policy would have barred a claim by the defendant. It may be that the defendant could not have insisted on the building society applying the policy money in discharge of the indebtedness secured on 38 Salisbury Road. That is the view expressed in MacGillivray and Parkington, *Insurance Law*, 8th edn, 1988, London: Sweet & Maxwell, para 485. The reasoning is that, although public policy does not bar the innocent mortgagee from recovering the policy money, it does bar the criminal mortgagor from obtaining a direct benefit from the policy money by requiring the mortgagee to credit the policy money towards repayment of the secured debt. But in the present case the building society has applied the policy money towards the payment of the secured debt. It has executed a vacating receipt on the legal charge acknowledging that it has received all moneys thereby secured. So, submitted counsel, it was irrelevant that public policy would have prevented the defendant from requiring the building society to do so. All that is left, he submitted, is the defendant's claim to 15/34ths of the net proceeds of sale, a claim made not in reliance on his criminal act but made pursuant to the proprietary interest that he acquired in 1983.

This is a forceful argument, but I am not satisfied that it is sound. In particular, the argument does not, and cannot, deal with the inescapable fact that if the defendant can claim the £7,011 he will be claiming a fund that would not have come into existence but for his criminal act. To allow him to claim the fund would, in my opinion, run counter to the reasoning that underlies the rule of public policy discussed in the authorities to which I have referred …

As between the defendant and the plaintiffs, the defendant is, in my judgment, barred by public policy from claiming to have supplied the policy money that was paid on the death of his victim, and was applied in reduction of his indebtedness …

APPENDIX 3.11

Gray and Another v Barr (Prudential Assurance Co Ltd, Third Party) [1971] 2 Lloyd's Rep 1, CA

Lord Denning MR: Mr Barr was tried at the Central Criminal Court for the murder of Mr Gray. His defence was that the fatal shot was an accident. The judge directed the jury that if they thought that it might have been an accident, they should acquit him. They did so. They found him 'Not guilty of murder'. Also, 'Not guilty of manslaughter'. He was thereupon discharged.

Now, Mrs Gray, the widow of Mr Gray, has brought this action against Mr Barr under the Fatal Accidents Act 1846–1969. She claims that Mr Barr wrongfully killed her husband and is liable to pay her and her children the pecuniary loss they have suffered by his death. Mr Barr admits that he is liable to compensate her, but he says that he is entitled to be indemnified by the Prudential Assurance Co Ltd. Mrs Barr had taken out a 'hearth and home' policy under which the company agreed to indemnify the insured and any member of her household against all sums which such person 'shall become legally liable to pay as damages in respect of ... bodily injury to any person ... caused by accidents'. On this claim against the Prudential, two points arise: (1) Was the death of Mr Gray 'caused by accident'? (2) Is the claim of Mrs Gray barred by public policy? The judge ... has held that Mr Gray's death was caused by accident, but that the claim is barred by public policy ...

Each one of us would readily forgive Mr Barr. He was distraught, fearful, anxious, provoked beyond endurance, quite beside himself with the thought that his wife had gone back to this man once again. Yet his conduct walking up the stairs with the loaded gun was no accident. It was deliberate. He was determined to get into the bedroom to see if his wife was there. It was the dominant cause of the death. It is not covered by the wording of the policy of insurance.

IS THE CLAIM BARRED BY PUBLIC POLICY?

In case I am wrong about this, I turn to the next question. Is it against public policy to allow Mr Barr to recover on the insurance?

There is no doubt, to my mind, that Mr Barr was guilty of manslaughter. I know that at the criminal trial he was acquitted altogether. But that was a merciful verdict, and in this civil action we must, when called upon, give the true decision according to law ...

... Does this manslaughter mean that, as matter of public policy, Mr Barr is not to be allowed to recover on the policy? In the category of manslaughter which is called 'motor manslaughter', it is settled beyond question that the insured is entitled to recover: see *Tinline v White Cross Insurance Association Ltd* [1921] 2 KB 327; *James v British General Insurance Co Ltd* [1927] 2 KB 311. But, in the category which is here in question, it is different. If his conduct is wilful and culpable, he is not entitled to recover: see *Hardy v Motor Insurers' Bureau* [1964] 2 QB 745 ...

... In my opinion, therefore, Mr Barr cannot recover on the policy. It was not an 'accident', and also he is defeated by 'public policy'. It will be noticed by the observant that the two questions raise one and the same point of 'causation'. If the death of Mr Gray was caused by the deliberate act of Mr Barr in going up the stairs with a loaded gun, it was no accident, and it would, in any case, be against public policy to allow him to recover indemnity for the consequences of it ...

APPENDIX 3.12

Tinline v White Cross Insurance Association Ltd [1921] 3 KB 327

Bailhache J: In this case, the plaintiff claims a declaration that he is entitled to be indemnified against the consequences of an accident ... He ran into three persons who were crossing the road, injuring two and killing the third. In respect of this occurrence the plaintiff was prosecuted for manslaughter. The crime of manslaughter in a case like this consists in driving a motor car with gross or reckless negligence. Ordinary negligence does not make a man liable for manslaughter ...

The policy sued on indemnifies the assured against sums which he shall become legally liable to pay to any other person as compensation for 'accidental personal injury'. A man does not become liable to pay compensation for accidental personal injury unless the accident is due to his negligence. The policy therefore is one which insures against the consequences of negligence, including personal negligence. The defendants say however that where the negligence is so gross and excessive that as a result of it a man is killed and the crime of manslaughter is committed the assured cannot claim an indemnity, for it is said it is against public policy to indemnify a person against the civil consequences of his criminal act.

So far as I know, this is the first time this defence has been raised upon an indemnity policy. Speaking generally, it is true to say that it is against public policy to indemnify a man against the consequences of a crime which he knowingly commits, and, in the word 'crime', I include the breach of any statutory duty which renders a man liable to fine or imprisonment. In motor accidents where the assured is the driver of the motor car, I suppose that in the great majority of cases the accident is due to the breach by the driver of some enactment. Many of these accidents are due to driving at excessive speed. That was the case here. Driving at an excessive speed – exceeding the speed limit – is a breach of an enactment which subjects the person guilty of it to fine or imprisonment; and if the ordinary law were to be applied to cases of this kind it would be a defence to say that the assured, although he did not intend to commit manslaughter, committed it by violating an enactment – namely, by driving in excess of the speed limit, or by driving to the danger of the public. But it is notorious that the defence is never raised. In *Quinn v Leathem* [1901] AC 495, Lord Halsbury said that the law is not always logical, and every one concerned with the administration of the law knows this. If the law is not logical, public policy is even less logical, for, by common consent, these third party indemnity insurances have been treated as valid and effective. There can be no doubt that if none of the three persons who were knocked down had been killed but all had been injured there would have been no defence to this action. In my opinion, the fact that one of the persons was killed makes no difference for this purpose. The policy is against claims for accidents due to negligence, because without negligence there is no liability. Precisely the same negligence which injured the two persons killed the third, but to hold that there is any difference in the liability to indemnify would be to hold that the indemnity depends upon the nature and result of the injury sustained by the person who is knocked down, or, to put it in another way, that it depends in some degree upon the amount of the assured's negligence. That will not do, because there is very often quite as much negligence in knocking down a person who is not killed as there is in knocking down a person who is killed and whose death makes the person who has knocked him down and killed him guilty of manslaughter. The fact that one of the three persons was killed is, as I have said, really immaterial for the purposes of this case; it was the incident of the accident, or the accident of the accident, an accident due, it is true, to gross negligence, but the policy is an insurance against negligence whether slight or great, and it seems to me that it covers this case. It must, of course, be clearly understood that if this occurrence had been due to an intentional act on the part of the plaintiff, the policy would not protect him. If a man driving a motor car at an excessive speed intentionally runs into and kills a man, the result if not manslaughter, but murder. Manslaughter is the result of an accident and murder is not, and it is against accident and accident only that this policy insures. The point, as I have said, is a novel one, but, for the reasons I have given, it fails and the plaintiff is entitled to the declaration asked for.

APPENDIX 3.13

Hardy v Motor Insurers' Bureau [1964] 2 QB 745, CA

Lord Denning MR: The policy of insurance which a motorist is required by statute to take out must cover any liability which may be incurred by him arising out of the use of the vehicle by him. It must, I think, be wide enough to cover, in general terms, any use by him of the vehicle, be it an innocent use or a criminal use, or be it a murderous use or a playful use. A policy so taken out by him is good altogether according to its terms. Of course, if the motorist intended from the beginning to make a criminal use of the vehicle – intended to run down people with it or to drive it recklessly and dangerously – and the insurers knew that that was his intention, the policy would be bad in its inception. No one can stipulate for iniquity. But that is never the intention with which such a policy is taken out. At any rate, no insurer is ever party to it. So the policy is good in its inception. The question only arises when the motorist afterwards makes a criminal use of the vehicle. The consequences are then these: if the motorist is guilty of a crime involving a wicked and deliberate intent, and he is made to pay damages to an injured person, he is not himself entitled to recover on the policy. But, if he does not pay the damages, then the injured third party can recover against the insurers under s 207 of the Road Traffic Act 1960; for it is a liability which the motorist, under the statute, was required to cover. [See now s 151 of the Road Traffic Act 1988.]

The injured third party is not affected by the disability which attached to the motorist himself.

So here the liability of Phillips to Hardy was a liability which Phillips was required to cover by a policy of insurance, even though it arose out of his wilful and culpable criminal act. If Phillips had been insured, he himself would be disabled from recovering from the insurers. But the injured third party would not be disabled from recovering from them. Seeing that he was not insured, the Motor Insurers' Bureau must treat the case as if he were. They must pay the injured third party, even though Phillips was guilty of felony. I would therefore dismiss the appeal.

APPENDIX 3.14

Gardner v Moore [1984] 1 All ER 1100, HL

Lord Hailsham of St Marylebone LC:

THE QUESTION FOR APPEAL

The sole question for decision by the House is accordingly whether *Hardy v Motor Insurers' Bureau* [1964] 2 QB 745 was correctly decided. This depends primarily on the true construction of the agreement relating to uninsured drivers of 22 November 1972, between the appellants and the Secretary of State for the Environment ('Motor Insurers' Bureau (Compensation of Victims of Uninsured Drivers)') ('the MIB agreement'), Pt VI of the Road Traffic Act 1972, and the proper application of any relevant rule of law or public policy arising from the fact that the actions alleged against the first defendant were not caused by negligence or recklessness but by his deliberate act amounting to an offence under s 18 of the Offences against the Person Act 1861.

Before proceeding further, it is perhaps relevant to point out the function of the MIB agreement and the sister and similar agreement of the same date between the same parties relating to untraced drivers. Part VI of the Road Traffic Act 1972 is designed to protect the innocent third party from the inability to pay of a driver who incurs liability by causing him death or personal injuries. This it does partly (ss 143 and 145) by imposing an obligation on all drivers to insure against third party liability under sanction of the criminal law, and partly by conferring on a successful plaintiff a right of direct recourse in the civil courts against the judgment debtor's insurers if he is insured in the manner prescribed (for example, ss 148 and 149). This, by itself, leaves a gap in the protection afforded to the innocent third party by Pt VI, since a guilty driver may either be uninsured altogether or turn out to be untraceable so that it is not known whether he is insured or not and if so by whom. It is to fill this gap that the two agreements between the Motor Insurers' Bureau and the Secretary of State for the Environment have been voluntarily entered into. Their foundations in jurisprudence are better not questioned any more than were the demises of John Doe and the behaviour of Richard Roe in the old ejectment actions ...

The MIB agreements impose on the appellants an obligation to underwrite this liability so far as regards uninsured or untraceable tortfeasors. The two agreements were intended precisely to protect the innocent third party either because the insurer did not choose or was not able to discharge his liability under s 149, or where the wrongdoer was not covered by a relevant policy of insurance at all (which is the present appeal) or was untraceable. To invoke, as the Motor Insurers' Bureau now do, the well known doctrine of public policy, that a man may not profit by the consequences of his own wrongdoing, seems to me to stand the principle of public policy on its head. There are no socially desirable consequences flowing from its application in the sense contended for by the appellants. On the contrary, all the pointers in ss 143 and 145 read alone, or in ss 143 and 145 as read in conjunction with ss 148 and 149, seem to me to point exactly in the opposite direction. The construction of the MIB agreement contended for by the appellants is contrary to the grammatical sense of the agreement, read, as it must be read, in the context of the statute, and the construction of the statute contended for by the appellants is contrary both to its manifest grammatical meaning and to the policy illustrated by its more mature articulation ...

APPENDIX 3.15

Marcel Beller Ltd v Hayden [1978] 1 QB 694

Edgar Fay J: This case raises important questions in insurance law which have not hitherto been directly decided in this country, although there have been decisions in not dissimilar situations here and in other common law jurisdictions ...

... I think it is important to keep distinct the two causative elements, namely, the immediate cause which is the deceased's manner of driving and the predisposing cause which is his drinking. If the first alone is regarded, the crash was accidental. It has long been established and was accepted by counsel that the assured's negligence does not deprive a happening of the character of accidental. But ought I to regard it in isolation? Here, I must pay attention to *Gray v Barr* [1971] 2 Lloyd's Rep 1 ...

... I may be risking misinterpreting the ordinary meaning of 'accident', but I am firmly of the view that the word covers the happening with which I am dealing. In drafting the narrative part of this judgment I have avoided pre-empting the decision by using the word 'accident', but I have been conscious that wherever I have used the neutral terms 'crash' or 'what happened' or 'catastrophe' it would have been better English usage to call it an accident. I am convinced that the man in the street would say that Mr McCredie died in a motor accident. A further reason for adopting this view is that had some other person been killed by Mr McCredie's driving this would have been an accident within the meaning of his own motor policy: see *Tinline v White Cross Insurance Association Ltd* [1921] 3 KB 327. If the same offence killed both a driver and a bystander, it is the kind of decision that brings the law into disrepute, to call one an accident and the other not an accident ...

... It seems to me that a clear distinction can be drawn between cases where the predisposing cause is the deliberate taking of an appreciated risk and the cases, such as the present, where the predisposing cause, although it leads to the taking of risks, involves risk which was neither deliberately run nor actually appreciated. I find this death to have been accidental.

The remaining questions arise under the exclusions clause which reads in part as follows:

> The underwriters shall not be liable for death or disablement directly or indirectly resulting from ... deliberate exposure to exceptional danger (except in an attempt to save human life) or the insured person's own criminal act ...

I am disposed to think it would be right to find an implied term limiting that phrase so as to exclude acts of inadvertence or negligence. But I can find no justification for confining it to cases where a subjective test of conscious wrong doing is applied, as I have applied it to the phrase 'deliberate exposure to exceptional danger'. The fact that the word 'deliberate' qualifies the one exception but not the other points to an element of deliberation not being a necessary ingredient of the criminal act. In my judgment, I am concerned with criminal acts other than those of inadvertence or negligence. If I were wrong and the limitation upon the criminal acts was that they be crimes of moral culpability or turpitude, I am satisfied that the offences of dangerous driving and driving while under the influence of drink are sufficiently serious to qualify. In my judgment, wherever the line is to be drawn these offences are on the exemptive side of it ...

APPENDIX 3.16

Geismar v Sun Alliance and London Insurance Ltd and Another [1978] QB 383; [1977] 3 All ER 570

Talbot J: Applying these cases to the present problem it would seem that a contract of insurance, which is separate and apart from the illegal act, is not rendered unenforceable, but if the contract of insurance purports to cover property which the law forbids him to have, then the contract is directly connected with the illegal act and is unenforceable. In the present case, it is argued that the plaintiff's contract of insurance purports to cover property which the law forbids him to have, then the contract is directly connected with the illegal act and is unenforceable. In the present case, it is argued that the plaintiff's contract of insurance is quite apart from and does not in any way spring from his illegal act of importation of some of the articles insured under the policy. Moreover, the law of this country does not forbid possession of property brought in from foreign countries. What it requires is that the importer shall pay for its importation. The fact that property is liable to confiscation under the relevant Act does not negative the plaintiff's right of property in it until the act of confiscation is carried out.

All these authorities, with their application to problems related to the present one, though of assistance, do not cover the precise point. I start with the fact that the contracts of insurance are separate from the illegal importation. Next, there is no contractual point taken here and there has been no repudiation of the contracts by the defendants. It is clear that the plaintiff has an insurable interest in the property, though subject to defeasance. It is also clear that to allow the plaintiff to recover under the policies would be to allow him to recover the insured value of the goods which might have been confiscated at any moment and which, therefore, were potentially without value to him.

So far as the defendants were concerned, they being unaware of the illegal importation, the policies were not tainted with illegality, but the question is: ought the court to enforce these policies against them in favour of the plaintiff?

It seems to me that, from what Lord Denning MR said in *Mackender v Feldia AG* [1967] 2 QB 590, the policies would be unenforceable, provided that to enforce them would conflict with public policy. So these smuggled articles are in the same category as the forbidden cargo in *Parkin v Dick* (1809) 11 East 502. No new area of public policy is involved here. The plaintiff is seeking the assistance of the court to enforce contracts of insurance so that he may be indemnified against loss of articles which he deliberately and intentionally imported into this country, in breach of the Customs and Excise Act 1952.

I am not concerned with cases of unintentional importation or of innocent possession of uncustomed goods. I would think that different considerations would apply in those cases. But where there is a deliberate breach of the law I do not think the court ought to assist the plaintiff to derive a profit from it, even though it is sought indirectly through an indemnity under an insurance policy ...

APPENDIX 3.17

Euro-Diam Ltd v Bathurst [1988] 2 All ER 23, CA

Kerr LJ: I propose to refer to the submissions raised on behalf of the defendant in this case compendiously as the '*ex turpi causa* defence'. In my view, the relevant principles can then be summarised as follows:

(1) the *ex turpi causa* defence ultimately rests on a principle of public policy that the courts will not assist a plaintiff who has been guilty of illegal (or immoral) conduct of which the courts should take notice. It applies if, in all the circumstances, it would be an affront to the public conscience to grant the plaintiff the relief which he seeks because the court would thereby appear to assist or encourage the plaintiff in his illegal conduct or to encourage the plaintiff in his illegal conduct or to encourage others in similar acts: see para (2)(iii) below.

The problem is not only to apply this principle, but also to respect its limits, in relation to the facts of particular cases in the light of the authorities;

(2) the authorities show that in a number of situations the *ex turpi causa* defence will *prima facie* succeed. The main ones are as follows:

   (i) where the plaintiff seeks to, or is forced to, found his claim on an illegal contract or to plead its illegality in order to support his claim ...;

   (ii) where the grant of relief to the plaintiff would enable him to benefit from his criminal conduct ...;

   (iii) where, even though neither (i) nor (ii) is applicable to the plaintiff's claim, the situation is nevertheless residually covered by the general principle summarised in (i) above ...;

(3) however, the *ex turpi causa* defence must be approached pragmatically and with caution, depending on the circumstances ...

This applies, in particular, to cases which at first sight appear to fall within para (2)(i) or (ii) above.

Thus:

(i) situations covered by para (2)(i) above must be distinguished from others where the plaintiff's claim is not founded on any illegal act, but where some reprehensible conduct on his part is disclosed in the course of the proceedings, whether by the plaintiff himself or otherwise ...

Nor will it succeed where the defendant's conduct in participating in an illegal contract on which the plaintiff sues is so reprehensible, in comparison with that of the plaintiff, that it would be wrong to allow the defendant to rely on it ...

But, where both parties are equally privy to the illegality, the plaintiff's claim will fail, whether raised in contract or tort ...

And an action on a contract the terms of which are falsely recorded in documents intended to conceal the true agreement between the parties may be defeated by the *ex turpi causa* defence …

(ii) In situations covered by para (2)(i) and (ii) above the *ex turpi causa* defence will also fail if the plaintiff's claim is for the delivery up of his goods, or for damages for their wrongful conversion, and if he is able to assert a proprietary or possessory title to them even if this is derived from an illegal contract …;

(4) most of the situations and authorities referred to in paras (1) to (3) above have no direct application between Euro-Diam and the insurers in the present case, because the insurers were obviously entirely innocent throughout, and because the contract of insurance sued on by Euro-Diam was, in itself, wholly unaffected by any illegality. But they were nevertheless debated on this appeal, for two reasons. First, an illegality involving one contract or transaction can have the effect of tainting the plaintiff's claim under another related contract, so that the *ex turpi causa* defence still has to be considered in relation to his claim under the latter contract …

For that purpose it is relevant to consider the effect of the understated invoice on the contract between Euro-Diam and Verena …

The decision of Talbot J in *Geismar v Sun Alliance and London Insurance Ltd* [1977] 3 All ER 570; [1978] QB 383 … was counsel for the defendant's sheet-anchor …

I therefore conclude that *Geismar v Sun Alliance and London Insurance Ltd* was correctly decided on the basis of the principle and the authorities referred to in para (2)(ii) above. Furthermore, from the point of view of public policy the plaintiff's position in *Geismar*'s case was obviously very different from the position of Euro-Diam in the present case. The plaintiff was in possession of goods which he had effectively smuggled into this country, and on which he had evaded customs duty which he made it clear he would not pay. By his claim, he sought to recover the value of these goods in this country, which would presumably include the unpaid duty. Euro-Diam, on the other hand, did not smuggle the diamonds into Germany and did not themselves make use of the understated invoice; they were not liable for the underpaid tax; and they did not have the goods in their possession at any relevant time.

For all these reasons, I am in full agreement with the judge that the *ex turpi causa* defence fails …

MISREPRESENTATION AND NON-DISCLOSURE

INTRODUCTION

Misrepresentation and non-disclosure are topics which loom large in any discussion on insurance contract law. While misrepresentation is covered in any course on general contract law, non-disclosure is very much special to insurance law. Both topics pose major danger areas for the proposer when seeking insurance cover whether he is a consumer, businessman or insurer seeking reinsurance. What is forgotten by insurers when defending the rules relating to these topics is that they themselves often fail to meet the high standards they expect from others when they are seeking reinsurance (see *Pan Atlantic*, Appendix 4.24).

Insurance contracts are contracts requiring utmost good faith – *uberrima fides* – from both parties. The reasons for describing such contracts in this way are explained by Lord Mansfield in *Carter v Boehm* (1766) 3 Burr 1905 (Appendix 4.1). Distinguishing between a misrepresentation and non-disclosure is not always easy and in the latest House of Lords judgment in this area there was a tendency to merge the two topics (*Pan Atlantic*).

For the purpose of this chapter, misrepresentation is used to describe situations where the wrong or misleading answer has been given to questions posed of the applicant for insurance. Non-disclosure describes a situation where no answer has been volunteered to the insurer because no specific question was asked. Thus, the danger presented by the requirements of non-disclosure are usually greater than the requirements of misrepresentation. A further problem in insurance contract law, unlike the general law of contract, is that it does not matter whether the proposer is acting innocently or negligently. If the information is inaccurate, then the insurer is said to have been prejudiced by the inaccuracy. There are, however, exceptions to this for consumer insureds by virtue of the Statement of General Insurance Practice, (Appendix 4.10) and the approach used by the Insurance Ombudsman Bureau (see Chapter 11). It must be stressed that neither have the force of law and not all insurers have agreed to abide by the self-regulatory processes.

MISREPRESENTATION AND NON-DISCLOSURE

(See Bennett, 'Mapping the doctrine of utmost good faith in insurance contract law' [1999] LMCLQ 165, Appendix 4.36.)

In general contract law, for a misrepresentation to be actionable, there must be:

- a statement of fact and not opinion or law;
- it must be untrue or inaccurate;
- it must be material to the making of the contract (but see the basis of the contract clause, below and in Chapter 5);
- it must be a statement of present fact and not as to the future (but see the section on warranties in Chapter 5);
- it must have induced the innocent party into making the insurance contract on the terms on which it was made (but see the difficulties arising from the decision in *Pan Atlantic* (Appendix 4.24)).

Why utmost good faith? The classic case on the subject of the duty of good faith (does 'utmost' add anything to the meaning of 'good faith'?) is Lord Mansfield's judgment in *Carter v Boehm* (above) (see Appendix 4.1). It is the decision inevitably relied upon by insurers when resisting a claim, although they often appear to forget the actual outcome of the litigation. The insured was the Governor of Fort Marlborough on the island of Sumatra in the East Indies and the insurance was against the fort being taken by a foreign enemy. It was in fact attacked and taken by the French. The insurers, in refusing to pay on the policy, argued that there had been a concealment (thus, this is probably a case of non-disclosure rather than misrepresentation) relating to the weaknesses of the fort and the likelihood of attack by the French. Lord Mansfield set out the reasons why insurance contracts required good faith from the insured:

> The special facts, upon which the contingent chance is to be computed, lie most commonly [note that he does not say 'always'] in the knowledge of the insured only: the underwriter trusts to his representation, and proceeds upon confidence that he does not keep back any circumstances in his knowledge, to mislead the underwriter into a belief that the circumstance does not exist ... The policy would equally be void ... if the [underwriter] concealed [note: as to the insurer's duty of good faith, see below].

The classic extract appears to lean heavily in favour of the underwriter. The jury of merchants who heard the case found for the insured and Lord Mansfield agreed with the verdict in refusing a retrial. Why? The reason given by Lord Mansfield was that the underwriter in London could judge much better the probability of the French attacking outlying installations. The knowledge was based on the state of the war in Europe and the strength of the French fleet. The Governor did not have this information.

Unfortunately, the decision was interpreted in later cases as placing a very heavy burden of disclosure on the insured. See Hasson, 'The doctrine of *uberrima fides* in insurance law – a critical evaluation' (1969) 32 MLR 615 (Appendix 4.2), who argues that Lord Mansfield's judgment was misinterpreted leading to an entirely different doctrine and one largely fashioned during the 20th century. Inevitably, Hasson calls for and suggests method of reform. (See also Hodgin, 'The early development and rationale of utmost good faith in insurance law', in *Corporate and Commercial Law: Modern Developments*, 1996, London: LLP, Chapter 14.) Lord Mansfield also set out the occasions when the insured need not disclose information to the underwriter and these form the basis of s 18(3) of the Marine Insurance Act (MIA) 1906 (Appendix 4.3).

Timing of good faith. When does the duty to disclose arise? Section 18(1) of the MIA 1906, states 'the assured must disclose to the insurer, before the contract is concluded, every material circumstance which is known to the assured'. It may be thought, therefore, that changes in circumstances that occur after the inception of the contract need not be later declared until renewal time. The problem is that s 17 of the MIA 1906 states simply that the contract is based on utmost good faith and, if that is not observed, then the innocent party may avoid the contract. In practical terms, particularly in relation to commercial insurance contracts, as opposed to consumer contracts, insurers are likely to ask, by way of warranties, for information affecting changes of circumstance. It may even be that, without such a requirement, the change is so great that the original contract no longer can be said to cover the new risk (see *Hussain v Brown* [1996] 1 Lloyd's Rep 627, Appendix 5.7). To demand a constant updating of the circumstances in consumer contracts would lead to administrative burdens that no insurer would wish upon himself: for the insured, it is unlikely that many would remember that there was such an ongoing obligation and, even if he did remember, then all of the problems of what amounts to material change would have to be faced.

In a non-consumer setting, the Court of Appeal in *New Hampshire Insurance Co v MGM* [1997] LRLR 24, Staughton LJ, giving the judgment of the court, said:

> While there are no doubt cases where a defence of non-disclosure is fully justified, there are also in our experience some where it was not. We should hesitate to enlarge the scope for oppression by establishing a duty to disclose throughout the period of a contract of insurance, merely because it contains (as is by no means uncommon) a right to cancellation for the insurer.

German law approaches the problem of 'increase of hazard' somewhat differently. Thus, Law Concerning the Insurance Contract (VVG) states, in para 23: 'After the making of the contract the policyholder may not, without the insurer's approval, effect an increase of the hazard ... he must without delay inform the insurer.' The insurer then has the right to cancel within one month of the notification, but not after. However, the insurer's liability continues, if the increase in the hazard has had no effect on the occurrence of the insured event and on the extent of the insurer's obligation. Thus, there is a requirement of a causal connection, something which is unfortunately absent in English law, generally, when dealing with the good faith requirement, subject to the Statements of Insurance Practice discussed later.

French law on the other hand requires the insured to notify the insurer of material changes and on such notification the policy may be terminated or a higher premium charged (Code d'assurance, Article L.113-2-3).

The question of a continuing duty and the ambit of s 17 have now been considered by the House of Lords in *Manifest Shipping Co Ltd v Uni-Polaris Shipping Co Ltd (The Star Sea)* [2001] 1 All ER 743 (Appendix 4.35).

Insurers insured numerous ships owned by the insured. A fire broke out and the ship in question was a total loss. The insurers argued that the insureds were in breach of utmost good faith. This alleged breach referred to the fact that after the fire but before trial, in other words during negotiations of the claim, the insured failed to disclose information/reports relating to similar fires in other ships in the insured's fleet. (There was another defence based on aspects specific to marine insurance which we are not covering here.)

All three courts found the insurers liable. The duty on an insured during the claim period was not to be fraudulent. It was not enough to prove that the insured might have been negligent. The duty should not be widened to include culpable behaviour.

It is at least clear from this decision that while it might be said that there was a duty of good faith that existed during the currency of the policy it was not the onerous duty that we shall see below that exists during the negotiations leading up to the formation of the policy. In the words of Lord Hobhouse:

> ... the content of the obligation to observe good faith has a different application and content in different situations. The duty of disclosure as defined by ss 18–20 only applies until the contract is made ... The right to avoid referred to in s 17 ... applies retrospectively. It enables the aggrieved party to rescind the contract *ab initio*. Thus he totally nullifies the contract ... This is appropriate where the cause, the want of good faith, has preceded and been material to the making of the contract. But, where the want of good faith first occurs *later*, it becomes anomalous and disproportionate that it should be so categorised and entitle the aggrieved party to such an outcome (that is, rescission) ... The result is effectively penal ... This cannot be reconciled with principle ... Where an insured is found to have made a fraudulent claim ... the insurer is obviously not liable for the fraudulent claim ... The law is that the insured who has made a fraudulent claim may not recover the claim which could have been honestly made.

If insurers are unhappy with the interpretation of the House of Lords in *The Star Sea* then they will find little joy in the Court of Appeal decision in *K/S Merc-Scandia v Certain Lloyd's Underwriters* [2001] Lloyd's Rep IR 802. Here, under a liability policy, the insured had written a fraudulent letter during the negotiations leading to a claim. This letter however had nothing to do with the substantive claim and its falsity was discovered long before the claim was duly processed. (In fact it was a claim against the insured that the insurers were seeking to defend after the insured had gone into liquidation and thus it was not a 'claim' by the insured at all.) The insurer sought to avoid on the grounds of fraud arguing that *The Star Sea*, while rejecting a right to avoid merely because there may have been culpable behaviour at the claims stage, had implied that fraud would be an example of breach of good faith post-contract.

It was held that the insurer was liable. Longmore LJ explained that it was well recognised that, before a contract could be avoided for pre-contract non-disclosure or misrepresentation, the fact not disclosed or misrepresented had first to be material from the point of view of a prudent insurer when assessing the risk and second it must have induced the actual insurer to write that risk. There was no reason why these ingredients should not also be the test where an insurer seeks to avoid liability for lack of good faith or fraud in relation to post-contractual matters. In particular the requirement of inducement which exists for pre-contractual lack of good faith must exist in an appropriate form before an insurer can avoid the entire contract for post-contract lack of good faith. In this way the requirement of inducement for pre-contract conduct resulting in avoidance is then made to tally with post-contract conduct said to enable the insurer to avoid the contract. The conduct of the assured which is relied on by the insurer must be causally relevant to the insurer's ultimate liability or, at least, to some defence of insurers before it can be permitted to avoid the policy. 'This is ... the same concept as that insurers must be seriously prejudiced by the fraud complained of before the policy can be avoided.'

Some examples of the good faith requirements in operation

(a) No requirement to disclose that which you did not or could not know: the leading case is *Joel v Law Union and Crown Insurance Co* [1908] 2 KB 863 (Appendix 4.4). In an application for life insurance, X was asked if she had ever suffered from mental illness. She answered in the negative, unaware that she had been treated for acute mania. She later committed suicide. The court refused the jury's finding and held that the insurers were liable on the policy. In the words of Fletcher Moulton LJ: 'The duty is to disclose, and you cannot disclose what you do not know.' He went on to stress that the applicant's view of what was material was not however important. Thus, if you have been treated, but consider yourself to be cured, you would still need to disclose that earlier illness.

(b) Moral hazard: this is a favourite phrase of insurers. What amounts to a moral hazard, however, is not always easy for the insured to define and it is not helped when underwriters' views may vary.

In *Roselodge Ltd v Castle* [1966] 2 Lloyd's Rep 113 (Appendix 4.5), the plaintiff insured against loss of diamonds. There was no question asked of him relating to previous convictions of his employees. No disclosure was made that one director had been found guilty of bribing a policy officer, 18 years earlier, and another employee had been convicted of smuggling diamonds into the United States eight years earlier. The insurers refused a claim on the theft of diamonds. The court found for the insurers. It was held that the bribery conviction did not need to be disclosed, but the smuggling conviction, for which a prison sentence had been imposed, should have been disclosed. (Brief mention was made in Chapter 3 as to the placing of business at Lloyd's. In the present case the defendant was a Lloyd's underwriter who had subscribed to the slip for four 848ths or for £73 of the £304,590 loss – the case lasting for 43 days!) One of the underwriters giving evidence as to his understanding of moral hazard, stated that it was his view that if a man stole apples at the age of 17 and lived a blameless life for 50 years, he was so much more likely to steal diamonds at the age of 67; and that if he had told him this when he was putting forward a proposal at the age of 67, he would not have insured him. The judge explained that such an extreme view was unacceptable to him.

In *Roselodge*, the smuggling conviction when insuring in a commercial policy against loss of diamonds is clearly one that any reasonable person would expect to have to declare, even though no specific question had been asked. One would have thought, however, that any competent insurer dealing in this type of insurance would have had the sense to ask a specific question. Failure to do has never been successfully raised by an insured as an example of breach of good faith by the insurer.

A much harsher situation and one of great potential difficulty for a consumer insured is illustrated in *Lambert v Co-operative Insurance Society Ltd* [1975] 2 Lloyd's Rep 485 (Appendices 4.6 and 4.7). The plaintiff took out an 'all risks' policy on her and her husband's jewellery. There were no questions relating to previous convictions. To the plaintiff's knowledge her husband had been convicted for receiving stolen cigarettes. The policy contained a provision that it would be void for failure to disclose any material fact. The policy was renewed for nine years. Just prior to the last renewal her husband was sentenced for two offences of dishonesty. No mention was made of this on renewal. The plaintiff's claim for loss of £311, was rejected by the insurer. The Court of Appeal found for the insurers. Relying on such decisions as *Joel* and *Roselodge*, above, this was an inevitable outcome. But, clearly, Mackenna LJ was not comfortable with the outcome. He said, at the end of his judgment:

> The present case shows the unsatisfactory state of the law ... she is not an underwriter and presumably has no experience in these matters. The

> defendant company would act decently if, having established the point of principle, they were to pay her. It might be thought a heartless thing if they did not, but that is their business, not mine.

Lord Justice Lawton stated: 'Such injustices as there are must now be dealt with by Parliament, if they are to be got rid of at all.' Suggestions for reform were made by the Law Commission in 1980 (Appendix 4.8), but no legislation has been forthcoming, unlike the situation in Australia (Appendix 4.9).

While German law adopts a similar approach to present English law, para 18 of the VVG, states that where the insured has been asked to supply answers to written questions, the insurer may not rescind the contract if there was no question about the particular matter in question, unless there was a fraudulent concealment.

The closest thing to reform in this area is the self-regulatory Association of British Insurers' Statement of General Insurance Practice (Appendix 4.10), which is discussed below. Paragraph 1(d) states that those matters which insurers have found generally to be material will be the subject of clear questions in proposal forms. Will it be breach of insurers' good faith if the relevant question is not asked? The Insurance Ombudsman Bureau would probably say 'yes' – but what of commercial contracts?

(c) Rehabilitation of Offenders Act 1974: *Roselodge* and *Lambert* refer to past convictions. What part, if any, does the Rehabilitation of Offenders Act 1974 have to play?

The purpose of this Act is to wipe the slate clean for certain offenders, whereby they need not divulge previous convictions. The scope of the Act is limited to offences that do not exceed 30 months' imprisonment, and the rehabilitation period, after which they need not declare the previous conviction, ranges from three years to 10 years. For our purposes, therefore, an insured would not need to declare on the proposal form, or in any pre-insurance contract negotiations, any conviction which has become 'spent'. But this is perhaps an oversimplification, because of s 7(3) of the Act. This states that, if a court is satisfied that justice cannot be done in the case before it unless evidence is admitted relating to a person's spent convictions, then the court may require that such information be divulged. There are no examples of where this sub-section has been directly relevant in an insurance case, although it was referred to in one of the cases below.

In *March Cabaret Club and Casino v London Assurance* [1975] 1 Lloyd's Rep 169, the plaintiff owned premises in which he ran a Casino. He obtained a Traders Combined Policy with the defendant insurers covering the buildings and contents against fire risks. There were no questions on the proposal relating to moral hazards. A fire claim for £27,000 was made and rejected by the insurers on the basis that there had been a non-disclosure of an earlier conviction by one of the two directors, for handling stolen goods. The facts of these convictions were that on 14 June 1969 the director was charged; on 28

November 1969 he was committed for trial; he was convicted on 22 June 1970. The insurance contract was renewed on 20 June 1970. The question therefore was whether the arrest and committal should have been declared to the insurers, even though renewal was prior to the date of conviction. The High Court thought that it should have been and therefore the insurers were entitled to avoid liability. What may have influenced the minds of the court was that, in evidence, the insurers were able to show that this type of insurance was unattractive unless they were convinced that the management of such clubs was 'well established, reputable, clubs where the management is known to be of a high standard'. The implications that come from the decision are more worrying. It appears that an applicant for insurance must declare matters for which he has not been convicted, if he knows that he did in fact commit that offence. The judge placed importance on the fact that the director had admitted to a police officer that he was indeed guilty of the offence in question. This seems to imply that technical acquittals are irrelevant so far as insurers are concerned and must, therefore, be declared. May J said:

> Have the defendant insurers satisfied me on the balance of probabilities that immediately before the renewal of the policy in April 1970 the fact that Mr Skoulding had since the previous year's renewal committed the criminal offence ... was a material fact which it was necessary to disclose to insurers? I have no doubt at all on the evidence before me that the insurers have so proved.

The judge admitted that he was concerned with the apparent inconsistency between his approach and the presumption of innocence, which is a foundation of English criminal law. He went on to say, however, that his worries were based upon a fallacy; namely that there is nothing to prevent one party to a civil action attempting to prove that the other party had indeed committed the crime of which he had been acquitted. This means that even if there had been an acquittal, in Skoulding's case, the insurers would have been at liberty to attempt to prove that he was in fact guilty.

One needs, immediately, to compare this approach with the later case of *Reynolds and Anderson v Phoenix Assurance Co Ltd* [1978] 2 Lloyd's Rep 440 (Appendix 4.11). The two plaintiffs purchased premises for £16,000. They insured the premises for £18,000 and three years later increased the cover to £500,000 (1972). A year after that the cover was further increased to £628,000 made up of £500,000 premises, £28,000 machinery and £5,000 stock. A fire occurred and the problem of indemnity arose. After the commencement of the action it was discovered that one of the plaintiffs was faced with proceedings relating to a conspiracy to defraud. The insurer asked for leave to amend their defence to include this charge on the grounds of non-disclosure. Leave was granted but subsequent to the insurance hearing that plaintiff was acquitted of that charge. During the criminal trial, evidence showed that there was also a conviction of the insured dating from 1961. This also had not been disclosed and in the insurance hearing the non-disclosure of the 1961 conviction was also raised as a defence. The trial judge refused to allow this second amendment. The insurers appealed. The Court of Appeal allowed the appeal to amend, but left it to the trial judge as to whether he would exercise his discretion under s 7(3) of the Rehabilitation of Offenders Act 1974. The trial judge in the later trial found for the plaintiffs on the grounds that neither matters were ones which needed to be disclosed. With regard to the conviction in 1961, that is, 11 years earlier, the trial judge agreed that it was a 'spent' conviction under the 1974 Act but he was also of the opinion that s 7(3) gave him the discretion to consider that earlier conviction. He went on to argue that the offence itself was immaterial to the risk, and therefore there was no need to give a view as to the exercise of the discretion under s 7(3). But he gave guidance as to the position he would have taken if he had thought it necessary to exercise that discretion. His answer was that such a conviction should be disclosed if the expert witnesses had convinced him that insurers would want to know about this 1961 offence.

As to the non-disclosure of the allegation of conspiracy to defraud (of which he was later acquitted) the judge rejected the argument that this should be disclosed. He explained:

> I have no doubt that every insurer would like to have the most complete information about the moral make up of each proposer, but that is not the test. The test is whether the circumstances in question would influence his judgment in determining whether he will take the risk. The insurer's thirst for knowledge, however understandable, is not, therefore, the required criterion. A good example of what I have in mind is that many of the witnesses maintained that any allegation of fraud made against a proposer must be disclosed even though it had no foundation; the reason being that it must be for the insurer to investigate such allegations and decide on their truth ... I find this attitude wholly unacceptable.

In arriving at this decision, the judge is declining to follow the views expressed above in the *March Cabaret* case. It is the commission of the offence that must be disclosed, whether of not he was found guilty. The mere allegation of the offence to which the accused pleads innocent or when he is later acquitted because he did not commit it need not be disclosed. The implication, however, of this statement is that an insured should disclose an offence which he indeed committed, even though he has not been prosecuted or has been acquitted.

The Rehabilitation of Offenders Act 1974 is only of limited effect. It will only avail those people whose convictions were relatively trivial. If the applicant for insurance cannot bring himself within the Act, then the general rules of disclosure and materiality will come into play.

Woolcott v Sun Alliance and London Insurance Ltd [1978] 1 All ER 1253 illustrates yet another harsh aspect of these two requirements. The plaintiff obtained a mortgage to buy a house. It is customary, in this situation, for the building society advancing the loan to arrange for the insurance of the property, acting as the link between the insured and the insurer. This is done by means of a block policy whereby many insureds are dealt with in the same policy. The building society sent the insured a form. There were no questions concerning moral hazard, but there was one question: 'Are there any other matters which you wish to be taken into account?' The insured answered, 'no', thereby omitting to mention that he had been sentenced to 12 years' imprisonment for armed robbery 12 years before his present application for a mortgage. Two years later, the insured made a claim on the fire policy. The insurers rejected the claim on the basis of the non-disclosure, and succeeded on the basis of *Lambert*'s case. The worrying aspect of this decision is that the insured was not completing an insurance proposal form; that the type of cover could be said not to be affected by this type of conviction; that mortgages are normally tied to obtaining insurance in this way; that it implies that anyone who cannot come within the 1974 Act would be unable to obtain a loan to purchase property; that there must be statistically, many people in the insured's position at the present time, but unaware of the potential results if and when in the future they do need to make a claim.

(d) Previous refusals: previous refusals by insurers need to be disclosed. If another underwriter has made the decision that the applicant is unworthy of cover there should be a warning light for the next insurer who is approached. That is not to say that some insurers do not specialise in hard risks, at a greatly enhanced premium (for example, drink driving offenders).

In *Glicksman v Lancashire and General Assurance Co Ltd* (1927) 26 Ll L Rep 69 (Appendix 4.12), the problem was one of previous refusal combined with potential ambiguity of the questions on the proposal form (see Chapter 7 for construction problems). The plaintiff wanted to insure his stock in trade. He completed the proposal in his own name. In answer to a question relating to earlier refusals, he stated that he had refused an offer from another insurer. In fact, he had also been refused cover by another insurer, when insuring in the name of another company being run from the present premises. The House of Lords found for the insurers, reversing the Court of Appeal, but with some regret and sympathy for the claimant. Lord Atkinson was of the view that it was a lamentable thing that insurers could not frame questions in clear and unambiguous language. Lord Wrenbury added that it was a mean and contemptible policy on the part of an insurer that he should take the premium and refuse to pay upon a ground that was not really material on the facts. If the mistake was not material, how, then, could the policy be avoided? The answer is to be found in the use of the basis of the contract provision, which elevates all answers to conditions precedent to liability, and is discussed in the next chapter.

Is it necessary to declare an earlier refusal, the subject matter of which is unconnected with the present application? The question is answered in *Locker and Woolf Ltd v Western Australian Insurance Co Ltd* [1936] 1 KB 408 (Appendix

4.13). The plaintiff was seeking fire cover for their premises. One question asked if any other insurance application had been declined. The plaintiff did not declare that a motor application had been rejected on the grounds of misrepresentation and non-disclosure. The claim on the fire policy was also successfully avoided. The result is justified in that a specific question relating to past refusals had been incorrectly answered. But is the duty to disclose wider still? Should the proposer have to offer up information relating to other types of insurances from the one he now seeks? The approach of the judges in *Locker* leaned heavily in that direction. However, in *Ewer v National Employers Mutual General Insurance Association Ltd* [1937] 2 All ER 193 (Appendix 4.14), the insurers argued for this heavy duty of disclosure, namely that the proposer should, even when no questions were asked, declare every claim he had ever made on any other insurance policy whatever the subject matter be and state every refusal by an insurer that had ever been made. The court rejected such a requirement describing it as of great gravity and a complete novelty. The need to declare earlier refusals does not, however, apply to marine insurance. In *Glasgow Assurance Corporation Ltd v Symmonds* (1911) 16 Com Cas 109, Scrutton J said:

> The ordinary businessman would, I am sure, think it material to know that the underwriter wanting to reinsure thought so badly of the risk that he was ready to pay a higher premium to get [it]; but no one has ever suggested that need be disclosed.

(e) Knowledge of an agent: this topic is covered in detail in Chapter 6, but two cases can be referred to here to provide an illustration of the approach of the court.

In *Ayrey v British Legal and United Provident Assurance Co Ltd* [1918] 1 KB 136 (Appendices 4.15 and 6.12), the proposer sought life cover and one question inevitably asked for his occupation, which he correctly stated as fisherman. He was also a member of the Royal Naval Reserve, which he did not declare on the proposal form, but which he verbally relayed to the district manager of the insurers, who then accepted his premiums. Nearly two years later, the insured was drowned at sea, although the circumstances of his death were not known. The court found against the insurer. The company was held to have waived its rights to avoid the policy by continuing to accept premiums after it had become aware of the insureds' involvement in the Royal Naval Reserve. It was sufficient that a senior officer of the insurer had that information. There is danger for the insured, however, where the agent does not have authority to receive such information (see Chapter 6).

An independent intermediary, for instance a registered insurance broker, is the agent of the insured and not the insurer. Information passed to the broker is not therefore information in the hands of the insurer. For criticism of this rule, see *Roberts v Plaisted* [1989] 2 Lloyd's Rep 341 (Chapter 6).

(f) Waiver by insurer: it may be that the insurer by his behaviour can be said to have waived his rights to further information. This was part of the reason for the decisions in *Ayrey* and *Roberts* (above). The application of waiver is described in MacGillivray, *Insurance Law*, 9th edn, 1998, London: Sweet & Maxwell, in this way (paras 17–78):

> The test appears to be as follows: the assured must perform his duty of disclosure properly by making a fair representation of the risk proposed for insurance. If the insurers thereby receive information from the assured or his agent which taken on its own or in conjunction with other facts known to them or which they are presumed to know, would naturally prompt a reasonably careful insurer to make further inquiries, then if they omit to make the appropriate check or inquiry, assuming it can be made simply, they will be held to have waived disclosure of the material fact which that inquiry would necessarily have revealed.

(See Appendix 5.16.)

It is clear from this extract that waiver will not be lightly applied by the courts to relieve the proposer from his basic burden of good faith. The fact that the burden remains heavily on his shoulders is illustrated by the majority decision of the Court of Appeal on *Malhi v Abbey Life Assurance Co Ltd* [1996] LRLR 237 (Appendix 4.16). Do you prefer the dissenting judgment? M took out a joint life policy. He disclosed that he suffered from asthma and high blood pressure, but failed to disclose that he suffered from alcoholism and malaria. The policy lapsed due to failure to pay the premiums but was reinstated on the signing of a statement that health had remained good. The insurers avoided the policy on the death of M but his wife argued that the insurers had waived their rights. This argument was based on the fact that, at a later date, M had applied to the same insurer for a further joint life policy, which had been refused when a medical report had identified these two crucial medical histories. The insurer, however, had continued to accept premiums in relation to the first policy. The Court of Appeal held (2:1) that the plaintiff failed. The insurer had received different information in relation to different applications at three different times and this was insufficient to find that the insurers had waived the rights in relation to the first policy. Nor was there constructive knowledge. The majority distinguished *Evans v Employers Mutual Insurance Association Ltd* [1936] KB 505 (Appendix 5.11). In an age of computerisation of records the decision seems unfortunate. It is unfortunate that the court was prepared to accept expert evidence, admittedly evidence from experts from both sides, that it is not the practice of insurers to check earlier policies and that the pressure of work is such that it would make such a practice impracticable. If records are computerised, then surely it is possible in a second or so to call up all that is known about a customer. It surely would be done when an insurer is seeking evidence on which to reject a claim?

What would happen today if the insurers were subscribers to the Insurance Claims and Underwriting Exchange (CUE) (Appendix 4.17)? Surely information held on that system should not be used only as a defensive mechanism? Surely it is a potential infringement of the good faith requirement by insurers if they do not access the information at the underwriting stage? In fact, the very title of the system implies that this will be done? Subscribers to the system usually inform proposers that they are members and that they can retrieve earlier histories. Would it be wrong for insurers to claim that this only refers to claims histories?

(g) Half truths: failure to tell the whole truth will usually amount to non-disclosure unless the question can be interpreted as requiring less than that. In motor insurance it is common for insurers to ask for the claims history for the last, say, five years. This would mean that a catastrophic claim seven years earlier would not need to be declared. Asking about motor claims would not require disclosure of non-motor claims. Where the question on the proposal is ambiguous, the court will interpret it *contra proferentem* and therefore against the insurer who has framed the ambiguous question (see Chapter 7).

In *Roberts v Avon Insurance Co Ltd* [1956] 2 Lloyd's Rep 240 (Appendix 4.18), the proposer was faced with a question on the proposal form which was put in the following way: 'I have never sustained a loss in respect of any of the contingencies specified in this proposal except ... Note – Give date, amount and name of insurers in respect of such loss.' The 'question' was left unanswered. On the claims form, which often tends to elicit the same type of information as the proposal form and thus provides a very effective way for the insurer to cross check for inadequacies of information, and thereby raise the defence of breach of good faith, the insured also stated that he had no previous claims history. The insurers discovered from other insurers that he had made a claim within the last three years. The insurers were able to avoid the claim, the court holding that the unanswered question did amount to a non-disclosure. There was no ambiguity in the question as read by a reasonable proposer. Section 27 of the (Australian) Insurance Contracts Act 1984 (Cth) (Appendix 4.9) states in stark contrast to the common law position that an applicant shall not be taken as having made a misrepresentation by his failure to answer a question on a proposal form. The duty is placed on the insurer in such circumstances to make further enquiries. After all, that is what the art of underwriting is all about – asking the right questions and evaluating the answers!

(h) Duty of good faith on the insurer: there is no doubt that the duty of good faith requirement is reciprocal. Lord Mansfield said as much in *Carter v Boehm* (1766) 3 Burr 1905 (Appendix 4.1). 'The policy would be equally void, against the underwriter, if he concealed ...' Although that has been the requirement for more than 200 years there have been almost no cases illustrating the point. This could mean that all insurers during this period of time have attained such impeccable standards that the question has never been worth litigating. It could, on the one hand, mean that the expense of litigation for the privately insured is so great that no one has thought it worthwhile taking the point particularly, if successful, the remedy will turn out to be disastrously ineffectual, as will be seen below.

There is one case that does illustrate an insurer in breach of the duty, but one that has not been built upon. In *Horry v Tate and Lyle Refineries Ltd* [1982] 2 Lloyd's Rep 416 (Appendix 4.19), the plaintiff was injured at work and the employer's insurers took over the negotiations and a settlement was reached which clearly was at a figure below what that injury required. The plaintiff successfully argued that he was not bound by the earlier settlement because there was a fiduciary duty of care owed to him by the insurers. Their desire to keep the figure to a minimum clearly clashed with the plaintiff's requirement to be fairly compensated (see how the Ombudsman deals with disputed motor vehicle valuations in Chapter 11).

The extent of the insurer's duty of good faith and the remedy available should there be such a breach was dealt with in the voluminous litigation in *La Banque Financière de la Cité SA v Skandia (UK) Insurance Ltd* [1990] 2 Lloyd's Rep 377 (Appendix 4.20; see also Appendices 4.21 and 4.22). The question for present discussion can be reduced to the following: does an insurer who knows that his insured has received fraudulent advice from his broker owe a duty, based on good faith, to inform his insured? The answer was that there was no duty on a party to disclose that the other party's agent had committed breaches of his duty to his principal. In the present case the insurer had made no representations to the insured. The House of Lords decision, which did not refer to *Carter v Boehm*, is largely concerned with the question of causation, which is beyond the scope of the present discussion. It is necessary to look back to the Court of Appeal's judgment ([1988] 2 Lloyd's Rep 513) for guidance as to when a duty of good faith on the part of an insurer to his insured might arise. Lord Bridge approved of the following statement by Slade LJ:

> In our judgment, the duty falling on the insurers must at least extend to disclosing all facts known to him which are material either to the nature of the risk sought to be covered or the recoverability of a claim under the policy which a prudent insured would take into account in deciding whether or not to place the risk for which he seeks cover with that insurer.

Thus, it would appear that the insurer's duty of good faith is to be kept in rather narrow bounds. But even if it could be shown that the insurers were liable what would be the remedy? The Court of Appeal explained that the duty of disclosure 'is neither contractual, tortious, fiduciary or statutory but based on the original jurisdiction of the court of equity and therefore did not give rise to an award of damages ... the only remedy was rescission'. That, of course, is the remedy when the insured is in breach and leads to the insurer not paying out on the policy. But, when used the other way round, it means that all that a successful insured would be able to recoup would be a return of his premiums!

(i) Materiality and inducement: the most crucial question that faces the proposer in his uphill struggle to meet the requirements of good faith is, what exactly is it that must be disclosed? The answer is – all things that are material to the risk sought to be covered. That will inevitably be followed by a second question – what is material? The answer should be found by applying s 18 of the MIA 1906 (Appendix 4.3). Unfortunately, that section has provided much uncertainty in its interpretation. The crucial phrase is 'Every circumstance is material which would influence the judgment of a prudent insurer in fixing the premium, or determining whether he will take the risk'. The cause of the uncertainty is the Court of Appeal decision in *CTI v Oceanus Mutual* [1984] 1 Lloyd's Rep 476. For a critique of the judgment, see Appendix 4.23.

The insurers were able to avoid their liability on the grounds of non-disclosure and misrepresentations relating to previous claims history. This looks like a straight application of s 18(2) of the Marine Insurance Act 1906. The problem, however, was that it was said that the word 'influenced' in that sub-section means that 'the disclosure is one which would have an impact on the formation of his opinion and on his decision making process in relation to the matter covered by s 18(2)' (*per* Kerr LJ). Thus, a fact is material, even though it would not have caused the insurer, if the fact had been disclosed, to reject the proposer or to have increased the premium. It is still material and therefore needs to be disclosed if it is something which a prudent insurer would have wanted to know. To be material it need not be something which would have decisively influenced the underwriter. This interpretation appears to increase considerably to burden on the proposer.

In *Pan Atlantic Insurance Co Ltd and Another v Pine Top Insurance Co Ltd* [1994] 3 All ER 581 (Appendix 4.24), the House of Lords were presented with the opportunity of reassessing the *CTI* decision. *Pan Atlantic* was a case of reinsurance, where the reinsurers successfully avoided liability on the grounds that the reinsureds had not fully disclosed earlier losses at the time of concluding the present contract. It is worth stressing at this point that this is, therefore, a case of insurers (admittedly, through their brokers) themselves failing the test of good faith in their dealings with other insurers.

The two crucial questions for the court were the interpretation of s 18 of the MIA 1906 and whether a material fact had to induce the actual insurer into making the contract on the relevant terms.

To answer the first question it was necessary to analyse the *CTI* decision. Lord Mustill set out in some detail the criticism that had been made of *CTI* in the intervening years. Despite the weight of these criticisms, the court held, by a majority (3:2), that *CTI* was correctly decided and that to be material the fact need not have a decisive influence on the mind of the prudent insurer, it was sufficient if it was a matter about which he would like to have known. Lord Mustill argued that s 18(2) did not say 'decisively' influence, but left the word 'influence' unadorned. The question was asked earlier in the chapter whether the word 'utmost' adds anything to the phrase 'good faith'. So here one can ask whether 'decisively' adds anything to the word 'influence'. Surely neither 'utmost' nor 'decisively' adds anything to the meaning of the other words. Surely Lord Lloyd's dissent on this point is the more convincing? (See Appendix 4.25 for criticisms of the majority view.)

The majority refused to input a new word into s 18(2), but by a unanimous decision the House decided to read into the Act a requirement that a material fact must have influenced the actual underwriter into making that particular contract. 'If this requires the making of new law, so be it' (*per* Lord Mustill). In so doing the House overruled *CTI* on this particular point. This inducement test is taken from the general law of contract. Even a fraudulent misrepresentation, in the general law of contract, is not actionable if there is no causal connection between it and the making of the contract.

The remaining question is – on whose shoulder does the inducement test lie? It is for the insurer to show that there has been a breach of good faith according to the standards of a prudent insurer. It is then necessary to move to the inducement test. Lord Mustill, on more than one occasion, talks of a presumption of inducement, which would mean that the insured would have the task of rebutting that presumption. Lord Lloyd, however, put the questions in reverse order. He said:

> (a) Did the misrepresentation or non-disclosure induce the actual insurer to enter into the contract on those terms?
>
> (b) Would the prudent insurer have entered into the contract on the same terms if he had known of the misrepresentation or non-disclosure immediately before the contract was concluded? ...
>
> The evidence of the insurer himself will normally be required to satisfy the courts on the first question. The evidence of an independent broker or underwriter will normally be required to satisfy the court on the second question.

How have subsequent cases interpreted *Pan Atlantic*? In *St Paul's Fire and Marine Insurance v McConnell Dowell Constructors Ltd and Others* [1995] 2 Lloyd's Rep 116 (Appendix 4.26), the insured had described a particular building method that was to be used for a development in the Marshall Islands. A Contractors All Risk policy was issued on the basis that piled foundations were to be used. Before the contract was concluded, difficulties of terrain subsequently required the construction to be built on spread foundation, but this change was not notified to the insurers. A subsidence claim was successfully avoided for the innocent non-disclosure. As to the test of materiality Evans LJ, quoting from *Edgington v Fitzmaurice* (1885) 19 Ch D 459 (a non-insurance case), said that it was not necessary to show that the misrepresentation was the sole cause of acting in a particular way. Thus, any statement that would have had a material influence on the decision making of a prudent insurer in relation to that particular risk will lead to avoidance if the test of inducement of the actual insurer is shown. The 'insurer must prove that he was induced by the non-disclosure or misrepresentation' (*per* Evans LJ). However, where the evidence as to the materiality is strong, it seems that there will be a presumption of inducement. In the present case, there were four insurers of whom only three gave evidence. There was, however, 'no evidence to displace a presumption that Mr Earnshaw, like the other three was induced by the non-disclosure or misrepresentation'.

There must surely be situations where different underwriters act differently on the face of the same set of facts. There must surely be cases where an underwriter has an 'off-day'. How strong need be the evidence to lead to a presumption of inducement?

Marc Rich and Co AG v Portman [1997] 1 Lloyd's Rep 225 (Appendix 4.27) was a complex case of marine insurance. The underwriter sought to avoid liability *inter alia*, on the grounds of non-disclosure of the poor claims experience of the insured. The insured argued that such non-disclosures that had occurred had not induced the making of the contract. How could a poor claims record not lead to a presumption of inducement? The reason was, argued the insured, that the particular underwriter had little or no understanding of the type of risk that he was initialling. The court agreed with the assessment of the particular underwriter's professional competence. The insurers were, however, not liable on the policy. How did the court reach that conclusion? The loss experience was so poor that the burden of disclosure was clearly on the insured. If he had spelt out, in detail, the previous history then even this underwriter would have been put on the alert, whereby he would have referred the matter to the senior underwriter. Thus, a highly negligent underwriter (a description used by the trial judge) was saved by the failure of the insured to meet the high standards of the good faith requirements. This view, coupled with a presumption of inducement seen in the *St Paul's* case seem to minimise, for the insured, the assumed advantages of the creation of the inducement test in *Pan Atlantic*.

If the courts too readily apply the 'presumption of inducement' test then the Pan Atlantic decision will not have as much impact in this area of law as some had hoped. Where numerous insurers are on risk it may happen that one underwriter's reputation has the effect of others readily agreeing to sign. In such a situation the followers can not say that they have been induced by any breaches by the insured. This is what happened in *Sirius International Insurance Corp v Oriental Assurance Corp* [1999] Lloyd's Rep IR 343 where only the lead reinsurer was able to avoid but not the other two reinsurers.

The 'all or nothing' remedy available to insurers by virtue of s 18(1) of the MIA 1906 when there has been a breach of utmost good faith has led, in certain areas of insurance at least, to the insureds demanding a 'softer' approach. Thus in professional indemnity insurance it is not unusual to find that the insurer will not avoid on the grounds of innocent or negligent breach by the insured. Even fraudulent behaviour by the assured's agent, but not by the assured himself, can be excluded although the wording would have to be clear on this matter. It is obvious that where such insurance is required by virtue of membership of a professional body the reason is that an innocent victim of that professional's negligence is deserving of compensation. If the PI cover could be avoided the PI cover would not produce the required result.

It is possible for the insured to attempt to negotiate a 'softer' treatment from the insurer in any branch of insurance law. In *HIH Casualty and General Insurance Ltd v Chase Manhattan Bank and Heath North America Ltd etc* [2001] Lloyd's Rep IR 703 the policies in issue were financial contingency cover relating to the financing of film production. Such policies were taken out by the insured defendant through the defendant brokers who were themselves the architects of such policies. The variously worded exclusions of responsibility found in the policies (known as 'truth of statement' clauses) were such that the insured was not to be liable for any mistakes made by others who had completed part of the proposal and such immunity expressly covered statements made by the brokers. The complex facts were reduced to two main issues in the Court of Appeal. In the face of alleged fraudulent, reckless or negligent non-disclosures or misrepresentations by the brokers were the insurers entitled, despite the exclusion clauses, to avoid or rescind the contracts against the insured and were the insurers entitled to damages for misrepresentation or non-disclosure from the insured and/or were the insurers entitled to damages from the brokers?

The court held (Rix LJ giving the only judgment) that it was possible to exclude misrepresentation/non-disclosure committed by the brokers and that had been achieved by the wording used here. But the particular wording would not extend to save the insured from any claim by the insurer to avoid, rescind and/or claim damages in relation to any fraud or deceit committed by the brokers. Would it be possible to find a wording that did exclude fraud? The basic rule is that a person can not exclude their own fraudulent behaviour. But is it possible to exclude the fraud of one's agents? After an extensive review of case law Rix LJ came to the conclusion that there was no legal principle why it should not be possible, although he was of the view that it might be very difficult to find a wording that would be acceptable to the other party at the time of making the contract. The use of the word 'fraud' in the exclusion would almost appear to be axiomatic to achieve the desired immunity. It would appear to be a somewhat startling clause and one which no court has previously been asked to consider.

Reform

It is clear from the cases discussed earlier in the chapter that insurance contracts have been marked out for special treatment. The reason for this is said to stem from Lord Mansfield's views in *Carter v Boehm* (1766) 3 Burr 1905 (Appendix 4.1), although, as Hasson (Appendix 4.2) has argued, Lord Mansfield's judgment has been over-enthusiastically developed in later cases. The opportunity for the House of Lords to modernise the subject of good faith in *Pan Atlantic* (Appendix 4.24) has been largely wasted (Birds and Hird, Appendix 4.25; but note the concluding remarks of Lord Hobhouse in Appendix 4.35). Ultimately, it will probably require Parliament to consider the matter, but, based on past experience relating to insurance law reform, that looks a long way off. After all, this is a highly successful industry and complaints about certain unfairness will probably be subservient to the economic advantages created by the insurance industry. In the remaining part of this chapter, reference is made to attempts to change the law in this country, in Australia and in the United States.

Reform in England and Wales

An early attempt at reform was made by the Law Reform Committee in their Fifth Report, *Conditions and Exceptions on Insurance Policies*, Cmnd 62, 1957, London: HMSO. This relatively short report was referred to in the much more detailed consideration given to the subject by the Law Commission (*Insurance Law Non-Disclosure and Breach of Warranty*, Cmnd 8064, Law Comm 104, 1980, London: HMSO (Appendix 4.8)). This report dealt with the alleged defects in the law of non-disclosure; the Statement of General Insurance Practice (see below); the proportionality principle as applied in Sweden and France; warranties in insurance contracts and the basis of the contract clause (see Chapter 5). The Law Commission's work was probably hindered rather than assisted by the fact that at the same time there was a draft Council Directive seeking to co-ordinate the insurance contract laws of Member States, which was ultimately shelved (see Chapter 1). In relation to our present topic of the duty of disclosure, the recommendation was that it should be limited to those material facts:

> (a) which are actually known to the proposer or which ... he is assumed to know; and
>
> (b) which a reasonable man in the position of the proposer would disclose to the insurer, having regard to the nature and content of the insurance cover which is sought and the circumstances in which it is sought.

A fact was considered to be material if it would influence the judgment of the prudent insurer:

> (a) in deciding whether to offer insurance against the risks covered by that contract; or

(b) in deciding the premium or other terms on which he would be prepared to offer that insurance.

Such a recommendation, if implemented, would have modified the present law in favour of the proposer, but not to the extent achieved by the (Australian) Insurance Contracts Act 1984 (Cth) (see below).

With the Australian Act very much in mind, the National Consumer Council issued their Insurance Law Reform publication in 1997 (Appendix 4.28). The Association of British Insurers (ABI) (1997) responded to the NCC Report (Appendix 4.29), the basic premise of which was that 'the overall case for comprehensive legislative reform of insurance law has not been made out'. In relation to the suggested changes to the good faith doctrine made by the NCC Report, the ABI was of the view that there was nothing new and that their own Statement of General Insurance Practice (Appendix 4.10) dealt with most of the criticisms. The Statement has inevitably been strongly relied upon by the ABI to deflect criticisms since its introduction.

Originally, there were three Statements. These covered general insurance business, long term business (that is, life policies) and industrial assurance. The category of industrial assurance was absorbed into the Statement concerned with long term practice in 1986.

The first two Statements were issued in 1977 and have undergone revision in the light of criticisms and evaluation. Their present revised wording dates from 1986 for the General and Life Statements.

The Statement of General Insurance Practice is concerned with all types of insurance cover, which a person resident in the United Kingdom would take out in their private capacity, other than long term policies such as life insurance.

The thrust of consumer protection is to protect people contracting in their private capacity. This has the effect of putting into a special and unprotected category the corner shop owner who is by definition equated with major national chain outlets. This is obviously unfair, in that the latter has the money and expertise, through legal or insurance advisers, to negotiate his insurance requirements. The former may not have such assistance at hand. From another viewpoint, it also means that a private individual who has great experience in the business or legal world will be given the same sympathetic treatment (as a private person) as one who is unwary of business techniques. This is one of the difficulties of consumer protection. It has, for the sake of a workable rule, usually tended to use the private-commercial division as its dividing point.

The first section of the Statement is concerned with proposal forms. It is the longest section reflecting, as it does, that in reality this is the area most fraught with danger for the policyholder.

Section 1(a) states that: '... the declaration at the foot of the proposal from should be restricted to completion according to the proposer's knowledge and belief.' This is intended to deal with the criticism of one of the more notorious areas of insurance law. At the foot of the proposal form, the proposer was usually told that his signature would mean that all the answers he had given would now become the basis of the contract between him and the company. Thus, if any answer was later found to be incorrect, the proposer would have broken the contract and the company could avoid liability.

The present paragraph attempts to resolve the issue of unfairness. If the proposer honestly believed his answer was accurate, then that is all he is verifying. To be fair to insurers, some companies did, before the 1977 Statement, use words that implied that the answers were correct 'to the best of my knowledge'.

Section 1(b) states:

> ... neither the proposal form nor the policy shall contain any provision converting the statements as to past or present fact in the proposal form into warranties. But insurers may require specific warranties about matters which are material to the risk.

Breach of a warranty in insurance law, unlike other aspects of contract law, allows the insurer to avoid his liabilities under the policy, irrespective of how important a particular breach might be. Thus, it was the blanket defence of 'breach of warranty' that was criticised as being so unfair. This paragraph, therefore, explains that while the use of warranties is permitted, they must be specifically referable to material risks in that type of policy. The company will still, however, remain the first judge of what is material and it may not necessarily be clear to the proposer the importance of the question or the dire results that may follow should the warranty be broken. The Law Commission had suggested that the insurer should be obliged to supply the insured with a written document setting out the warranty within a reasonable time after completing the contract. In this way, an additional attempt would have been made to bring the matter to the attention of the insured. Where this is not done, the Law Commission suggested that the insurer should be precluded from relying on any breach of such warranty. Unfortunately, the Statement does not reflect this suggestion. It would clearly be possible, however, for forward-looking companies to adopt the Law Commission's recommendations irrespective of what the Statement requires.

Section 1(c) states that:

> ... if not included in the declaration, prominently displayed on the proposal form should be a statement:
>
> (i) drawing the attention of the proposer to the consequences of the failure to disclose all material facts, explained as those facts an insurer would regard as likely to influence the acceptance and assessment of the proposal;
>
> (ii) a warning that if the proposer is in any doubt about facts considered material, he should disclose them.

This sub-section immediately raises the problem of how to define 'material'. As we have seen earlier, the standpoint in English insurance law has always been that of the insurer rather than that of the insured. The inevitable problem, therefore, is how will the average insured know what is material and what is not material? Insurance practice reflects insurance knowledge. That knowledge is based on the information from millions of policies and thousands of claims. It is clearly impossible for the insured to appreciate precisely what the company regards as material. Some information is clearly relevant to most types of insurance (for example, past criminal convictions are material). In house contents insurance, it is material to the insurer to know whether or not the insured takes in lodgers. Someone who, having been insured with the same company for many years and now, due to financial necessity or even a desire for companionship, takes in a student lodger, may not receive the insurer's sympathy when failing to declare this new situation on renewal.

To some extent, s 1(d) tries to deal with this by stating that: '... those matters which insurers have found generally to be material will be the subject of clear questions in proposal forms.' Each insurer will be free to decide whether a particular matter is material to them. There is no suggestion that a particular branch of insurance should be governed by a uniform proposal form. Although many insurers have, in recent years, attempted to improve and simplify the language of their documentation, the problem of 'clear questions' still remains. Insurers are understandably loath to increase the length of their proposal forms for fear that this will intimidate the applicant. On the other hand, the attempted brevity can lead to complex, convoluted and, thus, ambiguous questions. Insurers must keep their forms under regular review and make changes based on the experience of problems that have arisen. It has been suggested above that failure to ask obviously relevant questions might be breach of the duty of good faith on the part of the insurer.

Section 1(e) states that:

> ... so far as is practicable, insurers will avoid asking questions which would require expert knowledge beyond that which the proposer could reasonably be expected to possess or obtain or which would require a value judgment on the part of the proposer.

The basic thrust of the section is an attempt to help the proposer but the phrase, 'so far as is practicable', must surely have an important limiting effect. If technical questions need to be answered, how can the average insured, lacking in technical know-how, be expected to answer?

Although the above sections of the Statement go some way to simplifying matters for the insured, much of it is undone by the continued requirement that full information affecting the risk must be disclosed, even though no specific questions are asked relating to that particular point. The Law Commission Working Paper, the forerunner of the 1980 Report, had suggested abolishing this requirement. Their final report, however, changed direction. They explained that this was seen to be necessary in the light of comments made by the insurance industry. These comments concentrated on the argument that proposal forms would need to be more lengthy, detailed and complex and that there might be occasions when even an average proposer would know that he should divulge information, which was perhaps not covered by a specific question.

The only hope that insurers can have of not being unfairly caught by the residual requirement, 'declare all', is that some of the earlier sections of the Statement set out above, will be used to minimise the failure to divulge more information. Thus, if s 1(d), 'ask material questions' and s 1(c) 'prominent statement of failure to disclose all material facts' are honoured by insurers, there should only be the rare occasion when the residual requirement defence could be used. If that assumption is correct, then it would have been tidier if the Law Commission had advocated the abolition of the requirement altogether and the Statement varied. If the assumption is not correct, then the residual requirement is a problem that needs to be looked at again.

Section 1(f) deals with imparting information about the policy to the insured. It states that:

> ... unless the prospectus or the proposal form contains full details of the standard cover offered, and whether or not it contains an outline of that cover, the proposal form shall include a prominent statement that a specimen copy of the policy form is available on request.

It has to be said that, even when the full policy wording is available at the time the applicant completes the proposal, he will probably find such a document daunting in length and in complexity. But, clearly, it is his right to have it instantly available should he wish to inform himself of what is and is not included. Many companies have managed to produce useful prospectuses setting out, often in different colours, the main areas of cover and useful lists of what is not covered. A constant striving for greater simplicity in the policy itself should, however, remain a continuing priority. (See also the Unfair Terms in Consumer Contract Regulations 1999, Appendix 7.1.)

Section 1(g) advises that:

> ... proposal forms shall contain a prominent warning that the proposer should keep a record (including copies of letters) of all information supplied to the insurer for the purposes of entering into the contract.

This is obviously good advice in order to simplify problems that might arise in the future. Numerous arguments ensue, sometimes reaching the courts, because of disagreements between the parties on whether or not a particular communication had been made. The high technology office is no guarantee that proper or efficient records will be kept.

The proposal form shall also:

> ... contain (s 1(h)) a prominent statement that a copy of the completed form: (i) is automatically provided for retention at the time of completion; or (ii) will be supplied as part of the insurer's normal practice; or (iii) will be supplied on request within a period of three months after its completion.

The preceding sections emphasise the crucial importance of the questions and answers on the proposal form. The availability of option (iii) seems, therefore, to be completely out of place. The insured should automatically receive a copy of the form unless there are technical reasons why option (ii) should apply. If this rule applied, there would then be no necessity for s 1(i) which states that 'an insurer shall not raise an issue under the proposal form, unless the policyholder is provided with a copy of the completed form'.

Section 2 of the General Insurance Practice Statement is concerned with the handling of insurance claims.

Section 2(a) states that:

> ... under the conditions regarding notification of a claim, the policyholder shall not be asked to do more than report a claim and subsequent developments as soon as reasonably possible except in the case of legal processes and claims which a third party requires the policyholder to notify within a fixed time where immediate advice may be required.

Insurance companies understandably want to know as soon as possible when a loss has occurred. In this way, they are in a position to investigate the claim. Unfortunately, it was not unknown for some insurers in the past to insist upon time clauses with which it was difficult if not impossible for the insured to comply. The first half of this section now eases that burden and asks no more than that they be told within a reasonable time. It should be noted, however, that the policy may demand notification of any 'accident' covered by the policy. Unfortunately, it does not usually say 'whether or not a claim will follow'.

The second part of this sub-section is cumbersomely worded and does no credit to the industry when trying to put its own proposal and policy wording in order. It refers to situations where the insured may be sued or prosecuted. Immediate investigation and asking for witnesses' statements, may be crucial to a successful defence or claim.

Perhaps a 'reasons why' clause should be added for greater clarity.

Section 2(b) explains that:

> ... an insurer will not repudiate liability to indemnify a policyholder:
>
> (i) on the grounds of non-disclosure of a material fact which a policyholder could not reasonably be expected to have disclosed;
>
> (ii) on grounds of misrepresentation unless it is a deliberate or negligent misrepresentation of a material fact;

(iii) on grounds of a breach of warranty or condition where the circumstances of the loss are unconnected with the breach unless fraud is involved.

Paragraph 2(b) does not apply to marine and aviation policies.

Section 1(c) requires that the insurer warns the insured of the need to disclose material facts and, if in doubt as to whether something is material or not, then to divulge it. The problem with this, as explained above, is that it is the insurer's and not the insured's definition of what is material that counts. This might be said to be somewhat mitigated by s 2(b)(i) in that there will be no repudiation of liability if the insured could not reasonably have appreciated that he was under a duty to disclose that particular fact. Again, however, the problem is in defining when the insured would have been acting reasonably. The insurer in the first instance will be the judge of that.

To penalise the insured for a deliberate misrepresentation of a material fact is understandable. To extend the right of repudiation to negligent misrepresentation is a little harsher. This is especially so when cases from contract law generally display some difficulty in distinguishing negligent from innocent misrepresentation. This section unfairly equates the deceitful person with the negligent person in denying cover to both.

Section 2(b)(ii) answers the criticism that it was possible for an insurer to avoid liability for breach of a condition or breach of warranty even in circumstances where the breach had nothing to do with the actual loss. Thus, it is a normal requirement that a motor vehicle should be kept in a roadworthy condition. If the insured parks his car on his driveway, knowing that both rear lights are not working, but intending to repair them the following day, and the car is stolen during the night, s 2(b)(iii) states that the insurer will not repudiate liability.

Where the insurer alleges fraud against the insured then s 2(b)(iii) will not operate. The Law Commission's criticism of this part of the section was that insurers might allege fraud, even though not able to prove it, and thus withdraw the safety net of the section.

Section 2(c) states that: '... liability under the policy having been established and the amount payable by the insurer agreed, payment will be made without avoidable delay.' It is not known to what extent late payments have been a problem. The inclusion of this sub-section will, however, act as a reminder to any insurer that dilatoriness is an unacceptable ploy.

Section 3 is concerned with the all-important question of renewals. The section states that:

(a) renewal notices shall contain a warning about the duty of disclosure including the necessity to advise changes affecting the policy which have occurred since the policy inception or last renewal date, whichever was the later;

(b) renewal notices shall contain a warning that the proposer should keep a record (including copies of letters) of all information to the insurer for the purposes of renewal of the contract.

This section should be read in conjunction with s 1(b) (above). Renewals represent a dangerous time for the insured. He is, in effect, making a new contract, but without the need for completing a proposal form. Therefore, he is not asked to concentrate his mind on the task in hand. It would be unusual for the information previously given to remain unchanged in its entirety. Changing occupations may well have an important effect on motor insurance. Recently purchased additions to the home will increase the house contents valuation. As explained above, it is a drawback that s 1(b) allows alternative modes of informing the insured of the answers he originally gave on the proposal form. He should automatically receive a copy and the renewal notice should ask him to check his earlier answers and sign a statement that he has so checked. It would also improve matters if the renewal notice contained a section where changes could be entered. Renewal notices could include examples, varying with the type of insurance about to be renewed, which highlight the more important changes that affect insurer's decision making.

Section 4 states that: '... any changes to insurance documents will be made as and when they need to be reprinted, but the Statement will apply in the meantime.'

Section 5 explains that: '... insurers will continue to develop clearer and more explicit proposal forms and policy documents whilst bearing in mind the legal nature of insurance contracts.'

Both sections have brought about a marked change in the format of insurance documentation, although the changes obviously vary from company to company. It would be interesting to know how much, if any, consumer input went into the new models. The second half of s 5 seems to imply that because it is a legal document, it will inevitably have some complexities. It seems to reflect a defeatist approach to the problem. Section 6 states that the:

> ... provisions of the Statement shall be taken into account in arbitration and any other referral procedures which may apply in the event of disputes between policyholders and insurers relating to matters dealt with in the Statement.

While the Statement does not have the force of law and will not, therefore, be directly relevant in the few cases where the insured can afford to take his insurer to court (but see *Economides v Commercial Union Assurance Co plc* [1997] 3 All ER 636: Appendix 8.9), it will at least provide the basis on which the Insurance Ombudsman will deal with complaints.

The Statements represented an attempt by the insurance industry to avoid what were perceived as the possible rigours of the Unfair Contract Terms Act 1977. The changes brought about in 1981 and revised, in their latest format, in 1986 were due largely to the adverse criticisms levelled at them by the Law Commission Report in 1980 and other commentators.

It is understandable that the industry should seek to avoid legislation that would restrict their practices. In particular, being subjected to the Unfair Contract Terms Act 1977 may well have produced an increase in cases testing the reasonableness of many well used clauses. But, however understandable their worries may have been, the Government's decision to permit this method of side-stepping such legislation is certainly unacceptable. No good reason has been shown for treating insurance contracts in any special way.

More specific criticisms can be made. Not all insurers are members of the ABI and, therefore, they are not subject to the Statements. Some members of the ABI are not members of the Insurance Ombudsman's Bureau and, therefore, those sections of the Statements referring to this possible avenue of dispute resolution are not necessarily applicable.

The contents of the Statements are largely unknown to insureds. Although some sections act to change the insurance documentation, others equally refer to matters which are of little use to the insured if he knows nothing of them, for instance, timely payments and, again, dispute resolution.

The language of the Statements is far from satisfactory. Admittedly, it is largely aimed at the insurer in order to convince him to change his practices in relation to his customer. But the language does, at times, seem at variance with the Statements' desire to aim for clearer terminology generally.

There is no method of enforcing compliance with the spirit of the Statements by the insurer in question, unless he is a member of the Bureau and the insured knows both this fact and knows of the existence of the Statement.

On the positive side, many companies have changed their ways in response to the Statements. This can be seen from the improved wording now being used by many companies. But, while companies spend vast sums in media advertising, it seems odd that they should have fought so determinedly against legislation which must have the effect of raising the customers' suspicions that all is not what it should be (see Appendices 4.30 and 4.31).

Ultimately, only legislation can effectively bring about serious change to the many outdated principles of English insurance law (see Appendix 4.37).

Australian statutory reforms

(See Tarr and Tarr, 'The insured's non-disclosure in the formation of insurance contracts: a comparative perspective' (2001) 50 ICLQ 577.)

Reference is made on numerous occasions in this book to the (Australian) Insurance Contracts Act 1984 (as amended). The Act grew out of the Law Reform Commission Report No 20, published in 1982 (ALRC 20). The terms of reference required the Commission to consider, *inter alia*, the relative bargaining power between insurer and insured; the need for contracts of insurance to strike a fair balance between the interests of insurer and insured; the desirability of ensuring that the manner in which insurance contracts are negotiated and entered into is not unfair, and the desirability of ensuring that there are no unfair provisions in insurance contracts. The only types of contracts that were excluded from the terms of reference were marine insurance, workers compensation and compulsory third party insurance. One of the driving forces behind the review of Australian insurance law was a desire to clarify uncertainties, which had been developed over more than 200 years by common law judges, and also to seek to establish rules for the modern relationship between insurer and insured. In relation to the present chapter, ss 21, 21A, 22, 27–29 and 31 are of special importance (see Appendix 4.9). These sections are set out in the Appendices but here a brief overview will help. Section 21 (the insured's duty of disclosure) predates *Pan Atlantic* (above), by introducing the requirement of inducement. This is achieved by the simple process of using the phrase 'the insurer' rather than 'the prudent insurer' as used in s 18(2) of the MIA 1906. You will remember that there was judicial creativity in *Pan Atlantic* to arrive at the inducement test. Section 21(3) also states that the insurer will be deemed to have waived the duty of disclosure where he has offered insurance, even though the proposer has failed to answer a question on the proposal form, or where he had given an incomplete or ambiguous answer. Section 27 reinforces this last point.

A new s 21A was added by the Insurance Law Amendment Act 1998. The section refers to new contract for insurance on motor vehicles, homebuildings and contents, sickness and accident, consumer credit and travel insurance. The thrust of the new section is to place responsibilities on insurers to bring home to the applicant those matters which the insurer considers to be important to his decision making. Failure to do this will amount to waiver on the part of the insurer. Section 22 requires the insurer to provide the applicant with a prescribed written explanation of the requirements of disclosure.

Sections 27–29 and 31 are concerned with the remedies available for non-disclosure and misrepresentation. Important limitations are introduced to the 'all or nothing' approach that exists in English law. Thus, English law allows the insurer to avoid the contract if there is a material misrepresentation, etc, irrespective of whether it be innocent, negligent or fraudulent. Section 28 allows avoidance for fraudulent misrepresentation or non-disclosure, subject to s 31, below. The section introduces the concept of proportionality. This concept has different meanings in those countries which recognise it. In England, the Law Commission had, in 1980, rejected French and Swedish principles, on the grounds of commercial uncertainty as to its application. The Australian approach is very different. The section states that, in a non-fraudulent situation, the insurer's liability is reduced to the amount that would place him in the position in which he would have been if the failure had not occurred. This is clearly a difficult concept to put into practice. The Australian Law Reform Committee set out their interpretation as follows:

(i) where the insurer can prove, and the burden is on the insurer, he would not have accepted the risk at all then no claim is possible;

(ii) where the insurer would have accepted the risk then he should pay out on the policy after deducting the additional premium that he would have charged;

(iii) where he would have accepted the risk but would have been able to introduce clauses which would have reduced his exposure then he can deduct from his liability those excesses or apply those exclusions.

There is no doubt that the implementation of the sub-section is fraught with difficulties. But some sort of proportionality is preferable to the all or nothing approach presently in use in England. The English position is that where the proposer pays a premium of £1,000 per annum, but would have paid a premium of £2,000 per annum if he had correctly divulged all material information, and the loss is £100,000 he will receive nothing (although the insurer may offer an *ex gratia* payment). The Australian answer is that he will receive £100,000 minus the £1,000 per annum of which the insurer has been deprived. The French system of proportionality is very different in that it would say that the insurer has been deprived of 50% of his premium and therefore the insured is entitled to 50% of his loss. Sections 29 and 30 deal with non-disclosure and misrepresentation in relation to life insurance and a more detailed proportionality formula is used.

Section 31 allows the court to disregard even fraudulent misrepresentation, if it would be harsh and unfair to allow avoidance and to substitute a sum which it believes to be just and equitable in the circumstances. Such a discretion is unknown in English law.

The Australian Act has now been in operation for a sufficient period of time to allow judicial interpretation. Such cases are beyond the scope of this book but they would repay a detailed study. (See Appendix 4.32 for a general overview and Tarr and Tarr, 'The insured's non-disclosure in the formation of insurance contracts: a comparative perspective' (2001) 50 ICLQ 577.)

French law is more concerned with bad faith. Thus innocent mistakes are not treated with the same severity as English law does. Article L-113-9 of the French insurance Code reads:

> The omission or inaccurate description on the part of the insured whose bad faith is not established will not cause the nullity of the contract.
>
> If the omission or the inaccurate description is ascertained before the loss, the insurer has the right to either maintain the contract subject to the insured agreeing to pay an increased premium or terminate the contract ten days after having notified the insured by registered letter to that effect and refund the portion of the premium already paid for the period during which insurance will no longer run.
>
> In case the omission or the inaccurate declaration is ascertained after the loss, the indemnity shall be reduced in proportion to the rate of premiums paid

> bears to the rate of premiums which should have been claimed if the risks had been completely and exactly declared.

This, the Law Commission was convinced, was far too great a problem for it to be recommended as a reform to English law. It is no surprise that the draft Insurance Contract Directive 1980 (see Chapter 1) was doomed from the start!

The United States of America

Texts on Insurance Law in the United States still refer to early English cases. But things moved on at an early stage, certainly as early as the last century. Many of the English rules have been discarded, where those rules militated unfairly against the insured. Thus, Hasson:

> The American rules ... are more favourable to the insured than the English rules ... Not only that; the English rules of insurance law are more oppressive to the insured than are the ordinary rules of the law of contract [Appendix 4.33].

We have seen above, in Chapter 2, how the American definition of insurable interest is more favourably disposed to insureds. In relation to the present topic, the American preference is to change the emphasis from requiring good faith from the insured to showing bad faith by the insured (see Appendix 4.34) where, in 1896, Taft J was of the view that:

> We think the modern tendency ... is to require that a non-disclosure of a fact not inquired about shall be fraudulent, before voiding the policy; and as already stated, the view is founded on the better reason.

For a view 100 years later see, 'The duty of utmost good faith in marine insurance law: a comparative analysis of American and English law' (1998) 29 Journal of Maritime Law and Commerce 1 (Schoenbaum).

This brief survey of the state of affairs in Australia and United States illustrates how far there is to go in the modernisation of English law in the area of good faith.

CHAPTER 4

MISREPRESENTATION AND NON-DISCLOSURE

APPENDIX 4.1

Carter v Boehm (1766) 3 Burr 1905

Lord Mansfield: The special facts, upon which the contingent chance is to be computed, lie most commonly in the knowledge of the insured only: the underwriter trusts to his representation, and proceeds upon confidence that he does not keep back any circumstance in his knowledge, to mislead the underwriter into a belief that the circumstance does not exist, and to induce him to estimate the risque, as if it did not exist.

The keeping back such circumstance is a fraud, and therefore the policy is void. Although the suppression should happen through mistake, without any fraudulent intention; yet still the underwriter is deceived, and the policy is void; because the risque run is really different from the risque understood and intended to be run, at the time of the agreement.

The policy would equally be void, against the underwriter, if he concealed; as, if he insured a ship on her voyage, which he privately knew to be arrived, and an action would lie to recover the premium.

The governing principle is applicable to all contracts and dealings.

Good faith forbids either party by concealing what he privately knows, to draw the other into a bargain, from his ignorance of that fact, and his believing the contrary.

But either party may be innocently silent, as to grounds open to both, to exercise their judgment upon ...

This definition of concealment, restrained to the efficient motives and precise subject of any contract, will generally hold to make it void, in favour of the party misled by his ignorance of the thing concealed.

There are many matters, as to which the insured may be innocently silent – he need not mention what the underwriter knows ...

An underwriter can not insist that the policy is void, because the insured did not tell him what he actually knew; what way soever he came to the knowledge.

The insured need not mention what the underwriter ought to know; what he takes upon himself the knowledge of; or what he waves being informed of.

The underwriter needs not be told what lessens the risque agreed and understood to be run by the express terms of the policy. He needs not to be told general topics of speculation: as for instance – the underwriter is bound to know every cause which may occasion natural perils; as, the difficulty of the voyage – the kind of seasons – the probability of lightning, hurricanes, earthquakes, etc. He is bound to know every cause which may occasion political perils; from the ruptures of states from war, and the various operations of it. He is bound to know the probability of safety, from the continuance or return of peace; from the imbecility of the enemy, through the weakness of their counsels, or their want of strength, etc ...

Men argue differently, from natural phenomena, and political appearances: they have different capacities, different degrees of knowledge, and different intelligence. But the means of information and judging are open to both: each professes to act from his own skill and sagacity; and therefore neither needs to communicate to the other.

The reason of the rule which obliges parties to disclose, is to prevent fraud, and to encourage good faith. It is adapted to such facts as vary the nature of the contract; which one privately knows, and the other is ignorant of, and has no reason to suspect.

The question therefore must always be:

> ... whether there was, under all the circumstances at the time the policy was under written, a fair representation; or a concealment; fraudulent, if designed; or, though not designed, varying materially the object of the policy, and changing the risque understood to be run ...

The underwriter at London, in May 1760, could judge much better at the probability of the contingency, than Governor Carter could at Fort Marlborough, in September 1759. He knew the success of the operations of the war in Europe. He knew what naval force the English and French had sent to the East Indies. He knew, from a comparison of that force, whether the sea was open to any such attempt by the French. He knew, or might know everything which was known at Fort Marlborough in September 1769, of the general state of affairs in the East Indies, or the particular conditions of Fort Marlborough, by the ship which brought the orders for the insurance. He knew that ship must have brought many letters to the East India Company; and, particularly, from the governor. He knew what probability there was of the Dutch committing or having committed hostilities.

Under these circumstances, and with this knowledge, he insures against the general contingency of the place being attacked by a European power. If there had been any design on foot, or any enterprise begin in September 1759, to the knowledge of the governor, it would have varied the risk understood by the underwriter; because not being told of a particular design or attack then subsisting, he estimated the risk upon the foot of an incertain operation, which might or might not be attempted.

But the governor had no notice of any design subsisting in September 1759. There was no such design in fact: the attempt was made without premeditation, from the sudden opportunity of a favourable occasion, by the connivance and assistance of the Dutch, which tempted Count D'Estaigne to break his parol.

These being the circumstances under which the contract was entered into, we shall be better able to judge of the objections upon the foot of concealment.

The first concealment is, that he did not disclose the condition of the place.

The underwriter knew the insurance was for the governor. He knew the governor must be acquainted with the state of the place. He knew the governor could not disclose it, consistent with his duty. He knew the governor, by insuring, apprehended at least the possibility of an attack. With this knowledge, without asking a question, he underwrote.

By so doing, he took the knowledge of the state of the place upon himself. It was a matter as to which he might be informed in various ways: it was not a matter within the private knowledge of the governor only …

There is no imputation upon the governor, as to any intention of fraud. By the same conveyance, which brought his orders to insure, he wrote to the company every thing which he knew or suspected: he desired nothing to be kept a secret, which he wrote either to them or his brother. His subsequent conduct, down to the 8 February 1760, shewed that he thought the danger very improbable.

The reason of the rule against concealment is, to prevent fraud and encourage good faith.

If the defendant's objections were to prevail, in the present case, the rule would be turned into an instrument of fraud.

The underwriter, here, knowing the governor to be acquainted with the state of the place; knowing that he apprehended danger, and must have some ground for his apprehension; being told nothing of either; signed this policy, without asking a question …

APPENDIX 4.2

Hasson, R, 'The doctrine of *uberrima fides* in insurance law – a critical evaluation' (1969) 32 MLR 615

... it is surely remarkable that the insured's duty to disclose material facts to the insurer on his own initiative – the so called *uberrima fides* principle – has been subjected to virtually no critical assessment by either English courts or commentators. In this paper, an attempt will be made to suggest that the current English principle is thoroughly unsatisfactory in that it does not reflect the 'reasonable expectations' of insurer and insured and in that it is a rule that works against 'fairness' in the insurance contract.

An attempt will also be made to show that the classical doctrine on this subject as stated in the leading case of *Carter v Boehm* (1766) 3 Burr 1905, has been misunderstood and misapplied by English courts. By way of sharp contrast American courts in the 19th century correctly understood and interpreted the case ...

The conflict between the 'broad' and the 'narrow' duty of disclosure may fairly be said to have been finally resolved in favour of the former theory by the decision of the Court of Appeal in *Joel v Law Union and Crown Insurance* [1908] 2 KB 863. Since the date of that decision, the only question has been as to the breadth of the duty to disclose. In *Joel* itself, the Court of Appeal drew a distinction: the assured was under no duty to disclose facts he did not know of, since, as Fletcher Moulton LJ put it, 'you cannot disclose what you do not know'. On the other hand, if the assured knew of a fact, his duty to disclose was not affected by the fact that he (the assured) thought the fact was not a material one ...

It is now proposed to examine some of the case law with regard to the duty to disclose four allegedly material facts. These particular facts have been chosen both for their importance in practice and also because they demonstrate very clearly the unfortunate results that are liable to occur when it is sought to apply an unsatisfactory rule.

(1) THE CLAIMS HISTORY OF THE INSURED – INCLUDING NOTICE OF REJECTION

The law in this area shows a remarkable cleavage between marine insurance situations (where the duty to disclose is extremely narrow) and the situation prevailing in other fields of insurance law where an unfairly broad duty of disclosure applies.

Thus, although it would be fatal to the assured's claim in a marine insurance situation to represent untruthfully that previous underwriters have taken the proposed risk at the same or at a lower premium, yet the insured is not bound to disclose the fact that the other underwriters have previously declined to accept the same risk. Similarly, the insured is under no duty to report any apprehensions that may have been expressed about the subject matter of the insurance by other underwriters, or by foreign correspondents.

By way of sharp contrast, it is now settled by the decision of the Court of Appeal in *Locker and Woolf Ltd v W Australian Insurance Co* [1936] 1 KB 408 that an insured must report a rejection with regard to an entirely different type of insurance (for example, fire insurance) from the type he has now applied for (for example, motor insurance). The Court of Appeal in *Locker* seems to have been so impressed by the incantation of the phrase *uberrima fides* that it did not bother to deal with the highly relevant argument advanced by counsel for the insured: 'If the insurance companies desire to have information as to other insurances, they should make this clear ...'

... In the first place, a distinction should be drawn between on the one hand the insured's duty to give details of previous refusals to insure him (or his property), and on the other the insured's duty to give details of previous losses suffered by him (the insured). With regard to the first duty, it is submitted that the marine insurance rule, which does not recognise this duty, should be applied across the entire field of insurance law. This is so because information with regard to a refusal only tells the insurer to investigate his risk with great care. But this, one should have thought, only describes the insurer's duty at the present time with regard to the investigation of all risks. In short, if an applicant for insurance has been rejected by a previous insurer for arbitrary or capricious reasons, it is monstrous to penalise such a person further by holding that his subsequent insurance is void because of his (the applicant's) failure to disclose an earlier capricious refusal! On the other hand, if the applicant was rejected by an earlier insurer for good and sufficient reasons, it is presumably open to the subsequent insurer to ascertain by intelligent and searching questions what those reasons were.

It does not require much argument to establish that an insured's accident history will often be of greatest importance to an insurer. This fact, however, does not argue for a broad duty of disclosure; on the contrary, it is submitted that the duty of disclosure should be a very narrow one. In the first place, the information allegedly withheld must be closely related to the circumstances of the present loss in the manner described by Scrutton LJ in *Becker v Marshall* (1922) 11 Ll L Rep 114. Second, an insurer's failure to ask questions with regard to losses should be regarded as a waiver of this information, as should the insurer's acceptance of blank replies to questions in the proposal form (regardless of the form of the question). Further, an insurer should not be allowed to take advantage of ambiguous questions in the proposal form. Finally, the insurer should not be able to render immaterial information material by the simple expedient of using a 'basis of the contract clause'. This alternative, unhappily appears to be open to an insurer.

(2) CRIMINAL CONVICTIONS

The small body of case law requiring the insured to disclose previous criminal convictions is worthy of note, principally because it illustrates the ludicrously unjust results that are liable to occur from the application of an unsound rule ...

Happily, in ... *Roselodge Ltd v Castle* [1966] 2 Lloyd's Rep 113, some limit seems to have been set to the duty to disclose in this area. In this case, the insurer refused to indemnify the plaintiffs, diamond merchants, who had insured diamonds against all risks on the ground that these facts had not been disclosed: (i) that R, the principal director of the company seeking to effect the insurance, had been convicted of bribing a police office in 1946; and (ii) that M, the plaintiffs' sales manager, had been convicted of smuggling diamonds into the United States in 1956.

Two of the three underwriters called by the insurer stated their view of the duty to disclose previous convictions in terms that can fairly be described as being outrageously broad. Thus, according to Mr Archer, one of the experts in question, a man who had stolen apples when he was 17, after which time he lived a blameless life for 50 years, was more likely to steal diamonds at the age of 67 than someone who had not committed this youthful indiscretion.

Essaying his own evaluation of the materiality of the two convictions, McNair J decided that R's conviction in 1946 was not material, since it had 'no direct relation to trading as a diamond merchant'. His Lordship held that in the case of M's conviction there was such a 'direct relationship' and it must be regarded as material. Although this holding obviously represents a more enlightened approach than that demonstrated in the two earlier cases discussed in this section, it is submitted that, on the facts in *Roselodge Ltd v Castle*, the insurer should have been held to have waived the information relating to M's previous conviction. Remarkably enough (given the type of insurance involved in this case), the insurer in *Roselodge Ltd v Castle* did not ask M any questions relating to moral hazard. To require the court to step into the breach, as it were, means that in the first place, the court may have to make an extremely difficult decision with regard to the materiality of a particular fact when it lacks both the requisite knowledge to make this determination, as well as adequate means for obtaining such knowledge. Secondly, and perhaps even more seriously, permitting a judge to 'second guess' an insurer tends to dilute the well established and essential duty of the insurer to make the relevant inquiries of the insured ...

Critique

It is now possible to summarise briefly the various defects of the *uberrima fides* as it exists today. In the first place, current doctrine, so far from representing a restatement of classical doctrine as set out in decisions such as *Carter v Boehm*, sets out an entirely different principle, one largely fashioned during the present century. It is respectfully submitted that *Carter v Boehm* was correctly read by a number of American courts in the 19th century who read the case as stating a 'narrow' rule of disclosure.

More seriously, it is clear (in words of the Law Reform Committee Report *Conditions and Exceptions in Insurance Policies*) that 'a fact may be material to insurers ... which would not necessarily appear to a proposer for insurance, however honest and careful, to be one which he ought to disclose'. Further, the doctrine seems to work harder against laymen than against professionals. The 'marine' professional is in the strongest position: in the first place, he does not, as we have seen previously, have to disclose information that has to be disclosed by other classes of applicants. Secondly, it would appear that the courts are more ready to infer a waiver of information by the insurer in a marine insurance situation than in other insurance situations. The land based professional does not occupy as privileged a position as his marine cousin but he would still appear to be in a stronger position with regard to the working of the doctrine than in the layman who applies for, for example, life insurance. In the first place, the professional is more likely to know that a duty to disclose exists and to know also what information the insurer needs to know, than is likely in the case with a lay applicant for life insurance. Secondly, it is likely that an applicant for life insurance will be asked more questions (some of them relating to his health, a matter in which he has no expertise) than will be true in the case of a businessman taking out a policy against fire or burglary.

Thirdly, the doctrine is in error in assessing the strength of the parties with regard to knowledge. The doctrine assumes that the insured is in a stronger position than the insurer because he (the insured) has more knowledge than the insurer. But the possession of greater knowledge, it is submitted, puts the insured in a weaker position, since he (the insured) does not know which parts of that information the insurer wishes to have. It is submitted, however, that it is the insurer who should be seen as the stronger party, since he (the insurer), is aware of what information he seeks to have. As against this, the insured, even under the limited formulation of the doctrine, requiring him to disclose only facts within his knowledge, may well be in the position of either not knowing, or else being uncertain as to the materiality of a particular fact.

In short, current doctrine as applied seems to assume that the purchase of insurance is some kind of *emptio spei*. Despite the various gambling analogies which invariably suggest themselves in any discussion of an insurance contract, it is submitted that such a contract is not analogous to, say, the entering of a football pool coupon. Even without the detailed regulation by both legislative and administrative agencies of the terms and conditions of an insurance policy such as exist in the United States, and every European country (with the exception of Holland), it would appear to be necessary to emphasise the fact that the purchase of insurance, whether by layman or by professional, represents a 'purchase' of the greatest importance. The failure of this 'purchase' will in most cases involve far more serious results for the 'purchaser' than is likely to be true in the event of any other defective goods or commodity the insured acquires.

Notes on reform

... Turning more specifically to the form revised disclosure provisions might take, it is submitted that, while foreign legislation should obviously be consulted, great care be taken in borrowing statutory provisions. The statutory provisions of many American States, to take but one example, are too brief for English conditions. The brevity of these statutory provisions is to be explained by reference to two very closely connected factors. In the first place, very often the statutory provision will represent no more than codification of the pre-existing common law position. But, even where this is not the case, a brief statutory provision will be interpreted in the light of a general judicial solicitude for the position of the insured.

The fact that these circumstances are not present in England makes it advisable that any statutory provisions go into far greater detail than any potential foreign model appears to do.

Without being exhaustive, a model disclosure statute might well provide for the following. In the first place, it might be desirable to provide that an insured is under no obligation to provide information with regard to certain matters. As examples of such 'classified' information could be included an applicant's race or nationality; further, the insured should be deemed to be under no obligation to reveal that he has previously been refused insurance.

The key provision in the statute should state in the clearest possible language that any failure by an insurer to ask of an insured information customarily sought by insurers in the type of policy in question should be deemed a waiver of such information. The burden of proof to show that a particular piece of information was so esoteric as not to have been ascertainable by ordinary inquiry should again clearly be placed on the insurer.

The adoption of the above-described waiver principle should reduce the insured's duty of disclosure to (justly) narrow limits. With regard to the disclosure of this 'unascertainable' information, the insured should be penalised only if he acted in 'bad faith,' ie, if he knew, or had very good cause to believe that a particular piece of information would in fact be material to the insurer. The burden of showing 'bad faith' should again be placed on the insurer.

The insured's duty of disclosure should also be recognised in another situation, namely, when the insured comes into possession of material information between the time of the application for a policy and the time the policy is issued. If American case law is any guide, disputes arise more frequently over the duty to disclose in this situation than is true of the insured's duty to disclose 'unascertainable' information. The duty to disclose such information should be recognised (as it is in American law), except that the policy should be made to spell out clearly that such an obligation exists. It is, it is submitted, all too easy for an insurance applicant to think that a contract has been concluded at the time the policy was applied for.

Again, it might be desirable to expressly provide for the *contra proferentem* principle in a separate provision. Perhaps more valuable than such a provision would be one stating that the insurer is responsible for any ambiguities in questions asked in the application. Indeed, the situation in *Glicksman v Lancashire and General Insurance Co* (1927) 26 Ll L 69, could be set out, with, of course, a different outcome indicated.

Finally, even with a much limited duty of disclosure, it is still desirable to provide that an insurer prove clearly the materiality of some particular piece of information that has been withheld. In particular, serious consideration should be given to reforming the manner in which expert evidence is given, so that the responsibility for ascertaining insurance practice become the responsibility of the court, instead of being left, as at present, to the unequal struggle between the parties. Such a system would not attain complete objectivity since obviously most expert testimony will continue to be given by underwriters, but it will at least make it impossible for an insurer to hand pick his experts or to call 'experts' from the insurer's own company.

Would be reformers frequently make the claim that the changes they propose in any given area of the law are conservative rather than radical in nature. That claim can, it is submitted, be made with special force in the present area. Changes of the kind indicated above would do no more than to bring present day English doctrine in line both with its 'classical' 18th century antecedents as well as the present day law in the United States and the various countries on the European continent.

APPENDIX 4.3

Marine Insurance Act 1906

DISCLOSURE AND REPRESENTATIONS

17 Insurance is *uberrima fides*

A contract of marine insurance is a contract based upon the utmost good faith, and, if the utmost good faith be not observed by either party, the contract may be avoided by the other party.

18 Disclosure by assured

(1) Subject to the provisions of this section, the assured must disclose to the insurer, before the contract is concluded, every material circumstance which is known to the assured, and the assured is deemed to know every circumstance which, in the ordinary course of business, ought to be known by him. If the assured fails to make such disclosure, the insurer may avoid the contract.

(2) Every circumstance is material which would influence the judgment of a prudent insurer in fixing the premium, or determining whether he will take the risk.

(3) In the absence of inquiry the following circumstances need not be disclosed, namely:

  (a) any circumstance which diminishes the risk;

  (b) any circumstance which is known or presumed to be known to the insurer. The insurer is presumed to know matters of common notoriety or knowledge, and matters which an insurer in the ordinary course of his business, as such, ought to know;

  (c) any circumstance as to which information is waived by the insurer;

  (d) any circumstance which it is superfluous to disclose by reason of any express or implied warranty.

(4) Whether any particular circumstance, which is not disclosed, be material or not is, in each case, a question of fact.

(5) The term 'circumstance' includes any communication made to, or information received by, the assured.

19 Disclosure by agent effecting insurance

Subject to the provisions of the preceding section as to circumstances which need not be disclosed, where an insurance is effected for the assured by an agent, the agent must disclose to the insurer:

(a) every material circumstance which is known to himself, and an agent to insure is deemed to know every circumstance which in the ordinary course of business ought to be known by, or to have been communicated to, him; and

(b) every material circumstance which the assured is bound to disclose, unless it come to his knowledge too late to communicate it to the agent.

20 Representations pending negotiation of contract

(1) Every material representation made by the assured or his agent to the insurer during the negotiations for the contract, and before the contract is concluded must be true. If it be untrue the insurer may avoid the contract.

(2) A representation is material which would influence the judgment of a prudent insurer in fixing the premium, or determining whether he will take the risk.

(3) A representation may be either a representation as to a matter of fact, or as to a matter of expectation or belief.

(4) A representation as to matter of fact is true, if it be substantially correct, that is to say, if the difference between what is represented and what is actually correct would not be considered material by a prudent insurer.

(5) A representation as to a matter of expectation or belief is true if it be made in good faith.

(6) A representation may be withdrawn or corrected before the contract is concluded.

(7) Whether a particular representation be material or not is, in each case, a question of fact.

APPENDIX 4.4

Joel v Law Union and Crown Insurance Co [1908] 2 KB 863, CA

Vaughan Williams LJ: I have now only to deal with the question whether the policy is vitiated by concealment or non-disclosure of facts material to the risk insured against. This, to my mind, is the most difficult question in this case. First, I ask myself, does the obligation to make full disclosure apply to a contract of life insurance in the same sense that it applies to a contract of marine insurance? In my opinion, it does. The judgment of Sir George Jessel in *London Assurance v Mansel* [(1879) 11 Ch D 363] shews that the principles which govern insurance matters, which are said to require the utmost good faith, *uberrima fides*, apply to all kinds of insurances. But the same judgment shews that there may be certain circumstances from the peculiar nature of marine insurance which require to be disclosed, and which do not apply to other contracts of insurance. I think also that the insurance office may, by the requisitions for information of a specific sort which it makes of the proposer, relieve him partially from the obligation to disclose by an election to make inquiries as to certain facts material to the risk to be insured against itself. It is worthy of observation that the obligation to disclose does not extend to matters equally within the knowledge of those granting the policy of insurance and the applicant for insurance. Thus, Lord Campbell in *Wheelton v Hardisty* [(1854) 8 E & B 232, at pp 269, 270] says:

> But the assurer and assured being equally ignorant of material facts to influence their contract, if the assurer asks for information, and the assured does his best to put the assurer in a situation to obtain the information, and to form his own opinion as to whether the information is sincere, can it be permitted, where the assurer, without any blame being imputable to the assured, has allowed himself to be deceived, that he shall be able to say to the assured, 'You warranted all the information I received to be true; and having received your premiums for many years, now the life drops, I tell you I was incautious, and the policy I gave you is a nullity'?

The *uberrima fides* is to be observed with respect to life insurances as well as marine insurances. The assured is always bound, not only to make a true answer to the questions put to him, but spontaneously to disclose any fact exclusively within his knowledge which it is material for the assurer to know; and any fraud by an agent employed to effect the insurance is the fraud of the principal; but there is no analogy between the statements of the 'life' or the referees in the negotiation of a life insurance and the statements of an insurance broker to underwriters, by which he induces them to subscribe the policy ...

Fletcher Moulton LJ: I am of the same opinion. The contract of life insurance is one *uberrima fides*. The insurer is entitled to be put in possession of all material information possessed by the insured. This is authoritatively laid down in the clearest language by Lord Blackburn in *Brownlie v Campbell* [(1880) 5 App Cas 925, at p 954]:

> In policies of insurance, whether marine insurance or life insurance, there is an understanding that the contract is *uberrima fides* [*sic* in the report], that, if you know any circumstance at all that may influence the underwriter's opinion as to the risk he is incurring, and consequently as to whether he will take it, or what premium he will charge, if he does take it, you will state what you know. There is an obligation there to disclose what you know, and the concealment of a material circumstance known to you, whether you thought it material or not, avoids the policy.

There is, therefore, something more than an obligation to treat the insurer honestly and frankly, and freely to tell him what the applicant thinks it is material he should know. That duty, no doubt, must be performed, but it does not suffice that the applicant should *bona fide* have performed it to the best of his understanding. There is the further duty that he should do it to the extent that a reasonable man would have done it; and, if he has fallen short of that by reason of his *bona fide* considering the matter not material, whereas the jury, as representing what a reasonable man would think, hold that it was material, he has failed in his duty, and the policy is avoided. This further duty is analogous to a duty to do an act which you undertake with reasonable care and skill, a failure to do which amounts to negligence, which is not atoned for by any amount of honesty or good intention. The disclosure must be of all you ought to have realised to be material, not of that only which you did in fact realise to be so.

But, in my opinion, there is a point here which often is not sufficiently kept in mind. The duty is a duty to disclose, and you cannot disclose what you do not know. The obligation to disclose, therefore, necessarily depends on the knowledge you possess. I must not be misunderstood. Your opinion of the materiality of that knowledge is of no moment. If a reasonable man would have recognised that it was material to disclose the knowledge in question, it is no excuse that you did not recognise it to be so. But the question always is: was the knowledge you possessed such that you ought to have disclosed it? Let me take an example. I will suppose that a man has, as is the case with most of us, occasionally had a headache. It may be that a particular one of those headaches would have told a brain specialist of hidden mischief. But to the man it was an ordinary headache undistinguishable from the rest. Now, no reasonable man would deem it material to tell an insurance company of all the casual headaches he had had in his life, and, if he knew no more as to this particular headache than it was an ordinary casual headache, there would be no breach of his duty towards the insurance company in not disclosing it. He possessed no knowledge that it was incumbent on him to disclose, because he knew of nothing which a reasonable man would deem material or of a character to influence the insurers in their action. It was what he did not know which would have been of that character, but he cannot be held liable for non-disclosure in respect of facts which he did not know.

Insurers are thus in the highly favourable position that they are entitled not only to *bona fides* on the part of the applicant, but also to full disclosure of all knowledge possessed by the applicant that is material to the risk. And, in my opinion, they would have been wise if they had contented themselves with this. Unfortunately, the desire to make themselves doubly secure has made them depart widely from this position by requiring the assured to agree that the accuracy, as well as the *bona fides*, of his answers to various questions put to him by them or on their behalf shall be a condition of the validity of the policy. This might be reasonable in some matters, such as the age and parentage of the applicant, or information as to his family history, which he must know as facts. Or it might be justifiable to stipulate that these conditions should obtain for a reasonable time – say, during two years – during which period the company might verify the accuracy of the statements which by hypothesis have been made *bona fide* by the applicant. But insurance companies have pushed the practice far beyond these limits, and have made the correctness of statements of matters wholly beyond his knowledge, and which can at best be only statements of opinion or belief, conditions of the validity of the policy. For instance, one of the commonest of such questions is: 'Have you any disease?' Not even the most skilled doctor after the most prolonged scientific examination could answer such a question with certainty, and a layman can only give his honest opinion on it. But the policies issued by many companies are framed so as to be invalid unless this and many other like questions are correctly – not merely truthfully – answered, though the insurers are well aware that it is impossible for any one to arrive at anything more certain than an opinion about them. I wish I could adequately warn the public against such practices on the part of insurance offices. I am satisfied that few of those who insure have any idea how completely they leave themselves in the hands of the insurers should the latter wish to dispute the policy when it falls in ...

APPENDIX 4.5

Roselodge Ltd v Castle [1966] 2 Lloyd's Rep 113

McNair J: Until about 100 years ago, it was commonly held that the fact of materiality could not be proved by expert evidence but must be determined by the jury as representing the reasonable business man – particularly apposite in the case of Lord Mansfield's jurymen; but it has long been the practice in our courts to allow proof of this fact by the evidence of independent underwriters ...

In the course of time, it was found that in many cases the evidence of underwriters if fully accepted would work serious hardship to assureds, particularly to dependents suing upon life policies, unless some check was imposed. Accordingly, though in some of the earlier cases to which I have been referred there are certain rather oblique references to the point, it was not until the case of *Joel v Law Union and Crown Insurance Co* [1908] 2 KB 863, that one finds in the judgment of Lord Justice Fletcher Moulton, at p 883, a passage ... in which the learned Lord Justice says this ...:

> ... There is, therefore, something more than an obligation to treat the insurer honestly and frankly, and freely to tell him what the applicant thinks it is material he should know. That duty, no doubt, must be performed, but it does not suffice that the applicant should *bona fide* have performed it to the best of his understanding. There is the further duty that he should do it to the extent that a reasonable man would have done it; and, if he has fallen short of that by reason of his *bona fide* considering the matter not material, whereas the jury, as representing what a reasonable man would think, hold that it was material, he has failed in his duty, and the policy is avoided. This further duty is analogous to a duty to do an act which you undertake with reasonable care and skill, a failure to do which amounts to negligence, which is not atoned for by any amount of honesty or good intention. The disclosure must be of all you ought to have realised to be material, not of that only which you did in fact realise to be so ...

In my judgment, on this review of the authorities the judgment of Lord Justice Fletcher Moulton in *Joel*'s case ... contains, if I may respectfully say so, a correct statement of the law on the topic. It has the merit, as Mr Caplan submitted, of emphasizing that even under the present practice of admitting expert evidence from underwriters as to materiality, the issue as to disclosability is one which has to be determined, as it was in Lord Mansfield's day, by the view of the jury of reasonable men ...

Each of these witnesses was emphatic in the view that in a jewellery insurance of this kind the moral hazard is important. Mr Archer defined the moral hazard as the risk of honesty and integrity of the assured, and, in the case of a company, the honesty and integrity of any executives or key personnel (though I think he meant the risk of dishonesty and lack of integrity). The moral hazard he considered of particular importance in the case of jewellery insurance, 'because of the smallness and little weight of the jewellery and because in jewellery insurance there is often a lack of adequate documentation and jewellery is very easily disposed of'. This seems to me to be a reasonable view, except that I observe in passing that in the policy sued upon the requirement to keep stock books had been deleted.

Turning now to the evidence of Mr Lindley and Mr Archer as to the materiality of Mr Rosenberg's conviction 20 years before, it is true that both these witnesses stated in plain terms that they would not have written the risk had that fact been disclosed; but they were driven in cross-examination to state such extreme views that I am unable to accept their evidence on this point. It is not necessary to cite specific examples of their extreme views. But I would mention one. Mr Archer stated that in his view a man who stole apples at the age of 17 and had lived a blameless life for 50 years is so much more likely to steal diamonds at the age of 67; that if he had told him this when putting forward a proposal at the age of 67, he would not have insured him. Many other instances of the like character can be cited from the transcript ...

In the result, I have come to the conclusion that it is not established to my satisfaction that Mr Rosenberg's offence and conviction on a matter which has no direct relation to trading as a diamond merchant was a material fact which would have influenced a product underwriter. Furthermore, if the test be that laid down by Lord Justice Fletcher Moulton in *Joel*'s case ... I am satisfied beyond any doubt that a reasonable business man would not have imagined for a moment that this was a matter which the proposer should have disclosed as material. If any relevant question had been asked in the proposal form and untruthfully answered the position would clearly be quite different.

I now turn to the question of Mr Morfett's conviction and engagement ...

As it seems to me, the position must be viewed as at the date when the 1964 insurance or possibly the 1963 insurance was put forward. Would a prudent underwriter, having heard the whole story, have declined the risk or altered the premium, or, applying the *Joel* test, would a reasonable man at that date have thought that this whole story was a matter which was material to be disclosed ...?

After anxious consideration of the matter in all its aspects, I have reached the conclusion and so find that the average reasonable business man, though no doubt impressed by Mr Rosenberg's charitable act in attempting and apparently succeeding in rehabilitating a man who had paid his penalty, would appreciate that Mr Morfett remained or might remain a security risk and that underwriters should have been given the opportunity to decide for themselves whether the story as a whole was one which would have influenced them in accepting the risk as offered for fixing the premium.

The non-disclosure places upon the underwriters the risk that Mr Rosenberg's estimate of Mr Morfett's rehabilitation might be wrong without their having been given an opportunity of considering it. Furthermore, if, contrary to my view, the *Joel* test is not the correct test, I would hold on balance of probabilities as a fact that the whole incident was a material fact which would have influenced the prudent underwriter.

Though with great reluctance, in view of the conclusion I have reached as to the honesty of the claim and as to Mr Rosenberg's charitable action towards Mr Morfett, I find that this plea of non-disclosure succeeds ...

APPENDIX 4.6

Lambert v Co-operative Insurance Society Ltd [1975] 2 Lloyd's Rep 485, CA

MacKenna LJ: This case concerns the duty of disclosure by an applicant for insurance. The question is whether, as the trial judge has held, he is bound to disclose every circumstance which would influence the judgment of a prudent insurer in fixing the premium or determining whether he will take the risk, or whether, as the appellant contends, the duty is the lesser one of disclosing such circumstances as a reasonable man might expect would influence that prudent insurer's judgment ...

Lawton LJ: I agree with the judgment which has been delivered by Mr Justice MacKenna. I do not consider it necessary to review the authorities in any detail because, in my judgment, the law as stated by the learned judge has been the law for a long time. It is not open to doubt at all. The courts have been concerned with the problem of what a proposer for insurance should disclose to the underwriter, for over 200 years. As far as the researches of counsel have gone, the first reported case on this topic was *Carter v Boehm* (1766) ...

... It was inevitable, as the years went by, that special cases would arise which would require the courts to inquire whether there had been a disclosure of material facts. Each case had to be decided on its own facts, as the problem before the court was essentially one of fact. In the course of giving judgment in many cases during the 19th century expressions were used by judges, which may have been apt for the particular case under consideration, but not perhaps apt for all cases. Indeed, as Mr Fawcett pointed out, one such case in which the words may have been apt for the particular problem under consideration but perhaps not apt for all cases was the decision of this Court in *Joel v Law Union and Crown Insurance Co* [1908] 2 KB 863 ...

As Mr Justice MacKenna has said, the law was put beyond any doubt at all by the Privy Council in *Mutual Life Insurance Co of New York v Ontario Metal Products Co Ltd* [1924] AC 334 ... If ever there had been any doubt about the application of that case to the law of this country, that was dissipated by the decision of this Court in the case of *Zurich General Accident and Liability Insurance Co v Morrison* ...

From time to time, counsel have sought to use some of the observations in cases before 1925 to support the theory that the test is not that adjudged to be so by the Privy Council in 1925, but that of the reasonable insured seeking to get insurance. Why is it that, on a number of occasions since 1925, if one can judge from law reports, this attempt has been made? The attempt seems to have made some impression upon Mr Justice McNair in *Roselodge Ltd v Castle* [1966] 2 Lloyd's Rep 113, to which Mr Justice MacKenna has already referred. Mr Justice Megaw in *Anglo-African Merchants Ltd and Another v Bayley and Others* [1970] 1 QB 311 ... seems to have thought the 'reasonable insured' test to be worth some consideration. The explanation for this desire to show that the test accepted by the Privy Council in 1925 in the clearest possible terms is not the true test may be because some lawyers are of the opinion that it is unfair to many policyholders. It was said by Mr Lewis, with some force, that when the law first began to develop in the 18th century those who sought to get the benefit of insurance cover were really acting with the same sort of knowledge and understanding as the underwriters from whom they were seeking cover. Nowadays when the ordinary citizen seeks to take out insurance cover for his house and belongings he is not acting on equal terms with the insurance companies. Much as I sympathise with the point of view which was put forward by Mr Lewis, I cannot accept that it can alter the law.

At the end of the 19th century, Parliament began to consider the injustices and hardships which could arise under the common law as it related to insurance. Acts of Parliament were passed relating to life assurance. In 1906, Parliament passed the Marine Insurance Act of that year. In 1934, an Act of Parliament was passed dealing with motor car insurance and, as has been pointed out, one section of that Act defined what was a material fact in terms identical with those in the Marine Insurance Act, 1906, and identical with pronouncements as to what the law was by such distinguished judges as Mr Justice Blackburn.

It is difficult to see how there can now be any room at all for any query of these statements as to what the law is. Mr Lewis accepted that so far as marine and motor car insurance are concerned, the rule with all its hardships applies to those branches of insurance, but he asked us to say that an exception should be made for the class of insurance with which we are dealing in this case. I can find nothing in the authorities to justify doing anything of the kind. Such injustices as there are must now be dealt with by Parliament, if they are to be got rid of at all. I would dismiss the appeal ...

APPENDIX 4.7

Merkin, R, '*Uberrima fides* strikes again' (1976) 39 MLR 478

There are certain statements used by lawyers which, in addition to presenting a fact, presume a conclusion and justify it as well. One such statement is: 'Contracts of insurance are contracts *uberrima fides*.' A plaintiff who hears a judge utter these words is best advised to ask for the costs bill and go home, for not only is he subject to the contractual duty to avoid material misrepresentation but also to the insurance rule to disclose material facts. All too often, judges have blindly used these words as an excuse for ignoring the merits of insurance claims. Consider the recent fate of Mr and Mrs Lambert ...

... The decision is highly unsatisfactory in four major aspects each of which demonstrates that insurance law as it at present stands is heavily loaded in favour of the insurer.

First, there is the doctrine of non-disclosure itself which, coupled with the prudent insurer test now adopted in *Lambert* [1975] 2 Lloyd's Rep 485, in practice, means that the insured person must possess clairvoyant powers to discover what a reasonable insurer would regard as material. Many of the matters that have been held material using this test would surely be regarded as nothing more than useless information by any reasonable proposer. Thus, criminal convictions are material even if they occurred 24 years previously and 'belonged to a dim and distant past' ... past refusals to grant a motor policy are material for the purposes of a fire policy; and a change in a man's name is material as well. The logical view to take is surely that if an insurance company thinks these things are material it should ask express questions about them, and for any matter not raised on the proposal form, a 'reasonable insured' test should be applied. However, the law is very different as summarised in *Schoolman v Hall* [1951] 1 Lloyd's Rep 139 – the court will presume that anything on the proposal form is material but it will not make the corresponding presumption that other matters are immaterial. Consequently, the insurers are protected whether or not they insert a question. While accepting that there is need for a disclosure requirement in certain exceptional cases, it is submitted that at its highest the test used should be that of the 'reasonable insured' along with a clear presumption of non-materiality ...

... Secondly, and closely allied to the first point, is the question of proof. A 'reasonable insured' test is not hard to apply for it is merely a reasonable man test which judges have, through practice, become fairly proficient in applying. But no judge can pretend to be a prudent insurer. The only way to discover what a prudent insurer considers material is to ask him, and this allows an insurance company to bring in the evidence of other insurers as to their views on the question ...

... Thirdly, the treatment of both convictions in *Lambert* as material is not necessarily consistent with authority. The leading cases do not attempt to formulate a guiding test but it is possible to glean three broad principles from them:

(a) if the type of crime is identical to the subject matter of the policy, then past convictions are relevant. Thus, in *Jester-Barnes v Licences and General Insurance*

(1934) 49 Ll L Rep 231, a previous conviction for drunken driving was material to a motor policy. Similarly, in *Roselodge v Castle* [1966] 2 Lloyd's Rep 113, diamond smuggling was relevant to a policy on diamonds, as was receiving stolen furs to a policy on furs;

(b) general dishonesty is relevant if it is serious and likely to have a direct effect on the type of policy taken out. In *Schoolman v Hall*, the assured had been convicted of a series of offences ranging over 10 years, and these were held material to a burglary policy. It is submitted that they would not have been material to a fire or motor policy;

(c) time is of no importance. The convictions in *Schoolman* had ended 15 years before the policy, and the gaps between conviction and policy in *Regina Fur* and *Roselodge* were 24 and 18 years, respectively ...

... Whatever the true position, the fundamental question still remains unanswered – why are criminal convictions regarded as material facts? At best they raise a presumption of further dishonesty ('moral hazard'), but, surely if fraud is suspected, it ought to be pleaded in court and not inferred from previous conduct. If it is in fact true that those with prior convictions do 'suffer' above average losses, then insurers ought to demand the information expressly, instead of later relying on devious defences.

Fourthly, there is the question of Mr Jacobs, stated in the report to be an insurance agent, which raises the whole issue of selling insurance. Many companies use untrained agents who are paid by results. It is the policy of certain companies to have the questions in the proposal form dictated to the proposer by the agent, for the agent to fill in the answers on the form, with the proposer signing the form after it has thus been completed. These factors make cutting corners by the agent almost inevitable. In practice, the agent is likely to inform the proposer that if he answers a few simple questions, insurance can be his. In such circumstances, it is plain that there is no room for a non-disclosure doctrine, for the agent (however innocently) is impliedly representing that answering the list of questions in the proposal form is exhaustive of the proposer's legal duty. For the company, at a later date, to claim that the policy is voidable for non-disclosure is extremely harsh, yet the law not only permits this, but goes much further – an insurance agent who fills in the proposer's oral answers is in law magically transformed from being the agent of the company to the agent of the proposer, so that any misstatements later discovered are deemed to be the responsibility of the insured. It is submitted that in such circumstances the reverse should be true both in fact and in law, that is, an agent should be regarded as the agent of the company only and he should either be properly trained to warn the proposer that the duty to disclose exists or the company should be estopped from denying the agent's implied representation ...

APPENDIX 4.8

Law Commission Report, *Insurance Law: Non-Disclosure and Breach of Warranty*, Cmnd 8064, Law Comm 104, 1980, London: HMSO

1.1 ... To consider the effect on the liability of an insurer, and on the rights of an insured, of:

(a) non-disclosure by, or on behalf of, the insured;

(b) misrepresentation by, or on behalf of, the insured;

(c) breach of 'warranty' by the insured;

(d) special conditions, exceptions and terms;

(e) increase and decrease of risk covered,

particularly in the light of the Fifth Report of the Law Reform Committee (1957) and the draft EEC Directive on the co-ordination of laws, regulations and administrative provisions relating to insurance contracts, and to make recommendations ...

3.14 The insured's duty of disclosure has been affected by recent legislation. The Rehabilitation of Offenders Act 1974 provides that an applicant is entitled to withhold from the insurers information about certain of his or her convictions. The purpose of the Act is, *inter alia*, 'to rehabilitate offenders who have not been reconvicted of any serious offence for periods of years'. This object is achieved by providing that after the expiry of the 'rehabilitation period' a conviction becomes 'spent'. There are different rehabilitation periods according to the seriousness of the sentence with which the offence is punishable. Under s 4, a spent conviction is to be treated 'for all purposes in law' as though it had never happened, and the person who has a spent conviction is to be treated as though he had not committed or been charged with the offence in question. In the result, the insurer will have no remedy if the insured has failed to disclose a spent conviction in an answer in a proposal form. Even if the insured has warranted the truth of all his answers, which thus become terms of the contract, the insurer is not entitled to treat the insured's failure to acknowledge a spent conviction as a breach of warranty entitling him to repudiate the policy or reject a claim made under it. As a result of s 4(3)(a), the proposer for insurance is relieved of any duty to disclose not only a spent conviction, but also the events (for example, a motor accident) out of which it arose.

3.15 The insured's duty of disclosure is also affected by the Sex Discrimination Act 1975 and the Race Relations Act 1976. Both enactments provide that it is unlawful for persons providing certain services or facilities to the public to discriminate against any person seeking them by failing to provide them on the same terms as those on which they are available to other members of the public. The provision of insurance cover is expressly included within the ambit of both Acts. The effect of these Acts is to make it unlawful for insurers to claim that the insured's sex or racial origins are material to the risk, with the result that they need not be disclosed by an applicant for insurance even if the insurers ask questions about them …

3.20 It has been pointed out that many laymen are not aware that a duty of disclosure exists and that it may be very difficult, if not impossible, for those who are aware of the duty to know what information would be regarded as material by a prudent insurer. This point was put to us forcefully on consultation mainly by those representing consumer interests. One writer has observed that the duty imposes an especially heavy burden on an insured who holds a policy which is renewable year by year since he is most unlikely to realise that the duty arises on each successive renewal. Another has raised the problem of the extent of the duty on an insured when he applies for cover over the telephone. Above all, the general rule of the present law whereby an insured is not relieved of his duty of further disclosure even when the insurer has asked questions of him in a proposal form, is open to the obvious criticism that the insured is thereby likely to be led to believe that no further information is required to be volunteered by him.

3.21 Under the present law, in order to determine disputes as to whether certain facts are material, the courts will hear the evidence of other insurers as expert witnesses. Such evidence will usually be readily available to the insurers who will have no difficulty in selecting appropriate witnesses. However, the insured will often be at a considerable disadvantage in finding expert witnesses prepared to challenge those of the insurer and the position of such witnesses is often invidious. Some judicial doubt has also been case on the cogency of such evidence …

COMMENTS ON THE STATEMENTS OF INSURANCE PRACTICE

3.27 The most important provision of both Statements is to the effect that insurers will not 'unreasonably' repudiate liability or reject a claim for non-disclosure or misrepresentation. In our working paper, we pointed out that this leaves insurers as the sole judges of whether repudiation or rejection is unreasonable in any given situation, and we indicated that in our view this was unsatisfactory. These Statements of Practice do not in themselves change the law but are intended merely to set out existing insurance practice. Thus, insurers are always entitled to invoke their strict legal rights to repudiate policies and reject claims for non-disclosure. However, we have already noted that the law as to non-disclosure in unfair and it seems to us unacceptable that insurers should have what is in effect a discretion to repudiate policies and reject claims on grounds which are in themselves unsatisfactory. On consultation, only very few of the commentators who were unconnected with the insurance industry disagreed with this conclusion. Even amongst the representatives of the insurance industry, a number of commentators conceded that some reform was necessary, although most of them would have restricted it to 'consumer' insurance.

3.28 We are accordingly not convinced by the objections to reform of the law raised by the industry. In our view the Statements of Insurance Practice are themselves evidence that the law is unsatisfactory and needs to be changed. As we have pointed out, the Statements lack the force of law, so that an insured would have no legal remedy if an insurer fails to act in accordance with them. Indeed, the liquidator of an insurance company would be bound to disregard them. We consider that the further protection which the insured needs should be provided by legislation. We are fortified in this view by the words of Lawton LJ in *Lambert v Co-operative Insurance Society* [1975] 2 Lloyd's Rep 485:

> Such injustices as there are must now be dealt with by Parliament, if they are to be got rid of at all.

We are also impressed by the fact that all those who commented on our working paper, other than those connected with the insurance industry, considered that the law ought to be changed.

3.29 There is one further point. The Statements of Practice are confined to policyholders effecting insurance in their 'private' capacity. We assume that this confines the application of the Statements to consumers. It seems to us, however, that the mischiefs in the present law which have just been described apply both to consumers and businessmen. It follows that even if the Statements are an effective means of protecting some insured, they leave others, many of whom are equally vulnerable, without the protection which they need.

3.30 Our conclusion is that the mischiefs which we have noted in the law relating to the duty of disclosure imposed upon applicants for insurance are not cured by the Statements of Insurance Practice. Part IV of this report is accordingly devoted to the examination of various ways in which the law of disclosure can be reformed. However, it will also be noted that many of our recommendations follow lines broadly similar to the provisions of the Statements of Practice, in particular with regard to proposal forms ...

TOTAL ABOLITION OF ANY DUTY OF DISCLOSURE

4.32 The second way in which the law might be reformed is by the abolition or attenuation of the duty of disclosure. In our working paper we rejected the suggestion that the duty should be abolished altogether. We pointed out that despite the radical changes since Lord Mansfield's judgment in *Carter v Boehm* (1766) 3 Burr 1905, and, in particular, the widespread use today of the proposal form as a means of eliciting from the insured information relevant to the risk, insurers still often rely, at least in part, on the insured's duty of disclosure as well as on their own means of information and enquiry. No one on consultation took the view that the duty to disclose should be abolished in all cases, but many commentators considered that the duty should be abolished or, at least, attenuated, with respect to consumers. In our working paper, we stated that it was significant that some duty of disclosure was imposed on the insured not only by the draft Directive but also by the laws of all the common law and civil law jurisdictions which we had been able to study. As we have seen, the proposed Directive continues to subject the insured to a wide duty of disclosure, and no one on consultation drew our attention to a system of law which dispenses with any such duty. We remain firmly convinced that the total abolition of any duty of disclosure would be undesirable and impractical. Two examples should help to make this clear. Suppose that a prospective insured's life has been threatened. If there were no duty to disclosure, he could then apply for life insurance, knowing this fact and knowing it to be material, and could say nothing about it unless he was asked, which would be unlikely to be the case. Again, a threat may have been made to burn down his premises. In the absence of any duty of disclosure, the insured could apply for a fire policy on his premises without revealing the threat unless he was asked. In both cases, it is clear that insurers must be told about the threats, and in both cases it would be unreasonable to expect them to ask the appropriate questions. Such undesirable results could only be avoided by compelling the use of long questionnaires in relation to all types of cover. It was made clear to us on consultation, and seems self-evident, that such a requirement would add substantially to administrative expenses and that it would interfere with normal and reasonable underwriting practice.

4.33 It was represented to us forcefully on consultation by representatives of the insurance industry that abolition of the duty of disclosure would mean that insurers would be unable to assess risks accurately and would accordingly be unable to differentiate in their premiums between good and bad quality risks. As we suggested in our working paper, the general body of honest and reasonable policyholders would then have to pay higher premiums to compensate for 'sharp practice' on the part of the few. It was also pointed out to us that the British insurance industry would then be unable to quote premiums that were competitive in the international market. We accept the force of those contentions. Whether they have the same force in relation to proposals to *attenuate* the duty of disclosure is another matter to which consideration is given below. We therefore *recommend* against total abolition of the duty of disclosure.

Abolition of the duty with respect to consumers

4.34 Having rejected the suggestion that the duty of disclosure should be totally abolished, we must now consider the proposal, which was advanced by some of those whom commented on our working paper, that it should be abolished with respect to consumers. These commentators urged that consumers as a group should be treated differently from commercial undertakings. In particular, it was suggested that consumers should be under no duty to volunteer material information to insurers and that if insurers wanted such information, they should ask for it. In the paragraphs which follow, we shall adapt the definition of 'consumer' used in s 12 of the Unfair Contract Terms Act 1977, in the case of contracts other than contracts for sale or hire purchase: we intend 'consumer' to mean a person who neither makes the contract in the course of a business nor holds himself out as doing so. Thus, a shopkeeper living in a flat above his shop would insure his shop and its contents as a businessman, but his flat and its contents as a consumer.

4.35 In our working paper, we rejected any distinction between consumers and non-consumers on the ground that the arguments in regard to 'sharp practice' against the total abolition of the duty of disclosure apply equally to the proposal that it be abolished with regard to consumers only. For example, in the absence of any duty of disclosure the insured could apply for cover on his premises without revealing that a threat had been made to burn them down. This result would be unacceptable even if the prospective insured were a consumer applying for insurance on his house.

4.36 The basis for any differentiation between consumers and non-consumers must be that the more lenient treatment of a particular category is justified because that category is in need of special protection. As explained in our working paper, there are certain mischiefs in the law of non-disclosure which apply equally whether the insured is a consumer or a businessman who is not constantly concerned in his business activities with the insurance market. Neither consumers nor ordinary businessmen who are not in the insurance market have the knowledge or experience to identify all facts which may be material to insurers. Both are therefore to this extent in need of protection and both may properly be regarded as consumers vis à vis insurers.

4.37 It may also be contended that it is unfair to consumers to subject them to a duty of disclosure since they may be totally unaware of the duty or of the consequences of breach of the duty. However, many small businesses are equally unlikely to be aware of the niceties of insurance law when applying for insurance. Similarly, consumers are on the whole considered less likely than businessmen to take advice – for example, from insurance brokers – which might reveal the existence and extent of the duty. But the well off or cautious consumer may as a matter of course seek the advice of an insurance brokers – which might reveal the existence and extent of the duty. But the well off or cautious consumer may as a mater of course seek the advice of an insurance broker when in need of cover, while the small businessman may not. It is however impracticable to draw a line between those who consult brokers and those who do not. This is not to say that a person's need for protection may not depend on his situation and the circumstances in which he enters into the contract. For example, if a large business corporation enters into a contract for the supply of goods or services it will usually appreciate the nature and consequences of the transaction far better than a small business or a private individual. Thus there may well be a sensible dividing line between those insured who are in need of special protection and those who are not, but in our view this dividing line should be between 'professionals' and 'non-professionals'. The exclusion of MAT [marine, aviation, transport] insurance from the scope of our recommendations reflects this distinction.

4.38 Furthermore, if a special regime were devised for consumers, there would be three categories of insured to each of which different rules would apply. Those insured against MAT risks would be excluded from the scope of our recommendations and would be regulated by the present law; non-consumers would be subjected to a modified duty of disclosure, and consumers would be exempted from any duty. This multiplication of legal categories would clearly be complex and undesirable.

4.39 A further reason against differentiating between consumers and non-consumers is connected with the fact that the vast majority of consumer insurance is written on the basis of proposal forms. As we point out below, the present law in relation to proposal forms is defective in certain respects. In particular, we think it likely that many applicants, regardless of whether they are consumers or businessmen, who have completed a proposal form may erroneously believe that they are under no duty to disclose further information, and, in our view, such a belief will usually be perfectly reasonable. For this reason, we have made detailed recommendations in this report in order to protect applicants for insurance who complete such forms. These recommendations are in effect measures of consumer protection. But the use of proposal forms and the mischiefs associated with them are not confined to consumer insurance; to this extent our recommendations also protect businessmen, and, in our view, it is right that they should do so.

4.40 Finally, if the duty of disclosure were to be wholly abolished for consumers, the granting of provisional insurance cover prior to the completion of a proposal form would give rise to difficulties. This type of cover is often granted to consumers. For example, insurance cover for motor vehicles is often granted over the telephone by a broker and a cover note is then issued. Similarly, house insurance cover is often granted over the telephone where the insured has just exchanged contracts for the purchase of a property. In the absence of any duty it would be open to a prospective insured to conceal any information which he knew to be material but which was unusual in its nature, so that the insurer or broker could not reasonably be expected to ask about it over the telephone. As we pointed out in our working paper, while insurers might not withdraw facilities for such cover they might well increase premiums, and might also insert a greater number of conditions and exceptions into their policies to narrow the scope of the risk covered.

Attenuation of the duty of disclosure with respect to consumers

4.41 It was suggested to us that in relation to cover obtained by consumers, insurers should not be entitled to repudiate a policy unless the non-disclosure was fraudulent. We think that it would only be in exceptional cases that an insurer would be able to discharge the onus of proving that an applicant for insurance omitted to volunteer a material fact with the intention of deceiving him. Even where there has been a misstatement in the proposal form, the onus of proving fraud is difficult to discharge. We think that such an attenuation would be unacceptable. Like the proposal to abolish any duty of disclosure with respect to consumers, it would create three categories of policy holders to each of which different rules would apply, with resultant multiplicity of legal categories and undesirable complexity. In any event, as a matter of underwriting practice, insurers must be able to rely upon a prospective insured to disclose those material facts which a reasonable man would in all the circumstances disclose to them: the duty merely not to act fraudulently would be virtually useless to them as a means of assessing the risk.

4.42 In the result, it seems to us that any separate regime for consumers and non-consumers would lead to anomalous results in practice. This can again be illustrated by a shopkeeper who lives above his shop. He applies for fire and burglary cover in respect of both his shop and his flat at the same time: the former application would be made in the course of a business, but the latter would not. It would be odd, to say the least, if the resulting contracts were subject to different vitiating factors. We are persuaded by all these cumulative considerations that there should be no special category of consumer insurance to which more lenient rules should apply, and we are reinforced in this conclusion by the attenuation of the general duty of disclosure which we recommend in the following paragraphs in relation to all insurance (other than MAT) ...

The duty of disclosure

4.47 We recommend that the duty of disclosure imposed on an applicant for insurance should be modified as follows. A fact should be disclosed to the insurers by an applicant if:

(i) it is material to the risk;

(ii) it is either know to the applicant or is one which he can be assumed to know;

(iii) it is one which a reasonable man in the position of the applicant would disclose to his insurers, having regard to the nature and extent of the insurance cover which is sought and the circumstances in which it is sought.

It will be seen that this formulation departs somewhat from that put forward in our working paper. In the following paragraphs, we will elaborate the elements of the modified duty of disclosure.

A fact which is material to the risk

4.48 A fact must be material to the risk before there can be any question of a duty to disclose it to the insurers. We propose that the definition of a material fact should remain substantially the same as in the present law. Thus a fact should be considered as material if it would influence a prudent insurer in deciding whether to offer cover against the proposed risk and, if so, at what premium and on what terms. This definition amplifies the present one, which only refers to the prudent insurer's decision to accept the risk and to his premium rating of the risk. Insurers may, however, react to the disclosure of material facts otherwise than by refusing the risk or altering the premium: they might, for example, insert additional warranties, increase the 'excess', or narrow the scope of the risk by exclusion clauses. The revised definition takes these additional factors into account by referring to terms other than the premium upon which the insurers would be prepared to offer cover.

A fact which is known to the proposer or which he can be assumed to know

4.49 No duty to disclose a material fact will arise unless that fact is known to the proposer or can be assumed to be known by him. The present law is uncertain as to whether the duty of disclosure extends beyond facts actually known by the insured, and in our view is in need of clarification. In marine insurance the rule is that, for the purpose of his duty of disclosure, the insured is to be treated as knowing facts if he ought to have known them in the ordinary course of business. It has not been clearly settled whether or to what extent this rule applies to non-marine insurance, but in life insurance cases there are *dicta* which suggest that the insured is only bound to disclose facts within his actual knowledge. Moreover, the words, 'in the ordinary course of business', are inappropriate to cover private individuals who obtain insurance otherwise than in the course of business. In one fairly recent case, the extent of the duty in non-marine insurances was left open. We do not consider that it would be acceptable for the insured to be required to disclose all material facts without regard to whether such facts were known or ought to have been known by him, since an insurer would then be entitled to repudiate the contract for the non-disclosure of a fact outside the insured's knowledge or means of knowledge. Equally, it seemed to us in the working paper that it would not be acceptable for the insured to be able to say that he has complied with his duty of disclosure if he did not actually know a fact, even when that fact was obviously relevant and easily ascertainable by him. On consultation, few commentators referred specifically to the question of constructive knowledge and opinion was divided amongst those who did.

4.50 In our view, an insured should not be entitled to say that he did not know facts which were obviously relevant and easily ascertainable by him. However, the insured should clearly not be obliged to mount elaborate investigations within the whole spectrum of material facts. What we recommend is that he should be assumed to know a material fact if it would have been ascertainable by reasonable enquiry and if a reasonable man applying for the insurance in question would have ascertained it.

A fact which a reasonable man in the position of the proposer would disclose to the insurer, having regard to the nature and extent of the insurance cover which is sought and the circumstances in which it is sought

4.51 Even if a fact is material to the risk and is known to the proposer or can be assumed to be known by him he will only be obliged to disclose it to the insurers if a reasonable man in his position would disclose it. The words, 'in the position of the proposer', would allow the courts to have regard to the knowledge and experience to be expected of a reasonable person in the position of the applicant. Thus, more would be expected of the large company with an insurance division than of the small shopkeeper. On the other hand, we would not wish the court to take account of the individual applicant's idiosyncrasies, ignorance, stupidity or illiteracy in determining whether a reasonable man in his position would disclose a know material fact. Our formulation would only direct the court's attention to the nature and extent of the insurance cover which is sought and to the circumstances in which it is sought. Thus, a reasonable man applying for life insurance would not disclose facts relevant to his house or his car. Equally, a reasonable man applying for householder's cover would not disclose facts relevant to his health. The court would also have regard to whether the cover applied for was only provisional or temporary, since a reasonable man would not necessarily disclose the full spectrum of known material facts when applying for merely temporary cover. In addition, the extent or magnitude of the proposed risk would be relevant. Thus more would be expected of a businessman applying for insurance on a factory full of machinery than would be expected from a householder insuring his house and its contents.

4.52 Our formulation would also concentrate the court's attention on the circumstances in which insurance cover was sought. Thus a reasonable man applying for insurance over the telephone might well address his mind to the disclosure of material facts to a different extent than if he were making a written proposal for insurance. Equally, in negotiating the cover the insurers may have given the insured the impression that on certain aspects material facts need not be disclosed in full or at all; in such cases the insured may assume that they are waiving disclosure of matters concerning which they appear to be indifferent or uninterested in an illness suffered six years ago. Another example of a case where waiver could be inferred is provided by 'coupon' insurance. This type of insurance can be obtained either by inserting the required amount of money into a machine, as happens mainly at airports, or by completing a very simple application form which asks only for the name, address and occupation of the applicant. The 'coupon' itself is a document which may either itself be a contract of insurance or an undertaking to issue a policy. In such cases there would seem to be no duty of disclosure, since the applicant is unlikely to have any occasion to disclose anything. By making an offer to the public which is capable of being accepted by anyone, the insurers in such cases in effect indicate that they are willing to insure anyone regardless of his antecedents or characteristics. Another example is provided by the issue of immediate or interim cover, usually in connection with motor vehicles. It is usual in such cases for insurers to require an applicant to complete a proposal form at a later stage, and a reasonable applicant might therefore assume that the insurers were at this stage not interested in the disclosure of material facts which would be relevant only to the premium-rating and not to the question whether the risk should be accepted. In all such cases, the position is that the insurers have adopted a procedure whereby cover is applied for and granted in such a way that a waiver as to the disclosure of material facts may be inferred. Under our recommendations, all such matters could be taken into account by the courts in determining whether or not there had been a material non-disclosure ...

The duty of disclosure in relation to proposal forms

4.56 A major criticism of the present law, as we have already noted in para 3.20, above, is that an insured may well be unaware that he is under a residual duty to disclose material facts to the insurer when he has answered a series of specific questions in a proposal form, because these could naturally lead him to believe that the questions cover all matters about which the insurer is concerned to be informed. Indeed, the very fact that specific questions are invariably asked in proposal forms, which is their essential purpose, may have the effect of creating a trap for the insured under the present law. We have no doubt that this is a mischief which requires reform for the protection of the insured.

4.57 In the working paper, we made the provisional recommendation that this protection should be provided by confining insurers to the answers to specific questions asked in proposal forms and that they should be treated as having waived the disclosure of any information to which no specific question had been directed. Consequentially to this, we also provisionally recommended that no general questions in addition to specific questions should be permitted, such as a question whether there were any other facts which might influence the judgment of a prudent insurer in accepting the risk and fixing the premium. The effect of these recommendations would be to confine insurers to specific questions in all cases in which proposal forms are used and to abolish any residual duty on the insured beyond answering the questions. We have given careful further thought to the desirability of resolving the problem by a recommendation which would have this effect, which at first sight is clearly one which appears attractive. However, in the light of the comments received on consultation from the insurance industry, and for other reasons explained in the following paragraphs, we have concluded that despite its attractions this solution would not be the right one and that the necessary protection for the insured can and should be provided by other means.

4.58 In the comments received on consultation, our provisional recommendations were criticised on the ground that the purpose of proposal forms was to elicit information of a standard nature and not to circumscribe the nature of the risk in all respects. It was pointed out that the effect of our provisional recommendations would be that proposal forms would inevitably have to become far more lengthy, detailed and complex than at present and, further, that proposers might well be aware of facts which any reasonable person would realise should be disclosed but about which insurers could not reasonably be expected to ask specific questions. We accept these criticisms. For instance, a person might take out product liability insurance when it appears to him that his quality control is inadequate but he does not know the reason, or a businessman might effect some special fire cover on his premises when he has reason to believe that they might be burned down. Such cases could not possibly be expected to be covered by specific questions in proposal forms. They would of course be covered by a general question, such as we have instanced above, which is indeed commonly included as normal underwriting practice in many kinds of proposal forms at present. The effect of a general question of this kind is that the insured is placed under a residual duty to volunteer further information, though with the advantage of having had his attention drawn specifically to this duty. On further consideration we see no reason to outlaw such general questions; indeed, it seems to us that they can be said to fulfill a useful purpose, and they may indeed be essential in many cases. This is the first reason why we consider that it would be impracticable to confine the duty of the insured in relation to proposal forms simply to supplying answers to specific questions and thus to eliminate any residual duty of disclosure.

4.59 The second crucial matter to bear in mind on the question whether it would be right to abolish any residual duty of disclosure in cases where proposal forms are completed is that the effect of the recommendations which we have already made is to reduce the level of the duty of disclosure to that of the reasonable insured in all cases (other than MAT insurances), whether proposal forms are used or not. It follows that, under our recommendations, no insured will have been in breach of his duty of disclosure in any event unless *ex hypothesi* he has fallen below this standard. The effect of this recommendation is therefore that it also greatly reduces the remaining problems concerning non-disclosure in cases of proposal forms. Nevertheless, there still remains the problem that in cases of proposal forms, particularly where no general question is asked in addition to specific questions, a proposer is likely to be unaware that he may be under a further residual duty to volunteer additional material information. It may well be, of course, that in the absence of a general question the courts might hold in the particular circumstances of some cases that a proposer could reasonably assume that he was under no further duty beyond answering the specific questions; on this basis the effect of our recommendations will be that in such cases he will have discharged his duty of disclosure by answering the questions. However, we do not think that this is sufficient; in our view, the interests of both parties require that various matters concerning the insured's obligations when he completes a proposal form should be drawn specifically and explicitly to his attention.

4.60 In our view, the solution to the foregoing problem lies in the requirement that all proposal forms should contain certain clear and explicit warnings to the insured, presented in a prominent manner, together with appropriate sanctions wherever such warnings have not been given. In many cases, proposal forms already contain some warnings of the kind which we have in mind, and we see no administrative or other difficulties in requiring them to be included as a matter of law and providing for appropriate legal consequences if they are omitted. However, before dealing with these matters at greater length we must deal with two further topics; the standard which should be required from an insured in answering questions in proposal forms, and the necessity to supply to the insured a copy of his completed proposal form for future reference, particularly in relation to renewals of the cover.

Standard of answers to questions in proposal forms

4.61 We turn first to the standard which should be required from an insured in answering specific questions in a proposal form. In our working paper, we pointed out that it followed from the principle of utmost good faith on the part of the insured that he should *prima facie* only be considered to have discharged his duty of disclosure if he had answered the questions in the proposal forms completely and accurately. However, we added the qualification that it would not be reasonable to expect an applicant always to given an objectively accurate answer to a question. We accordingly added that, if they could prove that he had answered a material question to the best of his knowledge and belief, having carried out all those enquiries which a reasonable man in his circumstances would have carried out, he should be considered to have discharged his duty of disclosure, notwithstanding that the answer was in fact inaccurate. On consultation, this proposal attracted some criticism because the words 'in his circumstances', were considered to import a subjective element into the nature of the enquiries which an individual applicant could be expected to make. As already mentioned, we consider this criticism to be well founded. We therefore *recommend* that an applicant for insurance should be considered to have discharged his duty of disclosure in relation to the answers to specific questions if, after making such enquiries as are reasonable having regard both to the subject matter of the question and to the nature and extent of the cover which is sought, he answers the questions to the best of his knowledge and belief. This formulation would allow the court to take account of the particular topic raised by a specific question when assessing what enquiries ought to have been made into that topic. Further, the nature of the topic itself would be relevant. Thus, enquiries as to the materials of which a factory roof is constructed would obviously need to be more extensive than those concerning the cubic capacity of the engine of a motor vehicle. Equally, it would clearly be reasonable to expect enquiries to be substantially more thorough if the cover applied for was on a factory worth several million pounds than if the subject matter of the insurance was a house. If it can be established by reference to this standard that the insured has discharged his duty of disclosure, then it would not matter if his answer turns out in fact to have been inaccurate. This recommendation is along lines similar to those suggested by the Law Reform Committee in their Fifth Report, in which the Committee formulated the following rule which, in their view, could be introduced into the law without difficulty:

> ... that, notwithstanding anything contained or incorporated in a contract of insurance, no defence to a claim thereunder should be maintainable by reason of any misstatement of fact by the insured, where the insured can prove that the statement was true to the best of his knowledge and belief.

4.62 In the foregoing paragraph, we dealt with the standard required from an insured when answering specific questions in a proposal form. To complete this aspect, it remains to mention the standard which is to be required from him when he answers a general question at the end, such as whether there are any other facts which might influence the judgment of a prudent insurer in accepting the risk and fixing the premium. We think that the standard required from the insured in answering such questions in proposal forms should be assimilated in all respects with out basic recommendation concerning the reduced standard required from proposers in relation to their general duty of disclosure: viz, they are under no higher duty than to disclose material facts which they know or are to be assumed to know and which would be disclosed by a reasonable person in the position of the proposer, having regard to the nature and extent of the insurance cover which is sought and the circumstances in which it is sought. Thus, for the avoidance of doubt we propose that the legislation which we recommend should also expressly provide that all general questions in proposal forms shall be construed as seeking no further information from the proposer than such information as he would be bound to disclose by virtue of the reduced duty of disclosure referred to above. We *recommend* accordingly.

Copies of proposal forms to be supplied to insured

4.63 Next, we turn to a problem which is of particular significance when an insured is attempting to fulfill his duty of disclosure on renewal of his insurance. It was forcefully represented to us on consultation that the insured will often no longer remember the information which he supplied to the insurers on his initial application and on subsequent renewals (if any), unless he is at least able to refer to a copy of his proposal form. In our view, insurers should be required to supply the insured with a copy of his completed proposal form. Insurers should be able to comply with this requirement by providing a carbon copy with the original proposal form which can be torn off and retained by the insured after completion. If a tear off carbon copy is not supplied, then as soon after he has submitted the original form as is practicable in the circumstances. In addition, the proposal form should warn the proposer of the importance of keeping a copy of the proposal form as supplied to him. Further, in some cases there may be further communications between the insurer and the insured after the proposal form has been filled in, in the course of which the insured may supply further written information to the insurer, either in amplification of an answer given or in regard to a matter not canvassed specifically in the proposal form. The insured should clearly also be able to refer to these matters on renewal, and we again consider that he should be warned of the importance of keeping copies for future reference of the information which he has supplied.

Warnings to be included in proposal forms

4.64 We have already explained that in our view all proposal forms should contain certain warnings to the insured and that these should be presented in a prominent manner. We can now summarise the warnings which we *recommend* should be required to be included in all proposal forms in this manner. These should warn the insured:

(i) that he must answer all questions to the best of his knowledge and belief, after making such enquiries as are reasonable in the circumstances;

(ii) that in relation to any matter which is not the subject of a question in the proposal form, he must disclose any matter which he knows or could ascertain by reasonable enquiry and which might reasonably be considered to influence the judgment of a prudent insurer in deciding whether or on what terms to provide the cover which is sought;

(iii) of the consequences to the insured of a failure to fulfill the obligations referred to in (i) and (ii) above, that is, of the insurer's right to repudiate the policy and to reject any claim which may have arisen; and

(iv) of the importance to the insured of keeping the copy of the completed proposal form which will have been supplied to him under our recommendations and of any additional information which he may give to the insurers.

Sanctions if any of the requirements concerning proposal forms are not complied with

4.65 We have already mentioned that it is clearly necessary to provide sanctions against insurers in cases in which any of the prescribed warnings are omitted or are not presented in a prominent manner. Similarly, sanctions will clearly also be necessary if an insurer fails to comply with the obligations which we have recommended to supply to the insured a copy of the completed proposal form. We therefore turn to this aspect.

4.66 Since we foresee no real difficulties for insurers in complying with the foregoing recommendations, which are in any event already widely adopted so far as concerns warnings about the duty of disclosure and the standard for answering questions in proposal forms, we consider that there should be a clear and substantial sanction for cases in which there is a failure to comply with these requirements. They are all directed to seeking to assist the proposer to discharge his obligation to disclose material facts to the insurer, whether by answering questions in proposal forms or by complying with any residual duty of disclosure which might still subsist. In these circumstances we consider that the appropriate sanction is that if there is a failure to comply with any of these requirements the insurer shall not be entitled to rely on any failure by the insured to disclose any material fact, and we so *recommend*.

4.67 However, there may be cases in which the stringency of this sanction would be inappropriate because it may be quite clear that some trivial failure on the part of the insurer will not have caused any prejudice to the insured in relation to any failure of disclosure on his part. For instance, the insurer may have failed to provide the insured with a copy of the proposal form, but the insured may have kept his own copy. Alternatively, although the absence of the warnings concerning the duty of disclosure and of answering questions in the manner required, as well as of the consequences of non-compliance by the insured with his duty of disclosure, is in virtually all cases likely to lead to the conclusion that the insured was thereby prejudiced, there might also be rare cases, particularly in commercial insurance, where this would not be so. For instance, a particular proposal form covering an important particular risk may have been settled in negotiations between the insurer and the proposer, perhaps with the assistance of a broker or even with lawyers, and one or more of the required warnings may have been accidentally omitted from the final form, even though the original form may have contained them or there may have been specific discussions about the insured's duty in relation to the completion of the form so as to make him fully aware of his obligations and of the consequences of any breach on his part. In such cases it may be quite clear that the non-disclosure of some material fact has had no connection with some particular failure on the part of the insurer to comply with the requirements. We think that some additional provision should be made for exceptional cases of this kind. We accordingly *recommend* that, where there has been a failure by the insured to disclose a material fact, in circumstances in which the court is satisfied that a failure on the part of the insurer to comply with the requirements did not cause any prejudice to the insured with regard to his obligation to disclose such fact, then the court may give leave to the insurer to rely on the non-disclosure in question ...

RENEWALS

Introduction

4.69 Having dealt with the topic of disclosure in the context of proposal forms we now turn to deal with it in relation to renewals. In this context, the topic is of great importance because the vast majority of insurance contracts made in England are by way of renewal of existing policies, with the result that the duty of disclosure will most often arise on applications for renewed cover. The reason is that most insurance policies in England, other than policies of life insurance, are contracts for a term of one year and are renewable annually. In relation to such contracts the parties usually envisage that the contract will be renewed each year. In law such renewal, even if it is taken for granted at the outset, is a new contract, with the result that the insured is under a fresh duty to disclose all facts which are material at the date of renewal. The extent of the duty is the same as on the original application. However, since the insured need not disclose facts which are known to the insurer, and on the assumption that the insured has complied with his duty of disclosure on the original application (and on any subsequent renewals), he will only be under a duty to disclose any material changes in circumstances that have occurred since the date of the initial application or the date of the previous renewal, as the case may be.

4.70 This situation gives rise to two major difficulties. First, it is most unlikely that the ordinary insured is aware of this somewhat technical rule of law, with the consequence that he will be unlikely to be aware of the existence of any duty of disclosure on renewal; further, even if he is aware of it he is unlikely to be aware of its extent. Secondly, even if the insured is aware of both the existence of his duty and of its extent, he is likely in many cases to find great difficulty in complying with the duty unless he is able to refer to the documents which record the information previously supplied by him to the insurer. This difficulty will increase on each successive renewal.

4.71 One possible solution would be to abolish the duty of disclosure on renewal. However, this would mean that the insurer could not rely on the volunteering of information relevant to the circumstances on which his assessment of the renewal of the risk depends. He would then either have to make fresh investigations each year, perhaps even by means of a fresh proposal form, thus increasing administrative costs, or to increase premiums generally to take account of the new material facts which would not have come to his notice. Clearly, either alternative would be undesirable. Our conclusion is that the reasons which led us to recommend that the duty of disclosure should not be abolished as regards original applications for insurance apply with equal force to renewals. However, the implications of this conclusion require further consideration.

Reform of the duty of disclosure on renewal

4.72 Earlier in this report we concluded that, to put it shortly, an insured should on an original application for insurance, be under a duty to disclose only those material facts which, having regard to the particular circumstances, a reasonable man would disclose. On this basis, we consider that it would be clearly unsatisfactory if an insured were under a more onerous duty of disclosure on renewal than when he made his original application, and in our view the same standard of duty should clearly apply. On the other hand, since an insured is under no obligation to disclose matters which are already known to the insurer, on renewal the insured will only be obliged to update the matters disclosed when the contract was concluded or on the occasion of the last renewal, as the case may be. The effect of this, and of our recommendation about the general duty of disclosure, will therefore be that on renewal the insured will have to disclose material facts which he knows or is assumed to know, which have not been disclosed by him and which would be disclosed by a reasonable insured in his position, having regard to the nature and extent of the cover which is renewed and the circumstances in which it is renewed. We *recommend* accordingly …

SHOULD THE INSURER'S RIGHTS IN RESPECT OF NON-DISCLOSURE BE FURTHER RESTRICTED?

Introduction

4.88 In the following paragraphs we will consider whether the balancing of the interests of the insurer and the insured requires that the insurer's rights in respect of non-disclosure by the insured should be still further restricted than on the basis of the recommendations which we have already made. We consider two possible further restrictions. The first would preclude the insurer from rejecting a claim if the insured could prove that there could have been no connection between his non-disclosure and the loss. The second would leave the remedy for non-disclosure to the discretion of the court and would thus allow the insured who is in breach to make partial or total recovery of his claim in some cases. We deal with proposals in turn.

CONNECTION BETWEEN THE NON-DISCLOSURE AND THE LOSS

4.89 In our working paper, we dealt with the question whether our provisional recommendations should go further to protect the insured on the basis that insurers should only be entitled to reject a claim on the ground of non-disclosure of a material fact if the undisclosed fact is in some way connected with the loss. We refer to this hereafter for convenience as a 'nexus test'. Our provisional conclusion was that our recommendations had already struck a fair balance between the interests of the insured and of the insurer, and that it was neither necessary nor desirable to introduce any further restriction on the insurer's rights in the event of non-disclosure. On consultation, a number of commentators took the view that a duty of disclosure coupled with a nexus test would provide a second best to abolition of the duty. Those who took this view appear to have made their comments mainly in the context of protecting consumers. We have already stated our reasons for rejecting the outright abolition of the duty of disclosure as well as any regime based on a 'consumer-non-consumer' dichotomy. However, in view of the support that was expressed for the adoption of a nexus test in non-disclosure we have reconsidered the possibility of introducing such a test in this context.

4.90 In our working paper, we provisionally recommended that the law of warranties should be reformed so that rejection of a claim for breach should only be allowed if there is a connection of some kind between the insured's breach and the loss. We adhere to this recommendation in this report. In the context of non-disclosure the precise formulation of a nexus test would require separate consideration, but for the purpose of the present discussion it is sufficient to put the issue in broad terms. Suppose that an insured has failed to disclose a material fact, that is, one which would have affected a prudent insurer's decision whether or not to accept the risk at all or, if so, at what premium and on what terms. Suppose also that a loss subsequently occurs which could not have had any connection with the undisclosed fact. Although the insurer would be entitled to repudiate the policy, should the insured nevertheless be entitled to recover his claim?

4.91 At first sight this result may appear to be just, as some of our commentators felt. However, on examination it is clear that the insurer would thereby be held to a contract which he would either not have accepted at all, or only at a higher premium or subject to different terms, or both. This would appear to be unfair. For this reason and for the reasons set out in the paragraphs below, we have concluded that, whatever superficial attraction the nexus test may have in the context of non-disclosure, it is misconceived and should not be adopted in this context.

4.92 One must begin by putting the issue into the perspective of our other recommendations in this report in order to see the extent of the problem which would remain if these are adopted. Our present law of non-disclosure has caused hardship and led to widespread criticism, as we have already pointed out. In particular, we have identified the following mischiefs with which we have already dealt, viz: (a) that the standard to be applied to the duty of disclosure is that of a prudent insurer and not of a reasonable insured; and (b) that in proposal form cases it may well not occur to the proposer that in addition to answering a large number of questions he is required to volunteer material information without his attention having been drawn to this obligation in any way. However, under our recommendations these mischiefs will disappear. By applying the test of a reasonable insured, many of the 'moral hazard' cases, which have been subject to particularly strong criticism, may in any event be decided differently. Further, in proposal form cases, which in the present context in our view present the greatest mischief in practice, the insured will have had his attention drawn expressly to his duty to volunteer material information. If the insurer has failed to give the necessary warning, he will not be entitled to rely on the non-disclosure of such information.

4.93 For present purposes one therefore starts with cases concerning proposers who will, *ex hypothesi*, not have acted in the way in which a reasonable person in the position of the insured would have acted. On this basis, the considerations of justice concerning the consequences of a non-disclosure at once assume a different aspect. But then one comes to a further consideration. Suppose that a proposer unreasonably fails to disclose some material fact under the rubric of 'moral hazard': how could the application of a nexus test work in practice? Suppose that an applicant fails to disclose a bad claims record or (unspent) convictions for dishonesty: such facts could, in practice, hardly ever be shown to have had any connection with a particular loss. The result would be that an insured who is unreasonably in breach of his duty of disclosure would, in such cases, virtually always recover. We do not think that this would be acceptable or that it strikes a fair balance between insured and insurer against the background of the reforms of the law of non-disclosure which we are recommending.

4.94 There is a further and perhaps even more fundamental objection to the introduction of a nexus test into the law of disclosure which applies whether or nor the undisclosed material fact concerns 'moral hazard'. This objection stems from comments which we received from the insurance industry on consultation which have greatly impressed us. Unlike cases of breach of warranty, in relation to which we are recommending that there must be a connection between the breach and the loss, all considerations relating to non-disclosure must focus on the moment when a proposal for insurance is put forward and either accepted on certain terms or rejected, in either event by reference to what the insurer judges to be the quality of the risk. The technique – one might almost say the art – of good underwriting is to judge all the factors affecting an offered risk at this moment, when the underwriter must then and there assess its quality on the basis of his experience, as though he were considering the overall impression given by a 'still photograph' of the risk at this point. In these respects, the implications of non-disclosure are quite different from those of breaches of warranties during the currency of the cover. As a result of the non-disclosure, the insurer will have accepted a risk which, had he known all the material facts, he would either not have accepted at all or would have accepted at a different premium or on different terms. In these circumstances, we see great force in the contention made on behalf of the industry that it would be wrong in principle to hold the insurer to the contract in such cases. Furthermore, under our recommendations made later in this report we severely curtail the rights of insurers to rely on 'basis of the contract' clauses as a means of avoiding liability, with the result that their rights in cases of non-disclosure would assume even greater importance than at present.

4.95 In addition, many underwriters are anxious to confine their portfolios to 'good risks', particularly in the context of large commercial insurances to which our recommendations would of course apply in the same way as to 'consumer' insurance. In such cases, the world wide insurance market in this country strongly relies for its competitiveness on the duty of a proposer to disclose material facts (which under our recommendations a reasonable insured would realise required disclosure) of which the insurer knows nothing and about which he could not in practice be expected to ask exhaustive questions. We have in mind matters such as the tests carried out in a manufacturing process in connection with liability insurance for defective products, or security aspects in businesses which are insured against a variety of risks (for example, the routes taken by vehicles carrying a firm's payroll in connection with insurance against theft and allied risks). We are satisfied that in relation to cover of these types, which provides premium income which is of great financial importance to this country, the introduction of a nexus test into the law of disclosure would prevent the insurer from quoting rates for 'good risks' which are competitive in comparison with those quoted by insurers operating under the present system, because he would be less able to identify which risks are good and which are bad and to adjust premium rates accordingly. Since it would clearly be unacceptable to erect protective walls around the market in which a nexus test prevailed, the British insurance industry might therefore suffer a substantial loss of competitiveness. For an international market, such as London, the consequences of this might be extremely serious.

4.96 Finally, let us take one extreme type of case in order to illustrate the difference between the superficial attraction of a nexus test in relation to non-disclosure and its deeper implications. Suppose that a person insures his life without disclosing that he is suffering from constant stomach ache. Some months later, he is killed in a railway accident. It is then discovered during the post mortem that he had been suffering from terminal cancer, and the insurers repudiate on the grounds of non-disclosure. Supporters of a nexus test might well say that this would be unjust, since the death clearly had no connection with the non-disclosure. At first sight, this may seem attractive, but only because one is reasoning with hindsight from the knowledge of a clearly unconnected loss. But suppose that the problem is put differently: suppose that one month after the conclusion of the contract the insurers learn that the insured is suffering from cancer and claim to cancel the policy because they would never have accepted the risk if the insured had disclosed its existence. Clearly, we think, they should be entitled to do so and not be held to a cover which they would never have accepted if the full facts had been disclosed. In our view, the death of the insured in the meantime should make no difference in principle and the insurer should be entitled to refuse to pay the sum assured.

4.97 For these reasons we *recommend* against the introduction of a nexus test in relation to non-disclosure ...

'BASIS OF THE CONTRACT' CLAUSES

The present law

7.1 We have seen that an insurer may avoid a contract of insurance for the non-disclosure of a material fact. However, insurers often pre-empt the issue whether a particular fact is material by including in the proposal form a declaration for signature by the proposer whereby he warrants the accuracy of all the answers to the questions asked: the usual formula is to provide that the proposer's answers are to form the 'basis of the contract' between the insurer and the insured. Sometimes, the policy itself contains a provision to the like effect. Such declarations and provisions are known as 'basis of the contract' clauses. Their effect in law is that all answers in the proposal form are incorporated into the contract as warranties and that, in the event of any inaccuracy in any one of them, the insurer may repudiate the contract for breach of warranty regardless of the materiality of the particular answer to the risk. Since, in cases where the answer related to past or present facts, the breach of warranty is committed at the moment when the contract is made, the effect is that the insurer may refuse to pay any claims under the policy. The fact that the insured may have answered the questions in good faith and to the best of his knowledge and belief does not help him if his answers are in fact inaccurate ...

REFORM OF THE PRESENT LAW

The mischief

7.5 It is clear from the foregoing criticisms that 'basis of the contract' clauses constitute a major mischief in the present law. These clauses, to the extent that they apply to statements of past or present fact in proposal forms, seem to us to be objectionable on three main grounds. First, they enable insurers to repudiate the policy for inaccurate statements even though they are not material to the risk. Secondly, they entitle insurers to repudiate the policy for objectively inaccurate statements of fact even though the insured could not reasonably be expected either to know or to have the means of knowing the true facts. Thirdly, the elevation *en bloc* of all such statements into warranties binding on the insured means that, if the insurers can establish any inaccuracy, however trivial, in any of the statements, they can exercise their right to repudiate the policy, even when the statement is not material to the risk and even when it concerned matters beyond the insured's knowledge of means of knowledge. Such a repudiation is often referred to as one example of a 'technical' repudiation.

7.6 Insurers contend (and indeed one sector of the insurance industry mentioned this on consultation) that in practice they only take advantage of technical defences, such as those founded on 'basis of the contract' clauses, to repudiate policies when they suspect fraud which they are unable to prove. However, we reiterate the view taken in the working paper that it is unsatisfactory for insurers to be able to repudiate policies on mere suspicion of fraud. It should be for the courts, and only for the courts, to make findings of fraud. It seems quite unacceptable that insurers should in effect in many cases have a discretion to repudiate policies on technical grounds; their entitlement in this regard should depend on the law and not on their discretion.

7.7 The first of the above objections to 'basis of the contract' clauses has already been met by our recommendation that no provision of a contract of insurance should be capable of constituting a warranty unless it relates to a matter which is material to the risk. This of itself does not however go far enough, since it does not meet the second and third objections made in para 7.5. Earlier in this report, we pointed out that it was unjust to the insured to require him, by means of a proposal form, to give objectively accurate answers to specific questions as to past and present facts which were outside his knowledge or means of knowledge. We accordingly reached the conclusion that such injustice could best be avoided by a provision that the insured should be treated as having discharged his duty of disclosure if he has answered any such questions to the best of his knowledge and belief, after making such enquiries as are reasonable, having regard both to the topics covered by the question and the nature and extent of the cover which is sought, even if his answer is *in fact* inaccurate. In our view it would be unacceptable if insurers were able to circumvent the protection thus afforded to the insured by obtaining from him, by way of a 'basis of the contract' clause, a warranty as to the accuracy of all or any of his answers. The Law Reform Committee undoubtedly had this mischief in mind when it suggested that a provision could be introduced into our law without difficulty whereby:

> Notwithstanding anything contained or incorporated in a contract of insurance, no defence to a claim thereunder should be maintained by reason of any misstatement of fact by the insured, where the insured can prove that the statement was true to the best of his knowledge and belief.

7.8 Accordingly, our recommendation is that any 'basis of the contract' clause should be ineffective to the extent that it purports to convert into a warranty any statement or statements by the insured as to the existence of past or present facts, whether the insured's statement is contained in a proposal form or elsewhere. However, it would defeat our recommendations if insurers were able to evade this ban on 'basis of the contract' clauses by obtaining from the insured a separate warranty as to past or present fact or a series of such warranties, either in proposal forms or in documents which refer to proposal forms. We therefore recommend that no provision in a proposal form whereby the insured promises that a state of affairs exists or has existed should be capable of constituting a warranty. This would mean, for instance, that a promise by the insured in a proposal form that his house is constructed of brick and slate would not constitute a warranty. Furthermore, any provision either in or referring to the proposal form whereby the insured purports to undertake the accuracy of a statement or statements in the proposal form concerning past or present fact should be ineffective to create a warranty. This would mean for example that a provision of the policy whereby the insured declares that answers to specific questions in the proposal form are true would not constitute a warranty.

7.9 The object of these recommendations is twofold. The first is to deny any legal efficacy to the 'basis of the contract' clause as regards warranties as to past or present facts. The second is to prevent the proposal form from being used as a vehicle for the creation of warranties as to past or present facts and to ensure that the parties' rights and duties as regards statements made by the insured in the proposal form as to past or present fact are governed exclusively by the recommendations we have made in Pt IV of this report.

Effect of our recommendation

7.10 We should, however, make it clear that we do not intend to ban specific undertakings by the insured as to the existence of past or present facts or to prevent such specific undertakings from constituting warranties in all cases. If insurers consider it necessary to obtain such undertakings, they should be able to do so by introducing them into the policy as individual specific warranties, always provided, however, that the formal requirements which we have recommended in regard to the creation of warranties are satisfied. Furthermore, we should point out that our other recommendations concerning warranties substantially restrict the present rights of insurers to reject claims for breach of a warranty.

7.11 We turn next to promissory warranties. If an answer in a proposal form relates to the future, then under the present law a 'basis of the contract' clause will elevate that statement into a promissory warranty. We do not see the same objection to this as in relation to statements as to past or present fact because the safeguards and precautions which can be created by promissory warranties are clearly necessary for insurers and unobjectionable, and there appears to be no reason to prevent their creation by means of 'basis of the contract' clauses as a matter of convenience. There is then the further possibility that, as noted above, an answer in a proposal form may relate to past and present fact as well as containing a reference to the future. In such cases a 'basis of the contract' clause will be effective under out recommendations only insofar as it creates a promissory warranty, and we consider this to be unexceptionable for the reasons stated above. Accordingly, we *recommend* that no change be made to this aspect of the present law. However, it is again necessary to point out that if insurers do create promissory warranties in this way they will still have to comply with the formal requirements we propose in relation to warranties, and that their right to reject claims for breaches of any such warranty would be restricted ...

APPENDIX 4.9

(Australian) Insurance Contracts Act 1984 (Cth) (as amended)

21 (3) Where a person:

(a) failed to answer; or

(b) gave an obviously incomplete or irrelevant answer to a question included in a proposal form about a matter, the insurer shall be deemed to have waived compliance with the duty of disclosure in relation to the matter ...

21A **Eligible contracts of insurance disclosure of specified matters**

(1) This section applies to an *eligible contract of insurance* unless it is entered into by way of renewal.

'Position of the insurer'

(2) The *insurer* is taken to have waived compliance with the *duty of disclosure* in relation to the contract unless the *insurer* complies with either subsection (3) or (4).

(3) Before the contract is entered into, the *insurer* requests the *insured* to answer one or more specific questions that are relevant to the decision of the *insurer* whether to accept the risk and, if so, on what terms.

(4) Before the contract is entered into, both:

(a) the *insurer* requests the *insured* to answer one or more specific questions that are relevant to the decision of the *insurer* whether to accept the risk and, if so, on what terms; and

(b) the *insurer* expressly requests the *insured* to disclose each exceptional circumstance that:

(i) is known to the *insured*; and

(ii) the *insured* knows, or a reasonable person in the circumstances could be expected to know, is a matter relevant to the decision of the *insurer* whether to accept the risk and, if so, on what terms; and

(iii) is not a matter that the *insurer* could reasonably be expected to make the subject of a question under paragraph (a); and

(iv) is not a matter covered by *subsection 21*(2).

(5) If:

(a) the *insurer* complies with subsection (3) or (4); and

(b) the *insurer* asks the *insured* to disclose to the *insurer* any other matters that would be covered by the *duty of disclosure* in relation to the contract,

the *insurer* is taken to have waived compliance with the *duty of disclosure* in relation to those matters.

'Position of the insured'

(6) If:

(a) the *insurer* complies with subsection (3); and

(b) in answer to each question referred to in section (3), the *insured* discloses each matter that:

(i) is known to the *insured;* and

(ii) a reasonable person in the circumstances could be expected to have disclosed in answer to that question,

the *insured* is taken to have complied with the *duty of disclosure* in relation to the contract.

(7) If:

(a) the *insurer* complies with subsection (4); and

(b) in answer to each question referred to in paragraph (4)(a), the *insured* discloses each matter that:

(i) is known to the *insured;* and

(ii) a reasonable person in the circumstances could be expected to have disclosed in answer to that question; and

(c) the *insured* complies with the request referred to in paragraph (4)(b),

the *insured* is taken to have complied with the *duty of disclosure* in relation to the contract.

'Onus of proof exceptional circumstance'

(8) In any proceedings relating to this section, the onus of proving that a matter is an exceptional circumstance covered by subparagraph (4)(b)(iii) lies on the *insurer.*

'Definition'

(9) In this section:

'eligible contract of insurance' means a contract of insurance that is specified in the regulations.

22 **Insurer to inform of duty of disclosure**

(1) The insurer shall, before a contract of insurance is entered into, clearly inform the insured in writing of the general nature and effect of the duty of disclosure and, if section 21A applies to the contract, also clearly inform the insured in writing of the general nature and effect of section 21A.

(2) If the regulations prescribe a form of writing to be used for informing an insured of the matters referred to in subsection (1), the writing to be used may be in accordance with the form so prescribed.

(3) An insurer who has not complied with subsection (1) may not exercise a right in respect of a failure to comply with the duty of disclosure unless that failure was fraudulent.

FAILURE TO ANSWER QUESTIONS

27 A person shall not be taken to have made a misrepresentation by reason only that he failed to answer a question included in a proposal form or gave an obviously incomplete or irrelevant answer to such a question.

DIVISION 3 – REMEDIES FOR NON-DISCLOSURE AND MISREPRESENTATION

General insurance

28 (1) This section applies where the person who became the *insured* under a contract of general insurance upon the contract being entered into:

(a) failed to comply with the *duty of disclosure*; or

(b) made a misrepresentation to the *insurer* before the contract was entered into,

but does not apply where the *insurer* would have entered into the contract, for the same premium or on the same terms and conditions, even if the *insured* had not failed to comply with the *duty of disclosure* or had not made the misrepresentation before the contract was entered into.

(2) If the failure was fraudulent or the misrepresentation was made fraudulently, the insurer may avoid the contract.

(3) If the insurer is not entitled to avoid the contract or, being entitled to avoid the contract (whether under subsection (2) or otherwise) has not done so, the liability of the insurer in respect of a claim is reduced to the amount that would place him in a position in which he would have been if the failure had not occurred or the misrepresentation had not been made.

Life insurance

29 (1) This section applies where the person who became the insured under a contract of life insurance upon the contract being entered into:

(a) failed to comply with the duty of disclosure; or

(b) made a misrepresentation to the insurer before the contract was entered into, but does not apply where;

(c) the insurer would have entered into the contract even if the insured had not failed to comply with the duty of disclosure or had not made the misrepresentation before the contract was entered into; or

(d) the failure or misrepresentation was in respect of the date of birth of one or more of the life insureds.

(2) If the failure was fraudulent or the misrepresentation was made fraudulently, the insurer may avoid the contract.

(3) If the insurer would not have been prepared to enter into a contract of life insurance with the insured on any terms if the duty of disclosure had been complied with or the misrepresentation had not been made, the insurer may, within three years after the contract was entered into, avoid the contract.

(4) If the insurer has not avoided the contract, whether under subsections (2) or (3) or otherwise, he may, by notice in writing given to the insured before the expiration of three years after the contract was entered into, vary the contract by substituting for the sum insured (including any bonuses) a sum that is not less than the sum ascertained in accordance with the formula SP/Q, where:

S is the number of dollars that is equal to the sum insured (including any bonuses);

P is the number of dollars that is equal to the premium that has, or to the sum of the premiums that have, become payable under the contract; and

Q is the number of dollars that is equal to the premium, or the sum of the premiums, that the insurer would have been likely to have charged if the duty of disclosure had been complied with or the misrepresentation had not been made.

(5) In the application of subsection (4) in relation to a contract that provides for periodic payments, 'the sum insured' means each such payment (including any bonuses).

(6) A variation of a contract under subsection (4) has effect from the time when the contract was entered into …

Court may disregard avoidance in certain circumstances

31 (1) In any proceedings by the insured in respect of a contract of insurance that has been avoided on the ground of fraudulent failure to comply with the duty of disclosure or fraudulent misrepresentation, the court may, if it would be harsh and unfair not to do so, but subject to this section, disregard the avoidance and, if it does so, shall allow the insured to recover the whole, or such part as the court thinks just and equitable in the circumstances, of the amount that would have been payable if the contract had not been avoided.

(2) The power conferred by subsection (1) may be exercised only where the court is of the opinion that, in respect of the loss that is the subject of the proceedings before the court, the insurer has not been prejudiced by the failure or misrepresentation or, if the insurer has been so prejudiced, the prejudice is minimal or insignificant.

(3) In exercising the power conferred by subsection (1), the court:

(a) shall have regard to the need to deter fraudulent conduct in relation to insurance; and

(b) shall weigh the extent of the culpability of the insured in the fraudulent conduct against the magnitude of the loss that would be suffered by the insured if the avoidance were not disregarded,

but may also have regard to any other relevant matter.

(4) The power conferred by subsection (1) applies only in relation to the loss that is the subject of the proceedings before the court, and any disregard by the court of the avoidance does not otherwise operate to reinstate the contract.

APPENDIX 4.10

Association of British Insurers, *Statement of General Insurance Practice*, 1986, London: ABI (replacing 1977)

The following statement of normal insurance practice, issued by the Association of British Insurers, applies to general insurances of policyholders resident in the United Kingdom and insured in their private capacity only.

(1) PROPOSAL FORMS

(a) The declaration at the foot of the proposal form should be restricted to completion according to the proposer's knowledge and belief.

(b) Neither the proposal form nor the policy shall contain any provision converting the statements as to past or present fact in the proposal form into warranties. But insurers may require specific warranties about matters which are material to the risk.

(c) If not included in the declaration, prominently displayed on the proposal form should be a statement:

   (i) drawing the attention of the proposer to the consequences of the failure to disclose all material facts, explained as those facts an insurer would regard as likely to influence the acceptance and assessment of the proposal;

   (ii) warning that if the proposer is in any doubt about facts considered material, he should disclose them.

(d) Those matters which insurers have found generally to be material will be the subject of clear questions in proposal forms.

(e) So far as is practicable, insurers will avoid asking questions which would require expert knowledge beyond that which the proposer could reasonably be expected to possess or obtain or which would require a value judgment on the part of the proposer.

(f) Unless the prospectus or the proposal form contains full details of the standard cover offered, and whether or not it contains an outline of that cover, the proposal form shall include a prominent statement that a specimen copy of the policy form is available on request.

(g) Proposal forms shall contain a prominent warning that the proposer should keep a record (including copies of letters) of all information supplied to the insurer for the purpose of entering into the contract.

(h) The proposal form shall contain a prominent statement that a copy of the completed form:

   (i) is automatically provided for retention at the time of completion; or

   (ii) will be supplied as part of the insurer's normal practice; or

   (iii) will be supplied on request within a period of three months after its completion.

(i) An insurer shall not raise an issue under the proposal form, unless the policyholder is provided with a copy of the completed form.

(2) CLAIMS

(a) Under the conditions regarding notification of a claim, the policyholder shall not be asked to do more than report a claim and subsequent developments as soon as reasonably possible except in the case of legal processes and claims which a third party requires the policyholder to notify within a fixed time where immediate advice may be required.

(b) An insurer will not repudiate liability to indemnify a policyholder:

(i) on grounds of non-disclosure of a material fact which a policyholder could not reasonably be expected to have disclosed;

(ii) on grounds of misrepresentation unless it is a deliberate or negligent misrepresentation of a material fact;

(iii) on grounds of a breach of warranty or condition where the circumstances of the loss are unconnected with the breach unless fraud is involved.

Paragraph 2(b) above does apply to marine and aviation policies.

(c) Liability under the policy having been established and the amount payable by the insurer agreed, payment will be made without avoidable delay.

(3) RENEWALS

(a) Renewal notices should contain a warning about the duty of disclosure including the necessity to advise changes affecting the policy which have occurred since the policy inception or last renewal date, whichever was the later.

(b) Renewal notices shall contain a warning that the proposer should keep a record (including copies of letters) of all information supplied to the insurer for the purposes of renewal of the contract.

(4) COMMENCEMENT

Any changes to insurance documents will be made as and when they need to be reprinted, but the Statement will apply in the meantime.

(5) POLICY DOCUMENTS

Insurers will continue to develop clearer and more explicit proposal forms and policy documents whilst bearing in mind the legal nature of insurance contracts.

(6) DISPUTES

The provisions of the Statement shall be taken into account in arbitration and any other referral procedures which may apply in the event of disputes between policyholders and insurers relating to matters dealt with in the Statement.

(7) EUROPEAN UNION

This Statement will need reconsideration when the draft EU Directive on Insurance Contract Law is adopted and implemented in the United Kingdom. [The draft has now been abandoned: see text, above.]

Association of British Insurers, *Statement of Long Term Insurance Practice*, 1986, London: ABI

This statement relates to long term insurance effected by individuals resident in the United Kingdom in a private capacity.

(1) PROPOSAL FORMS

(a) If the proposal form calls for the disclosure of material facts a statement should be included in the declaration, or prominently displayed elsewhere on the form or in the document of which it forms part:

  (i) drawing attention to the consequences of failure to disclose all material facts and explaining that these are facts that an insurer would regard as likely to influence the assessment and acceptance of a proposal;

  (ii) warning that if the signatory is in any doubt about whether certain facts are material, these facts should be disclosed.

(b) Neither the proposal nor the policy shall contain any provision converting the statements as to past or present fact in the proposal form into warranties except where the warranty relates to a statement of fact concerning the life to be assured under a life of another policy. Insurers may, however, require specific warranties about matters which are material to the risk.

(c) Those matters which insurers have commonly found to be material should be the subject of clear questions in proposal forms.

(d) Insurers should avoid asking questions which would require knowledge beyond that which the signatory could reasonably be expected to possess.

(e) The proposal form or a supporting document should include a statement that a copy of the policy form or of the policy conditions is available on request.

(f) The proposal form or a supporting document should include a statement that a copy of the completed proposal form is available on request.

(2) POLICIES AND ACCOMPANYING DOCUMENTS

(a) Insurers will continue to develop clearer and more explicit proposal forms and policy documents whilst bearing in mind the legal nature of insurance contracts.

(b) Life assurance policies or accompanying documents should indicate:

  (i) the circumstances in which interest would accrue after the assurance has matured; and

  (ii) whether or not there are rights to surrender values in the contract and, if so, what those rights are.

(Note: The appropriate sales literature should endeavour to impress on proposers that a whole life or endowment assurance is intended to be a long term contract and that surrender values, especially in the early years, are frequently less than the total premiums paid.)

(3) CLAIMS

(a) An insurer will not unreasonably reject a claim. In particular, an insurer will not reject a claim or invalidate a policy on grounds of non-disclosure or misrepresentation of a fact unless:

(i) it is material fact; and

(ii) it is a fact within the knowledge of the proposer; and

(iii) it is a fact which the proposer could reasonably be expected to disclose. (It should be noted that fraud or deception will, and reckless or negligent non-disclosure or misrepresentation of a material fact may, constitute grounds for rejection of a claim.)

(b) Except where fraud is involved, an insurer will not reject a claim or invalidate a policy on grounds of a breach of a warranty unless the circumstances of the claim are connected with the breach and unless:

(i) the warranty relates to a statement of fact concerning the life to be assured under a life of another policy and that statement would have constituted grounds for rejection of a claim by the insurer under 3(a) above if it had been made by the life to be assured under an own life policy; or

(ii) the warranty was created in relation to specific matters material to the risk and it was drawn to the proposer's attention at or before the making of the contract.

(c) Under any conditions regarding a time limit for notification of a claim, the claimant will not be asked to do more than report a claim and subsequent developments as soon as reasonably possible.

(d) Payment of claims will be made without avoidable delay once the insured event has been proved and the entitlement of the claimant to receive payment has been established.

(e) When the payment of a claim is delayed more than two months, the insurer will pay interest on the cash sum due, or make an equivalent adjustment to the sum, unless the amount of such interest would be trivial. The two month period will run from the date of the happening of the insured event (that is, death or maturity) or, in the case of a unit linked policy, from the date on which the unit linking ceased, if later. Interest will be calculated at a relevant market rate from the end of the two month period until the actual date of payment.

(f) In the case of a tax exempt policy with a friendly society, the total of the cash sum due and such interest to the date of the claim cannot exceed the statutory limit on such assurance.

(4) DISPUTES

The provisions of the Statement shall be taken into account in arbitration and any other referral procedures which may apply in the event of disputes between policyholders and insurers relating to matters dealt with in the Statement.

(5) COMMENCEMENT

Any changes to insurance documents will be made as and when they need to be reprinted, but the Statement will apply in the meantime.

Note regarding industrial assurance policyholders:

Policies effected by industrial assurance policyholders are included amongst the policies to which the above Statement of Long Term Insurance Practice applies. Those policyholders also enjoy the additional protection conferred upon them by the Industrial Assurance Acts 1923 to 1969 and Regulations issued thereunder. These Acts give the Industrial Assurance Commissioner wide powers to cover *inter alia* the following aspects:

(a) Completion of proposal forms.

(b) Issue and maintenance of premium receipt books.

(c) Notification in premium receipt books of certain statutory rights of a policyholder including rights to:

- (i) an arrears notice before forfeiture;
- (ii) free policies and surrender values for certain categories of policies;
- (iii) relief from forfeiture of benefit under a policy on health grounds unless the proposer has made an untrue statement of knowledge and belief as to the assured's health;
- (iv) reference to the Commissioner as arbitrator in disputes between the policyholder and the company or society.

The offices transacting industrial assurance business have further agreed that any premium (or deposit) paid on completion of the proposal form will be returned to the proposer if, on issue, the policy document is rejected by him or her.

APPENDIX 4.11

Reynolds and Anderson v Phoenix Assurance Co Ltd [1978] 2 Lloyd's Rep 440

Forbes J:

NON-DISCLOSURE

The defendants claim that they are entitled to avoid and have avoided the insurance policy on the ground of material non-disclosure. Two matters are alleged in the re-amended defence as being matters which the plaintiffs should have disclosed to defendants before entering into either of the contracts of insurance in this case. The first is in these terms ...

> ... (1) that, in about May 1971, the Colne Investment Corporation Ltd had alleged ... that the first named plaintiff had in 1968 and 1969 conspired with Mr Carroll to defraud and had defrauded the said company of the sum of £2,750.

It is convenient to refer to this as the 'Colne allegation'. The second is in sub-para (iii) ...

> ... that, in or about the year 1961, the first named plaintiff had been convicted of the offence of receiving property, namely two batteries, knowing the same to have been stolen for which offence the first named plaintiff had been fined £250.

Now, if the allegation made in this sub-paragraph were true the conviction would be a spent conviction under the provisions of the Rehabilitation of Offenders Act, 1974, from which certain consequences would follow, the principal of which is that no evidence of such a conviction is admissible and that the convicted person must be treated not only as one who has not been convicted of the offence but as one who has never in fact committed it. This is subject to a certain judicial discretion, exercisable under s 7(3) of the Act, and I shall have to return to consider this in more detail later. At this stage, it is sufficient to say that in exercising that discretion the court has to be ...:

> ... satisfied that justice cannot be done except by admitting evidence relating to a person's spent convictions.

This at once produces a difficulty because, as it seems to me, it is quite impossible to decide where the justice of the matter lies without considering at any rate some of the details of the conviction and of the offence which may have been committed. Particular difficulty arises in this case because one of the important arguments about non-disclosure is the question of the materiality of that which has not been disclosed. Again, any question of materiality may become difficult of solution unless details of the offence and conviction are before the court. Very sensibly, both counsel agreed that the evidence and argument on this aspect of the matter should proceed on the basis of an hypothesis, namely that Mr Reynolds, the first plaintiff, had been convicted in 1961 of the offence of receiving two stolen tractor batteries worth £10–12 knowing them to have been stolen, and was fined £250 by the magistrates for that offence ...

... I can find no special facts in this case to cause me to change my first impression which was similar to that of Lord Pearson, with this added facet that the conviction only resulted in a fine, the size of which might quite properly have been designed to reflect not the gravity of the offence but the fact that Mr Reynolds was a man of considerable means. Nor is there any unanimity among the experts. I conclude that the defendants have failed to prove to my satisfaction that this particular conviction 11 years previously was a material fact which would have affected the judgment of a reasonable or prudent insurer in fixing the premium or determining whether he will take the risk.

THE REHABILITATION OF OFFENDERS ACT 1974

In view of the conclusion to which I have come about the materiality of the conviction, it is probably unnecessary for me to consider the position under the 1974 Act. However, I feel that I should indicate the course I would have taken had I decided that the conviction was a material fact which should have been disclosed. This is because, it seems to me, that the terms in which the discretion to admit evidence concerning a spent conviction is given by the statute are such that it is virtually incumbent upon a judge of first instance to pass upon this matter. The relevant provision is s 7(3) of the 1974 Act. So far as is material it is in these terms ...:

> If at any stage in any proceedings before a judicial authority in Great Britain – the authority is satisfied in the light of any considerations which appear to it to be relevant *including any evidence which has been or may thereafter be put before it* that justice cannot be done in the case except by admitting or requiring evidence relating to a person's spent convictions or to circumstances ancillary thereto, that authority may admit or as the case may be require the evidence in question notwithstanding the provisions of sub-s (1) of s 4 above and may determine any issue to which the evidence relates in disregard, so far as necessary, of those provisions ...

Had I considered that the defendants had proved that the conviction was a material fact, it would have been because I would have accepted the evidence of those of the expert witnesses who maintained that the conviction was material. This, in its turn, would be because I accepted that it was the general practice among insurance companies to require such matters to be disclosed, to consider themselves entitled to refuse cover in such circumstances, and, and this is important, to avoid a policy on the ground of material non-disclosure in cases where no such disclosure was made. It would be against that background that I would have had to have judged whether or not I was satisfied that justice could not be done in the case except by admitting or requiring evidence of the spent conviction. It seems to me, on those hypotheses, that there is really only one conclusion to which I would have come. If the universal practice of insurance companies would involve the probable refusal of cover if the fact of a previous conviction had been disclosed, and in this case a material conviction was not so disclosed, then there would be no real injustice to the plaintiffs in requiring the conviction to be disclosed now because on this view they were bound to disclose it in 1972, did not do so, and therefore obtained a policy which otherwise they would probably never have obtained. On the defendants' side, on the other hand, there would be the gravest injustice because they would be prevented from avoiding a policy, which on this view of the evidence, it would be the universal practice of insurers to avoid in such circumstances, and would be bound to pay insurance moneys on a policy relating to a risk which … they would, by universal practice have been entitled to decline …

APPENDIX 4.12

Glicksman v Lancashire and General Assurance Co Ltd [1926] All ER Rep 161, HL; (1927) 26 Ll L Rep 69

Viscount Dunedin: The law has often been stated, but perhaps it is just as well to state it again. A contract of insurance is denominated a contract *uberrima fides*. It is possible for persons to stipulate that answers to certain questions shall be the basis of the insurance, and if that is done then there is no question as to materiality left, because the persons have contracted that there should be materiality in those questions; but quite apart from that, and alongside of that, there is the duty of no concealment of any consideration which would affect the mind of the ordinary prudent man in accepting the risk. Now, as I have said, upon this proposal two questions arose. First, the question arose upon what I call the plural and the singular. One of the learned judges in the Court of Appeal has said that he would like further to consider this. Roche J decided it in the sense that the question was really put in the plural, and that therefore there was no untrue answer. There were certain cases quoted to us which go to the same view. Two of the learned judges in the Court of Appeal took the other view. My Lords, I do not think it necessary that we should come to a conclusion on which of these views is right, and I therefore do not propose myself to express any opinion upon them, because I think the ground of judgment is quite clear on the other point. It is narrow enough, because when you come to the law as to materiality and concealment, of course there are certain circumstances which are so obviously material that it will not be taken from any man to say that he did not know it. If you are insuring a ship on a time policy and that ship had been badly knocked about three weeks before, of course you could not be heard to say that you did not think that was a material circumstance. But here the whole point really comes to turn upon this – and this is the ground of the judgment of the learned judges in the Court of Appeal – that, never minding the singular or the plural, the fact that a question of this sort was put showed that the insurance company thought it was material whether a proposal had been refused or not, and that that was brought to the knowledge of the claimant. My Lords, under the circumstances I have considerable doubts, but then I am not entitled to take any view of my own on that, because that is a fact and the arbitrator has found it as a fact and I cannot get beyond the arbitrator's finding. I think that the reasoning of the learned judges in the Court of Appeal is impeccable. This was brought to the knowledge of the claimant that it was a material fact, and he certainly did not disclose it, and, therefore, the policy is void.

Therefore, my Lords, with unfeigned regret, I move your Lordships that this appeal be dismissed ...

Lord Atkinson: My Lords, I concur. I wish to say one word in reference to the observations of Scrutton LJ. I think it is a lamentable thing that insurance companies will abstain from shaping the questions they put to intending insurers on these occasions in clear and unambiguous language.

For instance, in this particular case, all that it was necessary to ask was: 'Did you two or either of you make an application to the Sun Insurance Co for a policy against burglary?' This whole case and all the expense incurred in it would have been prevented had that simple method been adopted.

Lord Wrenbury: My Lords, it is with the very greatest reluctance that I concur in the motion which is proposed from the Woolsack. I think it a mean and contemptible policy on the part of an insurance company that it should take the premiums and then refuse to pay upon a ground which no one says was really material. Here, upon purely technical grounds, they, having in point of fact not been deceived in any material particular, avail themselves of what seems to me the contemptible defence that, although they have taken the premiums, they are protected from paying ...

APPENDIX 4.13

Locker and Woolf Ltd v Western Australian Insurance Co Ltd [1936] 1 KB 408, CA

Slesser LJ: When the policy was originally taken out by the partnership they had to answer certain questions in a proposal form, and although the provision so often found in insurance contracts that the answers shall form part of the contract is absent in this instance, it will not be necessary to decide definitely on the relation of the proposal form to the contract, inasmuch as we are of the opinion that there has here been such a non-disclosure of material facts as to make the contract voidable at the instance of the insurance company. The proposal form contained the following questions: 'Have you ever suffered loss by fire?' To which the answer given was: 'Yes, £5. Sea.' That, we are told, refers to a loss to the extent of £5 which was paid by the Sea Insurance Company. The answer, however, showed a considerable economy of the truth, for in reality one of the partners at a previous date had a very serious loss by fire; but the loss having been incurred by one only of the partners, the arbitrator found that in answering the question whether 'you' have suffered loss it was not untrue, inasmuch as 'you,' collectively as a partnership, had not suffered loss. Whether that view is right it is unnecessary for us finally to decide in this case, but it is a very arguable point whether to the question have 'you' suffered loss by fire the answer given was justified.

Another question in the proposal form was: 'Has this or any other insurance of yours been declined by any other company?' To which the answer given was: 'No.' The arbitrator came to the conclusion that that was a false answer and was the non-disclosure of a material fact, because a policy of insurance on the motor vehicles of Locker and Woolf had been declined by the National Insurance Company of Great Britain Ltd, and the two persons being then in partnership, to the question 'Has this or any other insurance of yours been declined by any other company?' the answer given was incorrect, and the arbitrator held that it was a non-disclosure of a material fact, and it is primarily on that determination that we have reached our conclusion ...

APPENDIX 4.14

Ewer v National Employers' Mutual General Insurance Association Ltd [1937] 2 All ER 193

MacKinnon J: All these matters that it is said the plaintiff fatally failed to disclose are all claims on different subject matters, and nothing to do with these particular premises, except the one which did involve a claim in regard to these particular premises, and about which the defendant company knew everything, because it paid the loss in regard to it. The proposition is that, when effecting the original insurance, the assured is bound to disclose any claim he has ever had on any other insurance policy, and, in each yearly renewal, any claim on any other insurance policy that he has had during the previous 12 months. As regards the original effecting of the policy, it apparently goes back to the whole of his life, because, when his disclosure about Mr Smart is brought in, the matter goes back to 1912 as the earliest date. The proposition is that he must disclose any claim he has ever had on any insurance policy. For that proposition in its bald form there is no authority whatever.

I have been referred by counsel for the defendant company to certain cases which, they suggest, establish it. In my judgment, they do not do that at all. The first case to which I was referred was *Becker v Marshall* (1922) 12 Ll L Rep 413. That was a case on a fire policy, in which, as so often happens, the company had required the assured to answer certain questions, and, among those questions, were questions as regards previous fire losses, which were answered by the card. By reason of the personality of the firm or its constituent partners, the insurers were able to say that this particular firm which was proposing this insurance had had losses, and as regards that Salter J says, at p 117:

> I am satisfied that the insurers do in fact rely on the answers to the questions in the proposal form, and that they rely on them throughout, and that the contract was made upon the faith of the accuracy of these answers, and that the accuracy of the answers was a condition of each of these contracts, I have, therefore, to ask myself whether question 10 was correctly answered, and in my opinion it was. The question is one on which minds might easily differ. I think it was correctly answered.

Question 10 was whether or not there had been previous burglaries. It was a policy in favour of Becker & Wise. Becker & Wise, or one of them, had had previous burglaries, but the ambiguity of the question is what Salter J, is referring to, when he says: 'The question is one on which minds might easily differ.' The ambiguity was as to whether you, as a firm, have had previous burglaries, or have either of you, or either of the constituent partners, had previous burglaries. He said that that was ambiguous, and that, upon its true construction, it was in fact correctly answered. But then he goes on to say that, having regard to the fact that these questions had been asked, and the fact that the insurance company plainly attached importance to the question whether there had been previous burglaries, he thinks it was a fact material for the assured to disclose:

> With regard to the three burglaries, I confess that I cannot have the shadow of a doubt that these are very material matters to be known to the insurers under the circumstances of the case.

The circumstances of the case clearly are the fact that those two questions had been asked ...

All I am concerned to say is that *Becker v Marshall* is no authority for the very wide and disastrously general proposition that is contended for in this case, namely, that one who is proposing an insurance upon any subject matter must reveal the fact that he has had, during the previous course of his life, claims on other policies, and other policies of every kind ...

Those cases are cited to me as the only authorities for this proposition, which I venture to characterise as of great gravity, and, so far as I know, complete novelty, namely, that, when any assured is effecting an insurance or renewing an insurance upon some subject matter, he has to disclose, first of all, every loss that he has had on any form of policy, and, secondly, the fact that any other insurance company on any other policy has either declined to renew or refused to insure it. In regard to that, by the way, I was told by one of the gentlemen who was called as an expert that there is some subtle difference between what he was pleased to call a declinature of a policy and its refusal. If a risk has been only refused, that, he says, need not be disclosed, but, if it has been declined, then it must be disclosed. I made strenuous efforts to try to get some explanation, from him and from the other gentleman who was called, as to what was the difference between declining and refusing a risk, and I am still in a state of complete ignorance as to what the difference is. It only adds to the gravity of the task which appears to be set before the would-be assured, that he has, first of all, to understand the difference between refusing and declining a risk, and then to bear in mind that, if the risk has been refused, he need not disclose it, and if it has been declined, he must. I think that the defendant company has failed to establish that there was any concealment of material facts by the plaintiff or his brokers, Messrs Muir, Beddall & Co, in the original effecting of this policy in February 1930, or its successive renewal each February up till 1936 ...

Then there is a second, comparatively unimportant point raised in the defence. It is said that the claim which was put forward was false and fraudulent ... The result figure of £900 [for the contents of the premises] looks preposterous, because nearly all these things are claimed at the cost price of new things bought from the makers. There is no deception about that. In the list, that was put down quite clearly, and I am satisfied it was done from the catalogues of the various makers, and, where there were no catalogues, by telephoning to the makers and asking the price. That was apparent on the face of it, because, to start with, the figures given are £14 10s each less 15% trade discount. That was the new price. Of course, these things were not worth that. It was one of those cases where the view of the assured as to what he was entitled to, or would like to recover, for the things that had been burned or damaged differed very much from the view of the insurance company as to the amount the assured would eventually be entitled to recover. These things were not new; they were all second hand, but, according to the plaintiff, they were efficient, and he could use them in his business. If the law were otherwise, that might be very reasonable, but all he can recover is the reasonable value of the second-hand goods that have been destroyed. The plaintiff here has put down the cost price of new things. I do not think he was doing that as in any way a fraudulent claim, but as a possible figure to start off with, as a bargaining figure. The plaintiff knew the claim would be discussed, and probably drastically criticised, by the assessors; he had been asked for invoices, and he started the bargaining with them by putting down the cost price of these articles as if they were new. Though I admit the resulting figure is preposterously extravagant, I do not think there was any fraud in putting it forward. The result is that, in my view, the plaintiff is entitled to the declaration that he asked for, namely, that this is a valid and subsisting policy …

APPENDIX 4.15

Ayrey v British Legal and United Provident Assurance Co Ltd [1918] 1 KB 136

Lawrence J: The assured was a fisherman, and the fact was stated in the proposal form, but he was also a member of the Royal Naval Reserve and had been called up for service. That fact was not stated in the proposal form, but it was communicated to one of the agents of the defendant company at the time the proposal form was signed, and subsequently to the company's superintendent, who was also their district manager. The question is whether the omission to state this fact in the proposal form invalidates the policy. I do not think it does. I think the company must be taken to have waived any objection to the validity of the policy founded upon that omission. It is true that the proposal form contained a declaration that if any information which ought to be disclosed to the company with reference to the proposed insurance had been withheld the policy would be absolutely void, and if the fact of the assured being a member of the Royal Naval Reserve had been concealed it would have invalidated the policy.

I also agree that the district manager has no authority to make a new contract on behalf of the company, but it is not necessary, in order to hold the company liable to the plaintiff, to regard the district manager as having made a new contract. It was the duty of the district manager to supervise the company's subordinate agents, and he was the means of communication between them and the head office. The district manager was told by the plaintiff that the assured was in the Royal Naval Reserve and had been called up for service, and it was a reasonable thing for her to assume that the making of that communication to the district manager was equivalent to informing the company's head office. It was not necessary, in my opinion, that the communication should have been made direct to the head office or to the company's general manager. It is clear that the plaintiff believed that the communication to the district manager would be passed on by him to the head office, because on being told by him that the fact of the assured being in the Royal Naval Reserve was immaterial she continued to pay the premiums. The evidence of the plaintiff was uncontradicted, for the defendants called no witnesses. In my opinion the receipt of premiums by the district manager with full knowledge of the facts was a waiver by the company of the objection that there had been a concealment of a material fact. There was no new contract entered into by the district manager, but there was a waiver of the objection to the existing contract. The plaintiff was, therefore, entitled to judgment, and this appeal must be allowed.

Atkin J: I agree ... For the purpose of the operation of the principle of estoppel it must of course be shown that the company knew that the condition precedent had not been performed, and that depends on whether the knowledge of the district manager must be imputed to the company. I think it must be. I have great difficulty in seeing how an assured who desired to impart information to the company could reasonably be supposed to do so otherwise than by giving the information to the district manager. He is the person who is named on the premium card as the district manager of the company, and, in my opinion, it must be implied that the person holding that position is the person who has authority to receive on behalf of the company information as to all matters affecting a policy issued by the company, and that it was his duty to pass on to the company such information as he might receive. I think, therefore, that the knowledge of the district manager that there had been a breach of a condition by reason of the concealment of a material fact was the knowledge of the company. The remaining question to be considered is whether the company led the plaintiff to believe that they did not intend to treat the contract as at an end. In my opinion, nothing could have been more likely to induce that belief in the mind of the plaintiff than the fact that the district manager to whom she had disclosed the facts which showed that the conditions of the proposal form had not been complied with continued to receive payment of the premiums from her week by week for a period of at least 18 months …

APPENDIX 4.16

Malhi v Abbey Life Assurance Co Ltd [1996] LRLR 237, CA

Rose LJ: Accordingly, I agree with Miss Belson that *Evans v Employers' Mutual* [1936] KB 505 is the most closely relevant of her authorities. I am unable to accept, however, that that case is authority for the proposition that the defendants in the present case should have imputed to them knowledge of the contents of all the documents in their records in relation to insurance business proposed by the deceased, regardless of when, to whom and in what circumstances those documents were supplied.

In my judgment, the provision of information to an insurance company does not necessarily afford to that company knowledge sufficient to found waiver by election: whether it does afford such knowledge depends on the circumstances of its receipt and how it is dealt with thereafter. In particular, information will not give rise to such knowledge unless it is received by a person authorised and able to appreciate its significance. In the present case that necessarily involved the correlation of information received by the defendants at three different times for three different purposes ...

... In my judgment, the principal *ratio* of *Evans v Employers' Mutual Insurance Association Ltd*, to be found in all three judgments, is that Mitchell's knowledge was to be imputed to the company because he had the duty of comparing the documents and did so. A second *ratio*, in the judgments of Lords Justices Greer and Roche is that the company could not be heard to say that it did not know the information in the claim and proposal forms which they had invited and which had been communicated to them in the manner invited. The first *ratio* is pertinent in the present case. The sub-underwriter with the duty to compare did so. In relation to the second *ratio*, it is to be noted that the facts of the present case are very different. Information here was contained in a proposal for a life policy in 1984, a health declaration in 1985 and a proposal for a different policy in 1986. The judge found on the evidence before him that no comparison of these documents was properly to be expected at the time of, or in relation to, the 1986 proposal. Significantly, as in *Evans v Employers' Mutual Insurance Association Ltd*, such a comparison was first made when in 1988, a claim was made ...

McCowan LJ (dissenting): I fail to see why the information ... was not in the knowledge of the company in September 1986, every bit as much as in May 1988 when the company used that knowledge to repudiate the policy. here is no question at either date of the information having been forgotten or lost ...

APPENDIX 4.17

Bowyer, LM, 'The Insurance Claims and Underwriting Exchange and the duty of disclosure' (1995) 89 BILA Jo 45

Insurance companies have finally begun to utilise information technology in the fight against fraud. The Claims and Underwriting Exchange (CUE) is provided by Equifax on behalf of Insurance Database Services Ltd to household insurers.

The system, which went on-line at the end of November last year (1994) enables insurers to sift through past claims records of other insurers to check for any duplicate payments made to policy holders. This may occur where the insured in question has taken out other insurance on the goods and then in the event of a loss claimed on both policies without notification to either insurer of the other policy. Whilst the law allows multiple cover, provided that obligations as to notification are met, multiple claims for the same loss are not. This is in line with the principle of indemnity, whereby, under typical contracts of insurance the insured must be fully indemnified but never more than fully indemnified. In addition, insurance companies usually require proposers to declare whether the goods in question are already insured elsewhere when they fill in the proposal form. Any concealment of such a fact may suggest fraudulent intention, whereby the insurance is taken out with a view to making a future claim, as opposed to merely transferring the risk to the insurer for a period.

Insurance companies have opened up their records to this national database with a view to avoiding payment of fraudulent claims and also to act as a deterrent to such in the future. In addition, insurers may also have the opportunity to reopen settled claims through retrospective searching on CUE. To carry out this type of search insurers would have to obtain the consent of the insured. In practice, it is unlikely that insurers will engage in such activity, partly because of the bad publicity it would attract and also because of the problems in recovering the monies paid.

The Association of British Insurers (ABI) issued a document to is members entitled, 'The CUE Code' which sets out the type of notices to be added to the proposal form, claim form, and renewal form. Below is the notice to be incorporated into proposal forms:

> Insurers and their agents share information with each other to prevent fraudulent claims and for underwriting purposes via the Claims and Underwriting Exchange register, operated by Insurance Database Services Ltd A list of participants is available on request. In dealing with your application this register may be searched. In the event of a claim, the information relating to the claim, will be put on the register and made available to participants.

Another system to cover motor policies will be set up ... and the customer development manager of Equifax is reported as estimating that, by the end of 1995, CUE will cover more than 60% of the motor market and 80% of the household ...

However, while insurance companies are without doubt set to gain from the use of CUE by avoiding fraudulent claims, and one hopes that this will be reflected by lower premiums being imposed on honest policyholders, there are other aspects to consider. It may be that the advantages of such a system are matched by implications for insurers at the underwriting stage and beyond. An underwriting manager for personal insurances was reported as saying: 'We may have to search every proposal – or possibly lose the right to ask questions subsequently. But, overall, I believe the benefits of CUE will outweigh its disadvantages.' It had already been acknowledged by some that insurers may face problems in denying claims on the basis of information revealed on the database if such information was not utilised when the policy was effected. Former Insurance Ombudsman Dr Julian Farrand had warned that he did not want to see underwriting at the claims stage.

The question asked in this paper is to what extent does the information revealed to insurers on CUE affect the legal rights of the parties to a contract of insurance ...?

If the underwriter has used, or indeed should have used CUE, does this have any effect on the insured's duties, in particular that of disclosure and secondly are additional obligations imposed on the insurers?

As regards the first issue, there appears to be plenty of scope for a defence based on estoppel to prevent the insurer from relying on the non-disclosure or misrepresentation when a claim is made, if having been aware of the material facts when the policy was proposed they still accepted it. The argument is that the silence of the insurer at the underwriting stage is a representation that the details revealed on CUE which contradict or add to those provided on the proposal form will not be used against the insured in the event of a claim. Of course, such a claim would only succeed where the insurer has notified the proposer that CUE will be utilised so that the reliance element is satisfied.

In addition, in the light of the *dicta* of the Court of Appeal in *Malhi v Abbey Life Assurance Co Ltd* [1996] LRLR 237 there may be room for an argument based on imputed or constructive knowledge coupled with subsequent waiver to use against an insurance company which attempts to rely on a misrepresentation or non-disclosure ...

Surely, with the provision of CUE and the use of IT in general to document company records, insurance companies will find themselves in a position whereby it could be regarded as very easy for them to check such details, thus giving rise to imputed or constructive knowledge of the material facts. A subsequent acceptance of the policy would then amount to a waiver of the non-disclosure.

This submission appears more acceptable to the situation created by CUE than that which existed in the Malhi case. In that case, the acquisition of imputed or constructive knowledge, if such had been established, happened some time after the policy was effected. At that point the insurer had the option of avoiding the policy but it is difficult to appreciate how their inaction could affect the formation of the contract that took place in 1984 and 1985. With the introduction of CUE, the acquisition of knowledge would have or should have occurred at the proposal stage, with the subsequent waiver by acceptance of the policy resulting in a valid contract, at least to the extent that the insurer would be unable to avoid for non-disclosure of the material facts revealed on CUE. The employment of CUE at the underwriting stage is therefore important to this argument. Finally, it should be noted that the *Malhi* case involved a life policy. Life policies once effected do not require renewal like other types of policies. Therefore, if CUE is utilised on renewal, the decision in the *Malhi* case should not prevent a claim of imputed or constructive knowledge, followed by waiver of any concealment ...

Moving onto the second issue, what effect do the facilities offered by CUE have on the obligations of the insurer?

It is recognised that the duty of disclosure applies to both the insurer and the insured and perhaps the information revealed on CUE will be construed as material facts which the insurers should disclose to the proposer.

The insured may benefit to know that having misrepresented or not disclosed claims made in the past, assuming this is unaffected by the suggestions made above, then the policy may be repudiated before, at the time or after a loss has occurred. Also, alongside data on previous claims which is deliberately sought, it may become apparent that the proposer has already insured the risk for which it now seeks cover. Should the concealment be fraudulent then the insured will not even be entitled to a return of the premiums paid ...

Even in the event of establishing that insurers have a duty to disclose details discovered on CUE, as the remedy for non-disclosure is avoidance or repudiation of the contract, the advantages of breach may only be open to the insurer, the only possible benefit to the insured of repudiation, being the return of the premium. However, if the remedy of damages were available the position would be quite different in that policyholders would become as active as the insurers in bringing an action for non-disclosure. Of course, it would not be as simple for the insured as it is for the insurance company, in that the latter merely refuse to pay the claims and wait for the insured to challenge that ...

APPENDIX 4.18

Roberts v Avon Insurance Co Ltd [1956] 2 Lloyd's Rep 240

... Declaration made by plaintiff in proposal form that:

(10) I have never sustained a loss in respect of any of the contingencies specified in this proposal except ...

NOTE – Give date, amount and name of insurers in respect of such loss.

(11) This declaration shall be the basis of the contract between me and the [defendants] whose policy subject to the terms and conditions thereof I am willing to accept ...

Conditions of policy providing (*inter alia*):

(6) This policy will be rendered void in the event of:

(a) any omission of a material fact or suppression misrepresentation or misstatement of any fact in the said proposal form notwithstanding that the fact omitted suppressed misrepresented or misstated may be disclosed rightly represented or rightly stated to any agent or agents of the company whether verbally or in writing;

(b) any misrepresentation or fraud committed in making or supporting any claim hereunder ...

Declaration No 10 in proposal from was left unanswered ...

Barry J: Looking at the matter in what I hope is a fair and reasonable way, I think there is really no ambiguity about this sentence 'in respect of any of the contingencies specified in this proposal'. I think it is clear that there are no contingencies expressed on the particular p on which the assured makes his declaration, but there are, of course, a very large number of contingencies referred to in the remainder of the document. I think that the meaning which any ordinary person would attribute to those words, and, indeed, the only reasonable interpretation that can be placed upon them, is that 'the contingencies specified in this proposal' means the risks, or events which may occur in the nature of those risks and perils, referred to in the document as a whole, and I am quite satisfied that any ordinary reasonable person reading that sentence would have no difficulty in reaching the conclusion that by this part of the declaration, namely, declaration No 10, he was required to disclose any previous losses from the type of peril, or perils, covered by the policy and described in the remaining portions of the document to which he was putting his signature.

In those circumstances, I do not think that there is any real ambiguity in the language used, and, assuming, as I must, that Mr Roberts is a reasonable person, capable of understanding the English language, I cannot find that he would have any difficulty in ascertaining from this paragraph the type of information required by the insurance company. He had had previous insurance experience and, as I have already pointed out, his application form to the Cornhill Insurance Company, in April 1948, contained a request – couched, it is true, in somewhat different language -which made it obvious that at that time, at least, it was desired to know the previous history of the assured with regard to losses from the perils in respect of which they were being asked to insure …

Perhaps the most formidable portion of Mr Platts-Mills's argument on this branch of the case was directed to the final words, or the final word, in this paragraph of the declaration, and the blank lines which follow. The declaration reads: 'I have never sustained a loss in respect of any of the contingencies specified in this proposal except,' and there are two blank lines, and, below, a note: 'Give date, amount and name of insurers in respect of each loss.'

The argument runs thus: the blank lines following the word 'except' have clearly been left blank; in those circumstances, says Mr Platts-Mills, the word 'except' not having been deleted, the proposed assured is stating quite definitely that there is an exception, an unspecified exception, to his declaration that he has never sustained a loss in respect of any of the contingencies specified in the proposal, and, with that unspecified exception, his contention is that the insurers are put upon inquiry, and if they fail to elicit further information from the applicant – in this case from the plaintiff – they cannot be heard to say that a false declaration in the proposal form has in fact been made. His submission is that the declaration was correct though incomplete …

Ingenious though that argument undoubtedly is, I am satisfied that it does not truly represent the meaning of the declaration made by the plaintiff in this case. I agree with Mr Mattar when he suggests that the inference to be drawn from leaving blank the two lines provided for the purpose of stating any exception can, to any reasonable applicant and to any reasonable insurer, have only one meaning, namely, that no exception exists …

It seems to me perfectly clear that any applicant for insurance, completing this form, would appreciate without any doubt or ambiguity that the insurers required particulars of any previous loss in respect of contingencies specified to be set out on the two blank lines left for that purpose, with the date, amount and the name of the insurers who were concerned in respect of each of those losses.

If that information is clearly required, it seems to me that the only inference, and the obvious inference, is that the applicant intended the blank lines to represent what I think has been described as a negative answer. As this statement is in a declaration, the obvious inference to be drawn from the applicant leaving those lines blank is that there was in fact no exception to his categoric statement that he has never sustained any loss in respect of any of the contingencies specified. I think that to give effect to Mr Platts-Mills's argument would be introducing far too great a refinement into business documents of this kind, and one which is really quite unrelated to the common sense of the situation.

I fully appreciate, and indeed I am not only bound by but would desire to follow, all those decisions cited to me where the dangers of ambiguous questions put by insurance companies in proposal forms have been the subject matter of judicial comment. Clearly, it is the duty of a company to make abundantly plain to those seeking insurance what information they do in fact require, but here, as I have said, looking at the matter from a reasonable business point of view, I think that the present defendants have made clear from this proposal that they do wish to know what are the losses the applicant has suffered in respect of any of the perils against which they are being asked to insure, and the applicant is expected to give particulars – the date, amount and the name of the insurers – in respect of each of those losses.

That, I think is quite obvious from this proposal form, and in my judgment an applicant who signs the declaration leaving those lines at the end of declaration No 10 blank is quite clearly intimating to the insurers that there is no exception to the generalities of his declaration in respect of previous losses …

One always has sympathy with an assured person who, having paid his premium and sustained a loss, then finds that his insurers refuse to grant him the indemnity to which he thought he was entitled under the terms of his policy. In the present case my natural regret at reaching that finding is somewhat tempered by the fact that, although there is no evidence to that effect, it is, as I have already indicated, very well known in insurance cases that particulars of previous losses are always required, by insurers before they undertake any particular risk …

APPENDIX 4.19

Horry v Tate and Lyle Refineries Ltd [1982] 2 Lloyd's Rep 416

Peter Pain J: So far as this case goes, I find that the plaintiff did rely on the guidance or advice of the Iron Trades as to the settlement of his claim. I find that the insurers knew that he so relied, and I find – this is perhaps almost a glimpse of the obvious – that they had an interest in the figure at which the claim was settled, and their interest conflicted with the plaintiff's interest.

Further, I find here that there was a quality of confidence between the plaintiff and the insurers, which extended beyond that inherent in the confidence that can well exist between trustworthy persons who in business affairs deal with each other at arm's length.

The relationship existed, of course, between the plaintiff and the Iron Trades, not between the plaintiff and Mr Oram personally, although, of course, Mr Oram was closely involved, because he was the agent through whom the Iron Trades acted.

On this basis, there was in my view a duty of fiduciary care lying upon the Iron Trades. They might have discharged that duty as late as January 28, if Mr Oram had said to the plaintiff: 'Look here, you really ought to get some independent advice about this before you settle.' But, that not having been done, in my view it was incumbent on the Iron Trades to have offered a figure which was considerably higher and towards the upper part of the bracket appropriate to hernia claims, in view of the severity of the hernia in this case.

Secondly, it was their duty to specify what reduction they were making which was inherent in their offer in respect of contributory negligence; that is to say, they should have made it clear what they thought the claim was worth *in toto* and how much they were deducting in respect of the plaintiff's contributory negligence. That could have been done of course, either by way of percentage or by way of figures.

I think that they should have supplied the plaintiff with a copy of the medical report which was provided by his doctor. It is all very well to read a report out to someone in an interview, but if he had got it to read it over and consider himself it makes a great deal more of an impression on the mind. Mr Oram told me that it was company policy not to hand such a document over to a claimant in person, although it would have been disclosed had the plaintiff been legally represented. The company policy to my mind provides no answer here. There is nothing whatever in this report which the plaintiff should not have seen and there seems to me to have been no good grounds for not giving him an opportunity to see exactly what the doctor said before he settled. I dare say that there was a fairly substantial reading of the report, but that is not sufficient.

Fourthly, they should have made sure that the plaintiff understood that this settlement, if entered into, was the end of the road and that no further claim could be made in respect of this accident, and in view of the fact that the risk of recurrence at 15%, was by no means insubstantial, they should have made sure that he understood that and that nothing further could be taken up if the injury did recur. As to that, as I have already said, I think they left the plaintiff in a state of considerable confusion.

Finally, I take the view that they should have advised the plaintiff to think the matter over and to delay until he had had an opportunity of testing himself back at work and had had a proper opportunity of considering the offer. I hold that the defendants were in breach of their duty of fiduciary care, in that they did none of these things and that therefore, in my view, they are no entitled to rely upon the settlement, or the alleged settlement of the plaintiff's claim.

In saying this, I ought to make it plain that I do not regard Mr Oram as someone who is morally to blame, as having overreached a simple man. He was a claims inspector settling a claim, but I think he failed to appreciate that if he encouraged a layman to act without independent advice, then he, Mr Oram put himself in a position quite different from the position he was in, in the ordinary way, when he is negotiating a claim with a man's trade union or solicitor.

I also want to say that I am not seeking to lay down any general principle with regard to insurance companies and claimants who act for themselves. The insurance company which encourages a layman with no legal knowledge to act for himself without advice clearly puts itself in a position of risk; but the decision I am giving is simply an exercise in applying the principles of *Lloyds Bank Ltd v Bundy* [1975] QB 326, as set out in Sir Eric Sach's judgment, to the facts of the present case.

In view of that finding, it is not strictly necessary for me to deal with the second question, but I think in defence to the arguments addressed to me I ought to do so. The second question is: did Mr Oram misrepresent to the plaintiff the nature and effect of the contract of settlement and was the plaintiff induced to enter into it by such misrepresentation? The word 'misrepresentation' has a nasty ring about it, but of course, I am here considering an innocent misrepresentation. What I have had some doubt about is whether Mr Oram's poor explanation causing a misunderstanding in the plaintiff ought properly to be regarded as a misrepresentation; but when I look at the way Lord Justice Denning dealt with matters in the case of *Curtis v The Chemical Cleaning and Dyeing Co Ltd* [1951] 1 KB 805, his judgment being at p 808, he said:

> In my opinion, any behaviour by words or conduct is sufficient to be a misrepresentation if it is such as to mislead the other party about the existence or extent of the exemption. If it conveys a false impression, that is enough. If the false impression is created knowingly, it is a fraudulent misrepresentation. If it is created unwittingly, it is an innocent misrepresentation; but either is sufficient to disentitle the creator of it to the benefit of the exemption.

Applying that to the present case, I hold that there was a misrepresentation by Mr Oram as to the nature and effect of the contract for settlement. However, that is not the end of the matter, because it has to be shown that that misrepresentation induced the plaintiff to enter into the settlement ...

On the evidence of Mr Oram, it clearly was an inducive act, because the whole point of making the confusing remarks which he made was to deal with what the position would be if there was a recurrence and to explain what the plaintiff's position would be ...

If there had been no question of undue influence and this matter had stood on its own, I feel that I would have come to the conclusion that there was a misrepresentation here as to the nature and effect of the settlement and that that misrepresentation was one of the factors that induced the plaintiff to enter into it; but I would have reached that conclusion, I am bound to confess, with some doubt. I find it much more satisfactory to put my decision as I have done, primarily, on the basis that there was here undue influence because of the Iron Trades' breach of the duty of fiduciary care ...

APPENDIX 4.20

La Banque Financière de la Cité v Westgate Insurance Co Ltd [1990] 2 Lloyd's Rep 377, HL

Lord Templeman: The proceedings before Mr Justice Steyn endured for 38 days ...

The appeal occupied 23 days before the Court of Appeal; 51 authorities are cited in the judgment of Lord Justice Slade, 74 additional authorities were cited in argument. A further 32 authorities were referred to in Counsel's skeleton arguments submitted in writing to the court. The grand total of 157 authorities appear in the report of the Court of Appeal judgment ...

Kusa submit that Hodge, as insurers, owed the banks, as the assured, a common law duty of care in negligence. Kusa also submit that Hodge, as insurers, owed the banks, as the assured, a duty of utmost good faith. Kusa assert that Hodge through their employee, Mr Dungate, committed a breach of the duties owed to the banks and continued in breach at all times after May, 1980 when he discovered but failed to disclose to the banks his knowledge that Mr Lee had issued fraudulent cover notes in January, 1980 ...

It would be strange if in these circumstances one party to a contract owed a duty in negligence to the other party, to warn the other party of his suspicions of former misconduct by the agent of that other party; it would be stranger still if the party who failed to disclose his suspicions were liable in damages for the misconduct of the agent thereafter. I am talking now about liability in law. Hodge, a firm of reputable insurers, might have thought it right to inform Notcutts of the suspicions which their employee, Mr Lee, had aroused. In the absence of a reasonable explanation, Hodge might have declined to have any dealings with Mr Lee. Notcutts, a reputable firm of insurance brokers, would no doubt have investigated any suspicions reported to them by Hodge and dismissed Mr Lee if those suspicions proved well founded. The judge held that Hodge were and Notcutts would have been under a legal duty to report the misconduct of Mr Lee to the banks even if that misconduct had been remedied by the completion of the first and second excess layers and even if Mr Lee had been dismissed from the employment of Notcutts. I do not agree. A professional should wear a halo, but need not wear a hair shirt.

No authority was cited for the proposition that a negotiating party owed a duty to disclose to the opposite party information that the agent of the opposite party had committed a breach of the duty he owed to his principal in an earlier transaction. The party possessing the information will no longer himself trust the agent and may refuse to deal with the agent. The party possessing the information must not himself become involved with any misconduct by the agent and the courts will naturally consider whether he is or has become involved. Subject to these reservations, a duty to disclose sounding in damages for breach would give rise to great difficulties. The information may be unreliable or doubtful or inconclusive. Disclosure may expose the informer to criticism or litigation ...

It would be strange if a breach of duty by Mr Dungate in failing to disclose the fraud of Mr Lee enabled the banks to claim damages which they would have been unable to recover if Mr Lee had not been fraudulent. It would be strange if the silence of Mr Dungate in failing to warn the banks that Mr Lee could not be relied upon to effect the third excess layer insurance enabled the banks to claim damages which they would not have been able to recover if the insurance had been effected. It would be strange if the banks, which as against Hodge, had, by the terms of the insurance policies, agreed to bear the risk of fraud by Mr Ballestero were enabled by Mr Dungate's silence recover from Hodge the loss suffered by banks as a result of the fraud by Mr Ballestero ...

The advance would have been lost whether the advance was insured or not because the banks had accepted and paid a premium for insurance which contained a fraud exemption clause. The fraud of Mr Ballestero caused the loss of the advance and caused the rejection by the insurers of any claim under the policy. The fraud of Mr Ballestero which caused the loss of the advance and the rejection of the claims under the insurance policies was, as the judge found, not foreseeable. The fraud of Mr Lee which caused the advance to be made did not affect the rights of the banks to recover their loss and therefore did not cause the loss of the advance. The policies of insurance did not or would not have protected the banks against the fraud of Mr Ballestero and his fraud was causative of the loss of the advance. Accordingly the failure by Mr Dungate to inform the banks of the fraud of Mr Lee was not causative of the bank's loss ...

In the circumstances, it is not necessary to consider whether Hodge were under a duty to disclose the misconduct of Mr Lee by reason of the obligation of an insurer to deal with the proposer of insurance with the utmost good faith. If Hodge were in breach of that duty no damage flowed from the breach for the reasons I have already given. But it may be helpful to observe that I agree with the Court of Appeal that a breach of the obligation does not sound in damages. The only remedy open to the insured is to rescind the policy and recover the premium. The authorities cited and the cogent reasons advanced by Lord Justice Slade are to be found in the report of the proceedings in the Court of Appeal, *Banque Keyser Ullmann SA v Skandia (UK) Insurance Co Ltd* [1988] 2 Lloyd's Rep 514 ...

Lord Jauncey of Tullichettle: What is said in this appeal is that when Dungate discovered in early June, 1980 that Lee had issued fraudulent cover notes in January of that year he, as insurer, came under a duty to disclose this fact to the banks. I do not consider that the obligation of disclosure extends to such a matter. Although there have been no reported cases involving the failure of an insurer to disclose material facts to an insured the example given by Lord Mansfield in *Carter v Boehm* (1766) 3 Burr 1905 is of an insurer who insured a ship for a voyage knowing that she had already arrived. Another example would be the insurance against fire of a house which the insurer knew had been demolished. In these cases, the undisclosed information would have had a material and direct effect upon the risk against which the insured was seeking to protect himself. Indeed, the insured would have said that the risk no longer existed. In the present case, the risk to be insured was the inability, otherwise than by reason of fraud, of Ballestero and his companies to repay the loan to the banks. Lee's dishonesty neither increased nor decreased that risk. Indeed it was irrelevant thereto. It follows that the obligation of disclosure incumbent upon Dungate, as the insurer, did not extend to telling the banks that their agent Lee was dishonest. If the obligation of disclosure incumbent upon parties to a contract of insurance could ever *per se* create the necessary proximity to give rise to a duty of care, a matter upon which I reserve my opinion, it is clear that the scope of any such duty would not extend to the disclosure of facts which are not material to the risk insured. It follows that the appellants' reliance on the duty of disclosure does not assist them to establish negligence on the part of Dungate.

APPENDIX 4.21

Trindade, F, 'The *Skandia* case in the House of Lords' (1991) 107 LQR 24

... In relation to the action based on the principle of *uberrima fides*, the House of Lords has now clearly indicated that the obligation of the utmost good faith, at least in an insurance context, is reciprocal and owed therefore both by the insured and the insurer to each other. This is bound to be of some significance for the future as counsel explore the scope of the duties which might be owed by *insurers* to their insured. The House of Lords has also clearly endorsed the view of the Court of Appeal that a breach of the obligation of the utmost good faith does not sound in damages. There does not appear to be, however, clear agreement among their Lordships on the ambit of the duty of the utmost good faith. Lord Bridge ... expresses his agreement with the view of the Court of Appeal that the duty falling upon the insurer:

> ... must at least extend to disclosing all facts known to him which are material either to the nature of the risk sought to be covered or the recoverability of a claim under the policy which a prudent insured would take into account in deciding whether or not to place the risk for which he seeks cover with the insurer': [1990] ...

But Lord Jauncey appears to confine the ambit of the duty to disclose only to those facts:

> ... which are material to the risk insured, that is to say, facts which would influence a prudent insurer in deciding whether to accept the risk and, if so, upon what terms and a prudent insured would take into account in deciding whether or not to place the risk for which he seeks cover with the insurer ...

As Lord Brandon and Lord Ackner express their agreement with the speeches of both Lord Bridge and Lord Jauncey it is difficult to state the ambit of the duty of the utmost good faith, in the insurance context, with any degree of confidence, particularly as Lord Templeman does not appear to advert to the duty or its ambit at all ...

... The complexity of this case is matched only by the incongruities occasioned by it. First, Ballestero and his fraudulent associates were not parties to this complex litigation. Secondly, the action against the dishonest Lee for fraud, which was left for subsequent adjudication, will now certainly fail. If, as the House of Lords has held, Ballestero's fraud is the *only* cause of the loss then Lee's fraud cannot have caused the banks any loss for which they could successfully sue him. Thirdly, Notcutts (the reputable brokers) and their insurers, who paid the banks £10.5 m by way of settlement, must be wondering why they did so if, as the House of Lords has held, the only cause of the banks' loss, was Ballestero's fraud and not the dishonest conduct of Lee, one of Notcutt's employees ...

APPENDIX 4.22

Fleming, J, 'Insurer's breach of good faith – a new tort?' (1992) 108 LQR 357

With admirable open mindedness, Badgery-Parker J of the New South Wales Supreme Court has refused to dismiss summarily a claim of damages for an insurer's breach of good faith in processing and paying the plaintiff's workers' compensation claim: *Gibson v The Parkes District Hospital* [1991] Austr Torts Rep 81–140. Despite the absence of any English or Australian authority for such a cause of action in tort, he sought comfort in the sterling declaration by Glass JA on an earlier occasion that 'it is no longer appropriate to react with outraged dignity when a litigant propounds a novel theory judiciously constructed from elements of received doctrine' (*Champtaloup v Thomas* [1976] 2 NSWLR 264, p 271).

It is now well settled that the duty of good faith implicit in the insurance relation is mutual, binding insurer and insured alike. While the insured's duty to disclose relevant information has in the past received most attention, it was only recently confirmed by the House of Lords that a reciprocal duty rested on the insurer, for example, to share its knowledge of an agent's fraud practised on the prospective insured (*Banque Keyser Ullmann SA v Skandia (UK) Insurance Co Ltd*, below). However, the remedy has been assumed to be limited to rescission, not damages.

In the United States, breach of good faith has long attained a measure of legitimacy as a tort in the context, at least, of insurance. This development has been largely played out in California, although it is by no means confined to that state. Determined to play a part in discouraging the notorious dilatory and obstructive practices of the insurance industry in handling consumer claims, the courts decided to allow damages for mental distress, besides economic loss, as an appropriate corrective. These had perforce to sound in tort in order to sidestep the statutory limitation of damages for non-pecuniary losses to tort claims. This reductionist argument could be reinforced by the strong connotation of bad faith with tort. Later, punitive damages were added on additional proof of malice, which came to include conscious indifference to the plaintiff's rights. But the most profound impact on American tort practices resulted from the extension of the doctrine from first to third party claims. Failure by the tortfeasor's liability insurer to accept a fair settlement offer within policy limits (which are often very low) would, in case of a later award in excess of those limits, result in exposing the insured to excess liability; the tort defendant's claim against his own insurer could then be assigned to the plaintiff so as to enable him to recover the whole of his award from the insurer notwithstanding the policy limits. It has since become routine for the plaintiff's lawyer to send the defendant's insurer a letter warning against the risk of excess liability in case of refusal to accept the plaintiff's offer. (See Fleming, J, *The American Tort Process*, 1988, pp 181–86.)

Badgery-Parker J was much impressed by the American recognition of the tort. Unknown to him, however, its extension to other than insurance contracts was halted, indeed rolled back when the California court refused to apply it to wrongful dismissal, let alone to bad faith breach of any other contract (*Foley v Interactive Data Corporation* 47

Cal 3d 654 (1988); see (1990) 106 LQR 8). Its reasons for confining the action to insurance cases are revealing. We are not here concerned, the court said, with the implied covenant of good faith and fair dealing as a matter of general contract law, but with an exceptional departure to protect a 'general public policy interest not directly tied to the contract's purposes'. In three respects, the 'special relationship' of insurance fails to provide an analogous model for employment. First, breach does not place the employee in the same economic dilemma as it does to the insured, inasmuch as the employee can seek alternative employment, while the insured cannot find another insurance company to pay for his past loss. Secondly, the 'quasi-public' insurance company sells protection against the very loss, which the employer does not. Finally, in the insurance relationship the parties are financially at odds, in contrast to employment where the respective interests are usually aligned ...

... But what of *Banque Keyser Ullmann SA v Skandia (UK) Insurance Co Ltd* [1990] 1 QB 665; [1991] 2 AC 249? In that painful litigation, in so far as relevant here, Steyn J had held the insurer liable to the bank both for negligence and breach of the duty *uberrima fides* for failing to disclose the fraud of the plaintiff's agent. The Court of Appeal held the defendant not liable for negligence but liable for breach of their duty of good faith; it dismissed the claim however on the ground that the breach did not sound in damages. (See Trindade (1989) 105 LQR 191.) The House of Lords affirmed on the different ground that the breach of that duty had not caused the loss (criticised by Trindade (1991) 107 LQR 24 [Appendix 4.21, above]), but also *en passant* endorsed the conclusion of the Court of Appeal that the only remedy for breach of the duty of good faith was to rescind the policy and recover the premium ... But on closer reading it appears that Slade LJ's reasons for denying damages were focused on and germane only to a duty to disclose ... It is certainly arguable therefore that they did not preclude a tort duty such as that postulated in the instant case. Besides, of course, their endorsement by the House of Lords was clearly *dictum*. Badgery-Parker J, while noting the *Skandia* case, did not attempt to come to terms with it beyond reiterating that, in his and the American view, the duty did not rest on an implied term but was a 'true tort duty' ...

APPENDIX 4.23

Diamond, A (QC), 'The law of marine insurance – has it a future?' [1986] LMCLQ 25

1 NON-DISCLOSURE

The relevant law was formulated in the 18th century. The first important case on the subject, which remains one of the great leading cases on non-disclosure today, is the judgment of Lord Mansfield in *Carter v Boehm* (1766) 3 Burr 1905 in 1766. For present purposes, however, it is sufficient to take the law from the Act of 1906. The relevant provisions of the Act have recently been considered and construed by the Court of Appeal in the case of *CTI v Oceanus* [1984] 1 Lloyd's Rep 476, in a decision handed down in February 1984. This decision, which will not go to the House of Lords, has been met with almost universal concern and disappointment.

The Act provides that, with one or two exceptions, the assured must disclose to the insurer, before the contract is concluded, every material circumstance which is known to the assured. A circumstance is material if it would influence the judgment of a prudent insurer in fixing the premium or in determining whether he will take the risk. If the assured fails to make such disclosure, the insurer may avoid the contract.

Now this duty of disclosure exists, as everyone knows, because the relevant facts pertaining to any proposed insurance are in the knowledge of only one of the two parties to the insurance, the assured, and because the insurer might be misled in estimating the risk if he were not told of those facts before he made up his mind. So far, so good. It is possible for everyone to agree, at least, that the assured should not misrepresent material facts. Perhaps many would go further and agree that some duty of disclosure is called for.

The question then arises: 'What duty of disclosure?' The answer one might have expected is that the duty extends to not misleading the insurer so that he is induced to write the risk when he would not otherwise have written it, or so that he is induced to fix a lower premium instead of a higher premium. Even then many would be perplexed as to what the consequences of an innocent non-disclosure ought to be.

What do we find when we look at the relevant law as declared by the Court of Appeal? We find three somewhat disconcerting features:

(i) the concept of the 'prudent insurer';

(ii) the word 'influence';

(iii) the difficulty of distinguishing between material facts and all facts.

(i) The 'prudent insurer'

The person who has to be considered, say the Court of Appeal, is the hypothetical prudent insurer and no one else. Now the common law is quite accustomed to judging conduct by the standards of the reasonable man. The reasonable man exists even if he is to be found nowhere in particular, not even these days on an omnibus in Clapham. But, in connection with the duty of disclosure, it may not be sufficient for the assured to act as a reasonable man would act in his position and to disclose those facts which a reasonable assured would think it right to disclose. Nor is it even necessarily sufficient to disclose all facts that the actual underwriter would wish to know about before making up his mind. The assured may have to go further and disclose all facts that a prudent underwriter would wish to know about.

This test present some difficulty to the assured because he may not know what facts would influence the judgment of a prudent insurer and thus, through ignorance, he may fail in his duty of disclosure. But let us put this difficulty, important as it is, on one side for the moment. Suppose that you or I, as reasonable prospective assureds, were to go in search of the prudent insurer. He is to be found, if anywhere at all, in the Room at Lloyd's. So let us suppose that you or I were to go to Lime Street and were somehow lucky enough to be permitted to enter the Room and, having brought the business of insurance to a standstill, suppose we were to interrogate the working underwriters, or at least those of them that write marine business and are thus subject to the Act of 1906. What would we find if we began to ask a few questions? Surely we would find many prudent underwriters. But also, in all probability, even in that ancient institution, we would find some who are not prudent at all. And even the great majority who are without question prudent underwriters, would tell us, if we persisted in our questioning, that there are occasions when they simply cannot afford to be prudent. For example, one might say that he cannot afford not to write a fixed line on every risk presented by a certain broker; otherwise he would never see that broker again. Or another might tell us that he has on occasion to write 'loss leaders' knowing that the business will be unprofitable and in the hope of getting an entrée into a particular line of business in the future.

Should an underwriter who is not a prudent underwriter at all, or one who is not acting as a prudent underwriter when a particular risk is written, should he be entitled to complain of non-disclosure, when a claim arises, if he would not in fact have been influenced in any way by fact had it been disclosed? This question was considered by Mr Justice Kerr 12 years ago, in 1973, in *Berger v Pollock* [1973] 2 Lloyd's Rep 442. That judge regarded it as an 'absurd position' that the defendant underwriter could avoid the policy if he would not have been influenced by the undisclosed fact but the hypothetical prudent underwriter would have been so influenced. Unfortunately, however, the same judge, Lord Justice Kerr, as he now is, in the recent *CTI* case said he was wrong in the earlier case and his colleagues agreed. Who are we to compare his first thoughts with his second? If I had to venture an opinion, however, I have to say that I prefer the judgment of Mr Justice Kerr to that of Lord Justice Kerr. Surely it would be a fraud on the assured for an underwriter, who is more interested in collecting premium income than assessing a risk, to rely on non-disclosure simply because the prudent underwriter (which in this example he is not) would have wished to know about a certain fact before making up his mind ...

[Note: The author's view in this last paragraph has been endorsed by the House of Lords in the *Pan Atlantic* decision (see below).]

APPENDIX 4.24

Pan Atlantic Insurance Co Ltd and Another v Pine Top Insurance Co Ltd [1994] 3 All ER 581, HL

Lord Mustill:

THE QUESTIONS OF LAW

On these facts, two questions of law arise for decision:

(1) Where ss 18(2) and 20(2) of the 1906 Act relate the rest of materiality to a circumstance 'which would influence the judgment of a prudent underwriter in fixing the premium, or determining whether he will take the risk,' must it be shown that full and accurate disclosure would have led the prudent underwriter to a different decision on accepting or rating the risk; or is a lesser standard of impact on the mind of the prudent underwriter sufficient; and, if so, what is that lesser standard?

(2) Is the establishment of a material misrepresentation or non-disclosure sufficient to enable the underwriter to avoid the policy; or is it also necessary that the misrepresentation or non-disclosure has induced the making of the policy, either at all or on the terms on which it is made? If the latter, where lies the burden of proof? ...

CRITICISMS OF THE *CTI* CASE

In substance, this is an appeal against the decision in the *CTI* case [1984] 1 Lloyd's Rep 476. In his judgment, Steyn LJ said quite bluntly that *CTI* had proved to be a remarkably unpopular decision, not only in the legal profession but also in the insurance markets ... Whether this generalisation about the markets is correct I cannot judge, but the books and articles produced in argument all adopt a critical stance. Nevertheless, although the unanimous disapprobation of the *CTI* case is striking, equally striking is the lack of unanimity about what exactly was wrong with it. Space does not permit a full discussion of the diverse criticisms. The following appear to be the principal complaints:

(1) The law is too harsh, for it deprives the assured of a recovery for a genuine loss by perils insured against even if the misrepresentation or non-disclosure had no bearing on the risk which brought about the loss. There is practical force in this objection, but it is not consistent with general principle, for the vice of misrepresentation and non-disclosure is not that after the event the underwriter has suffered from having taken on a parcel of risks one of which led to a loss, but that a breach of the duty of good faith has led the underwriter to approach the proposal on a false basis ...

(2) The law is too harsh, for it deprives the assured of the whole of his recovery even if full and accurate disclosure would have done no more than cause the actual underwriter, or the hypothetical prudent underwriter, to insist on one rate of premium rather than another. The inflexibility of an 'all or nothing' rule has been present to the minds of all the courts which have heard these two cases, as the judgments of Kerr LJ

and Sir Donald Nicholls VC clearly demonstrate. It has been fully ventilated before your Lordships, and I acknowledge the attractions of a solution which involves an element of 'proportionality'. Whether such a solution would be practicable outside the field of consumer insurance is debatable ...

As early as 1808 it was stated in Marshall, *A Treatise on the Law of Insurance*, 2nd edn, Vol I, p 463; 'Nor can the insured, by tendering any increase of premium, require the insurer to confirm the contract'; and there has never subsequently been any suggestion that an intermediate solution of this kind was the common law. Moreover, the words of the 1906 Act are plainly inconsistent with any such rule. It may be that the question of a statutory change is due for reconsideration in the light of the last 20 years' experience, but this is not an area in which the courts have any freedom of choice.

(3) The law fails to take account of whether a reasonable person seeking insurance would appreciate that a particular circumstance was material and ought to be disclosed. Again, there is force in this submission, at least as regards those consumer cases where there is an imbalance of expertise and experience between the proposer and the insurer. The position is however quite different in a case like the present ... The assured here was an insurance company acting through an experienced broker. The performance of the latter in the episode of the long record shows that these were no shorn lambs who needed the winds of the common law rule to be tempered. The broker knew very well what he was doing, and took care about how he did it. But this is beside the point. The House has not been, and could not be, invited to introduce a wholly new doctrine, hinging upon what was, or could have been, or should have been, in the mind of the proposer. In the field of marine insurance, this would require a fundamental amendment of the 1906 Act, and in commercial insurance as a whole such a wholesale change to a central and long established first principle of insurance law could not have been made by the Court of Appeal in the *CTI* case any more than it can now be made by this House.

(4) The doctrine of the *CTI* case demands more of the assured than is feasible in modern trading conditions. This is the kind of criticism which it is hard for a court, and particularly for an appellate court, to assess. I would, however, make the following brief comments upon it. First, I believe that a substantial part of the criticisms, to the effect that the broker in order to play safe will be force to disclose hundreds of documents which are of no real interest to the insurer and which impede that speedy placing of risks which is such a positive feature of the London market, are based on an interpretation of Kerr LJ's pronouncements in the *CTI* case which is wider than the Lord Justice intended. Secondly, although the physical bulk of placing material is likely in modern times to have been swollen by photocopies, electronically transmitted documents and computer print outs there will, I believe, be many cases where the core of material of which good faith demands the disclosure is relatively small and easy to identify. The present case is a good example. Finally, some of the critics come close to saying that the central obligation of good faith and its embodiment in the 1906 Act are out of date in modern conditions. This was not an option open to the court in the *CTI* case, or to any other court. Undoubtedly, commercial law must be responsive to changes in commercial practices if it is not to founder, and established principles must be applied sensitively in new situations. Thus, once the court has reached a conclusion

on the true content of the obligations created by the Act, in the light of any relevant previous decisions, it must translate them into practice by reference to conditions prevailing, not in 1906, but at the time when the risk was written. But it was not for the Court of Appeal, any more than for this House, to alter the meaning of the statute. Only Parliament can do that.

(5) The effect of the *CTI* case has been to deter overseas interests from placing risks in the London market. Again, it is not possible to judge the factual accuracy of this complaint. The comment is however obvious that if overseas interests take business elsewhere because English law insists that they and their brokers make fair presentations in good faith this may be business which the London market can well do without; and there is no need to emphasise at the present time the dangers of judging the success of an insurance market by volume alone. Moreover, whilst I accept that if that good quality business is being driven away there is reason to look carefully at whether the rules are being properly applied, if the rules established by Act of Parliament are having a deleterious economic effect it is for Parliament, not the courts, to change them.

Thus far, I have summarised and briefly discussed various of the criticisms to show that, although they have not been overlooked, they do not point towards a solution of the problems now before the House. The literature does however also develop in considerable detail a number of other groups of criticism which are directly in point.

(6) The Court of Appeal in the *CTI* case set the standard of materiality too low. The law ought to be that a circumstance is material only if its disclosure would *decisively* have influenced the mind of the prudent underwriter; if it would have made all the difference to whether he wrote the risk, and if so at what premium. Alternatively, even if a circumstance can be material without being decisive, the law ought to require a greater potential effect on the mind of the hypothetical underwriter than was acknowledged in the *CTI* case.

(7) The decision in the *CTI* case that a defence of misrepresentation or non-disclosure can succeed even if the actual underwriter's mind was unaffected is contrary to commonsense and justice. Moreover, the rule is not correct in principle, since: (i) the juristic basis of the underwriter's ability to disclaim the policy is that the misrepresentation or non-disclosure vitiates the consent necessary for a binding contract, and consent cannot be vitiated if the underwriter would have made the same contract even if the circumstance in question had been properly disclosed; and (ii) to dispense with the requirement for inducement of the contract is inconsistent with the general law on misrepresentation.

(8) If the actual underwriter would not have been influenced by the information it cannot have been material, and hence the assured was under no duty to disclose it.

(9) The court in the *CTI* case failed to appreciate the importance of *Ionides v Pender* (1874) LR 9 QB 531 and associated cases …

MATERIALITY

This part of the case depends on the words 'which would influence the judgment of a prudent insurer in fixing the premium, or determining whether he will take the risk' (ss 18(2) and 20(2) of the 1906 Act).

The main thrust of the argument for Pan Atlantic is that this expression calls for the disclosure only of such circumstances as would, if disclosed to the hypothetical prudent underwriter, have caused him to decline the risk or charge an increased premium. I am unable to accept this argument.

In the first place I cannot find the suggested meaning in the words of the Act. This is a short point of interpretation, and does not yield to long discussion. For my part, I entirely accept that part of the argument for Pan Atlantic which fastens on the word 'would' and contrasts it with words such as 'might'. I agree that this word looks to a consequence which, within the area of uncertainty created by the civil standard of proof, is definite rather than speculative. But this is only part of the inquiry. The next step is to decide what kind of effect the disclosure would have. This is defined by the expression 'influence the judgment of the prudent underwriter'. The legislature might here have said '*decisively* influence'; or '*conclusively* influence'; or 'determine the decision'; or all sorts of similar expressions, in which case Pan Atlantic's argument would be right. But the legislature has not done this, and has instead left the word 'influence' unadorned. It therefore bears its ordinary meaning, which is not, as it seems to me, the one for which Pan Atlantic contends. 'Influence the judgment' is not the same as 'change the mind'. Furthermore, if the argument is pursued via a purely verbal analysis, it should be observed that the expression used is 'influence the judgment of a prudent insurer or [the underwriter] in ... determining *whether* he will take the risk'. To my mind, this expression clearly denotes an effect on the thought processes of the insurer in weighing up the risk, quite different from words which might have been used but were not, such as 'influencing the insurer *to take* the risk' ...

INDUCEMENT

I turn to the second question which concerns the need, or otherwise, for a causal connection between the misrepresentation or non-disclosure and the making of the contract of insurance. According to ss 17, 18(1) and 20(1) if good faith is not observed, proper disclosure is not made or material facts are misrepresented, the other party, or in the case of ss 18 and 20 the insurer, 'may avoid the contract'. There is no mention of a connection between the wrongful dealing and the writing of the risk. But for this feature I doubt whether it would nowadays occur to anyone that it would be possible for the underwriter to escape liability even if the matter complained of had no effect on his processes of thought. Take the case of misrepresentation. In the general law, it is beyond doubt that even a fraudulent misrepresentation must be shown to have induced the contract before the promisor has a right to avoid, although the task of proof may be made more easy by a presumption of inducement. The case of innocent misrepresentation should surely be *a fortiori*, and yet it is urged that so long as the representation is material no inducement need be shown. True, the inequalities of knowledge between assured and underwriter have led to the creation of a special duty to make accurate disclosure of sufficient facts to restore the balance and remedy the injustice of holding the underwriter to a speculation which he had been unable fairly to assess; but this consideration cannot in logic or justice require courts to go further and declare the contract to be vitiated when the underwriter, having paid no attention to the matters not properly stated and disclosed, has suffered no injustice thereby ...

A fact which at once captures attention is the existence, almost from the outset, of a controversy about the need for inducement. I have already given references to the conflicting views of the 19th century scholars. To modern eyes the controversy is puzzling. The doctrine that a contract of marine insurance is *uberrima fides* had been firmly established for decades. How could there still be any doubt as to a point which, although rarely arising in practice, was of fundamental theoretical importance, the more so given that it is nowadays a truism that an innocent misrepresentation will lead to rescission ...?

... My Lords, in my judgment little or nothing can be gleaned from twentieth century cases to indicate a solution to the problem of causation. Before stating my own opinion on this problem, there are two more points to be made.

First, one suggested explanation for the absence from s 20 of any requirement that the misrepresentation shall have induced the contract is that any such requirement had been swept away 30 years before in *Ionides v Pender* (1874) LR 9 QB 531. Consistently with the views already expressed, I am unable to accept this, and I should add that even if the effect of *Ionides v Pender* had been to make the influence on the hypothetical underwriter the benchmark of materiality I am unable to see why this should not have left behind such requirements of actual causation as had previously formed part of the common law. However, as I have said, although *Ionides v Pender* was an important case it did not in my opinion have the effect contended for.

Secondly, it has been suggested that the absence from the 1906 Act of any reference to causation stems from a disciplinary element in the law of marine insurance. The concept is that persons seeking insurance and their brokers cannot be relied upon to perform their duties spontaneously; that the criterion of whether or not the misrepresentation or non-disclosure induced the contract would make it too easy for the assured to say that the breach of duty made no difference; and that accordingly the law prescribes voidability as an automatic consequence of a breach by way of sanction for the enforcement of full and accurate disclosure. For my part, although I think it possible to detect traces of this doctrine in the earlier writings I can see nothing to support it in later sources; and I would unhesitatingly reject any suggestion that it should now be made part of the law. The existing rules, coupled with a presumption of inducement, are already stern enough, and to enable an underwriter to escape liability when he has suffered no harm would be positively unjust, and contrary to the spirit of mutual good faith recognised by s 17, the more so since non-disclosure will in a substantial proportion of cases be the result of an innocent mistake.

For these reasons, I conclude that there is to be implied in the 1906 Act a qualification that a material misrepresentation will not entitle the underwriter to avoid the policy unless the misrepresentation induced the making of the contract, using 'induced' in the sense in which it is used in the general law of contract. This proposition is concerned only with *material* misrepresentations. On the view which I have formed of the present facts, the effect of an immaterial misrepresentation does not arise and I say nothing about it.

There remain two problems of real substance. The first is whether the conclusion just expressed can be transferred to the case of wrongful non-disclosure. It must be accepted at once that the route via s 91(2) of the Act and the general common law which leads to a solution for misrepresentation is not available here, since there was and is no general common law of non-disclosure. Nor does the complex interaction between fraud and materiality, which makes the old insurance law on misrepresentation so hard to decipher, exist in respect of non-disclosure. Nevertheless, if one looks at the problem in the round, and asks whether it is a tolerable result that the Act accommodates in s 20(1) a requirement that the misrepresentation shall have induced the contract, and yet no such requirement can be accommodated in s 18(1), the answer must surely be that it is not the more so since in practice the line between misrepresentation and non-disclosure is often imperceptible. If the Act, which did not set out to be a complete codification of existing law, will yield to qualification in one case surely it must in common sense do so in the other. If this requires the making of new law, so be it. There is no subversion here of established precedent. It is only in recent years that the problem has been squarely faced. Facing it now, I believe that to do justice a need for inducement can and should be implied into the Act ...

CONCLUSION

For these reasons, although I differ in certain important respects from the view of the law which the Court of Appeal was constrained to apply I would dismiss the appeal. In conclusion I wish to acknowledge the painstaking research which founded the arguments addressed on appeal, and in particular the deployment of modern academic and other writings. Throughout its long history the law of marine insurance has owed as much to commentators as to the courts, and although the views of these writers are not fully reflected here, I have taken them carefully into account ...

Lord Lloyd (dissenting on the decisive influence test of the majority): My provisional conclusion, before coming to the authorities, is that Mr Beloff succeeds on the first half of his argument, and that in order to avoid a contract for non-disclosure it must be shown that a prudent insurer, if he had known of the undisclosed fact, would either have declined the risk altogether, or charged an increased premium. This goes further than Steyn LJ in the Court of Appeal, but not by much. For in all ordinary cases where the prudent insurer would have perceived an increase in the risk, he would presumably charge an increased premium. There might be special circumstances in which the *actual* insurer would decide, for his own reasons, to incur an increased risk at the same premium. But this consideration should not affect the objective application of the prudent insurer test. My reasons for preferring Mr Beloff's test are that it does full justice to the language of s 18 of the 1906 Act. It is well defined, and easily applied. It does something to mitigate the harshness of the all or nothing approach which disfigures this branch of the law, and it is consistent with the reasons given by the Court of Appeal for rejecting the test proposed by Mr Hamilton ...

... If your Lordships accept this conclusion, the position will be as follows. Whenever an insurer seeks to avoid a contract of insurance or re-insurance on the ground of misrepresentation or non-disclosure, there will be two separate but closely related questions: (1) Did the misrepresentation or non-disclosure induce the actual insurer to enter into the contract on those terms? (2) Would the prudent insurer have entered into the contract on the same terms if he had known of the misrepresentation or non-disclosure immediately before the contract was concluded? If both questions are answered in favour of the insurer, he will be entitled to avoid the contract, but not otherwise.

The evidence of the insurer himself will normally be required to satisfy the court on the first question. The evidence of an independent broker or underwriter will normally be required to satisfy the court on the second question. This produces a uniform and workable solution, which has the further advantage, as I see it, of according with good commercial commonsense. It follows that the *CTI* case was wrongly decided, and should be overruled ...

APPENDIX 4.25

Birds, J and Hird, N, 'Misrepresentation and non-disclosure in insurance law – identical twins or separate issues?' (1996) 59 MLR 285

In *Pan Atlantic Co Ltd and Another v Pine Top Insurance Co Ltd* [1994] 3 All ER 581, the House of Lords again tackled the vexed question of the meaning of materiality in English insurance law. The main point at issue was to determine the exact meaning of s 18(2) of the Marine Insurance Act 1906 …

The main reasons given by the majority for the rejection of the 'decisive influence' test were as follows. First, Lord Mustill discusses the difficulties facing both the court, and the prospective insured and insurer, if they have to decide before the risk is underwritten whether one particular fact, if undisclosed, will be decisive on the terms of the contract. This is surely to misunderstand the issue. The prospective insured does not sit down in conference with his underwriter to discuss all material facts, nor does he consciously sit down and think to himself: '... if I do not disclose this fact, will it make a difference to the risk?' If every prospective insured could be relied upon to do that, then there would not be many non-disclosure actions. It is far more likely that he does not think about it at all – we are not here discussing a fraudulent or deliberate concealment, but an inadvertent one. We are assuming that he is abiding by the duty of good faith to the best of his ability; questions of whether or not he realises that one concealed fact will sway the underwriter's opinion are surely, therefore, out of place here.

Secondly, Lord Mustill says:

> The argument for Pan Atlantic demands an assumption that the prudent underwriter would have written the risk at the premium actually agreed on the basis of the disclosure that was actually made. Yet this assumption is impossible if the actual underwriter, through laziness, incompetence or a simple error of judgment, has made a bargain which no prudent underwriter would have made, full disclosure or no full disclosure. This absurdity does not arise if the duty of disclosure embraces all materials which would enter into the making of the hypothetical decision, since this does not require the bargain actually made to be taken as the starting point.

This, with the greatest of respect, *must* be considered irrelevant. What can it matter what the actual underwriter would/might/should have done? The whole point of a prudent underwriter test is to bring objectivity and dispense with such subjectivity – if the prudent underwriter would not have made the bargain on the same terms without the non-disclosure. Then we can surely assume that he would not have made it had the fact been disclosed. If this is the case, then the fact is material on the decisive influence test and that is an end to it (assuming, of course, that any number of prudent underwriters could even be expected to agree on such a matter, which must surely, in itself, be overly optimistic). However, if the starting point for such a decision is not to be the bargain actually made, then where is it to be? There is surely no other place to start, nor probably to contemplate or finish!

The third reason for rejection bears greatly on the first and again assumes (wrongly, in our view) that the prospective insured weighs up the possible influence of the non-disclosed fact, and then deliberately chooses to conceal it not necessarily from any fraudulent motive, but because he objectively considers it to be unimportant or not weighty enough to bother the prudent underwriter. We have already given our opinion on whether the insured normally acts in such a conscious fashion – the more conscious that conduct becomes, the further away from inadvertent non-disclosure we travel, and we should keep in mind that it is only inadvertent conduct we are concerned with here.

Lord Lloyd, for the minority, has little difficulty in dismissing these arguments and presenting a different line of reasoning which leads, of course, to a different conclusion. He asks what is the central question, that is, the meaning of the words 'would influence the judgment of a prudent insurer', and gives the following answer:

> If I ask myself what the phrase as a whole means, I would answer that it points to something more than what the prudent insurer would want to know or take into account. At the very least, it points to what the prudent insurer would perceive as increasing or tending to increase the risk.

He goes on to tell us, correctly, that this also best ties in with the statement made by Lord Mansfield in *Carter v Boehm* (1766) 3 Burr 1905, which explicitly says that neither party is under any duty to disclose any fact which might diminish the risk. As *Carter v Boehm* is regarded by everybody as being the starting point for any discussion which centres on non-disclosure, we should take this point seriously. It also fits best with s 18(3)(a) of the Marine Insurance Act, which confirms this.

Lord Lloyd then analyses the phrase word by word, and not only reaches the same conclusion, but carries it one stage further. 'Influence,' on its ordinary meaning, is to affect or alter. Most of us would agree with this. 'Judgment' can have many meanings and is the most difficult to define out of context but, as he points out, in a commercial sense it is often used to mean 'assessment', as in the term 'market assessment'. This usually means a judgment as to what the market is going to do, not the process of arriving at that opinion. The word 'would' does not, and, in our view, cannot mean 'might'. It is a much more positive word than 'might.' It must be observed and, indeed, Lord Mustill paid great attention to this fact when it suited his purpose to do so, that Sir Mackenzie Chalmers, who drafted the 1906 Act, was an extremely precise draftsman – if he meant 'might', we can safely assume that he would have drafted 'might'.

In short, Lord Lloyd is simply saying that nothing can be properly described as 'influencing' anything, unless it does actually have a positive effect on behaviour, and it is surely very difficult to disagree with this analysis. Nevertheless, both arguments already have their respective supporters, and a trawl through early authority, both case law and commentary, provides no ready solution to the dilemma ...

INDUCEMENT

The second aspect of the *Pan Atlantic* decision is concerned with the idea that the misrepresentation or non-disclosure must have proved an actual inducement to the innocent party to enter that particular contract, if that party wishes to avoid. This is absolutely novel in relation to non-disclosure, although not of course to misrepresentation – inducement has always been a requirement for misrepresentation, at least in the general law of contract. Their Lordships were, on this point, unanimous in deciding that there should indeed be an inducement requirement for both misrepresentation and non-disclosure in the law of insurance.

The crux of the problem is not that those of us who ever think about such matters do not recognise the probable need for a causal link between the misrepresentation or non-disclosure and the assessment of the risk – such a link may be essential if the law in this area is to be rendered 'morally correct' – but that the relevant sections of the Marine Insurance Act 1906 contain no such requirement. Lord Mustill begins his analysis of inducement with just such an observation; that there is, strictly on the wording of the relevant sections of the Marine Insurance Act, no mention of a necessary causal link between the misrepresentation or non-disclosure and the writing of the risk. He then recognises that most interested observers will find this somewhat surprising:

But for this feature, I doubt whether it would nowadays occur to anyone that it would be possible for the underwriter to escape liability even if the matter complained of had no effect on his processes of thought.

He goes on to ask:

> How, then, does it happen that the 1906 Act seems to contemplate that once a material misrepresentation or non-disclosure is established, the underwriter has an invariable right to avoid?

With respect, this seems to us to be entirely self-explanatory. Plainly nobody should envisage the underwriter being allowed to escape liability when his thought processes, and therefore surely his actions, are unaffected by the misrepresentation or non-disclosure, and we would maintain that the Act supports no such thing. The Act, a codification of the existing case law, must have supposed that the test for materiality was exactly that which Lord Mustill and the majority of the House have expended much energy telling us it was not; namely, that the fact will not be considered material unless it affects the thought processes and, therefore, the actions of the underwriter, that is, the 'decisive influence' test just discarded by their Lordships. If one accepts that test, what need is there for an inducement requirement? Indeed, the whole issue is better resolved by the necessary effect being confined to materiality, because then we can remain in the realms of objectivity, having only to assess the effect on the prudent underwriter and not the actual underwriter, which is where we must look if an inducement requirement is introduced.

Lord Mustill obviously disagrees, but recognises that a rejection of this interpretation and the introduction of an inducement requirement needs some justification. One possibility that has been mooted, and which he considers and rejects, is that the requirement was simply omitted by the draftsman. We would also reject such a submission. Given that the draftsman of the Act was Sir Mackenzie Chalmers, it is highly improbable that a need for inducement, if the common law required it, would simply have been forgotten.

Lord Mustill therefore considers that there might be three reasons why the Act took the form it did. First, the common law did not require inducement and was correctly reproduced by the Act. Secondly, the common law did require inducement but the promoters of the Act wishes the law to be changed, and Parliament did change it. Thirdly, the common law did require inducement and the Act, properly understood, is to the same effect. He suggests that the way to make a choice is to look behind the Act to the developing history of marine insurance law and in particular, to the scholarly writings ...

... there are difficulties involved in treating misrepresentation and non-disclosure as the same creatures. The two are often pleaded indiscriminately and this is bound to become even more common the more the legal differences between the two are blurred. Yet there are differences – for example, an innocent misrepresentation can never be an actionable non-disclosure. A misrepresentation that the law deems to be innocent is a positive statement based upon the representor's genuine belief in its truth. A good example in insurance law is the declaring of losses by a prospective insured to his insurer. If the actual loss is more than that declared, albeit through no fault of the insured, this could as easily be termed a non-disclosure in the sense that an amount of actual loss remains hidden, and this is exactly what happened in *Pan Atlantic*. This situation cannot, however, technically be an actionable non-disclosure because, to be actionable, an innocent non-disclosure must involve the insured failing to disclose something which he knows, because he fails to realise it might be important to a prudent insurer. We must assume, in the given situation, that the insured is totally unaware of the true actual losses, otherwise the misrepresentation must be deemed to be fraudulent, a situation which the law treats very differently.

It is not difficult to imagine other situations where this may arise and it surely cannot be sensible for the law to attempt to merge these doctrines when they are, legally, quite separate entities.

Another difficulty arises conceptually when one talks of an insurer being induced into a contract by a non-disclosure. How can anyone really be induced by what amounts to silence? Of course, the non-disclosure could be framed in a different way, for example, had the undisclosed facts been disclosed, then the insurer would not have entered into this particular contract, but that is not quite the same as alleging that silence was the actual inducement, which is what should be proved in this situation. In our opinion, inducement does not make any real sense when non-disclosure is being alleged, unlike misrepresentation where it is easy to see how an incorrect positive statement can be an inducement. This difficulty may, in our opinion, be another nail in the coffin of a presumption that inducement was a requirement of either misrepresentation or non-disclosure in insurance law but, even if one accepts that it was a requirement of misrepresentation, it should be another argument in favour of keeping the two doctrines separate.

CONCLUSION

In *St Paul Fire and Marine (UK) Ltd v McConnell Dowell Constructors Ltd* [1995] 2 Lloyd's Rep 116, strictly a case of misrepresentation, the Court of Appeal were asked to clarify certain of the problems arising out of *Pan Atlantic*. It was argued that the test for materiality had still not been precisely determined and, concerning inducement, that is was not clear whether an actual insurer benefits from a *presumption* of inducement.

Evans LJ, who delivered the principal judgment in *St Paul*, had no hesitation that the proper test for materiality had been properly determined, and was only that the prudent insurer would have wished to know; this must mean that the 'decisive influence' test has now been absolutely discounted. As to the second limb, Lord Mustill alludes to a presumption of inducement at least twice in his judgment in *Pan Atlantic*, but it was firmly rejected by Lord Lloyd. The Court of Appeal in *St Paul* decided, however, that there was such a presumption in favour of the innocent party and, moreover, that it was enough for him to show that the misrepresented fact had proved *an* inducement, but not necessarily *the* inducement. One of us has already argued that if a presumption of inducement does exist, then the misrepresented fact must be shown to be the only inducement because anything less only aids the insurer, already subject to a very lenient test on materiality, however, such an argument has been firmly rejected, at least by this particular Court of Appeal.

It therefore appears that the law after *Pan Atlantic* is much the same as it was after the much criticised *CTI* decision, although it is arguable that it is worse in that it is no longer open to the insured to argue the 'increased risk' theory. The introduction of an inducement requirement has served only to muddy the waters, rather than clear them, which is what the House of Lords purportedly set out to do.

There must now be a very strong argument for referring this whole issued back to the House for clarification and resolution.

APPENDIX 4.26

St Paul Fire and Marine Insurance Co (UK) Ltd v McConnell Dowell Constructors Ltd and Others [1995] 2 Lloyd's Rep 116, CA

Evans LJ: The House of Lords decided unanimously in *Pan Atlantic Insurance Co Ltd v Pinetop Insurance Co Ltd* [1994] 3 All ER 581 ... that the insurer's right of avoidance arises only when the misrepresentation, or non-disclosure, induced him to make the contract. This is part of the general law of contract and although not stated expressly must be regarded as an implied qualification of the right to avoid the contract under the Act ...

In this respect, the Court of Appeal's decision in *Container Transport International Inc v Oceanus Mutual Underwriting Association (Bermuda) Ltd* [1984] 1 Lloyd's Rep 476 ... was reversed. In that case, the decision was that the insurer who sought to avoid the policy was under no obligation to prove that he, or the prudent insurer, was or would have been induced to enter into the contract. It was sufficient that the representation or non-disclosure was 'material' within the definition in the Act. Since the meaning given to the definition was regarded as being wide, and therefore generous to insurers, the decision caused much concern in commercial and legal circles (see *per* Lord Justice Steyn in *Pan Atlantic*, CA ... and Lords Mustill and Lloyd in *Pan Atlantic* ...). The reasons for this concern have been largely removed by the House of Lords decision and there is only a right to avoid when the misrepresentation or non-disclosure was 'material' *and* when the actual insurer was induced thereby to enter into the contract ...

The statutory definition of 'material' makes it necessary to have regard to the 'prudent insurer'. This person, in the words of Lord Radcliffe's celebrated *dictum* in *Davis Contractors Ltd v Fareham Urban DC* [1956] AC 696 ... is no more than the anthropomorphic conception of the standards of professional underwriting which the court finds it appropriate to uphold. Subject to the limitation that the standard must be established by evidence in the particular case:

> ... the materiality or otherwise of a circumstance should be constant and the actual underwriter should be held to the bargain unless something objectively material is not disclosed [*per* Lord Mustill] ...

This approach led to the conclusion of the majority in the House of Lords (Lords Goff, Mustill and Slynn) that it is not necessary for the insurer to show that the true facts, if they were disclosed and not misrepresented to the prudent underwriter, would have caused him either to refuse the risk or to require a different or a higher premium; the so called decisive influence test. The question of law was posed by Lord Mustill in these terms:

> ... must it be shown that full and accurate disclosure would have led the prudent underwriter to a different decision on accepting or rating the risk; or is a lesser standard of impact on the mind of the prudent underwriter sufficient; and if so, what is the lesser standard ...?

The short answer, after a detailed and authoritative review of the authorities, is this:

> A circumstance may be material even though a full and accurate disclosure of it would not in itself have had a decisive effect on the prudent underwriter's decision whether to accept the risk and if so at what premium ...

It is worth noting how far the definition of 'material' in *CTI* was affected by the court's decision was not relevant and that no question of inducement arose. This meant that regard was had only to the position of the prudent underwriter. Hence, the question arose whether it was necessary for the insurer to show that the notional prudent underwriter would have been *decisively* influenced in his judgment whether or not to accept the risk and if so on what terms. This is, in substance, the same question as inducement, and the need to ask it in relation to the prudent underwriter only arose because the actual underwriter, to whom it was more easily applied, was disregarded. The majority in the House of Lords in *Pan Atlantic* rejected the decisive influence test and a major factor in Lord Mustill's reasoning, which was echoed by Lord Goff, is the practical difficulty of inquiring after the event into what would have decisively influenced the judgment of a prudent underwriter ...

In retrospect, therefore, it can be seen that the 'decisive influence' test applied to the prudent underwriter came to be formulated in the light (or rather in the shadow) of the court's rejection of the role of the actual underwriter, and the prominence given to the prudent underwriter after *Ionides v Pender* (1874) LR 9 QB 531. Now that his role has been restored, and the qualification implied in the statutory provisions has been recognised, there is no practical need to define 'material' in terms of decisive influence or by reference to inducement. But the question remains, how then should it be defined?

It was thought that the Court of Appeal had given a wide meaning to 'material' in *CTI* This was defined by the Court of Appeal (*per* Lord Justice Steyn) in *Pan Atlantic* as follows:

> The first solution was that a fact is material if a prudent insurer would have wished to be aware of it in reaching his decision ...

One of the criticisms of the *CTI* decision to which Lord Mustill referred was that the requirement of disclosure was so widely defined that it:

> ... demands more of the assured than is feasible in modern trading conditions ...

In this context, Lord Mustill suggested that these criticisms 'are based on an interpretation of Lord Justice Kerr's pronouncements in the *CTI* case which is wider than the Lord Justice intended' ... This is a clear indication that Lord Mustill did not endorse the widest interpretations of the CTI judgments.

The alternative test was formulated by Lord Justice Steyn in *Pan Atlantic* ... as follows:

> The second solution involves taking account of the fact that avoidance for non-disclosure is the remedy provided by law because the risk presented is different from the true risk. But for the non-disclosure the prudent underwriter would have appreciated that it was a different and increased risk.

Lord Justice Steyn 'unhesitatingly' chose the second solution, and the Court of Appeal so held.

Lord Mustill commented as follows:

> In the Court of Appeal ... we find that court striving ... to find a workable understanding of the *ratio* of the *CTI* case which was consistent not only with the rejection of the decisive influence as the test for materiality but also with the rejection of any requirement of influence on the actions of the individual underwriter. It may well be that but for this second constraint, the court might have felt more free in its ruling on materiality.

This, in my judgment, reflects the passage from Lord Goff's speech ... and suggests that the crucial aspect of the *CTI* decision was not the definition of materiality but the rejection of the actual underwriter as playing any part in the process of establishing his own right to avoid the policy.

In the present case, Mr Phillips submits that the House of Lords judgments do not disapprove of Lord Justice Steyn's interpretation of the *CTI* decision as regards materiality, and that it should therefore stand as a definition tacitly approved by the House of Lords. If this is correct, then the test of materiality is only satisfied if the fact in question would have led the prudent underwriter to appreciate that the risk was: (a) different from; and (b) greater than he would otherwise have supposed.

I find it difficult to accept that Lord Mustill's speech omitted any clear statement of his conclusions on one of the major issues of law with which his researches were concerned, namely, the meaning of 'materiality', and in my judgment it did not ... His phrase 'all matters which would have been taken into account by the underwriters when assessing the risk' was clearly intended to reflect the extracts from text-book writers on the previous page, including Parsons ('naturally and reasonably influence the insurer in his estimate of the risk'), Duer ('regulating the underwriter's estimate of the premium') and Arnould ('underwriter's estimate of the risk'). The 'whole object of the rules is to enable the underwriters to judge accurately of the risk' (Lord Mustill) ...

This concept, in my judgment, is no different from the formulation in Lord Justice Steyn's judgment ('would have appreciated that it was a different ... risk'). To this extent, Lord Mustill expressly approved the Court of Appeal's definition and no 'gloss' (Mr Phillips' expression) on his formulation ... is necessary.

... The position is different, however, with regard to the suggested further requirement that the factor is only material if it would have increased rather then merely altered the perceived risk. That was a necessary qualification when the likely reaction of a prudent underwriter alone determined the actual insurer's right to avoid. Now that inducement of the actual underwriter must also be proved, there is no reason why 'material' should be limited to factors which are seen as increasing the risk, and in my judgment there are good reasons for not doing so. First, many factors may not be 'clear cut' in this way; the risk may be increased in some respects but decreased in others ... Secondly, the duty of disclosure operates both ways because the duty of good faith is reciprocal ... so the definition of 'material' is not concerned with the proposer of insurance alone. For these reasons alone, I would reject Mr Phillips' submission that the fact cannot be material unless the risk is thereby increased, and I would support this conclusion on the wider ground that 'material' like 'relevant' denotes a relationship with the subject matter rather than a prediction of its effect.

The conclusion is also supported, in my judgment, by the fact that s 18(3)(a) provides that the insured need not disclose 'any circumstances which diminishes the risk'. This means that the insurer has no right to avoid the policy on the ground that a circumstance of that sort was not disclosed, but it does not state that the circumstance is not 'material' within the definition in s 18(2). The contrary inference, if any, should be drawn. If the circumstance was not material, it would be unnecessary to provide that it should not be disclosed.

As regards inducement, it is common ground that the insurer must prove that he was induced by the non-disclosure or misrepresentation to enter into a contract on terms which he would not have accepted if all the material facts had been made known to him, and that the test of 'inducement' is the same as that established by many authorities in the general law of contract. These are summarised in *Halsbury's Laws of England*, 4th edn, Vol 31, para 1067 …

… If, therefore, the true facts had been disclosed, they would have been to the effect that the project included shallow/spread foundations, and that the ground conditions were such as to make it questionable whether those foundations without additional safeguards were an acceptable alternative to deep foundations for the site in question, and that conflicting views had been expressed by different experts. If these facts had been disclosed, then on the evidence they would certainly have affected the prudent underwriter's estimate or appreciation of the risk. Therefore they were material to be disclosed, alternatively the true facts were misrepresented, albeit mistakenly and innocently. In my judgment, the respondents are entitled to avoid the policy on these grounds, subject to proof that the actual underwriters were thereby induced to enter into the contract of insurance on the terms on which they did.

INDUCEMENT

Although the evidence of the actual underwriters was directed solely towards the views of the notional prudent underwriter, as was inevitable when the court had to apply the Court of Appeal decisions in *CTI* and *Pan Atlantic*, the evidence which they gave establishes beyond doubt, in my judgment, that if they had been informed not merely that the project included piled foundations but that the ground conditions were questionable, notwithstanding that spread foundations were proposed to be used, then they would have requested sight of the Worleys report and this would had led them to ask for the 1982 report also, because it is referred to by Worleys. They would have been more likely, in the circumstances of this case, to have refused cover than to seek expert technical advice of their own, but on no view, had those reports been disclosed to them, would they have underwritten the insurance at the same premium on terms which included the subsidence risk. I therefore consider that the necessary inducement of the three actual underwriters who gave evidence is sufficiently proved.

The position of the Prudential Assurance Co is different, for the reason indicated above. Their underwriter Mr Earnshaw was not called to give evidence although he was available to do so. These respondents are not entitled to avoid their contract unless there is a presumption upon which they can rely to discharge the burden of proving inducement which rests upon them.

The existence of such a presumption is recognised in the authorities: see *Halsbury's Laws*, Vol 31, para 1067, where the law is stated as follows:

> Inducement cannot be inferred in law from proved materiality, although there may be cases where the materiality is so obvious as to justify an inference of fact that the representee was actually induced, but, even in such exceptional cases, the inference is only a *prima facie* one and may be rebutted by counter evidence …

Here, the evidence of the three underwriters who did give evidence and of the expert witnesses was clear. If the underwriters had been told the true state of the ground conditions, as revealed by the 1982 report, and of the conflicting views expressed by the authors of that report and by Worleys, then they would have called for further information and in all probability either refused the risk or accepted it on different terms. In fact, all four underwriters including Mr Earnshaw accepted it without any relevant enquiries. There is no evidence to displace a presumption that Mr Earnshaw like the other three was induced by the non-disclosure or misrepresentation to give cover on the terms on which he did. In my judgment, these insurers also have discharged their burden of proof ...

APPENDIX 4.27

Marc Rich and Co AG v Portman [1997] 1 Lloyd's Rep 225, CA

Leggatt LJ:

PRESUMED KNOWLEDGE

In relation to presumed knowledge Mr Kealy argued first, in reliance on *Carter v Boehm* (1766) 3 Burr 1905, that an underwriter who insures a risk within a particular industry ought to know or find out the practices of the industry or trade, and the matters which are in general well known by persons in that trade. He also submitted that if an underwriter is writing a class of business he should be conversant with the course of losses affecting the types of risk which fall within that class, although he cannot be presumed to know about particular losses which specially affect particular assureds …

… Lord Mansfield spoke only of what the underwriter 'ought to know'. Underwriters were not bound to know the extent of the liability for demurrage which Marc Rich had incurred. The liability was not 'ordinarily inherent' in the risk. There was nothing that could be said to constitute 'the ordinary loss experience': the information required was about Marc Rich's 'actual loss experience'. That was not a matter of common knowledge …

… To suggest that all charterers who used the same ports had incurred losses comparable with those sustained by Marc Rich would be absurd. At the very least the underwriter was entitled to suppose that if the premium rate and the excess were both accepted, he would not be subjected to inevitable loss. Marc Rich's loss experience was peculiar to Marc Rich, and was not something of which an underwriter could have been aware unless it was disclosed. It was not …

WAIVER

… An insurer cannot waive a class of information that he does not know exists. That requires a fair presentation of the risk. It is obvious that a presentation cannot be fair if unusual facts are not disclosed. The insurer is entitled to assume the fairness of the presentation. Without it he cannot sensibly be said to refrain from asking questions. He must be on notice of the existence of information before he can be said to waive it …

In my judgment, a presentation cannot be fair if there is silence as to material losses, as there was here. Since Mr Gibson kept his broker in ignorance, he ensured that the resulting presentation was wholly unfair …

INDUCEMENT

… Mr Kealey submitted that there was no indication that Mr Overton did anything about understanding the risk which he was writing or about learning how he should rate it. He was unreliable, unsatisfactory and evasive. Neither could his first statement be relied on, nor could his understanding of the risk be accepted. In those circumstances, Mr Kealey contended, no inference could fairly be drawn that if Marc Rich's claims experience had been disclosed to him, Mr Overton would have read it, understood it or reacted to it. The burden of proof which lay upon the underwriters was therefore not satisfied.

When approaching the question of inducement, the judge had the evidence of Mr Portman as well as that of Mr Overton himself. and the evidence of the expert underwriters was that the losses were not only serious but were on such a scale as would have rendered the risk uninsurable. The judge reached the unchallenged finding that:

> ... neither Mr Hunter nor Mr Overton thought that the endorsement contemplated any major extension of the risk.

It is obvious that Marc Rich's massive loss experience would have completely abrogated that assumption. The judge's conclusion, at p 441, was therefore wholly supported, that if Mr Overton:

> ... had been shown or told that Marc Rich had a substantial record or experience of previously incurred demurrage, he would either have sought to confirm that that was no part of the cover or, at least, would have decided to discuss the matter with Mr Portman who would himself have checked it was nothing to do with the risk. In either event the risk would not have been written on the terms it was.

I see no warrant for interfering with that conclusion. No doubt there are good grounds for supposing that Mr Overton would have been unlikely to pay any attention to information about the causes of delay. But it is, in my judgment, probable, if not certain, that he would have reacted in the manner that the judge suggested to information which showed that, if the business was written on the terms proposed, substantial losses would inevitably be incurred not merely by Marc Rich but also by underwriters.

It follows that Marc Rich's grounds all fail, and I would dismiss the appeal ...

APPENDIX 4.28

National Consumer Council, *Report on Insurance Law Reform*, 1997, London: NCC

THE CONSUMER'S POSITION ON DISCLOSURE AND MISREPRESENTATION

Recommendation 4

We recommend reform of the law to require insurers to give notice to the buyer, in writing, of the general nature and effect of the duty of disclosure. In the event of failure to do this, the insurer should not be able to rely upon any defence other than fraudulent concealment by the policy holder.

Recommendation 5

The insured person's duty on disclosure and misrepresentation should be defined in law as follows:

(a) the insured consumer has a duty to disclose facts within his or her knowledge which *either* he/she knows to be relevant to the insurer's decision *or* which a reasonable person in the circumstances could be expected to know to be relevant;

(b) an untrue statement made by an insured person is not misrepresentation if he/she honestly believed it to be true, and is a misrepresentation in law only if the insured person knew, or a reasonable person in his position could be expected to have known, that the statement would have been relevant to the insurer's decision;

(c) if there has been a relevant non-disclosure or misrepresentation, the insurer has no remedy if its decision would not in fact have been any different;

(d) if a misrepresentation or non-disclosure is non-fraudulent, the insurer retains liability under the policy but is entitled to deduct the extra premium it would have charged had there been no non-disclosure or misrepresentation. The contract can be avoided only where there is fraudulent non-disclosure or misrepresentation or it would not have insured the risk.

THE PRINCIPLE OF UTMOST GOOD FAITH

Recommendation 6

We recommend legal codification of the principle of utmost good faith in insurance contracts, by defining it as follows:

(a) an insurance contract is a contract based on the utmost good faith, where it is implied that each party should act towards the other party, in respect of any matter arising under or in relation to it, with the utmost good faith;

(b) the duty includes the requirement that an insurer who unreasonably delays in paying a claim is liable for breach of contract;

(c) the duty includes the requirement that the insurer bring to the insured consumer's attention the general nature and effect of his/her obligations under the contract; failure to do so will mean the insurer cannot rely upon a breach by the insured;

(d) remedies for breach of the duty (other than those covered by (c) above) would include damages ...

APPENDIX 4.29

Insurance Law Reform, *The Response of the Association of British Insurers to the National Consumer Council Report 1997*, 1997, London: ABI

2 SUMMARY

2.1 To begin with, we argue that the overall case for comprehensive legislative reform of insurance law has not been made out.

2.2 Furthermore, in the main we do not support the specific recommendations made by the NCC. This is for a variety of reasons. these reasons can be grouped together as follows:

- where we do agree that there has been a problem in the past, we argue at a number of points that there is currently a working solution in place;
- where we agree that there is an ongoing, present problem or difficulty, we argue that its solution is not in reforming the law but in an alternative, more effective approach.

Section 1: general matters

3 WHY LAW REFORM?

3.1 The NCC report concludes that 'self regulation by the industry is simply not enough to protect the interests of the consumers of personal insurance' and that, therefore, comprehensive legislation reform of insurance law is required.

3.2 As the insurance industry's trade association, we have some experience of law reform. We know how legislative opportunity and Parliamentary time are severely limited and, therefore, at a premium. In our experience, legislative reform of the law can realistically be achieved only when there is a compelling need which can be demonstrated by reference to real, immediate and substantial problems with the existing law. Even then, it is our experience that the larger the law reform issue, the less realistic it becomes that it will be implemented in whole or even in part. There are also various unpredictable factors, such as the presence or imminence of European legislation …

3.5 To begin with, the NCC uses complaints statistics to try and demonstrate the size of the problem. For instance, the report refers to the fact that in 1996 the Insurance Ombudsman Bureau received 66,416 general enquiries of which 4,959 became new cases. The report also mentions that Citizens Advice Bureau in England and Wales in 1994–95 received 95,000 'insurance enquiries'.

3.6 The inference which the NCC would like to draw from these figures is that there is a very significant number of individuals suffering because of unfair insurance law. However, it would be unwise to draw this inference from the statistics quoted in the report for two reasons:

- first, because not all of the enquiries represented by the statistics will have involved insurance *law* as opposed to insurance selling or marketing or practice using 1995 figures and no scientific approach, of the 4,000 general cases received by the IOB, only around 40% will have involved insurance law, the bulk involved non-law issues such as failure in service, maladministration, disputes about no claims discounts or valuations, selling, lack of proof, delay and poor communication;
- secondly, because many, if not the majority, of the 'enquiries' will have been just that, certainly involving no unfairness; anecdotal evidence of this is provided by the ABI's own consumer line which receives about 12,000 'enquiries' every year approximately 60% of which are merely queries about insurance involving no dispute, let alone any unfairness.

3.7 The next argument the NCC report uses to support its call for comprehensive legislative reform of insurance law is that a MORI survey in 1995 'concluded that consumers felt they have too little protection' in insurance services.

3.8 It is difficult to see the substance in this argument. Consumers themselves are unlikely to give an objective view of the level of consumer protection in insurance services. More objectively, it is necessary merely to consider a few common linked transactions to see how well protected the insurance consumer is in comparison to other consumers:

- when an individual buys a holiday with travel insurance, there is more protection in relation to the insurance product ABI General Business Selling Code plus IOB/PIAS (Personal Insurance Arbitration Service) even though the holiday is by far the more expensive product;
- when an individual buys a used car with a warranty, there is normally a direct right of redress through the IOB/PIAS or through the courts against the warranty provider in the event that the warranty is unsatisfactory, but it is often much more difficult to take action in respect of the defects in the car (title, quality, etc) again despite the fact that the car will almost always be by far the more expensive product;
- similarly for home insurance compared to the property itself and loan protection insurance compared to the loan itself ...

3.9 The report states that the MORI survey findings are matched by other reports, including Risk Insurance and Welfare, published by the ABI. However, that publication does not call for comprehensive legislative reform of insurance law and indeed does not even consider it.

3.10 Thirdly, the report argues that there are gaps in the self-regulatory regime. The report commends the work of the IOB and states that the Ombudsman's decisions are 'likely to be radically changing the behaviour and practices of [...] insurers'. This is questionable considering that 60–70% of all IOB decisions confirm the insurer's decision, but nevertheless it is proper that the report should commend the work of the IOB. The report goes on, however, to identify what it calls a gap in the protection network – in that not all insurers belong to the ABI or the IOB. It notes that this gap could widen 'in the wake of the opening up of the "single European market". It describes it as a 'gaping hole in the safety net'.

3.11 In practice, ABI membership covers more than 95% of the UK insurance market and probably a greater percentage of the personal lines general business market. As far as the shortfall is concerned, the DTI encourages those companies to observe the ABI's self-regulatory mechanisms in the interests of the general good. The IOB membership also covers around 90% of these same markets. The shortfall is picked up by PIAS which the Consumers Association recognises as equivalent to the IOB. The 'gap', therefore, is very very small, certainly too small to justify comprehensive legislative reform of insurance law, and has shown no sign of widening in the three years since the opening-up of the single European market.

3.12 Lastly, the report argues that modern selling practices (by telephone/ machine) challenge existing insurance law concepts. We agree that some areas of insurance contract law need to revised in the light of recent developments in selling practices, but that itself does not prove that those areas of law are outdated or need to be reformed. In any event, the ABI has issued guidance to its members and to intermediaries on remote selling methods (telephone, internet, direct marketing) to ensure the consistent application of good selling practices. It is important to remember that consumers seem to want and prefer these modern selling practices – the growth of direct writers is evidence of that.

3.13 Overall, the report does not make out any case for comprehensive legislative reform of insurance law, a compelling substantiated one ...

9 CONCLUSION

9.1 Comprehensive legislative reform of insurance law would be a huge, very time consuming undertaking. It would soak up resources within the civil service, the Law Commission, the insurance industry and elsewhere. This cannot be justified and it is not realistic in the absence of a compelling case for comprehensive legislative reform supported and substantiated by immediate, real and sizable problems.

9.2 The NCC report does not make out such a case. In relation to many of the matters the NCC describes as ongoing problems, we take the view that there is no ongoing problem. Where there has been a problem in the past, we conclude that there is already a working solution in place. Where there is genuinely an ongoing problem, we take the view that it should be handled in isolation probably not even as a law reform issue ...

APPENDIX 4.30

Forte, A, 'The revised Statements of Insurance Practice: cosmetic change or major surgery?' (1986) 49 MLR 754

The last decade has witnessed mounting concern about certain aspects of the law of insurance and related practices of British insurers. The continued existence of the positive duty of disclosure of material facts, the testing of materiality by reference to the effect of non-disclosure 'on the judgment of the risk formed by a hypothetical prudent insurer', and the ability to avoid a contract for breach of warranty despite the absence of any nexus between the breach and the loss have all been subjected to sustained criticism. Both Law Commissions had proposed that insurance contracts should fall within the ambit of the controls for exclusion clauses ultimately prescribed in the Unfair Contract Terms Act 1977 but this suggestion was not implemented. Indeed, insurance contracts are specifically excluded from coverage by the Act. However, the possibility of legislative reform was enough to prompt the several professional bodies representing many companies to promulgate codes of practice for non-life and life insurance. Though yet another instance of the industry's tradition of self-regulation, the Statements received, on the whole, a cool reception, the leading work on insurance stating: 'We do not regard these statements of self-regulatory practice, as a substitute for reform of the law.' They have also been described as a mere 'token gesture to consumerism' effecting little change. The most potentially influential indictment of the Statements was voiced by the Law Commission in its report on non-disclosure and breach of warranty:

> In our view, the Statements of Insurance Practice are themselves evidence that the law is unsatisfactory and needs to be changed. As we have pointed out, the Statements lack the force of law so that an insured would have no legal remedy if an insurer failed to act in accordance with them. Indeed, the liquidator of an insurance company would be bound to disregard them. We consider that the further protection which the insured needs should be provided by legislation. We are fortified in this view by the words of Lawton LJ in *Lambert v Co-operative Insurance Society* [1975] 2 Lloyd's Rep 485: 'Such injustices as there are must now be dealt with by Parliament, if they are to be got rid of at all.'

So legislative reform was again put on the political agenda and in late April 1984 the Secretary of State for Trade and Industry was clearly considering statutory implementation of the Law Commission's recommendations. The prospect had receded somewhat by the end of the year when the Secretary of State announced that he was consulting the insurance industry to see if changes to the Statements might not resolve the matter. It ought not, therefore, to have come as a surprise when, on 21 February 1986, the Minister announced that the insurance industry had promulgated revised Statements of both General Insurance Practice and Long Term Insurance Practice, and that consequently:

> ... the case for legislation is outweighted by the advantages of self-regulation so long as this is effective' and so, 'there is [no] need for the moment to proceed with earlier proposals for a change in the law'.

For the present, and subject to the *caveat* that legislation will be reconsidered should problems continue to arise, the insurance industry has, once more, staved off the threat of statutory reform ...

CONCLUSION

The revised Statements represent a genuine attempt by the insurance industry to meet some of the criticisms levelled against it and it would be unduly cynical to describe them as mere tokenism. Nonetheless, by adhering closely to the Law Commission's proposals, on which any legislation would have been modelled, the Statements represent a minimalist attitude to the problem of abuses. They do not, for example, address themselves to the question of risk exclusion by means of 'excepted perils' clauses ...

... Although the Statements can be criticised, this does not mean that it is enough, or even sometimes fair, to confine one's criticisms to them. The Law Commission, for example, refused to countenance a separate regime for consumers, though the Statements have in fact created one. There has, rather, been a failure to resolve some of the more fundamental issues which flow from the existence of such codes. Why, for example, can there not now be a simple legislative change of the law abolishing the duty of disclosure? The spirit of the Statements is certainly inimical to its continued existence. And why should these particular codes be a substitute for legislation rather than, as in many other cases, a supplement to it? If insurers are prepared, under threat of legislation, to construct a regime which would substantially replicate, in unenforceable codes of practice, the broad proposals which might have been enacted, then why are they so concerned to avoid statutory regulation? The question is all the more intriguing when one considers the participation by British insurance companies in the United States where there is far greater legislative control over the use warranties and the notion of *uberrima fides* has all but disappeared.

For the immediate future, consumers must rest content with the voluntary adherence of insurers to the Statements. And it must be regarded as being fundamentally unsatisfactory that the consumer of insurance services continues to receive less favourable treatment than the consumer of goods and other services ...

APPENDIX 4.31

Cadogan, I and Lewis, R, 'Do insurers know best? An empirical examination of the extent that insurers comply with their Statements of Practice and whether they are a satisfactory substitute for reform of the law' (1992) 21 Anglo-Am L Rev 123

It is the aim of this article, by using the results of a small scale survey of insurers carried out by the authors, to assess whether the Statements of Practice are working effectively and to determine whether they represent a satisfactory substitute for reform of the law. In particular, it looks at the problems caused by enforcing the Statements.

A series of interviews were conducted with representatives of the Association of British Insurers, the Insurance Ombudsman Bureau, the former Law Commissioner responsible for insurance and five insurance companies. The companies were chosen to represent a cross-section of the insurance industry and included a composite, a mutual, a non-ABI and non-Insurance Ombudsman member. Their premium incomes in 1988 ranged from £22.5 m to £1,340.9 m. During the structured interviews, questions were asked with the aim of obtaining a realistic picture of the way in which the self-regulatory scheme is implemented. In addition, correspondence was conducted with the Department of Trade and Industry concerning the enforcement of the Statements. The overall result of this study offers an indication of the extent to which insurers adhere to their undertaking not to apply the strict laws of insurance. In addition, by comparing present day practice with what would have been the position had the proposals for reform been enacted, conclusions can be drawn as to whether the Statements provide adequate protection for the insurance consumer and whether legal reform is needed ...

(A) THE EXCLUSION OF COMMERCIAL INSURANCE

The Statement applies only to policyholders resident in the United Kingdom in so far as they are insured in their private capacity. Birds suggests that whilst this may not be 'harsh upon large commercial organisations, it is upon the small businessman'. In effect, the limit on the applicability of the Statement is to equate the sole trader's knowledge with that of a multi-national company. At the same time it provides protection to individuals who may be fully conversant with insurance law, whilst a sole trader, ignorant of insurance law, receives none.

The insurance companies interviewed all agreed that large commercial organisations contracted on 'equal terms' and ought to be aware of the law. With respect to small businesses, one company took the view that many of them were adequately protected because of their membership of various trade associations which often provide advice about insurance. Other companies similarly suggested that small businessmen were sufficiently protected because they normally arranged their commercial insurance through a broker, who ought to know the law.

The insurers surveyed were reluctant to extend the Statements of Practice to small businesses because of the problem of defining what constitutes a 'small business'. Underlying this unwillingness is also a recognition that liabilities under such policies are generally larger. Nevertheless, it seems that in practice the protection given by the Statements is sometimes extended to commercial policies. However, the survey showed that insurers were keen to safeguard their discretion here, and only wanted to extend the protection given by the Statements when they thought it appropriate to do so ...

Enforcement of the Statements of Practice

It is a condition of membership of the ABI that an insurer complies with the Statements of Practice. The ABI does not maintain an officer or department responsible for monitoring compliance, but their spokesperson said that this was done in a general way through 'eyes and ears'. If a member of the public or a member company complains that a particular insurer has not observed the Statements, the Association would investigate and, if necessary, request the company to ensure that it complies in the future. The Association say that this has happened in the past in relation to the warnings to be included on proposal forms and renewal documents. The ABI's experience is that the company concerned is usually embarrassed by any failure to comply and it rectifies the matter quickly. However, if a company refuses to do so then the matter would be referred to the Association's membership and disciplinary committee. They would review what had happened and make recommendations to the Board of the association. The ultimate sanction is expulsion from the ABI. To date, no company has been expelled for failure to comply with the Statements. Whilst loss of membership may give competitors little in the way of commercial advantage, the adverse publicity which would accompany an expulsion could be damaging to a company's reputation.

Membership of the ABI is not a prerequisite to transacting insurance business. A number of companies for various reasons have chosen not to become members and are therefore not bound as a condition of membership to adhere to the Statements of Practice. Despite this, the Secretary of State has stated:

> ... I look to all insurers, whether or not they belong to the ABI which promulgated the Statements, to observe both their spirit and their letter.

The Department of Trade and Industry is responsible for ensuring that non-members comply with the Statements. Although the Department receives complaints it deals with them only on an informal basis. The DTI states that:

> ... monitoring of compliance with the terms of the Statements is in the first instance a matter for the Association of British Insurers and Lloyd's. This Department does, however, take careful note of any complaint either received direct from members of the public or reported from other sources, which may indicate that there are problems over the way in which insurers deal with consumers. We have seen no evidence to suggest any significant failure to act in accordance with the terms of the industry's Statement of Practice.

Quite clearly, the ABI and DTI will only discover non-compliance when someone feels sufficiently strongly to make a complaint. This in turn assumes that the public are not only aware of the existence of the Statements, but also know where to complain. Whilst members show on all their literature that they belong to ABI, a policyholder of a non-member may not appreciate that the DTI is concerned with insurance matters.

It is apparent that there is no established body charged with monitoring the Statements of Practice even though bodies have been established to monitor other self-regulatory measures. This shortcoming was recognised by the Wilson Committee which expressed concern about the use of self-regulation in the context of insurance. They took the view that non-statutory regulation depends upon the existence of an institutional structure of some authority which those concerned are prepared to accept voluntarily. The Committee concluded that non-statutory regulation of insurance is not possible because there is no body with sufficient authority to enforce it. Based upon our responses from the relevant bodies, it is difficult to disagree with this view.

CONCLUSION

This article has examined the scope and actual operation of the Statements of Insurance Practice. We have shown that they differ in significant respects from the legislation that was proposed by the Law Commission in 1980, and that by comparison, they give consumers less protection. However, the real importance of our study is twofold: first, it evaluates the extent that the Statements are in fact complied with in practice; and secondly, it examines the procedures for enforcing the Statements.

We found that, by and large, insurers satisfied the basic requirements laid down by the Statements. However, the omission by one company to include certain warnings in its proposal form was an alarming discovery, especially since the Statements were originally introduced 14 years ago. Our survey also revealed that the manner in which the Statements are implemented varies from company to company. It is clear that some insurers go far beyond the minimum standards prescribed, and, for example, make a genuine effort to inform consumers of what is required of them, and what it is that they are buying. If a dispute occurs, such as insurer may go beyond both the letter of law and the Statements, and waive rights to avoid the policy. However, the discretion to do so lies entirely with the insurer; it is free to act without fear of legal interference. In making its decision it may rely upon factors with which many might disagree, but the lack of legal protection for consumers means that the decision can be reached in private. If called to account for its refusal of a claim, the insurer may ultimately refer to the strict legal position and not reveal its true reasons.

This reveals two major criticisms of the Statements: they do not reflect the better practice of many insurers, and they lack the force of law. In examining the enforcement of the Statements we exposed the inadequacies of relying upon the supervision exercised by the ABI and the DTI. The former Law Commissioner charged with responsibility for the 1980 report stated to us that the subject was too important to be left to self-regulation. He argued that if the law is defective it should be reformed.

Time will tell whether Parliament will intervene. Perhaps it will eventually be forced to do so by the European Community. Until such action is taken, the British insurance industry will continue to occupy in law a position of privilege. One result of this for the consumer is that when disaster strikes, its consequences may be more tragic than they should be.

APPENDIX 4.32

Derrington, J, 'Recent Australian insurance law reform: the intent and the result: a model for England?' (1996) 91 BILA Jo 19

Dramatic changes have been witnessed in the development of Australian insurance law in recent times. So similar are the values and legal culture of our countries that it would be surprising if England were not to respond to its perception of the successes of the Australian experiment. Favourable comments have already been generously bestowed on it by at least one English enquiry into the topic. This discussion is designed to stimulate further interest in its progress in the hope of spurring legislative action there, as some of my English friends fervently desire in the interest of this valuable social instrument ...

THE COMMON LAW

As a prefatory observation destined to show that serious reform is in the air, something more profound than the robust application of the *contra proferentem* principle or judicial tenderness towards the position of the insured, it is desirable to mention briefly one important recent development of the Australian common law in respect of insurance contracts.

In 1989, the High Court by a scholarly decision held (*Trident Insurance Co Ltd v McNeice Bros Ltd* (1988) 165 CLR 107) that at least in respect of contracts of liability insurance the doctrine of privity of contract in an insured person was not part of the common law of Australia. This meant that an insured person to whom the cover of a policy was extended could enforce the insurer's promises of indemnity in respect of his or her own cover despite that the person was not a party to the insurance contract, either directly or through agency or trust. This means that the insurer's discretion to dishonour the so called 'honour policies' does not exist and in such cases it is now dependent upon the merits of its contractual position. Few fair-minded people will mourn the departure of the former state of affairs that had attracted much judicial criticism ...

... the Insurance Contracts Act 1984. Although the relevant provision was expressly limited to insurance contracts, it reflected other legislation of general application that was already extant in some Australian states and in New Zealand. In brief it enables a person who has a beneficial interest in a policy but who is not a contracting party to enforce the interest directly against the insurer, subject otherwise to the terms of the policy.

THE 'BASIS' POLICY

Under the common law, another of the most unjust and criticised terms appearing in some policies was that whereby the insured warranted the truth of the answers in the proposal to the questions posited by the insurer. This was the 'basis' policy and despite the attempts by the courts to ameliorate its injustices by requiring strict compliance with certain qualifications before such a term could operate, there were many cases where it did so in a most undesirable way. An innocent error that was in fact totally immaterial to the insurer's decision as to whether to accept the proposal or similarly irrelevant to the subsequent claim would be used to avoid the policy and defeat the claim.

The Insurance Contracts Act ('the Act') has reformed this by substituting such a statement's status as a warranty with the status of a pre-contractual statement only. Read with the other provisions of the Act, including particularly those dealing with misrepresentation, this metamorphosis permits the insured's default to be treated on the merits according to its practical effects …

The Act has now remedied this in a simple direct and powerful way and the limits of the cure are still being worked out. In effect, it provides that where an insurer is entitled by reason of a post contractual act (which by definition includes an omission) of the insured or some other person to refuse to pay a claim, then it may not so refuse except to the extent proportionately that the act prejudiced the interests of the insurer. If the insurer proves that the act could reasonably be regarded as being capable of causing or contributing to an insured loss, the onus shifts to the insured to show either that no part of the loss was caused by the act or that some part of it was not so caused. In the latter case the insurer may not refuse to indemnify in respect of that part. The insurer may not refuse where the act was necessary to protect the safety of a person or to preserve property, or where it was not reasonably possible for the person not to do the act. It should be noted that the expression of this provision is not limited to conditions so that it avoids any circumvention by drafting.

The application of this remedy causes little difficulty in practice for courts are well versed in the art of attribution and the adjustment of rights according to the apportionment of causal responsibility. The difficulty comes when the act or omission is related to a feature that arguably goes to the description of the basic cover, as distinct from the exclusions and conditions that modify it.

UTMOST GOOD FAITH, DISCLOSURE AND MISREPRESENTATION

Disclosure and misrepresentation together form another area of fundamental upheaval through this legislation and its provisions on this subject constitute a code. The doctrine of utmost good faith is preserved as an implied term of the contract of insurance (which itself resolves some controversy as to the precise nature of the principle) and that behaviour is required of both parties in respect of any matter between them arising under or in relation to the contract. However, this is subject to the specific provisions controlling disclosure.

As to that the duty is still limited to disclosure, before the contract is entered into, of material matters that are known to the insured. It is the prescription of materiality that is interesting. It is any matter of relevance to the decision of the insurer whether to accept the risk and, if so, on what terms. This would seem to anticipate recent English developments for the matter need only be relevant to the insurer's decision. It need not be decisive.

The content of the change here is mostly obvious. Materiality is measured by reference to the significance of the relevant fact to the actual insurer, and while that quality was formerly a necessary element of actionable non-disclosure, the position now is that it is the only such element. There is no longer any reference to the materiality of the matter to a prudent insurer, though that issue may arise in an indirect and disguised form in respect of the question of imputed knowledge, which will be discussed shortly. No doubt, the view of a prudent insurer may also be adverted to, in order to test the truth of an assertion that the point was material to the actual insurer, but this is only a matter of circumstantial evidence and not one determinative of the relevant measure.

Materiality accepted, the recognition of it is a further element necessary in the duty of disclose. Under the Act, this knowledge can exist in two ways, either of which is sufficient – the insured may subjectively know it or a reasonable person in the circumstances could be expected to know it. Several possibilities are encompassed by this.

Some matters may be directly known from the circumstances to have specific relevance to the insurer. Other matters may not be so directly known to be material but in the circumstances should be deduced to be so by reason of the nature of the fact in the context of an insurance transaction and the nature of the particular cover sought. In such cases it should be inferred that insurers generally, including the actual insurer, would regard such a matter as material.

While the focus of the enquiry must always be directed to the actual insurer, absent any idiosyncratic circumstances to the contrary, in drawing such an inference a reasonable person would need to consider in the abstract the materiality of the matter to the insurer as a reasonable insurer and this is close in substance to the test of the prudent insurer. Consequently, this feature does not depart as significantly as may first seem from the former position. There may be some debate as to where an insurer has an easier task in proving that the reasonable person could be expected to know it rather than that such a person would know it.

There are specific exceptions to the general duty of disclosure. It is not required as to a matter that diminishes the risk, that is of common knowledge, that the insurer knows or should know in the ordinary course of its business; or whether there is waiver. These accord with earlier principle but waiver is also deemed where the insurer accepts an unanswered or obviously partly-answered response to a question in the proposal. Moreover, if the insurer fails to give antecedent written notice to the insured clearly informing of the nature and effect of the duty of disclosure then it cannot rely on any non-disclosure that is not fraudulent.

The materiality of a misrepresentation is defined in the same general terms as in the case of non-disclosure but such conduct is excused in certain circumstances based on objective reasonableness. And a non-answer or an obviously incomplete one cannot be a misrepresentation.

REMEDIES FOR NON-DISCLOSURE AND MISREPRESENTATION

More radical is the change effected through the remedies provided for non-disclosure and misrepresentation. The principal focus is on the distinction between fraud or mere error on the part of the insured, and the emphasis is on fairness. Needless to say, the insurer's right of avoidance of the contract is more extensive in the event of fraud but even then it is not absolute.

Even in that case the court may disregard the avoidance if it would be both harsh and unfair not to do so, but only if the court is of the opinion that in respect of the relevant loss the insurer has suffered only minimal, insignificant or no prejudice by the insured's fraud. In exercising this power, the court must have regard to the need to deter fraud in insurance business and must weigh the extent of the insured's culpability against the magnitude of the loss that would be suffered if the remedy were refused. The specification of these matters does not exclude the consideration of other relevant matters.

In any event, the insurer will not have any right to avoid the contract for non-disclosure or misrepresentation, even associated with fraud if knowing the truth of the relevant facts the insurer would still have entered into the contract for the same premium and on the same terms and conditions.

If the insurer is prevented or refrains from exercising its right to avoid the contract on any of these grounds, its liability in respect of a claim will be reduced so as to place it in the position that would have obtained if the insured's default had not occurred. It has been firmly established that this may reduce that liability to nil where, for example, the insurer would have declined the risk or would have inserted a term in the policy that would have allowed it to escape liability for the claim.

CLAIMS BY THIRD PARTIES DIRECTLY AGAINST INSURERS

Another useful provision allows a third party claimant to proceed directly against the insurer where the insured has died or cannot after reasonable enquiry be found. It is an extension to the remedy already available in England and Australia that provides similar direct recourse in the event of the bankruptcy of the insured. This extension of the facility is not unknown in existing compulsory insurance schemes.

CONCLUSIONS

That is enough for present purposes. These are but some examples of a wide ranging redefinition of the law that has been undertaken in this field. Its venture is bold while responsible and its cut is both wide and deep. The full flavour of the medicine can be discerned from this sample. Its efficacy is revealed in the results which the passage of time has uncovered in the judgments of the courts and the response of the industry.

Because of the general quality of its drafting and because the courts have willingly adopted the spirit of the reform, by searching for the resolution of any ambiguity through the purpose of the provision, with a few exceptions which were satisfactorily worked out within a short time, the results have generally conformed with expectation. The fairness which was the goal of the legislation for the conformity of the law to a just result is of importance to the judges, not least for its enhancement of public confidence in the legal system. They would be equally concerned with the converse.

While the beneficial reforms of the Act fell mostly to the insured side, the courts have not permitted them to become an instrument of unfairness to insurers. There have been several reported cases where the insurer has been successful because the courts have refused to lend themselves to an over-expansive interpretation of the sections of the Act invoked by overly hopeful but unmeritorious insured parties.

For example, although the Act does not say so, it has been held that in appropriate circumstances a non-contracting party to the insurance who enjoys the benefit of cover is affected by any breach by the contracting party of the duty in utmost good faith to make full disclosure and the insurer is entitled to its rights under the Act for any breach.

This has led to a general acceptance of the thrust of the reform by the industry so that there has been no noticeable movement towards amendment of the remedies that it provides. The imperative need for greater fairness to consumers in the areas affected was generally recognised and accepted. There will be the necessary emendation of the first version of the Act by way of fine tuning common to such sea changes in the law, but it is unlikely that any of the positions now established will be reversed or will be sought to be reversed.

Manifestly, the success of the Australian solution does not predicate that it is the only or the best one. No doubt when England is sufficiently stirred to move in the same direction some improvements will be found; but hopefully the Australian model will provide a useful paradigm, in the same way that English reform of the past has so often provided Australia with guidance of great value.

APPENDIX 4.33

Hasson, R, 'The special nature of the insurance contract: a comparison of the American and English law of insurance' (1984) 47 MLR 505

... But although insurance regulation has lost much of its impetus, the American rules developed in, say, the first three decades of this century are more favourable to the insured than are the English rules on the subject. Not only that; the English rules of insurance law are more oppressive to the insured than are the ordinary rules of the law of contract.

NON-DISCLOSURE

The insured's duty of disclosure is at the heart of the English law of insurance. It was not always thus. In a paper I wrote 15 years ago, I showed that Lord Mansfield had not formulated a wide duty of disclosure on the part of the insured. Indeed, neither I nor anyone else has, to my knowledge, been able to find a case where the defence of *uberrima fides* succeeded before Lord Mansfield. The duty of disclosure only became established firmly in 1907 with the Court of Appeal decision in *Joel v Law Union Insurance Co* [1908] 2 KB 863. Thus, for a century and a half, the insurance industry seems to have functioned very well without a duty of disclosure ...

... In their report on *Insurance Law: Non-Disclosure and Breach of Warranty* [Appendix 4.8], the Law Commission favoured the retention of a duty of disclosure because such a duty was recognised 'by the laws of all the common law ... jurisdictions which we have been able to study'. No authority is cited for this statement. In fact, the duty of disclosure occupies an insignificant role in the United States law of insurance. In the first place, most, if not all, jurisdictions in the United States require the insurer to show that the insured was fraudulently withholding information – a burden that is almost impossible to discharge. Further, in the United States, a life insurance contract cannot be challenged even for fraudulent misrepresentation (let alone fraudulent non-disclosure) after two years in most states and after one year in a minority of states.

The Law Commission was of the view that the duty of disclosure imposed on the applicant for insurance was 'defective'. At the same time, the Commission was opposed to both the abolition of the duty of disclosure or to 'a special attenuated duty'. The Commission thought all would be well if the applicant for insurance disclosed facts which a reasonable man as opposed to a reasonable insurer would think material. This is the same solution as was suggested by the Law Reform Committee in 1957.

The proposal ignores the fact that reasonable persons come in a wide variety of shapes and sizes. For our purposes, I will assume that there are two types of reasonable person:

(1) the first kind of reasonable person has a law degree or has an insurance qualification. Such a person is likely to know the duty of disclosure, although it is problematical if she or he knows of the extent of the duty;

(2) there is a second kind of reasonable person who may be very intelligent and highly educated and who has never heard of the duty of disclosure. Professor Atiyah, in a comment addressed to the Law Commission after their working paper had appeared, suggested that the Commission try to find out how many people without a legal training had any knowledge of the duty of disclosure. This the Commission did not do.

Thus, we have a rule which probably only a tiny fraction of the population know about, imposed on the entire population in the name of 'reasonableness'! I expect there to be little (if any) difference between the 'old' test and the 'new' test. I think that the courts will continue to penalise applicants for insurance who do not volunteer, for example, the information that they were refused insurance or had made prior claims.

The Law Commission uses more 'reasonableness' when it comes to deal with the duty of disclosure on renewals. In the Commission's words:

> ... on renewal the insured will have to disclose material facts which he knows or is assumed to know, which have not been disclosed by him and which would be disclosed by a reasonable insured, having regard to the nature and extent of the cover which is renewed and the circumstances in which it is renewed.

This is too vague to give anyone any guidance. Suppose an applicant takes an automobile policy with the Good Faith Company. The applicant answers truthfully 'No' to the question: 'Have you been involved in a car accident?' When does the applicant's duty of disclosure arise, assuming he does have an accident? Does it arise one year after the issuance of the policy? Five years? Ten years? A much simpler solution would be for the insurer to ask the insured to check the proposal form each year, or else to fill in a new one each year and issue a new policy ...

Misrepresentation

Misrepresentation in the law of insurance is quite unlike misrepresentation in the general law of contract. Throughout most of the law of insurance, insurers have removed the question of materiality from the law of misrepresentation by using 'the basis of the contract' clause. This clause enables insurers to avoid a policy without having to prove that the misrepresentation was material. The tactic was denounced by Fletcher Mounton LJ, who wished in 1908 he could 'adequately warn the public against such practices on the part of insurance offices' and by Lord Greene MR, who denounced it in 1942 as 'a vicious device'. Despite these criticisms, the doctrine is still with us ...

Policing unfairness in contracts

Every contract seems to have some device for policing unfair bargains. The law of unemployment has a whole range of statutory and common law devices to protect against unfair contracts. The law of consumer credit, and the law relating to sale of goods have devices to police unfair contracts. For other contracts, there is the Unfair Contract Terms Act 1977.

With the exception of some minor controls in the law of industrial life insurance, a cooling off period in the law of life insurance, and some provisions in motor vehicle and employers' liability policies, there is a remarkable lack of control over the terms of insurance contracts. Writing in 1957, Professor Gower said, 'there can be few countries ... where the insurance companies are allowed the same freedom to dictate their own terms' ...

... I do not favour policing insurance contracts by the use of devices such as 'unconscionability', 'unequal bargaining power' and the like, because they are too vague to offer much support for the insured. Secondly, even if the courts used their powers more generously than anyone could reasonably expect, there would still be delays and the insured may be in dire straits before relief comes.

I favour the enactment of statutory policies for the principal classes of insurance – for example, life, householders', employers' liability, etc. All other classes of insurance would have to be vetted by an Insurance Superintendent who would have to consult with consumers' groups both in drawing up statutory policies and in vetting new policies ...

... The Superintendent would also, in my scheme, have the responsibility for ensuring that 'all risks' policies and 'comprehensive' policies did provide the kind of cover their names suggested. It might be argued that this type of control is ultimately doomed to fail because of the power of the insurance industry. But much depends on the quality of the Insurance Superintendent and, perhaps, even more on the vigour of consumer organisations, including trade unions. Even with a heavy input from the insurance industry, I think this method of control is better than our threadbare system of control ...

CONCLUSION

American insurance law has been something of a pace setter for the general law of contract in that country. Even today, the adoption of statutory policies in many fields of insurance places the insured in a more favourable position than, say, someone making a purchase under a conditional sales contract. The English law of insurance rules, on the other hand, are more oppressive to the insured than are the rules governing the purchase of goods and services.

I think that there are two reasons which explain this disparity. In the United Kingdom, the insurance industry has, at least during this century, enjoyed a very high reputation for fair dealing and probity. The American insurance industry, on the other hand, came under fire from muckrakers, populists and other reformers. The criticisms of American insurers find no parallel in English writings, to the best of my knowledge. The American reformers were able to push through a number of important reforms between, say, 1900–40. During this period, the only significant English reforms in the law of insurance came in the field of motor vehicle insurance.

A second factor, probably more important, is the fact that by the time the principal English doctrines of insurance law had been established – say, by 1930, there was an embryo welfare state in existence. The existence of some sort of welfare state has, I believe, weakened the movement for insurance law reform. Private insurance has come to be seen as icing on the welfare state cake and social reformers have concentrated their energies on trying to improve the social – rather than the private – insurance schemes. The Beveridge Report, for example, dealt with private insurance for workers' compensation, sickness insurance, and with industrial life insurance, but did not deal with any other kind of insurance.

By way of contrast, there was no welfare state in America in 1930. Because of that fact, the regulation of private insurance became a necessity. By 1945, say, Americans had some kind of welfare state and it is significant that the reform of private insurance has lost a great deal of its momentum since then.

It seems to me to be crucial to examine private insurance as critically as we now examine social insurance. Failure to do so means that we shall continue to have an irrational and stunted social security system.

APPENDIX 4.34

Penn Mutual Life Insurance Co v Mechanics Savings Bank and Trust Co (1896) 72 F 423; on rehearing 73 F 653

Taft J: *Carter v Boehm* (1766) 3 Burr 1905 ... states the rule enforced by the courts of this country in cases of marine insurance is established by many decisions ... The very marked difference between the situation of the parties in marine insurance and that of parties to a fire or life policy has led many courts of this country to modify the rigor of the doctrine in its application to fire and life insurance, and to lean towards the view that no failure to disclose a fact material to the risk, not inquired about, will avoid the policy, unless such non-disclosure was fraudulent. In the marine insurance, the risk was usually tendered and accepted when the vessel was on the high seas, where the insurer had no opportunity to examine her, or to know the particular circumstances of danger to which she might be exposed. The risk in such a case is highly speculative, and it is manifestly the duty of the insured to advise the insurer of every circumstance within his knowledge from which the probability of a loss can be inferred, and he cannot be permitted to escape the obligation by a plea of inadvertence or negligence. In cases of fire and life insurance, however, the parties stand much more nearly on an equality. The subject of the fire insurance is usually where the insurer can send its agents to give it a thorough examination, and determine the extent to which it is exposed to danger of fire from surrounding buildings or because of the plan or material of its own structure. The subject of life insurance is always present for physical examination by medical experts of the insurer, who often acquire, by lung and heart tests, and by chemical analysis of bodily excretions, a more intimate knowledge of the bodily condition of the applicant than he has himself. Then, too, the practice has grown of requiring the applicant of both fire and life insurance to answer a great many questions carefully adapted to elicit facts which the insurer deems of importance in estimating the risk. In life insurance, not only is the applicant required to answer many general questions concerning himself and his ancestors, but he is also subject to an extended examination concerning his bodily history ... When the applicant has fully and truthfully answered all these questions, he may rightfully assume that the range of the examination has covered all matters within ordinary human experience deemed material by the insurer, and that he is not required to rack his memory for circumstances of possible materiality, not inquired about, and to volunteer them. He can only be said to fail in his duty to the insurer when he withholds from him some fact which, though not made the subject of inquiry, he nevertheless believes to be material to the risk, and actually is so, for fear it would induce a rejection of the risk, or, what it the same thing, with fraudulent intent. A strong reason why the rule as to concealment should not be so stringent in cases of life insurance as in marine insurance is that the question of concealment rarely, if ever, arises until after the death of the applicant, and then the mouth of him whose silence and whose knowledge it is claimed avoid the policy is closed. The application is generally prepared, and the questions are generally answered, under the supervision of an eager life insurance solicitor (for example, an agent). Only the barest outlines of the conversations between the applicant and the solicitor are reduced to writing. The applicant is likely to trust the judgment of the solicitor as to the materiality of everything not made the subject of express inquiry, and, with the solicitor's strong motive for securing the business, there is danger that facts communicated to him may not find their way into the application. With respect to a contract thus made, it is clearly just to require that nothing but a fraudulent non-disclosure shall avoid the policy. Nor does this rule result in practical hardship to the insurer, for in every case where the undisclosed fact is palpably material to the risk the mere non-disclosure is itself strong evidence of a fraudulent intent ... To hold that good faith is immaterial in such a case is to apply the harsh and rigorous rule of marine insurance to a class of insurance contracts differing so materially from marine policies in the circumstances under which the contracting parties agree that the reason for the rule ceases. The authorities are not uniform, and we are able to take that view which is more clearly founded in reason and justice ...

APPENDIX 4.35

Manifest Shipping Co Ltd v Uni-Polaris Shipping Co Ltd (The Star Sea) [2001] 1 All ER 743, HL

Lord Hobhouse:

Section 17: the legal problems

[41] Section 17 raises many questions. But only two of them are critical to the decision of the present appeal: the fraudulent claim question and the litigation question. It is, however, necessary to discuss them in the context of a consideration of the problematic character of s 17 which is overlaid by the historical and pragmatic development of the relevant concept both before and since 1906.

[42] The history of the concept of good faith in relation to the law of insurance is reviewed in the speech of Lord Mustill in *Pan Atlantic Insurance Co Ltd v Pine Top Insurance Co Ltd* [1994] 3 All ER 581; [1995] 1 AC 501 and in a valuable and well researched article (also containing a penetrating discussion of the conceptual difficulties) by Mr Howard N Bennett 'Mapping the doctrine of utmost good faith in insurance contract law' [1999] Lloyd's MCLQ 165. The acknowledged origin is Lord Mansfield CJ's judgment in *Carter v Boehm* (1766) 3 Burr 1905; [1558-1774] All ER Rep 183. As Lord Mustill points out, Lord Mansfield was at the time attempting to introduce into English commercial law a general principle of good faith, an attempt which was ultimately unsuccessful and only survived for limited classes of transactions, one of which was insurance. His judgment in *Carter v Boehm* was an application of his general principle to the making of a contract of insurance. It was based upon the inequality of information as between the proposer and the underwriter and the character of insurance as a contract upon a 'speculation' ...

[47] The arguments of counsel in the present case disclosed a certain amount of common ground between them. The principle of utmost good faith is not confined to marine insurance; it is applicable to all forms of insurance ... and is mutual as s 17 itself affirms by using the phrase 'if the utmost good faith be not observed by either party' and as was expressly stated by Lord Mansfield in *Carter v Boehm.*

[48] Secondly, both counsel submitted that the utmost good faith is a principle of fair dealing which does not come to an end when the contract has been made. A different inference might have been drawn both from the language of s 17 and from its place in the Act – beneath the heading 'Disclosure and Representations' and above ss 18 to 21 which expressly relate to matters arising before the making of the contract. But there is a weight of *dicta* that the principle has a continuing relevance to the parties' conduct after the contract has been made. Why indeed, it may be asked, should not the parties continue to deal with one another on the basis of good faith after as well as before the making of the contract? ...

[49] Thirdly, both counsel accept and assert that the conclusion of the Court of Appeal in the *Banque Financière* case is good law and that there is no remedy in damages for any want of good faith. Counsel also drew this conclusion from the second half of s 17

– 'may be avoided by the other party'. The sole remedy, they submitted, was avoidance. It follows from this that the principle relied upon by the defendants is not an implied term but is a principle of law which is sufficient to support a right to avoid the contract of insurance retrospectively ...

[51] The right to avoid referred to in s 17 ... applies retrospectively. It enables the aggrieved party to rescind the contract *ab initio*. Thus he totally nullifies the contract. Everything done under the contract is liable to be undone. If any adjustment of the parties' financial positions is to take place, it is done under the law of restitution not under the law of contract. This is appropriate where the cause, the want of good faith, has preceded and been material to the making of the contract. But, where the want of good faith first occurs later, it becomes anomalous and disproportionate that it should be so categorised and entitle the aggrieved party to such an outcome. But this will be the effect of accepting the defendants' argument. The result is effectively penal. Where a fully enforceable contract has been entered into insuring the assured, say, for a period of a year, the premium has been paid, a claim for a loss covered by the insurance has arisen and been paid, but later, towards the end of the period, the assured fails in some respect fully to discharge his duty of complete good faith, the insurer is able not only to treat himself as discharged from further liability but can also undo all that has perfectly properly gone before. This cannot be reconciled with principle. No principle of this breadth is supported by any authority whether before or after the Act. It would be possible to draft a contractual term which would have such an effect but it would be an improbable term for the parties to agree to and difficult if not impossible to justify as an implied term. The failure may well be wholly immaterial to anything that has gone before or will happen subsequently ...

[57] These authorities show that there is a clear distinction to be made between the pre-contract duty of disclosure and any duty of disclosure which may exist after the contract has been made. It is not right to reason, as the defendants submitted that your Lordships should, from the existence of an extensive duty pre-contract positively to disclose all material facts to the conclusion that post-contract there is a similarly extensive obligation to disclose all facts which the insurer has an interest in knowing and which might affect his conduct. The courts have consistently set their face against allowing the assured's duty of good faith to be used by the insurer as an instrument for enabling the insurer himself to act in bad faith. An inevitable consequence in the post-contract situation is that the remedy of avoidance of the contract is in practical terms wholly one-sided. It is a remedy of value to the insurer and, if the defendants' argument is accepted, of disproportionate benefit to him; it enables him to escape retrospectively the liability to indemnify which he has previously and (on this hypothesis) validly undertaken. Save possibly for some types of reinsurance treaty, it is hard to think of circumstances where an assured will stand to benefit from the avoidance of the policy for something that has occurred after the contract has been entered into; the hypothesis of continuing dealings with each other will normally postulate some claim having been made by the assured under the policy ...

Fraudulent claims

[61] This question arises upon policies which up to the time of the making of the claim are to be assumed to be valid and enforceable. No right to avoid the contract had arisen. On ordinary contractual principles it would be expected that any question as to

what are the parties' rights in relation to anything which has occurred since the contract was made would be answered by construing the contract in accordance with its terms, both express and implied by law. Indeed, it is commonplace for insurance contracts to include a clause making express provision for when a fraudulent claim has been made. But it is also possible for principles drawn from the general law to apply to an existing contract – on the better view, frustration is an example of this, as is the principle that a party shall not be allowed to take advantage of his own unlawful act. It is such a principle upon which the defendants rely in the present case. As I have previously stated there are contractual remedies for breach of contract and repudiation which act prospectively and upon which the defendants do not rely. The potential is also there for the parties, if they so choose, to provide by their contract for remedies or consequences which would act retrospectively. All this shows that the courts should be cautious before extending to contractual relations principles of law which the parties could themselves have incorporated into their contract if they had so chosen. The courts should likewise be prepared to examine the application of any such principle to the particular class of situation to see to what extent its application would reflect principles of public policy or the overriding needs of justice. Where the application of the proposed principle would simply serve the interests of one party and do so in a disproportionate fashion, it is right to question whether the principle has been correctly formulated or is being correctly applied and it is right to question whether the codifying statute from which the right contended for is said to be drawn is being correctly construed.

[62] Where an insured is found to have made a fraudulent claim upon the insurers, the insurer is obviously not liable for the fraudulent claim. But often there will have been a lesser claim which could properly have been made and which the insured, when found out, seeks to recover. The law is that the insured who has made a fraudulent claim may not recover the claim which could have been honestly made. The principle is well established and has certainly existed since the early 19th century ... This result is not dependent upon the inclusion in the contract of a term having that effect or the type of insurance; it is the consequence of a rule of law. Just as the law will not allow an insured to commit a crime and then use it as a basis for recovering an indemnity (see *Beresford v Royal Insurance Co Ltd* [1937] 2 All ER 243; [1937] 2 KB 197), so it will not allow an insured who has made a fraudulent claim to recover. The logic is simple. The fraudulent insured must not be allowed to think: if the fraud is successful, then I will gain; if it is unsuccessful, I will lose nothing ...

[72] For the defendants to succeed in their defence under this part of the case the defendants have to show that the claim was made fraudulently. They have failed to obtain a finding of fraud. It is not enough that until part of the way through the trial the owners (without fraudulent intent) failed to disclose to the defendants all the documents and information which the defendants would have wished to see in order to provide them with some, albeit inadequate, evidential support for their alleged defence under s 39(5). The defence under s 17 fails. It must be added that, on the facts found, had the defendants' defence succeeded it would have produced a wholly disproportionate result. The defence under s 39(5) failed after a full disclosure and investigation of all the material evidence. The claim was in fact a good one which the owners were, subject to quantum, entitled to recover under the policy. The defendants were liable to pay it. The policy was valid and enforceable. For the defendants

successfully to invoke s 17 so as to avoid the policy *ab initio* and wholly defeat the claim would be totally out of proportion to the failure of which they were complaining. Fraud has a fundamental impact upon the parties' relationship and raises serious public policy considerations. Remediable mistakes do not have the same character ...

Conclusion

[79] I have in the course of this speech referred to some cases from other jurisdictions. It is a striking feature of this branch of the law that other legal systems are increasingly discarding the more extreme features of the English law which allow an insurer to avoid liability on grounds which do not relate to the occurrence of the loss. The most outspoken criticism of the English law of non-disclosure is to be found in the judgment in the South African case to which I have already referred, *Mutual and Federal Insurance Co Ltd v Oudtshoorn Municipality* 1985 (1) SA 419. There is also evidence that it does not always command complete confidence even in this country (see *Container Transport International Inc v Oceanus Mutual Underwriting Association (Bermuda) Ltd* [1984] 1 Lloyd's Rep 476; *Pan Atlantic Insurance Co Ltd v Pine Top Insurance Co Ltd* [1994] 3 All ER 581; [1995] 1 AC 501). Such authorities show that suitable caution should be exercised in making any extensions to the existing law of non-disclosure and that the courts should be on their guard against the use of the principle of good faith to achieve results which are only questionably capable of being reconciled with the mutual character of the obligation to observe good faith ...

APPENDIX 4.36

Bennett, H, 'Mapping the doctrine of utmost good faith in insurance contract law' [1999] LMCLQ 165

[Note: This is a long, closely reasoned article which should be referred to in greater detail.]

E SUMMARY AND CONCLUSIONS

A central theme of this article is that the rhetoric of 'utmost good faith' must never substitute for a careful consideration of what is good law in the particular and modern context. The Statements of Practice of the Association of British Insurers constitute an acceptance by the insurance industry that the traditional principles of insurance contract law, developed when the industry was dominated by commercial policies of marine insurance, are not appropriate for all sectors of the modern industry. The future development of the doctrine of utmost good faith must take place against an evaluation of the extent to which it continues to be appropriate for parties to insurance contracts, in practice, usually the insurers, to occupy a privileged position as opposed to all other contracting parties and litigants.

It may be useful to summarise the main arguments advanced:

1 The Marine Insurance Act 1906, s 17 provides expressly for the remedy of avoidance of the contract for breach. This means retrospective avoidance of the entire contract. The extent to which s 17 should be viewed as the basis of all aspects of the doctrine of utmost good faith depends on whether some measure of flexibility in the remedies for breach or standard of conduct is viewed as appropriate.

2 Section 17 is the basis of the entirety of the reciprocal pre-formation duties of utmost good faith resting upon the insurer and assured. Section 18 and s 20 to the extent that it applies to the assured provide details of the two main aspects of the assured's pre-formation duty under s 17.

3 Outside of and independently from the assured's duty of utmost good faith, an insurer is entitled to avoid the policy for pre-formation non-disclosure under s 19 and misrepresentation under s 20 by an agent to insure. In all probability, this aspect of the pre-formation doctrine does not fall within s 17.

4 The reasoning of the Court of Appeal in *Skandia* reveals a tenable justification for denying a damages remedy for breach of the duty of utmost good faith. However, breach of a contractual term implied in law need not sound in damages. The wording of the Marine Insurance Act, previous authority and the origin of the doctrine of utmost good faith are all perfectly compatible with an implied term basis for the duty. The law of assignment supports such an analysis. The doctrine of utmost good faith developed by the common law courts and codified in the Marine Insurance Act is a common law doctrine and the juristic basis of the duties generated by the pre-formation doctrine is a contractual contingent condition precedent to the enforceability of the contract implied in law.

5 The heterogeneity of the various duties to which the post-formation doctrine of utmost good faith gives rise requires flexibility in scope, standard and remedies. The unequivocal availability of retrospective avoidance as a remedy for any breach of s 17 denies any possibility of remedial flexibility. Consequently, it is suggested that the post-formation doctrine of utmost good faith lies entirely outside s 17.

6 The flexibility required by the heterogeneity of the various duties generated by the post-formation doctrine requires also a flexible juristic basis for the doctrine. The law of assignment again supports a contractual basis. Accordingly, each duty within the post-formation doctrine may be the subject of a separate contractual term implied in law, the precise properties of which may be moulded by the courts as appropriate to the duty in question.

7 In principle, the post-formation doctrine of utmost good faith attaches to all terms of insurance contracts under which the assured is required by the policy to give the insurer information relevant to fixing the terms on which cover is granted or to be extended and to the making of claims. Outside of such matters, however, there is no duty to disclose information simply because it would be of value to the insurer.

8 With respect to the giving of information or notice pursuant to express contractual terms, such as held covered clauses, the post-formation duty is strict liability in nature but moulds itself to its context in terms of scope and, it is suggested, remedy. Breach entitles the insurer to avoid such extension of cover as the insurer has been induced to grant by the breach.

9 The development of the order for ship's papers is consistent with a doctrine of utmost good faith but the order was probably not part of the doctrine. It was certainly no part of the s 17 duty of utmost good faith.

10 The fraudulent claims jurisdiction is part of the post-formation duty of utmost good faith. An assured who makes a fraudulent claim is liable, at the insurer's option, to forfeit the entire benefit of the policy. The insurer has the choice either to reject the entire claim, even if the fraud affects only part, or retrospectively to avoid the entire policy. It is possible also that a fraudulent claim may constitute a repudiatory breach of contract so that the insurer also has the option to elect to treat his liability under the contract as prospectively discharged.

11 The apparent harshness of a retrospective remedy in the event of a fraudulent claim is fully justified in all areas of insurance by the policing function of the doctrine of utmost good faith in that particular context. However, the argument that the realities of insurance practice justify a strict liability duty at the claims stage attracting a retrospective remedy is not immediately apparent in the modern world.

12 If the duty attaching to the making of claims is confined to the avoidance of fraud, a strict liability duty of utmost good faith may still attach to contracts of compromise of claims on insurance policies, although there is little authority for such a duty at present and, again, it is not immediately apparent why compromises of insurance contracts should be singled out for special treatment. Any such duty, if broken, should permit avoidance only of the compromise, not the entire policy.

APPENDIX 4.37

Longmore LJ, 'An Insurance Contracts Act for a new century?' (2001) 106 BILA 18; [2001] LMCLQ 356

Longmore LJ:

There are numerous areas where reform would be useful and some where it is essential. Piecemeal proposals for reform have not worked well in the past; reform elsewhere in the world is made more difficult by the fact that the City of London remains the leading insurance and reinsurance centre of the world. Other countries are somewhat reluctant to adopt reforms if the risk is likely to be reinsured by a significantly different law. The time has come when, in my view, both the law and the market should adopt sensible reform across the board. There has been some reform in the area of what I may call insurance by consumers as a result of the Unfair Terms in Consumer Contracts Regulations 1994/9 but it does not extend to business insurance or to the general law of avoidance for non-disclosure or misrepresentation; proposals for reform of business insurance have fought shy of reforming marine and aviation insurance as well ...

Codification or Piecemeal Reform?

There is an argument for codification of insurance law in general just as Chalmers codified the law of marine insurance in 1906. I would have no principled objection to such a proposal but it would be an enormous task and invite yet further delay. In this context, Sir Mackenzie Chalmers' own thoughts are worth reading. The Marine Insurance Bill was first introduced to Parliament in the early 1890's. It took 12 years to reach the statute book. He published the originally proposed Bill as a Digest of the law relating to marine insurance. In 1901 he said this:

> The future which awaits the Bill is uncertain. Mercantile opinion is in favour of codification, but probably the balance of legal opinion is against it. As long as freedom of contract is preserved, it suits the man of business to have the law stated in black and white. The certainty of the rule is more important than its nicety. It is cheaper to legislate than to litigate; moreover, while a moot point is being litigated and appealed, pending business is embarrassed. The lawyer, on the other hand, feels cramped by codification ... No code can provide for every case that may arise, or always use language which is absolutely accurate. The cases which are before lawyers are the cases in which the code is defective. In so far as it works well it does not come before them. Every man's view of a question is naturally coloured by his own experience, and a lawyer's view of insurance is perhaps affected by the fact that he sees mainly the pathology of business. He does not often see its healthy physiological action.

I would prefer the Law Commission to consider what reform is really necessary and attempt to re-engage Government to enact those reforms. I suggest 6 topics in particular:

1 Whether a doctrine of the utmost good faith should be retained and, if so, what , its content should be.

2 The appropriate test for an insurer or reinsurer who wishes to defend a claim on the basis of non-disclosure and misrepresentation before formation of the contract.

3 The remedies which should be open to an insurer or reinsurer if he wishes to defend a claim on the ground of non-disclosure or misrepresentation.

4 The right approach to breach of warranty by the insured.

5 The right approach to proposal forms and answers given being declared to be the basis of the contract.

6 The question whether damages should be payable for insurers' refusal to pay a valid claim.

I have said enough already on the first topic of the utmost good faith. But I would like to say something more about the appropriate test for evidence of non-disclosure and misrepresentation.

Test for Avoidance

The current law in relation to the objective part of the test is settled by *Pan Atlantic v Pine Top* and I hope I summarise it correctly by saying it is whether the non-disclosed or misrepresented fact would have been taken into account by a prudent insurer when assessing the risk.

My own view is that, even after the addition of the subjective part of the test (actual inducement), this tilts the matter too heavily in the insurers' favour ...

Any rational discussion of this thorny topic needs to take into account alternative formulations. Six possible alternative formulations spring to mind and, no doubt, others can be considered:

1 Whether a prudent insurer would have considered that, if the relevant matter had been disclosed, the risk was a different risk; this is the formulation preferred by the Court of Appeal in *St Paul Fire and Marine v McConnell* (1995); they obviously did not consider it any different from the *Pan-Atlantic* test; but I do wonder; a prudent insurer may take something into account without it being a factor that would make the risk different in any sensible use of the word 'different'.

2 Whether, if the matter had been disclosed, the prudent insurer would have declined the risk or written it in different terms (the decisive influence test which was espoused by the minority but rejected by the majority in *Pan Atlantic v Pine Top*).

3 Whether a reasonable insured would have considered the undisclosed matter to be material to a prudent insurer. (This is the solution adopted by statute in Australia and was recommended here by our own Law Commission.)

4 Whether the actual insured ought to have considered the undisclosed matter to be material to a prudent insurer.

5 Whether the undisclosed matter was a matter which a reasonable insured would realise was within the knowledge only of himself (or those for whom he is responsible) rather than a matter which could have been independently investigated and verified by insurers.

6 Whether the duty on an insured should be merely to answer correctly any question asked by the insurer; this would be to abandon any requirement of disclosure at all.

While I would not favour the total abolition of the requirement of disclosure, my own view for what that is worth is that option 5 has much to commend it viz that the insured should only be expected to disclose what a reasonable insured in his position should have appreciated was material and within his own knowledge rather than a matter which could have been independently verified.

This seems to have been the law in the aftermath of Lord Mansfield's famous decision in *Carter v Boehm* (1760) in which, it is sometimes forgotten, the insured actually succeeded. In 1817, it was expressly held in *Friere v Woodhouse*:

> What is exclusively known to the assured ought to be communicated; but what the underwriter, by fair inquiry and due diligence, may learn from ordinary sources of information need not be disclosed.

Of course, ordinary sources of information are far more extensive now than in the early 19th century but that seems to me to make stronger rather than weaker the case for a professional underwriter having to equip himself with knowledge of matters that can be independently investigated and verified.

Remedies

I have already remarked that one of the difficulties about a doctrine of avoidance for non-disclosure and representation in insurance law is that it is such an extreme remedy. That was a major reason why the House of Lords in *The Star Sea* declined to extend the doctrine of good faith in its widest form to post-contract dealings. The remedy would be worse than the disease.

The remedy may, however, be equally extreme in relation to pre-contract non-disclosure and misrepresentation. This was, of course, considered by the Law Commission in their 1980 report. They rejected, for good reasons as it seems to me, the notion of proportionality as espoused in some European countries and in the then proposed European directive. But I feel they may have rejected too readily the idea that the court should be vested with a discretion in a suitable case to adjust the parties' respective responsibilities. It is a concept that appealed to at least one member of the Court of Appeal when it decided *Pan Atlantic*. It would not be so necessary, no doubt, if there were to be reform of the law to adopt the reasonable insured test since, if an insured cannot recover on that test, he would only have himself to blame; it may well be for this reason that the Law Commission did not consider the proposal in any substantial detail. But if the tests for disclosure and misrepresentation are to remain as they are, a discretionary apportionment of the loss has much to recommend it. It would, of course, lead to some uncertainty but that, after all, was a reason against the introduction of the concept of contributory negligence which, in the event, is a concept that has worn the test of time very well. In these days when the incidence of costs in litigation may depend on well or ill-informed guesses made by the litigant, at the time they are obliged to serve pre-action protocols, uncertainty is endemic, yet the court, and litigants, are quite good at getting used to it. Moreover, the Insurance Ombudsman Bureau apparently uses its discretion on occasion to apportion the loss and appears to have no difficulty with the concept.

I do not think I need to say anything in particular about the 4th and 5th topics on my list; breach of warranty and basis of the contract clauses. The evils of the present law are, I think, well enough known and universally acknowledged and it is about time that the law was changed to accord with an ordinary person's expectations ...

The question of delay in paying valid claims is a newer topic, which, it seems to me, does merit consideration. The courts have set their face against there being an implied term of an insurance contract that valid claims will be met and thus do not award damages against an insurer even if his delay in negotiating the claim means that the insured goes out of business. In a sense this is part of a wider point viz whether interest is truly compensation for delayed payment of claims for damages. But it has always been an oddity that a claim under an insurance policy is treated by the law as a claim for damages rather than a straight debt. This is a doctrine that could be usefully considered, I suggest, by the Law Commission.

Where Do We Go From Here?

In terms of legal principle and abstract justice, the case for reform in the areas about which I have been talking is extremely strong.

Opposition to reform may come from the insurers' side of the insurance industry who like to rely on the content of the present law and, perhaps, from Government on the grounds of inertia rather than principle. Siren voices will say 'Show us the law is working unjustly in practice before we take any interest in proposals for reform'. On the assumption that, unlike Odysseus's crew, we should not consent to have our ears stopped with sealing wax, there are perhaps two separate ways to deal with these siren voices.

The first is to do some empirical research in order to discover whether insureds have suffered injustice in the areas I have been considering. In this respect the records of the Ombudsman Bureau will be an early port of call. The experience of other Law Commissions, eg, in Australia and Canada can be investigated. London firms of insurance brokers and of solicitors will be able to help, but it may be even more important to consult out of London brokers and solicitors. Barristers will be much less help because for every insured whom counsel has, regretfully or otherwise, to advise that he is likely to lose, there will be many insureds who have already given up the struggle in correspondence, well before there is any question of obtaining counsel's opinion. The judiciary is even less well placed to give examples of injustice since no insured will want to fight a case he knows he will probably lose. Despite the difficulties, I would urge the Law Commission to undertake a research project. I doubt if they would find that there is any widespread devotion to the present state of the law.

But secondly there is the question of principle. How can it be right that a lawyer insuring his home and household possessions can rely on a more relaxed test of non-disclosure under the Statements of Practice, but the small trader, eg, the garage owner or the fishmonger insuring his premises, cannot. The truth is that the same standard should apply to both and it should, at least, be the standard of the reasonable insured.

The very fact that insurance companies are so anxious to persuade people that the best form of self-regulation is to ensure that the law is not enforced in its full rigour shows that insurers are worried that, if the law is reformed, they would have to pay more claims. If they accept that for the consumer, why should the law not be the same for the small business as indeed a wealthy business? The very acceptance by the insurance industry of the Statement of Practice shows that the law ought to be different from what it is. If even insurers accept that, surely it is time that the rights of not merely consumers but of all insured persons should be enforceable as a matter of right not as a matter of discretion. Surely we should be able to look forward to a better day. ...

WARRANTIES AND CONDITIONS

INTRODUCTION

In general contract law, terms of the contract have traditionally been divided into conditions and warranties. Breach of a condition is regarded as a major fault and breach of a warranty is regarded as a minor fault. The resulting effect is that breach of condition permitted the innocent party to rescind the contract while breach of warranty saw the contract continue but the innocent party could sue for damages.

However, this strict division tied the courts to the remedies above which were not necessarily appropriate to the seriousness of the particular breach. The courts created the concept of an innominate term, something that was midway between a condition and a warranty which then gave the court a flexibility with regard to remedies. The concept of the innominate term is now to be seen in an insurance setting (see below). Section 15A of the Sale of Goods Act 1979 also reflects the same concern by allowing breach of a condition to be treated as a breach of warranty in certain circumstances.

There are two specific problems in relation to insurance law in this area. Warranties are regarded as major terms of the insurance contract seemingly reversing the general contract position and thus care must be taken when reading the cases. Breach of warranty can lead to unfair penalisation of the insured; reform of this situation has been called for, but with only limited success (see below). Meanwhile, the courts appear to be taking a more active role in their handling of allegations of breaches of warranty concerned by the 'draconian remedy' that follows in its wake.

WARRANTIES

Types of warranties

There are two main types of warranties: those which refer to past or present state of affairs and those which relate to the future, usually referred to as 'promissory warranties'.

Section 33 of the Marine Insurance Act 1906 states:

(1) A warranty ... means a promissory warranty, that is to say, a warranty by which the assured undertakes that some particular thing shall or shall not be

done, or that some condition shall be fulfilled, or whereby he affirms or negatives the existence of a particular state of facts ...

(3) A warranty, as defined above, is a condition which must be exactly complied with, whether it be material to the risk or not. If it be not so complied with, then subject to any express provision in the policy, the insurer is discharged from liability as from the date of the breach of warranty, but without prejudice in any liability incurred by him before that date.

Strict compliance necessary

Section 33(3) illustrates two problems. First, the use of the word 'condition' is equated to the word 'warranty' which adds confusion to the discussion, a confusion to which many cases over the years have added. Second the strictness of application of breach of warranty can lead to harsh results.

Two early cases illustrate the harshness. In *Pawson v Watson* (1778) 2 Cowp 786 (Appendix 5.1), a ship had been described to the first underwriter as mounting 12 guns and 20 men. To the defendant underwriter the representation had been made that she was a ship of force. The ship was taken by an American privateer when she had crew of 27, of whom 16 were men, the remainder being boys. She did however have a range of guns in excess of the 12 originally mentioned. The defence was that the original description amounted to a warranty, which had not been exactly complied with and therefore the defendant should not be liable on the policy. The plaintiff argued that the description did not amount to a warranty but to a representation. Lord Mansfield was of the opinion that it was only a representation and therefore the defendant was liable on the policy. The judge explained that if the description had been entered into the policy wording then exact compliance would have been necessary.

Lord Mansfield returned to this situation in *De Hahn v Hartley* (1786) 1 Term Rep 343 (Appendix 5.2), where the crew had been described in the margin to the policy as being 50 strong on a voyage from Liverpool to the West Indies. The ship sailed from Liverpool with 46 crew and six hours later put in at Anglesey and picked up six more crew. Even though the ship was not captured until five months later and the shortage of crew for six hours could make no obvious difference, the underwriter was not liable on the policy.

This decision helps form the basis of s 34(2) of the Marine Insurance Act, which states: 'Where a warranty is broken, the assured cannot avail himself of the defence that the breach has been remedied, and the warranty complied with, before loss.'

A non-marine insurance case shows that these marine rules similarly apply. In *Codogianis v Guardian Assurance Co Ltd* [1921] 2 AC 125 (Appendix

5.3) on a fire proposal form the proposer was asked if he had ever made a claim on a fire policy and if so to give particulars. The proposer declared an earlier claim but did not mention a further claim. The proposal form contained a basis of the contract clause (see below) the effect of which is to elevate all answers into warranties. There was a clear breach of this warranty and the insurer was not liable on the policy. The important point here is that there is no room for the insured to argue that the omission is not material to the risk. It is a matter of strict compliance.

Creation of a warranty

For insurers the safest thing is to make certain that the warranty appears in the policy. As *Codogianis* shows, another method is to refer to answers in the proposal form and to use those as a basis of the contract clause (see below). However it is not necessary to use the word warranty or warranted. In that situation the court may decide that the answer or commitment given is not in fact a warranty.

In *Provincial Insurance Co Ltd v Morgan and Another* [1933] AC 240 (Appendix 5.4), the plaintiff completed a proposal to insure his lorry. One question asked for the purposes for which the lorry would be used and a second question asked the nature of the goods to be carried. The answers were 'delivery of coal' and 'coal'. The main purpose was indeed delivery of coal but occasionally the owner transported timber. There was a claim for an accident that took place while the lorry was carrying coal but as it had transported timber earlier in the day the insurers argued that that had been a breach of warranty. The House of Lords found for the insured and Lord Russell was unhappy that insurers did not always use clear unambiguous language to achieve what they wanted. As will be seen in Chapter 7, ambiguity will allow the court to interpret policies against the party responsible for the confusion, invariably the insurer. Here, it was necessary to interpret the questions and answers on the proposal form; the conditions and warranties and the endorsements on the policy. As Lord Russell said: 'It may be that we have here some form of commercial shorthand which an expert could transcribe into a contractual obligation. I am unequal to the task.' The judgment may also illustrate the court's reluctance to invalidate a policy for a minor technical breach. A clear use of the word warranty would, however, have prevented the court from finding for the insured.

A similar approach can be seen in *Shaw v Robberds, Hawkes and Stone* (1837) 6 Ad & El 75 (Appendix 5.5), a decision referred to in *Morgan*'s case. Here the insured had described, for the purposes of a fire policy, the building as one used for storing and drying corn. The policy stated that it would be void if the building and use was wrongly described and that no alteration of use was permissible unless an indorsement to that effect was granted. The insured allowed a merchant to dry oak bark in his kiln, after a barge carrying the bark had sunk nearby. A fire started while this process was ongoing. It was agreed that drying bark was more hazardous than drying corn. The insurers repudiated liability for breach of warranty and for change of usage. They failed on both points. The court was not prepared to interpret the various conditions or warranties as applying to the facts.

With regard to alleged breach of a promissory warranty, the language of all of the relevant documentation, taken together, will need to be construed by the court. Two more recent examples can be used.

In *Hair v The Prudential Assurance Co Ltd* [1983] 2 Lloyd's Rep 669 (Appendix 5.6), a claim was made on a house policy for damage caused by fire. An array of defences was raised which the court struck down. Of special importance here was the question relating to occupation: 'To what extent are the premises ... left unattended regularly apart from holidays?' Answer: '8 hours daily approximately (weekdays).' The insurer argued that the premises had been left unoccupied for many months prior to the fire and thus the warranty relating to occupation had been broken. This was also rejected. The true construction of the question called for a statement of present fact. The answer was true. The language did not call for a promissory warranty from the insured. The matter might have been differently answered, if it could have been shown that the insured knew, at the time at which the question was answered, that the premises were soon to become unoccupied. The insured's knowledge, however, may not be fatal if the language of the question appears to steer him in a particular direction.

In *Hussain v Brown* [1996] 1 Lloyd's Rep 627 (Appendix 5.7), the plaintiff insured his premises against fire. One question asked if an intruder alarm was fitted and the insured said that it was. The proposal contained a basis clause (see below), and a statement that the answers were warranted. There was a fire and when making the claim the insured admitted that he knew that the alarm had not been operational for two or three months, but this was after the contract had been concluded. The Court of Appeal found for the insured. Again, as in *Hair*, the question and answer were construed as applying to a present state of affairs rather than reading into them a promise for the future. It would be easy for the insurer to have obtained a commitment as to the future by using language such as, 'The insured warrants that the alarm is operational throughout the currency of the policy'. This is a modern Court of Appeal decision and not one involving a consumer insured. It is worth quoting here a passage from Saville LJ's judgment:

> ... it must be remembered that a continuing warranty is a Draconian term ... the breach of such a warranty produces an automatic cancellation of the cover, and the fact that the loss may have no connection at all with that breach is simply irrelevant. In my view, if underwriters want such protection, then it is up to them to stipulate for it in clear terms.

This trend has continued in the latest cases. The courts appear prepared to construe strictly against the insurer the alleged warranty or condition precedent behind which the insurer hides and determine whether or not it should be classified as a defence allowing such a drastic remedy.

Thus, in *Kler Knitwear Ltd v Lombard General Insurance Co Ltd* [2000] Lloyd's Rep IR 47 the insured's policy was subject to a sprinkler installations warranty. This required that within 30 days of renewal the system would be inspected by an engineer and repaired if necessary. Breach of the warranty was stated as relieving the insurer of any liability whether or not it was material or whether or not it increased the risk. The inspection took place after 60 days. Storm damage occurred after five months and insurers sought to avoid. The insurers were held liable.

If the court had been convinced that the clause was a warranty then the insurers could have avoided even though it would have been harsh and unfair and there was no causative link. But here the court decided that the clause was not a warranty but a suspensive condition which means that had a loss occurred before the insured had carried out the policy requirements such loss would not have been paid.

Because breach of warranty produces the draconian remedy of avoidance the insurer must make that clear. The use of the words 'warranty' and 'warranties' was an indication of such intention but as insurers often misused them it was open to the court to decide in particular cases whether or not that was the intention. It was absurd, in the view of the judge, and against business commonsense to reject the property damage claim because the inspection requirement was late.

Again in *Virk v Gan Life Holdings plc* [2000] Lloyd's Rep IR 159 the Court of Appeal held that where the policy either made no mention of what clauses were to be regarded as conditions precedent or where some clauses were so labelled and others were not then the court could apply its own construction to the policy. It would be a different matter if the court was convinced that care and logic had been used by the insurer in its choice of terms.

However it is not easy to predict when and how the court will adopt a pro-active stance in this area. Thus, in *Alfred McAlpine plc v BAI (Run Off) Ltd* [2000] Lloyd's Rep IR 352 (see Davey [2001] JBL 179) a workman was injured and his injuries were covered by RCCL's insurers, BAI. RCCL however failed to give timely notification to BAI. RCCL went into liquidation. McAlpine wished to claim against RCCL and advised them to notify BAI. McAlpine obtained judgment against RCCL by which time BAI had also been wound up and McAlpine sought to proceed as statutory assignees under the Third Parties (Rights Against Insurers) Act 1930 (see Chapter 10, below).

BAI's defences were that there had been breach of a condition precedent (failure to notify); that there had been repudiation of the policy by RCCL caused by their failure to conform with the notice provisions and BAI had accepted that repudiation.

Both the trial court and the Court of Appeal found BAI liable on the policy. As to the argument that the time clause was a condition precedent the court held that for a clause to be classified as a condition precedent it had very clearly to state that it was so. Where some clauses did so state but others did not then the court would not allow the insurer to argue that a clause should be construed as a condition precedent when it had not said so in the policy. If the insurer could show that breach of the clause had caused damage to the insurer then any such sum could be set off against any policy claim.

As to the repudiation defence the court found that condition 1(a) was an innominate term (ie, a term that the court is not prepared to describe either as a condition or a warranty). Breach of it, however serious, would be unlikely to amount to repudiation of the whole contract of insurance. But a breach which demonstrated an intention not to continue with the claim or which had very serious consequences for BAI should be treated such as to entitle BAI to defeat the claim. But that did not apply to these facts.

A similar approach is seen in the Court of Appeal decision in *Jacobs v Coster* [2000] Lloyd's Rep IR 506. The claimant fell over on the defendant/ insured's petrol station forecourt. The defendant could find nothing untoward with the area of the accident. Seven months later the claimant sued for negligence, alleging oil on the forecourt. Insured gave insurers notice within 13 days of receipt of the claim.

A policy condition stated: 'If any event gives or is likely to give rise to a claim, the Insured must ... report the details immediately to the Company and send a written claim within 30 days.' This was stated to be a condition precedent.

The Court of Appeal held the insurers liable.

What is the meaning of the trigger word 'likely'? The court said that it meant that it was 'more likely than not' that a claim would ensue, that is, more than a 50% chance. Also the insured's inspection detected no obvious danger and no immediate allegation of blame had been levelled at the insured. Thus there had been no need to give any earlier notification.

In *Printpak v AGF Insurance Ltd* [1999] Lloyd's Rep IR 542 the insured held a commercial policy with defendant insurers. A fire claim was rejected for alleged breach of warranty the insurers arguing that s 33 of the Marine Insurance Act 1906 states that a warranty 'must be exactly complied with, whether it be material to the risk or not ... the insurer is discharged from liability as from the date of the breach of warranty'.

The insurers alleged that the insured warranted that a burglar alarm was fully operational at all times when the premises were closed. It was common ground between the parties that the alarm was not operating at the time having been switched off during building work. Each type of insured risk was dealt with in different sections of the policy and with differing wording.

The Court of Appeal found for the insured. The alarm was in that part of the policy dealing with 'theft' situations. The present claim was in that part of the policy dealing with fire.

Lord Justice Hirst quoted the concerns about 'draconian remedies' from *Hussain v Brown* [1996] 1 Lloyd's Rep 627 (Appendix 5.7), referred to above.

It may be however that the wording of a policy, while harsh in its results, is sufficiently clear and beyond any 'robust' interpretation by the courts. This was seen in *Kazakstan Wool Processors (Europe) Ltd v Nederlandsche Credietverzekering Maatschappij NV* [2000] Lloyd's Rep IR 371. The insured exported washed wool from Kazakstan and took out credit insurance with the defendant insurer. The policy wording provided that every stipulation in the policy was to be a condition precedent to any liability (Art 13(1)) and should there be any breach then the insurer could retain any premium paid together with terminating the policy and all liability (Art 13(2)). The premiums were to be based on monthly returns made by the insured relating to the value of goods despatched and if there were no sales in any month then a nil return was to be made.

The insurers paid out on a claim but some months later the insured failed to send in a nil return because they had ceased to trade. Other claims were however in the pipeline prior to the insured's breach. The insurers gave notice of termination, denied any liability and requested the return of the earlier payment. The insured argued that it was an unreasonable interpretation of the policy to disallow claims relating to matters that had attached before their breach of the condition.

The Court of Appeal held that Art 13(1) should be interpreted as meaning that the insurers were not liable for any claim where there had been a breach of condition by the insured in relation to that claim. Thus it was not for the insurers to argue that they were entitled to a return of monies paid out for earlier losses when there had been no breach by the insured. Any other interpretation would have a draconian effect in that relatively minor breaches could also lead to termination of the policy.

However, by a majority and with regret, the Court held that Art 13(2) did permit the insurers to serve notice of terminating all liability under the policy. It was still a matter of construction as to the meaning to be attached to that phrase. It was held that all liabilities that had accrued prior to the breach and had been paid were not to be repaid; any sums that should have been paid prior to the breach but had not been, for instance, because of delay by the insurer, should be paid; the premium could be retained even though the policy was terminated because although it was an unattractive solution it was not sufficiently outrageous based on the wording used. Crucially however the insurers were not liable to pay future or contingent losses.

This meant that the insurers were relieved from paying sums for losses that had occurred prior to the breach but which under the policy wording did not fall due for payment until a six month period had elapsed.

Basis of the contract clause

A particularly potent method of creating a warranty, as illustrated in some of the cases above, is the use of the 'basis of the contract' clause that may appear on proposal forms. The technique deserves separate mention. In Chapter 4, it was explained that, for an insurer to avoid liability for alleged breach of good faith, it is now necessary (post-*Pan Atlantic*) for it to be shown that the misrepresentation or non-disclosure would have influenced a prudent insurer and that it induced the actual insurer into making that particular contract. Thus, 'materiality' plays a crucial role.

The basis of the contract clause, however, does away with the materiality requirement. In a variety of phrases, depending on which insurer one is considering, it will say, usually just above the proposer's signature, that the answers given above shall form the basis of the contract between the parties. An incorrect answer, whether fraudulent, negligent or innocent and whether material or not will allow the insurer to avoid liability.

One of the leading cases is the House of Lords decision in *Dawsons Ltd v Bonnin and Others* [1922] All ER Rep 210 (Appendix 5.8). A firm wished to insure a lorry. In answer to the question, 'where will the lorry be usually garaged?', it was stated 'see above' which related to the business address of the firm which was in Glasgow. The lorry was usually garaged on a farm on the outskirts of Glasgow. This was an innocent misstatement. There was a fire at the garage, which damaged the lorry. If the case had been defended by the insurer on the grounds of breach of good faith, it might have been possible for the insured to argue that the farm address was more beneficial to the insurer than central Glasgow. However, the defence rested on the fact that there was a basis clause and that the insured had warranted the address as correct. The House of Lords, by a 3:2 majority, allowed the defence. Viscount Haldene explained that the result may be technical and harsh, but if the parties have so stipulated then there was no alternative and hard cases must not be allowed to make bad law. Lord Wrenbury, dissenting, thought that the insurer's defence was neither creditable nor capable of being sustained. Which view do you prefer?

An earlier House of Lords decision arrived at a similar conclusion as in *Dawson's* case. In *Thomson v Weems and Others* (1884) 9 App Cas 671 (Appendix 5.9), the proposer applied for a life policy. The question was asked as to whether he was temperate in his habits and whether he had always been so. He answered in the affirmative and signed the form, which contained a basis clause. The insurer successfully avoided liability for breach of an express warranty. Lord Blackburn explained that this technique had been in existence for at least 50 years and though it might be seen as hard on an insured who had been innocent in his answers, once he warranted the answer he was bound by its consequences. It was argued for the insured that the questions were ones of opinion and not fact but it was decided that they were facts and that the insured must have known of his predilection for alcohol. His death was due to alcohol.

Calls for reform of the basis of the contract procedure are referred to below.

Effect of breach of warranty

The onus of proving the breach of warranty rests on the insurer. Until recently it was thought that the effect of such breach was to allow the option to the insurer whether or not to repudiate his liability from the date of the breach. However, the leading authority is now that in *Bank of Nova Scotia v Hellenic Mutual War Risks Association (The Good Luck)* [1991] 3 All ER 1, a case involving marine insurance. The language of Lord Goff, who gave the only judgment, is, however, of general application to the issue under consideration. The short answer to the effect of breach of a promissory warranty is that the insurer is discharged from liability automatically and irrespective of any decision by him. In greater depth, Lord Goff explained the situation in these words, having quoted from Lord Blackburn in *Thomson v Weems*, above:

> ... if a promissory warranty is not complied with the insurer is discharged from liability as from the date of the breach of the warranty, for the simple reason that fulfilment of a warranty is a condition precedent to the liability or further liability of the insurer. This, moreover, reflects the fact that the rationale of warranties in insurance law is that the insurer only accepts the risk provided that the warranty is fulfilled. This is entirely understandable; and it follows that the immediate effect of a breach of a promissory warranty is to discharge the insurer from liability as from the date of the breach. In the case of a condition precedent, the word 'condition' is being used in its classical sense in English law, under which the coming into existence of (for example) an obligation, or the duty or further duty to perform an obligation is dependent upon the fulfilment of the specified condition. Here, where we are concerned with a promissory warranty, that is, a promissory condition precedent, contained in an existing contract of insurance, non-fulfilment of the condition does not prevent the contract from coming into existence. What it does ... is to discharge the insurer from liability as from the date of the breach. Certainly it does not avoid the contract *ab initio*. Nor, strictly speaking, does it have the effect of bringing it to an end. It is possible that there may be obligations of the assured under the contract, which will survive the discharge of the insurer from liability, as for example a continuing liability to pay a premium.

(See case notes: (1991) 107 LQR 540; [1991] LMCLQ 437; [1991] JBL 598.)

The effect of breach of warranty described above is special to insurance law and would not therefore apply to other commercial contracts. The next question is whether it is special to marine insurance (ie, the facts of *The Good Luck*) or of application to insurance policies generally. In *HIH Casualty and General Insurance Ltd v Axa Corporate Solutions* [2001] All ER (D) 384 (Appendix 5.16, for the underlying facts of the litigation see Chapter 4), the court held that the automatic cessation of cover on breach of a promissory warranty did extend to all types of insurance.

Section 34 of the Marine Insurance Act 1906 in excuses this automatic remedy in certain situation. The one that concerned the court in *HIH* was s 34(3), a breach of warranty may be waived by the insurer. What amounts to waiver or promissory estoppel by the insurer sufficient for it to provide the other party with a defence against the automatic cessation argument? It must be a clear and unequivocal representation, with full knowledge of the facts, that the insurer will not use the automatic cessation right and the other party must be aware of this. Thus there needs to be some form of mutuality. Merely because the insurer continues to act in a way that is in keeping with the continuance of the policy does not necessarily amount to waiver. Here the parties continued their relationship unaware of the effect of the automatic cessation point and thus the insurer could not be said to be willing to forgo its rights. This did not amount to waiver on the facts.

CONDITIONS

Numerous cases referred to above have intermingled the word warranty with condition. Policy wording often does the same. MacGillivray, *Insurance Law* 9th edn, London: Sweet & Maxwell, talks mainly of warranties in Chapter 10 and so, too, Clarke, in *Law of Insurance Contracts*, 3rd edn, London: LLP, in Chapter 20, while Ivamy, in *General Principles of Insurance Law*, 6th edn, London: Butterworths, talks mainly of conditions in Chapter 30. Even when the word 'condition' is used, the court may construe it as not having the effect that breach of condition would normally have (see below).

Thus, in *Re Bradley and Essex and Suffolk Accident Indemnity Society Ltd* [1911–13] All ER Rep 444 (Appendix 5.10), the insured took out a policy against his potential liability under the Workmen's Compensation Act. The policy contained several conditions, which the policy described as conditions precedent to liability. One requirement of the policy was that the insured kept a wages book, which should include the names of all employees and their individual earnings. The insured had only one employee, his son, and he did not maintain a wages book. The insurer refused to pay on the policy alleging breach of condition. The Court of Appeal, by a 2:1 majority, allowed the insured's claim. The majority considered that the condition in question was ambiguously worded and that the wages book requirement was part of a longer section of the policy of which the other parts, by their nature, could not be regarded as conditions precedent. Lord Justice Farwell, finding for the insured, considered that it was:

> ... scarcely honest to induce a man to propose on certain terms and then accept that proposal and send a policy [which] ... contains numerous provisions not mentioned in the proposal which operate to defeat any claim ...

Surely, however, that is exactly what does happen on countless thousands of occasions? Do you find the dissent of Fletcher-Moulton LJ more convincing? The majority are clearly attempting to do justice to the insured in a situation where they feel that the insurer is attempting to use a technicality. Such attempts by the courts clearly cause confusion in the law's application. Such attempts however have a long history. Thus, Vance, 'The history of the development of the warranty in insurance law' (1911) 20 Yale LJ 523, was forced to complain:

> The unseemly struggle that ensued between unwise insurers who sought to frame their policies so as to compel the courts to allow them the benefits of forfeitures unsuspected by the insured, and the courts who sought by liberal construction, and sometimes distortion of the language of policies, to do justice in spite of the warranties, resulted in a mass of litigation and confused precedent, the likes of which cannot be found in any other field of law.

Perhaps you feel that some of the decisions in this chapter reflect this view.

There are two major types of conditions. The first can be described as a condition precedent to the effectiveness of the policy, such as the requirement in a motor policy that the vehicle be kept in a roadworthy condition. The second type can be called a condition precedent to liability. Thus, a motor policy will contain such conditions requiring notification of loss within a certain period of time or as soon as is reasonably practical (see Statement of General Insurance Practice, Appendix 4.10).

It is possible for the insurer to waive breach of condition. Thus, in *Evans v Employers' Mutual Insurance Association Ltd* [1936] 1 KB 505 (Appendix 5.11), the proposer for a motor policy stated in the proposal form that he had held a driving licence and had practical experience of driving for five years. When he later made a claim he stated on the claims form that he had been driving for six weeks. The claims clerk noticed the discrepancy but considered it to be unimportant. Part of the claim was paid before a senior investigator realised that the discrepancy was sufficient to seek to avoid on grounds of the misrepresentation. The court held that the insurers had waived their right to avoid the policy.

Care must be taken, however, not to infer waiver over-enthusiastically. Simply because, somewhere in the insurer's files, there is evidence that might look like a waiver on the part of the insurer, it will not necessarily mean that there is a waiver. See the decision *in Malhi v Abbey Life* [1996] LRLR 237 (Appendix 4.16), in which the Court of Appeal dealt with *Evans* in detail, but came to the conclusion that there was no waiver. In *Evans*, the clerk had the duty to compare the proposal and claims form answers. No such duty of comparison existed in *Malhi*.

Reform

The brief discussion above shows that there are problems for insureds in relation to the effect that breach of warranty or condition may have on claims on the policy. The two main problem areas are the use of the basis of the contract clause whereby even innocent mistakes on the proposal form are elevated to the standing of warranties and the strict compliance required by warranties such that even non-material breach of a warranty will invalidate the insured's claim.

England and Wales

In 1957, the Law Reform Committee presented a brief report, *Conditions and Exceptions in Insurance Policies*, Cmnd 62, in which they discussed non-disclosure, conditions and the position of insurance agents. Nothing was done. In 1980, the Law Commission published their report, *Insurance Law: Non-Disclosure and Breach of Warranty*, Cmnd 8064. Their views on non-disclosure appear in Chapter 4 (Appendix 4.8). The report also tackled the problem of warranties and the basis of the contract technique (Appendix 5.12). The Law Commission view was that there was a 'formidable case for reform'. In the draft Bill that was attached to the report, cl 8 reads:

8 (1) A provision of a relevant contract of insurance whereby the insured:

(a) affirms or denies the existence of, or gives his opinion with resect to, any fact or state of affairs at any time (whether past, present or future); or

(b) undertakes that any particular state of affairs will continue or that a particular course of action will or will not be taken,

shall not be capable of constituting a warranty unless it relates to a matter which is *material* [emphasis added].

(2) An insurer shall not be entitled to rely for any purpose on a breach of warranty in a relevant contract of insurance unless, at or before the time the contract was entered into or as soon thereafter as was practicable in the circumstances of the case, a written statement of the provision which constitutes the warranty was supplied to the insured.

(3) If the insurer under a relevant contract of insurance seeks for any purpose to rely on a breach of a provision of the contract as a breach of warranty then, unless the contrary is proved, that provision shall be presumed to be material.

Section 8(3) clearly puts the burden of proof on the insured. This is a reversal of the original recommendation in Working Paper No 73.

The report deals with the basis of the contract clause in cl 9. This reads:

9 (1) Without prejudice to s 8 above, if, in connection with a relevant contract of insurance the insured makes a statement affirming or denying the

existence of, or giving his opinion with respect to, any fact or state of affairs at any time past or present, that statement:

(a) shall not be capable of constituting a warranty if it is contained in, or is made by reference to any provision of, a proposal form; and

(b) shall not be capable of being converted into a warranty by means of any provision purporting to incorporate it into the contract, either alone or together with other statements (and whether by declaring the statement to form the basis of the contract or otherwise).

(2) Nothing in the section relates to promissory warranties, that is to say, warranties consisting of undertakings such as are mentioned in s 8(1)(b) above and warranties relating to any fact or state of affairs which may or may not come into existence at a future time.

Clause 10 deals with the effect of breach of warranty and suggests important changes to the present law not least of which is the reversal of the decision in *West v National Motor Insurance Union* [1955] 1 All ER 800, CA.

Clause 10 states:

10 (1) If an insurer seeks to avoid a relevant contract of insurance in reliance on a breach of warranty, the repudiation shall not be effective with respect to any time prior to the date on which notice in writing of the repudiation is served on the insured.

(2) The following provisions of this section apply where:

(a) the insured under a relevant contract of insurance is in breach of a warranty in that contract; and

(b) after the date of the breach an event occurs which gives rise to a claim under the contract.

(3) If, in a case falling within sub-s (2) above:

(a) the insurer seeks to avoid the contract in reliance on the breach; but

(b) by virtue of sub-s (1) above, the effective date of the repudiation is after the date of the event which gives rise to the claim,

then, notwithstanding that the relevant contract of insurance continues in force until the date of the service of the notice of repudiation, the insurer shall not be liable to meet the claim unless the case falls within sub-s (5) below.

(4) If, in a case falling within sub-s (2) above, the insurer:

(a) does not seek to avoid the contract as mentioned in sub-s (3) above; but

(b) seeks to reject the claim by notice given to the insured,

the contract of insurance shall continue in force but the insurer shall not be liable to meet the claim unless the case falls within sub-s (5) below.

(5) In a case to which sub-s (3) or sub-s (4) above applies the insurer shall be liable to meet the claim if the insured proves either:

(a) that the warranty concerned was intended to safeguard against, or was otherwise related to, the risk of the occurrence of events of a description which does not include the event which gave rise to the claim; or

(b) that the breach of warranty could not have increased the risk that the event which gave rise to the claim would occur in the way in which it did in fact occur [see Appendix 5.13].

Despite the detailed report, no legislative reform has taken place. What we do have, however, is the self-regulatory Code of practice formulated by the Association of British Insurers referred to elsewhere in this book (Appendix 4.10). The Law Commission Report was critical of the ABI Statement for a number of reasons. The most important of which were: it is applicable only to consumer insurance contracts; not all insurers are members of the ABI; the Statement still allows insurers to repudiate on technical grounds. The report's view was that protection of the insured requires more than measures of self-regulation. In the light of some of the recommendations in the report, the wording of the Association of British Insurers' Statement was redrafted, but the full breadth of the criticisms have not been met (Appendices 4.30 and 4.31). Of crucial importance however is that the Statement does appear to ban the use of the basis of the contract formulation and calls for a causal connection between breach of condition and avoidance.

While the ABI may attach great weight to their self-regulatory Codes one has seriously to doubt whether their members attach a similar importance in their working practices. The independent audit carried out in relation to the ABI General Business Code of Selling (see Chapter 6 and Appendix 6.5) illustrated a very poor uptake of that Code by ABI members. There is no good reason to suppose that the basis clause is not 'alive and well' in many consumer proposal forms today. See Adams, 'Basis of the contract clauses and the consumer' [2000] JBL 203 where the writer's own researches bear this out. He also goes on to suggest that the language of the typical clause, although fully understood to the insurer, could well fall foul of the Unfair Terms in Consumer Contracts Regulations 1999 (Appendix 7.1), as being 'unintelligible to the overwhelming majority of consumers'.

See the suggestions, in this area, of the National Consumer Council Report in 1997 (Appendix 5.14).

Australia

The Law Reform Commission Report, *Insurance Contracts*, ALR 20, called for a causal connection between breach and avoidance and, as with the English Law Commission, they were critical of the use of the basis of the contract clause.

The reforms appear in the (Australian) Insurance Contracts Act 1984 (Cth) (Appendix 5.15).

WARRANTIES AND CONDITIONS

APPENDIX 5.1

Pawson v Watson (1778) 2 Cowp 786; [1778] 98 ER 1361, HL

Lord Mansfield: This was an action upon a policy of insurance. At the trial it appeared in evidence, that the first underwriter had the following instructions shown him: 'Three thousand five hundred pounds upon the ship *Julius Caesar*, from Halifax, to touch at Plymouth, and any port in America: she mounts 12 guns and 20 men.' These instructions were not asked for or communicated to the defendant; but the ship was only represented generally to him, as a ship of force: and a thousand pounds had been done, before the defendant did anything upon her. The instructions were dated the 28 June 1776, and the ship sailed on the 23 July 1776; and was taken by an American privateer. That at the time of her being taken, she had on board six four pounders, four three pounders, three one pounders, which are called swivels, and 27 men and boys in all, for her crew; but of them, 16 only were men, (not 20, as the instructions mentioned,) and the rest, boys. But the witness said, he considered her as being stronger with this force, than if she had 12 carriage guns and 20 men: he also said (which is a material circumstance) that there were neither men nor guns on board, at the time of insurance. That he himself insured at the same premium, without regard or enquiry into the force of the ship. Other underwriters also insured at the same premium, without any other representation than that she was a ship of premium, without any other representation than that she was a ship of force. That to every four pounder there should be five men and a boy. That in merchant ships, boys always go under the denomination of men. This was met by evidence on the part of the defendant, saying, that guns mean carriage guns, not swivels, and men mean able men exclusive of boys. There were three causes of the same nature, depending upon the same evidence: the defence in each was, that these instructions were to be considered as a warranty, the same as if they had been inserted in the policy; though they were not proved to have been shown to any but the first underwriter. In all the three cases, the question reserved for the opinion of the court is: '... whether the written instructions which were shown to the first underwriter, are to be considered as a warranty inserted in the policy, or as a representation, which would only avoid the policy, if fraudulent?' ...

At the trial, I was of opinion that it would be of very dangerous consequence to add a conversation that passed at the time, as part of the written agreement. It is a collateral representation: and if the parties had considered it as a warranty, they would have had it inserted in the policy. But, secondly, if these instructions were to be considered in the light of a fraudulent misrepresentation, they must be both material and fraudulent: and in that light, I held, that a misrepresentation made to the first underwriter, ought to be considered as a misrepresentation made to every one of them, and so would infect the whole policy. Otherwise, it would be a contrivance to deceive many: for where a good man stands first, the rest underwrite without asking a question; and if he is imposed upon, the rest of the underwriters are taken in by the same fraud. The case was left to the jury under that direction …

There is no distinction better known to those who are at all conversant in the law of insurance, than that which exists, between a warranty or condition which makes part of a written policy, and a representation of the state of the case. Where it is a part of the written policy, it must be performed …

The question then is: 'whether in this policy, the party insuring has warranted that the ship should positively and literally have 12 carriage guns and 20 men?' That is: 'whether the instructions given in evidence are a part of the policy?' Now, I will take it by degrees. The two first underwriters before the court are Watson and Snell. Says Watson, 'It is part of my agreement, that the ship shall sail with 12 guns and 20 men; and it is so stipulated, that nothing under that number will do. Ten guns with swivels will not do'. The answer to this is, 'read your agreement; read your policy'. There is no such thing to be found there. It is replied, yes, but in fact there is, for the instructions upon which the policy was made, contain the express stipulation. The answer to that is, there never were any instructions shown to Watson, nor were any asked for by him. What colour then has he to say, that those instructions are any part of his agreement. It is said, he insured upon the credit of the first underwriter. A representation to the first underwriter, has nothing to do with that which is the agreement, or the terms of the policy. No man who underwrites a policy, subscribes, by the act of underwriting, to terms which he knows nothing of. But he reads the agreement, and is governed by that. Matters of intelligence, such as that a ship is or is not missing, are things in which a man is guided by the name of a first underwriter, who is a good man, and which another will therefore give faith and credit to; but not to a collateral agreement, which he can know nothing of. The absurdity is too glaring, it cannot be. By extension of an equitable relief in cases of fraud, if a man is a knave with respect to the first underwriter, and makes a false representation to him in a point that is material; as where having notice of a ship being lost, he says she was safe; that shall affect the policy with regard to all the subsequent underwriters, who are presumed to follow the first. How, then, do Watson and Snell underwrite the ship in question? Without knowing whether she had any force at all. That proves the risk was equal to a ship of no force at all; and the premium was a vast one – eight guineas. So much therefore for those two cases. The third case is that of Ewer, who saw the instructions, with the representation which they contained. Did the number of guns induce him to underwrite the policy? If it did, he would have said 'put them into the policy; warrant that the ship shall depart with 12 guns and 20 men'. Whereas, he does no such thing, but takes the same premium which Watson and Snell did, who had no notice of her having any force. What does that prove? That he is paid and receives a premium, as if it were a ship of no force at all. The representation amounts to no more than this, 'I tell you what the force will be, because it is so much the better for you'. There is no fraud in it, because it is a representation only of what, in the then state of the ship, they thought would be the truth. And in real truth, the ship sailed with a larger force: for she had nine carriage guns, besides six swivels. The underwriters, therefore, had the advantage by the difference. There was no stipulation about what the weight of metal should be. All the witnesses say, 'she had more force than if she had had 12 carriage guns, both in point of strength, of convenience, and for the purpose of resistance'. The supercargo in particular says, 'he insured the same ship and the same voyage, for the same premium, without saying a syllable about the force'. Why, then, it was a matter proper for the jury to say, whether the representation was false? or whether it was in fact an insurance, as of a ship without force? They have determined, and I think very rightly, that it was an insurance without force. Ewer makes an objection that the representation ought to be considered as inserted in the policy; but the answer to that is, he has determined whether it should be inserted in the policy or not, by not inserting it himself. There is a great difference, whether it shall be considered as a fraud. But it would be very dangerous to permit all collateral representations to be put into the policy. I am extremely glad to hear that a great many of the underwriters have paid. Mr Thornton has paid, who was the first person that saw the instructions. Shall the rest refuse then? As to Watson and Snell, they have no pretence to refuse, for there is not a colour for the objection made by them. As to Ewer, we are all satisfied with the determination of the jury against him …

APPENDIX 5.2

De Hahn v Hartley (1786) 1 Term Rep 343; [1786] 99 ER 1130

Lord Mansfield CJ: There is a material distinction between a warranty and a representation. A representation may be equitably and substantially answered: but a warranty must be strictly complied with. Supposing a warranty to sail on the 1st of August, and the ship did not sail till the 2nd, the warranty would not be complied with. A warranty in a policy of insurance is a condition or a contingency, and unless that be performed, there is no contract. It is perfectly immaterial for what purpose a warranty is introduced; but, being inserted, the contract does not exist unless it be literally complied with. Now in the present case, the condition was the sailing of the ship a certain number of men; which not being complied with, the policy is void.

Ashurst J: The very meaning of a warranty is to preclude all questions whether it has been substantially complied with; it must be literally so.

Buller J: It is impossible to divide the words written in the margin in the manner which has been attempted; that part of it which relates to the copper sheathing should be a warranty, and not the remaining part. But the whole forms one entire contract, and must be complied with throughout.

Judgment for the plaintiff …

APPENDIX 5.3

Codogianis v Guardian Assurance Co Ltd [1921] 2 AC 125, PC

Lord Shaw of Dunfermline: Among the questions in the appellant's fire insurance proposal to the respondents was the following: 'Has proponent ever been a claimant on a fire insurance company in respect of the property now proposed or any other property? If so, state when and name of company.' To this the answer was given: 'Yes. 1917. "Ocean".'

This answer was in a literal sense true – that is to say, it was true that the proposer had in the year 1917 made a claim against the Ocean Insurance Co in respect of the burning of a motor car. He omitted, however, to state what was also the fact – namely, that in the year 1912 he had made another claim against the Liverpool and London and Globe Co in respect of the burning of a motor car owned by him ...

It is unnecessary to state that the answer given by the appellant in the proposal falls clearly within the express declaration which is now to be quoted. The terms of that declaration are as follows:

> This proposal is the basis of the contract and is to be taken as part of the policy and (if accepted) the particulars are to be deemed express and continuing warranties furnished by or on behalf of the proponent; and any questions remaining unanswered will be deemed to be replied to in the negative. The proposal is made subject to the company's conditions as printed and/or written in the policy to be issued hereon, and which are hereby accepted by the proponent.

The case accordingly is one of express warranty. If, in point of fact, the answer is untrue, the warranty still holds, notwithstanding that the untruth might have arisen inadvertently and without any kind of fraud. Secondly, the materiality of the untruth is not in issue; the parties having settled for themselves – by making the fact the basis of the contract, and giving a warranty – that as between them their agreement on that subject precluded all inquiry into the issue of materiality. In the language of Lord Eldon in *Newcastle Fire Insurance Co v Macmorran* (1815) 3 Dow 255 ...:

> It is a first principle in the law of insurance, on all occasions, that where a representation is material it must be complied with – if immaterial, that immateriality may be inquired into and shown; but that if there is a warranty it is part of the contract that the matter is such as it is represented to be. Therefore the materiality or immateriality signifies nothing.

This rule has been repeated over and over again, and is too well settled to be questioned: *Anderson v Fitzgerald* (1853) 4 HL Cas 584 ... and the judgments of Lord Blackburn and Lord Watson, in particular, in *Thomson v Weems* (1884) 9 App Cas 671 ...

The more serious proposition arose on the construction of the question and answer. In a contract of insurance, it is a weighty fact that the questions are framed by the insurer, and that if an answer is obtained to such a question which is upon a fair construction a true answer, it is not open to the insuring company to maintain that the question was put in a sense different from or more comprehensive than the proponent's answer covered. Where an ambiguity exists, the contract must stand if an answer has been made to the question on a fair and reasonable construction of that question. Otherwise, the ambiguity would be a trap against which the insured would be protected by courts of law. Their Lordships accept that doctrine to the full, and no question is made of the soundness of it as set forth in many authorities ...

But, upon the other hand, the principle of a fair and reasonable construction of the question must also be applied in the other direction – that is to say, there must also be a fair and reasonable construction of the answer given; and if, on such a construction, the answer is not true, although upon extreme literalism it may be correct, then the contract is equally avoided. These principles seem to be entirely in accord with Lord Watson's view in *Thomson v Weems*, which was thus expressed: 'Notwithstanding that the warranty is express there still remains for consideration what must be held to be the subject matter of the warranty. That is a point to be determined in each case, according to the just construction of the question and answer taken *per se* and without reference to the warranty given.' ...

With these matters in view, what is a just and reasonable construction of the words in the question, 'Has proponent ever been a claimant on a fire insurance company? If so, state when and name of company'?

It is not to be wondered at that this was made the basis of the contract, because insurance companies might hesitate long before entering into a contract with an insurer who had been formerly a claimant upon companies, and they would have been put upon their inquiry as to what these claims were and how they had been settled and what were the circumstances of these former transactions. The importance of the question might be increased by the number of times in which such transactions had taken place ...

When that question is reasonably construed, it points to the insurer getting the benefit of what has been the record of the insured with regard to insurance claims. This was distinctly its intention and in their Lordships' opinion is plainly its meaning. To exclude, however, from that record what might in the easily supposed case be all its most important items, however numerous these might be, and to answer the question in the singular, which again in the easily supposed case might be a colourless instance favourable to the claimant, would be to answer the question so as to misrepresent the true facts and situation and to be of the nature of a trap.

On this simple ground, which is in accord with the spirit and principle of insurance law as frequently laid down, their Lordships see no occasion for interfering with the judgment of the majority of the court below ...

APPENDIX 5.4

Provincial Insurance Co Ltd v Morgan and Another [1933] AC 240, HL

Lord Russell of Killowen: It appears to me that the result of this appeal depends solely upon the true construction of the documents.

There is no need for me to recapitulate the facts. It is sufficient to say that the appellant insurance company claim that the policy by its terms provides that if at any time during its currency the assured used the vehicle in question for any purpose other than the delivery of coal, or carried in it goods other than coal, no liability on the part of the insurance company would arise thereunder.

The foundation of this contention is as follows: The proposal form requires the proposer (among other things) to state: (a) the purposes (in full) for which the vehicle will be used; and (b) the nature of the goods to be carried. The proposer stated: (a) delivery of coal; (b) coal; and they signed a declaration that the questions were fully and truthfully answered. The policy refers to the proposal and declaration, which (it provides) shall be deemed to be of a promissory nature and effect and shall be the basis of the contract as if incorporated in the policy. One of the conditions indorsed on the policy runs thus:

> 6 It is a condition precedent to any liability on the part of the company under this policy:
>
> (i) that the terms, provisions, conditions, and indorsements hereof, so far as they relate to anything to be done or complied with by the insured, are duly and faithfully observed; and
>
> (ii) that the statements made and the answers given in the proposal hereinbefore referred to are true, correct, and complete.

It is contended by the appellants that the statement above referred to constituted a statement: (a) that during the currency of the policy the vehicle would never be used for any purpose other than the delivery of coal; and (b) that during the currency of the policy coals, and coals only, would be carried in the vehicle. They then say that these statements are incorporated into the policy as contractual provisions relating to something to be done or complied with by the insured, the due and faithful observance of which is, under condition 6, a condition precedent to any liability on their part, and that the vehicle having, in fact, been used during the currency of the policy for the purpose of carrying timber no liability can attach to them. Alternatively, it was said that the answer given in the statement was not true, correct, or complete, because the vehicle had in fact subsequently carried timber; with the result of freedom from liability to the appellant insurance company under the second part of condition 6.

This argument, in my opinion, breaks down at the outset. I cannot read the above statements in the proposal form as being more than statements by the proposers of their intentions as to the user of the vehicle and the goods to be carried in it, and so as descriptive of the risk. If it had really been the intention of the appellants that the carrying of goods other than coal at any time should free them from liability in respect of an accident happening subsequently, it was incumbent on them to make that abundantly clear to the proposers. On the construction which I give to the statements, there is no scope for the operation of condition 6 in favour of the appellants. It is not shown that there has been any failure of the insured to observe any provision relating to anything to be done or complied with by them, or that their answers were not true, correct, and complete …

For myself, I think it is a matter of great regret that the printed forms which insurance companies prepare, and offer for acceptance and signature by the insuring public, should not state in clear and unambiguous terms the events upon the happening of which the insuring company will escape liability under the policy. The present case is a conspicuous example of an attempt to escape liability by placing upon words a meaning which, if intended by the insurance company, should have been put before the proposers in words admitting of no possible doubt …

I would dismiss this appeal …

APPENDIX 5.5

Shaw v Robberds, Hawkes and Stone (1837) 6 Ad & El 75, CA

Lord Denman CJ (now delivered the judgment of the court): This was an action upon a policy of insurance against fire. There were two subjects of insurance: certain buildings including a dwellinghouse, 'and also a kiln for drying corn in use, attached to the outward walls of the granary and communicating therewith by one door, the kiln built entirely of brick and iron'. Both were destroyed by the fire. The policy was subject to the usual conditions: amongst which, the third provided that, if there were any misrepresentation in the description of the premises, the policy should be void; and the sixth that, if any alteration were made, either in the buildings or the business carried on therein, notice should be given to the insurers, an additional premium, if required, paid, and an indorsement made on the policy; otherwise the policy should be void.

It appeared in evidence that the kiln had been constantly used for the purpose of drying corn only; but that, in the year 1832, a vessel laden with bark having been sunk in the river near the premises, and the bark wetted, the plaintiff had allowed the bark to be dried in his kiln, as a favour to the owner of it. No notice was given to the insurers. No greater fire than usual had been made; but, in the course of drying the bark, the kiln took fire, and both the kiln and the other premises were burned down.

The jury found that corn drying and bark drying are different trades, that the latter is more dangerous than the former, and that the loss happened from the use of the kiln in drying the bark. A verdict was entered for the defendants, with leave to the plaintiff to move to enter a verdict for him, either for the whole amount of the loss, or, at least, for the value of the kiln.

The third and sixth conditions were relied on in argument by the defendants; and it was contended that the facts here were either a misdescription of the kiln within the third condition, or a change of business within the sixth. The two conditions together were also said to amount to a warranty that nothing but corn should ever be dried in the kiln; and what has occurred was likened to a deviation in the case of marine insurance. It was proved, at the trial, that a much higher premium was regularly exacted by insurance offices for a bark kiln than for a malt kiln. The argument, therefore, was, that the premises were not truly described in the policy, or that the trade carried on there had been altered at the time of the fire without notice to the insurance office.

We are, however, of opinion that neither of the conditions applies to this case. The third condition points to the description of the premises given at the time of insuring; and that description was in this instance perfectly correct. Nothing which occurred afterwards, not even a change of business, could bring the case within that condition, which was fully performed when the risk first attached.

The sixth condition points at an alteration of business, at something permanent and habitual; and, if the plaintiff had either dropped his business of corn drying, and taken up that of bark drying, or added the latter to the former, no doubt the case could have been within that condition. Perhaps, if he had made any charge for drying this bark, it might have been a question for the jury whether he had done so as a matter of business, and whether he had not thereby (although it was the first instance of bark drying) made an alteration in his business, within the meaning of that condition. But, according to the evidence, we are clearly of opinion that no such question arose for the consideration of the jury; and that this single act of kindness was no breach of the sixth condition ...

One argument more remains to be noticed, viz, that the loss here arose from the plaintiff's own negligent act, in allowing the kiln to be used for a purpose to which it was not adapted. There is no doubt that one of the objects of insurance against fire is to guard against the negligence of servants and others; and, therefore, the simple fact of negligence has never been held to constitute a defence. But it is argued that there is a distinction between the negligence of servants or strangers and that of the assured himself. We do not see any ground for such a distinction; and are of the opinion that, in the absence of all fraud, the proximate cause of the loss only is to be looked to.

For these reasons, we are of the opinion that the rule must be made absolute, to enter a verdict for the plaintiff for the whole loss, as having been produced by causes which do not prevent the policy from attaching.

APPENDIX 5.6

Hair v The Prudential Assurance Co Ltd [1983] 2 Lloyd's Rep 669

Woolf J: This is an action under a policy of insurance where the insurers are refusing liability on the basis that there was a breach of a warranty of the policy which entitles them to take that course, and, secondly on the basis that there has been a failure to disclose material matters. The case, because it raises these issues, is of greater significance than the amount at stake would otherwise indicate. When a responsible insurer such as the defendant takes that course it is indicating that it is regarding the case as one where as a matter of principle it should not be regarded as under any liability, and where this is the case the amount of the claim reduces in significance …

I was helpfully referred to the relevant passages in MacGillivray's *Insurance Law*, 7th edn, London: Sweet & Maxwell, and I will confine myself to drawing attention to the four questions posed at para 754, in determining whether a clause should be construed as a continuing warranty. I bear in mind those considerations. Having done so, it seems to me that the proper way to regard the questions and the answers is to treat them as being an indication of the state of affairs which existed at the time that the answers were given, or was going to exist within the immediate future thereafter and was going to continue so far as the insured was concerned for the period of the policy, but they did not amount to a warranty that no change would occur. They were doing no more than indicating the situation as the plaintiff then understood it would be and was going to continue to be, but they did not amount to an assurance that there would not be change during the period of insurance. To regard them as a continuing obligation to have a named individual in occupation throughout the period, seems to me to be putting an unreasonable interpretation upon the effect of the questions and answers there appearing. Approaching the matter on this interpretation which I would apply to the questions and the answers which were given, it appears that the plaintiff has, again, established on a balance of probability that she was not in breach of warranty.

That leaves the question of the closing order. So far as the closing order was concerned, I have no doubt that was something which was known to the plaintiff. Mr Pelling submits that it was material to be known to him and he indicates what the Prudential's attitude would be if the matter had been drawn to their attention. Again, I obtain assistance from MacGillivray's *Insurance Law*. The relevant paragraph is para 626. It reads:

> It is more likely, however, that questions asked will limit the duty of disclosure, in that, if questions are asked on particular subjects and the answers to them are warranted, it may be inferred that the insurer has waived his right to information either on the same matters but outside the scope of the questions or on kindred matters to the subject matter of the question. Thus, if an insurer asks 'How many accidents have you had in the last three years?', it may well be implied that he does not want to know of accidents before that time, though these would still be material. If he were to ask whether any of the proposer's brothers or sisters had died of consumption or had been inflicted

> with insanity, it might well be inferred that the insurer had waived similar information concerning more remote relatives, so that he could not void the policy for non-disclosure of an aunt's death of consumption or an uncle's insanity. Whether or not such waiver is present depends on a true construction of the proposal form, the test being: Would a reasonable man reading a proposal form be justified in thinking that the insurer had restricted his right to receive all material information and consented to the omission of the particular information in issue?

Approaching the matter on the basis of that paragraph and, in particular, the final sentence of that paragraph, it is important to draw attention to the fact that where the proposer signed the proposal form this appears:

> I wish to insure as above with the Prudential Assurance Company Limited in the usual form for this class of insurance and warrant that all the information entered above is true and complete and that nothing materially affecting the risk has been concealed.

Reading that sentence as a whole, coming as it does at the end of the proposal form, it appears to me that it is reasonable to regard the question as requiring the proposer to make it clear that he or she has given a true and complete answer to the questions which appear above, and, what is more, the risk with regard to matters on which he is being questioned. I am bound to say, that, if it was intended that an assured should answer matters even though he is not being questioned about them, I would expect a different form of statement from the one to which I have just made reference. I would have expected something to be said which clearly indicated to a proposer that, although they had not been asked any specific question about the matter, if there was something which was relevant to the risk which they knew of, but which was not covered by the questions, they should still deal with it, and leave a space for them to do so ...

I have come to the conclusion that the plaintiff, despite her conduct which I have fully in mind and to which I have already made reference, is entitled to succeed on the claim ...

APPENDIX 5.7

Hussain v Brown [1996] 1 Lloyd's Rep 627, CA

Saville LJ: The warranty question arises out of a proposal form completed by the plaintiff and signed on 9 June 1992. Question 9 of this form was as follows:

> Are the premises fitted with any system of intruder alarm?
>
> If 'yes', give name of installing company. (Please provide a copy alarm specification if applicable.)

The plaintiff answered this question 'yes' and 'See specification'. Accompanying the proposal form, when it was offered to underwriters' agents, was a specification for a proposed security alarm dated 2 February, 1990 and a survey report dated 11 April, 1990. By the date of the report, the security alarm had been fitted and the report recorded that certain modifications were to be made to the system. Underwriters' agents were informed when the risk was presented that these modifications had in fact been carried out. Underwriters accepted the proposal and the insurance incepted on 14 July 1992.

The proposal form contained the following declaration:

> I/We the Proposer warrant that the above statements are true and that they shall be the basis of the contract between me/us and the Underwriters and will be incorporated into such contract.

The insurance itself, which was in the form of a Lloyd's certificate dated 18 December, 1992, also provided that the proposal and the declaration I have just quoted were to be the basis of and form part of the certificate ...

The underwriters' submission is that the answer given to question 9 in the proposal form, amounted to a continuing warranty that the premises were fitted with an intruder alarm, that the alarm was operational and/or would be habitually set by the plaintiff when the premises were unattended. Assuming for the moment that this is the true meaning and effect of the answer, there is no dispute that on ordinary principles of insurance law, the admissions made by the plaintiff would mean that the underwriters were discharged from liability from the date of the breach, which in this case (on the assumption made) was before the date of the fire, and that it was immaterial whether or not the breach had anything to do with the fire. The question, therefore, is simply whether the answer to question 9 amounts to a continuing warranty of the kind suggested by the underwriters ...

In my judgment ... there is no special principle of insurance law requiring answers in proposal forms to be read, *prima facie* or otherwise, as importing promises as to the future. Whether or not they do depends upon ordinary rules of construction, namely consideration of the words the parties have used in the light of the context in which they have used them and (where the words admit of more than one meaning) selection of that meaning which seems most closely to correspond with the presumed intentions of the parties ...

In the present case, the question posed for the potential insured was in the present tense. In addition, it did not seek on its face any information as to the practice of the proposer with regard to the alarm, for example, whether it was set when the premises were left unoccupied. The construction contended for by Mr Brodie involves not only reading the present tense as referring to the future, but also as importing into the question an inquiry whether the alarm would be kept operational, and/ or (to use the words in Mr Brodie's skeleton argument) 'habitually set by the plaintiff' when the premises were left unattended. I can see nothing in the words of the simple question posed, or to be gleaned from the context, which begins to suggest that what an affirmative answer entails is an undertaking as to the future along these lines.

Mr Brodie sought support for his construction by suggesting that to confine the question to the state of affairs existing when it was answered, would be of no assistance to underwriters and would therefore be absurd, so that to give any sense it must have been intended to refer to the future. I disagree …

It is, in my view, of value to underwriters to know whether or not an alarm is fitted, for depending on the answer, underwriters could require one to be fitted, or indeed seek a continuing warranty or decline the risk …

It must be remembered that a continuing warranty is a draconian term. As I have noted, the breach of such a warranty produces an automatic cancellation of the cover, and the fact that a loss may have no connection at all with that breach is simply irrelevant. In my view, if underwriters want such protection, then it is up to them to stipulate for it in clear terms. A good example of the way this can be done is in fact to be found in the standard printed terms incorporated into the certificate itself when dealing with theft risks, though, of course, these are not directly relevant to the insurance under discussion which was limited to fire risks. The fact that such a warranty would be likely to give underwriters more protection than a warranty as to the existing state of affairs, as importing warranties as to the future …

APPENDIX 5.8

Dawsons Ltd v Bonnin and Others [1922] All ER Rep 210

Viscount Haldane: My Lords, the reply of the appellants, the insured, on this point was that the question whether the motor vehicle was to be stored at Dovehill or at Cadogan Street was not a material one. The chief risks covered by the policy were in the main wholly unconnected with fire at the garage, and the percentage of the premium to be allocated to that risk was very small. The respondents called evidence to prove that they did consider that the question was one of importance, and the learned judges in the court below appear to have given credence to that evidence and to have attached weight to it. This is an important fact, and I am reluctant to differ from them. But I think that, notwithstanding some differences in the way in which they cross-examined the witnesses called for the respondents, the appellants have sufficiently proved by testimony which commends itself that in all probability no importance would have been attached to any answer to the fourth question in the proposal form to the effect that Dovehill was to be the place of garage.

But that does not dispose of the case. For if the respondents can show that they contracted to get an accurate answer to this question, and to make the validity of the policy conditional on that answer being accurate, whether the answer was of material importance or not, the fulfilment of this contract is a condition of the appellants being able to recover.

My Lords, for this reason it appears to me that the question which really lies at the root of the matter in dispute is one of construction simply ...

If there are statements in the answers to the questions in the proposal form which are in this way constituted by special stipulation conditions, they are therefore unaffected by the subsequent and independent condition dependent on materiality ...

The proper significance of the word in the law of England is an agreement which refers to the subject matter of a contract, but, not being an essential part of the contract either intrinsically or by agreement, is collateral to the main purpose of such a contract. Yet, irrespective of this, the word came to be employed in England when what was really meant was something of wider operation, a pure condition. If goods tendered in performance of a contract did not satisfy the conditions stipulated for, the buyer may reject them; but he may alternatively accept the goods and claim damages for breach of the stipulated condition, thus treating his claim as one for damages for a breach of warranty, sufficiently so constituted. The condition is thus wider than the warranty strictly so called, but may be founded on as giving rise to a contract of warranty ...

As Lord Blackburn observed in *Thomson v Weems* (1884) 9 App Cas 671:

> It is competent to the contracting parties, if both agree to it and sufficiently express their intention so to agree, to make the actual existence of anything a condition precedent to the inception of any contract; and if they do so the non-existence of that thing is a good defence. And it is not of any importance whether the existence of that thing was or was not material; the parties would not have made it a part of the contract if they had not thought it material, and they have a right to determine for themselves what they shall deem material ...

It is clear that the answer was textually inaccurate. I think that the words employed in the body of the policy can only be properly construed as having made its accuracy a condition. The result may be technical and harsh, but if the parties have so stipulated we have no alternative, sitting as a court of justice, but to give effect to the words agreed on. Hard cases must not be allowed to make bad law. Now the proposal, in other words the answers to the questions specifically put in it, are made basic to the contract. It may well be that a mere slip, in a Christian name, for instance, would not be held to vitiate the answer given if the answer were really in substance true and unambiguous. '*Falso demonstratio non nocet*.' But that is because the truth has been stated in effect within the intention shown by the language used. The misstatement as to the address at which the vehicle would usually be garaged can hardly be brought within this principle of interpretation in construing contracts. It was a specific insurance, based on a statement which is made foundational if the parties have chosen, however carelessly, to stipulate that it should be so. Both on principle and in the light of authorities such as those I have already cited, it appears to me that when answers, including that in question, are declared to be the basis of the contract this can only mean that their truth is made a condition exact fulfilment of which is rendered by stipulation foundational to its enforceability ...

Lord Wrenbury (dissenting): It is a document whereby the proposer makes certain statements of fact, and if those statements are inaccurate or misleading the proper consequences will follow which result from misstatement made in inducing a contract. In order to see what these are in this case, it is necessary to look further. The second part consists of the operative body of the policy, consisting of recital and operative words of obligation. By way of recital this document states that the proposer has made a proposal which is to be 'held as incorporated herein'. As this proposal was a unilateral document signed by the proposer only, it can be incorporated only by way of recital. When I have incorporated it, I find only that the policy says that the proposer had made certain statements, and so he had. As further part of the recital under review, the document runs 'which proposal shall be the basis of this contract'. The whole effect of these words I think is to state that the proposal is to be taken to be the initiation and foundation of the contractual relation, and the statements contained in the proposal are to be statements on the faith of which the insurers are prepared to contract. The statements in the proposal are thus made material. I must look at the contract to see what effect is to be given to their materiality. To see what is to ensue if any of them are inaccurate, I have therefore still to look further.

If a contract is induced by misrepresentation, the misrepresentation does not necessarily render the contract void. It may render the contract voidable at the instance of the contracting party who proves that he was misled. This differs *toto caelo* from a case in which the contract itself provides that if a certain alleged fact is not true the contract shall be void. In that case, the contract becomes contractually void, because the contract itself provides that in that event it shall be void. In the former case, the contract remains an operative obligation, but one from which the party misled may be in a position to relieve himself, because he cannot be held to a contract which was tainted at its source.

The question here is what was, in this case, the position of the insurers in this respect? This brings me to the third part of the contract – namely, the 'conditions of insurance'. By the operative words of the policy the obligation of the insurers is 'subject to the conditions on the back hereof, the due observance of which is a condition precedent to all liability of the underwriters hereunder'. The fourth condition is 'Material misstatement or concealment of any circumstance by the insured material to assessing the premium herein, or in connection with any claim, shall render the policy void'. As matter of construction, I hold that this means 'Material misstatement, by which I mean misstatement material to assessing the premium'. Further, I think that the sentence is a pregnant sentence, and by providing that certain statements shall render the policy void, thus excluding a construction which would give to other statements the effect of a warranty. Misstatements not material to assessing the premiums are not to render the policy contractually void, but their effect is to be determined by the considerations relevant to misstatement as distinguished from warranty ...

I can have no doubt that the insurers attributed no importance at all to this question of construction: that at most they asked for and obtained information as to locality of which they might have availed themselves if they attributed importance to construction, but that they never did so.

My Lords, in my opinion the resistance of the insuring office (who have taken the premium) to satisfy the claim of the assured upon his policy is neither creditable nor capable of being sustained. I think the assured is entitled to succeed on this appeal.

APPENDIX 5.9

Thomson v Weems and Others (1884) 9 App Cas 671, HL

Lord Blackburn: It became usual, I do not know when, but at least for the last 50 years, to insert a term in the contract, that if the statements were untrue the premiums should be forfeited.

That, no doubt, is a hard bargain for the assured if he has innocently warranted what was not accurate, but if he has warranted it, 'untruth', without any moral guilt, avoid the insurance; and in *Duckett v Williams* (1834) Cr & M 348, in 1834, it was held, on reasoning to my mind irresistible, that in a declaration substantially as far as regards this point the same as this, what was untrue so as to have the effect of avoiding the insurance was also untrue so as to cause the forfeiture of the premium.

In *Anderson v Fitzgerald* (1853) 4 HL Cas 484, Lord St Leonards points out very strongly that where such a consequence would follow from a warranty, before a contract is held to have the effect of a warranty it is necessary to see that the language is such as to shew that the assured as well as the insurer meant it, and that the language in the policy being that of the insurers, if there is any ambiguity, it must be construed most strongly against them. But he never questioned that if it was a warranty and it was not fulfilled, it avoided the policy ...

The Lord Advocate argued very powerfully that the truth of that statement involved questions of degree and of opinion, and therefore could not, he argued, be warranted. But the most familiar instance of a warranty (implied on every voyage policy) is that of seaworthiness, involving in it questions of degree and opinion to quite as great an extent as a warranty of temperate habits. I think, therefore, whilst I agree that the burden is on the insurers, and that they must prove drinking carried on before the date of the declaration, 9 November 1881, to such an extent as to amount to intemperance, and so often and continuously as to amount to habits of intemperance, they are not obliged to prove anything more.

The object of the insurance company was to know that the life to be insured was not merely not rendered already diseased by drinking, but that his habits were so temperate that there was no unusual risk that he should become a drunkard, and they took the warranty that they might safely dispense with any further inquiry on that point ...

Lord Watson: When the truth of a particular statement has been made in the subject of warranty, no questions can arise as to its materiality or immateriality to the risk, it being the very purpose of the warranty to exclude all controversy upon that point. As the Lord Chancellor (Cranworth) said in *Anderson v Fitzgerald* ...:

> Nothing, therefore can be more reasonable than that the parties entering into that contract should determine for themselves what they think to be material, and if they choose to do so, and to stipulate that unless the assured shall answer a certain question accurately, the policy or contract which they are entering into shall be void, it is perfectly open to them to do so, and his false answer will then avoid the policy.

It would, in my opinion, be equally subversive of the contract which the parties make for themselves, to hold (as Lord Young apparently does) that there can be no breach of such a warranty, unless it is proved that the answer of the assured, being untrue was made by him either wilfully and in the knowledge of its untruth, or inexcusable, in the sense of its having been a blameably reckless or careless assertion.

APPENDIX 5.10

Re Bradley and Essex and Suffolk Accident Indemnity Society Ltd [1911–13] All ER Rep 444

Farwell LJ: Contracts of insurance are contracts in which *uberrima fides* is required not only from the assured but also from the company insuring. It is the universal practice for the companies to prepare both the forms of proposal and the form of policy. Both are issued by them on printed forms kept ready for use. It is their duty to make the policy accord with and not exceed the proposal, and to express both in clear and unambiguous terms, lest, as Fletcher-Moulton LJ says, quoting Lord St Leonards in *Joel v Law Union and Crown Insurance Co (No 2)* [1908] 2 KB 886, provisions should be introduced into policies which:

> ... unless they are fully explained to the parties will lead a vast number of persons to suppose that they have made a provision for their families by an insurance on their lives, and by payment of perhaps a very considerable portion of their income, when in point of fact from the very commencement the policy was not worth the paper on which it was written.

It is especially incumbent on insurance companies to make clear both in their proposal forms and in their policies the conditions which are precedent to their liability to pay. For such conditions have the same effect as forfeiture clauses and may inflict loss and injury on the assured and those claiming under him out of all proportion to any damage that could possibly accrue to the company from non-observance or non-performance of the conditions. Accordingly, it has been established that the doctrine that policies are to be construed *contra proferentes* applies strongly against the company ... It has been further held that if the proposal be in one form and the office draws up the policy in a different form, varying the rights of the assured, courts of equity would rectify the policy so as to make it accord with the proposal ... and, in cases like the present, where the proposal is 'considered as incorporated' in the policy, the court will, on construction of the two documents read together, give effect to the proposal as overriding the policy where they differ ...

Tens of thousands of small shopkeepers with one assistant, lodging house keepers and other with one 'general', small farmers, tenants of small holdings and the like with one man are driven to insure. They receive a printed form of proposal, and it is reasonable to assume that they read and rely on it, and they receive in exchange for the form signed by them a policy which they are entitled to assume, and do assume in most cases without careful perusal of the document, to accord with the proposal form. It is, in my opinion, incumbent on the company to put clearly on the proposal form the acts which the assured is by the policy to covenant to perform and to make clear in the policy the conditions, non-performance of which will entail the loss of all benefit of the insurance. It is contended that it is of the utmost importance to insurance companies that they should be able to defend themselves against fraud by inserting conditions precedent, such as keeping wage-books and the like. Be it so. There is no objection whatever to the insertion of such conditions so long as the intending assurer [*sic*] has full and fair notice of them and assents to them. This can easily be done by stating them shortly in the proposal form with the addition that payment may be refused if they or any of them are not complied with. But it is, in my opinion, scarcely honest to induce a man to propose on certain terms and then to accept that proposal and send a policy as in accordance with it when such policy contains numerous provisions not mentioned in the proposal which operate to defeat any claim under the policy, and all the more so when such provisions are couched in obscure terms.

In the present case both proposal forms and policy offend against both the requirements to which I have referred; and the form of policy is to my mind very objectionable …

I turn to the policy and I find a provision that may be common, but is, in my opinion, most objectionable. The policy states that the due observance and fulfilment of the conditions of this policy 'shall be a condition precedent to any liability of the society under this policy'. The policy then sets out in small print eight clauses, of which it is admitted that several are not conditions precedent, and some are not conditions at all. Clause 5 contains the provision relied on by the society. It is in the middle of a clause the first and last provisions of which are clearly not conditions precedent. The first paragraph is not a condition at all, and the last is obviously subsequent because the amount due on the policy may become due before the event happens. Bray J has held that the provision for keeping a proper wages-book, inserted as it is in the middle of cl 5, cannot fairly be read as an independent condition precedent, but is merely machinery for that ascertainment and adjustment of premium which is mentioned in the proposal form. I agree with him because I think that reading the policy with the proposal form (in accordance with the provision in the form that the form is incorporated in the policy) and construing the policy most strongly against the society in the interests of honesty and fair dealing, this is the better construction. Any other construction would convict the society of having issued a tricky policy calculated to deceive and entrap the unwary, and of insisting on the success of their devices. I think it is the duty of all insuring companies to state in clear and plain terms as conditions precedent, those provisions only which are such, not to wrap them up in a number of clauses which are not conditions precedent at all, and I think further, that it is their duty to call attention to such conditions in their forms of proposal so as to make sure that the insurers understand their liabilities …

Fletcher-Moulton LJ (dissenting): I come now to the main question as to the due observance and fulfilment of cl 5 being a condition precedent to the liability of the society under the policy. It is clearly and unmistakably pronounced to be so in the policy itself, and I ask myself whether there is any reason why we should declare it to be otherwise. I can see none. The clause appears to me to be a most reasonable precaution necessary for the protection of the society, and wisely made by it a condition precedent. By the scheme of insurance the premium is fixed, not at the inception of the risk, but after it is over, and the amount of the premium is calculated upon the total of the wages actually paid within the year. It follows that if there is any omission either of persons employed or of wages paid to them in calculating the adjustment the society gets a diminished premium. By the time the adjustment has to be made the risk is over, and therefore, it is directly to the interest of the insured to make such omissions. But if the insured is bound to keep a contemporary record of the names of his employees and the wages paid to them there is no such temptation to him to fail in his duty because the risk is not then over, and as he wishes to be covered for all his employees he necessarily has an interest in entering them as such at the time. It will be seen, therefore, that the duty of making contemporary records of the names of the employees and of the wages paid is a most valuable protection to the society against fraud or forgetfulness on the part of the insured. I may go further and say that it is in substance their only protection. It would be impossible for them actually to check the correctness of the statements as to the employees and their wages which are rendered to them by the insured at the end of the year since they probably have many thousands of policies. But by making it a condition that all wages shall be duly recorded in a proper wages-book, and that such wages book shall at all times be open to the inspection of the society, the latter has a really effective check upon the insured. It becomes much too dangerous to leave unrecorded the wages paid, and in this way the insured are spared the temptation of omitting to make records of wages paid to persons with regard to whom the risk is over, such as persons taken on temporarily whose period of service has expired. To my mind, a provision such as this is precisely correlative to a condition that notice of an accident shall be given as soon as practicable. The latter protects the society from unfounded claims of liability by putting it in the best position for testing the justice of the claims, and the former protects the society from loss on its premiums by providing that it shall have the best material for checking their correctness. And these two conditions are alike in another respect. However vital to the society their observance may be they can only be rendered effective by stipulating that they shall be conditions precedent, that is, that a claimant, in order to make good his claim must aver and prove their performance down to the date of bringing his action. If they are merely independent obligations the breach of which gives ground for a cross claim in damages they might as well be struck out of the policy because from their nature it is impossible to establish the quantum of damages resulting from a breach. The conditions, therefore, seems to me to be one of such a nature that it can be made, and would naturally be made, and by the language of the policy has expressly been made a condition precedent, and inasmuch as *ex concessis* it has not been performed in this case, I am of the opinion that the liability of the society under the policy has ceased ...

APPENDIX 5.11

Evans v Employers' Mutual Insurance Association Ltd [1936] KB 505; [1935] All ER Rep 659

Slesser LJ: In my opinion, the fundamental question in this case is whether the knowledge which Mr Mitchell acquired in comparing the claim with the proposal form thereby became the knowledge of the respondent company.

It is true that in *Houghton's Case* [1928] AC 1 ... Lord Sumner points out that 'the mind, so to speak, of a company is not reached or affected by information merely possessed by its clerks'. And, again, 'the knowledge, which is relevant, is that of directors themselves, since it is their board that deals with the company's rights'. But it must depend upon the facts of each case, where the matter is not specially determined by the articles, by what particular means of information and in what circumstances a company may properly be said to acquire knowledge, or have knowledge thrust upon them. In this case, as to the two documents themselves, the proposal form and the claim form, it cannot in any view be said that the company did not know their several contents since both were addressed to the company; but the correlation of the two, leading to discrepancy and consequent falsity of the claimant's first statement, depended solely upon the investigations of Mr Mitchell. Now, Mr Mitchell was not a mere clerk: it was his specific duty to do the very act of comparison which here resulted in his ascertainment of the conflict between the claimant's two statements. He carried out his duty and he made the comparison, and the fact that he did not think fit to convey the information so obtained to Mr Morice or Mr Last, who were the persons who properly decided that the company should deal with the matter, does not enable the company, in my judgment, to deny that they were bound by the knowledge which he obtained in carrying out duties entrusts to him, albeit negligently performed, by the company through Mr Morice ...

Roche LJ: In *Bentsen v Taylor, Sons and Co* [1893] 2 QB 274 ... Bowen LJ stated the principles governing waiver in such a case, in language that has often been quoted with approval, as follows:

> In order to succeed, the plaintiff must show, either that he has performed the condition precedent, the onus being on him, or that the defendants have excused the performance of the condition, and we have to consider whether the plaintiff has sustained that burden, so that no reasonable man could doubt that there has been a waiver of the condition or an excuse of its performance. In other words, did the defendants by their acts or conduct lead the plaintiff reasonably to suppose that they did not intend to treat the contract for the future as at an end, on account of the failure to perform the condition precedent, but that they only intended to rely on the misdescription as a breach of warranty, treating the contract as still open for further performance? Did the defendants lead the plaintiff to believe that they intended to treat the misdescription as a breach of contract only, and not as a failure to perform a condition precedent ...?

Certain material questions contained in the claim were directed to ascertaining whether the statements in the proposal form were true. The answers stated the truth and showed that the statements in the proposal form were untrue in the sense that they were inaccurate. I agree with my Lord that if such information is invited by a company and is given and communicated to that company in the manner invited, that fact alone would be sufficient …

The company therefore acquired the knowledge through the very person appointed to acquire it, and if it failed to use it the failure was due to that person's default. Cases in which knowledge was acquired by a company for other purposes and by other persons than those concerned with the particular matter under enquiry have no application to the present case …

APPENDIX 5.12

Law Commission, *Insurance Law: Non-Disclosure and Breach of Warranty*, Cmnd 8064, Law Com 104, 1980, London: HMSO

WARRANTIES

Defects in the present law

6.9 Later we set out our view on the defects in the rules of law which give insurers the right to create warranties as to past or present fact by means of 'basis of the contract' clauses. There are however in our view four major defects in the present law of warranties which derive from the characteristics of warranties and the ways in which they are created:

(a) it seems quite wrong that an insurer should be entitled to demand strict compliance with a warranty which is not material to the risk and to repudiate the policy for a breach of it;

(b) similarly, it seems unjust that an insurer should be entitled to reject a claim for *any* breach of even a material warranty, no matter how irrelevant the breach may be to the loss;

(c) material warranties are of such importance to the insured that in our view he ought to be able to refer to a written document in which they are contained;

(d) as we have already mentioned, we deal below with the mischiefs which arise from the creation of warranties by the use of a 'basis of the contract' clause in a proposal form.

Is reform of the law necessary?

6.10 In our view the defects in the present law just described show a formidable case for reform. On consultation there was general agreement that the law of warranties was in need of reform ...

Reform of the law of warranties

Introduction

6.11 ... warranties are of two types: warranties as to past or present fact, and promissory warranties. In view of the recommendations which we make as regards 'basis of the contract' clauses insurers wishing to introduce warranties of the first type will no longer be able to do so either by the use of appropriate words in a proposal form or by a provision which refers to a proposal form. Insurers will have to introduce them individually in compliance with the formal requirements set out in paras 6.14 and 7.10 ... However, we anticipate that as a matter of underwriting practice insurers will find it necessary to introduce such warranties in relatively few cases, usually in relation to large commercial risks and normally as a result of negotiations with the insured. Thus, although the recommendations in this part are intended to apply both to warranties as to past or present fact and to promissory warranties, they will be applicable in the main to promissory warranties.

A modified system of warranties

6.12 In our view, the system of warranties in English insurance law should be modified to the extent necessary to eradicate the defects we have described. The first defect in the present law noted above was that a breach of any warranty entitles the insurer to repudiate the policy whether or not the warranty was material to the risk. We consider that insurers should not be entitled to repudiate the policy for the breach of an undertaking which is immaterial to the risk, even if the word 'warranty' is used or if the true construction of the contract provides the insurer with the right to repudiate for any breach of warranty even if immaterial. Accordingly, we recommend that a term of the contract should only be capable of constituting a warrant if it is material to the risk, in the sense that it is an undertaking relating to a matter which would influence a prudent insurer in deciding whether to accept the risk and, if he decides to accept it, at what premium and on what terms.

6.13 In our working paper, we took the provisional view that since the materiality or otherwise of a particular warranty depends on its influence on the judgment of a prudent insurer it would be inappropriate and unduly harsh on the insured if the onus of disproving materiality were placed on him, and that the onus should accordingly be on the insurer to prove that the warranty broken was material to the risk. However, we have reconsidered this. We now consider that if the insurer has complied with the formal requirements recommended in the next paragraph, so that the insured is made aware of his obligations, but the insured nonetheless acts in breach of any such obligation, it is inappropriate that the insurer should also have to prove the materiality of the obligation to the risk as a condition of being entitled to avoid the policy. We accordingly *recommend* that there should be a presumption that a provision in a contract of insurance, which possesses the attributes of a warranty at common law, is material to the risk. The insured can rebut this presumption by showing that the provision in question relates to a matter which would not have influenced the judgment of a prudent insurer in assessing the risk. It is to be noted that this recommendation is along the same lines as that made in relation to the materiality of questions in proposal forms.

6.14 It will be convenient to discuss next the third of the defects relating to warranties which we noted in para 6.9. This concerns the desirability of the insured being able to refer to a written document containing the warranties by which he is bound. In our view the insurer should be obliged, as a condition precedent to the legal effectiveness of the warranty, to furnish the insured with such a document at least as soon as practicable after the insured gave the warranty in question. If the insured has completed a proposal form and has given answers to certain questions relating to the future, these answers will often have the force of promissory warranties because of the inclusion of a 'basis of the contract' clause. The insurer would accordingly be able to comply with this obligation by furnishing the insured with a copy of the completed proposal form. Where no proposal form has been completed, and the insured has given a promissory warranty, we consider that it should be incorporated as an individual term on the face of the policy or in an endorsement thereon. However, we are aware that in some cases, for example where short term cover is granted, no policy is ever issued and that in others, for example where provisional cover is granted, a policy may not be issued within a reasonable time of the warranty having been given. In the case of provisional cover, a warranty may often be given over the telephone. In all such cases the insurer should be required to confirm in writing the warranty given by the insured as soon as is practicable in the circumstances. This may be done in a cover note, in a certificate of insurance or even by letter. If the insurer fails to comply with these formal requirements he should in our view be precluded from relying on a breach of the warranty in question in order to repudiate the policy or reject a claim. Nevertheless, if a loss should occur in the interim, before it has become practicable for the insurer to provide such written confirmation, then the insurer should be entitled to rely on an oral warranty as this will then still be fresh in the mind of the insured.

The legal effect of a breach of warranty

6.15 We must now deal with the second, and perhaps the most important of the defects in the law of warranties which we have described. The effect of our recommendations so far is that if the insured is in breach of a term of the contract which possesses the attributes of a warranty at common law and has failed to rebut the presumption that it relates to a matter which is material to the risk, and the insurer has complied with the formal requirements set out in the preceding paragraph, then the insurer will be able to repudiate the policy for breach of warranty. Under the present law, the insurer's repudiation relates back to the date of the breach with the result that he can also reject all claims for losses occurring thereafter. One of the mischiefs in the present law of warranties to which we have drawn attention is that insurers are thus able to base their refusal to pay a claim on a breach of warranty which may be totally unconnected with the loss. We are told that insurers usually only make use of this type of 'technical repudiation' if they suspect but are unable to prove some other ground for repudiation. In our working paper our provisional view was that an insurer should not be entitled to reject the claim unless he is able to prove a valid ground for rejection. Our provisional recommendation was that the insurer's right to reject a claim for a loss occurring after the date of the breach should be restricted.

6.16 On consultation, it was put to us that such a restriction would result in the erosion of safety standards by removing or reducing the incentive for compliance with warranties many of which are in the nature of undertakings on the part of the insured to observe precautions. We think it unlikely that a restriction of the insurer's rights of rejection would remove or reduce the incentive to comply with warranties: it may well be that many insureds observe prescribed precautions not out of any considerations relevant to their rights against the insurers but simply because they wish to preserve their persons or property from loss or damage.

6.17 On consultation the majority of those who commented agreed that the insurers' rights to reject claims should be restricted but some of them raised minor points as to how the restriction proposed in the working paper would work in practice. In order to meet these points, we have attempted, in the following paragraphs, to improve our formulation. We also recommend some changes in the present law relation to the effect of repudiation which would necessarily follow from introductions of our proposed restrictions ...

Our recommendation

6.22 Our recommendation is that in cases of breach of warranty the insurer should *prima facie* be entitled to reject claims in all cases which occur after the breach provided that the formal requirements enumerated in para 6.14 have been complied with. However, if the insured can show either:

(a) that the broken warranty was intended to reduce (or prevent from increasing) the risk that a particular type of loss would occur and the loss which in fact occurs is of a different type; or

(b) that even though the loss was of a type which the broken warranty was intended to make less likely, the insured's breach could not have increased the risk that the loss would occur in the way in which it did in fact occur,

then the insured should be entitled to recover; but in such cases the insurer should remain entitled to repudiate *the policy* for the future on account of the breach of warranty which has occurred. The reason for the latter qualification is that in our view insurers should not be compelled to continue to cover insureds who have committed breaches of warranty; they should remain liable for prior claims on the basis of the nexus test referred to above, but subject to this they should be entitled to discontinue to cover. These recommendations necessitate some minor changes in the law relating to the effect of repudiation for breaches of warranty; we discuss these in the next paragraph.

The effect or repudiation for breach of warranty

6.23 The recommendations made above to restrict the insurers' right to reject claims for breach of warranty could not work if the present law as to the retrospective effect of repudiation remains unchanged. If the insurer's repudiation operated retrospectively to the date of breach, then the contract of insurance would cease to exist from that date, with the result that the insurer would be entitled to reject all claims for subsequent losses. As pointed out in para 6.6, under the present law it is unclear whether insurers have a right to reject claims without at the same time repudiating the policy. However, under the above mentioned recommendations, an insured who has committed a breach of warranty will nevertheless be entitled to recover claims if he can satisfy the nexus test. This right, and the consequent liability of the insurer, can co-exist if the contract of insurance remains in existence. We accordingly *recommend* that if insurers exercise their right to repudiate a policy for breach of warranty, that repudiation should take effect for the future only and should no longer be retrospective to the date of the breach. The effective date of repudiation should be the date on which the insurer serves a written notice of repudiation on the insured. In the result, the insurer would remain on risk between the date of the breach and the effective date of repudiation, but would be entitled to reject all claims which occur during that period unless the insured could satisfy the nexus test. We *recommend* accordingly. Further, for the avoidance of doubt, and as a consequence of the foregoing proposals, we *recommend* that rejection of claims on account of breaches of warranty should not necessarily also involve repudiation of the policy: insurers should be free to reject a particular claim without also repudiating the policy. It should, in our view, be open to insurers to make independent decisions as to whether or not to reject individual claims and as to whether or not to continue on risk for the remainder of the policy period, without having to make these decisions in tandem. We believe that this reflects the present practice of the industry, but since the present law is uncertain we make an express recommendation to cover this point.

APPENDIX 5.13

Birds, J, 'Warranties in insurance proposal forms' [1977] JBL 231

Among the many problems which may face insured persons in understanding the full range of their rights and duties under their insurance policies are the full meaning and consequences of the questions, answers and declarations in the proposal form. Normally only filled in at the very inception of the insurance, its contents often, one suspects, forgotten, nevertheless the slightest inaccuracy in it may debar a claim on the policy many years later. Generally inaccuracies will relate to incorrect answers to specific questions, but proposal forms often also contain declarations as well as the questions and answers are capable of amounting to warranties – exact truth is then a condition precedent to the validity of the policy.

Unfortunately, insurers do not always draft these clauses as clearly as they might, nor do they make it entirely clear to the layman exactly what are the consequences of even the slightest inaccuracy ...

It seems appropriate first to review briefly the legal status of the different answers and statements to be found:

(1) the most straightforward example is the question and answer which, taken together, clearly warrant the truth of particular facts at the date the proposal form is completed. The classic example is the leading case of *Dawsons Ltd v Bonnin* [1922] All ER Rep 210, where the immaterial inaccuracy as to where the insured lorry was garaged was held by the House of Lords to entitle the insurer to avoid the policy *ab initio*;

(2) insurers can make statements as to future facts or future states of affairs into warranties, that is, a warranty that a certain state of facts will or will not exist at some time in the future or will or will not continue to exist for the future. The best description of this type of warranty is perhaps a continuing warranty. The effect of a breach would seem to be that the insurer can avoid the policy from the date of breach;

(3) something which may be very difficult to distinguish from the continuing warranty is the clause in the proposal form which is merely 'descriptive of the risk', sometimes, rather unfortunately, referred to as a warranty describing the risk. Such a clause is held to describe those times, and those times only, when the insurer will be at risk. A breach will not avoid the policy, but merely relieve the insurer from liability if the clause is not being complied with at the time of loss ...

SUGGESTIONS FOR REFORM

... this raises the question as to how far insurers should be allowed to create continuing warranties. Even if the language is clear, there may be warranties of a totally immaterial character ... however material the warranty, do many insured persons realise the obligations they may be under? They do not generally see the proposal form after it has been filled in at the inception of the insurance ... True, in law the contents of the proposal form are invariably incorporated into the policy which contains the terms of the generally annually renewed contract. But it is difficult enough to understand and remember all the matters in the policy itself, regardless of those in the once seen proposal form.

It is submitted that legislative action is desirable to mitigate this harshness, in addition to the Law Reform Committee recommendations ... Insurers should be obliged specifically to incorporate in the policy those questions and answers and declarations intended to be continuing warranties. Further, there should be a clear statement in bold type or differently coloured ink emphasising the effects of a breach of warranty. And it might also be useful to require insurers, when sending out renewal notices or accepting renewal premiums, to stress in writing to the insured the continuing importance of these warranties as well as the other terms and conditions of the insurance policy ...

APPENDIX 5.14

National Consumer Council, *Report on Insurance Law Reform*, 1997, London: NCC

BASIS OF THE CONTRACT CLAUSES

Recommendation 7

We recommend a legal prohibition on 'basis of the contract' clauses.

TERMS AND CONDITIONS: CONTROLLING THE INSURER'S RISK

Recommendation 8

We recommend reform of the law to restrict the insurer's right to deny a claim on the grounds that the policy has been breached because of some act or omission of the insured or some other person:

(a) where conduct cannot cause a loss, the insurer cannot refuse to pay the claim; subject to the insurer's right to claim damages for any loss it can prove it has suffered;

(b) where the policyholder's act or omission was reasonably capable of causing or contributing to the loss, the insurer may refuse to pay the claim unless one of the following three qualifications applies:

  (i) if the policyholder can prove that no part of the loss was actually caused by his act or omission, the insurer cannot refuse to pay the claim;

  (ii) if (i) applies in relation to a part of the loss, the insured can recover for that part;

  (iii) if the act or omission was necessary to protect the safety of a person or to preserve property or where compliance with the policy was not reasonably possible, the insured may recover.

Recommendation 9

We recommend law reform to make the following terms void:

(a) mandatory arbitration for disputes about liability or amount of a claim;

(b) exclusions from, or limitations on, cover in respect of sickness or disability (for insurance of a person) or in respect of pre-existing defects or imperfections (for insurance of a thing) of which the insured was reasonably unaware at the time of entry into the contract ...

APPENDIX 5.15

(Australian) Insurance Contracts Act 1984 (Cth) (as amended)

WARRANTIES OF EXISTING FACTS TO BE REPRESENTATIONS

24 A statement made in or in connection with a contract of insurance, being a statement made by or attributable to the insured, with respect to the existence of a state of affairs does not have effect as a warranty but has effect as though it were a statement made to the insurer by the insured during the negotiations for the contract but before it was entered into ...

[This would then throw the insurer back to the remedies available for misrepresentation which themselves were seriously curtailed by ss 28–30 (Appendix 4.9).]

APPENDIX 5.16

HIH Casualty and General Insurance Ltd v Axa Corporate Solutions [2001] All ER (D) 384

The Law

Sher J: Accordingly, it is quite plain and it is common ground before me that there was a breach of warranty (with regard to the number of films) in the case of each primary insurance contract as well as each reinsurance contract. It is also common ground before me that the effect of the breach of warranty in the case of each insurance and reinsurance contract was to discharge the liability of the insurer (or reinsurer) under that policy. The warranty relating to the number of films to be produced was in the nature of a promissory warranty which, in accordance with the *Bank of Nova Scotia v Hellenic Mutual War Risks Association (Bermuda) Limited (The 'Good Luck')* [1991] 2 Lloyd's Rep 191, is to be treated as a condition precedent to liability under the policy. The breach of warranty will have occurred at the latest at the end date in respect of each slate, that being the date at which the comparison has to be made under the policy between the aggregate revenues generated by the slate and the insured sum in order to determine the shortfall, if any. The moment that breach occurred the insurance cover was automatically discharged without any action or election by the insurer (or reinsurer) to accept the breach as a repudiatory breach discharging the contract of insurance (or reinsurance). This is the effect of the decision in the House of Lords in *The 'Good Luck'*. That of course was a decision based upon the Marine Insurance Act 1906. It is, however, common ground before me that this principle of automatic cessation of cover on breach of a promissory warranty in an insurance or reinsurance contract is not restricted to policies in the field of marine insurance and applies in the instant case to the insurances [that are] the subject of this litigation.

The Marine Insurance Act, however, provides that a breach of warranty may be waived by the insurer. It is common ground before me that the automatic discharge of the cover under the insurances and reinsurances in these cases could be waived by the insurer or reinsurer concerned. The allegation, put forward by HIH in its Reply, is indeed that the breach of warranty has been waived ...

The evidence before me comes from the solicitors on each side. There is no evidence from the representatives of HIH and Axa who were involved at the relevant times. Despite this it is quite apparent from the correspondence between the parties that neither side realised that the failure to produce six films in the 7.23 slate and 10 in the Rojak slate might have the consequence that cover was wholly and automatically discharged on the grounds of breach of warranty. That realisation came, it seems, at or about the time of the defences in each action and the point is taken in the defences filed in each case. The important point to make, however, is that HIH do not assert that Axa (or, indeed, HIH themselves) were aware that the reinsurance (and insurance) cover had (or even might have) been discharged as a result of breach of warranty in relation to the number of films produced in each slate ...

The plea is put in terms of waiver or estoppel. It is necessary to distinguish two, quite different, concepts that lie behind these words. The first is waiver by election. The second is waiver by estoppel. The traditional common law concept of waiver by election involves a choice by the waiving party between two inconsistent courses of action. Outside the insurance sphere, when there has been a repudiatory breach of a promissory warranty by one party the other has a choice whether to accept the breach as discharging the contract or to waive it and affirm the contract. If he does not accept it the contract continues in force. That is an example of a true election between two inconsistent courses. In the case of an insurance contract, on the other hand, breach of the promissory warranty discharges the cover (though not, technically, the entire contract) automatically, without any action or election on the put of the insurer. There is no choice involved at all. There is no decision to be made. So much comes out of *The 'Good Luck'* and is not disputed before me as applicable to the insurances and reinsurances here. It follows that waiver by election can have no application in such a case and the waiver, therefore, referred to in s 34(3) of the Marine Insurance Act 1906 must encompass waiver by estoppel, the second of the two concepts abovementioned, rather than waiver by election ...

Waiver by estoppel or promissory estoppel, as it is more commonly described, involves a clear and unequivocal representation that the reinsurer (or insurer) will not stand on its right to treat the cover as having been discharged on which the insurer (or insured) has relied in circumstances in which it would be inequitable to allow the reinsurer (or insurer) to resile from its representation. In my judgment it is of the essence of this plea that the representation must go to the willingness of the representor to forego its rights. If all that appears to the representee is that the representor believes that the cover continues in place, without the slightest indication that the representor is aware that it could take the point that cover had been discharged (but was not going to take the point) there would be no inequity in permitting the representor to stand on its rights. Otherwise rights will be lost in total ignorance that they ever existed and, more to the point, the representee will be in a position to deny the representor those rights in circumstances in which it never had any inkling that the representor was prepared to waive those rights. It is of the essence of the doctrine of promissory estoppel that one side is reasonably seen by the other to be foregoing its rights. There is nothing improbable in such a foregoing of rights. It might, for example, be prompted by considerations as to the preservation of future goodwill.

I am greatly assisted in the conclusions I have come to on this point by the decision in *Youell and Others v Bland Welch and Co Ltd ('The Superhulls Cover')* (No 2) [1990] 2 Lloyd's Rep 431 where, at 450, Philips J said this:

> A party can represent that he will not enforce a specific legal right by words or conduct. He can say so expressly – this of course he can only do if he is aware of the right. Alternatively he can adopt a course of conduct which is inconsistent with the exercise of that right. Such a course of conduct will only constitute a representation that he will not exercise the right if the circumstances are such as to suggest either that he was aware of the right when he embarked on a course of conduct inconsistent with it or that he was content to abandon any rights that he might enjoy which were inconsistent with that course of conduct.

...

At all events, Mr Flaux contends that his position is supported by *Motor Oil Hellas Corinth Refineries SA v Shipping Corporation of India ('The Kanchenjunga')* [1990] 2 Lloyd's Rep 391 at 399 where Lord Goff in contrasting waiver by election with equitable estoppel said this:

> Election is to be contrasted with equitable estoppel, a principle associated with the leading case of *Hughes v Metropolitan Railway Co* (1877) 2 App Cas 439. Equitable estoppel occurs where a person, having legal rights against another, unequivocally represents (by words or conduct) that he does not intend to enforce those legal rights; if in such circumstances the other party acts, or desists from acting, in reliance upon that representation, with the effect that it would be inequitable for the representor thereafter to enforce his legal rights inconsistently with his representation, he will to that extent be precluded from doing so.
>
> There is an important similarity between the two principles, election and equitable estoppel, in that each requires an unequivocal representation, perhaps because each may involve a loss, permanent or temporary, of the relevant party's rights. But there are important differences as well. In the context of a contact, the principle of election applies when a state of affairs comes into existence in which one party becomes entitled to exercise a right, and have to choose whether to exercise the right or not. His election has generally to be so informed choice, made with knowledge of the facts giving rise to the right. His election once made is final; it is not dependent upon reliance on it by the other party. On the other hand, equitable estoppel requires an unequivocal representation by one party that he will not insist upon his legal rights against the other party, and such reliance by the representee as will render it inequitable for the representor to go back upon his representation. *No question arises of any particular knowledge on the part of the representor*, and the estoppel may be suspensory only. Furthermore, the representation itself is different in character in the two cases. The party making his election is communicating his choice whether or not to exercise a right which has become available to him. The party to an equitable estoppel is representing that he will not in future enforce his legal rights. His representation is therefore in the nature of a promise which, though unsupported by consideration, can have legal consequences; hence it is sometimes referred to as promissory estoppel.

The emphasis has been added by me, as it has by Mr Flaux, to identify the point he is making, which is that he does not have to show any particular knowledge on the part of Axa (and the insured financier would not have to show any particular knowledge on the part of HIH). I cannot accept Mr Flaux's submission. It appears to me that all Lord Goff is doing in the sentence underlined is emphasising that in the case of equitable estoppel what matters is how the representation appeared to the representee, as opposed to election where the concentration is upon the knowledge of the representor. It is plain from the passage cited from Lord Goff that the representation, in the case of equitable estoppel, must be that the representor 'will not insist upon his legal rights against the other party'. It seems to me that this sentence makes it clear that the representation must be that the representor is prepared to forego his legal rights. This is particularly so when this language is compared with Lord Goff's reference a few lines before to the case of election in which the representor has to make an informed choice 'made with knowledge of the facts giving rise to the rights'. At any rate, in my judgment, Mr Flaux can gain no comfort from the passage he cited from Lord Goff's speech in *The Kanchenjunga*.

INSURANCE INTERMEDIARIES

CLASSIFICATION AND SUPERVISION OF INSURANCE INTERMEDIARIES

Since the 1970s there has been considerable confusion, not to say chaos, with regard to the classification of those who are involved in the advising on, selling of and servicing of insurance. A common sense division would have been to divide such people into two groups: those who worked for insurers and those who were truly independent of insurers. Instead of that division the Insurance Brokers (Registration) Act 1977 sought to supervise only those who chose to be registered brokers leaving independent advisers subject to no authority. Employees were also not subject to any supervision other than that of the insurer for whom they worked and such supervision was rather wide ranging in efficiency. The 1977 Act has now gone. It was repealed by the Financial Services and Markets Act 2000 (FSMA). No statutory replacement was planned under that Act. Instead the concept of self-regulation was considered adequate to control this all important area of insurance.

In 2000 the General Insurance Standards Council (GISC) was formed. This is a self-regulatory body open for membership to both insurers and intermediaries but on a voluntary basis. Internal disputes within the intermediary sector in 2001 brought about the (very) early death warrant for the GISC. It is now expected that by 2004 the work of the GISC will be taken over by the Financial Services Authority (FSA) under the FSMA. Thus ultimately and very much unintentionally there will be a form of statutory control over this crucial sector of insurance.

The GISC has published two Codes of Conduct (Appendix 6.1) and, at the moment, there is no reason to believe that these will not continue to be appropriate at least in forming the basis, perhaps subject to refinements, for the scheme after the takeover in 2004.

The 1977 Act provided supervision only for registered brokers. Therefore the Association of British Insurers (ABI), a body representing only insurers and again only if the insurer chooses to join, produced their own Code (Appendix 6.5) in an attempt to govern the working practices of their member's employees and non-brokers. In other words the Code was aimed at all who were not subject to the 1977 regime. The GISC Codes are expected to replace the ABI Codes at some point in time.

In addition to the above there have been EU Directives in this area (77/92/EEC; 92/48/EEC and a new proposal for a Directive on insurance mediation 2000) which, of course, should be implemented into our own domestic law!

Confused? That is what the opening sentence states!

Despite any such confusion it should be stressed that little of the above makes much difference to the legal content of an intermediaries responsibilities. However to be able to discern for whom an intermediary is acting at any particular moment in the insurance transaction is crucial, as we will see below.

The following topics are discussed:

- employees of insurance companies;
- independent intermediaries, commonly now called 'brokers';
- Lloyd's brokers;
- European dimensions.

AGENCY LAW AND THE INTERMEDIARY

It is necessary to deal briefly with certain aspects of agency law which more directly affect the present topic and which will be taken up more specifically below.

Commercial life is impossible without reference to agency. Insurance is sold by means of agents, claims are settled by means of agents. An explanation of how the principal-agent relationship is created is called for together with a brief explanation of the legal relationships between the principal, the agent and third parties.

Creation of agency

There are four main methods of establishing a principal-agent relationship: (a) by an agreement between the two parties; (b) by ratification; (c) by estoppel; (d) by operation of law. Only the first three really concern insurance intermediaries.

The normal situation is that the insurer will either have a contract of employment with his employees or an agency agreement with independent agents and brokers. The contents of that agreement and the construction given to it by the courts, in case of conflict between the parties, will be the main determining factors on which will hang the rights and duties of the parties.

It is possible for someone to act on behalf of another person without sufficient authority and for that person to ratify what has been done in his name or on his behalf. This may be done both where the agent has some authority from the principal but exceeds it, and also where he had no authority at all to act as an agent for that person.

Thus, an intermediary may hold an agency from an insurer which is limited in certain ways, such as the types of insurance that he may market or the limits within which he may operate. If he deals in classes of insurance beyond his mandate, the insurer can, if he so wishes, ratify what the intermediary has done. If he holds no agency agreement with that insurer, but the customer presses for cover with that particular company, any resulting arrangement can be ratified if the company so wishes. When this is done, the ratification clothes the agent with authority from the time he so acted on behalf of the principal.

The Privy Council decision in *Siu Yin Kwan v Eastern Insurance Co Ltd* [1994] 1 All ER 213 (Appendix 6.2) throws an interesting light on the question of the rights of undisclosed principals. A shipping company appointed A as their worldwide agents and this included obtaining their various insurance requirements. A particular ship was insured by A and this included the compulsory employers' liability cover for its employees. However, A did not declare the name of the shipowner and A signed the proposal form in their own name. The insurers were unsuccessful in their attempts to avoid their liability. An undisclosed principal could sue and be sued on a contract made by its agent when acting within the scope of his authority, if there was nothing in the contract that prevented this. It is, perhaps, crucial to the decision that the trial judge found that the insurers had no real interest in knowing the real identity of the shipowner. As long as the questions on the proposal form relating to past insurance history were correctly stated, there was no material breach of good faith. In some classes of insurance, the identity of the insured is crucial to the underwriter. In such a situation, it may well be that the present decision would be inapplicable.

Ratification may be express or implied. Implied ratification arises where the conduct of the principal shows that he adopts or recognises the transaction.

Agency by estoppel arises where one person represents to another person, either by words or conduct, that a particular individual is his agent in such a way that it would be inequitable for the person making such representations to deny the agency. It arises in situations where there is no formal agency agreement and also where the authorised agent has been permitted to go beyond his original remit.

It might be argued that, by arming an intermediary with proposal forms and explanatory literature, an insurer should be stopped from denying most things that are said by the salesman while attempting to convince the customer to enter into the contract. This view is rarely adopted by the courts and, therefore, the buyer of the policy will often find himself without an effective remedy in situations where he has been misled by inaccurate statements and predictions. One reason is that the proposal wording may state specifically that the intermediary has limited powers. A more worrying reason is that such words of caution only appear in the policy documentation, but by the time this reaches the customer, the harm has been done. It may be that the Unfair Terms in Consumer Contracts Regulations 1999 (Appendix 7.1) will change this approach.

Thus, in *Comerford v Britannic Assurance Co* (1908) 24 TLR 593, a superintendent of one of the defendant company's branch offices discussed a policy that the plaintiff wished to take out on her husband. An indorsement to the policy stated that it would pay out certain sums in each of the first five years of cover up to a final total of £150. The superintendent, however, told the plaintiff that the full £150 would be payable at any time within the first five years, if death resulted from an accident. The assured drowned after two years and the company was held liable to pay only £75 on the grounds that the advice given could not contradict the wording of the policy and that it was not normal for a local superintendent to have authority to validate such promises as he had made.

Hard though it may be on contracting parties, there can be no doubt that English law does allow later documentation to include the core of the contractual agreement, as long as reference is made to its existence in the earlier negotiations. American law has gone a long way in protecting the insured in such situations of misleading statements by intermediaries, by what has been termed the doctrine of detrimental reliance.

It is difficult to see how English law can change without legislative action. This has been done in Australia (see Appendix 6.3).

An additional problem for the customer is where the proposal/policy wording sets out different (and probably more limited) powers and duties for the agent and this information is contractually relayed to the insured in the (later) policy wording. Where the intermediary is an independent adviser, the insured may be able to sue him for negligent advice or for breach of his contract to effect insurance. Because of professional indemnity insurance, the chances are that, if successful in his allegation, the insured will recover his losses. The real problem is where the intermediary is really classed as an employee of the insurer. Although it would be possible to sue him directly, there will be less chance of any legal success translating itself into monetary compensation.

It may be, however, that the Unfair Terms in Consumer Contracts Regulations 1999 could be of some importance here. Schedule 3, entitled 'Indicative and illustrative list of terms which may be regarded as unfair', provides, in illustration (n), that it will be unfair where the term limits:

> ... the seller's or supplier's obligation to respect commitments undertaken by his agents or making his commitments subject to compliance with a particular formality.

Where the agency relationship is clear cut, there will almost always be a prohibition on delegating the authority to others. This is an obvious business necessity. If the insurer has trained his employee or has carefully vetted the independent intermediary, it would be to no avail if the work could then be passed down to others not known to the insurer.

Duties owed by agent to his principal

The contract of employment or the agency agreement will provide the basis of the relationship and therefore the rights and duties between the principal and his agent. Some documentation may be detailed, leaving little room for uncertainty. But, with the modern tendency in many commercial areas to simplify matters in an attempt to set out clearly the relationship, ambiguities and uncertainties often creep in, thus thwarting the original desired aim for simplicity.

The basic duties owed by the intermediary to his principal include obeying any specific instructions given to him and carrying out those instructions with reasonable skill and judgment. He must deal honestly with his principal and account for any money received by him for his principal. It will be a matter of fact in each case whether or not the intermediary has reached the required standard.

The crucial factor will be the precise requirements placed by the principal on him. As long ago as 1833, in *Chapman v Walton* (1833) 10 Bing 57, the court stated that the test of reasonable and proper care, skill and judgment was to ask whether other persons exercising the same profession or calling would or would not have come to the same conclusion as did the individual in question. It may be that the relationship between the parties points to the intermediary doing the best he can in the circumstances, rather than guaranteeing to achieve a specific result. But there is little doubt that the burden of professional competence on the independent intermediary is an increasingly heavy one, following the House of Lords decision in *Hedley Byrne v Heller and Partners* [1964] AC 465. This decision, however, must be read in the light of the more recent House of Lords decision in *Caparo Industries plc v Dickman* [1990] 1 All ER 568.

Agent's rights against his principal

An agent has the right to expect a payment, normally in the form of commission, for the work he has done. The principal should not put obstacles in his way preventing him from earning his remuneration. The method of calculating the remuneration will normally be set out in the agreement between the parties, but custom or usage in a particular branch of insurance may also have its part to play (see *Great Western Insurance Co v Cunliffe* (1874) 9 Ch App 525).

Problems can arise in the case of commissions for renewals. Normal practice is for the intermediary to receive commission at each renewal, but this is obviously a reflection of the work done by the intermediary.

Agency agreements usually spell out the renewal commission conditions, but even where this is not the case, an agent would be entitled to claim a *quantum meruit* for a payment to reflect the amount of work he had done.

In *McNeil v Law Union and Rock Insurance Co Ltd* (1925) 23 Ll L Rep 314 (Appendix 6.4), the plaintiff broker was instrumental in setting up and renewing annually an employer's liability policy. After several years, problems arose concerning the collection of premiums and the broker asked the insurers to send one of their inspectors to see the insured. This was done, but only on the basis that the arrangement then became an 'own case' agency. By this method, the commission was paid to the inspector who, in turn, was contractually obliged to return it to the insurers. No commission was paid to the broker, who then sued the insurers. The court said that if the broker could be described as actively participating in the renewal, which on the facts he could, then he was entitled to his commission. This must be the correct approach. Any other technique could lead effectively to eliminating the intermediary once he had completed the initial burdensome task of setting up the policy in the first year.

Thus, in *Gold v Life Assurance Co Pennsylvania* [1971] 2 Lloyd's Rep 164, it was held that an agent was entitled to the commission on the first year's premium, even though his agency had been terminated prior to the payment of that premium.

Termination of agency

An agency agreement would normally set out the circumstances in which the agency comes to an end. Possible examples would include failing to meet the minimum standards of competence as required by the insurer; legislation or applicable Codes of Practice; failing to service and develop and realise the full potential of the agency from the point of view of the insurer; deliberately overcharging a policyholder; failure to keep proper accounts or mishandling the insurer's money; and backdating or otherwise falsifying cover notes.

THE INSURANCE EMPLOYEE

In this part we are not concerned with truly independent intermediaries. The Financial Services Act 1986 and now the FSMA brought about changes in terminology and will require changes in business practice. It is necessary to emphasise here that if the insurance business transacted is not classified as 'investment business' under the 2000 Act then the idea of 'tied' agents survives. By 'tied' agent we refer to those who have agency agreements with one or more insurers. This category will include those working on a part time basis.

Also included in this category is the employee-agent of the insurance company. He is now referred to as a company representative, under the 1986 Act, and that phrase will also include a previously independent agent who decides to forgo that independence and transact investment business with one insurer only.

The legal position of these agents will clearly depend on their contract of employment or their agency agreement. It is usual however to incorporate into those contracts the relevant 'Codes' that have been established in recent years aimed at providing the public with a sounder basis for their insurance dealings with the industry.

The Codes of the Association of British Insurers

(See Appendix 6.5.)

Note: as explained above, the assumption is that these Codes will be withdrawn when the GISC/FSA regime is fully implemented at a date in the future. Strictly speaking, it is perhaps incorrect to call an employee of an insurance company an intermediary. He certainly does not stand between insurer and assured in the same way as a broker. He clearly is the representative of the company. However, the Life Association's Code of Selling practice for non-registered intermediaries defines 'intermediaries' as 'all those persons, including employees of a life office, selling life assurance'. The Association of British Insurers' *General Business Code of Practice* does not attempt any definition, although it specifically excludes registered insurance brokers. Both Codes add a further classification complication by differentiating between intermediaries and introducers; the latter's function is merely to introduce a prospective policyholder to a company and then take no further part in the selling transaction.

Both Codes provide useful guidelines as to the responsibilities expected of the agent. It must be stressed, however, that neither Code has the force of law (see *Harvest Trucking Co Ltd v PB Davis Insurance Services* [1991] 2 Lloyd's Rep 638; Appendix 6.6) and the policing of them is left in the hands of the particular company concerned. Thus, an individual insurer's sense of professionalism and what image it wishes to create in the minds of the public will be the main control mechanism. In the first 10 years of the Code's life there was no independent method of verifying its effectiveness. In 1996 an independent firm of auditors was appointed to carry out compliance monitoring. The initial findings were a great cause for concern and its findings were contrary to the ABI's own earlier internal monitoring. The findings led to a number of agency agreements being cancelled. Hopefully close future monitoring (and of the ultimate successor to the ABI Code, the GISC Codes) will bring home to intermediaries that high levels of professionalism are required.

A major concern, in addition to enforcing the Code in a general way, is what, if anything, can be done about an intermediary who is found to be failing in his duties as set out in the Code. The Code is silent on this point. Responsibility falls on the shoulders of the insurers to see that as much compliance as possible is maintained.

The Insurance Ombudsman (see Chapter 11) referred in some detail to the Code in his 1993 Annual Report. Until 1998, the Insurance Ombudsman Bureau's jurisdiction concerns only insurance companies (and Lloyd's) and then only those companies who have chosen to join the Bureau. In 1998, it was decided that independent intermediaries could become members of the Insurance Ombudsman Bureau.

The Life Associations (and also the Financial Services Act and its successor the FSMA requirements) spell out in more detail the agent's responsibilities when explaining life assurance contracts. The Code covers industrial and ordinary long term insurance, including all types of annuities, pension contracts and permanent health insurance. In particular, the agent should explain the meaning and effect of long term policies and the problems posed by early discontinuance and surrender values. Of the greatest importance is the explanation of how future benefits are calculated and that variations in both directions are possibilities. It is this area of advice that presents a legal minefield for agents and has led to large payments made by the Investors Compensation Scheme (if the matter is covered by the FSMA).

Both Codes appear to place a great burden of professional competence on the shoulders of agents. As policies become more sophisticated and numerous that burden increases in complexity. The problem is particularly acute for those giving advice within the terms of the FSMA.

The effect of the general Code was referred in *Harvest Trucking Co Ltd v Davis* (Appendix 6.6). The plaintiff was a haulage contractor who had arranged his various business insurance needs through the agency of the defendant insurance intermediary. One of the plaintiff's lorries was stolen and the insurers successfully avoided liability on the grounds that one of the policy conditions was not met. In earlier years of the policy, both plaintiff and defendant had successfully negotiated that the conditions should be omitted from the policy on the grounds that it was impracticable for the plaintiff to conform with it. However, when the plaintiff expanded his business and purchased two larger lorries capable of carrying a more expensive load, the conditions had been reintroduced.

The plaintiff argued that the defendant intermediary had either failed to renegotiate successfully on his behalf or had failed to inform him of the conditions. On the evidence before the court the plaintiff succeeded.

Codes of the General Insurance Standards Council

(See Appendix 6.1.)

As explained on the first page of this chapter the creation of the GISC in 2000 was expected to be provide a cohesive single regulatory non-statutory body that would provide insurers and intermediaries with standards which would be monitored by the Council in all areas of general insurance. Insurance that could be classified as investment business is subject to the FSMA requirements. The GISC has published two Codes, one governing commercial insurance and one concerned with consumer insurance, both are set out in Appendix 6.1.

Problems in 2001 brought about a change of thinking. The role of the GISC will be taken over by the FSA (just as the Insurance Ombudsman Bureau (Chapter 11) has been similarly absorbed). This may take place in 2004. In the meantime the present Codes apply to those who chose to join the GISC and it may be that the Codes will form the basis of any arrangements that the FSA implement. Any future regime will have to take into account EU innovations in this area (see below).

(For a discussion of the GISC as of 2001, see Burling, 'The impact of the GISC' [2001] JBL 646.) In the interim period the Codes are therefore in operation. It must be remembered however that while they remain self regulatory they do not carry the authority of law although they may be referred to, as have other Codes, by the courts as an aid to their decision making.

The GISC Commercial Code

It is intended here to give a brief overview of the contents of the Code.

The word 'Member' in the Code refers to insurers and to insurance intermediaries.

The Code is divided into a number of sub-headings and starts with *Core Principles* which, like so many other self-regulatory Codes, exhort its Members to be professionally competent; observe high standards; know their customers' requirements; present information in a way that will allow the customer to make an informed choice; safeguard information and property handled by the Member and to handle complaints fairly and expeditiously.

Thereafter appears guidance on specific topics. Those more specifically referrable to intermediaries are reviewed here.

Arranging insurance. The intermediary must explain to the commercial customer on whose behalf the intermediary is acting: insurer or customer (this is no easy matter as this chapter illustrates). It stresses that there should be a written follow up of what has been agreed and, in particular, what advice the customer has rejected. Unfortunately the paragraph contains the phrase 'where it is reasonably practical'. In fact the requirement should be a basic working practice for intermediaries. The advice given by Cresswell J in *Aneco* (see below) should be ignored at the intermediaries' peril even if intermediaries believe that this is not the way insurance business can be transacted, ie, because of the need for speed and urgency.

Customer requirements. The intermediary should attempt to understand each customer's needs, their understanding of risk and their knowledge of insurance products.

Information about the proposed insurance. Customers must be placed in a position where they can make an informed choice.

This would require a review of what is available in the insurance market and what would be most appropriate for the customer's needs.

Under this heading comes perhaps the most onerous of all the requirements of the Code although it probably reflects what the common law would expect of an intermediary. The intermediary must explain the extent of the cover, the effect of the exclusion/limitations and the obligations that rest on the insured. The commercial customer's awareness of the situation will have an effect on this burden of disclosure.

Advice and recommendations. The above burdens are heavy and therefore an intermediary should only be prepared to advise where it has sufficient professional competence to do so.

Costs and remuneration. The intermediary must disclose fully the cost of the policy. On request there must be disclosure of commission and any other benefits received.

Duty of disclosure. As we have seen in detail in Chapter 4 the burden of disclosure and the dire consequences that flow from failure to disclose lie at the heart of English insurance law. This paragraph requires the intermediary to explain such obligations, that apply both before and during the policy cover, and the consequences that follow if the duty is breached.

The customer must be warned that all answers on proposals, claims forms or on any related communications are the customers own responsibility. This would seem to reinforce all the old (bad?) law whereby intermediaries can avoid the consequences of their own professional neglect (assuming of course that the courts will agree with the wording of the Code).

Intermediaries should cease to act for the customer where the customer appears not to be willing to act in good faith.

Confirming cover. There should be prompt confirmation of cover and prompt notification of any changes followed by written confirmation of any changes.

Ongoing services. An important point here is that a Member should give notice of renewal dates and early enough for the customer to consider the new quotation. This would seem to be an obligation that exceeds common law requirements (although it is the law of Australia: see Appendix 3.3).

Claims. Where the intermediary is involved in claims handling it must handle the claim without delay and advise the customer how to pursue the claim.

The GISC Private Customer Code

This is for private customers and is said to state the minimum standards of good practice in relation to the whole range of general insurances. The wording is much more directed to the consumer than the commercial Code whose wording appears to be directed to the Member.

The content is very much along the lines of the commercial Code. The emphasis is on explaining for whom the intermediary is acting, explaining the contents and limitations of the policies on offer and advising on what is the most appropriate in the circumstances. Commission must be declared if the customer so requests. The complaints procedures available must be explained.

A 'cooling off' period of 14 days is introduced for the first time in general insurance (as opposed to that which exists with regard to investment products under the FSMA). It applies where the intermediary has failed to supply information required by the Code. It would allow the customer to cancel the policy. If it can be shown that the customer did not require the information required by the Code then no cooling off period applies.

With regard to renewal, notice must be given to the customer in good time for the customer to make a decision and the intermediary must give information about any changes in cover and explain the renewed duty to disclose relevant facts. Assistance with claims handling is required as with the commercial customer Code, above.

Cases involving the insured

The following cases involve both the employee/agent of particular insurers and the 'tied' agent of one or more insurers. It is convenient to group the decisions under three main agency functions: (a) failure to follow the customer's instructions to insurers; (b) advising the customer as to his particular insurance requirements; (c) completing the proposal form.

Failure to follow the customer's instructions

We saw earlier that an agent owes a number of duties to his principal. These include a duty to carry out the transaction; a duty to obey instructions; and a duty to act with reasonable skill and to exercise reasonable judgment. The first problem that arises is that an agent may owe these duties to both insurer and customer, depending on the particular task he is performing. Thus, it is possible that a 'tied' agent may have a contract with the customer to oversee his insurance requirements.

Advising the customer as to his particular insurance requirements

Here, we have an area fraught with difficulties and dangers, although, as the cases illustrate, it is often the customer who suffers. In these cases, the agent is usually the agent of the insurer. The problem stems from the fact that many agents who have contact with the customer have much more limited powers of negotiation than the public think they have. When the agent exceeds the authority given to him by his principal he no longer binds the principal to the contract.

It would be possible, under *Hedley Byrne v Heller*, to sue the agent in negligence. But if the agent does not carry professional indemnity insurance it may prove to be an illusory legal remedy, although the Association of British Insurers' Code of Selling (Appendix 6.5) does require the intermediary to carry professional indemnity insurance.

The main hope of the customer is that the agent is clothed with sufficient authority to bind his principal. That is a matter of construction of his agency agreement. But, as we have seen above, the normal terms of the agreement limit his powers.

In *Kettlewell v Refuge Assurance Co* [1908] 1 KB 545 (Appendix 6.8), a policyholder who intended to give up her policies was persuaded by the company agent that if she continued with them she would be eligible for a free policy. The court found that this was a fraudulent statement and she was entitled to a refund on the premiums paid to the company.

Another area of difficulty, and yet one which must commonly face both 'tied' agents and independent intermediaries, is where the customer asks for help in understanding the policy wording. It can be seen in *Horncastle v Equitable Life* (1906) 22 TLR 735 that the insured is often prevented from successfully alleging that he has been misled by the agent by the simple argument that the policy states clearly that it can not be altered without senior management approval. But what of the situation where help is requested in determining the meaning of words in phrases in the policy?

In *Re Hooley Hill Rubber and Chemical Co Ltd and Royal Insurance Co Ltd* [1920] 1 KB 257 (Appendix 6.9), manufacturers of explosives discussed with the insurer's agent the extent of the policy and particularly the meaning of exclusion clauses in the policy. The manufacturers alleged that they had been misled by the agent's answers, and therefore the insurers were estopped from denying that the policy had the meaning given to it by the agent.

The judge rejected this defence. He did so even though he was of the opinion that an intelligent businessman would have been misled by the statements made by the agent. The difficulty confronting the judge was the rule that while misleading statements of fact may allow one party a remedy, a misstatement of law will not. He had the further difficulty of deciding whether the statements were ones of fact or law. He considered that the matter was finely balanced, but what tipped the decision against the insured was that the agent made specific references to one of the conditions in the policy and in so doing he was giving his view as to the interpretation of the legal document. The decision has been doubted by some writers. In consumer contracts, the Association of British Insurers' Statements of Insurance Practice place a clear burden on the intermediary to explain the policy wording. The Statements are discussed elsewhere (see Chapter 4, Appendix 4.10).

Completing the proposal form

If the last section exposes the customer to difficulties in his relationship with the insurers, then the present topic illustrates an even more lamentable situation. The agent may well be individually liable, but again this may be of little comfort to the customer, unless the agent holds indemnity insurance.

There is a considerable conflict of judicial opinion in the cases that follow. The basic factual situation is one that must occur on a regular basis. The customer is faced with a proposal form for completion. Although there has been an attempt in recent times to simplify such forms, many customers still find them a trying experience. The agent, eager to help or perhaps eager to speed up the exercise, often offers to complete the form for the customer. Wrong answers are entered and, when a claim is later made, the insurers plead misrepresentation or non-disclosure by the customer.

There are various permutations possible. It may be that correct answers were given by the customer to the agent but he, innocently, negligently or fraudulently, entered an incorrect answer. The position of the agent may be that of either limited powers or he may be vested with authority to complete proposals. The proposal form may contain a proviso that, if an agent assists in completing the form, he is to be treated as acting as agent of the customer and not the agent of the insurer for this purpose.

The starting point in analysing the cases is *Bawden v London, Edinburgh and Glasgow Assurance Co* [1892] 2 QB 534 (Appendix 6.10). In completing a proposal for accidental injury cover, the plaintiff stated that he had no physical infirmity and that there were no circumstances that rendered him peculiarly liable to accidents. In fact, the plaintiff was blind in one eye. The agent knew this, but did not relay the information to the insurers. The court was given no explanation as to the terms of the agency agreement. The court found for the plaintiff. Lord Esher MR explained the situation clearly. He said that the agent was the agent of the company. His function was to negotiate terms with a view to completing a contract. He was not merely an agent to take a piece of paper to the company. Knowledge that he possessed was deemed to be the knowledge of the company. This common sense description of an insurance agent must surely commend itself as a reflection of what the general public believe to be the situation (see *Roberts v Plaisted*, below).

Unfortunately for insureds, *Bawden* was soon distinguished in later judgments. In *Biggar v Rock Life Assurance Co* [1902] 1 KB 516 (Appendix 6.11), the customer gave the correct answers to the agent who incorrectly transcribed them. The customer did not check over the completed form. He failed in his action against the insurer. The decision in this, and later cases, is based on the argument that one is bound by one's signature and failing to read over a document before signing it is a fault that should rest squarely on that person's shoulders.

As a general statement of legal principle, such an argument is unassailable. But does it reflect the reality of insurance sales using proposal forms? Surely the agent knows that reliance is being placed on him and, having carelessly or negligently filled in answers which had been correctly given, it does not seem to reflect the public's reasonable expectations when the courts reject claims. The judge did show some sympathy with the plaintiff when he said that the most that the plaintiff could ask for was that the contract be declared void on the grounds of fraud, if proved, or mistake. But, even if this could be done, only the return of premiums would be possible and not a claim to the insurance money.

In *Ayrey v British Legal and United Provident Assurance Co Ltd* [1918] 1 KB 136 (Appendix 6.12), on an application for a life policy the proposer correctly stated that he was a trawlerman. But he also told the agent that he was a member of the Royal Naval Reserve. The agent referred the matter to the district manager and the policy was issued without alteration. Despite the fact that the policy stated that the agent was to be regarded as the insured's agent when receiving information, the court found that the policy was valid. It was considered to be a reasonable expectation that, when information is given to a person with the status of district manager, this is equivalent to informing head office. The acceptance of premiums by the district manager with full knowledge of the facts amounted to a waiver by the company of any objection by them that there had been a concealment of a material fact.

Here, the court is using two methods to place responsibility on the company for their agent's neglect. The first is to look closely at the status of the agent and determine whether or not he is sufficiently senior, so that knowledge on his part can be regarded as knowledge of the company. The other technique used is that of waiver or estoppel. This arises where the insurers, in full knowledge of the facts, act in such a way as to show that they are not intent on raising any objections and thereby convince the insured that he is fully covered.

Keeling v Pearl Assurance Co Ltd [1923] All ER Rep 307 (Appendix 6.13) provides another illustration of these techniques. The agent discussed with a wife life assurance on the life of her husband. True answers were given to health questions, but the agent filled in incorrect answers. There was also an inconsistency between the 'date of birth' and the 'age next birthday' questions. The company attempted to avoid liability on the death of the husband.

The court rejected the defence. It was found that the agent had authority from the company to negotiate and complete proposal forms and was therefore the agent of the insurer for this purpose. The discrepancy between the date of birth and age answers was something which the company should have detected. It was a glaring inaccuracy and if companies insist that the answers are crucial to their judgment of the risk, they cannot avoid the consequences of their own negligence in not recognising the mistake.

Any glimmer of hope, from these two cases, that an agent may be regarded as agent of the insurer when completing proposal forms and that this was to be the way forward, was, however, crushed by the Court of Appeal, in *Newsholme Bros v Road Transport and General Insurance Co Ltd* [1929] 2 KB 356 (Appendix 6.14).

The agent discussed insurance of the plaintiff's motor bus. The customer gave the agent correct answers which the agent incorrectly entered on the proposal form. The court found for the insurer. The agent had authority to obtain completed proposal forms, and to receive premiums. But he had no authority to complete the forms and no authority to issue cover notes. In completing the form he was, according to Scrutton LJ, the amanuensis of the customer.

The conflict between the earlier cases was explained as a desire, in some situations, to hold an insurer liable for anything that an agent does in procuring business and a desire, in other cases, to uphold the contention that a person who signs a promise, that his written statements are true and are to be regarded as the basis of his contract, cannot then vary his contract by omitting that promise and disclaiming misstatements. The court distinguished *Bawden*'s case by arguing that it did not apply where the agent completed the proposal at the request of the customer. If that is the situation, then according to Scrutton LJ, the agent must be the agent of the customer for that specific purpose.

Insurance companies are quick to learn from any adverse judicial decisions and to adapt their approach accordingly. While *Newsholme* clearly favoured them, it still left open the problem that, in certain circumstances, as in *Keeling*, an agent might have authority to complete answers and thus remain the agent of the insurer. The modern technique, therefore, used by many insurers, is to state on the proposal form that, when an agent helps to complete a proposal, he is to be regarded as the agent of the customer. The form must be signed by the customer and thus he assents to this role of the agent.

This is what happened in *Facer v Vehicle and General Insurance Co Ltd* [1965] 1 Lloyd's Rep 113. The plaintiff wanted to insure his car. He did not have a great ability in completing forms. The sub-agent of the insurer's agent completed the form and no mention was made of the fact that the plaintiff had lost one eye. The plaintiff argued that this fact was well known to the sub-agent, as he had known him for 18 months prior to his application for insurance and, consequently, the knowledge of the agent should be imputed to the insurers.

The court was faced with the *Bawden-Newsholme* conflict. Marshall J found that *Bawden* had not been followed in English cases and had been criticised in Scotland, Ireland and in America. *Newsholme,* on the other hand, had been accepted as correctly stating the law. In addition, the signed agreement stating that the agent was to be regarded as the customer's agent put the matter beyond doubt and the plaintiff's claim failed.

While the courts seemed to accept the correctness of *Newsholme*, the decision is clearly so contrary to what the general public would expect the legal position to be that it was inevitable that, in the days of mounting demands for consumer protection, a change should be advocated. This was first seen as far back as 1957 in a Law Reform Committee Report. The recommendation was that:

> ... any person who solicits or negotiates a contract of insurance shall be deemed for the purpose of the formation of the contract, to be the agent of the insurers, and that the knowledge of such person shall be deemed to be the knowledge of the insurers.

In 1976, a Committee of Inquiry into the Insurance Industry in Ireland proposed similar changes to Irish law.

The (Australian) Insurance (Agents and Brokers) Act 1984 (Cth) (Appendix 6.3) introduced these changes (see also Appendix 6.27).

Section 11 states that an insurer is responsible for the conduct of his agent or employee where the customer could reasonably be expected to rely and did rely in good faith on any matter relating to the insurance. This liability applies even where the agent has acted outside the scope of his authority. The insurer cannot avoid this obligation in any way. Where the customer has been misled in these circumstances, the insurer must make good any losses. Section 13 goes on to penalise any misrepresentations made by agents and employees of insurers and also of insurance intermediaries. The type of conduct covered is where misleading statements are made about premiums and other amounts payable in respect to an intended contract, and also situations where the agent or employee misleads the customer as to his duty to disclose or as to the content of his duty of disclosure. However, the liability only covers situations where the agent or employee's conduct has been wilful, with an intent to deceive.

New Zealand legislated to change the situation in their Insurance Law Reform Act 1977 along lines similar to the English Law Reform Committee's recommendations. Canadian provinces have also enacted changes that shift the burden onto the shoulders of the insurers. It is surely impossible to criticise such proposals and reforms. But in England nothing has been done legislatively to implement the suggested changes of 1957. In 1997, the National Consumer Council Report called *Report on Insurance Law Reform*, has again called for the 1957 approach to be adopted (Appendix 6.15).

The only inroad into the *Newsholme* rule has been made by the Court of Appeal in *Stone v Reliance Mutual Insurance Society Ltd* [1972] 1 Lloyd's Rep 469 (Appendix 6.16). The appellant insured his flat against fire and theft with the respondent insurers, the premiums paid weekly to collectors. A year later, a fire occurred and the appellant was indemnified. The policy later lapsed and an inspector visited the appellant with a view to reviving the policy. He convinced the appellant's wife to renew. The inspector was empowered to complete proposal forms and amazingly he did not record the earlier claim or that the original policy had lapsed. When a later theft occurred, the appellant declared on his claims form both the fire and the lapse of policy. An assessor was sent and a figure agreed.

Premiums were collected for a further three months before the respondent insurers rejected the claim on the grounds of non-disclosure. To avoid the negligence of their own inspector, they argued that the proposal form contained a declaration stating that:

> I further declare insofar as any part of this proposal is not written by me the person who has written same has done so by my instructions and as my agent for that purpose.

In other words, it was a *Facer* defence. Oddly enough, *Facer* (see above) was not referred to in the judgment.

The problem now remains as to the present state of the law with regard to answers filled in erroneously by agents. In *Stone*, the agent had such authority to complete the answers, and that is often not the case. Will the case be extended to this wider area? In *Stone*, the company had records showing the earlier claim, and although waiver was not pleaded by the customer, the fact must have been in the mind of the court.

In Australia, the High Court showed a dislike of the *Newsholme* decision (although they now have their 1984 legislation; Appendix 6.3) and, in Canada, a similar preference for the *Stone* approach has been seen in *Blanchette v CIS Ltd* 36 DLR (3rd) 561 (1973), a decision of the Supreme Court of Canada.

These conflicting decisions clearly demonstrate the urgent need for legislative reform. In an age of consumer protection, it is surprising that nothing has been achieved. The Law Reform Committee recommendations of 1957 gather dust. But, in New Zealand and Australia, the necessary changes were introduced in 1977 and 1984. Section 10 of the New Zealand Insurance Law Reform Act 1977 states:

(1) A representative of an insurer who acts for the insurer during the negotiation of any contract of insurance, and so acts within the scope of his actual or apparent authority, shall be deemed, as between the insured and the insurer and at all times during the negotiations until the contract comes into being to be the agent of the insurer.

(2) An insurer shall be deemed to have notice of all matters material to a contract of insurance known to a representative of the insurer concerned in the negotiation of the contract before the proposal of the insured is accepted by the insurer.

The Insurance Ombudsman in this country has made reference to the difficulties of the present legal position:

> Whether a remark uttered in the heat of the sales pitch can be binding on the insurer is sometimes an exceedingly nice question, in the philosophical sense. It turns on the extent, to which, if at all, the agent – which can in certain circumstances include a so called independent – 'holds himself out', by express words or conduct, as speaking, on behalf of the company or underwriter [1988 Report].

With the Court of Appeal criticism in *Roberts v Plaisted* (see Chapter 4) in mind, he said:

> I am now prepared, in appropriate cases, to hold insurers responsible for the defaults of intermediaries. Speculation as to exactly what will prove an appropriate case appears fruitless [1989 Report].

And, in his 1992 Report, he commented:

> A complaint against an insurer on these grounds (wrong advice) will not ... be upheld as valid if the warning or advice was given (or not) by an independent intermediary or other person for whom the insurer has no responsibility.

Since 1998, however, the Insurance Ombudsman Bureau will have jurisdiction over independent intermediaries, or at least over those firms which elect to become members of the Insurance Ombudsman Bureau.

THE INDEPENDENT ADVISER

While the Insurance Brokers (Registration) Act 1977 provided a major reform in this area, it also had the side effect of creating an additional group of intermediaries who were not eligible for registration as brokers or who chose not to register even if eligible. This was the major reason for the repeal of the Act by the FSMA and the setting up of the GISC as a self-regulatory replacement (see above).

We are here concerned with the legal position of anyone who can truly be described as 'independent' of a particular insurer in the sense that he has no employment contract with an insurer. Lloyd's brokers, because of the working practices at Lloyd's are dealt with separately below.

It is commonly said that the insurance adviser is the agent of the insured. That being so, then there would normally be a contractual relationship between the two parties. But the cases below show that, in certain aspects of a tripartite insurance transaction, the insurance adviser may also act as agent of the insurer and is thus contractually bound also to that insurer.

However, it is the possible tortious relationship between the insurance adviser and others that is the more potentially dangerous for the adviser, because this liability is more difficult to define and, potentially, more wide ranging in effect.

We need now to examine further the extent of the duty of care in negligence in the area of independent insurance advisers. The answer depends on what the courts consider to be reasonable in the circumstances of the case.

The broker's closest relationship is usually the one he has with his assured, and we will consider the extent of his duty in this area first. We will then look at the relationship between insurance adviser and insurer and, finally, whether or not a duty is owed beyond this close circle of connected parties.

The insurance adviser and his client

Normally, the insurance adviser's relationship with his client is in both contract and tort. But it rarely happens that a formal contract is made between the adviser and the lay client and, therefore, it might be easier for the client to argue that the adviser was in breach of a duty of care owed towards him in tort.

The cases that follow show the standard that the courts have perceived to be necessary from insurance advisers. But it should be remembered that the GISC also gives guidance to which the courts will, presumably, pay some heed in future cases.

The general principles of professional conduct expressed in the GISC Codes (Appendix 6.1) are stated to be that brokers shall at all times conduct their business with the utmost good faith and integrity; that they shall do everything to satisfy the insurance requirements of their clients and thus place these requirements above all other considerations; and that brokers must avoid all misleading or extravagant advertising. One example given in the Code concerns the matter of 'disclosure'. It is a basic requirement of insurance contract law (see *Carter v Boehm* (1766) 3 Burr 1905, Appendix 4.1) that the insured disclose all facts which would be considered by a prudent insurer as material to his judgment of the risk. The close relationship that might exist between client and broker, perhaps built up over many years, may lead the broker to possess information about his client that conflicts with the information now being given by the client about the risk to be insured. The broker should advise the client of the need to show good faith in the answers (see below).

Another illustration is that the broker shall use his skill objectively in selecting an insurer suitable to the best interests of his client. This could be widely interpreted, especially where the client's interests are themselves wide ranging. Certainly, it would be a requirement of the broker, that he should not recommend any insurer over whom hangs any solvency or trading doubts.

The present commercial Code follows the line taken by the earlier statutory Codes under the, now defunct, Insurance Brokers (Registration) Act 1977, namely that it will remain the insured's responsibility to see that all answers given on a proposal form, claim form or in any other material document remain the responsibility of the insured. The consumer Code does not expressly set out a similar statement but merely says that 'We will explain your duty to give insurers information before cover begins and during the policy, and what may happen if you do not'.

It could be argued that when an applicant chooses to approach a broker rather than a company agent, they do so partly because they want more detailed professional assistance.

The guidance given to the broker in the commercial Code is to avoid completing the form himself and to throw that burden on to the client's shoulders. While it may be good advice in helping to avoid accusations of negligence, just how practical is it? An independent adviser may feel that he should assist in the completion of forms because he knows this is one reason why many clients choose to approach him in the first place. Sometimes, the adviser may choose to do so merely to speed up the transaction. Presumably, the example was drafted with the many cases in mind where the adviser has been held liable for negligently completing insurance forms. Assuming that many advisers will still choose to maintain their existing work methods, it is important that they realise that by so doing they risk the accusation of negligence being levelled at them by their client.

It is submitted that this advice is not in the best interests of the profession's image. If the advice is that the broker throws back on the client the responsibility of accuracy in completing the documentation, then the broker absolves himself from liability in that part of the transaction that is potentially the most traumatic for the average client. The suggestion here is not that the broker should be liable for misrepresentations made by the client to the broker, but that the broker should be liable to the client for any negligence that derives from the broker's own failure to maintain professional standards.

A good illustration is provided by the Irish Supreme Court decision in *Chariot Inns Ltd v Assicurazioni Generali SpA and Coyle Hamilton Phillips Ltd* [1981] Lloyd's Rep IR 199.

The plaintiff had stored part of his furniture at another party's premises. A fire destroyed the premises and the insurers of those premises paid out a sum which included the value of the plaintiff's property. This sum was paid over to the plaintiff. At a later date the plaintiff instructed brokers to obtain fire cover for his own premises. The broker knew of the earlier fire. The proposal form asked questions relating to claims experience during the last five years. The broker when completing the form himself failed to declare the earlier fire apparently on the grounds that he did not consider that it was material to the present application. The Supreme Court found the insurers not liable on the grounds of non-disclosure and misrepresentation but held the broker liable for breach of contract and in negligence to their client. The view of expert witnesses was that even if the particular broker did not consider that the earlier fire was material to the risk, it would be normal practice to have disclosed it. The court also rejected the broker's argument that if they were negligent then the plaintiffs were equally culpable since it should have been obvious to them that the earlier fire should have been disclosed. The court was of the opinion that the plaintiffs having employed brokers as their professional advisers were entitled to rely on any advice given to them in relation to the completion of the proposal form. 'The reasonable man who goes to the trouble of obtaining professional advice normally acts in accordance with it.'

According to one decision of the Court of Appeal, even that standard may not be as high as the client would have hoped. In *O'Connor v Kirby and Co* [1971] 2 All ER 454, the plaintiff approached the defendant broker to arrange motor insurance. The broker completed the proposal based on questions and answers between him and the client. It was stated on the form that the car was garaged, whereas it later transpired that it was parked on the street. The insurers avoided liability and the client sued the brokers and failed.

The court considered that the duty owed by the broker was to take reasonable care in the circumstances. The client had given the correct answer to the broker and then had been asked to read the completed form before signing, but he failed to detect the broker's mistake. The court's view was that the duty of care did not extend as far as guaranteeing that every answer was correctly recorded.

Care should be taken in assessing the value of this decision. If the broker's mistake was due to an act that could be classed as less than negligent, then the decision is sound. It may well be that the court was influenced by the hint of a conspiracy between broker and client at the time of the claim against the insurer, and felt that in the circumstances the loss should remain on the car owner.

If the general attitude towards negligent advice displayed by the courts in various professional cases is anything to go by, then insurance advisers who negligently, and thus incorrectly, enter client's accurate answers to questions will be liable for any losses suffered, and thus, *O'Connor*'s decision should be limited in its interpretation.

United Mills Agencies Ltd v Harvey Bray and Co [1952] 1 All ER 225 (Appendix 6.17) looks at the intermediaries' duties from a different angle. Here, the question was how pro-active an intermediary should be in advising his client on his insurance needs. The plaintiff required insurance for goods destined for export. The policy arranged by his intermediary covered the goods from 'warehouse to warehouse'. This description did not include the time while the goods were at the packers' place of business. A fire at these premises destroyed the plaintiff's goods. The plaintiff's argument really came down to the complaint 'you failed to advise us properly, as to our real insurance requirements'. The judge rejected the argument in strong terms. His view was that an intermediary should be able to expect that a businessman conducts his business in a prudent fashion, and that he has sufficient insurance to cover those parts of his business which are not subject to the specific instructions given at a particular time. In the light of developments from the late 1970s onwards, whereby there has been an effort to 'professionalise' the insurance intermediaries' role by means of various Codes of conduct, the decision in *United Mills* looks somewhat outmoded. In advising the client on insurance of his goods for export, it is not appropriate or necessary, for instance, to review the client's vehicle insurance. But, where policies draw lines at points which would not automatically be clear, even to an alert businessman, then perhaps more should be expected of an insurance adviser.

It must be stressed that references to Codes are merely by way of example of what might be considered as negligent by the courts. It is now necessary to look at past situations on a more general basis as reflections of what the courts have considered to be negligent behaviour. The main areas are where the insurance adviser fails to carry out the client's instructions or fails to instruct the client as to his true needs. It should act as a general warning to the adviser that often the cause of complaint stems from poor office practices.

In *Cherry Ltd v Allied Insurance Brokers Ltd* [1978] 1 Lloyd's Rep 274 (Appendix 6.18), the defendant brokers had handled the plaintiff company's business for over 50 years. The plaintiffs were unhappy at the size of the premium in the light of a low claims record. They instructed the brokers to terminate all policies and informed them that they intended putting their business in the hands of other brokers. New policies were arranged by the new brokers, when the defendant brokers reported that the present insurers would not agree to cancel mid-term. The plaintiff being double insured cancelled the new policies but did not inform the defendants. At a later date, the original insurers agreed to cancel, but the defendants did not relay this fact to the plaintiffs who were now uninsured. A major loss occurred and the plaintiffs claimed in negligence from the defendant brokers who were held liable.

It is interesting to note that neither party told the other of the changed circumstances but clearly the court's view was that the brokers were professional advisers and it was their negligence that was the sole cause of the loss. The measure of damages was the amount covered by the original, cancelled policy.

A matter closely related to the termination of the cover is the question of renewals and the insurance adviser's duty towards his client. This is not an easy area wherein precise rules can be stated. The relationship between insurer and insurance adviser, set out in contractual terms, will be a deciding factor. This may indicate whether or not days of grace apply and the method of account between the two is also an important indicator of whether late renewals will be valid.

This relationship is crucial to the adviser/client relationship and will help dictate the extent of the duty owed by the insurance adviser to his client. The first question to ask is what is the extent of the adviser's duty at renewal time? Assuming that the insurance contract is for a set period of time, usually for one year, there is no legal obligation on the insurers to advise the insured that the policy is due for renewal. The situation would be different if the policy expressly stated that the insurers would give such notice. But does the adviser have a greater duty to warn the client about renewal dates? *Cherry*'s case would imply that such a duty exists. Section 58 of the (Australian) Insurance Contracts Act 1984 (Cth) is of interest in that it requires an insurer to give at least 14 days' notice that a policy is to expire. If he fails to do so and the insured has not arranged insurance elsewhere, the original policy is automatically renewed on the same terms. It could be implied from the Statement of General Insurance Practice (Appendix 4.10), that insurers must send renewal notices to the insured. The Statement does not, however, have legal force. Both the GISC Codes contain an obligation on its members, insurers and intermediaries, to give customers adequate warnings relating to renewal dates. The question remains, however, what would be the legal responsibility of a member towards a (former) customer who suffered an uninsured loss.

Further guidance can be taken from the Court of Appeal decision in *Fraser v BN Furman (Productions)* [1967] 3 All ER 57; [1967] 2 Lloyd's Rep 1 (Appendix 6.19). The plaintiffs instructed their brokers to arrange employer's liability insurance and it was common ground between the parties that the Eagle Star Insurance Co would be the insurers. The brokers failed to arrange cover. The plaintiffs were ordered to pay damages to an injured employee and, on seeking an indemnity, discovered that they were uninsured. They commenced proceedings against their broker for breach of contract. The brokers argued that an exclusion clause in the Eagle Star policy would have allowed the insurers to avoid liability and, therefore, the broker's omission had not caused any loss to the plaintiffs.

The court rejected their argument on the grounds that it was:

> ... highly improbable that, as a matter of business, a company of high reputation, wishing to obtain business, would conceivably take the wholly unmeritorious point in a claim of this kind.

The court awarded the plaintiffs damages representing the total sum that had been awarded against them in the employee's claim.

Here, the failure was to obtain the initial cover required by the client, but it would not stretch the principle too far to add that the insurance adviser should continue to see that his client's insurance requirements were up to date. Inevitably, there is a limit to such a duty. If the adviser sends his client renewal questions and these are unanswered by the client, then there would seem to be no answer to the adviser's claim that he had done all that was reasonable in the circumstances.

A further illustration of renewal problems can be seen in *Mint Security v Blair* [1982] 1 Lloyd's Rep 188. This case is also concerned with the problem of possible sub-agency when more than one broker is used. The third defendant brokers were instructed by the clients to obtain cash in transit cover. They, in turn, asked the second defendant broker to approach the market and a slip was initialled by the first defendant insurers. The policy contained a limitation of £50,000 on any one vehicle. The policy was renewed. During the second year of the policy, the plaintiffs decided to expand their business and again all the above parties were approached, as before, with a view to increasing cover. The insurers were only prepared to take part of the enlarged risk, but the third defendant broker failed to inform the client of the limitation. The addition to the new slip was dated to incorporate the original policy specifications in relation to the original vehicles. Again, the clients were not informed of this. A loss of £85,000 occurred. The plaintiffs were unsuccessful in their claim against the insurers, because of breach of policy warranties.

In the alternative, the plaintiff sued both sets of brokers. The second defendants were held to be in breach of their duty of care in that no copy of the slip had been passed on. The third defendants were not liable because there was no breach of duty on their part. The damages were limited to £20,000 as set out on the policy. But why were the third defendants not liable for the negligence of the second defendants? This was answered by Staughton J in the following way:

> There might have been an interesting question as to whether the second defendants were true sub-agents, owing a duty to the third defendants only; or whether they were agents of the plaintiffs appointed as such by the third defendants on the plaintiff's behalf. However, the second defendants accept that in the circumstances of the case and in particular in view of the fact that

> they issued a brochure jointly with the third defendant they owed a duty of care directly to the plaintiffs, both in contract and tort. Nobody else has argued otherwise. I am the last to complain that an interesting academic issue does not need to be decided. If the second defendants had been true sub-agents, the third defendants would have been vicariously liable for the second defendant's negligence.

The approach used in *Fraser v Furman*, whereby the court made an assessment of what insurers might have done in a given situation, was adopted in *Dunbar v A and B Painters Ltd and Others* [1986] 2 Lloyd's Rep 38.

The plaintiff was an employee of the first defendant. The employer had for a number of years obtained his employer's liability policy from the Eagle Star Group. When his premium doubled the employer instructed his brokers, the third defendants, to insure elsewhere. His insurance was placed with the Economic Insurance Co. In completing the proposal form, serious misstatements were made. It was stated that no insurer had ever asked for an increased premium and two earlier claims for £10,000 and £20,000 were shown as claims for £5,000 and £250.

The exact circumstances whereby these answers were given are not clearly set out in the judgments, but in the trial court the deputy judge held the brokers at fault on the grounds that, although they were endeavouring to negotiate cover at the cheapest rates for their clients, they unfortunately allowed their standards to fall below that which was acceptable. But the brokers then raised a defence similar to that in *Fraser*'s case. The policy with Economic contained an exclusion clause, which stated that no indemnity would be paid if the employee was injured while working at a height in excess of 40 feet. The plaintiff received serious injuries, compensated by an award of £125,000, when he fell from a height a little in excess of 40 feet. The brokers therefore argued that even if they had correctly completed the proposal form the employer would not have obtained his indemnity from Economic.

The trial court rejected this argument on the basis that no respectable insurance company would have taken the height defence in these circumstances. The Court of Appeal, while agreeing with the trial judge's decision on the facts, stated that the correct approach would be for the judge to assess the chances that the insurers might attempt to utilise their exclusion clause to negotiate a settlement. In which case, the brokers should be made liable for whatever assessment the judge estimated as a likely outcome of such negotiations. Here, the brokers were liable for the full compensation awarded to the plaintiff employee.

Fraser and *Dunbar* were relied on in *O and R Jewellers v Terry* [1999] Lloyd's Rep IR 436. The second defendant brokers had arranged jewellery cover for the plaintiffs. Following a major loss, the insurers raised a number of defences. One defence related to the fact that previous criminal convictions of one of the senior executives had not been declared. The matter was known to the brokers and therefore the plaintiffs alleged that the brokers had been negligent in not advising the insured that the matter was crucial and that the executive should have been dismissed in order to facilitate the obtaining of the insurance. The brokers argued that the insurers had other defences available to them and therefore even if the brokers were negligent it was not their negligence that caused the loss.

The court explained that in such a situation it was for the judge to decide the chances that the insurers would have relied on their other defences. (See *Mallet v McMonagle* [1969] 1 Lloyd's Rep 1270.) In coming to that evaluation the judge said that it was a matter of taking into account all the ifs and buts and then come to a comprehensive estimate of the chance. Having done so, he decided that the plaintiffs had lost a 30% chance of recovering their full loss due to the negligence of their broker and thus awarded them that percentage of the total insured loss. The wide variation in these three cases shows how difficult, or hit and miss, the court's final calculation may be.

The placing of the heavier burden on the shoulders of the broker, rather than equally or more so on the client, is further illustrated by the Court of Appeal decision in *Warren v Henry Sutton and Co* [1976] 2 Lloyd's Rep 276.

The plaintiff planned a driving holiday in France and wanted a friend included as an additional driver. This was arranged for an additional premium of £2 and, presumably, the brokers received the relevant commission. The additional driver was represented as having a clean driving record, which was not the case. The insurers were able to avoid their liability for the property damage that followed on the grounds of the misrepresentation. The plaintiff sued his brokers arguing that they were responsible for the misrepresentation, in that they had failed to ask the relevant questions concerning the claims history of the additional driver. The brokers defended by arguing that it was not they who had made the misrepresentation, but the plaintiff, and it was for him to have divulged his friend's bad driving record.

The Court of Appeal, by a majority, decided the brokers were liable. The representation was made by the brokers over the telephone to the insurers without first checking with the plaintiff. The brokers had volunteered the statement 'no accidents, convictions or disabilities'. Because of the dilatoriness of the brokers, the plaintiff had also contacted the insurers but no questions had been asked of him concerning his friend and no information volunteered. The question then remained as to whether the plaintiff should have told the brokers what he knew of his friend's previous record or whether the brokers should have asked.

The majority of the court felt that the misrepresentation was due to the brokers' failure to ask the client the relevant questions. Lord Denning MR, in a strong dissent, argued that it was the duty of the client not to mislead the broker and that, by failing to inform the broker, he was the author of his own misfortune. The financial implications of this decision presumably go beyond the cost of the repair damages. The accident involved a personal injury claim. The insurers were bound to pay that by virtue of their membership of the Motor Insurers' Bureau. But, having paid out, they would look to the car owner for an indemnity who in turn would add this to his claim against the brokers.

The true extent to which the client places himself in the hands of his adviser, and relies on him for professional advice, extends to conversations prior to actually filling in the proposal. This clearly is a potentially dangerous period for the adviser.

In *McNealy v Pennine Insurance Co Ltd and West Lancashire Insurance Brokers Ltd* [1978] 2 Lloyd's Rep 18 (Appendix 6.20), the plaintiff approached brokers to arrange comprehensive motor insurance. The Pennine were offering motorists special low rates. The plaintiff was a property repairer and qualified for their insurance. He was also a part time musician and this made him unacceptable to the insurers. The brokers knew of the insurers' rejection list of certain occupations but they failed to ask the plaintiff whether he had any part time occupation. When an accident occurred, the insurers were able to repudiate liability for non-disclosure. The brokers, however, were held liable. Knowing of the insurers' condition concerning certain part time occupations, it was not sufficient for them merely to accept the plaintiff's main trade. They should have gone one step further and questioned him as to any part time work. The brokers had completed the proposal and the plaintiff had signed it. No questions as to part time work appeared on the form and the plaintiff's answer 'property repairer' to the occupation question was correct on the face of it. There was nothing that should have put him on the alert. The prohibited occupations only appeared in the insurer's instructions to brokers.

Lord Denning MR also gave judgment in this case. But, unlike *Warren*'s case, he had no criticisms of the plaintiff. Full responsibility fell on the brokers. The brokers should have gone through the list of unacceptable occupations with the client. In failing to do so they did not do all that was reasonable to see that their client was properly insured.

A decision which illustrates a number of problems arising from the adviser-client relationship referred to above, can be seen in *Sharp v Sphere Drake Insurance plc* [1992] 1 Lloyd's Rep 501 (Appendix 6.21). The decision covers a number of insurance questions, including wrongful signing of the proposal form.

In part, it was alleged that there had been a non-disclosure in that the proposal form had never been signed by the applicant for insurance, but by an employee of D3, the brokers. The court found for the insurers but against the brokers.

In order to answer the question whether or not the broker had fallen below the required standard, it was important to evaluate what information he had at hand and how he came to have it. The plaintiff and the broker spoke over the telephone. The broker did not read over all of the questions. They spoke in general terms about living abroad and on that information the broker considered that a negative answer should be given to the question relating to the 'house boat' clause. The plaintiff, however, alleged that the broker had failed properly to construe that clause, and failed to give to it the importance it deserved.

The difficulties of watching over the affairs of clients who are at a distance and, particularly, where communication is difficult, led the brokers in the present case to take an unfortunate and expensive shortcut. It would seem, at least from one expert witness, that one way out would be to explain the situation fully to the underwriters and ask for them to hold cover while the completed proposal form finds its way from one party to the other. On the facts of the present case, however, even that solution would not avail the broker if he falls below the standard of professional competence in the way he construes the questions on the proposal form and fails to instruct or advise his client as to their true meaning.

One of the most basic tasks falling on the shoulders of the intermediary is to explain the contents and implications of the wording of the policy. The problem is in assessing the needs of the customer. How much help does the customer require? Can one assume that a business person is sufficiently acquainted with insurance terminology not to need help beyond a certain point. Such an emphasis appears in the GISC Commercial Code. Would it be possible to argue, in the face of an allegation of negligence by the customer, that the customer was also contributorily negligent?

These matters were addressed in *Bollom v Byas Mosley* [1999] Lloyd's Rep PN 598 (Appendix 6.7). The defendant brokers had arranged the plaintiff company's insurance affairs for more than 30 years. The policy in question required, as a condition precedent, that whenever the premises were closed for business all security devices were operational. A fire occurred when the alarm was not switched on. It had been switched off due to complaints from neighbours on the occasions when it had malfunctioned. The insurers, who probably could have avoided for breach of the condition precedent, came to a settlement with the insured and the present action was against the brokers to recover the balance (£2.5 m). The plaintiff's argument was that the importance of the condition precedent had not been adequately explained to them by the brokers. The judge agreed. He said that the broker's duty was to take reasonable steps to see that the client was aware of the nature and terms of the policy and in particular to draw the client's attention to and if necessary to explain to him any terms which might invalidate the cover. This the brokers had failed to do in relation to the alarm requirements. Even if the brokers had explained the significance would the client have activated the alarm? The court thought that he would and therefore there was sufficient causation between the broker's breach and the loss suffered.

Two other defence arguments were raised by the brokers. They argued that if they were liable then the client had been contributorily negligent in not setting the alarm and also that the sum insured was inadequate. Both defence arguments were rejected by the judge who explained:

> When a person engages a professional man to provide specialist services the law will not ordinarily impose a duty on that person to take steps to protect himself against negligence on the part of someone who has himself undertaken to act with all reasonable skill and care. Negligence involves a failure to guard against a risk that is reasonably foreseeable and there cannot therefore be contributory negligence in a case of this kind unless the plaintiff ought reasonably to have foreseen that his adviser might fail to carry out his responsibilities.

The judge also dealt with the question of valuation at some length (see generally Chapter 8). He found that the plaintiff was underinsured by about 25% on an indemnity basis and by over 50% on a reinstatement basis. The question then was to determine what duty was owed by a broker to see that a client was adequately insured with regard to valuation. The court considered that a broker was not a professional valuer but that they should be certain that the client understands the concept and the working rules that govern how an insurer approaches paying compensation based on reinstatement or replacement of property. A broker should therefore explain the significance of average clauses. In the present case there was no evidence that the brokers had explained these essential details to their clients. If they had done so the court found that the insureds would have increased the valuations and thus again there was sufficient causation. The brokers were therefore also in breach of their duty under this heading.

The scope of the duty of care owed by a professional is usually to be tested by the contract of retainer. Where the wording is found wanting (often because of its brevity and possibly lack of thought to tailoring it to the specific needs of the situation) then the court will have to decide, usually on tort principles, what that duty is by looking at how the parties dealt with each other and what reasonable expectations were created. The leading case is the House of Lords decision in *SAAMCO v York Montague Ltd* [1997] AC 191. That decision is referred to in their Lordships' decision in a broker setting in *Aneco Reinsurance Underwriting Ltd v Johnson and Higgins Ltd* [2002] Lloyd's Rep 157 (Appendix 6.28).

The facts also provide an example of the pivotal role that brokers can play in creating a market for insurance.

Aneco were interested in participating in certain types of excess of loss accounts of marine syndicates. However they were not prepared to do so until they could be sure that there was sufficient reinsurance interest elsewhere in the market. This is not an unusual scenario. The defendants were brokers whose task it was to test the market for that cover. It was explained to them that the reinsurance was crucial to Aneco's decision whether or not to enter the market. The brokers said that such was obtainable and Aneco entered into the excess of loss treaty. In time Aneco were faced with considerable claims and they turned to their reinsurers who were able, however, to avoid their liability on the grounds of a negligent presentation of the risk by the brokers. It was also agreed that if the risk had been correctly presented there would have been no reinsurance available because this type of risk (facultative/obligatory and not quota share treaty) was regarded as highly unattractive in the market. The question on appeal related to the quantum of damages, the choice being either the value of the lost reinsurance cover (the defendant broker's position) or the full loss suffered by Aneco thus including the losses on the primary insurance .

The House of Lords and the Court of Appeal reversing the trial court held that the full losses suffered by Aneco were to be awarded on the grounds that the defendants knew that on their advice hinged Aneco's decision whether or not to enter this market. In holding that the defendants were to be held liable for the whole of the loss suffered the House came to the opposite conclusion on the facts, that the House had reached in *SAAMCO* where negligent valuers were not liable for the full losses suffered by the lender when the borrowers failed to repay the loans and there was then a fall in property values at the time of the forced sales. The reason for the difference was that the scope of the duty on the defendants in the two cases was not the same.

The duty in the present case was considerably more onerous than in the *SAAMCO* case.

Thus it is crucial for brokers, and other professionals, to seek a clear understanding of either what is expected of them or to make clear the limits of what they are prepared to do for the other party. To that end parties should heed the words of the trial judge Cresswell J who stated: 'It is highly desirable that means be found of recording (in a form which precludes later dispute) what was said between broker and underwriters at the time of the presentation of the risk.' If this means that market practices should be re-examined and more time given to thinking through a relationship, then doing so might prevent what Cresswell J described as inadequate standards of broking.

The insurance adviser and the insurer

In the above section, the question was whether or not the adviser was liable to the client when the insurers were able to avoid their liability to the 'assured'. In this section, we are concerned with situations where the insurer is liable but is entitled to turn on the adviser and seek indemnification on the ground of the adviser's negligence or breach of agency.

The cases show that this is possible and they thus illustrate that the adviser owes a duty of care to both parties whom he is attempting to put into a contractual relationship. But the situation is not without its complications as to whose agent the adviser is at a particular time during the transaction. The problem is particularly acute when cover notes are being issued by an adviser, or when he is dealing with changes to existing cover. It is more likely than not that he is acting as agent of the insurers for part of this time. If this is the case and any negligence occurs on the part of the adviser, then the insurers will be liable to the assured, but, in all probability, the insurer can seek reimbursement from the adviser for any breach of their relationship.

In *Stockton v Mason and Vehicle and General Insurance Co and Arthur Edward (Insurance) Ltd* [1978] 2 Lloyd's Rep 430 (Appendix 6.22), the first defendant's father had his Ford Anglia insured with the second defendant, Vehicle and General, through the agency of the third defendants. The owner's wife telephoned the brokers to explain that her husband had sold the Anglia and had replaced it with an MG Midget. She asked for the insurance to be transferred. A clerk in the broker's office told her that everything would be all right and that they would see to it. The owner took this to mean that the same terms and conditions applied as previously. A week later the brokers informed the owner that driving must be restricted to the owner only. A few hours before that information reached the owner, his son negligently caused an accident while driving the car, and damages of £46,000 were awarded to the plaintiff. Who was to pay?

The difficulty of analysing the legal position of the broker in this transaction is reflected in the fact that the county court judge's view was overruled by the Court of Appeal. What was the role of the broker at the moment he gave information over the telephone to Mrs Mason? The judge considered that he was not yet acting as an agent of the insurers. The broker owed a personal duty of care to the client and was in breach of that. The Court of Appeal saw it differently. The relationship between insurer and broker in non-marine insurance is such that the broker can have implied authority to enter into interim insurance and to issue cover notes.

The vast majority of the motoring public believe that a telephone call to a broker will result in immediate temporary cover, sufficient to drive a newly acquired car immediately. The industry practice reflects those assumptions and, therefore, the broker's conversation with Mrs Mason had the effect of granting temporary cover and therefore they were agents of the insurers. The plaintiff's case against the insurers succeeded and the court's earlier judgment against the brokers was reversed.

It is clear that in the client-broker relationship much will depend on what was said and understood. That is a matter of evidence for the court to deal with having seen and heard the witnesses. In *Stockton*'s case, the decision hinges on the court's interpretation of a telephone conversation that can only have lasted a minute or two.

In the broker-insurer relationship, there is more chance that conversations will have been written down or recorded in some way. This may present the court with clearer evidence on which to base their decision. But even here inadequate office administration can lead to unhappy results for one of the parties.

In *Stockton* (see also *Hadenfayre Ltd v British National Insurance Society* [1984] 2 Lloyd's Rep 393), the disputed statements were made in what one might call 'office hours and office environment'. But the broker would not deny that his working environment goes beyond those parameters. So too do his legal responsibilities to both insurer and client.

This is well illustrated in *Woolcott v Excess Insurance and Others* [1979] 1 Lloyd's Rep 23, CA; and see also *Woolcott v Sun Alliance* [1978] 1 Lloyd's Rep 629. The plaintiff had a number of criminal convictions, including one of 12 years' imprisonment for armed robbery. He set up a business and several insurance policies were effected for the business through the third party defendant brokers. The business was put into a creditors' voluntary liquidation. But, before this occurrence, the plaintiff asked the brokers to arrange a household comprehensive policy. This was placed with the first party defendant insurers in accordance with the authority given to the brokers, by the insurers. When a subsequent loss occurred due to fire the insurers repudiated liability on the grounds of non-disclosure of the plaintiff's criminal record.

The plaintiff argued that the brokers were aware of his previous record and, consequently, as agents of the insurers, in effecting the policy the brokers' knowledge was imputed to the insurers. If that argument was sound, then the insurers argued that the brokers were liable to indemnify them for failing to relay this crucial information. This the brokers were obliged to do, by virtue of the 'binding authority' issued by the insurers to the brokers whereby it was an implied term of that authority that such matters as previous criminal convictions must be brought to the attention of the insurers. What, then, was the extent of the brokers' knowledge and by what means were they in possession of it? The plaintiff first argued that, when the brokers visited his company, prior to its liquidation, it was common knowledge among the company's employees that the plaintiff had a criminal record. This knowledge came into the possession of the broker. Secondly, it was argued that, on a social occasion, this knowledge had also been passed on to the broker when dancing with a lady later to become the plaintiff's wife. The resolving of these crucial issues led to a judgment by the High Court, an appeal to the Court of Appeal and an order by them for a retrial.

This sequence of events, while not unheard of, is certainly unusual, and expensive in a civil matter. No intricate question of law was involved, only the evaluation of the witnesses' evidence. In the retrial, the judge admitted as much when he confessed that 'the decision ultimately depends on my human and, therefore, fallible judgment as to which of two witnesses I believe' (referring to the testimony of the broker and Mrs Woolcott). The judge preferred the evidence of Mrs Woolcott that on a social occasion she had confirmed the broker's suspicions of the plaintiff's previous criminal record. This knowledge was therefore imputed to the insurers by the finding by the court that the brokers were acting as agent of the insurers under their binder with them. This being the case, the brokers were in breach of their contract of agency with the insurer. Why they did not pass on this important information to the insurers was, as the judge said, 'one of the mysteries and tragedies of this case'. The outcome then was that the plaintiff succeeded in his claim against the insurers, while the insurers were successful in their claim for an indemnity from the brokers.

There is no doubt however that the 'classical' relationship between potential policyholder, independent adviser and insurer is that the adviser is the agent of the policyholder. This reflects the fact that the customer approaches the adviser with a request that the adviser arrange a policy on his behalf. But the policyholder is well aware that he does not pay directly for this service, at least not in normal consumer insurance. Every party to the transaction knows that commission is paid by the insurer to the adviser. It is therefore not surprising that the policyholder thinks that the information he has given to the adviser should automatically be implied to the insurer. The above case illustrates that this can be the situation in certain circumstances, especially where the adviser has the right to issue cover notes, or acts under a binder.

The Court of Appeal decision in *Roberts v Plaisted* [1989] 2 Lloyd's Rep 341, however, contains strong criticism of the so called 'classical' position. Although the court found that the insured was not in breach of the duty of disclosure, and therefore the insurers were liable for fire damage to a hotel complex, one of the plaintiff's arguments in the alternative was that the broker had sufficient knowledge of the risk for this to be imputed to the insurers. Lord Justice Purchas dealt with the argument in the following way:

> Full and frank disclosure to the Lloyd's broker concerned in presenting on behalf of the proposed assured the proposal to the insurers as against an insurer who complains of non-disclosure and repudiates on that ground avails the proposed insured in no sense at all. To the person unacquainted with the insurance industry it may seen a remarkable state of the law that someone who describes himself as a Lloyd's broker who is remunerated by the insurance industry and who presents proposals and suggested policies on their behalf should not be the safe recipient of full disclosure; but that is, undoubtedly, the position in law as it stands at the moment. Perhaps it is a matter which might attract the attention at an appropriate moment of the Law Commission.

The insurance adviser and third parties

Perhaps another significant impact of the *Hedley Byrne* decision, for brokers, is the potential liability that it may place on them when dealing with third parties. At the same time, it must be admitted that there are few cases that so far illustrate this point. We have seen above that the relationship that binds the broker to his client and to the insurer may be contractual as well as tortious. Here, we are concerned with situations where no contractual relationship can be shown between the parties.

The extent of the broker's duty of care to third parties has been considered by the Court of Appeal in *Punjab National Bank v De Boinville and Others* [1992] 3 All ER 104 (Appendix 6.23). The decision was referred to by the House of Lords in *White v Jones* [1995] 1 All ER 691 when the House, by a 3:2 majority, extended the liability of a solicitor to a non-client 'beneficiary' under a will.

THE LLOYD'S BROKER AND THE LAW

Broking insurance business at Lloyd's requires separate treatment to reflect the unique rules that apply (although many of the cases referred to above also concern Lloyd's brokers).

'Rules' may in fact be a misleading word, as much of what goes on is governed by usage and custom stretching back over several centuries. In recent years however there has been a flood of Lloyd's byelaws and regulations following various working party reports and recommendations (see *Lloyd's Acts, Byelaws and Regulations*, London: LLP; and Ellis, *Regulation of Insurance*, Dordrecht: Kluwer, both looseleaf).

Lloyd's brokers are subject to the supervision of the Lloyd's Act 1982, and the byelaws made under the Act. All Lloyd's brokers were instructed to join the GISC by September 2000 if they wished to continue as Lloyd's brokers.

Major changes affecting Lloyd's brokers were implemented during 2000. Several byelaws have been revoked and a new Brokers byelaw implemented (Byelaw 17 of 2000). The aim is to widen the access to the products available in the market place and the main route for this is to allow a wider range of intermediaries to become Lloyd's brokers. The former method of access to the market by means of umbrella arrangements has been revoked.

In placing personal lines business, commercial life business and commercial motor business it is not necessary to be a Lloyd's broker.

The present principal regulatory byelaw is the Lloyd's Brokers Byelaw 2000. This has made radical changes to the previous broker arrangements at Lloyd's. The Council still has control over the registration of those who wish to be Lloyd's brokers and the criteria for such registration must satisfy the requirements of either engaging in insurance activities from a permanent place of business in the United Kingdom and be a member of the General Insurance Standards Council or if the applicant does not meet the residence requirement it must demonstrate that it meets the GISC requirements and rules.

Custom and usage

The earliest references to Lloyd's Coffee House date from around 1688 and it is understandable that early transactions were governed by the usages and customs existing between merchants trading together in London, where the subject matter invariably referred to marine risks, often involving foreign parts.

What is clear is that the usages may apply between underwriter and broker, but do not necessarily affect the rights of the insured. This is partly because a Lloyd's broker is treated as a principal by the underwriter and not merely as an agent of the client. More importantly, usage cannot bind a person who is not conversant with such usage or custom.

Necessity of using a Lloyd's broker

It is commonly stated that business can only be placed at Lloyd's through a Lloyd's broker because only such a person has access to the underwriting room.

If a client in Manchester, who normally uses a local broker, wants to place some of his business at Lloyd's, or his local broker advises that this is the most appropriate place for a particular risk, then the local broker must contact a Lloyd's broker for this purpose. The commission will be shared between them on an agreed basis. Each would owe the other a duty of care in the work undertaken. However, as seen above, the intention is to provide easier access to the Lloyd's market.

The slip

(For detailed analysis, see Bennett, 'The role of the slip in marine insurance law' [1994] LMCLQ 94.) The formation of the insurance contract at Lloyd's is unique and, therefore, so too is the broker's role. A number of recent cases have helped to clarify previously unclear areas. The broker is the agent of the client and must divulge all relevant facts to the underwriter when seeking cover. Thus, despite his description of 'Lloyd's broker', it does not mean that information that he possesses will be implied to the underwriter.

The procedure for obtaining cover is that the broker prepares a 'slip', which is a document setting out the main aspects of the risk requiring cover. The information entered on the slip obviously varies from one class of business to another and, even then, the language is heavily abbreviated.

The broker should have a professional view of the various areas of specialisation offered by certain syndicates and will then approach an underwriter offering the class of business required. The first signature to the slip will usually become the lead underwriter and his initialling will help to convince others who are approached by the broker to follow his lead.

Each underwriter will accept a percentage of the total cover. It is possible that a subsequent subscriber will take a larger percentage than the lead underwriter.

It is also possible for later underwriters to add amendments to the wording of the original cover and then problems arise as to the position of the earlier subscribers. The amendments would be shown to them in the expectation that they will accept the modifications. If this is not done, it may be necessary for the broker to prepare more than one contract on differing terms.

It is also possible for the slip to be oversubscribed in which case it will be necessary for the broker to arrange a proportional scaling down.

Where the slip is under subscribed, then the policy will go ahead for only a proportion of the originally desired cover and the insured is deemed to be his own insurer for the balance.

The slip or slips are then sent to the Lloyd's Policy Signing Office, where language which is almost unintelligible from the client's point of view, is put into a formal policy which should be intelligible.

Throughout the operation, the broker is clearly required to act with the highest professional competence and integrity in order to acquaint the various underwriters with all details of the risk he is attempting to place. Failure to meet the high standards required will expose him to an accusation of negligence by the underwriters. Failure to meet the legitimate expectations of the client will similarly place him in a potentially dangerous legal situation.

It is instructive to look, in some detail, at the cases involving Lloyd's brokers and, more generally, at the formation of a contract at Lloyd's because of some of the unusual features described above.

In *Rozanes v Bowen* (1928) 32 L1 L Rep 98 (Appendix 6.24), Scrutton LJ went out of his way to explain the placing of business at Lloyd's on the grounds that the plaintiff was a foreign national who would probably be unfamiliar with the system.

In *American Airlines Inc v Hope* [1974] 2 Lloyd's Rep 301, Lord Diplock's judgment provides an excellent review of the Lloyd's broker's position in the market. He said:

> Contracts of insurance are placed at Lloyd's by a broker acting exclusively as agent for the assured. It is he who prepares the slip in which he undertakes in the customary 'shorthand' to obtain the cover that the assured requires. He takes the slip in the first instance to an underwriter whom he has selected to deal with as leading underwriter, that is, one who has a reputation in the market as an expert in the kind of cover required and whose lead is likely to be followed by other insurers in the market. If it is the first contract of insurance covering that risk in which a particular underwriter has acted as leading

> underwriter it is treated as an original insurance. The broker and the leading underwriter go through the slip together. They agree on any amendments to the broker's draft and fix the premium. When agreement has been reached, the leading underwriter initials the slip for his proportion of the cover and the broker then takes the initialled slip round the market to other insurers who initial it for such proportions of the cover as each is willing to accept. For practical purposes all the negotiations about the terms of the insurance and the rate of premium are carried out between the broker and the leading underwriter alone. Where, as is often the case, the slip gives the assured options to cover additional aircraft or additional risks during the period of cover, it does so on terms to be agreed with the leading underwriter.

Lord Diplock also dealt with renewals of an original cover. He explained that, where there are no substantial alterations, the expiring slip is shown to the lead underwriter and the only matter for negotiation is usually the renewal premium. In such cases, it is normal practice for the broker to indicate that no substantial changes are required by adding the words 'as expiring' to the renewal slip.

It is the broker's obvious duty to inform that underwriter of any changes, just as it is his duty to inform him fully of all relevant details when negotiating the original cover. Brokers keep copies of all slips and policies issued to their clients, whereas it is not customary for the leading underwriter to do so.

The *Fennia Patria* case [1983] 2 Lloyd's Rep 287 helps to clear up earlier doubts relating both to the contractual position of the parties to a partially subscribed slip, or where later underwriters made amendments to the wording of the slip.

Jaglom v Excess Insurance Co Ltd [1971] 2 Lloyd's Rep 171 had suggested that, where the slip was not fully subscribed, there was no concluded contract between the various underwriters and the assured. The *Fennia Patria* case, however, has stated that each signature to the slip concludes a binding contract between the parties for the percentage of the risk shown, assuming of course, that the underwriter has not attached any conditions to his acceptance. There must be an unqualified acceptance.

If the underwriter does amend the broker's details on the slip, this becomes a counter-offer and the broker will be put in a position, as agent of the intending assured, to accept or reject the alteration. Before reaching his decision, he should refer back to his principal (the 'assured') for instructions or explain the situation to him.

Would the assured be in a position to withdraw from the contract prior to the slip being fully subscribed? The Court of Appeal recognised that underwriters often permit the assured to do this but added that such a practice did not have the force of law and was not therefore a binding custom.

Settlements and claims

Another area of potential conflict between the broker's own interest and his duty to his client, the assured, is in the handling of claims.

Lloyd's practice in this matter has been seriously criticised by the courts. The practice has been for the underwriter to discharge his liability to the assured by altering the running account that he has with the broker. Thus, the underwriter credits the account of the broker, thus debiting that amount from what the broker owes the underwriter by way of premiums. Such practice dates back a long way, but, for more than 160 years, it has been criticised by the courts.

Conflict of interest arises at Lloyd's when there is a dispute as to liability on the policy. In such a situation it is customary for the broker to handle the claim, apparently for both protagonists.

In *Anglo-African Merchants Ltd and Exmouth Clothing Co Ltd v Bayley* [1969] 1 Lloyd's Rep 268 (Appendix 6.25), a claim was made under a theft policy and the underwriters argued non-disclosure by the assured. During the investigation of the claim, the assured's brokers had made their files available to the underwriters and their solicitors, but when asked by the assured's solicitors for the same facility, this was refused.

Megaw J considered that such behaviour was not justified and that such a sorry state of affairs should not be allowed to arise again. He reinforced the general rule that a broker is the agent of the assured when placing business. The underwriters agreed, but argued that, when it came to claims, the broker also could and usually did act for the underwriter. Megaw J reasoned that this view was only acceptable in the very precise circumstances where the broker, before he accepts instructions to place the insurance, discloses to his client that he wishes to be free to act in this dual role. Even then, it must be shown that the assured fully appreciates the implications of such a collaboration between the two parties. Without evidence of such express and fully informed consent, it would amount to a breach of duty on the part of the broker.

Without such requirements, potential dangers and undesirable consequences might well follow. In the words of Megaw J: 'Such a relationship with the insurer inevitably invites suspicion that the broker is hunting with the hounds whilst running with the hare.' The way to avoid these problems is for the underwriter to appoint his own assessors or investigators. Even if it could be shown to be a generally accepted method of dealing with claims, the court considered that such a custom could not be upheld by the courts in this country, because it is in direct violation of one of the basic rules of the law of agency: that an agent may not serve two masters when in actual or potential opposition to one another.

The matter was again dealt with in *North and South Trust Co v Berkeley* [1970] 2 Lloyd's Rep 467 (Appendix 6.26), and the strictures of Megaw J were approved. The plaintiffs insured goods in transit from Buenos Aires to Paraguay. A local agent arranged the cover using a Lloyd's broker. The underwriters rejected a claim and, when pressed by the plaintiffs, they instructed the brokers to arrange for assessors to investigate the claim.

In accordance with Lloyd's practice, the report went direct to the underwriters while the brokers kept a copy for their files. The claim was again rejected. In the action on the policy, the underwriters claimed that the assessors' report was privileged and need not be disclosed to the plaintiffs. The plaintiffs therefore asked their brokers for their copy of the report and the underwriters sought an injunction preventing such disclosure.

The court strongly criticised the practice adopted by Lloyd's – of using brokers in this way – but, at the same time, held that the brokers need not divulge the contents of the report. This was because the report was not acquired in the service of the plaintiffs or in discharge of any duty to them.

Despite the lack of success by the plaintiff, the importance of the decision is the attack on the broker's role in the claim settlement process. Donaldson J explained that there was ample evidence that the practice was widespread, not only at Lloyd's but in the insurance industry generally. It was only in 1969, in *Bayley*'s case, that the practice was challenged. Donaldson J expressed surprise that the Committee of Lloyd's had not immediately reacted to the criticisms, either by requiring an alteration to the practice or by means of a friendly test action to seek the views of the Court of Appeal. The judge expressed the hope that now that he was adding his support to the views of Megaw J the changes would be forthcoming.

INSURANCE INTERMEDIARIES AND THE EUROPEAN UNION

(See Devine, *Insurance Intermediaries in the EEC*, 1998, London: LLP.) In 1976, the European Union introduced the Insurance Intermediaries Directive to take effect from June 1978. One of the great strengths of the United Kingdom insurance market is the expertise and international orientation of its sales force, in particular insurance brokers and more particularly, Lloyd's brokers. It is, therefore, of the greatest importance to them that the European Union markets should be open to their skills. This Directive helps to achieve those goals by introducing measures to allow freedom of establishment and freedom to provide services by such persons.

Article 4 calls for the mutual recognition of academic qualifications or work experience. In fact the United Kingdom's Insurance Brokers (Registration) Act 1977 requires more stringent requirements for registration of a United Kingdom broker than those called for by the Directive. Proof of compliance with the conditions required for recognition as an insurance broker, agent or sub-agent, shall be a certificate issued by the competent authority or body in the Member State of origin. Each State must inform the others as to which bodies have the power of granting such certificates of competency. The Directive is transitional in nature in that it will remain applicable only until there is a co-ordination of national rules concerning the taking up and pursuit of these activities.

In December 1991, the European Union published its Recommendation on Insurance Intermediaries (92/48/EEC). A Recommendation does not have binding force on Member States, but it clearly has the psychological effect of directing their minds towards what the Commission would like to see happen in a particular case. The Recommendation is of special importance, in that the European Single Market for insurance is now complete with the adoption of the Third Non-Life Directive in June 1992 and the Third Life Directive in November 1992 (see Chapter 1). These Directives should lead to a fully competitive market in insurance and, therefore, methods of distribution of insurance within the European Union are of crucial importance.

Insurance intermediaries are defined in Art 2, para 1(a)–(c) of the Insurance Intermediaries Directive. Article 2 of the present Recommendation states that all such insurance intermediaries are subject to the Recommendation, other than those who offer cover against loss or damage to goods supplied by that person and where the principal professional activity of that person is other than providing advice on and selling insurance. The example given in the Department of Trade and Industry Consultative Document is where an optician sells cover for loss of contact lenses. The argument is that such selling requires no detailed insurance ability on the part of the seller. However, a car salesman selling motor insurance would not be exempt from meeting the Recommendation's requirements on the grounds that this type of insurance cover is more complex in its nature.

Article 2.3 requires the management of an undertaking exercising the activity of an insurance intermediary to have an adequate number of persons who have commercial and professional knowledge and ability. There is, however, no definition of what is envisaged by the phrase 'adequate number'. The article calls upon such undertakings to provide relevant basic training for those employees involved in advising on insurance products. Article 4 elaborates on this requirement. Intermediaries must possess general, commercial and professional knowledge and ability although this may vary depending on the type of intermediary involved. Crucially, the standard of such ability shall be determined by the Member States. However, these standards can also be determined and administered by professional organisations recognised by Member States. It is assumed by the UK government that the GISC can perform this function. An insurance agent working for a specific insurance company, which has assumed responsibility for that person can, subject to the supervision of the Member State, undertake this obligation in relation to that agent.

The intermediary must have professional indemnity insurance or the undertaking accepting responsibility for that person must provide such cover. No explanation is given as to the required level of such professional indemnity cover.

The intermediary must be of good repute and must not be a declared bankrupt.

Article 5 requires that all intermediaries who fulfill the requirements of professional competence set out in the previous article must be registered in their Member State. Such registration is a prerequisite to pursuing the activity of an insurance intermediary. It is the responsibility of each Member State to appoint a competent body to administer such registration. Such competent bodies can include professional bodies and insurance undertakings where relevant. Registers of intermediaries shall be available to the Member States' administrative bodies. Intermediaries must inform the public that they are so registered. If one central register exists it must distinguish between independent and dependent intermediaries.

Adequate sanctions must exist in Member States, which can be applied to those who act as insurance intermediaries without proper registration.

Article 3 refers to independent intermediaries. It requires them to divulge to prospective policyholders any direct or economic connections they have with an insurance undertaking or any shareholding in or by such undertakings. It is also required that such intermediaries declare to the competent authority the spread of their business with different insurance undertakings over the previous year.

The great majority of the requirements set out in the Commission's Recommendation are already in place in the United Kingdom. However, the sources of such requirements are something of a mish-mash. Some are statutory in nature, while some are on a voluntary basis. If the United Kingdom intends to implement the Recommendation it will require the political will power to reorganise the present system and to put it on a more coherent footing.

There is a proposal (2002) for a draft Directive on 'insurance mediation' which, if implemented would replace the above Directive and Recommendation.

It is intended to remove the existing barriers which some Member States still have which prevent insurance intermediaries from operating freely throughout the community and thus prevent a single market in insurance. It will require Member States to nominate a body which will act as a central registry for all intermediaries within that State. The body will be required to see that such registered people have general, commercial and professional knowledge and ability suitable to the type of insurance with which they wish to be involved. They must be of good repute and have no criminal record connected with offences against property or financial activities and they must not have been declared bankrupt, unless rehabilitated by national law. They must have professional indemnity insurance at a minimum level of EUR1 m. Arrangements must be in place for keeping separate accounts for clients and the intermediary must have a sound financial base. There must be in force penalties against anyone acting without registration. There must be a complaints procedure in place for customers and Member States must encourage the setting-up of effective procedures for out-of-court settlement of disputes. The intermediary must make information available to the customer that explains his role as an intermediary. When in force it would seem that the FSA, once the GISC has been absorbed into it, will be the body charged with the responsibility of implementation.

INSURANCE INTERMEDIARIES

APPENDIX 6.1

General Insurance Standards Council Codes

A The Commercial Code

1 The Commercial Code introduction

Within this Commercial Code 'Member' means a Member of GISC (an Insurer, Intermediary (including broker) or agent), and anyone acting on its behalf, with whom the Commercial Customer deals.

Core principles

In the course of their General Insurance Activities Members should:

1.1 act with due skill, care and diligence;

1.2 observe high standards of integrity and deal openly and fairly with their Commercial Customers;

1.3 seek from Commercial Customers such information about their circumstances and objectives as might reasonably be expected to be relevant in enabling the Member to fulfil their responsibilities to them;

1.4 take reasonable steps to give Commercial Customers sufficient information in a comprehensible and timely way to enable them to make balanced and informed decisions about their insurance;

1.5 take appropriate steps to safeguard information, money and property held or handled on behalf of Commercial Customers;

1.6 conduct their business and organise their affairs in a prudent manner;

1.7 seek to avoid conflicts of interest, but where a conflict is unavoidable or does arise, manage it in such a way as to avoid prejudice to any party. Members will not unfairly put their own interests above their duty to any Commercial Customer for whom they act; and

1.8 handle complaints fairly and promptly.

PRACTICE NOTES

1 It is GISC's intention to promote standards of professional conduct for Members.

These Practice Notes represent statements of reasonable practice which Members will be expected to follow generally in adhering to the Core Principles.

2 A failure on the part of a Member to observe the standards set out in these Practice Notes shall not of itself constitute a breach of the Rules but any such failure may in disciplinary proceedings be relied upon by GISC or any party to the proceedings as tending to establish or to negate any liability which is in question in those proceedings.

Marketing

3 Members will ensure that all their advertising and promotional material is clear, fair and not misleading.

Arranging the insurance

Commercial Customer relationship

4 Members will advise their Commercial Customers of the nature of their service and their relationship with them, in particular, whether they act on behalf of an Insurer or act independently on behalf of the Commercial Customer as an Intermediary. They will also make it clear if they operate as an agent of another Intermediary.

5 Members will, where it is reasonably practical, confirm in writing instructions to act on behalf of a Commercial Customer and this will include appropriate reference to any recommendations made by the Member but declined by the Commercial Customer.

Commercial Customer requirements

6 Members will take appropriate steps to understand the types of Commercial Customers they are dealing with and the extent of their Commercial Customers' awareness of risk and General Insurance Products and take that knowledge into account in their dealings with them.

7 Members will seek from Commercial Customers such information about their circumstances and objectives as might reasonably be expected to be relevant in enabling them to identify the Commercial Customer's requirements and fulfil their responsibilities to their Commercial Customers.

Information about proposed insurance

8 Members will provide adequate information in a comprehensive and timely way to enable Commercial Customers to make an informed decision about the General Insurance Products or General Insurance Activity – related services being proposed.

9 If they are acting on behalf of the Commercial Customer, Members will explain the differences in, and the relative costs of, the types of insurance, which in the opinion of the Member, would suit the Commercial Customer's needs. In so doing, Members will take into consideration the knowledge held by their Commercial Customers when deciding to what extent it is appropriate for their Commercial Customers to have the terms and conditions of a particular insurance explained to them.

10 Members will advise Commercial Customers of the key features of the insurance proposed, including the essential cover and benefits, any

significant or unusual restrictions, exclusions, conditions or obligations, and the period of cover. In so doing, Members will take into consideration the knowledge held by their Commercial Customers when deciding to what extent it is appropriate for Commercial Customers to have the terms and conditions of a particular insurance explained to them.

11 If Members are unable to match Commercial Customers' requirements they will explain the differences in the insurance proposed.

Advice and recommendations

12 Members should only discuss with or advise Commercial Customers on matters in which they are knowledgeable and seek or recommend other specialist advice when necessary.

13 Members will take reasonable steps to advise Commercial Customers if any General Insurance Products or General Insurance Activity – related services being offered or requested are not covered by this Commercial Code and any possible risks involved. In so doing, Members will take into consideration the knowledge held by their Commercial Customers in deciding to what extent such advice may be necessary.

Information about costs and remuneration

14 Members will provide details of the costs of each General Insurance Product or General Insurance Activity – related service offered.

15 Members will not impose any fees or charges in addition to the premium required by the Insurer without first disclosing the amount and purpose of the charge. This will include charges for policy amendments, claims handling or cancellation.

16 Members who are acting on behalf of a Commercial Customer in arranging their insurance will, on request, or where they are legally obliged to do so, disclose the amount of commission and any other remuneration received for arranging the insurance.

17 Members will disclose to Commercial Customers any payment they receive for providing to, or securing on behalf of, their Commercial Customers any additional General Insurance.

Activity-related services

Duty of disclosure

18 Members will explain to Commercial Customers their duty to disclose all circumstances material to the insurance and the consequences of any failure to make such disclosures, both before the insurance commences and during the policy.

19 Members will make it clear to Commercial Customers that all answers or statements given on a proposal form, claim form, or any other material document, are the Commercial Customer's own responsibility. Commercial Customers should always be asked to check the accuracy of information provided.

20 If Members believe that any disclosure of material facts by their Commercial Customers is not true, fair or complete, they will request their Commercial Customers to make the necessary true, fair or complete disclosure, and if this is not forthcoming must consider declining to continue acting on their Commercial Customer's behalf.

Quotations

21 When giving a quotation, Members will take due care to ensure its accuracy and their ability to place the insurance at the quoted terms.

Placement

22 Members who act on behalf of Commercial Customers when arranging their insurance will use their skill objectively in the best interests of their Commercial Customers when choosing Insurers.

23 Where two or more Members are acting jointly for a Commercial Customer when placing an insurance, Members will take appropriate steps to see that they and their Commercial Customers know their individual responsibilities and duties.

24. Members will inform and seek from their Commercial Customers written acknowledgement where they are instructed to place an insurance which is contrary to the advice that has been given by the Member.

Confirming cover

25 Members will provide Commercial Customers with prompt written confirmation and details of the insurance which has been effected on their behalf.

26 Members will identify the Insurer(s) and advise any changes once the contract has commenced at the earliest opportunity.

27 Members will forward full policy documentation without avoidable delay where this is not included with the confirmation of cover.

Providing ongoing service

28 Members will respond promptly to Commercial Customers' queries and correspondence.

29 Members will deal promptly with Commercial Customers' requests for amendments to cover and provide them with full details of any premium or charges to be paid or returned.

30 Members will provide written confirmation when amendments are made.

31 Members will remit any return premium and charges due to Commercial Customers without avoidable delay.

32 Members will notify Commercial Customers of the renewal or expiry of their policy in time to allow them to consider and arrange any continuing cover they may need.

33 Members will remind Commercial Customers at renewal of their duty to disclose all circumstances material to the insurance.

34 On expiry or cancellation of the insurance, at the written request of the Commercial Customer, Members will promptly make available all documentation and information to which the Commercial Customer is entitled.

Claims

Where Members handle claims:

35 Members will, on request, give their Commercial Customers reasonable guidance in pursuing a claim under their policy.

36 Members will handle claims fairly and promptly and keep their Commercial Customers informed of progress.

37 Members will inform Commercial Customers in writing, with an explanation, if they are unable to deal with any part of a claim.

38 Members will forward settlement of a claim, without avoidable delay, once it has been agreed.

Documentation

39 Members will reply promptly or use their best endeavours to obtain a prompt reply to all correspondence.

40 Members will forward documentation without avoidable delay.

41 Members should not withhold from their Commercial Customers any written evidence or documentation relating to their contracts of insurance without their consent or adequate and justifiable reasons being disclosed in writing and without delay. If Members withhold a document from their Commercial Customers by way of a lien for monies due from those Commercial Customers they should provide advice of this to those Commercial Customers in writing at the time that the documents are withheld. If any documentation is withheld Members will ensure that Commercial Customers receive full details of the insurance cover and any documents to which they are legally entitled.

Conflicts of interest

42 Members will seek to avoid conflicts of interest, but where this is unavoidable, they will explain the position fully and manage the situation in such a way as to avoid prejudice to any party.

43 Members will not put their own interests above their duty to any Commercial Customer on whose behalf they act.

Confidentiality and security

44 Members will ensure that any information obtained from a Commercial Customer will not be used or disclosed except in the normal course of negotiating, maintaining or renewing insurance for that Commercial Customer, unless they have their Commercial Customer's consent, or disclosure is made to enable GISC to fulfil its regulatory function, or where the Member is legally obliged to disclose the information.

45 Members will take appropriate steps to ensure the security of any money, documents, other property or information handled or held on behalf of Commercial Customers.

Complaints

46 Members will provide details of their complaints procedures to Commercial Customers, and details, if appropriate, of any dispute resolution facility which is available to them.

47 Members will handle complaints fairly and promptly.

Commercial Code

48 Members will provide, on request, a copy of this Commercial Code to Commercial Customers or anyone acting on their behalf.

49 The Commercial Code forms part of the Membership Contract between Members and GISC which is governed by English law. Nothing in the Commercial Code or in the Membership Contract between Members and GISC will give any person any right to enforce any term of the Membership Contract between Members and GISC (including the Commercial Code) which that person would not have had but for the Contracts (Rights of Third Parties) Act 1999.

B The GISC General Insurance Code for private customers

The General Insurance Standards Council (GISC) is an independent organisation which was set up to regulate the sales, advisory and service standards of members (insurers, intermediaries (including brokers) and agents and anyone acting for them). Its main purpose is to make sure that general insurance customers are treated fairly.

The Private Customer Code

This Private Customer Code sets the minimum standards of good practice which all members of GISC must follow when they deal with private customers. It gives you important protection and should help you to understand:

(i) how insurers, intermediaries and agents, and anyone acting for them, must deal with you;

(ii) what information you should receive before you commit yourself to buying any insurance; and

(iii) how your insurance should be dealt with once it is in place.

Insurance products and services covered by the Private Customer Code

The Private Customer Code covers all types of general insurance products and services that are sold to private customers, including:

(i) motor insurance;

(ii) home insurance – buildings and contents;

(iii) insurance for caravans, boats, pets and other property;

(iv) travel insurance;

(v) private medical and dental insurance;

(vi) personal accident insurance;

(vii)extended warranty and breakdown insurance;

(viii)legal expenses insurance; and

(ix) payment protection insurance for mortgages and other loans.

Understanding the Private Customer Code

Within the Private Customer Code, 'you' means the private customer and 'we' and 'us' means the member of GISC (an insurer, intermediary or agent), and anyone acting for them, who you deal with.

Contents

1 Our commitments

1.1 As members of GISC, we promise that we will:

(i) act fairly and reasonably when we deal with you;

(ii) make sure that all our general insurance services satisfy the requirements of this Private Customer Code;

(iii) make sure all the information we give you is clear, fair and not misleading;

(iv) avoid conflicts of interest or, if we cannot avoid this, explain the position fully to you;

(v) give you enough information and help so you can make an informed decision before you make a final commitment to buy your insurance policy;

(vi) confirm your insurance arrangements;

(vii) make sure that our service meets GISC's standards;

(viii) handle claims fairly and promptly;

(ix) make sure you receive all the documentation you need;

(x) protect any personal information, money and property that we hold or handle for you; and

(xi) handle complaints fairly and promptly.

2 Marketing

Advertising

2.1 We will make sure that all our advertising and promotional material is clear, fair and not misleading.

3 Helping you find insurance to meet your needs

We will give you enough information and help so you can make an informed decision before you make a final commitment to buy your insurance policy.

Explaining our service

3.1 We will explain the service we can offer and our relationship with you, including:

(i) the type of service we offer;

(ii) whether we act for an insurer or act independently for you as an intermediary;

(iii) whether we act as an agent of another intermediary or agent; and

(iv) the choice of products and services we can offer you.

Matching your requirements

3.2 We will make sure, as far as possible, that the products and services we offer you will match your requirements:

(i) If it is practical, we will identify your needs by getting relevant information from you.

(ii) We will offer you products and services to meet your needs, and match any requirements you have.

(iii) If we cannot match your requirements, we will explain the differences in the product or service that we can offer you.

(iv) If it is not practical to match all your requirements, we will give you enough information so you can make an informed decision about your insurance.

Information about products and services

3.3 We will explain all the main features of the products and services that we offer, including:

(i) who the insurer is;

(ii) all the important details of cover and benefits;

(iii) any significant or unusual restrictions or exclusions;

(iv) any significant conditions or obligations which you must meet; and

(v) the period of cover.

Information on costs

3.4 We will give you full details of the costs of your insurance, including:

(i) separate insurance premiums for each of the individual products or services we are offering;

(ii) details of any fees and charges other than the insurance premium, and the purpose of each fee or charge (this will include any possible future fees or charges, such as for changing or cancelling the policy or handling claims);

(iii) when you need to pay the premiums, fees and charges, and an explanation of how you can pay; and

(iv) if we are acting on your behalf in arranging your insurance, if you ask us to, we will tell you what our commission is and any other amounts we receive for arranging your insurance or providing you with any other services.

Advice and recommendations

3.5 If we give you any advice or recommendations, we will:

(i) only discuss or advise on matters that we have knowledge of;

(ii) make sure that any advice we give you or recommendations we make are aimed at meeting your interests; and

(iii) not make any misleading claims for the products or services we offer or make any unfair criticisms about products and services that are offered by anyone else.

Customer protection information

3.6 We will explain the customer protection benefits under our GISC membership, including:

(i) our complaints procedures, together with details of who you should contact first if you want to make a complaint; and

(ii) whether any of the products or services we are offering you are not covered by this Private Customer Code.

Your duty to give information

3.7 We will explain your duty to give insurers information before cover begins and during the policy, and what may happen if you do not.

Quotes

3.8 If you want to consider the products or services we have offered you, we will:

(i) confirm how long you have to take up your insurance on the terms we have quoted to you;

(ii) give you a written quote if you ask for one, including all the information you need to make an informed decision; and

(iii) give you a sample policy if you ask for one.

Cooling-off period

3.9 Under the Private Customer Code, we have to give you certain information before you make your decision. If we have not given you this information when you buy your insurance (and you have not told us you do not want it), we will allow you a 'cooling-off period' of at least 14 days from the time you receive the information. If you do not want to continue with the insurance, you may cancel your cover within this period and get all your money back (as long as you have not made any claims).

Choosing to receive limited information

3.10If you want to buy your insurance without receiving all the information about the products and services that the Private Customer

Code requires, we will keep a record of your agreement to this and there will not be a 'cooling-off' period.

4 **Confirming your cover**

We will confirm your insurance arrangements and provide you with full policy documentation.

Confirming your cover

4.1 When we put your insurance arrangements in place, we will give you written confirmation of cover, including:

(i) enough information so you can check the details of your cover;

(ii) the date when your cover starts and the period of cover;

(iii) any certificates or documents which you need to have by law; and

(iv) details of any 'cooling-off' period.

Proof of payment

4.2 We will make sure that you have proof that you have paid the premiums, fees and charges.

Full policy documents

4.3 We will send you full policy documentation promptly.

5 **Providing our service to you**

We will make sure that our service meets the GISC's standards.

Questions

5.1 We will answer any questions promptly and give you help and advice if you need it.

Changes to your policy

5.2 We will deal with any changes to your insurance policy promptly. We will:

(i) give you written confirmation of any changes to your policy;

(ii) give you full details of any premiums or charges that you must pay or we must return to you;

(iii) give you any certificates or documents that you need to have by law;

(iv) make sure that you have proof that you have paid extra premiums, fees and charges; and

(v) send you any refunds of the premiums, fees or charges that are due to you.

Notice of renewal

5.3 We will tell you when you need to renew your policy, or that it will end, in time to allow you to consider and arrange any continuing cover you may need. We will:

(i) explain the renewal terms (if offered);

(ii) tell you about any changes to the cover, service or insurer being offered;

(iii) explain your continuing duty to give insurers information; and

(iv) send you any certificates or documents that you need to have by law.

Expiry or cancellation

5.4 When your policy ends or is cancelled, we will send you all the documentation and information that you are entitled to, if you ask for it.

6 Claims

We will handle claims fairly and promptly.

Information on claims procedures

6.1 When you first become a customer, we will give you details of how you can make a claim and tell you what your responsibilities are in relation to making claims.

If you make a claim

6.2 If you make a claim:

(i) we will respond promptly, explain how we will handle your claim and tell you what you need to do;

(ii) we will give you reasonable guidance to help you make a claim under your policy;

(iii) we will consider and handle your claim fairly and promptly, and tell you how your claim is progressing;

(iv) we will tell you, in writing, and explain why, if we cannot deal with all or any part of your claim; and

(v) once we have agreed to settle your claim, we will do so promptly.

7 Documentation

We will make sure you receive all the correct documentation you need.

Information in writing

7.1 We will give you information in writing, especially if there is a lot of information or if it is very complicated.

Standards of written information

7.2 We will make sure that all the written information and documents we send you are clear, fair and not misleading.

Sending you documentation

7.3 We will send you all the documentation you need promptly.

Withholding documentation

7.4 We will not withhold any insurance documentation from you without your permission, unless we are allowed to do so by law. If we do withhold any documents, we will make sure that you receive full details of your insurance cover and any documents that you need to have by law.

8 Confidentiality and security

We will protect your personal information, money and property.

Confidentiality

8.1 We will treat all your personal information as private and confidential to us and anyone else involved in providing your insurance, even when you are no longer a customer.

We will not give anyone else any personal information about you, except:

(i) when you ask us to or give us permission;

(ii) if we have to because we are a member of GISC; or

(iii) if we have to by law.

Security

8.2 We will take appropriate steps to make sure that any money, documents, other property or information that we handle or hold for you is secure.

9 Complaints

We will handle complaints fairly and promptly.

Information on complaints procedures

9.1 When you first become a customer, we will give you details of our complaints procedures in our policy or service documentation.

If you make a complaint

9.2 If you make a complaint:

(i) we will acknowledge it promptly, explain how we will handle your complaint and tell you what you need to do; and

(ii) we will consider and handle your complaint fairly and promptly, and tell you how your complaint is progressing.

Dispute resolution scheme

9.3 We are a member of a recognised independent dispute resolution scheme. If you are not happy with our final response to your complaint, we will tell you how you can contact this scheme.

10 Other information

GISC monitoring

10.1 We are monitored independently by GISC to make sure that we meet the standards of this Private Customer Code. If we do not satisfy the requirements of the Private Customer Code, we may face a penalty.

The Private Customer Code and your legal rights

10.2 The Private Customer Code forms part of the Membership Contract (which is governed by English law) between GISC and us. Nothing in the Private Customer Code or in our Membership Contract with GISC will give any person any right to enforce any term of our Membership Contract which they would otherwise have under the Contracts (Rights of Third Parties) Act 1999.

Copies of the Private Customer Code

10.3 You can get a free a copy of the Private Customer Code if you ask any GISC member, or from GISC at the address below.

More information

10.4 If you want to check that we are members of GISC, or if you have any questions about the Private Customer Code, you can contact GISC at the address below.

General Insurance Standards Council

110 Cannon Street

London

EC4N 6EU

Telephone: 020 7648 7810

Fax: 020 7648 7808

Email (general enquiries): enquiries@gisc.co.uk

Or, you can access the GISC website at: www.gisc.co.uk

APPENDIX 6.2

Siu Yin Kwan v Eastern Insurance Co Ltd [1994] 1 All ER 213, PC

Lord Lloyd (at p 220): The main features of the law relating to an undisclosed principal have been settled since at least at the end of the 18th century. A hundred years later, in 1872, Blackburn J said that it had often been doubted whether it was originally right to hold that an undisclosed principal was liable to be sued on the contract made by an agent on his behalf, but added that 'doubts of this kind come now too late'.

For present purposes, the law can be summarised shortly as follows:

(1) an undisclosed principal may sue and be sued on a contract made by an agent on his behalf, acting within the scope of his actual authority;

(2) in entering into the contract, the agent must intend to act on the principal's behalf;

(3) the agent of an undisclosed principal may also sue and be sued on the contract;

(4) any defence which the third party may have against the agent is available against his principal;

(5) the terms of the contract may, expressly or by implication, exclude the principal's right to sue, and his liability to be sued. The contract itself, or the circumstances surrounding the contract, may show that the agent is the true and only principal.

APPENDIX 6.3

(Australian) Insurance (Agents and Brokers) Act 1984 (Cth) (as amended)

INSURANCE INTERMEDIARIES OTHER THAN BROKERS TO OPERATE UNDER WRITTEN AGREEMENTS

(1) An insurance intermediary (other than an insurance broker) shall not arrange, or hold the intermediary out as entitled to arrange, a *contract of insurance* as agent for an insurer unless an agreement in writing between the intermediary and the insurer authorizes the intermediary to arrange:

(a) that contract;

(b) any contracts of insurance; or

(c) a class of contracts of insurance in which that contract is included,

as agent for that insurer.

(2) An insurer shall not cause or permit an insurance intermediary (other than an insurance broker) to arrange, or hold the intermediary out as entitled to arrange, a contract of insurance as agent for that insurer unless an agreement in writing between the insurer and the intermediary authorizes the intermediary to arrange:

(a) that contract;

(b) any contracts of insurance; or

(c) a class of contracts of insurance in which that contract is included,

as agent for that insurer.

(2A) An agreement referred to in this section must specify whether an insurance intermediary can appoint a person as the intermediary's agent for the purposes of the agreement.

(3) Subsections (1) and (2) do not apply in relation to any act or thing done by an employee of an insurer in the course of performing his or her duties as such an employee.

(4) Where an insurance intermediary to whom subsection (1) applies proposes, or holds the intermediary out as entitled, to arrange, or has arranged, a *contract of insurance* as agent of an insurer. ASIC, or the intending insured or the insured, may request the intermediary to give ASIC, the proposed insured or the insured a copy of the agreement authorizing the intermediary to arrange that contract, and, if such a request is made, the intermediary shall comply with the request within seven days after the day on which the request is received by the intermediary.

(5) ASIC may request an insurer to give ASIC a copy of the agreement referred to in subsection (2) that is in force between the insurer and an

insurance intermediary referred to in the request, and, if such a request is made, the insurer shall comply with the request within seven days after the day on which the request is received by the insurer.

(6) The validity of a contract of insurance is not affected by a contravention of this section.

LIABILITY OF INSURER FOR AGENTS AND EMPLOYEES

11 (1) This section applies to any conduct of an employee or agent of an insurer:

(a) on which a person in the circumstances of the insured or intending insured could reasonably be expected to rely; and

(b) on which the insured or intending insured in fact relied in good faith.

(1A) An insurer is responsible, as between the insurer and the insured or intending insured, for the conduct of an employee of the insurer in relation to any matter relating to insurance, whether or not the employee acted within the scope of his or her employment.

(1B) If a person is the agent of one insurer only, the insurer is responsible, as between the insurer and the insured or intending insured, for the conduct of the agent in relation to any matter relating to insurance, whether or not the agent acted within the scope of the authority granted by the insurer.

(1C) If:

(a) a person who is the agent of more than one insurer is the agent of one insurer only in respect of a particular class of insurance business; and

(b) the person engages in the conduct in relation to any matter relating to that class of insurance business; the insurer who granted the agency agreement in respect of that class of insurance business is responsible for the conduct, as between the insurer and the insured or intending insured, whether or not the agent has acted within the scope of the authority granted by the insurer.

(1D) If:

(a) a person is the agent of more than one insurer in respect of a particular class of insurance business; and

(b) the person engages in the conduct in relation to any matter relating to that class of insurance; the insurers are jointly and severally responsible for the conduct, as between themselves and the insured or intending insured, if the agent has acted beyond the scope of the authority granted by any of the insurers.

(1E) If:

(a) a person is the agent of more than one insurer in respect of a particular class of insurance business; and

(b) the person engages in the conduct in relation to a matter relating to that class; and

(c) the person, in so engaging, has acted within the scope of the authority granted by one only of those insurers; that insurer is responsible for the conduct, as between the insurer referred to in paragraph (c) and the insured or intending insured.

(1F)If:

(a) a person is the agent of more than one insurer in respect of a particular class of insurance business; and

(b) the person engages in the conduct in relation to a matter relating to that class; and

(c) the person, in so engaging, has acted within the scope of the authority granted by some only of those insurers; the insurers referred to in paragraph (c) are jointly and severally responsible for the conduct, as between themselves and the insured or intending insured.

(1G)If:

(a) a person is the agent of more than one insurer; and

(b) the person engages in the conduct in relation to any matter relating to a class of insurance business in which the person is not the agent of any of those insurers; the insurers are jointly and severally liable for the conduct, as between themselves and the insured or intending insured, despite the fact that the agent acted outside the scope of the authority granted by any of the insurers.

(1H)If:

(a) a person (the 'principal agent') is the agent of an insurer; and

(b) the principal agent appoints a second person (the 'sub-agent') to act as agent of the principal agent; then, for the purpose of determining the ultimate responsibility of the insurer under this section, the actions of the sub-agent are to be taken to be the actions of the principal agent:

(c) whether the agency agreement entered into between the principal agent and the insurer permitted or forbade the principal agent to appoint the sub-agent; and

(d) whether or not the sub-agent acted within the scope of his or her authority.

(1J) If:

(a) a person is the agent of at least one insurer in respect of life insurance business; and

(b) the person is the agent of at least one other insurer in respect of another class of insurance business ('general insurance business'); the provisions of this section do not operate:

(c) if the person engages in the conduct in relation to life insurance business so as to make any insurer referred to in paragraph (b) responsible for the conduct; and

(d) if the person engages in general insurance business so as to make any insurer referred to in paragraph (a) responsible for the conduct.

(2) The responsibility of an insurer under sub-ss (1A), (1B), (1C), (1D), (1E), (1F), (1G) or (1H) extends so as to make the insurer liable to an insured or intending insured in respect of any loss or damage suffered by the insured or intending insured as a result of the conduct of the agent or employee.

(3) Subsections (1A), (1B), (1C), (1D), (1E), (1F), (1G), (1H) and (1J) and (2) do not affect any liability of an agent or employee of an insurer to an insured or intending insured.

(4) An agreement, in so far as it purports to alter or restrict the operation of subsections ((1A), (1B), (1C), (1D), (1E), (1F), (1G), (1H), (1J) or (2), is void.

(5) An insurer shall not make, or offer to make, an agreement that is, or would be, void by reason of the operation of subsection (4).

Penalty ...:

CERTAIN INSURANCE INTERMEDIARIES TO BE AGENTS OF INSURERS

12 (1) Subject to this section, an insurance intermediary shall be deemed, in relation to any matter relating to insurance and as between an insured or intending insured and an insurer, to be the agent of the insurer and not of the insured or intending insured.

(2) Subsection (1) does not apply to a general insurance broker in relation to any matter relating to general insurance business.

(3) Subsection (1) does not apply to a life insurance broker in relation to any matter relating to life insurance business.

(4) Subsection (1) does not affect any liability to which, if that subsection had not been enacted, an insurer would have been subject in respect of the conduct of an insurance intermediary.

REPRESENTATIONS, ETC, BY INTERMEDIARIES

13 (1) A person to whom this section applies shall not wilfully and with intent to deceive make a false statement, being a statement that the person making the statement intends to be acted upon:

(a) as to any amount that would be payable in respect of a proposed contract of insurance; or

(b) as to the effect of any of the provisions of a contract of insurance or of a proposed contract of insurance.

(2) A person to whom this section applies shall not wilfully and with intent to deceive, in relation to a proposed contract of insurance:

(a) write on a form, being a form that is given or sent to the insurer, matter that is material to the contract and is false or misleading in a material particular;

(b) omit to disclose to the insurer matter that is material to the proposed contract;

(c) advise or induce the intending insured to write on a form, being a form that is given or sent to the insurer, matter that is false or misleading in a material particular; or

(d) advise or induce the intending insured to omit to disclose to the insurer matter that is material to the proposed contract.

(3) A person to whom this section applies shall not wilfully and with intent to deceive, in relation to a claim under a contract of insurance:

(a) fill up, in whole or in part, a form, being a form that is given or sent to the insurer, in such a way that the form is false or misleading in a material particular;

(b) omit to disclose to the insurer matter that is material to the claim;

(c) induce the insured to fill up, in whole or part, a form, being a form that is given or sent to the insurer, in such a way that the form is false or misleading in a material particular; or

(d) advise or induce the insured to omit to disclose to the insurer matter that is material to the claim.

(4) An act done in contravention of subsections (1) or (2) constitutes an offence against the sub-section concerned notwithstanding that a contract of insurance does not come into being.

(5) The persons to whom this section applies are:

(a) insurance intermediaries; and

(b) agents and employees of insurance intermediaries and of insurers.

Penalty ...:

EFFECT OF PAYMENTS TO INTERMEDIARIES

14 (1) Where a contract of insurance is arranged or effected by an insurance intermediary, payment to the insurance intermediary of moneys payable by the insured to the insurer under or in relation to the contract, whether in respect of a premium or otherwise, is a discharge, as between the insured and the insurer, of the liability of the insured to the insurer in respect of those moneys.

(2) Payment to an insurance intermediary by or on behalf of an intending insured of moneys in respect of a contract of insurance to be arranged or effected by the intermediary, whether the payment is in respect of a premium or otherwise, is a discharge, as between the insured and the insurer, of any liability of the insured under or in respect of the contract, to the extent of the amount of the payment.

(3) Payment by an insurer to an insurance intermediary of moneys payable to an insured, whether in respect of a claim, return of premiums or otherwise, under or in relation to a contract of insurance, does not discharge any liability of the insurer to the insured in respect of those moneys.

(4) An agreement, in so far as it purports to alter or restrict the operation of subsections (1), (2) or (3), is void.

(5) Subsection (4) does not render void an agreement between an insurance intermediary and an insured in so far as the agreement allows the insurance intermediary to set off against moneys payable to the insured moneys payable by the insured to the insurance intermediary in respect of premiums.

LIABILITY IN RELATION TO BINDERS

15 Where a contract of insurance is entered into, or a claim under a contract of insurance is dealt with or settled, by an insurance intermediary who acted under a binder in relation to the contract or claim, the intermediary shall, with respect to the contract or claim, and with respect to all matters relating to the contract or claim, be deemed to be the agent of the insurer and not of the insured for all purposes, including the operation of section 11, and, if the insured in fact relied in good faith on the conduct of the insurance intermediary, shall be so deemed notwithstanding that the intermediary did not act within the scope of his authority under the binder.

DISCLOSURE BY PERSONS ACTING UNDER BINDERS IN RESPECT OF INSURANCE CONTRACTS

16 (1) An insurance intermediary who intends to act under a binder in effecting a contract of insurance on behalf of his principal shall:

(a) subject to paragraph (b), give notice to the intending insured, before he enters into the contract, that, in effecting the contract, he will be acting under an authority given to him by the insurer to effect the contract and that he will be effecting the contract as agent of the insurer and not of the intending insured; or

(b) if it is not practicable for him to comply with paragraph (a), give notice to the insured, as soon as is reasonably practicable after he has effected the contract, that, in effecting the contract, he acted under an authority given to him by the insurer to effect the contract and that he effected the contract as agent of the insurer and not of the insured.

Penalty ...:

DISCLOSURE BY PERSONS ACTING UNDER BINDERS IN RESPECT OF CLAIMS

17 (1) An insurance intermediary who intends to act under a binder in dealing with or settling a claim under a contract of insurance shall not deal with or settle the claim on behalf of his principal unless he has first informed the insured that, in dealing with or settling the claim, he will be acting under an authority given to him by the insurer to deal with or settle the claim and that he will be dealing with or settling the claim as agent of the insurer and not of the insured.

Penalty ...:

(2) A settlement of a claim made in contravention of subsection (1) is voidable at the option of the insured, subject to:

(a) the rights of parties acquired without notice and for good or valuable consideration; and

(b) compliance with the principles of common law and of equity with respect to the avoidance of contracts.

BROKERS TO GIVE CERTAIN INFORMATION

32 (1) Where an insurance broker arranges or effects a contract of insurance:

(a) he shall, as soon as it is reasonably practicable for him to do so, give to the insured particulars in writing of any fees or other amounts charged by the insurance broker in respect of his services in connection with the contract; and

(b) if requested to do so by the insured, he shall, as soon as it is reasonably practicable for him to do so, give to the insured particulars of any commission or other remuneration or benefit received by him from the insurer in respect of his services in arranging or effecting the contract ...

(5) An insurance broker shall, as soon as is reasonably practicable after he has arranged or effected a contract of insurance (including a contract of insurance effected by him under a binder), inform the insured of the name of the insurer and of a place of business of the insurer.

(6) It is a sufficient compliance with so much of subsection (5) as requires the insurance broker to inform the insured of the name of the insurer if, in relation to a contract of insurance with Lloyd's underwriters, or with Lloyd's underwriters and others, the insurance broker informs the insured that the contract was arranged or effected with 'Lloyd's', or with 'Lloyd's' and other specified insurers, as the case may be ...

[Now read Appendix 6.27.]

APPENDIX 6.4

McNeil v Law Union and Rock Insurance Co Ltd (1925) 23 Ll L Rep 314

Branson J: Where an agent is asking for commission upon a certain transaction, he has got to show that he was an efficient cause of the transaction coming about. It is not enough to show that he was the introducer of the two parties because that is merely a *causa sine qua non* and may not be the efficient cause.

Now, in the present case, it is said on behalf of the plaintiff that he was the efficient cause of the bringing about of this renewal. There is no doubt that he did a good deal of work, and, among other things, he was pointing out to the Expanded Metal Co the reason why the defendants were in difficulties about further reducing their premiums. That was an argument which they thought was sufficiently material to hand over to the plaintiff to pass on to the Expanded Metal Co. He did pass it on and he went and saw the company about it; and his efforts, in my view of the facts, were an efficient cause in the ultimate renewal of this policy. They were not the only cause, but they were an efficient cause. I do not think it is right to say, as Mr Norman Birkett says, that the plaintiff's efforts entirely failed, and that the policy was only renewed by reason of a completely fresh basis having been arrived at between the parties. My reason for declining to follow that view of the facts is the evidence which has been given, from which I think that it emerges beyond any doubt whatever that this question of the allowance of a premium to Mr Linnett was a mere – I do not want to use a word which would indicate that I think there was anything underhand in it – pretence in order to enable the company to get its insurance for a smaller sum than they otherwise would have done. It may be that the defendants' reason for doing the business in this way was that, being a tariff company with fixed rates, they had some hesitation in reducing their rates; but the fact remains, and nobody was under any illusion about it, the result and the intended result of this arrangement was that the Expanded Metal Co should get their cover for £25 odd, whatever the amount of the commission was, less than they would otherwise have had to pay. It is not a case of principals who have been introduced by an agent and brought to a certain point in negotiations setting out for themselves on a new tack altogether.

In my view the case is exactly on all fours with the one that I put to Mr Norman Birkett in argument, namely, the case of a man who employs an agent to go and try to sell something for him. The agent finds a purchaser but the purchaser will not pay the price which the vendor requires; he is willing to pay something a little bit less, but the price that he is asked he will not pay. The agent then goes to the vendor and tells him that. The vendor goes in turn to the person introduced by the agent and they agree that the sale shall take place at the less figure. The agent is entitled to his commission. The result is, in my view, that the plaintiff is entitled to succeed. The actual amount I understand has been agreed.

APPENDIX 6.5

Association of British Insurers, *General Insurance Business Code of Practice for All Intermediaries (Including Employees of Insurance Companies) Other than Registered Insurance Brokers,* 1989, London: ABI

Note: The expectation is that this Code will be withdrawn at some date when the GISC Codes are sufficiently widely applicable (Appendix 6.1).

INTRODUCED JANUARY 1989 (REPLACING EARLIER VERSIONS)

This code applies to general business as defined in the Insurance Companies Act 1982, but does not apply to reinsurance business. As an condition of membership of the Association of British Insurers, members undertake to enforce this code and to use their best endeavours to ensure that all those involved in selling their policies observe its provisions.

It shall be an overriding obligation of an intermediary at all times to conduct business with the utmost good faith and integrity.

In the case of complaints from policyholders (either direct or indirect, for example, through a trading standards officer or citizens advice bureau) the insurance company concerned shall require an intermediary to co-operate so that the facts can be established. An intermediary shall inform the policyholder complaining that he can take his problem direct to the insurance company concerned.

PART I

This part applies to the selling and servicing of general business insurance policies, but not where the intermediary is acting solely as an introducer.

A General sales principles

1 The intermediary shall:

(i) where appropriate make a prior appointment to call. Unsolicited or unarranged calls shall be made at an hour likely to be suitable to the prospective policyholder;

(ii) when he makes contact with the prospective policyholder, identify himself and explain as soon as possible that the arrangements he wishes to discuss could include insurance. He shall make it known that he is:

(a) an employee of an insurance company, for whose conduct the company accepts responsibility;

(b) an agent of one or a number of companies (as the case may be) for whose conduct the company/companies accept responsibility; or

(c) an independent intermediary seeking to act on behalf of the prospective policyholder, for whose conduct the company/companies do not accept responsibility:

(iii) ensure as far as possible that the policy proposed is suitable to the needs and resources of the prospective policyholder;

(iv) give advice only on those insurance matters in which he is knowledgeable and seek or recommend other specialist advice when necessary; and

(v) treat all information supplied by the prospective policyholder as completely confidential to himself and to the company or companies to which the business is being offered.

2 The intermediary shall not:

(i) inform the prospective policyholder that his name has been given by another person unless he is prepared to disclose that person's name if requested to do so by the prospective policyholder and has that person's consent to make that disclosure;

(ii) make inaccurate or unfair criticisms of any insurer; or

(iii) make comparisons with other types of policies unless he makes clear the differing characteristics of each policy.

B Explanation of the contract

The intermediary shall:

(i) identify the insurance company;

(ii) explain all the essential provisions of the cover afforded by the policy, or policies, which he is recommending so as to ensure as far as possible that the prospective policyholder understands what he is buying;

(iii) draw attention to any restrictions and exclusions applying to the policy;

(iv) if necessary, obtain from the insurance company specialist advice in relation to items (ii) and (iii) above;

(v) not impose any charge in addition to the premium required by the insurance company without disclosing the amount and purpose of such charge; and

(vi) if he is an independent intermediary, disclose his commission on request.

C Disclosure of underwriting information

The intermediary shall, in obtaining the completion of the proposal form or any other material:

(i) avoid influencing the prospective policyholder and make it clear that all the answers or statements are the latter's own responsibility;

(ii) ensure that the consequences of non-disclosure and inaccuracies are pointed out to the prospective policyholder by drawing his attention to the relevant statement in the proposal form and by explaining them himself to the prospective policyholder.

D Accounts and financial aspects

The intermediary shall, if authorised to collect monies in accordance with the terms of his agency appointment:

(i) keep a proper account of all financial transactions with a prospective policyholder which involve the transmission of money in respect of insurance;

(ii) acknowledge receipt (which, unless the intermediary has been otherwise authorised by the insurance company, shall be on his own behalf) of all money received in connection with an insurance policy and shall distinguish the premium from any other payment included in the money; and

(iii) remit any such monies so collected in strict conformity with his agency appointment.

E Documentation

The intermediary shall not withhold from the policyholder any written evidence or documentation relating to the contract of insurance.

F Existing policyholders

The intermediary shall abide by the principles set out in this code to the extent that they are relevant to his dealings with existing policyholders.

G Claims

If the policyholder advises the intermediary of an incident which might give rise to a claim, the intermediary shall inform the company without delay, and in any event within three working days, and thereafter give prompt advice to the policyholder of the company's requirements concerning the claim, including the provision as soon as possible of information required to establish the nature and extent of the loss. Information received from the policyholder shall be passed to the company without delay.

H Professional indemnity cover for independent intermediaries

The intermediary shall obtain, and maintain in force, professional indemnity insurance in accordance with the requirements of the Association of British Insurers as set out in the Annex, which may be updated from time to time.

I Letters of appointment

This code of practice shall be incorporated verbatim or by reference in all letters of appointment of non-registered intermediaries and no policy of the company shall be sold by such intermediaries except within the terms of such a letter of appointment.

ANNEX

Code of practice for the selling of general insurance

Professional indemnity cover required for non-registered independent intermediaries

As from 1 January 1989 (new agents) and by 1 July 1989 (existing agents) all non-registered independent intermediaries must take out and maintain in force professional indemnity cover in accordance with the requirements set out below.

The insurance may be taken out with any authorised UK or EEC insurer who has agreed to:

(a) issue cover in accordance with the requirements set out below;

(b) provide the intermediary with an annual certificate as evidence that the cover meets the ABI requirements, this certificate to contain the name and address including postcode of the intermediary, the policy number, the period of the policy, the limit of indemnity, the self insured excess and the name of the insurer;

(c) send a duplicate certificate to ABI at the time the certificate is issued to the intermediary;

(d) inform ABI, by means of monthly lists, of any cases of non-renewal, cancellation of the cover mid-term or of the cover becoming inadequate.

The requirements are as follows:

A *Limits of indemnity*

The policy shall at inception and at each renewal date, which shall not be more than 12 months from inception or the last renewal date, provide a *minimum limit* of indemnity of either:

(a) a sum equal to three times the annual general business commission of the business for the last accounting period ending prior to inception or renewal of the policy, or a sum of £250,000, whichever sum is the greater.

In no case shall the minimum limit of indemnity be required to exceed £5 m, and a minimum sum of £250,000 shall apply at all times to each and every claim or series of claims arising out of the same occurrence; or

(b) a sum equal to three times the annual general business commission of the business for the last accounting period ending prior to inception or renewal of the policy, or a sum of £500,000 whichever sum shall be the greater. In no case shall the minimum limit of indemnity be required to exceed £5 m.

B *Maximum self insured excess*

The maximum self insured excess permitted in normal circumstances shall be 1% of the minimum limit of indemnity required by para A(a) or A(b) above as the case may be. Subject to the agreement of the professional indemnity insurer, the self insured excess may be increased to a maximum of 2% of such minimum limit of indemnity.

C *Scope of policy cover*

The policy shall indemnify the insured:

(a) against losses arising from claims made against the insured:

(i) for breach of duty in connection with the business by reason of any negligent act, error or omission; and

(ii) in respect of libel or slander or in Scotland defamation, committed in the conduct of the business by the insured, any employee or former employee of the insured, and where the business is or was carried on in partnership any partner or former partner of the insured; and

(iii) by reason of any dishonest or fraudulent act or omission committed or made in the conduct of the business by any employee (other than a director of a body corporate) or former employee (other than a director of a body corporate) of the insured; and

(b) against claims arising in connection with the business in respect of:
   (i) any loss of money or other property whatsoever belonging to the insured or for which the insured is legally liable to consequence of any dishonest or fraudulent act or omission of any employee (other than a director of a body corporate) or former employee (other than a director of a body corporate) of the insured; and
   (ii) legal liability incurred by reason of loss of documents and costs and expenses incurred in replacing or restoring such documents.

D General business only

The above requirements relate only to the intermediary's general insurance business.

APPENDIX 6.6

Harvest Trucking Co Ltd v PB Davis Insurance Service [1991] 2 Lloyd's Rep 638

Diamond J: In this action, the plaintiffs, Harvest Trucking Co Ltd, a company which carried on business as haulage contractors, make a claim for damages against their insurance intermediary for professional negligence.

THE ISSUES

The issues raised in the action fall into three main heads. First, what duty, whether in contract or in tort, did the defendant owe the plaintiffs in and about the effecting of the goods in transit liability insurance? Second, has there been a breach of that duty? Third, if so, what is the amount of the plaintiffs' loss?

The plaintiffs in para 1(2) of their statement of claim plead that:

> The defendant acted as broker on behalf of the plaintiffs in obtaining insurance cover including insurance cover against loss of goods and liability which the plaintiffs as bailees might incur to the owners of fashion garments while the same were in the plaintiffs' possession.

I should add that this allegation is not in dispute, save, of course, that the defendant would say that he acted as an insurance intermediary and not as a broker.

In para 2 of the statement of claim, the plaintiffs allege that the defendant owed a duty of car in the following terms:

(1) To use all reasonable skill and care to ensure that the plaintiffs were properly covered by goods in transit insurance obtained on their behalf.

(2) To use all reasonable skill and care to obtain goods in transit insurance which adequately met the plaintiffs' requirements and in particular provided cover for the actual circumstances in which the plaintiffs' vehicles were operated.

(3) To inform the plaintiffs of any onerous and/or unusual term in the goods in transit insurance by means of referring specifically to the same and explaining its full import and requirements.

(4) To understand the full terms of the goods in transit insurance and to alert the plaintiffs to any unusual and/or specific requirements or condition precedent to indemnity therein.

WHAT DUTY, WHETHER IN CONTRACT OR TORT,
DID THE DEFENDANT OWE TO THE PLAINTIFF?

A broker or other insurance intermediary is employed to act as a middle man between the person employing him – normally the person requiring insurance – on the one hand, and the proposed insurer or insurers on the other. The broker or other intermediary is normally the agent of the assured. This arises because he is normally employed by the client to obtain insurance. That is not to say that he may not, in some instances, act as agent for the insurer. In the present case, however, it is common ground that the ordinary situation applies, that Mr Davis acted as agent for the plaintiffs.

The ordinary function of the insurance broker or other intermediary is to receive instructions from his principal as to the nature of the risk or risks and the rate or rates of premium at which he wishes to insure, to communicate the material facts to the potential insurers and to obtain insurance for his principal in accordance with his principals' instructions and on the best terms available. The liability of an insurance agent to his employer for negligence is comparable to that of any agent. He is bound to exercise reasonable care in the duties which he has undertaken. In no case does the law require an extraordinary degree of skill on the part of the agent, but only such a reasonable and ordinary degree as a person of average capacity and ordinary ability in his situation and profession might fairly be expected to exert.

The precise extent of the insurance intermediary's duties must depend in the last resort on the circumstances of the particular case, including the particular instructions which he has received from his client. In many cases, those duties will include advising his client on the type of insurance best suited to his requirements and, subject to his client's instructions, exercising reasonable care to obtain insurance which will best meet those requirements. It is normally not an ordinary part of the broker's or intermediary's duty to construe or interpret the policy to his client, but this again is not of course a universal rule. If a broker or intermediary is asked to explain the terms of a policy to his client and does so, then he must exercise due care in giving an accurate explanation. Again if the only insurance which the intermediary is able to obtain contains unusual, limiting or exempting provisions which, if they are not brought to the notice of the assured, may result in the policy not conforming to the client's reasonable and known requirements, the duty falling on the agent, namely, to exercise reasonable care in the duties which he has undertaken, may in those circumstances entail that the intermediary should bring the existence of the limiting or exempting provisions to the express notice of the client, discuss the nature of the problem with him and take reasonable steps either to obtain alternative insurance, if any is available, or alternatively to advise the clients to the best way of acting so that his business procedures conform to any requirements laid down by the policy.

All this stems from the duty falling upon any agent to act with reasonable care in the duties which he had been engaged to perform. I should mention that, in a recent case, it was held that an insurance broker's duties include the following (and this was put as a general proposition): (1) he must ascertain his client's needs by instruction or otherwise; (2) he must use reasonable skill and care to procure the cover which his client has asked for either expressly or by necessary implication; (3) if he cannot obtain what is required, he must report in what respects he has failed and seek his client's alternative instructions. (See the *Superhulls Cover* case [1990] 2 Lloyd's Rep 431 ...)

[The judge then quoted paragraphs from the Association of British Insurers' Code of Practice.]

I have to remember that this code has no statutory force and it does not, therefore, assist me greatly in the task which I have to perform in assessing whether there has been any negligence on the part of Mr Davis. This has to be assessed purely on the basis of the principles of law to which I have already referred.

At the same time, I found the reference to the code not unhelpful for two reasons. First, because it was part of the context in which an intermediary such as Mr Davis had to operate. Second, because in deciding whether a professional man has been negligent, a court has to be careful not to adopt too high or perfectionist a standard, and to some extent it may be helpful to refer to the code to ensure that the standard of care which the court is otherwise minded to apply is not considered unrealistic in the industry.

It is not unfair to infer that if he applied his mind to the security requirement, given his knowledge of the plaintiffs' business, Mr Davis ought to have appreciated the significance of a requirement that at all times there was to be no cover for the theft of property from the larger vehicle unless it was individually attended. The stringency of the security requirement must have alerted a reasonably competent and experienced intermediary to the necessity of ensuring that this clause confirmed with his client's requirements and that its terms could be fulfilled in practice. Mr Davis, by this stage, had extensive experience of the plaintiffs' mode of operation and indeed had visited their premises.

In my judgment, it does not amount to the adoption of too high a standard of care to conclude that on receipt of Mr Turley's renewal terms, including the application of VSR 7 to the larger vehicle, there was a duty on Mr Davis either to obtain the cover which he had been asked to obtain, which would of course not have included this requirement, or else to exercise reasonable care to bring the insurers' terms to the express notice of his clients, to ascertain in some detail whether the clause complied with their insurance requirements and, depending on the practicalities at the time, to obtain their further instructions. In the course of doing this and in order to obtain his clients informed consent to any further course of action, it may well have been necessary for Mr Davis to explain the effect of the clause, particularly in relation to lorries left unattended at night, since the regime for such lorries had, to Mr Davis's own knowledge, been the subject of detailed consideration during the renewal negotiations the previous year in May to July 1984.

[The judge then addressed the question of whether there had been a breach of duty by Mr Davis.]

In my judgment, it was clearly not a sufficient performance on Mr Davis's duty as intermediary merely to pass the endorsement and letter dated 20 June 1985 and the endorsement of 14 November 1985 to the client. There are several reasons for this. First, the insurance documents would take some time to prepare and a loss might occur before they were received.

Secondly, however, and much more importantly, the individually attended clause imposed quite a different and far more onerous regime on the assured in relation to the larger vehicles than the security arrangements for the previous year, which had been negotiated in some detail. There was an obvious risk that any assured would file away the insurance documents without carefully reading them, perhaps assuming that they would have been checked on his behalf by the intermediary.

Thirdly, although the documents clearly specified that there would be a different regime for the two large vehicles as compared with the three others, it would not necessarily strike the eye of the layman precisely what was the meaning of the limitation that no claim for theft would be admitted from any vehicle which was not individually attended. Nor would it have necessarily struck the eye of the layman that the assured's practice of leaving a loaded lorry inside the locked and alarmed warehouse overnight was no longer adequate to comply with the policy requirements.

I have, therefore, come to the clear conclusion for these and other reasons that Mr Davis failed in his duty to draw his client's attention to the existence or significance of the insurers' security requirement for the larger vehicle in May 1985. If he did not do so for this vehicle, it must follow that he did not do so in relation to the second large vehicle which was later added to the policy and on which the goods were loaded at the time of the loss.

It must follow from this, and I so find, that Mr Davis committed a breach of his duty on receipt of Mr Turley's renewal terms either to obtain the cover which his clients had requested him to obtain or else to exercise reasonable care to bring the insurers' terms to the express notice of his clients and to obtain their further instructions. I find that his failure to do either of these things and his further failure to obtain his clients' informed consent to any further course of action amounted to negligence on his part.

WHAT LOSS HAS BEEN SUFFERED BY THE PLAINTIFFS?

In my judgment, it is clearly established on a balance of probabilities that if Mr Davis had performed his duty in May 1985 the plaintiffs would, at worst, have renewed the policy on the terms which they were able to negotiate with the National Transit after the loss occurred in May 1986. These terms included a separate limit of liability for each vehicle including the larger ones of £50,000, no warranty that more valuable loads would not be carried, no condition of average and, of course, no term corresponding to VSR 7.

APPENDIX 6.7

Bollom v Byas Mosley [1999] Lloyd's Rep PN 598

Moore-Bick J:

Were the brokers in breach of duty?

When the insurers took a stand on their right to repudiate liability for the damage caused by the fire they did so on the grounds that Bollom were in breach of one or other or both of the Alarm and Protections clauses quoted earlier and it was on that basis that Bollom, on the advice of leading counsel accepted the sum of £5m in settlement of their claim under the policy. In these circumstances Bollom's primary complaint against Byas Mosley is that they failed to take reasonable steps to draw their attention to the presence in the policy of those clauses or to ensure that they understood their meaning and the effect, especially in relation to the yard alarm. An insurance broker owes a duty to his client to exercise reasonable skill and care in and about effecting insurance on his behalf. Mr Seymour, QC relied on the cases of *Youell v Bland Welch and Co Ltd (The 'Superhulls Cover')* Case (No 2) [19901 2 Lloyd's Rep 431; *Harvest Trucking Co Ltd v PB Davis* [1991] 2 Lloyd's Rep 638; and *Paul Tudor Jones II v Crowley Colosso Ltd* [1996] 2 Lloyd's Rep 619, but it is unnecessary for me to refer to them in any detail because it was common ground that in a case such as the present the broker's duty extends to taking reasonable steps to ensure that the client is aware of the nature and terms of the insurance and, in particular, to drawing to his attention (and if necessary explaining) any terms the breach of which might result in his being uninsured ...

Mr Hughes, QC on behalf of Byas Mosley accepted at the outset that his clients were in breach of duty in failing to take adequate steps to draw Bollom's attention to the terms and effect of the two Alarm and Protections clauses which formed part of the new LIRMA policy. In my judgment he was right to do so.

...

Would Bollom have set the yard alarm on 3 August?

It is not enough, of course, for Bollom simply to establish a breach of duty on the part of Byas Mosley; they must also show that that breach of duty caused their loss. The critical question in the present case is whether, if the brokers had taken proper steps to alert them to the significance of the Alarm and Protections clauses in the policy, Bollom would have set the yard alarm on 3 August. Mr Seymour suggested that it should be for the defendants in a case such as this to show that the yard alarm would not have been set, basing himself on the well known *dictum* of Diplock LJ in *Allen v Sir Alfred McAlpine and Sons Ltd* [1968] 2 QB 229 at pp 256–57 and the old authority of *Armory v Delamirie* (1721) I Stra 505, but although that may reflect a common sense approach to the evidence, it does not in my view reflect the legal burden on the plaintiff to prove the causative link between the defendant's breach of duty and his loss: see *Wilsher v Essex AHA* [1988] 1 AC 1074. However, in the light of the evidence this is not in my view an issue in relation to which the burden of proof has any significant part to play. I have little doubt that if Bollom had been aware that a failure to put all their alarms into operation would entitle their insurers to repudiate liability for any loss or damage to property at the Beckenham site, steps would have been taken to ensure that the yard alarm was set. The importance of setting the main intruder alarm to the buildings within the site (the 'central alarm') was well understood and although there were no formal written instructions covering the setting of that alarm, the evidence indicates that it was established practice to set it whenever the premises were closed. Indeed, the contrary was not suggested. At the time of the change in insurers Bollom already had it in mind to consolidate and modernise the central alarm system and following the survey by LUTS the insurers made it a requirement of cover that the specification of the revised system should be submitted to them for approval. The importance of that system was therefore clearly brought to Bollom's attention in the spring of 1994. The yard alarm had been treated quite differently, however. Although it had been installed in 1985 neither General Accident nor AXA Re had shown any interest in it and over the years prior to July 1996 it had ceased to function efficiently. Neither insurer required the provision of a perimeter alarm. Rightly or wrongly Bollom thought that the yard alarm was of no interest to insurers one way or the other and it is hardly surprising, therefore, that they did not attach the same degree of importance to setting it. In my view the fact that the decision not to set the yard alarm over the weekend of 3–4 August could be, and was, taken by someone of Mr Brasier's level of seniority in the company is more an indication of the lack of importance which was attached to that alarm than of any general indifference on the part of Bollom to the need to comply with the requirements of the policy. The fact that there had been five false alarms during the previous 10 days and that these had given rise to several complaints from local residents, at least one of which was of quite an aggressive nature, clearly weighed heavily with him. Nonetheless, if Bollom had been aware of the potential consequences of failing to set the yard alarm I have little doubt that the importance of doing so would have been communicated to Mr Brasier. In those circumstances I am satisfied that he would not have taken it upon himself not to set it. On the contrary, I am satisfied that he would have set the alarm in the usual way despite all the problems. In these circumstances, although it is no doubt true that Mr Hemphill and Mr Bollom expected the alarm to be set, it is no answer to say that the failure to set the alarm resulted from an unauthorised act on the part of Mr Brasier, it was a direct consequence of the brokers' breach of duty.

...

A second breach of duty?

This makes it necessary for me to consider whether there was a second and quite separate breach of duty on the part of Byas Mosley which resulted in Bollom's being under-insured in relation to both buildings and plant and machinery.

There was no dispute that one of the duties of an insurance broker is to take reasonable steps to ensure that his client understands the basis on which the insurance is written and the consequences of under-insurance. That is perhaps particularly important in a case where property insurance is written on a reinstatement basis because the historical cost of buildings, plant and machinery will often fall well below the cost of reinstatement or replacement. Brokers are not professional valuers and no one suggests that they should take it upon themselves to advise their clients what value should be placed on any particular item of property. They should, however, take reasonable steps to ensure that the client understands that under a policy of that kind the insurers will pay for reinstatement or replacement of the property insured provided the value for which it is insured represents the full cost of reinstatement or replacement. Similarly, it was not disputed that when several items of property are covered under the same policy the broker should take reasonable steps to ensure that the client is aware of the existence and effect of any average clause ...

...

As time passed Bollom's continued failure to request a general increase in the sums insured ought to have provoked a more explicit enquiry from Mr Winfield. The fact that there had been a general economic recession during the previous few years did not provide sufficient grounds for assuming that by 1996 the cost of rebuilding factories, offices and warehouses, and particularly the cost of replacing manufacturing plant and machinery, had not risen significantly since 1990. Although it was not his responsibility to advise Bollom on the extent to which costs had changed, it was part of his responsibility to draw their attention to the need to investigate the position, and if necessary take professional advice, if he had reason to think that they were unaware that they ran the risk of being under-insured. One particular matter which arose in connection with the renewal in 1996 ought to have altered [*sic*] Mr Winfield to the fact that Bollom' s senior management were confused about the basis on which the company's property was insured.

...

In my judgment by the end of February 1996 at the latest any grounds for believing that Mr Hemphill and Mr Bollom understood the nature of the policy, the effect of the average clauses and what that meant for the proper calculation of the sums insured had disappeared. Mr Winfield ought to have realised that there was at least a serious risk that neither of them properly appreciated that buildings, plant and machinery ought to be insured for their full replacement cost and that unbeknown to them there was, therefore, a risk that Bollom were significantly under-insured. In my judgment he should have drawn these things to their attention and had he done so I have no doubt that steps would have been taken to ensure that adequate cover was put in place without delay. I am satisfied, therefore, that insofar as Bollom's claim fell to be reduced as a result of under-insurance that was a consequence of a breach of duty on the part of Byas Mosley. In those circumstances the measure of Bollom's damages in the present case does not fall to be reduced as a result of that under-insurance ...

...

Contributory negligence

Mr Hughes submitted that Bollom were themselves negligent both in relation to the failure to set the yard alarm and in relation to the adequacy of the sums insured and that their negligence played an important part in causing the eventual loss. The essence of contributory negligence is that the plaintiff has failed in a duty imposed on him by law to take steps to protect himself from another's negligence. Mr Seymour submitted that the court must therefore first be satisfied that it is proper to impose such a duty on the plaintiff which will very much depend on the circumstances of the case: see the observations of Atkin LJ in *Ellerman Lines Ltd v H and G Grayson Ltd* [1919] 2 KB 514 at pp 535–36. When a person engages a professional man to provide specialist services the law will not ordinarily impose a duty on that person to take steps to protect himself against negligence on the part of someone who has himself undertaken to act with all reasonable skill and care. Negligence involves a failure to guard against a risk that is reasonably foreseeable and there cannot therefore be contributory negligence in a case of this kind unless the plaintiff ought reasonably to have foreseen that his adviser might fail to carry out his responsibilities ...

In my view, therefore, this is not a case in which Bollom were under a duty to guard against negligence on the part of their brokers. In any event, however, given the history of the yard alarm, I do not think that either of them could reasonably have been expected to regard it as having any bearing on the validity of the insurance unless Mr Winfield had specifically drawn their attention to it. Accordingly, even if they had read and understood that particular section of the document they would not have been negligent in failing to relate it to the yard alarm. It follows that I am unable to accept that they were in breach of any duty by failing to impress upon Mr Brasier the need to inform Byas Mosley of any alteration, modification or disconnection of that alarm.

As far as under-insurance is concerned, both Mr Hemphill and Mr Bollom remained ignorant of matters which it was essential for them to know if they were to make a proper assessment of the sums to be insured. The fact that they did remain ignorant was, as I have held, the fault of Byas Mosley. Mr Hughes submitted that there was a culpable failure on their part to heed the advice contained in the Schedules of Insurance that:

> ... it is vital that those sums insured that are subject to average represent the full value of the interest to be insured in accordance with the basis on which cover is arranged,

but that passage is rather opaque unless the reader understands clearly the basis of cover and the meaning of 'average'. This argument is tantamount to saying, contrary to my finding, that under-insurance was the result of a failure on the part of Mr Hemphill and Mr Bollom properly to review the sums insured rather than a failure of Mr Winfield to take proper steps to enable them to do so.

APPENDIX 6.8

Kettlewell v Refuge Assurance Co [1908] 1 KB 545, CA

Lord Alverstone CJ: We all think that the judgment appealed from is right but I am not sure that we are agreed as to our reasons. In this case the plaintiff, in February 1901, effected a policy with the defendants under circumstances to which no exception could be taken, and for rather more than 12 months she continued to pay the premiums. In April 1902, she was about to drop the policy, when a representation was made to her by one of the defendants' agents that if she went on paying for a certain time she would get a free policy, and a similar representation was made to her later by another of the defendants' agents. Those representations were untrue, and, relying upon them, the plaintiff was induced to continue payment of the premiums. Under those circumstances, she claims to be entitled to recover back the premiums paid since April 1902. Now, as a general rule, it is clear that where money is paid in reliance upon a fraudulent misrepresentation it can be recovered back. But it is said that that does not apply to policies of life insurance, because, inasmuch as the insurance company would not be allowed in an action on the policy to set up their own agents' wrong and allege that the policy was void, they must have been under a contingent liability to pay the sum assured during the whole time that the premiums were being paid and the policy was in existence, and that consequently, as they had been at risk during the whole of that time, the contract was no longer executory, and it was too late for the defrauded party to rescind. With that contention I cannot agree. In my opinion, it is not right to speak of a mere risk of that kind, which has not produced any benefit in fact to the assured, as being a part performance of the contract. I agree in the view that that is a state of things which arises in every case in which a contract is voidable, the one party being bound and the other not. I think this case is governed by the decision of the Court of Appeal in *British Workman's and General Assurance Co v Cunliffe* (1874) 9 Ch App 525 ... It is quite true that in that case the objection to the policy, namely, that the assured has no insurable interest, was one which made the policy void, and not merely voidable. But I think the principle of the judgment would equally apply to a case in which the fraudulent representation made the contract voidable only, because the assured would, in that case, be equally entitled to say that she would never have entered into the contract if she had known the truth. I am of opinion, therefore, that the plaintiff may recover back the premiums paid by her as money had and received to her use. I desire to add that the money can, in my judgment, be also recovered back as damages in an action of deceit, the measure of the damages in such an action being the amount of the premiums paid. It was contended, indeed, by Mr Manisty that an action of deceit would not lie under the circumstances of the case. In the first place, he said that the agent, in making the representation, was acting outside the scope of his authority. But there are a number of cases which shew that, if the agent is there to do the business for the benefit of the principal, the principal is responsible for representations made by the agent in the course of the business. Then it was said that the representation was not one as to an existing fact, but a mere promise as to what would be done *in futuro*. But it seems to me that it was a statement as to the course of the company's business, according to which the payment of five years' premiums was followed by a free policy. That is a statement of an existing practice, and, therefore, a representation as to a present existing fact. On both these grounds, I think the plaintiff is entitled to recover back the premiums paid.

APPENDIX 6.9

Re Hooley Hill Rubber and Chemical Co Ltd and Royal Insurance Co Ltd [1920] 1 KB 257

Bailhache J: The second question, which affects the Royal Insurance Company only, is whether the company are by reason of certain representations made by their manager estopped from denying that their policy covers the loss which happened. In order to ascertain whether there is an estoppel I have to consider the letters which passed between the assured and the company's manager ... Now, what meaning would those letters convey to an ordinary intelligent business man? I think they would convey the impression that such a loss as in fact happened was covered by the ordinary form of policy. It is true that the assured are referred to condition 3, but having regard to the earlier letters and to the fact that they were referred to that clause when asking about an incendiary bomb, I think an ordinary business man would understand the letters to mean that he was covered if a fire occurred which caused an explosion, but that he was not covered if the explosion was due to an incendiary bomb. If that is the meaning of the letters or is the sense in which they ought to be understood, does that create an estoppel? If the statement was a statement of an existing fact, independent of any question of construction of a written document which would be a question of law, or partly of law and partly of fact, I think there would be an estoppel. But in my judgment, though the matter does not seem to me to be free from doubt, the writer of the letters was putting a construction upon the ordinary form of his company's policy and he was telling the assured that in his opinion the policy did cover such an explosion as occurred in this case. If he had merely said that the ordinary form of policy did cover it, and had not referred to condition 3, I should have had even more doubt about the matter. But while expressing his opinion about it, and saying that as a matter of construction the assured were covered, he referred them to the very clause which, according to the construction placed upon it in *Stanley v Western Insurance Co* (1868) LR 3 Exch 71 ... does not cover the loss in question. I think the true position is that the writer was not stating a positive existing fact, but that he was giving his view as to the meaning of a policy which contained this particular clause. His view was a mistaken one, but the assured accepted it as accurate, and indeed if it were not for *Stanley*'s case ... I think there would be a good deal to be said in support of that view. I think that the arbitrator was right in holding that there was no estoppel. The award will therefore stand. I express no opinion as to whether the assured could successfully claim rectification of the policy.

Award upheld.

[The Court of Appeal dismissed the appeal, but without reference to the agency point.]

APPENDIX 6.10

Bawden v London, Edinburgh and Glasgow Assurance Co [1892] 2 QB 534, CA

Lord Esher MR: We have to apply the general law of principal and agent to the particular facts of this case. The question is, what was the authority of such an agent as Quin? His authority is to be gathered from what he did. He was an agent of the company. He was not like a man who goes to a company and says, I have obtained a proposal for an insurance; will you pay me commission for it? He was the agent of the company before he addressed Bawden. For what purpose was he agent? To negotiate the terms of a proposal for an insurance, and to induce the person who wished to insure to make the proposal. The agent could not make a contract of insurance. He was the agent of the company to obtain a proposal which the company would accept. He was not merely their agent to take the piece of paper containing the proposal to the company. The company could not alter the proposal; they must accept it or decline it. Quin, then, having authority to negotiate and settle the terms of a proposal, what happened? He went to a man who had only one eye, and persuaded him to make a proposal to the company, which the company might then either accept or reject. He negotiated and settled the terms of the proposal. He saw that the man had only one eye. The proposal must be construed as having been negotiated and settled by the agent with a one eyed man. In that sense the knowledge of the agent was the knowledge of the company. The policy was upon a printed form which contained general words applicable to more than one state of circumstances, and we have to apply those words to the particular circumstances of this case. When the policy says that permanent total disablement means 'the complete and irrecoverable loss of sight in both eyes', it must mean that the assured is to lose the sight of both eyes by an accident after the policy has been granted. The contract was entered into with a one eyed man, and in such a case the words must mean that he is to be rendered totally blind by the accident. That, indeed, would be the meaning in the case of a man who had two eyes. If the accident renders the man totally blind, he is to be paid £500 for permanent total disablement. Quin, being the agent of the company to negotiate and settle the terms of the proposal, did so with a one eyed man. The company accepted the proposal, knowing through their agent that it was made by a one eyed man, and they issued to him a policy which is binding upon them, as made with a one eyed man, that they would pay him £500 if he by accident totally lost his sight, that is, the sight of the only eye he had. In my opinion, the plaintiff is entitled to recover £500 for the total loss of sight by the assured as the direct effect of the accident.

Lindlay LJ: I am of the same opinion. The case turns mainly upon the position of Quin. What do we know about him? The company have given us no information about the terms of his agency. In the printed form of proposal he is described as the agent of the company for Whitehaven, and it is admitted that he was their agent for the purpose of obtaining proposals. What does that mean? It implies that he sees the person who makes the proposal. He was the person deputed by the company to receive the proposal, and to put it into shape. He obtains a proposal from a man who is obviously blind in one eye, and Quin sees this. This man cannot read or write, except that he can sign his name, and Quin knows this. Are we to be told that Quin's knowledge is not the knowledge of the company? Are they to be allowed to throw over Quin? In my opinion, the company are bound by Quin's knowledge, and they are really attempting to throw upon the assured the consequences of Quin's breach of duty to them in not telling them that the assured had only one eye. The policy must, in my opinion, be treated as if it contained a recital that the assured was a one eyed man. The £500 is to be payable in case of the 'complete and irrecoverable loss of sight in both eyes' by the assured. If the assured has only one eye to be injured, this must mean the total loss of sight. Within the true meaning of the policy, as applicable to a one eyed man, I think the plaintiff is entitled to recover £500.

Kay LJ: I agree. The defendants are a limited joint stock company, and the principal question is, whether the knowledge of their agent is to be imputed to them. I am clearly of opinion that it is. The agent, when he obtained the proposal, knew that this man had only one eye. It appears on the face of the proposal that Quin was the agent of the company for the Whitehaven district. What was he agent for? The company have given no evidence about this, but we cannot have better evidence than what the agent actually did. It was his duty to obtain proposals for assurances, and to send them to the company. It was his duty to get the form of proposal filled up and signed by the proposer, and to see that this was done correctly. Then he goes to a man who has obviously only one eye – he knows that he has only one eye – and he induces him to sign a proposal. The agent fills up the blanks in the proposal in his own handwriting, and it is sent in to the company. In the margin of the form is printed this note: 'If not strictly applicable, particulars of any deviations must be given at back,' which must mean that if the printed statements in the form are not strictly applicable to the particular case, the respects in which they are not, so are to be stated on the back of the proposal. If Quin had performed his duty to the company, who would have written at the back of the proposals the 'deviations' in the case of Bawden? I think it was Quin's duty to do this, and to point out to Bawden that without it the form would not be properly filled up. So far as we know, Quin did not convey to the company his knowledge of the fact that Bawden had only one eye; and it is argued that, the policy having been entered into by the company, and the premiums paid to them for some time, the policy is either void, or the company are only liable for a partial disablement of the assured. How is it possible for us to say that the knowledge of Quin is not to be imputed to the company? That knowledge was obtained by him when he was acting within the scope of his authority, and it must be imputed to the company. This is an answer to the argument that the policy is to be treated as void, because the statements in the proposal are not accurate. In my opinion, the condition that the statements in the proposal are to form the basis of the contract does not apply at all, because knowledge is to be imputed to the company of the fact that Bawden had only one eye.

Then it is said that the plaintiff can recover only for partial, not for total, permanent disablement. But, treating the company as knowing that Bawden had only one eye, how ought the policy to be construed? The material words are, 'complete and irrecoverable loss of sight in both eyes'; and, in my opinion, they ought to be construed as meaning that the company are to pay £500 in case the assured completely loses his sight by means of an accident. This is what has happened in the present case; and, therefore, in my opinion, the plaintiff is entitled to recover £500.

Application refused.

APPENDIX 6.11

Biggar v Rock Life Assurance Co [1902] 1 KB 516

Wright J: It is plain that the policy is *prima facie* avoided, for some of the particulars and statements in the answers, the correctness of which was a condition precedent to the validity of the policy, were false; Biggar, therefore, cannot recover unless he is able to shew that the insurance company is prevented from setting up that ground of avoidance by reason of its agent, Cooper, having acted in fraud of his principals.

If a person in the position of the claimant chooses to sign without reading it a proposal form which somebody else filled in, and if he acquiesces in that being sent in as signed by him without taking the trouble to read it, he must be treated as having adopted it. Business could not be carried on if that were not the law. On that ground, I think the claimant is in a great difficulty. But, further, it seems to me that here, as in the case of *New York Life Insurance Co v Fletcher* 117 US 519 (1885) ... it would be wrong to treat Cooper, the company's agent, as their agent to suggest the answers which Biggar was to give to the questions in the proposal. Cooper was an agent to receive proposals for the company. He may have been an agent, as Lindley and Kay LJJ put it in *Bawden v London, Edinburgh and Glasgow Insurance Co* [1892] 2 QB 534 ... to put the answers in form; but I cannot imagine that the agent of the insurance company can be treated as their agent to invent the answers to the questions in the proposal form. For that purpose, it seems to me, if he is allowed by the proposer to invent the answers and to send them in as the answers of the proposer; that the agent is the agent, not of the insurance company, but of the proposer. I cannot put the doctrine better than in the language of the Supreme Court in *New York Life Insurance Co v Fletcher* ... of the case referred to, where they are citing from and adopting previous decisions of the Supreme Court. They say (speaking of another case):

> The application was signed without being read. It was held that the company was not bound by the policy; that the power of the agent would not be extended to an act done by him in fraud of the company and for the benefit of the insured, especially where it was in the power of the assured by reasonable diligence to defeat the fraudulent intent; that the signing of the application without reading it or hearing it read was inexcusable negligence; and that a party is bound to know what he signs.

Then, speaking of the agent's conduct, they say:

> His conduct in this case was a gross violation of duty, in fraud of his principal, and in the interest of the other party. To hold the principal responsible for his acts, and assist in the consummation of the fraud, would be monstrous injustice. When an agent is apparently acting for his principal, but is really acting for himself or third persons and against his principal, there is no agency in respect to that transaction, at least as between the agent himself, or the person for whom he is really acting, and the principal ... The fraud could not be perpetrated by the agent alone. he aid of the plaintiff or the insured, either as an accomplice or as an instrument, was essential.

Then they go on:

> She says that she and her husband signed the application without reading it and without its being read to them. That of itself was inexcusable negligence. The application contained her agreements and representations in an important contract. When she signed it she was bound to know what she signed. The law requires that the insured shall not only in good faith answer all the interrogatories correctly, but shall use reasonable diligence to see that the answers are correctly written. It is for his interest to do so, and the insurer has a right to presume that he will do it. He has it in his power to prevent this species of fraud, and the insurer has not.

That doctrine of the Supreme Court of the United States seems to me to be good sense and good law. Even if those doctrines are not to be applied to their full extent, still I cannot conceive how this policy can be held to be binding on the company. The very basis of the policy is the statements in the proposal. These statements are false in several material respects. How, then, can the policy be binding on the company? If the plaintiff is entitled to anything, I think that the most he could ask for would be that the court should say that the contract is void on the ground of either fraud or mistake, with the consequence, perhaps, that he may be entitled to recover back the premium that he paid; but I cannot see how it can be held under these circumstances that the company is bound by the policy. I see no equity against the company in this case – no equity, for instance, such as might exist on the ground of receipt of premium with knowledge of the falsity of the statements. They never knew of the falsity of the statements, and they never knew that the proposal form had been filled in with answers invented by the person purporting to act as their agent. I think the answer to the question asked by the learned arbitrator must be that the facts stated shew a defence in law.

Judgment for the company.

APPENDIX 6.12

Ayrey v British Legal and United Provident Assurance Co Ltd [1918] 1 KB 136

Atkin J: On the point which seems to have been mainly argued before the county court judge, I think his decision was right in so far as it proceeded upon the footing that the officials of the defendant company had no authority to vary the terms of the contract which the assured had entered into. But that is not decisive of the case. The company seek to invalidate the policy on the ground that there was a concealment of material facts by the assured. The evidence shows that the company's agent was told by the assured that he was a member of the Royal Naval Reserve and therefore liable to be exposed to special risks, but he was described in the policy as a fisherman. The county court judge has found as a fact that that description was correct. Speaking for myself, I am not satisfied that there was, within the meaning of the clause in the policy or of the ordinary law of insurance, any concealment of the fact that the man's calling exposed him to special perils. The questions in the proposal form were all answered correctly, and I have great difficulty in seeing how it can be said that an assured, who correctly answers the questions in the proposal form and declares all the facts truly to an agent of the insurance company, has been guilty of concealing material facts, though, having regard to condition 2 of this policy, it may be doubtful whether statements as to material facts made to an agent can be treated as if made to the company. But the decision of this case does not depend upon the meaning or effect of condition 2, for it is clear from the evidence that before any premiums had been paid, and after the question of the assured being in the Royal Naval Reserve had been mentioned to the agent, he reported the matter to one of the company's superintendents who was also the district manager. The latter, having been informed as to all the facts, told the representative of the assured that the policy was valid. In so far as the plaintiff's case rests upon any supposed variation of the contract by the district manager, it must fail, because it is quite clear that the district manager had no power to vary the terms of the contract. But, after he had been told the true facts, he accepted payment of the premiums under the policy for two years, and in determining the question whether the company can now take advantage of a concealment of a material fact it is necessary to consider the question of estoppel.

The true principle to be invoked is best stated in the judgment of Bowen LJ in *Bentsen v Taylor* [1893] 2 QB 274 ... where he said:

> Did the defendants by their acts or conduct lead the plaintiff reasonably to suppose that they did not intend to treat the contract for the future as at an end, on account of the failure to perform the condition precedent?

That passage was cited by Viscount Reading CJ in *Panoutsos v Raymond Hadley Corporation of New York* [1917] 2 KB 473 ... and applied to a case where the question was whether the defendants were entitled to take advantage of a breach of a condition precedent in a contract, and the question as stated by Bowen LJ is the question which arises in this case.

For the purpose of the operation of the principle of estoppel, it must, of course, be shown that the company knew that the condition precedent had not been performed, and that depends on whether the knowledge of the district manager must be imputed to the company. I think it must be. I have great difficulty in seeing how an assured who desired to impart information to the company could reasonably be supposed to do so otherwise than by giving the information to the district manager. He is the person who is named on the premium card as the district manager of the company, and, in my opinion, it must be implied that the person holding that position is the person who has authority to receive on behalf of the company information as to all matters affecting a policy issued by the company, and that it was his duty to pass on to the company such information as he might receive. I think, therefore, that the knowledge of the district manager that there had been a breach of a condition by reason of the concealment of a material fact was the knowledge of the company. The remaining question to be considered is whether the company led the plaintiff to believe that they did not intend to treat the contract as at an end. In my opinion, nothing could have been more likely to induce that belief in the mind of the plaintiff than the fact that the district manager to whom she had disclosed the facts which showed that the conditions of the proposal form had not been complied with continued to receive payment of the premiums from her week by week for a period of at least 18 months.

For these reasons I think that the decision of the county court judge must be reversed and judgment entered for the plaintiff.

Appeal allowed.

APPENDIX 6.13

Keeling v Pearl Assurance Co Ltd [1923] All ER Rep 307; (1923) 129 LT 573

Bailhache J: The remaining question is one which, in these cases, always seems to me to be one of very considerable difficulty. It is:

> Is the assured barred because the person who negotiated on behalf of the insurance company with Mrs Keeling, for this insurance on her husband's life, had inserted in the proposal form answers which are untrue?

No doubt, if the answers had been given by the assured, or by her husband, the policy would be void, but the agent in this case has inserted answers which are not consistent with, and in one case are certainly directly contrary to, the information which he had from the husband. If the knowledge of the agent is to be imputed to the insurance company, or if, in filling up the proposal form, he was acting as the agent for the insurance company, then, in as much as the answers are his own answers and not the answers of the assured, the policy is undoubtedly good.

There have been a large number of cases cited to me on one side and the other. Perhaps the most illuminating, on the one hand, is that of the one eyed man, *Bawden v London, Edinburgh and Glasgow Assurance Co* [1892] 2 QB 534, and on the other hand, the case before Wright J, of *Biggar v Rock Life Assurance Co* [1902] 1 KB 516, each of them coming to a different conclusion. In *Bawden*'s case, it was held that the knowledge of the insurance agent that the assured had only one eye was to be imputed to the company, although in the filling up of the proposal form it was stated that he was not suffering from any physical defect – statement which, obviously, having regard to the fact that the man had only one eye, was untrue. In *Biggar*'s case, the answers were manufactured by the insurance agent, and were manufactured in fraud of the insurance company. In that case, it was held that the policy was void, and that the insurance agent, in manufacturing those answers, was not acting as the agent for the insurance company. A good many cases have been decided, some falling on one side of the line, and some on the other. The learned arbitrator has found that, in this particular case, the agent, Mr Allen, who filled up these forms, and particularly when he is more than a mere collector – when he is an inspector whose business it is, as Mr Allen says, to negotiate these contracts, and, as I gather, to fill up these forms for people who cannot fill them up for themselves – then, when one finds that the answers which the agent puts down are contrary to the facts which are stated to him by the assured-in such cases as that and in view of the finding of the learned arbitrator that Mr Allen was in fact the agent of the insurance company, I have come to the conclusion that in this case the line of cases to be follows is the *Bawden* line of cases rather than the *Biggar* line of cases. Having arrived at that conclusion, I see no reason to differ from the finding of the learned arbitrator in his award. The result is that Mr Allen was the agent of the insurance company in the matters to which I have alluded, and I answer the question submitted to me – whether the insurance company are liable to pay Mrs Keeling the £500 under the policy – in the affirmative.

Award affirmed.

APPENDIX 6.14

Newsholme Bros v Road Transport and General Insurance Co Ltd [1929] 2 KB 356, CA

Scrutton LJ: The difficulty on the authorities arises from the alleged conflict between the decisions of the English Court of Appeal in *Bawden v London, Edinburgh, and Glasgow Assurance Co* [1892] 2 QB 534 ... and the decisions of Wright J in *Biggar v Rock Life Assurance Co* [1902] 1 KB 516 ... and of Wills and Phillimore JJ in *Levy v Scottish Employers Insurance Co* (1901) 17 TLR 229 ... It is more important that this conflict should be determined because:

(1) Wright J acted on and followed a decision of the Supreme Court of the United States in *New York Life Insurance Co v Fletcher* ... the reasoning in which is not easy to reconcile with *Bawden*'s case ...;

(2) the Scottish courts in *McMillan*'s case ... and *Yule*'s case ... have declined to follow *Bawden*'s case ... and have expressed their preference for *Biggar*'s case ... and *Fletcher*'s case ...; (3) the Irish courts by the mouth of Palles CB have expressed a similar preference in *Taylor v Yorkshire Insurance Co* [1913] 2 IR 1 for *Bawden*'s case ... to quote the present Lord Chancellor, who, as a Lord Justice, was present at the first hearing of this case, is therefore a very 'distinguished' case.

In my view, the important question for the decision of this case is whether the knowledge of the agent, acquired in filling up the proposal for the assured, is to be taken as the knowledge of the company. If the person having authority to bind the company by making a contract in fact knows of the untruth of the statements and yet takes the premium, the question may be different. Even then, I see great difficulty in avoiding the effect of the writing signed by the proposer that the truth of the statements is the basis of the contract. But where the person contracting for the company has no actual knowledge, but only constructive notice, the difficulties of the proposer are greater. In commercial matters, the doctrine of constructive notice is not favoured: see the explanation by Lindley LJ *Manchester Trust v Furness* [1895] 2 QB 539 ... *Blackburn, Low and Co v Vigors* (1887) 12 App Cas 531 ... a broker employed to effect an insurance, heard of a fact affecting the risk, and did not tell his principal. That broker did not effect that insurance, but, later, the principal did effect an insurance on that risk. On a loss occurring, the underwriters alleged that the knowledge of the first broker was the knowledge of the principal, and as the principal had not disclosed a fact he must be taken to have known, the insurance was void. The House of Lords held that this contention was erroneous; that while it was true that if the first broker had effected a policy, he would have been bound to disclose his actual knowledge to the underwriters, he was not so bound to disclose his knowledge to his principal that his principal, though it was not disclosed, must be taken to know it.

In my view, the decision in *Bawden*'s case ... is not applicable to a case where the agent himself, at the request of the proposer, fills up the answers in purported conformity with information supplied by the proposer. If the answers are untrue and he knows it, he is committing a fraud which prevents his knowledge being the knowledge of the insurance company. If the answers are untrue, but he does not know it, I do not understand how he has any knowledge which can be imputed to the insurance company. In any case, I have great difficulty in understanding how a man who has signed, without reading it, a document which he knows to be a proposal for insurance, and which contains statements in fact untrue, and a promise that they are true, and the basis of the contract, can escape from the consequences of his negligence by saying that the person he asked to fill it up for him is the agent of the person to whom the proposal is addressed.

In my view, the judgment of Rowlatt J was right and the appeal must be dismissed with costs.

APPENDIX 6.15

National Consumer Council, *Report on Insurance Law Reform*, 1997, London: NCC

OUR RECOMMENDATIONS

Selling by intermediaries

Recommendation 1

We recommend amendment of the Insurance Brokers Registration Act 1977 to require all independent intermediaries:

- to be registered as brokers;
- to demonstrate their independence and competence; and
- to be subject to sanctions under the Act.

For the purposes of this amendment, a broker will be anyone who carries on the business of arranging contracts of insurance as the agent of intending policy holders. Where a broker acts with authority from an insurer to enter into or deal under insurance contracts, the broker should be statutorily deemed to be the agent of that insurer.

Recommendation 2

We recommend reform on the law on insurance to provide that:

(a) intermediaries who are not registered brokers are deemed to be the agent of the insurer in any matter relating to insurance between an insured (or intending insured) consumer and the insurer; and

(b) the insurer is responsible, and liable for damages, for the conduct of its agents in connection with any matter relating to insurance where:
   - a person in the circumstances of the insured (or intending insured) could reasonably be expected to rely on the agent; and
   - where the insured (or intending insured) consumer did in fact and in good faith rely on the agent.

Recommendation 3

On the question of whether a policy has been missold, we recommend that the seller must, by law, be able to demonstrate that the buyer received a clear explanation of the cover, the risk attached to non-disclosure and any important policy restrictions. The remedy for misselling a policy should be that, for the duration of the policy, the reasonable expectation of the policy holder will be met in any claim ...

APPENDIX 6.16

Stone v Reliance Mutual Insurance Society Ltd [1972] 1 Lloyd's Rep 469, CA

Lord Denning: What then is the legal position? It is quite clear that, in filling in the form, the agent here was acting within the scope of his authority. He said: 'It is company policy that I should put the questions, writing down answers.' This distinguishes the present case from *Newsholme*'s case [1929] 2 KB 356, where the agent had no authority to fill in the proposal forms: and it was held that he was merely the amanuensis of the proposer. The present case is more like *Bawden v The London, Edinburgh and Glasgow Assurance Co* [1892] 2 QB 534 ... where Bawden was an illiterate man who had lost one eye. The agent filled in the proposal form and put it before Bawden for signature. He signed it. The agent made a mistake in filling in the form because he ought to have stated in the 'particulars of deviations' the fact that Bawden had only one eye: but he failed to do so. There was the usual claim that the proposal was the basis of the contract. Bawden afterwards lost the other eye. It was held that Bawden was entitled to recover on the policy. That case was adversely commented on in *Newsholme*'s case, but I think it was correctly decided. It would have been most unjust if the company had been allowed to repudiate liability.

The case presents itself to my mind like this: the society seeks to repudiate liability by reason of the untruth of two answers in the proposal form. They seek to fasten those untruths onto the insured. They do so by virtue of a printed clause in the proposal form. They make out that it was the insured who misled them. Whereas the boot is on the other leg. The untrue answers were written down by their own agent. It was their own agent who made the mistake. It was he who ought to have known better. It was he who thereby represented to her that the form was correctly filled in. But it was a mistake induced by the misrepresentation of the agent, and not by any fault of hers. Neither she nor her husband should suffer for it. No doubt, it was an innocent misrepresentation for which, in former times, the only remedy would be to cancel the contract and get back the premiums. But, nowadays, an innocent misrepresentation may give rise to further or other relief. It may debar a person from relying on an exception. Likewise, in this case, it disentitles the insurance company from relying on the printed clause to exclude their liability. Their agent represented that he had filled in the form correctly: and, having done so, they cannot rely on the printed clause to say that it was not correctly filled in. So they are liable on the policy.

APPENDIX 6.17

United Mills Agencies Ltd v Re Harvey Bray and Co [1952] 1 All ER 225

McNair LJ found that the insurance brokers had no knowledge that the goods in the hands of packers were uninsured and that they were not negligent in not insuring them in the hands of packers or in not informing the insured that they had not so insured them. The insured contended that it was the duty of the brokers to cause the insured to be notified promptly of all the terms as soon as they had arranged the insurance and that there had been a failure on the part of the brokers to do so. Evidence had been called from an independent broker and substantially agreed to by the defendant brokers' witness – that it was the practice of, at any rate, those two offices of insurance brokers (and he (his Lordship) had no doubt the practice of brokers as a whole) that, when cover had been placed, the clients were notified as soon as possible. That seemed to be good business and prudent office management, but, on the evidence, he (his Lordship) was completely unable to hold that it was part of the duty owed by the broker to the client so to notify him, in the sense that a failure to do so would involve him in legal liability. No case was cited in which any broker had ever been held liable or had ever paid any client money in respect of such a failure. It seemed to him (his Lordship) to put an intolerable unreasonable burden on a broker to say that as a matter of law, apart from prudent practice, he was bound to forward the cover note as soon as possible. It was, no doubt, prudent to do so, both to allay the client's anxiety and possibly to enable the client to check the terms of insurance, but that was very different from saying it was part of the broker's duty. He (his Lordship) doubted whether, even if the cover had been in the insured's hands on 3 April, action appropriate to the circumstances would have been taken, but he did not found his judgment on that point because he was left in very considerable doubt on it. The insured failed on whichever of the three alternative ways they put their case, and there must be judgment for the brokers with costs.

APPENDIX 6.18

Cherry Ltd v Allied Insurance Brokers Ltd [1978] 1 Lloyd's Rep 274

Cantley J: It is contended that they had no duty to be careful. I think in the circumstances of this case they had. The meeting of 13 August was a mutual business meeting from the point of view of both parties; there was nothing casual about it. They were giving information within their specialised knowledge and they knew or ought to have known that it would be taken seriously and acted upon in a transaction of importance. Whatever may have been the position in contract, the situation seems to me to have been covered by the principles as stated by Lord Morris of Borth-y-Gest in the well known case of *Hedley Byrne and Co Ltd v Heller and Partners Ltd* [1964] AC 465 ... where he said:

> I consider that it follows and that it should now be regarded as settled that if someone possessed of a special skill undertakes, quite irrespective of contract, to apply that skill for the assistance of another person who relies upon such skill, a duty of care will arise. The fact that the service is to be given by means of or by the instrumentality of words can make no difference. Furthermore, if in a sphere in which a person is so placed that others could reasonably rely upon his judgment or his skill or upon his ability to make careful inquiry, a person takes it upon himself to give information or advice to, or allows his information or advice to be passed on to, another person who, as he knows or should know, will place reliance upon it, then a duty of care will arise.

APPENDIX 6.19

Fraser v BN Furman (Productions), Miller Smith and Partners (A Firm, Third Party) [1967] 3 All ER 57; [1967] 2 Lloyd's Rep 1, CA

Diplock LJ: The only point argued on this appeal has been that the employers sustained no damage as a result of the breach of contract. What is said is that, if the brokers had performed their contract, the employer's liability indemnity policy of Eagle Star, under which the employers would have been insured, would not have covered their liability to Miss Fraser, because the insurers, Eagle Star, would have been entitled to rely upon non-performance of the contract by the employers of condition 4 of the policy, a condition which is stated to be a condition precedent to any liability of the insurers under the policy and is in these terms: 'The insured shall take reasonable precautions to prevent accidents and disease.' That is a common form condition in many policies of this type.

The breach of contract in not obtaining an employer's liability indemnity policy is admitted. The employers are accordingly entitled to be put in the same position, so far as money can do so, as if the contract had been performed by the brokers. No question of remoteness of damages obviously arises in this case. If the contract had been performed by the brokers, the employers would have been parties to a policy of insurance against employer's liability in standard form underwritten by a first-class insurance company of the highest reputation. As a result of the breach, they were not insured at all.

What damage they have suffered does not depend upon whether Eagle Star would have been entitled as a matter of law to repudiate liability under their standard policy, but whether as a matter of business they would have been likely to do so. What the employers have lost is the chance of recovering indemnity from the insurers. If Eagle Star would not have been entitled to repudiate liability in law ... the damages recoverable would amount to a full indemnity. Even if they would have been entitled in law, however, to repudiate liability, it does not, in my view, follow that the employers would be entitled to *no* damages. The court must next consider in that event, what were the chances that an insurance company of the highest standing and reputation, such as Eagle Star, notwithstanding their strict legal rights, would, as a matter of business, have paid up under the policy.

In my view, therefore, the court has to consider whether or not, in the circumstances of this case, and assuming that I am wrong in the construction which I have put upon condition 4, the particular insurers contemplated as such by the contract between the employers and the broker, namely, the Eagle Star Insurance Company Ltd, would have sought to rely upon this condition to repudiate their liability under the contract.

It is right that I should make it perfectly clear that no evidence was called from Eagle Star to suggest that that company would ever have thought of taking such a course. The imputation which has been suggested by the broker alone without any evidence from Eagle Star or from anyone else in the insurance world, nor were other brokers called to support it.

In considering the likelihood that such a point would have been taken, even if it were open, one must, in my view, bear in mind, first, the character and reputation of the insurance company which was contemplated by the third party, one of the great insurance companies in this country with a high reputation. One must also bear in mind that, if the insurers were to take this point, they would have to take it at an early stage as soon as the facts were known to them, and before the action by Miss Fraser against the employers was tried, because one of the terms of the policy is that the insurers take over the conduct of the action, and, if they did so and failed to repudiate with knowledge of the facts, they would be estopped from doing so thereafter. In such an action, if they took the point, the onus would lie upon them of proving that the conduct of the insured did fall within the condition. That is itself a matter which the argument in this court has shown is one of considerable difficulty. The view which I have expressed in this court as to the meaning of the condition (which was, I think, also accepted by the judge) indicates that it is arguable that the condition would not exempt them from liability. The prospect of success in taking the point, therefore, even if they knew the facts, would be, to say the least of it, dubious.

APPENDIX 6.20

McNealy v Pennine Insurance Co Ltd and West Lancashire Insurance Brokers Ltd [1978] 2 Lloyd's Rep 18, CA

Lord Denning MR: The broker knew all about those exclusions. He knew perfectly well that part time musicians were not acceptable risks. Nevertheless, when Mr McNealy went to see him, he simply asked him: 'What is your occupation?' Mr McNealy said 'Property repairer'. The proposal form asked for 'Full details of occupation'. The answer was simply 'Property repairer'. At the trial a question arose as to how and when the proposal form was filled in, but we need not go into it. The form produced to the court was filled in by the broker himself: but it was signed by Mr McNealy or on his behalf. The important thing is that Mr McNealy was simply asked 'What is your occupation?', and he said 'Property Repairer'. On that answer, the risk was acceptable at low rates. The insurance company accepted it. Mr McNealy believed himself to be covered by a comprehensive insurance which also covered passengers.

At the trial of the case, it was accepted by both sides that the insurance company were not liable. The reason for their non-liability was because the broker was the agent of the assured. It is well settled that in all matters relating to the placing of insurance the insurance broker is the agent of the assured, and of the assured only, see *Rozanes v Bowen* (1928) 32 Ll L Rep 98. In the present case, the broker knew perfectly well that a part time musician was excluded from this risk. Then I go on to ask: ought that to have been disclosed to the insurance company? Clearly, it should have been. It was a most material fact. All facts are material which are, to the knowledge of the proposed assured, regarded by the insurers as material: and that extends to the knowledge of his broker also. Mr Carnell, the broker, knew that it was very material for the insurance company to know that Mr McNealy was a part time musician. If the insurance company had known that he was a part time musician, they would not have given him cover at this low premium. They would not have given him any cover at all.

Not having a remedy against the insurance company, Mr McNealy said: 'If that is so, surely the broker, my agent, is liable.' Certainly, he is liable. It was clearly the duty of the broker to use all reasonable care to see that the assured, Mr McNealy, was properly covered. An obvious step in the course of doing his duty would have been to say to Mr McNealy: 'The Pennine will not cover you if you are a full or part time musician, a bookmaker, a jockey, or anything to do with racing.' He ought to have gone through the whole list with Mr McNealy and said: 'You are not going to be accepted if you are one of these categories because, if you are, the insurance company can get out of it.' I am afraid the broker did not do his duty. He did not go through that list with Mr McNealy at all. He simply asked him what was his occupation, and Mr McNealy said 'property repairer'. The broker ought to have gone on and asked 'Have you ever been or are you a full or part time musician?' and the answer would certainly have been 'yes'. On the answer being 'yes', the broker should have said: 'It is no good trying to insure with the Pennine. You had better go to one of the companies who are ready to insure full or part time musicians, but that will no doubt be at a higher premium.' The broker did not do that at all. In other words, he did not do all that was reasonable to see that Mr McNealy was properly covered.

It seems to me that that quite clearly was a breach of duty, and that breach of duty was the cause of all the trouble that Mr McNealy found himself in. I think the judge was quite right. The broker was liable for not taking proper care to effect the insurance, and he is therefore liable for the full amount of the claim.

APPENDIX 6.21

Sharp v Sphere Drake Insurance plc [1992] 2 Lloyd's Rep 501

Mr AD Colman QC:

2 THE BOGUS SIGNATURE

The proposal form was completed by the brokers, the third defendants, and sent to GJW on 8 January 1987. It was not seen by Mr Sharp before being sent. Nor was it signed by him. Instead, it was completed by Mrs Sharp, an employee of the brokers on the basis of information provided to her mainly, if not wholly, by Mr Cleverdon. The brokers were under great pressure to perfect the cover because the insurers were holding covered only until 12 January 1987 and Mr Cleverdon was aware that Mr Sharp intended to sail the vessel from Majorca to Puerta Banus before 15 January 1987. The problems of communicating with Mr Sharp were considerable. The post was very slow and the telephone could be difficult. I infer that it was for such reasons that Mrs Sharp wrote alongside 'signed' at the bottom of the proposal form 'AJ Sharp' in a form which has the appearance of a signature but is indeed quite different from that of Mr Sharp. She wanted, I infer, to save time, to get the document to the insurers as quickly as possible and without having to make further contact with Mr Sharp. This, however, would only be a fruitful exercise if the insurers were led to believe that the form had indeed been signed by the would be assured. In substance, therefore, the proposal form by implication represented that it had been signed by Mr Sharp personally.

The insurers contend that for the brokers to issue the proposal form with that apparent signature was in gross breach of the duty of the utmost good faith owed by the assured's agents to the insurers and that they are accordingly entitled to avoid the policy. Since the renewal was based on the information imported by the original proposal, they contend that they are entitled to avoid the policy as renewed.

The evidence from the expert witnesses was strongly that the insurer to whom a proposal was presented was entitled to expect that the form had been signed by and only by the proposer. Mr Knox-Johnson called by the plaintiffs was adamant that the proper way was for the proposer to sign the proposal form. He rarely completed forms on behalf of clients but, when he did so, he always made it clear that he was doing it as agent and subsequently asked the client to sign it. He would never sign it instead of the client. He could not recall ever having signed 'pp the assured'. If he sent to insurers an unsigned form he would always tell them that he was sending it to the client for signature and would then pass it to the insurers. He did not consider that an insurer would issue a policy without a proposal signed by the proposer even if told by the broker that all the answers had come directly from the assured. A proposal form which bore a signature purportedly that of the assured but put on by someone else would not be a satisfactory proposal form because it had not been signed by the proposer. He would never send such a form to an underwriter and he would expect the underwriter to return it to him if told that this had been done and to request that the proposer should sign it before the underwriter entertained the proposal. If the underwriter found out how the proposal came to be signed in that way:

> ... because it would be so unusual for a broker to sign a proposal form, I would expect the underwriter to request that the proposal form was not correctly done to rectify the contract and also to check with the broker to find out whether this was the sort of thing they thought right ...

The check would be made because:

> It's not the sort of thing which should be done. I mean, if it's a one-off aberration one would do one's best to make sure the broker was aware it should not be done.

Mr Dillow-Prior, the broker called on behalf of the insurers, was firmly of the view that the fact that the signature was not that of the proposer ought to be disclosed to underwriters. Such fact was material even if all the information was true and factual:

> ... because it is misleading the underwriters in so far as the proposal form purports to have been produced by the assured ...

He later said that if they found out what happened:

> ... I would think that the underwriters would certainly enquire of the broker as to exactly what is going on [– because –] as far as I can see, you are submitting a document which has a declaration on it to say that everything is correct and true and it has been signed in a way so as to certainly deceive underwriters as to who produced it ...

If a broker did sign a proposal 'pp' the proposer he would expect the underwriter to contact the broker: '... and find out why it was done in that way ...'

Even if, in such a case, the underwriter was told by the broker that all the answers came from the proposer he would want the proposer's signature before writing the risk ...

The general effect of the evidence from the expert witnesses to whose evidence I have referred is that the information that the signature of the proposer on the proposal had been forged by the brokers would have caused the prudent underwriter to refuse to insure until the insured had confirmed the proposal in writing. That being so, I conclude that the fact that the signature of Mr Sharp had been forged ought to have been disclosed on behalf of the insurers ...

THE HOUSE BOAT CLAUSE DEFENCE

It was strongly contended by Mr Flaux on behalf of the plaintiffs that Mr Cleverdon ought to have read over on the telephone to Mr Sharp the proposal form question on houseboat use as printed on the form and should have explained to him its proper meaning, namely whether the vessel would be used by anybody as living accommodation while laid up. As it is, Mr Cleverdon assumed that the question had a meaning which it did not have and based on that assumption he asked Mr Sharp the question to which I have already referred, thereby suggesting the answer 'No' to the question. This submission necessarily involves that it was Mr Cleverdon's duty as a broker to arrive at the correct construction of the clause and to tell Mr Sharp what it was.

There is no doubt that a broker is not necessarily in breach of his duty of professional skill and care merely because he has given to a document relevant to the placing of the risk a meaning which on its proper construction such a document does not bear. This has long been settled law and finds its most explicit expression as far back as the judgment of Tindal CJ in *Chapman v Walton* (1833) 10 Bing 57 ... The essential point is not whether the broker arrived at the correct construction but 'whether other persons exercising the same profession or calling, and being men of experience and skill therein, would or would not have come to the same conclusion'. The decision of Mr Justice Roche in *James Vale and Co v Van Oppen and Co Ltd* (1921) 37 TLR 367 ... applies the same principle. That was a case involving the meaning of instructions by a would-be assured to his broker but the principle must be equally applicable to the broker's understanding of and conduct in relation to any document relevant to the placing of the risk, including the proposal form. However, in cases where the meaning of the document in question is clear and incapable of being understood in more than one sense, it will be difficult if not impossible for the broker who has misunderstood the meaning to assert that he has, nonetheless, exercised reasonable skill and care: see *Chapman v Walton* ... In those cases where the words used are of obscure meaning or are strongly arguably ambiguous, the broker may be able, possibly with the help of expert evidence, to refute the allegation that in arriving at a meaning other than what in the final analysis the court holds to be the ordinary and natural meaning, he has failed to exercise reasonable skill and care ...

Having regard to what is, in my judgment, the ordinary and natural meaning of the houseboat question in the proposal and further taking into account the expert evidence I hold that it was the professional duty of a non-specialist broker dealing with a client's proposal for yacht insurance on the basis of this proposal form and with reference to this form of policy to advise his client that the underwriters must be told if *anyone*, including a permanent crew, was to use the vessel as living accommodation during the period of lay up. If there was any doubt in his mind as to the matter, it was the duty of the broker to ask the insurers or GJW what meaning they attached to the question and house boat exclusion. Accordingly, in asking Mr Sharp the questions which he did ask about house boat use, framed in the way in which they were, I hold that Mr Cleverdon failed to exercise the standard of car to be expected from a professional broker, and was thereby in breach of contract and of duty to Mr Sharp ...

THE BOGUS SIGNATURE DEFENCE

I have already dealt fully with the aspect of materiality of the fact that the signature on the proposal was not that of Mr Sharp, but had been inserted by the brokers without his authority to appear as if he had signed the form. This conduct, as I have held, represented on the evidence a radical departure from the standard of practice of insurance brokers. It was conduct designed to mislead those at GJW responsible for underwriting the risk. It entitled the underwriters to avoid the policy for the reasons I have given, namely non-disclosure of material facts and misrepresentation.

The course which the brokers took of forging the signature of the assured in order to provide a signed proposal within the time limited by GJW for holding covered should not have been adopted. The correct course on the evidence was at the very least to sign the proposal in the brokers' name 'pp Mr Sharp' and on that basis to enable Mr Sharp to verify or alter where appropriate the answers in the proposal and to sign the proposal form in his own hand. I hold that had that course been adopted GJW would have continued to hold covered until the time when they received a satisfactory proposal signed by Mr Sharp himself.

In these circumstances, the brokers ought to have appreciated that their conduct was incompatible with proper broking practice. Moreover, they were knowingly misrepresenting to GJW what I have held to be a material fact. In so doing, they were guilty of a want of proper skill and care in the course of placing the risk and that want of skill and care has had the consequence that the insurers are entitled to avoid the policy on that ground.

Accordingly, I conclude that the brokers failed to exercise reasonable skill and care both in relation to the preparation of the proposal as regards the question relating to houseboat use and in relation to the presentation of GJW of the proposal bearing a bogus signature. That failure to exercise reasonable skill and care has caused Mr Sharp to be deprived of insurance cover which would otherwise have been available to him because the insurers are entitled to avoid the policy *ab initio* on the basis of non-disclosure and misrepresentation (the bogus signature defence) or to rely on the protection of cl 2(a)(ii) (the house boat clause defence).

APPENDIX 6.22

Stockton v Mason and Vehicle and General Insurance Co and Arthur Edward (Insurance) Ltd [1978] 2 Lloyd's Rep 430, CA

Diplock LJ: The point of insurance law on which this appeal turns arises out of the tripartite legal relationship between an insurance broker, the insurer and the assured in the field of non-marine insurance.

The principle of law involved in this relationship is one which is well established so far as the brokers' agency on behalf of the insurers is concerned. A broker in non-marine insurance has implied authority to issue on behalf of the insurer or enter into as agent for the insurer contracts of interim insurance, which are normally recorded in cover notes. The essential nature of the contract of interim insurance is that it is for a temporary period, generally, a maximum of 30 days or so, but is terminable by notice by the insurer at any time during that period. The implied authority of the broker does not extend to entering into the complete policy of insurance which is substituted for the temporary one and is for a fixed period ...

So it comes down to a very short point – whether those words, in reply to a request for substitution of the Midget for the Ford Anglia, 'Yes, that will be all right. We will see to that, Mrs Mason', were said as agent for the insurance company, or simply meant that the brokers, as agents for Mr Mason, would try and get the cover.

Bearing in mind the ordinary relationship between brokers and insurance companies in non-marine insurance as respects the implied authority to enter into contracts of interim insurance and to issue cover notes, it seems to me to be quite unarguable that, in saying, 'Yes, that will be all right. We will see to that, Mrs Mason', the brokers were acting as agents for the insurance company and not merely acknowledging an order or a request by Mr Mason to negotiate a contract with the insurance company on his behalf.

There must be every day thousands of cases, not only in motor insurance but in other forms of non-marine insurance, where persons wishing to become insured or wishing to transfer an insurance ring us their brokers and ask for cover or ask for fresh cover or ask to transfer the cover from an existing vehicle to another. In every case they rely upon the broker's statement that they are covered as constituting a contract binding upon the insurance company. In that sort of conversation, they are speaking, in the absence of any special circumstances, to the broker as agent for the insurance company, and the broker in dealing with the matter, is acting as agent for the insurance company and not as agent for the person wishing to have insurance. Of course, there may be exceptional cases. There was nothing exceptional about this. A contract of insurance of this kind can be made orally, it can be made informal, colloquial language, and this, in my view, is a very simple and clear example of that kind of legal situation.

I would, therefore, allow this appeal. The effect of that is, I think, that the judgment must be against the first third party, the insurance company, and the judgment against the second third party, the brokers, must be discharged.

APPENDIX 6.23

Punjab National Bank v De Boinville and Others [1992] 3 All ER 104; [1992] 1 Lloyd's Rep 7

Staughton LJ:

(E) IN THE ABSENCE OF A CONTRACTUAL RELATIONSHIP, DID ANY OF THE RELEVANT DEFENDANTS OWE A DUTY OF CARE TO THE BANK?

In the light of my earlier conclusions, this question arises in the case of Fieldings for the period between 24 May 1983 and some date in July, when they first entered a contractual relationship with the bank; and in the case of Mr De Boinville and Mr Deere, throughout the broking history, since nobody suggests that they entered into any contract with the bank.

We are concerned, yet again, with economic loss. The outline argument of counsel for Fieldings submits that whether they owed a non-contractual duty of care to the bank depends on whether the relationship between them: (1) falls within a recognised category in respect of which it has been held that a duty exists; or (2) should fall within a recognised category by a justifiable increment to an existing category ...

What then are the existing categories where a duty of care to avoid economic loss has been recognised? Mr Milligan, for Fieldings and the two individual defendants, submits that there are three: (i) the case where a professional man provides services to a client; (ii) agency, whether contractual or gratuitous; and (iii) negligent misstatement within *Hedley Byrne and Co Ltd v Heller and Partners Ltd* [1964] AC 465 ... I am not altogether sure that the categories should be stated in such broad terms. Lord Oliver of Aylmerton gave examples of categories in the *Caparo* case [1990] 1 All ER 568 ... But perhaps it does not matter whether one states a few broad categories or a larger number of small ones. Either way, one must consider whether the present case is within some recognized class, or is a justifiable increment.

Lord Bridge of Harwich in the *Caparo* case said ...:

> In advising the client who employs him the professional man owes a duty to exercise that standard of skill and care appropriate to his professional status and will be liable both in contract and in tort for all losses which his client may suffer by reason of any breach of that duty.

I would hold that this principle applies as much to insurance brokers as to those who exercise any other professional calling, and to other professional activities which they carry on, besides giving advice: see the judgment of Mr Justice Phillips in *Youell and Others v Bland Welch and Co Ltd* [1990] 2 Lloyd's Rep 431 ...

The question then is whether the bank were the clients of Fieldings. This has to be answered by reference to the period when Fieldings were placing the third and fourth policies without the bank's knowledge, and were not yet (as I have held) in a contractual relationship with the bank. In my opinion the bank were not the clients of Fieldings during that period. They were not to their knowledge giving instructions to

Fieldings, they were not to be an assured under the third and fourth policies, and they had no contract with Fieldings.

Is it, then, a justifiable increment to extend the professional category (or the insurance broker category, if a narrower classification is preferred) to this case? At this stage, I must revert to the finding of Mr Justice Hobhouse that:

> ... it was known by all relevant parties that financially the bank was at risk and that the bank would be taking an assignment of the relevant policies.

It must indeed have been plain to all that the bank has *some* financial interest in the transaction; if they were to confirm the letter of credit and honour bills drawn under it, their money would be at risk. But even if all the defendants knew of a right of recourse in the bank against Esal, I doubt if that would be determinative; to hold that a substantial creditor of an insurance broker's client is necessarily owed a duty of care in tort might well be more than a justifiable increment. So it is important to decide whether the judge was right to find that all relevant parties knew of the intended assignment to the bank of the third and fourth policies ...

I consider that the judge was justified in finding that Mr Deere knew of the impending assignment. From the time when he became employed by Fieldings, his knowledge should be attributed to them, and they too must be taken to have known of it.

In those circumstances, it seems to me a justifiable increment to hold that an insurance broker owes a duty of care to the specific person who he knows is to become an assignee of the policy at all events if (as in this case) that person actively participates in giving instructions for the insurance to the broker's knowledge. In such a case there is a rather greater degree of proximity than that which existed between the solicitor and the beneficiary under the will in *Ross v Caunters* [1980] Ch 297, for the beneficiary may have known nothing of the will or the solicitor and would not have derived any benefit from it if it had later been revoked. I hold that Fieldings owed a non-contractual duty of care to the bank ...

APPENDIX 6.24

Rozanes v Bowen (1928) 32 Ll L Rep 98, CA

Scrutton LJ: Sir Henry Maddocks admits, and I agree, that in the case of marine insurance there is not the slightest doubt, and never has been the slightest doubt, that the broker is not the agent of the underwriter. On that there is the opinion that was read in the judgment below, and which is referred to in some of the authorities, of Kennedy J, in the *Empress Assurance Corp v Bowring Co Ltd* (1905) Com Cas 107 …

I know of no case or legal authority which can be cited to show that the broker who is instructed to effect a marine insurance, either directly by the person intending to insure or indirectly through another broker, becomes for any part of the business of effecting the insurance the agent also of the underwriter. If such were the case the curious inference, I suppose, would follow that the knowledge of the broker would be the knowledge also of the underwriter.

Kennedy J, speaks of it as a 'curious inference', meaning so curious that he thinks it impossible; but, curiously enough, that is the inference that we are asked to draw in this case.

An attempt is made to suggest that that merely applies to marine insurance. That suggestion is quite contrary to my own experience, and, I believe, to all business experience in London. Companies not members of Lloyd's do have agents with whom they have agreements, and difficult questions may arise sometimes when the agent of a company fills up a form when the assured comes to him to get a policy. But no such difficulty arises in Lloyd's cases. When a broker is asked to get an insurance at Lloyd's he has no idea what member of Lloyd's will insure. He takes a slip round which is a proposal to A, who refuses, to B, who refuses, to C, who underwrites for his Names to D, who underwrites for his Names; but until he goes to Lloyd's he will have no idea for whom he is acting except that it will be a member of Lloyd's if he can get anybody to accept his proposal.

When it is suggested in this case that M Hacco in Paris is an agent of Lloyd's, I ask, for what member of Lloyd's was he an agent when he drew up this proposal? He did not know. The proposal was going to be submitted to any number of members of Lloyd's, and some of them might refuse; but M Hacco was not in any sense an agent of the individual members of Lloyd's to whom ultimately the proposal was going to be submitted by a Lloyd's broker.

APPENDIX 6.25

Anglo-African Merchants Ltd and Exmouth Clothing Co Ltd v Bayley [1969] 2 All ER 421; [1969] 1 Lloyd's Rep 268

Megaw J: There is, however, another matter with which I am bound to deal, even though in the end it does not affect the result of this case. It involves the legal position, the rights and duties of insurance brokers.

The plaintiffs have asserted, and by their amended points of reply have reiterated the assertion, that Sir William Garthwaite (Home and Overseas) Ltd – I shall call them Garthwaites and Mr Evans and Mr Mew, employed by that company or an associated company, were acting as agents, not of the plaintiffs, the assured, but of the defendant underwriters. This assertion was put forward, not as involving a general principle, but as being related to the special facts of this case: namely events which had occurred, at the instance of the defendant's solicitors, with regard to discovery after this action had been commenced. In his final speech, counsel for the plaintiffs did not seek to adduce any argument in support of the contention, but he did not abandon it. I have therefore to deal with it. The answer put forward by counsel for the defendant, rebutting the suggestion that Garthwaites were agents for the defendant in the placing of this contract of insurance, in its turn raised a question of much wider and more general importance as to the position of insurance brokers. With that question, also, I must concern myself.

Both Wilson Dean Ltd and Garthwaites saw fit to make their files, with regard to this insurance, available to underwriters and to underwriters' solicitors. So far as Garthwaites are concerned, further, they refused to make their file available to the plaintiffs or to the plaintiffs' solicitors. This attitude, it should be said, was taken because the defendant's solicitors advised Garthwaites that it was the right and proper attitude to take. The defendant's solicitors further asserted in a letter to the plaintiffs' solicitors that Garthwaites were not the plaintiffs' agents.

The action taken with regard to the files cannot be justified; and, indeed, counsel for the defendant did not seek to argue that it was correct; though he maintained, as I shall have to mention hereafter, that certain documents in Garthwaites' file were the property of the underwriters and that, despite Garthwaites' position as agents for the assured, the assured were not entitled to see documents in possession of their own agents.

I do not propose to go into all the complications which have bedevilled this particular action as a result of these matters. In the end, the plaintiffs' advisers have been enabled – though belatedly – to see all relevant documents which should have been available to them from, or before, the outset of the action; they have not, in the end, been prejudiced by the belatedness of discovery, nor by the fact that documents which were in the possession of the plaintiffs' agents were unjustifiably made available to the defendant and his advisers at a time when the agents, acting on the advice of the solicitors for the opposite party, were refusing them to their own principals and their principals' legal advisers. It is to be hoped that this sorry state of affairs will not arise again.

I cannot, however, leave this matter there. Counsel for the defendant conceded that, in all matters relating to the placing of insurance, the insurance broker is the agent of the assured, and of the assured only. I do not think that this proposition of law has ever been in doubt among lawyers. I hope it is not in doubt among insurance brokers or insurers. More than 40 years ago, Scrutton LJ said:

> ... I agree, that in the case of marine insurance there is not the slightest doubt, and never has been the slightest doubt, that the broker is not the agent of the underwriter ...

The learned Lord Justice then went on to say that in his experience it would be quite wrong to say that this applies merely to marine insurance. See *Rozanes v Bowen* (1928) 32 Lloyd's Rep 98 ...

Counsel for the defendant, however, submitted, on instructions, that while this principle applies to the placing of the policy (be it noted that Scrutton LJ expressed no such limitation), yet when a claim arises under a policy the insurance broker who placed the policy may thereupon become an agent of both parties in certain respects. This, says counsel, is not merely the practice at Lloyd's; it is the practice also in the non-Lloyd's insurance market in this country; indeed, it is said, it is world-wide practice in the insurance business. When a claim arises, it is asserted, the insurer – Lloyd's underwriters or other insurers – may, and commonly do, instruct the insurance broker who placed the insurance to obtain a report from assessors as to the claim. The broker is, apparently, entitled to accept these instructions without a by your leave from his principal, the assured, and without the principal being told by the agent that he is accepting instructions from the adverse, or potentially adverse, party. The assessors' report, unless it contains allegations of fraud, goes from the assessors to the insurer via the broker. The broker sees the report and keeps a copy on his file. But the broker may not disclose the contents of the report to the assured or to the assured's legal advisers, without the express consent of the insurer. The report is the insurer's document ...

The law, again, has been stated with clarity and precision in the judgment of Scrutton LJ in *Fullwood v Hurley* [1928] 1 KB 498:

> No agent who has accepted an employment from one principal can in law accept an engagement inconsistent with his duty to the first principal ... unless he makes the fullest disclosure to each principal of his interest, and obtains the consent of each principal to the double employment ...

If an insurance broker, before he accepts instructions to place an insurance, discloses to his client that he wishes to be free to act in the say suggested, and if the would-be assured, fully informed as to the broker's intention to accept such instructions from the insurers and as to the possible implications of such collaboration between his agent and the opposite party, is prepared to agree that the broker may so act, good and well. In the absence of such express and fully informed consent, in my opinion it would be a breach of duty on the part of the insurance broker so to act.

The potential dangers and undesirable consequences are obvious in any case where, as here, an agent permits himself, without the express consent of his principal, to make a compact with the opposite party whereby he is supplied with information which he is, or may be, precluded from passing on to his principal. Such a relationship with the insurer inevitably, even if wrongly, invites suspicion that the broker is hunting with the hounds while running with the hare. It readily leads to consequences such as occurred in this case where a broker refused to comply with a proper request from his principal's solicitors, but sought or accepted advice from the adverse party's solicitors as to how he should act vis à vis his principal. If the insurer desires to obtain an assessor's report, he can obtain it through some other channel than the assured's agent, the broker who has placed the insurance. If the insurer thinks it would be helpful in arriving at a fair and proper settlement of a claim that the assured's broker should see the whole or part of the assessor's report, he can disclose it to the broker; but not, in the absence of the express consent of the assured, subject to a condition that the agent shall withhold relevant information from his principal.

It was said by counsel, on instructions, that the practice which he described is common knowledge, not only as being the practice of Lloyd's brokers, but as being general practice in the insurance market. I find it remarkable, if so, that there is no reference to it – none so far as I am aware, and none to which counsel could refer me – in any decided case or in any of the well known textbooks dealing with insurance law, some of which deal at length with the practice of the insurance market and the position of insurance brokers. Even if it were established to be a practice well known to persons seeking insurance – not merely to insurers and brokers – I should hold the view ... that a custom will not be upheld by the courts of this country if it contradicts the vital principle that an agent may not at the same time serve two masters – two principals – in actual or potential opposition to one another: unless, indeed, he has the explicit, informed, consent of both principals. An insurance broker is in no privileged position in this respect.

APPENDIX 6.26

North and South Trust Co v Berkeley [1970] 2 Lloyd's Rep 467

Donaldson J: Lloyd's underwriters, in common with other insurers, employ firms of claims assessors to investigate and report upon claims. For many years it has been their practice to use the Lloyd's broker who placed the insurance as their channel of communications with the assessors. In these proceedings, the plaintiffs challenge the propriety of this practice and call for the delivery up to them of the assessors' report on their claim. The issues raised are thus of considerable general importance and interest …

Whatever else may be in doubt, it is clear beyond a peradventure that the parties would not have found themselves in their present situation but for the existence of the practice of Lloyd's underwriters and Lloyd's brokers to which I referred at the beginning of this judgment. This practice was condemned by Mr Justice Megaw (as he then was) in *Anglo-African Merchants Ltd v Bayley* [1969] 2 All ER 421 … and, in the light of that judgment, Mr MacCrindle, who appeared for the defendant, did not seek to persuade me that it constituted a lawful usage binding upon the plaintiffs. He asked, however, to be allowed to reserve the point for argument should this case be considered by a higher court. The evidence of the practice in that case does not seem to have extended much beyond the submissions of counsel for the defendant underwriter made on instructions. Bearing in mind that the practice is not referred to in any decided case or any of the well known text books on insurance law, it is perhaps understandable that Mr Justice Megaw expressed surprise when told that it was a matter of common knowledge and indeed was not only the practice of Lloyd's underwriters but also of the insurance companies in this country and throughout the world.

In present proceedings there is ample evidence that the practice exists amongst Lloyd's underwriters and brokers and it is clear that, strange as it may seem, its propriety was never challenged until this was done in *Anglo-African Merchants Ltd v Bayley*.

The propriety of the practice is fundamental to my decisions on the issues and, whether right or wrong, my views are not *obiter dicta*. Furthermore, I wish to make it abundantly clear that, whilst I have in the end been no more impressed with the propriety of the practice than was Mr Justice Megaw, I have approached the matter independently and without reliance upon his judgment, save to the extent that I should in any matter, and in particular one in the field of commercial law, pay the most careful regard to anything which he said. Above all, I wish to make it clear that despite the absence of active support for the practice from the defendant underwriter, I have given most careful consideration to all the evidence and views which have been put before me in affidavits and in the correspondence …

I appreciate that Mr Bayley, having succeeded in the action brought by Anglo-African Merchants Ltd, could not appeal against the judgment of Mr Justice Megaw. Nevertheless, I confess to a sense of very real surprise that, bearing in mind the strong terms in which that judgment was couched, the Committee of Lloyd's did not think it proper either to require an alteration in the practice or to take prompt steps by means of a friendly test action to seek the views of the Court of Appeal. Twelve months elapsed before the present dispute arose and it is now nearly two years since the judgment was given, yet the practice continues. I trust that the views which I express when added to those of Mr Justice Megaw will suffice to produce either a change of practice or a rapid sorties to the Court of Appeal. If the Committee wish to adopt the latter course, they will have my fullest co-operation.

If a usage is to have effect in law it must at least be notorious, certain and reasonable. On the evidence before me, it may be certain, despite the extension of which I think only Mr Winmill speaks. For my part, I entertain doubts whether it is sufficiently notorious, since I have no evidence that any assureds, who form the class of person who enter into the contracts affected by it, have ever heard of it. Mr Goff, for the plaintiffs, would also have wished to argue, and its at liberty to do so on any appeal, that a practice which only applies to Lloyd's is no more than the practice of a single business house or congeries of houses and cannot be said to be sufficiently widespread to amount to a market usage. It is sufficient for present purposes to say that I regard the practice as wholly unreasonable and therefore incapable of being a legal usage.

The general principle was stated by Lord Hanworth MR, in *Fullwood v Hurley* ... as being:

> ... if and so long as the agent is the agent of one party, he cannot engage to become the agent of another principal without the leave of the first principal with whom he has originally established his agency.

And by Scrutton LJ on the same page of the report as:

> No agent who has accepted an employment from one principal can in law accept an engagement inconsistent with his duty to the first principal from a second principal, unless he makes the fullest disclosure to each principal of his interest, and obtains the consent of each principal to the double employment ...

Underwriters and brokers would, I think, concede that the position of the Lloyd's broker is inconsistent with this general principle, but would contend that there are special features of the business of Lloyd's which take the Lloyd's broker outside the general principle. What are these special features?

It is true that Lloyd's are short of space both for staff and the storage of documents, but are they unique in this? Much modern technological research is devoted to enabling business enterprises to be directed from small centres remote from the main body of their staff and records. Lloyd's themselves have established outside departments, such as that concerned with claims recoveries, to operate in fields in which their interests cannot effectively be served by brokers.

What other advantages accrue? If, as in this case, the broker concerned with the claim instruct the assessor, the underwriter can be certain that the assessor fully understands the nature and details of the claim. The same result, however, could be achieved by instructing the assessor direct and inviting the assured and his broker to submit the claim to the assessor. If the broker goes further, the advantages to the underwriter are more obvious at the propriety of the practice becomes more dubious. The underwriter will, in many cases, wish the assessor to investigate the character, reliability and honesty of the assured and the broker must instruct the assessor accordingly. What happens then? Is it really to be thought that the broker can simply pass on the instructions and say nothing, although he knows that the assured is of the highest character? Of course not. But what if he knows of something to the detriment of the assured? Is he then to remain silent and, if so, will the assessor fail to draw his own conclusions? In some cases the activities of the brokers do not stop at the instruction of the assessors, but include the instruction of solicitors to resist the assured's claim. The claim itself will by then have been defined by letters from the assured's solicitors, so that the broker can add nothing on behalf of the assured. But he, above all, knows the full background of the claim, including its weaknesses. Is he to mislead underwriters' solicitors by giving them only half the story?

In the context of settlement negotiations, it is said to be a positive advantage to the assured that his broker shall have confidential information on the strength of underwriters' defence. But how can he use this information when advising his client? Again, underwriters may be denying liability on the basis of a wholly misconceived, but apparently correct, appraisal of the facts by the assessors. The broker must treat this appraisal as confidential and is therefore unable to inquire from the assured whether there may not be a fallacy. And what happens if the assured, taking a pessimistic view of the strength of his claim, indicates to his broker that he is prepared to accept a low figure in settlement, when the broker, having seen the assessor's report in confidence, knows that underwriters must be prepared to settle for a high figure.

Mr Boag assures me that part of the training of the broker is to act properly in the dual capacity and that he has never known insurance brokers to use their dual position improperly. But how do you train anyone to act properly in such a situation? What course of action can possibly be adopted which does not involve some breach of the duty to one principal or the other? I yield to no one in my admiration for the skill and honesty of the insurance brokers and other men of business of the City of London, but neither skill nor honesty can reconcile the irreconcilable.

The watch words of the business of insurance are '*uberrima fides*' and it is astonishing that Lloyd's should have evolved a practice which renders the maintenance of the utmost good faith so fraught with difficulty. The fact that the practice was impugned for the first time last year is in part attributable to the utter integrity of those involved and in part attributable to the fact that it was unknown to the public. The integrity remains, but the practice is now becoming common knowledge. Even if those who are members of Lloyd's or Lloyd's brokers still think on reflection that the practice is fair and reasonable, they and the Committee of Lloyd's may wish to consider whether in the changed circumstances that is now sufficient or whether, to adapt a precept which the court seeks to apply in relation to their own business, the practices of Lloyd's must not only be reasonable, but must be seen to be reasonable ...

Lamberts, in acting for the defendant, were undertaking duties which inhibited the proper performance of their duties towards the plaintiffs, but, in so far as they acted for the defendant underwriter, they were not acting in the discharge of any duty towards the plaintiffs. Lamberts wore the plaintiffs' hat and the underwriter's hat side by side and in consequence, as was only to be expected, neither hat fitted properly. The plaintiffs had a legitimate complaints on this account and can claim damages if and to the extent that the partial dislodgment of their hat has caused them loss or damage.

But what the plaintiff ask in these proceedings is to be allowed to see what Lamberts were keeping under the underwriter's hat and for that there is no warrant.

Before leaving this matter I should make a brief further mention of *Anglo-African Merchants Ltd and Another v Bayley and Others*, because it may be suggested that Mr Justice Megaw in that case was expressing a view which was inconsistent with that which I have expressed. The learned judge said that the refusal of the brokers to make their files available to the assured could not be justified, but that in the end they had been allowed to see all that should have been available to them from the outset. The documents in fact made available included a great deal of material to which the assured was plainly entitled and in addition an assessor's report and, it may be, other similar underwriters' documents. For my part, I do not believe that Mr Justice Megaw in that passage had in mind whether different considerations might or might not apply to the classes of document with which I have been concerned. His remarks were directed to the general conduct of the brokers which could not have been justified even on the basis of the practice upon which they relied, and which he condemned.

APPENDIX 6.27

Tarr, AA, 'Insurance law and the consumer' (1989) 1 Bond LR 79

LIABILITY FOR AGENTS AND BROKERS

Insurance agents and brokers perform vitally important functions in the insurance arena. However, in the performance of their various tasks a number of major problems have arisen.

First and foremost has been the difficulty in determining whose agent in law a particular intermediary is. This question is of particular significance where a misstatement in a proposal or non-disclosure derives from an agent's fraud or recklessness, or incompetence in performing the task undertaken. For example, in *Jumna Khan v Bankers and Traders Insurance Co Ltd* (1925) 37 CLR 451 an illiterate insured effected insurance through an agent of the defendant insurer. At the request of the agent, he signed a blank proposal form. Without asking the insured any questions, the agent then filled in the form and neglected to disclose the occurrence of a previous fire and a refusal of cover. The full court of the Supreme Court of New South Wales upheld the insurer's right to repudiate liability when a loss occurred. Street CJ held that the insured's illiteracy did not relieve him of his duty to exercise care and, by signing the proposal, the proponent had adopted it as his own. This decision was upheld by the High Court. Misstatements attributable to an agent's fraud or recklessness have also been resolved against an insured on the basis that the agent's authority from the insurer is regarded as an authority to receive the proposal, and in so far as the agent writes down the answers the agent is seen as the agent or amanuensis of the insured – in treating the agent as no more than the right hand of the insured for the purpose of completing the proposal the unfortunate consequences of agents' misguided actions have been visited upon insureds. The courts have in more recent times endeavoured to attribute to the insurer the responsibility for the agent's conduct in completing the proposal form – for example, in *Stone v Reliance Mutual Insurance Society and Deaves v CML Fire and General Insurance Co Ltd* [1972] 1 Lloyd's Rep 469 – but, generally speaking, the common law is unsatisfactory in this area and this is compounded by insurance industry practice of protecting itself by contractual provisions excluding the insurer's responsibility for the conduct of its agents.

The basic rule of agency that the principal is bound by any of the acts of the agent within the scope of the agent's actual or apparent (ostensible) authority and by any unauthorised act which the principal chooses to ratify, is departed from in the Insurance (Agents and Brokers) Act 1984 (Cth). One of the most far reaching provisions of the Act is s 11(1), which provides as follows:

> An insurer is responsible, as between the insurer and an insured or intending insured, for the conduct of his agent or employee, being conduct:
>
> (a) upon which a person in the circumstances of the insured or intending insured could reasonably be expected to rely; and

> (b) upon which the insured or intending insured in fact relied in good faith,
>
> in relation to any matter relating to insurance and is so responsible notwithstanding that the agent or employee did not act within the scope of his authority or employment, as the case may be.

A number of points must be made in relation to this section. First, as far as the scope is concerned it should be borne in mind that it deals with the responsibility of the insurer for the conduct of its agent or employee. The identification of these persons is made much easier by further reforms. The Act defines a broker as 'a person who carries on the business of arranging contracts of insurance, whether in Australia or elsewhere, as agent for intending insureds'. Insurance agents are not expressly defined in the Act but their identification is greatly facilitated by s 10 (which came into operation on 1 July 1986), as this section makes it mandatory for persons who arrange or hold themselves out as entitled to arrange contracts of insurance as agents for insurers to operate under a written agreement with the insurer or insurers in questions. This written agreement will clearly evidence an agency to arrange insurance cover on behalf of an insurer and it will be an offence not to comply with this provision. A complement to s 10, is s 12. This section (which commenced on 1 August 1988) deems insurance intermediaries, other than brokers, to be agents of the insurer 'in relation to any matter relating to insurance and as between an insured or intending insured and an insurer'. The conjoint effect of ss 10 and 12 is to require insurance agents to operate under written agreements and to fix the insurer in role of principal as far as the agent's insurance dealings with insureds are concerned. Moreover, the particular situation of intermediaries acting under binders has not escaped the legislature's attention. The conjoint effect of ss 9 and 15 of the Act is to deem a broker to be an agent of the insurer when exercising final underwriting or claims settlement functions pursuant to binder agreements.

Secondly, the statutory responsibility imposed upon the insurer by s 11(1) for the conduct of its agent or employee is in relation to conduct: (a) upon which a person in the circumstances of the insured or intending insured could reasonably be expected to rely; and (b) upon which the insured or intending insured in fact relied in good faith'. The expression 'in the circumstances of the insured' takes account of the personal idiosyncrasies of the particular insured such as background, illiteracy, or blindness, but there must be a reasonable expectation of reliance on the conduct by a person in the circumstances of the insured, and actual reliance in good faith must be shown. The kinds of conduct caught by s 11(1) are limited only by the words 'in relation to any matter relating to insurance'. This casts a very wide net and would, it is submitted, make an insurer responsible for its agent's or employee's advice as to investment or tax advantages associated with life insurance.

Thirdly, of vital importance are the concluding words to s 11(1) which provide that the insurer is 'responsible, notwithstanding that the agent or employee did not act within the scope of his authority or employment, as the case may be'. This represents a total departure from the common law position, and the Australian Law Reform Commission in advocating this step had the following to say:

> In dealing with an insurance agent, a member of the public is likely to rely exclusively upon the agent's knowledge and experience. He is not in a position to know, or to become informed of, the mysteries relating to the scope of an agent's authority. The present law determines the rights of insurer and insured

> partly by reference to arrangements between insurer and agent and partly by reference to the authority which persons in the agent's position normally have. Each of these is beyond the knowledge and experience of many members of the public. What is within their knowledge and experience is what an insurance agent represents to them as being within his authority. To place restrictions by reference to an agent's actual and apparent authority is necessarily to discriminate against those persons in the community who, by reason of their background, education and training, are lacking in knowledge, are most in need of advice and assistance and are most likely to rely uncritically on the advice of the insurer's agent. They are likely to constitute a large number of the insuring public, including a sizable proportion of the migrant population. A rule which requires the conclusion reached in *Jumma Khan* has little claim to respect. For this reason, the Commission suggested in its discussion paper that responsibility be imposed on an insurer for its agent's conduct, irrespective of any limitation which might be suggested by the present requirement of actual or apparent authority.

The Life Insurance Federation of Australia was, and presumably is still, critical of this reform as being 'too far reaching'; the specific example of an agent giving unauthorised and faulty advice on the making of a will while negotiating life cover was cited by this organisation. Moreover, NRMA Insurance Limited argued that small country agencies could depart from providing very limited insurance facilities and types of cover, into the unauthorised areas of livestock or worker's compensation insurance and the insurer would be held accountable. In essence, the Australian Law Reform Commission's unsympathetic response to the arguments put forward by LIFA and NRMA suggested that careful drafting of the statutory provisions would resolve the LIFA situation, and that reliance in the situation put forward by NRMA would be difficult to prove. With respect, by attributing responsibility to an insurer for conduct of an agent or employee 'in relation to any matter relating to insurance' it is difficult to see how an insurer can avoid responsibility, for example, for a life agent's estate planning or property settlement advice when allied to the negotiation of life cover, given that investment linked life cover (unbundled insurance) dictates that discussion should range into financial matters, the insurer is doubly hard pressed to escape liability. Moreover, it does not seem unfeasible that because conduct is to be assessed by reference to the personal idiosyncrasies of the particular insured that many instances of insurer liability could arise in situations outlined by NRMA. The requirement of reliance will not be too difficult to satisfy. However, the value judgment has been made that insurers should bear responsibility for the conduct of their agents – even outside the scope of their actual or apparent authority or employment – on the basis that the imposition of additional cost on the industry and, ultimately, on the public at large, is preferable than for it to be borne by a small number of insureds for whom the burden may be ruinous.

Section 11(2) provides that 'the responsibility of an insurer under sub-s (1) extends so as to make the insurer liable to an insured or intending insured in respect of any loss or damage suffered by the insured or intending insured as a result of the conduct of the agent or employee'. This statutory liability in damages does not require that the agent's or employee's conduct is tortious – all that is required is conduct in relation to a matter relating to insurance causing loss or damage. Contractual provisions designed to limit or exclude the insurer's responsibility for the conduct of his agent are ineffective, and, in addition to proceeding against the insurer, the insured's right to take action against the agent or employee is not affected. Finally, not only is any attempt to contract out of the responsibilities allocated by s 11 ineffective, it is an offence to seek to avoid such responsibilities through an agreement or contractual stipulation.

Section 11 is, therefore, a very far reaching provision and has a significance far beyond its relative obscurity in the midst of a statute which is basically about occupational licensing. Section 11 will override the express terms of any agency or employment document as far as an insured's reliance on an agent's or employee's conduct is concerned – save where the conduct is so outrageous that a person in the circumstances of the insured could not reasonably be expected to rely, or where there is no actual reliance, or bad faith. Insurers will have to exercise greater care in the selection and training of their agents if they are to avoid an unwanted acquaintance with the rigours of s 11 ...

APPENDIX 6.28

Aneco Reinsurance Underwriting Ltd v Johnson and Higgins Ltd [2002] Lloyd's Rep 157, HL

Lord Steyn: My Lords:

(1) The shape of the Appeal

20 The central issue in this case is not one of high legal principle but an evaluative one involving matters of fact and degree. This would not have been fully apparent when the Appeal Committee granted leave to appeal. The broad question is whether London reinsurance brokers, who were in breach of duty to a Bermudan reinsurance company, are liable only for the reinsurance cover which the company lost (US$11 m), or for the total losses which the company suffered on the transaction (US$35 m). This in turn depends on an assessment whether on the facts of the case it is governed by the 'scope of the duty' principle applied by the House in *Banque Bruxelles Lambert SA v Eagle Star Insurance Co Ltd* [1997] AC 191 also known as *South Australia Asset Management Corp v York Montague Ltd, ('SAAMCO')* or whether the brokers had undertaken or assumed a duty to advise the company as to what course of action they should take.

...

23 Johnson and Higgins were acting as Mr Bullen's brokers in the first or (from Aneco's point of view) inwards transaction and as Aneco's brokers in the second or outwards transaction. Mr Forster knew from the start that if satisfactory outwards reinsurance was not available in the market Aneco would not have proceeded. Mr Forster said in due course at the trial that 'the whole thing would have collapsed' ...

...

26 Unfortunately Mr Forster negligently failed properly to present the risk to Aneco's reinsurers some of whom subsequently avoided the policies as they were entitled to do. Euphemistically Mr Forster represented to Aneco's reinsurers that the Bullen treaty was a quota share treaty when it was in fact a fac/oblig treaty. The difference is that a quota share treaty is not facultative as far as the reassured (a person in the position of Bullen) is concerned: he must cede a set proportion of every risk which falls within the limits of the contract so that everything which meets those criteria is automatically ceded. By contrast fac/oblig treaties are plainly open to abuse. The reassured is able to put onto his reinsurer the least attractive pieces of qualifying business in his book while keeping what he considers to be the best business for himself. A reinsurer will tend only to reinsure another underwriter on fac/oblig terms if he has considerable trust in the way that his reassured will use it. It is common ground now that Mr King would not have agreed to lead the reinsurance of a fac/oblig treaty and that on a proper presentation of the risk it would have been impossible to get enough underwriters to subscribe the reinsurance slip so that the

reinsurance that Mr Crawley desired was never available in the market. If Mr Forster had made the enquiries, presentation and disclosure that he should have made he would have discovered that the outwards reinsurance cover on which Mr Crawley to his knowledge relied from the start was never available. In the event Aneco suffered a loss on the Bullen treaty of more than US$35 m of which they would have recovered US$11 m from their reinsurers if the reinsurance which Aneco had asked for and which Johnson and Higgins claimed to have obtained had been effective.

27 The brokers received the usual three per cent brokerage under the Bullen treaty and 10 per cent in respect of the six excess of loss contracts ...

28 Aneco sued the brokers in negligence. Aneco formulated its claim for damages on two alternative bases. Its primary case was a claim for all losses which it had in fact suffered by entering into the reinsurance of the Bullen treaty. Aneco put forward this claim on the basis that the brokers had wrongly advised them that the reinsurance was available in the market and that this advice led them to enter into the Bullen treaty. An indispensable part of this way of putting the claim was that in truth alternative security was never available. The secondary case of Aneco was a claim for all the sums which would have been payable under the outwards reinsurance if it had been in place.

...

V The issues before the House

32 Before the House the Court of Appeal's conclusions on the non-availability of alternative reinsurance cover was accepted it follows that Mr Forster's advice to Aneco that reinsurance cover was available in the market was wrong and was negligently given.

33 In these circumstances the principal question is: is the correct measure of damages all of Aneco's losses under the Bullen treaty or is the correct measure equal to the recovery which Aneco would have made under the reinsurance contracts but was unable to make to the extent that those have been avoided?

...

VII The law

36 Given that this case can be decided by applying settled principles, I do not propose to examine any problems which do not arise. Nevertheless, I must set out, without examination, the contours of established doctrine.

37 In the leading judgment in *SAAMCO* [1997] AC 191 Lord Hoffmann illustrated 'the scope of duty' concept with an example. He said, at p 213D:

> A mountaineer about to undertake a difficult climb is concerned about the fitness of his knee. He goes to a doctor who negligently makes a superficial examination and pronounces the knee fit. The climber goes on the expedition, which he would not have undertaken if the doctor had told him the true state of his knee. He suffers an injury which is an entirely foreseeable consequence of mountaineering but has nothing to do with his knee.

Lord Hoffmann said that on the usual principle the doctor is not liable. Lord Hoffmann supported his reasoning saying that, if the contrary were the case the paradoxical situation would arise that the liability of a person who warranted the accuracy of the information would be less than that of the person who gave no such warranty but failed to take reasonable care: at pp 213H–214A. Lord Hoffmann generalised the principle as follows, at p 213C–F:

> It is that a person under a duty to take reasonable care to provide information on which someone else will decide upon a course of action is, if negligent, not generally regarded as responsible for all the consequences of that course of action. He is responsible only for the consequences of the information being wrong. A duty of care which imposes upon the informant responsibility for losses which would have occurred even if the information which he gave had been correct is not in my view fair and reasonable as between the parties. It is therefore inappropriate either as an implied term of a contract or as a tortious duty arising from the relationship between them.
>
> The principle thus stated distinguishes between a duty to *provide information* for the purpose of enabling someone else to decide upon a course of action and a duty to advise someone as to what course of action he should take. If the duty is to advise whether or not a course of action should be taken, the adviser must take reasonable care to consider all the potential consequences of that course of action. If he is negligent, he will therefore be responsible for all the foreseeable loss which is a consequence of that course of action having been taken. If his duty is only to supply information, he must take reasonable care to ensure that the information is correct and, if he is negligent, will be responsible for all the foreseeable consequences of the information being wrong.

The House has twice followed and applied the law all stated in *SAAMCO*: see *Nykredit Mortgage Bank Plc v Edward Erdman Group Ltd (No 2)* [1997] 1 WLR 1627; and *Platform Home Loans Ltd v Oyston Shipways Ltd* [2000] 2 AC 190. In the latter case Lord Hobhouse of Woodborough summarised the *SAAMCO* principle by saying 'it is the scope of the tort which determines the extent of the remedy to which the injured party is entitled': at p 209B ...

40 The starting point of the enquiry is not in doubt. If the brokers had carefully performed their duty to report on the availability of reinsurance they would inevitably have reported to Aneco that reinsurance cover was not available in the market. In that event, Aneco would not have entered into the Bullen treaty. The issue is simply: Did the brokers undertake a duty to advise Aneco as to what course of action they should undertake'? The argument on behalf of the brokers was that they only undertook a duty to exercise reasonable care to obtain the reinsurance ordered and to report the result of their endeavours. Lord Justice Evans, who has vast experience of the way in which reinsurance business is transacted, gave the answer to this argument. He observed that it would be 'highly artificial to derive from the evidence any suggestion that Mr Forster was not advising

Mr Crawley what course to take': at para 78. There was ample material to support this conclusion. Only one item of evidence need be cited. In his evidence Mr Forster accepted that the brokers were advising Mr Crawley as to what reinsurance was available and as to the state of the market. He said:

> [A] Yes, I think we were advising him of what was available then, and we were advising him about the state of the market at that time as well.
>
> [Q] Yes, quite, you were advising him as to the state of the market? [A] Yes.

The core of the reasoning of Lord Justice Evans was at paras 82–84 ...

> ... the fact that no reinsurance cover was available in the market is important, because it introduces an additional head of breach of duty by Johnson and Higgins. They are liable not merely for failing to obtain effective cover on the terms which they reported to Aneco, but also for failing to report that no cover could be obtained.
>
> The last factor in particular means in my judgment that the Banque Bruxelles principle – compensating the claimant only for the consequences of the advice or information being wrong – fails to provide proper compensation in the present case. Aneco is also reasonably entitled to compensation for Johnson and Higgins' failure to report correctly the current market assessment of the reinsurance risks which Aneco was proposing to undertake. Those risks were central to Aneco's decision and Mr Forster took it upon himself to advise Mr Crawley with regard to them. This is far removed from the lender/valuer relationship and even from the client/professional adviser relationship to which the Banque Bruxelles case applies, and even more so from the doctor and mountaineer.
>
> I therefore would hold that Aneco is entitled to recover damages for the whole of the losses which it suffered in consequence of entering into the Bullen treaty, acting on Johnson and Higgins' advice with regard to the availability of reinsurance (retrocession) and therefore on the current market assessment of the risk.

For my part this reasoning is convincing ...

41 The contrary reasoning of Lord Justice Aldous, and the arguments of Counsel for the brokers, are in my view based on an artificial and unrealistic distinction between reporting on the availability of reinsurance in the market and reporting on the assessment of the market on the risks inherent in the Bullen treaty. These are two sides of the same thing they are inextricably intertwined. If the brokers had advised Aneco of the non-availability of reinsurance cover in the market, that would inevitably have revealed to Aneco the current market assessment of the risk. There was no other credible reason for reinsurance being unavailable. On the evidence Lord Justice Evans was correct to conclude that the brokers' breach of duty was their negligent advice 'with regard to the availability of reinsurance (retrocession) and therefore on the current market assessment of the risk'.

In my view the conclusion of Lord Justice Evans is supported by the commercial realities and inherent probabilities in the relationship between broker and reinsured revealed by the documentary and oral evidence.

42 Counsel for the brokers placed great weight on the argument that the conclusion of the majority places a broker, circumstanced in a dual capacity as Mr Forster was, in an invidious position. He argued that the difficulty lies in holding that the broker, who owes a duty to the insured to place the insurance, is simultaneously under a duty of care to the insurer to provide advice to him on whether or not to write the insurance at all. The answer is clear. Any problem of the brokers arising from the performance of their dual functions in this case was entirely of their own making. It cannot divert the House from arriving at the inescapable conclusion on the facts that the brokers assumed a duty to advise Aneco as to what course to take. In the result the brokers' failure to advise that reinsurance was unavailable in the market resulted in a recoverable loss of US $35 m. The width of the duty assumed by the brokers is determinative of this being the correct measure of damages.

43 Ultimately, on matters of fact the question is on which side of the line drawn in *SAAMCO* the present case falls. In my view the majority of the Court of Appeal came to the correct conclusion. The brokers were fortunate in obtaining leave to appeal to the House on what turned out to be issues of fact. Nevertheless, it was necessary to give the closest attention to all the arguments deployed during a three day hearing. Having done so my view is that the arguments of the brokers must be rejected.

...

CONSTRUCTION OF THE POLICY

INTRODUCTION

> The instant case presents yet another illustration of the dangers of the present complex structuring of insurance policies. Unfortunately, the insurance industry has become addicted to the practice of building into policies one condition or exception upon another in the shape of a linguistic Tower of Babel. We join other courts in decrying a trend which both plunges the insured into a state of uncertainty and burdens the judiciary with the task of resolving it. We reiterate our pleas for clarity and simplicity in policies that fulfil so important a public service [*Insurance Co of North America v Electronic Purification Co* 67 Cal 2d 679 (1967); 433 P 2d 174 (1967)].

Two hundred years earlier, Lord Mansfield said:

> It is amazing when additional clauses are introduced, that the merchants do not take advice in framing them, or bestow more consideration upon them themselves. I do not recollect an addition made which has not created some doubts on the construction of it [*Simond v Boydell* (1779) 1 Doug 268].

An important contribution to the approach that should be used in the construction of contracts generally was made by Lord Hoffmann in *ICS v West Bromwich BS* [1998] 1 All ER 98 building on the approach of Lord Wilberforce in *Prenn v Simmonds* [1971] 3 All ER 237. The case concerned home income plans and complex issues of interpretation under the Financial Services Act 1986 and schemes set up under it. His Lordship explained that almost all the old intellectual baggage of 'legal' interpretation has now been discarded in favour of an approach where common sense principles should be the guide. He summarised those principles as:

- To seek to discover what the document would mean to an ordinary person who had all the background knowledge that would be available to someone involved in that particular contract.
- That background is the 'matrix of fact' and that is to include everything of which the reasonable person would have knowledge.
- However from this background is to be excluded previous negotiations of the parties and their declarations of subjective intent. Such is available but only in cases of rectification.
- The meaning to be given to a document is not the same as the meaning of its words. The latter is the dictionary meaning of words, while the more important approach is what those words mean to the reasonable person who has the 'matrix of fact'.

- The rule that words should be given their natural and ordinary meaning (see below) is the common sense recognition that people did not normally make mistakes in formal documents. However if the words would appear to fly in the face of common sense then the court may choose a different interpretation. (See generally McMeel, 'The rise of commercial construction in contract law' [1998] LMCLQ 382.) The Hoffmann guidelines were adopted in the insurance case of *Kumar v AGF* [1998] 4 All ER 788 which concerned the interpretation of solicitors' professional indemnity insurance. The background used to aid construction was that the Solicitors' Indemnity Fund Rules were aimed at providing an indemnity to clients who suffered losses caused by a solicitor's negligence. Thus an interpretation that fails to provide that protection would be difficult to justify.

Even when spurred on by the desire to 'read-in' the surrounding circumstances and thus to provide clarity where there is considered to be none, would you have reached the same conclusion as the Court of Appeal in *Sargent v GRE (UK) Ltd* [2000] Lloyd's Rep 77? Here the insured had a personal accident policy which would provide £10,000 if the insured suffered 'permanent total disablement from attending to any occupation'. An accident necessitated the amputation of the insured's right index finger. He could not continue his occupation as a line jointer but he could have carried out many other types of work, for instance he could drive a lorry. The court found for the insured construing the above phrase as meaning that he qualified for payment if he could not continue the specific occupation that he was pursuing at the time of the injury.

As we will see at the end of the chapter, American courts have taken a pro-active stance towards the construction of policy wording. The main part of the chapter, however, is concerned with the position in England. Attempts have been made in the recent past to simplify documentation and to aim for a 'plain English' approach. The problem is that policies do not cover every eventuality that may befall an insured, even though he thinks they should, and thus the exceptions and limitations of coverage are all part of the underwriter's art.

It must not be thought that only consumers suffer from difficulty of understanding. Those with commercial insurance and indeed insurers themselves, as reinsureds, also find construction difficulties. In *Youell v Bland Welch and Co* [1992] 2 Lloyd's Rep 127, nine experienced underwriters admitted that they had had difficulties in understanding the scope of the reinsurance cover that they had obtained. The evidence came close to showing that they had not read the wording, a favourite allegation made by insurers against consumer and commercially insureds.

This chapter is concerned with the Unfair Terms in Consumer Contracts Regulations 1999; construction guidelines and the American approach.

UNFAIR TERMS IN CONSUMER CONTRACTS REGULATIONS 1999

The Regulations are set out in Appendix 7.1. They apply only to consumer contracts and unlike the Unfair Contract Terms Act 1977 they apply to insurance contracts, perhaps because they derive from a Directive rather than from London! The 1977 Act uses the term 'reasonableness' as the basic test, whereas the 1999 Regulations use the phrase 'good faith'. Thus, there will be an unfair term where it causes a significant imbalance in the parties' rights and obligations under the contract to the detriment of the consumer. If there is an unfair term then the contract continues, but the unfair term is not binding on the consumer. Of particular importance to the present topic are regs 5 and 6 which state:

> Reg 5(1) A contractual term which has not been individually negotiated shall be regarded as unfair if , contrary to the requirement of good faith, it causes a significant imbalance in the parties' rights and obligations arising under the contract, to the detriment of the consumer.

This obviously will cover all types of consumer insurance policies. However insureds should note that reg 6(2) states that 'in so far as it is in plain and intelligible language, the assessment of fairness of a term shall not relate: (a) to the definition of the main subject matter of the contract; or (b) to the adequacy of the price or remuneration, as against the goods or services supplied in exchange'.

Thus it will not be possible to argue that the policy does not cover that which the insured wanted or expected as long as what it does cover is set out in plain English, nor can one complain about the price paid. This is a crucial defensive point for insurers for they understandably argue that at times the customer expects too much from a particular policy sold at a particular price.

The first part of the above regulation is to be found in the Association of British Insurers' Statement of General Insurance Practice, but not the remedy (Appendix 4.10). The Association of British Insurers' response to the original 1994 Regulations under the title 'Plain language' was to refer to the advances made in the Statement, but the view was expressed that:

> ... in practice it is difficult to explain certain aspects of a policy to a consumer in plain English. It may be particularly difficult to provide a plain English explanation of many medical terms. It is much easier to explain other aspects of a policy, such as policy charges, in plain English.

Does this response adequately deal with the problems that appear below under 'Construction guidelines'?

As yet there are no reported cases on the 1999 Regulations dealing with insurance policy wording. Regulation 8(1) empowers the Director General of Fair Trading to consider complaints made to him that a term is unfair. In the Office of Fair Trading Bulletin for the three month period October–December

2000, reference is made to 355 consumer complaints relating to non-life insurance under the heading of unfair terms and conditions and 827 complaints related to selling techniques. This is not to say that the complaints were upheld, but it does give an indication of the volume of perceived grievance under these two sub-headings. (There were in fact 2,607 non-life insurance complaints in this particular three month period.)

CONSTRUCTION GUIDELINES

The doctrine of precedent is part of the bedrock of English law. If a word or phrase in a policy has been given a particular meaning then there will be an endeavour by the court to follow that interpretation. Inevitably, however, precedent depends on like facts being decided alike and it is not unreasonable for an insurer to argue, sometimes successfully, that the circumstances appertaining to the earlier case involved a different type of policy than the present case.

In *De Souza v Home and Overseas Insurance Co Ltd* [1995] LRLR 453 (Appendix 7.2, discussed below), Mustill LJ warned:

> The cases ... are difficult if not impossible to reconcile. Some of them would, I believe, be regarded by at least some lawyers as wrong. Others would perhaps be differently decided in today's different social context, and even at the time it is plain that the judges were not all of a like mind ... In these circumstances, I think it better to withdraw a little from the authorities to the firmer ground of *this* policy and *these* facts, and to look critically at each authority to see whether it really leads inexorably to a solution of our present problem, or indeed, lends us any help at all.

Another problem is to decide what documentation should be taken into account for the construction. Obviously, the policy itself is the core document. But we have seen elsewhere that proposal form questions and answers may be part of the agreement by virtue of the technique of the basis of the contract clause. At Lloyd's the slip may be the only evidence of the contract.

Assuming a decision can be made as to what documentation is to be taken into consideration, the question then arises as to the guidelines used by the courts to arrive at a solution. Ivamy, *General Principles of Insurance Law*, 6th edn, London: Butterworths, lists 13 principle rules of construction. This might be seen as an over elaboration and the cases which follow are discussed under four general sub-headings: (a) the ordinary natural meaning of words; (b) the technical meaning of words; (c) the *eiusdem generis* rule and *noscitur a sociis*; (d) the whole policy.

The ordinary natural meaning of words

This is the main guiding force for the courts. There should be an attempt to interpret words or phrases in a manner which is acceptable to the ordinary reasonable insured who has applied for that type of cover. That sounds simple enough. The following cases, however, show that matters may be far from easy.

JC Thompson v Equity Fire Insurance Co [1910] AC 592 (Appendix 7.3) involved a fire policy wherein it was stated that no gasoline was stored or kept on the premises. The insured owned a cooking stove which contained about a pint of gasoline. Did this amount to 'storing and keeping' gasoline? The Privy Council were of the opinion that it did not.

In *Leo Rapp v McClure* [1955] 1 Lloyd's Rep 292 (Appendix 7.4), the reasonable insured was not so fortunate. This was a burglary, theft and fire policy which covered quantities of metal 'whilst in warehouse'. The goods were in a lorry parked in a compound with high walls, topped with barbed wire, gates locked, engine immobilised and surrounded by other vehicles as a means of protection. The lorry and contents were stolen. The insured lost. Warehouse imports the notion of a building and the lorry was not in a building. It might well be that the lorry was as secure or more secure than it might have been if it had been in a warehouse. That, however, was not the point. The words were clear and the insured was in breach.

Reasonable care requirements are commonly found in many types of policies. The interpretation will depend on the type of policy in question as the following two cases illustrate.

In *Fraser v BN Furman (Productions) Ltd* [1967] 3 All ER 57 (Appendix 7.5; see also Appendix 6.19, for another aspect of the decision), a worker was injured at work. Had his employers taken reasonable precautions to prevent such an accident? The trial judge found that the employers had not appreciated the risk of such an accident. The purpose of the insurance was to compensate employers who were negligently liable for injuries to their employees. Thus, in finding for the insured employer Diplock LJ was of the opinion that the insured was reasonable as long as he did not deliberately court the danger. Thus, to be unreasonable in the context of this policy meant acting recklessly.

The decision in *Sofi v Prudential Assurance Co Ltd* [1993] 2 Lloyd's Rep 559 (Appendix 7.6) is one which has been instrumental in recent years in assisting the Ombudsman in arriving at his decisions when faced by the reasonable care requirement. The plaintiff had a house contents policy and a travel policy both with the defendant insurers. He decided to take jewellery worth £42,000 with him on holiday in the belief that it was safer than leaving it at home. The jewellery was locked in the car's glove compartment while the insured made a brief visit to Dover castle while awaiting his ferry. The car was broken into and the jewellery stolen together with other items of luggage. The insurer argued that the insured had not taken reasonable precautions. The Court of Appeal found for the insured, following *Fraser*, and thus equating the requirement of recklessness for liability insurance with that for property insurance. The division between negligence and recklessness may not be easy and in some cases the reasonable observer (or the attentive visitor from Mars as Scarman LJ once said in a vicarious liability case) might be inclined to the view that some judges used a different approach when dealing with consumer policies.

Thus, in *Morley and Another v United Friendly Insurance plc* [1993] 3 All ER 47 (Appendix 7.7), X had a personal accident policy with the defendants. He got out of a car to relieve himself and when approaching the vehicle his fiancée drove off slowly. X stepped onto the rear bumper, the driver slowly increased speed, zig-zagging and throwing X to his death. The claim on the accident policy was rejected by the insurers on the grounds that there was an exception clause which read: 'No accident benefit shall be payable if death ... results directly or indirectly from or be accelerated by ... wilful exposure to needless peril.' The Court of Appeal, reversing the trial judge, found against the insurer. Lord Justice Neill explained that it was necessary to take into account the commercial purpose of the policy; it clearly covered negligence and as, at the moment he stepped onto the bumper, the car was hardly moving, this was not an indication of 'wilful exposure to needless peril'.

Compare that approach with that in *Amey Properties Ltd v Cornhill Insurance plc* [1996] LRLR 259 (Appendix 7.8), where the insured's tractor caused $2 m damage when it collided with a United States Airforce TRI aircraft (on the ground!). The policy covered accidental damage but contained a condition requiring the tractor to be kept in an efficient and roadworthy condition. There were faults in the clutch and hand brake. The court found for the insurers. The judge held that the roadworthy condition requirement was not repugnant to the commercial object of the policy. The judge had no difficulty in distinguishing *Fraser* (above). What the cases show is that courts take differing approaches to construction depending on the nature and purpose of the policy in question. There was a difference between the negligent use of a vehicle, which would be covered, and the negligent maintenance of a vehicle, which would not.

The following four cases all revolve around the meaning of the same, seemingly straightforward phrase, 'left unattended'. The cases are taken in chronological order and in that way we can test the influence of precedent as an aid to construction.

In *Starfire Diamond Rings Ltd v Angel* [1962] 2 Lloyd's Rep 217 (Appendix 7.9), the plaintiff jeweller had a policy covering theft from a vehicle which excluded liability should the vehicle be left unattended. The driver went 37 feet along a lane to relieve himself. The jewellery was stolen from the locked vehicle. The insured's claim was dismissed, the Court of Appeal reversing the trial judge. What impressed Lord Denning was the distance the driver had gone. The trial judge considered that the car was still within the driver's superintendence and that more stringent words were required in the policy to relieve the insurer. Which view do you prefer? What was the driver to do, in his predicament, in order to conform with the 'not left unattended' requirement?

The case of *Ingleton of Ilford Ltd v General Accident Fire and Life Assurance Corp Ltd* [1967] 2 Lloyd's Rep 179 (Appendix 7.10) is a lot more straightforward. A transit policy to cover wines and spirits transported in a van required the van not to be left unattended in a public place unless securely locked. The driver left the van unlocked for 15 minutes while he went into a shop and for good measure he left the keys in the ignition. The insurers were not liable on the policy.

We return to jewellers' policies in the following two cases.

In *Langford v Legal and General Assurance* [1986] 2 Lloyd's Rep 103, the insured was a market trader specialising in jewellery. On arriving home, she parked and locked her car in the driveway while she first deposited her shopping in the house intending immediately to return to the car to retrieve two cases of jewellery. She could see the car and she saw the thief. She ran out and, in trying to prevent the theft, was injured. Were the goods attended as required by the policy provision? Faced with the *Starfire* judgment, much attention was placed on distances. The car was 17 feet from the front door. Faced with the *Ingleton* judgment, time of absence was also taken into consideration. Here she was absent from the car for a few seconds. Taking a 'practical, common sense view of these matters' the judge found for the insured.

In *O'Donoghue Ltd v Harding* [1988] 2 Lloyd's Rep 281 (Appendix 7.11) the insured claimed on his Jewellers' Block Policy the sum of £145,803, when a case of jewellery was stolen from his employee at a petrol station. The employee left the jewellery in the locked car, took petrol from the nearest pump to the kiosk and kept an eye on the car for most of the time. The court found for the insured. Referring to the three earlier cases, Otton J explained:

> He was not far away for the purpose of urinating ... nor was he away for a substantial period of time chatting ... The case was nearer to *Langford*.

These four decisions, involving a similar point of construction, utilise purpose, time and distance as tools to reach a decision – so we are back to where we started, namely that each case depends largely on its particular facts.

Two Court of Appeal cases involving the definition of accidental personal injury can be taken together.

In *De Souza v Home and Overseas Insurance Co Ltd* [1995] LRLR 453 [Appendix 7.2], X had travel insurance which covered 'accidental bodily injury caused solely and directly by outward violence and visible means ...'. X died, probably from heat exhaustion, while on holiday in Spain. The Court of Appeal, reversing the trial judge, found for the insurers. Where, asked Mustill LJ, was the 'injury', where was the element of 'accident', where was the 'violent' event? 'Nowhere, so far as I can see.'

The approach used in *De Souza* was followed in *Dhak v Insurance Co of North America (UK) Ltd* [1996] 1 Lloyd's Rep 632 (Appendix 7.12). X had a personal accident policy which covered bodily injury resulting in death if caused by 'accidental means'. X, who was a nursing sister, injured her back at work. Despite treatment the pain persisted and she took to drinking large quantities of gin to relieve the pain. She died in her sleep and the inquest found that she had died from 'acute alcoholism' and 'misadventure'. The court found for the insurers. Although she had died from bodily injury, such injury had not been caused by accidental means.

Where there is a true ambiguity in the word or phrase in dispute, the *contra proferentum* rule will be used. But one should be alert to the fact that, merely because there is a conflict, it does not automatically signify ambiguity. If the *contra proferentum* rule is applicable, then the party responsible for it will have the ambiguity interpreted against it. The cases cited above were not cases involving ambiguity. It should also be remembered that in some complex policies negotiated by brokers it is the broker who sometimes drafts the wording. In such cases, as the broker is the agent of the insured (see Chapter 6), the insured cannot complain that the insurer is at fault with regard to the ambiguity.

We can refer back to *Codogianis v Guardian Assurance Co Ltd* [1921] 2 AC 125 (Appendix 5.3). There the fact that a question on the proposal form was stated in the singular did not mean that it was ambiguous. Good faith clearly required that the answer should reveal all claims that had previously been made.

In re Etherington and Lancashire and Yorkshire Accident Insurance Co [1909] 1 KB 591 (Appendix 7.13) was a case of accident insurance that would pay out on death caused by accident, but not where it was caused by disease or other intervening cause. The insured fell heavily while hunting, was soaked to the skin but continued. The shock and the wetting lowered his defences and he died a week later from the complications of pneumonia. The fact that the policy would pay out if death followed within three months from the date of the accident indicated that sudden death following the accident was not a requirement. The Court of Appeal was of the opinion that the policy was ambiguous and should be construed *contra proferentum* against the insurer. Again, in *English v Western Insurance Co* [1940] 2 KB 156 (Appendix 7.14), a 17 year old took out a motor policy which excluded liability (as was possible in those days) for negligently causing injury 'to any member of the assured's household'. He injured his sister, who lived with him in the father's house. The Court of Appeal (by a 2:1 majority), reversing the trial judge, regarded the clause as ambiguous on the grounds that it could mean a household of which he was the head, or a household of which he was a member. The insurers were liable. The cases under this sub-heading cover a wide range of policy types. They illustrate judgments reversing lower courts and, when on appeal, they sometimes include dissents. While it is easy to say that the dominant rule of construction is to apply the reasonable interpretation of words, it is sometimes far from easy to put that into practice.

The technical meaning of words

Words or phrases may have technical meanings, which clash with what might be thought of as the ordinary meaning of the words. If the technical meaning is given to them then guideline (a), above, will not work. Whether or not the court applies the technical, rather than the ordinary, meaning will depend on the circumstances of the particular policy. The fact that the insured is unaware of the technical meaning will not sway the court in his favour, if it is clear that the technical interpretation is appropriate in that type of policy.

In *Young v Sun Alliance* [1976] 3 All ER 561, one of the insured's ground floor rooms was three inches deep in water caused by an underground watercourse. A claim was made on the household policy for damage caused by flood. Was there a flood? There was no previous case dealing with the definition of flood. Lawton LJ stated in his short judgment: 'This appeal raises a semantic problem which has troubled many philosophers for centuries, and it can, I think, be expressed in the aphorism that an elephant is difficult to define but easy to recognise.' There was no flood, which must have come as a nasty surprise to the insured. The word 'flood' always appears alongside the words 'storm' and 'tempest' and thus involves violence in atmospheric conditions. Thus, flood was held to import the notion of large quantities of water, abnormal and violent.

Twenty years later the Court of Appeal revisited the question of 'flood' in *Rohan Investments Ltd v Cunningham* [1999] Lloyd's Rep IR 190 (Appendix 7.15). Water from a flat roof entered the insured's premises due to a blockage of the drainage system caused by twigs and leaves. The court found for the insured stating that the word 'flood' should be given its ordinary and natural meaning and that the test used in *Young* should not be too rigidly followed. The court however recognised that in insurance construction attempts at uniformity should be made to see that words are given similar meanings but this should stop short of giving words some kind of statutory effect. This approach of the court is more in keeping with what the Americans would call the reasonable expectations of the insured.

The application of the technical guideline to interpretation has often concerned words or phrases having a criminal law meaning (Appendix 7.16). Three cases can be used as illustrations.

In *London and Lancashire Fire Insurance Co Ltd v Bolands Ltd* [1924] AC 836 (Appendix 7.17), the plaintiff had insured his bakery, in Dublin, to include losses due to burglary. The policy contained a typical clause which excluded loss due to riots. Four armed men held up the staff and stole money. Had there been a riot, as alleged by the insurer? The House of Lords said there had been, interpreting riot according to its definition in the criminal law (under the Public Order Act 1986, riot now requires a minimum of 12 people to be involved). In *Young*, the court looked at the surrounding words as an aid to interpretation. A typical clause within which 'riot' is to be found usually includes, as did the one in *Bolands* the words: invasions; hostilities; acts of foreign enemy; strikes; civil commotions; rebellions; insurrections; military or usurped power; martial law. An armed robbery does not seem to fit in here. However, the House held that there was no ambiguity and therefore the criminal law definition had to prevail. A victim of riot damage does, however, have a claim for compensation under the Riot (Damages) Act 1886, the compensation coming from police funds.

In *Dino Services Ltd v Prudential Assurance Co Ltd* [1989] 1 All ER 422 (Appendix 7.18), the insured held a business insurance policy which covered loss due to theft if entry was 'by forcible and violent means'. Thieves stole the keys to the premises from the insured's car and entered the premises at night. Had there been forcible and violent means used? The Court of Appeal held there had not and the insurer was not liable on the policy. Violent was an ordinary word (so perhaps this case is merely an illustration of guideline (a), above), which imports some kind of force being used. Merely because the entry was unlawful it did not mean that it was a violent entry as required by the policy. The court was of the opinion that as the plaintiff had taken reasonable care and the case was a novel one then it might be appropriate for the insurer to consider making an *ex gratia* payment.

The third case in this group is the House of Lords decision in *Deutsche Genossenschaftsbank v Burnhope* [1995] 4 All ER 717. The insured bank had cover against 'theft, larceny or false pretences, committed by persons present on the premises of the ['bank']'. A customer, who was the chairman of a company, persuaded the bank to release certain securities valued at £9 m and in exchange he agreed to deposit other securities later in the day. A junior employee of the customer innocently took delivery of the documents on the bank's premises. The other securities were never delivered, the company was suspended from trading three days later for fraud and the money was never repaid. Faced with a claim on the policy, the insurers argued that there had been no theft committed on the bank's premises. The House (by a 4:1 majority), reversing the Court of Appeal (a 2:1 majority), who had allowed an appeal from the trial judge, held that the insurers were not liable. No cases were cited by the four majority judges while five cases were cited by Lord Steyn in the minority. Lord Keith explained that the clause was obviously intended to limit the insurers liability in some way:

> What precisely was in contemplation is a matter of conjecture. It may have been some form of abstraction by electronic means, carried out by persons operating away from the bank's premises.

The majority of risks covered were the 'old fashioned crimes' that are committed on the premises. Theft, however, was more difficult, because in modern times this can be committed by the perpetrator while never physically being in the bank. Coverage for such a crime is possible in the market, obviously at an increased premium. Lord Steyn, dissenting, said:

> It is true the objective of the construction of a contract is to give effect to the intention of the parties. But our law of construction is based on an objective theory. The methodology is not to probe the real intentions of the parties but to ascertain the contextual meaning of the relevant contractual language. Intention is determined by reference to expressed rather than actual intention ... The word 'theft' must be accorded the technical meaning given to theft in the criminal law ...

It is suggested that the majority of the House would not have disagreed with this approach. The disagreement comes from the following interpretation of Lord Steyn:

> The company was present at the bank's premises through its innocent agent ... who was duly authorised by the company to receive the securities ... the company was present at the bank's premises ...

Lord Steyn was of the view that the insurer's argument led to absurd consequences, which demonstrated the uncommercial nature of their interpretation. No one was able to decide exactly what purpose the clause in question was intended to achieve. It would have been easy to clearly exclude all forms of electronic theft. This method had not been used and one would have thought that the clause was sufficiently obscure or ambiguous to have merited a *contra proferentum* approach in favour of the bank. Perhaps the sloppiness (or even gross negligence) of the bank's method of dealing had an unexpressed effect on the minds of the majority.

The *eiusdem generis* rule and *noscitur a sociis*

These two Latin phrases can be used as aides to construction. The *eiusdem* rule can be applied in a situation where a list of words is followed by words such as 'or other'. The 'or other' is then restricted to words similar to those previously listed. The simplest example is 'cats, dogs and other animals'. Cats and dogs being domestic animals, the 'other' can only include other domestic animals.

In *King v Travellers Insurance Association* (1931) 48 TLR 53, the plaintiff held a policy which required 'jewellery, watches, field glasses, cameras and other fragile or specially valuable articles' to be separately declared and valued. A fur coat was lost from her baggage and as this item had not been separately declared the insurers declined to pay. Applying the *eiusdem* rule the court found for the insured. The question that had to be asked was whether the fur coat was in the same category of objects as expressly set out in the policy. It was not. A more difficult application of the rule is seen in *Mair v Railway Passengers Association Co* (1877) 3 LT 356, where, in an accident policy, there was an exclusion if the insured wilfully exposed himself to any unnecessary danger or peril. The insured accosted a woman in the street and was knocked down by her male companion and died. In deciding whether this fell within the above exception, Lord Coleridge LJ looked at other instances set out expressly in the proviso. These included fighting, suicide, war, invasion, entering or leaving a train while in motion or riding steeplechases. The behaviour that led to his death could not be brought within the same class of behaviour listed above. The insurers were therefore liable on the policy. Mr Justice Denman, however, was not prepared to go as far as saying that the *eiusdem* rule would exclude the insured's behaviour.

The *noscitur* rule is rarely referred to in the cases, perhaps because it is merged with the *eiusdem* rule. The court looks to the other surrounding words in the sentence, paragraph or proviso to see whether that will assist in defining the troublesome word. This approach can be seen in *Young*'s case (above), although there was no specific reference to this particular rule.

The whole policy

We saw at the start of the chapter that more than one document may have to be taken into consideration in construing the meaning of words. Under the present heading, the guideline is that the whole policy can be looked at and not merely the paragraph or section in which the troublesome words are located. There should be an attempt to give a word the same interpretation throughout the policy, unless that is clearly inappropriate.

In *Hamlyn v Crown Accident Insurance Co* [1893] 1 QB 750, the plaintiff had an accident policy which covered 'any bodily injury caused by violent, accidental external and visible means'. The policy was not to cover injuries that arose from 'natural disease of weakness' (the proviso contained 188 words!). The insured stooped down to pick up a marble and dislocated a knee cartilage. The insurers argued there was no violence, it was not accidental because the insured did what he intended to do and there was no external or visible means. The court found for the insured. Lopes LJ explained that attention should not be confined to that clause alone, but that the whole policy should be taken into account. When that was done it could be seen that many of the exclusions were directed at internal problems from which an insured might suffer. The present injury was externally caused.

POLICY INTERPRETATION IN THE UNITED STATES

Insurance is a world wide industry and it is of importance to know what other jurisdictions' approaches are to common problems. The courts in the United States have a long history of attempting to interpret policy wording in such a way as to meet the reasonable expectations of the insured (Appendix 7.19).

A short American judgment reported in *Lloyd's Reports* can be used here to illustrate this approach. In *Gerhardt v Continental Insurance Cos and Firemen's Insurance Co of Newark* [1967] 1 Lloyd's Rep 380 (Appendix 7.20), the insured's domestic servant was injured in the house and the insured claimed on her houseowner's comprehensive policy. The insurers argued that workman's compensation claims were not covered by the present policy. The insured's claim was successful.

Insurers, however, have responded by attempting to draft their policies with greater precision (Appendix 7.21).

Do courts in England respond in the same way as the United States courts (Appendix 7.22)? They do not, although there are occasional examples of impatience by the judiciary when faced with what it considers to be an unfair stance taken by an insurer in an unmeritorious situation. The Insurance Ombudsman (Chapter 11) has much greater flexibility.

CONSTRUCTION OF THE POLICY

APPENDIX 7.1

1999 No 2083

CONSUMER PROTECTION

Unfair Terms in Consumer Contracts Regulations 1999

Whereas the Secretary of State is a Minister designated for the purposes of section 2(2) of the European Communities Act 1972 in relation to measures relating to consumer protection:

Now, the Secretary of State, in exercise of the powers conferred upon him by section 2(2) of that Act, hereby makes the following Regulations:

Citation and commencement

1 These Regulations may be cited as the Unfair Terms in Consumer Contracts Regulations 1999 and shall come into force on 1 October 1999.

Revocation

2 The Unfair Terms in Consumer Contracts Regulations 1994 are hereby revoked.

Interpretation

3 (1) In these Regulations–

'the Community' means the European Community;

'consumer' means any natural person who, in contracts covered by these Regulations, is acting for purposes which are outside his trade, business or profession;

'court' in relation to England and Wales and Northern Ireland means a county court or the High Court, and in relation to Scotland, the Sheriff or the Court of Session;

'Director' means the Director General of Fair Trading;

'EEA Agreement' means the Agreement on the European Economic Area signed at Oporto on 2 May 1992 as adjusted by the protocol signed at Brussels on 17 March 1993;

'Member State' means a State which is a contracting party to the EEA Agreement;

'notified' means notified in writing;

'qualifying body' means a person specified in Schedule l;

'seller or supplier' means any natural or legal person who, in contracts covered by these Regulations, is acting for purposes relating to his trade, business or profession, whether publicly owned or privately owned;

'unfair terms' means the contractual terms referred to in regulation 5.

(2) In the application of these Regulations to Scotland for references to an 'injunction' or an 'interim injunction' there shall be substituted references to an 'interdict' or 'interim interdict' respectively.

Terms to which these Regulations apply

4 (1) These Regulations apply in relation to unfair terms in contracts concluded between a seller or a supplier and a consumer.

(2) These Regulations do not apply to contractual terms which reflect–

(a) mandatory statutory or regulatory provisions (including such provisions under the law of any Member State or in Community legislation having effect in the United Kingdom without further enactment);

(b) the provisions or principles of international conventions to which the Member States or the Community are party.

Unfair terms

5 (1) A contractual term which has not been individually negotiated shall be regarded as unfair if, contrary to the requirement of good faith, it causes a significant imbalance in the parties' rights and obligations arising under the contract, to the detriment of the consumer.

(2) A term shall always be regarded as not having been individually negotiated where it has been drafted in advance and the consumer has therefore not been able to influence the substance of the term.

(3) Notwithstanding that a specific term or certain aspects of it in a contract has been individually negotiated, these Regulations shall apply to the rest of a contract if an overall assessment of it indicates that it is a pre-formulated standard contract.

(4) It shall be for any seller or supplier who claims that a term was individually negotiated to show that it was.

(5) Schedule 2 to these Regulations contains an indicative and non-exhaustive list of the terms which may be regarded as unfair.

Assessment of unfair terms

6 (1) Without prejudice to regulation 12, the unfairness of a contractual term shall be assessed, taking into account the nature of the goods or services for which the contract was concluded and by referring, at the time of conclusion of the contract, to all the circumstances attending the conclusion of the contract and to all the other terms of the contract or of another contract on which it is dependent.

(2) In so far as it is in plain intelligible language, the assessment of fairness of a term shall not relate–

(a) to the definition of the main subject matter of the contract; or

(b) to the adequacy of the price or remuneration, as against the goods or services supplied in exchange.

Written contracts

7 (1) A seller or supplier shall ensure that any written term of a contract is expressed in plain, intelligible language.

(2) If there is doubt about the meaning of a written term, the interpretation which is most favourable to the consumer shall prevail but this rule shall not apply in proceedings brought under regulation 12.

Effect of unfair term

8 (1) An unfair term in a contract concluded with a consumer by a seller or supplier shall not be binding on the consumer.

(2) The contract shall continue to bind the parties if it is capable of continuing in existence without the unfair term.

Choice of law clauses

9 These Regulations shall apply notwithstanding any contract term which applies or purports to apply the law of a non-Member State, if the contract has a close connection with the territory of the Member States.

Complaints – consideration by Director

10 (1) It shall be the duty of the Director to consider any complaint made to him that any contract term drawn up for general use is unfair, unless–

(a) the complaint appears to the Director to be frivolous or vexatious; or

(b) a qualifying body has notified the Director that it agrees to consider the complaint.

(2) The Director shall give reasons for his decision to apply or not to apply, as the case may be, for an injunction under regulation 12 in relation to any complaint which these Regulations require him to consider.

(3) In deciding whether or not to apply for an injunction in respect of a term which the Director considers to be unfair, he may, if he considers it appropriate to do so, have regard to any undertakings given to him by or on behalf of any person as to the continued use of such a term in contracts concluded with consumers.

Complaints – consideration by qualifying bodies

11 (1) If a qualifying body specified in Part One of Schedule 1 notifies the Director that it agrees to consider a complaint that any contract term drawn up for general use is unfair, it shall be under a duty to consider that complaint.

(2) Regulation 10(2) and (3) shall apply to a qualifying body which is under a duty to consider a complaint as they apply to the Director.

Injunctions to prevent continued use of unfair terms

12 (1) The Director or, subject to paragraph (2), any qualifying body may apply for an injunction (including an interim injunction) against any person appearing to the Director or that body to be using, or recommending use of, an unfair term drawn up for general use in contracts concluded with consumers.

(2) A qualifying body may apply for an injunction only where–

(a) it has notified the Director of its intention to apply at least 14 days before the date on which the application is made, beginning with the date on which the notification was given; or

(b) the Director consents to the application being made within a shorter period.

(3) The court on an application under this regulation may grant an injunction on such terms as it thinks fit.

(4) An injunction may relate not only to use of a particular contract term drawn up for general use but to any similar term, or a term having like effect, used or recommended for use by any person.

Powers of the Director and qualifying bodies to obtain documents and information

13 (1) The Director may exercise the power conferred by this regulation for the purpose of–

(a) facilitating his consideration of a complaint that a contract term drawn up for general use is unfair; or

(b) ascertaining whether a person has complied with an undertaking or court order as to the continued use, or recommendation for use, of a term in contracts concluded with consumers.

(2) A qualifying body specified in Part One of Schedule 1 may exercise the power conferred by this regulation for the purpose of–

(a) facilitating its consideration of a complaint that a contract term drawn up for general use is unfair; or

(b) ascertaining whether a person has complied with–

(i) an undertaking given to it or to the court following an application by that body; or

(ii) a court order made on an application by that body,

as to the continued use, or recommendation for use, of a term in contracts concluded with consumers.

(3) The Director may require any person to supply to him, and a qualifying body specified in Part One of Schedule 1 may require any person to supply to it–

(a) a copy of any document which that person has used or recommended for use, at the time the notice referred to in paragraph (4) below is given, as a pre-formulated standard contract in dealings with consumers;

(b) information about the use, or recommendation for use, by that person of that document or any other such document in dealings with consumers.

(4) The power conferred by this regulation is to be exercised by a notice in writing which may–

(a) specify the way in which and the time within which it is to be complied with; and

(b) be varied or revoked by a subsequent notice.

(5) Nothing in this regulation compels a person to supply any document or information which he would be entitled to refuse to produce or give in civil proceedings before the court.

(6) If a person makes default in complying with a notice under this regulation, the court may, on the application of the Director or of the qualifying body, make such order as the court thinks fit for requiring the default to be made good, and any such order may provide that all the costs or expenses of and incidental to the application shall be borne by the person in default or by any officers of a company or other association who are responsible for its default.

Notification of undertakings and orders to Director

14 A qualifying body shall notify the Director–

(a) of any undertaking given to it by or on behalf of any person as to the continued use of a term which that body considers to be unfair in contracts concluded with consumers;

(b) of the outcome of any application made by it under regulation 12, and of the terms of any undertaking given to, or order made by, the court;

(c) of the outcome of any application made by it to enforce a previous order of the court.

Publication, information and advice

15 (1) The Director shall arrange for the publication in such form and manner as he considers appropriate, of–

(a) details of any undertaking or order notified to him under regulation 14;

(b) details of any undertaking given to him by or on behalf of any person as to the continued use of a term which the Director considers to be unfair in contracts concluded with consumers;

(c) details of any application made by him under regulation 12, and of the terms of any undertaking given to, or order made by, the court;

(d) details of any application made by the Director to enforce a previous order of the court.

(2) The Director shall inform any person on request whether a particular term to which these Regulations apply has been–

(a) the subject of an undertaking given to the Director or notified to him by a qualifying body; or

(b) the subject of an order of the court made upon application by him or notified to him by a qualifying body,

and shall give that person details of the undertaking or a copy of the order, as the case may be, together with a copy of any amendments which the person giving the undertaking has agreed to make to the term in question.

(3) The Director may arrange for the dissemination in such form and manner as he considers appropriate of such information and advice concerning the operation of these Regulations as may appear to him to be expedient to give to the public and to all persons likely to be affected by these Regulations.

The functions of the Financial Services Authority

16 The functions of the Financial Services Authority under these Regulations shall be treated as functions of the Financial Services Authority under the Financial Services Act 1986.

Kim Howells

Parliamentary Under-Secretary of State for Competition and Consumer Affairs, Department of Trade and Industry.

22 July 1999

SCHEDULE 1

Regulation 3

QUALIFYING BODIES

PART ONE

1 The Information Commissioner.

2 The Gas and Electricity Markets Authority.

3 The Director General of Electricity Supply for Northern Ireland.

4 The Director General of Gas for Northern Ireland.

5 The Director General of Telecommunications.

6 The Director General of Water Services.

7 The Rail Regulator.

8 Every weights and measures authority in Great Britain.

9 The Department of Enterprise, Trade and Investment in Northern Ireland.

10 The Financial Services Authority

PART TWO

11 Consumers' Association.

SCHEDULE 2

Regulation 5(5)

INDICATIVE AND NON-EXHAUSTIVE LIST OF TERMS WHICH MAY BE REGARDED AS UNFAIR

1 Terms which have the object or effect of:

(a) excluding or limiting the legal liability of a seller or supplier in the event of the death of a consumer or personal injury to the latter resulting from an act or omission of that seller or supplier;

(b) inappropriately excluding or limiting the legal rights of the consumer vis à vis the seller or supplier or another party in the event of total or partial non-performance or inadequate performance by the seller or supplier of any of the contractual obligations, including the option of offsetting a debt owed to the seller or supplier against any claim which the consumer may have against him;

(c) making an agreement binding on the consumer whereas provision of services by the seller or supplier is subject to a condition whose realisation depends on his own will alone;

(d) permitting the seller or supplier to retain sums paid by the consumer where the latter decides not to conclude or perform the contract, without providing for the consumer to receive compensation of an equivalent amount from the seller or supplier where the latter is the party cancelling the contract;

(e) requiring any consumer who fails to fulfil his obligation to pay a disproportionately high sum in compensation;

(f) authorising the seller or supplier to dissolve the contract on a discretionary basis where the same facility is not granted to the consumer, or permitting the seller or supplier to retain the sums paid for services not yet supplied by him where it is the seller or supplier himself who dissolves the contract;

(g) enabling the seller or supplier to terminate a contract of indeterminate duration without reasonable notice except where there are serious grounds for doing so;

(h) automatically extending a contract of fixed duration where the consumer does not indicate otherwise, when the deadline fixed for the consumer to express his desire not to extend the contract is unreasonably early;

(i) irrevocably binding the consumer to terms with which he had no real opportunity of becoming acquainted before the conclusion of the contract;

(j) enabling the seller or supplier to alter the terms of the contract unilaterally without a valid reason which is specified in the contract;

(k) enabling the seller or supplier to alter unilaterally without a valid reason any characteristics of the product or service to be provided;

(l) providing for the price of goods to be determined at the time of delivery or allowing a seller of goods or supplier of services to increase their price without in both cases giving the consumer the corresponding right to cancel the contract if the final price is too high in relation to the price agreed when the contract was concluded;

(m) giving the seller or supplier the right to determine whether the goods or services supplied are in conformity with the contract, or giving him the exclusive right to interpret any term of the contract;

(n) limiting the seller's or supplier's obligation to respect commitments undertaken by his agents or making his commitments subject to compliance with a particular formality;

(o) obliging the consumer to fulfil all his obligations where the seller or supplier does not perform his;

(p) giving the seller or supplier the possibility of transferring his rights and obligations under the contract, where this may serve to reduce the guarantees for the consumer, without the latter's agreement;

(q) excluding or hindering the consumer's right to take legal action or exercise any other legal remedy, particularly by requiring the consumer to take disputes exclusively to arbitration not covered by legal provisions, unduly restricting the evidence available to him or imposing on him a burden of proof which, according to the applicable law, should lie with another party to the contract.

2 Scope of paragraphs 1(g), (j) and (l)

(a) Paragraph 1(g) is without hindrance to terms by which a supplier of financial services reserves the right to terminate unilaterally a contract of indeterminate duration without notice where there is a valid reason, provided that the supplier is required to inform the other contracting party or parties thereof immediately.

(b) Paragraph l(j) is without hindrance to terms under which a supplier of financial services reserves the right to alter the rate of interest payable by the consumer or due to the latter, or the amount of other charges for financial services without notice where there is a valid reason, provided that the supplier is required to inform the other contracting party or parties thereof at the earliest opportunity and that the latter are free to dissolve the contract immediately.

Paragraph l(j) is also without hindrance to terms under which a seller or supplier reserves the right to alter unilaterally the conditions of a contract of indeterminate duration, provided that he is required to inform the consumer with reasonable notice and that the consumer is free to dissolve the contract.

(c) Paragraphs l(g), (j) and (l) do not apply to:

- transactions in transferable securities, financial instruments and other products or services where the price is linked to fluctuations in a stock exchange quotation or index or a financial market rate that the seller or supplier does not control; contracts for the purchase or sale of foreign currency, traveller's cheques or international money orders denominated in foreign currency.

(d) Paragraph 1(l) is without hindrance to price indexation clauses, where lawful, provided that the method by which prices vary is explicitly described.

APPENDIX 7.2

De Souza v Home and Overseas Insurance Co Ltd [1995] LRLR 453, CA

Mustill LJ: During August 1984, Mr S de Souza went on holiday with his wife to Torremolinos. He was insured with Home and Overseas Insurance Company Limited, under a holidays policy, s 5 of which provided that:

> If the Insured Person shall sustain accidental bodily injury caused solely and directly by outward violence and visible means and such injury shall within 12 months be the sole and direct cause of death or disablement the Company will pay to the Insured Person or his legal personal representatives the under mentioned benefits.
>
> 1 Death … £15,000.

On 3 September, Mr de Souza died. His wife claimed under the policy. The insurers denied liability, and Mrs de Souza commenced proceedings …

To arrive at a conclusion on whether the claim under the contract should succeed the decision maker needs only to form an opinion about the categories of event which are covered, and then inspect the event which happened here to see whether it can properly be placed in one of those categories. If the matter were not encrusted with authority, he would begin by asking what in everyday terms had happened on the de Souzas' holiday. The answer would, I believe, be that Mr de Souza had suffered a sudden, acute and fatal illness through becoming overheated and dried out in a hot climate. If one then asked an ordinary literate lay member of the public whether this sad event entailed that Mr de Souza had been the victim of an accidental bodily injury, I believe that he or she would say: '... of course not.' If the question were amplified by adding a requirement of outward violent and visible means the answer would be doubly negative. If attention were then drawn to the policy conditions as a whole, where the clearest possible distinction is made between accident and injury on the one hand, and illness on the other, the answer would seem clearer than ever. Here we have a policy written in everyday language designed to tell the holiday maker what benefits he obtains from payment of his modest premium. On a fair reading of its clear words I think it is obvious that, in a case where the holiday maker becomes ill and dies, the section of the policy entitled 'Medical and other expenses' will bear the cost of doctors and nursing, together with a limited sum for funeral expenses, or the repatriation of the body; and equally obvious that the part of the policy entitled 'personal accident' will not yield a lump sum payment of £15,000. I doubt whether it would ever occur to people without knowledge of insurance law that the unhappy consequences of Mr de Souza's holiday might justify a claim under an accident policy.

It is easy to discern from the judgment now under appeal that this was how the matter struck the trial judge at first sight. Since we are here concerned with a well written consumer document, one might expect his common sense reading to prevail. Yet, in the end, the judge arrived at the opposite conclusion. How did this come about? Because after a careful examination of 16 reported cases and three textbooks he felt himself driven to that conclusion.

I will say at once that I do not criticise the learned judge for entering into the books in the way that he did. The English authorities and the Scottish cases in the House of Lords were all binding upon him, and he was, therefore, obliged either to make a synthesis of them, or to reject those which he regarded as inconsistent with higher authority and adopt the rest; and, having done so, apply the principles which they appeared to embody to the facts as found, whether he regarded the conclusion as sensible or not. Nor do I criticise counsel for citing these authorities (and more, on appeal). The cases are there in the textbooks, and could not be ignored. Indeed, the citation could have been much more copious, if counsel had not sensibly pruned it. Nevertheless, I believe that all concerned in this case (and for that matter the text writers) have come close to being mired in the Serbonian bog of which Cardozo J warned in *Landress v Phoenix Mutual* 192 US 491 (1934), at p 499. The cases, regarded simply as decisions, are difficult if not impossible to reconcile. Some of them would, I believe, be regarded by at least some lawyers as wrong. Others would perhaps be differently decided in today's different social context, and even at the time it is plain that the judges were not all of a like mind. In many instances I venture to detect, not a chain of reasoning leading inexorably to a conclusion, but the intuitive choice of a solution, followed by efforts to rationalise it. Again, as reported case succeeds reported case even finer distinctions of language are drawn: sometimes so fine that, approaching them with all the respect due to their authors I find them either impossible to understand, or to reconcile with statements by other judges worthy of equal respect.

In these circumstances, I think it better to withdraw a little from the authorities to the former ground of *this* policy and *these* facts, and to look critically at each authority to see whether it really leads inexorably to a solution of our present problem, or indeed lends us any help at all. In carrying out this task, we are, I believe, free to adopt a rather more summary (although I hope not cavalier) approach than was the learned judge in the county court; and, parting company with the trial judge I consider that we should look at the cases, not in chronological order, but according to subject matter …

THE INSURANCE CASES

Much closer to home are the decisions on accident insurance, albeit mainly concerned with policies whose wording was not precisely similar to the present. We were referred to a dozen or so of these in argument, and there are many more. In the light of the careful submissions addressed I had begun to attempt a synthesis when the occasion arose to consult Welford … whose summary of the law … I could not hope to better, and which I adopt as representing my own opinion:

> The word 'accident' involves the idea of something fortuitous and unexpected, as opposed to something proceeding from natural causes; and injury caused by accident is to be regarded as the antithesis to bodily infirmity by disease in the ordinary course of events.
>
> An injury is caused by accident in the following cases, namely:
>
> (1) Where the injury is the natural result of a fortuitous and unexpected cause, as, for instance, where the assured is run over by a train, or thrown from his horse whilst hunting, or injured by a fall, whether through slipping on a step or otherwise; or where the assured drinks poison by mistake, or is suffocated by the smoke of a house on fire or by an escape of gas, or is

> drowned whilst bathing. In this case the element of accident manifests itself in the cause of the injury.
>
> (2) Where the injury is the fortuitous and unexpected result of a natural cause, as, for instance, where a person lifts a heavy burden in the ordinary course of business and injures his spine, or stoops down to pick up a marble and breaks a ligament in his knee, or scratches his leg with his nail whilst putting on a stocking, or ruptures himself whilst playing golf. In this case the element of accident manifests itself, not in the cause, but in its result.
>
> On the other hand, an injury is not caused by accident when it is the natural result of a natural cause as, for instance, where a person is exposed in the tropical sun and in consequence suffers from sunstroke, or where a person with a weak heart injures it by running to catch a train, or by some other intentional act involving violent physical exertion. In this case the element of accident is broadly speaking absent, since the cause is one which comes into operation in the ordinary course of events, and is calculated, within the ordinary experience of mankind, to produce the result which it has in fact produced.
>
> In considering whether an injury is caused by accident, it is necessary to take into consideration the circumstances in which the injury is received. Similar natural causes may produce similar physical effects in two different persons; yet the element of accident may be present in the one case and absent in the other. Thus, a sailor on duty on the bridge of a ship may suffer serious bodily injury or even death through exposure to the violence of a winter gale; but the injury or death is not caused by accident within the meaning of the policy. Where, on the other hand, the sailor is shipwrecked and is afterwards exposed in an open boat to the inclemency of the weather, the element of accident intervenes, and the result of the exposure, whether injury or death, falls within the policy …

The author then continues:

> The same principles apply where the injury is the result, not of natural causes, but of the intervention of human agency. Two cases have to be distinguished, namely:
>
> (1) Where the injury is caused by the act of a third person …
>
> (2) Where the injury is caused by the act of the assured himself. An injury may be caused by accident within the meaning of the policy, although it is caused by the act of the assured. The following cases must be distinguished, namely …:
>
> (ii) an injury which is the natural and direct consequence of an act deliberately done by the assured is not caused by accident. A man must be taken to intend the ordinary consequences of his acts, and the fact that he did not foresee the particular consequence or expect the particular injury does not make the injury accidental if, in the circumstances, it was the natural and direct consequence of what he did, without the intervention of any fortuitous cause. Thus, where physical exertion, deliberately intended, such as, for instances, running to catch a train, throws a strain upon his heart at a time when it is in a

> weak and unhealthy condition in consequence of which the assured dies, his death is not to be regarded as accidental merely because the assured did not know his condition and therefore did not foresee the effect, provided that it was the natural and direct consequence of a strain being put upon a heart in that condition ...

In these circumstances, I adhere to the summary given by Mr Welford, which lends no support to the submission that the present policy should be read otherwise than in its natural sense ...

A RETURN TO THE WORDS OF THE POLICY

Is there anything in the authorities which compels the court to read the present policy as meaning anything other than what it appears to say? In my view there is not ... I pay careful regard to the accident insurance cases, and regard them as exemplifying ways of interpreting various forms of policy summarised in the passages from Welford which I have quoted. These tend strongly towards the conclusion that the present claim falls outside the policy, but do not demand it. So I think it right to return to the precise words of the policy under which the claim is brought. Did Mr de Souza suffer an 'injury'? I cannot see that he did. To my mind he unfortunately became ill and died. Where was the element of 'accident' in his illness? The plaintiff has never identified what the accident was, or when it happened. So far as we know, there was normal sun, normal heat, and normal exposure to them, which for some reason sadly led to Mr de Souza's death. Where was the 'violent' event? Nowhere, so far as I can see. On the evidence, there was ordinary Mediterranean summer weather, of which Mr de Souza, along no doubt with many others, gladly took advantage. The outcome was, of course, unexpected and unwished for, but this feature is not in my judgment enough to satisfy the clear words of the policy ...

APPENDIX 7.3

JC Thomson v Equity Fire Insurance Co [1910] AC 592, PC

Lord Macnaghten: The question is, Did the loss occur while gasoline was 'stored or kept' in the building? It is common ground that there was no gasoline in the building but what was in the stove, and it seems that the quantity of gasoline in the stove was about a pint.

What is the meaning of the words 'stored or kept' in collocation and in the connection in which they are found? They are common English words with no very precise or exact signification. They have a somewhat kindred meaning and cover very much the same ground. The expression as used in the statutory condition seems to point to the presence of a quantity not inconsiderable, or at any rate not trifling in amount, and to import a notion of warehousing or depositing for safe custody or keeping in stock for trading purposes. It is difficult, if not impossible, to give an accurate definition of the meaning, but if one takes a concrete case it is not very difficult to say whether a particular thing is 'stored or kept' within the meaning of the condition. No one probably would say that a person who had a reasonable quantity of tea in his house for domestic use was 'storing or keeping' tea there, or (to take the instance of benzine, which is one of the prescribed articles) no one would say that a person who had a small bottle of benzine for removing grease spots or cleansing purposes of that sort was 'storing or keeping' benzine.

The learned counsel for the respondents contended that the presence of gasoline on the premises was enough to bring the statutory condition into operation, and he referred to the accident which did happen as an example of the danger against which precautions are required. But it is obvious that the danger guarded against is not ignition caused by the article itself, but the risk of spreading or increasing the conflagration when once started and in progress by the presence of highly inflammable or explosive material. The fact that the fire in the present case was caused by the gasoline is irrelevant. And the fatal objection to the defendants' contention is that it gives no effect whatever to the words 'stored or kept'. The sentence would be complete and the meaning which the defendants seek to attribute to it might possibly or even probably prevail if the words in question had been omitted altogether, and the condition had excluded liability for 'loss or damage occurring while … gasoline … is … in the building insured'. Some meaning must be given to the words 'stored or kept'. Their Lordships think those words must have their ordinary meaning. So construing them their Lordships come to the conclusion that the small quantity of gasoline which was in the stove for the purpose of consumption was not being 'stored or kept' within the meaning of the statutory condition at the time when the loss occurred …

APPENDIX 7.4

Leo Rapp Ltd v McClure [1955] 1 Lloyd's Rep 292

Devlin J: In this case, the plaintiffs sue under a policy of insurance which was granted by Lloyd's underwriters and was expressed to insure the plaintiffs from:

> ... loss or damage by burglary, housebreaking, theft and/or larceny, with or without violence ... on stock of iron, steel, non-ferrous metals, whilst in warehouse anywhere in the United Kingdom,

and it is the words 'whilst in warehouse' and the application of them to the facts of this case which has constituted the dispute between the parties ...

The depot, so far as is material for this purpose, consists of an enclosed compound or yard with a high brick wall and barbed wire, and inside the yard there are two buildings, a furniture store, which I suppose is an enclosed building, and a covered space, that is a roof with no doors and open spaces in the yard itself. The lorry was put in one of the open spaces in the yard, and, notwithstanding the fact that it was enclosed by a high wall and barbed wire and that other precautions were taken – the lorry itself had its engine immobilised and there were other lorries placed round it – nevertheless, thieves broke into the depot, stole the keys to the gates, opened the gates, moved away the obstructing lorries, and, I suppose, got the engine of this lorry working and drove it away ... the sole question is whether at the time of the loss it was 'in warehouse'. If so, it was within the policy; if not, it was not.

It has been held over and over again, I think ever since the well known words of Lord Ellenborough (I think the case is *Robertson and Thomson v French* (1803) 4 East 130, at p 135) that, when the court is construing words in an insurance policy it must give them their ordinary natural meaning. The question is, therefore, what is the ordinary natural meaning of 'a warehouse'? It suggest to me some sort of building, and that view has been confirmed by the dictionary definitions to which Mr Raebury has referred and which all refer to as a building; and these goods were not in a building, but were in a yard, and upon that short ground I shall give my judgment ...

If one has regard as, of course, one is entitled to have regard, to what is the object of the policy, it is plain that the object of the policy is concerned with the question of security, not with the purpose of the store. It does not matter at all to the underwriters why the goods are to be stored there. What does matter to them is the nature of the place where the goods are being stored. It is quite plain that when they put the words 'whilst in warehouse', instead of saying 'whilst anywhere in the United Kingdom', the words 'whilst in warehouse' are there because they are insuring goods against the risk of burglary and because the risk of burglary may well be different in a building or warehouse than it might be in a yard. Of course, some yards may be just as secure as a warehouse. Perhaps this one was; but that is not the point. The point is that in the ordinary way, when Lloyd's are insuring, they do not know where the goods are going to be. They have got to define it in advance, and in the ordinary way if the goods are 'in warehouse' it offers some sort of security which in a yard they may not have. A warehouse is generally kept locked; there is very often a warehouseman in charge, a night watchman, a man who owed obligations, a warehouseman who in the conduct of the warehouse owes obligations which he has to fulfil to look after the goods. In a yard, which would have to be very much more closely defined than the mere use of the word, there is no such security …

APPENDIX 7.5

Fraser v BN Furman (Productions) Ltd, Miller Smith and Partners (A Firm, Third Party) [1967] 3 All ER 57, CA

Diplock LJ: The risks so specified, which are 'liability at law for damages', are liability for breach of statutory duty, for which the owner or occupier of the factory would always be personally liable, negligence at common law of the employer, for which he would be personally liable, and also the negligence of his servants, for which he would be vicariously liable. Therefore, when one approaches the construction of the condition, one does so in this context, and applies the rule that one does not construe a condition as repugnant to the commercial purpose of the contract …

Obviously, the condition cannot mean that the insured must take measures to avert dangers which he does not himself foresee, although the hypothetical reasonably careful employer would foresee them. That would be repugnant to the commercial purpose of the contract, for failure to foresee dangers is one of the commonest grounds of liability in negligence. What, in my view, is 'reasonable' as between the insured and the insurer, without being repugnant to the commercial object of the contract, is that the insured should not deliberately court a danger, the existence of which he recognises, by refraining from taking any measures to avert it. Equally, the condition cannot mean that, where the insured recognises that there is a danger, the measures which he takes to avert it must be as the hypothetical reasonable employer, exercising due care and observing all the relevant provisions of the Factories Act 1961, would take. That, too, would be repugnant to the commercial purpose of the contract, for failure to take such measures is another ground of liability in negligence for breach of statutory duty. What, in my judgment, is reasonable as between the insured and the insurer, without being repugnant to the commercial purpose of the contract, is that the insured, where he does recognise a danger should not deliberately court it by taking measures which he himself knows are inadequate to avert it. In other words, it is not enough that the employer's omission to take any particular precautions to avoid accidents should be negligent; it must be at least reckless, that is to say, made with actual recognition by the insured himself that a danger exists, and not caring whether or not it is averted. The purpose of the condition is to ensure that the insured will not, because he is covered against loss by the policy refrain from taking precautions which he knows ought to be taken …

It is right that I should make it perfectly clear that no evidence was called from Eagle Star to suggest that that company would ever have thought of taking such a course. The imputation which we are invited to make upon them is one which has been suggested by the broker alone without any evidence from Eagle Star or from anyone else in the insurance world, nor were other brokers called to support it.

In considering the likelihood that such a point would have been taken, even if it were open, one must in my view bear in mind, first, the character and reputation of the insurance company which was contemplated by the third party, one of the great insurance companies in this country with a high reputation. One must also bear in mind that, if the insurers were to take this point, they would have to take it at an early stage as soon as the facts were known to them, and before the action by Miss Fraser against the employers was tried, because one of the terms of the policy is that the insurers take over the conduct of the action, and if they did so and failed to repudiate with the knowledge of the facts, they would be estopped from doing so thereafter. In such an action, if they took the point, the onus would lie upon them of proving that the conduct of the insured did fall within the condition. That is itself a matter which the argument in this court has shown is one of considerable difficulty. The view which I have expressed in this court as to the meaning of the condition (which was, I think, also accepted by the judge) indicates that it is arguable that the condition would not exempt them from liability. The prospect of success in taking the point, therefore, even if they knew the facts, would be, to say the least of it, dubious ...

APPENDIX 7.6

Sofi v Prudential Assurance Co Ltd [1993] 2 Lloyd's Rep 559, CA

Woolf LJ: How finally does one apply that test of recklessness on the facts of the present case?

Mr Wadsworth argued that it was reckless of the plaintiff not to take the jewellery with him when he climbed the mound or not to have left somebody behind in the car, having regard to the value of the jewellery. I do not accept that submission. If the plaintiff had given no thought at all to the jewellery, the submission might have succeeded; or if, to take another example, the plaintiff had left the jewellery exposed to view. But here the plaintiff and his son-in-law considered together what was best to do. They were not going to be absent from the car for more than half an hour at the most. In the event, they were absent for much less than half an hour. They decided that, in the circumstances, the safest thing to do was to leave the jewellery in the locked glove compartment. I cannot regard that decision as having been taken recklessly.

To summarise, I agree with the test applied by the judge. Indeed, my only doubt is whether his reference to reasonable prudence in the passage which I have quoted may not be too favourable to the defendants. I agree also with his conclusion on the facts. It follows that I would dismiss the appeal.

Before leaving the case, I should refer briefly to the Annual Report of the Insurance Ombudsman for 1985. In that report the Ombudsman sets out certain guidance in relation to clauses such as general condition 2. At the end of para 2.5, he sets out certain questions which he says he usually asks himself when presented with a particular case. Those questions are as follows:

(a) What was the value of the goods at risk?

(b) What was the reason for having them in the place from which they were stolen?

(c) What precautions were actually taken to safeguard them?

(d) Where there any alternatives open to the policyholder?

Mr Legh-Jones, for the plaintiff, criticises those questions, and in particular asks us to say that on what he calls the subjective test stated by Lord Justice Diplock, the value of the goods is, strictly speaking, irrelevant.

I cannot go along with that submission. As a matter of common sense, the greater the value of the goods insured, the greater the risk that they will be stolen, and the easier it will be for the insurer to establish that the insured deliberately courted the risk, to use the language of Lord Justice Diplock, by taking measures which he knew to be inadequate. Further than that I am not prepared to go in defining the test of recklessness or commenting on the questions posed by the Insurance Ombudsman. I prefer to come to rest on the language of Lord Justice Diplock.

APPENDIX 7.7

Morley and Another v United Friendly Insurance plc [1993] 3 All ER 47, CA

Neill LJ: ... Clause 2 of the policy of insurance provided (so far as is material) as follows:

> 2 If the Insured shall within the United Kingdom sustain bodily injury caused by violent accidental external and visible means which injury shall solely and independently of any other cause result within seven days in his/her death ... the Company will upon production of reasonable proof of such injury pay to the Insured or in the event of death to his/her legal personal representatives the appropriate accident benefit ...

By an indorsement to the policy dated 21 October 1985, the deceased increased the amount payable on death to £3,000.

The policy provided that it was subject to the conditions therein contained. Paragraph 1 of the conditions set out special exclusions and provided, *inter alia*, as follows:

> No accident benefit shall be payable if death injury or incapacity shall result directly or indirectly from or be accelerated by any of the following causes ... (iii) Wilful exposure to needless peril (except in an attempt to save human life) ...

Having relieved himself the deceased crossed the railway by means of the footbridge ... As the deceased approached Miss Norrie started to move ... As she moved off, however, the deceased jumped or stepped onto the rear bumper of the car. It seems clear that Miss Norrie realised what had happened but instead of stopping the car she accelerated slightly and began to steer in a 'zig-zag fashion' ...

The case for the insurance company was put very succinctly. By stepping onto the rounded surface of the bumper of a moving car in the dark and when there were no handholds available the deceased exposed himself to the wholly unnecessary risk of a broken bone. The exposure was wilful because the deceased either knew the risk and accepted it or, if he did not consider the risk, was reckless. The risk of a broken or fractured bone was an obvious risk in the circumstances ...

How then is the phrase 'wilful exposure to needless peril' in this policy to be interpreted? It is clear, and indeed was accepted by counsel for the insurance company, that the words cannot be construed too strictly. Thus, they cannot be construed so as to remove insurance cover from an insured who engages in contact sports such as football. On the other hand, at the other end of the scale, the words would seem more than apt to cover the circumstances considered in the Canadian case of *Candler v London and Lancashire Guarantee and Accident Co of Canada* 40 DLR (2d) 408 (1963) ...

where the deceased, in order to demonstrate to a friend that he had not lost his nerve balanced himself on the coping of a hotel patio 13 floors above the street and fell to his death. The trial judge held that the event was not an accident within the meaning of the policy, but it is clear that, in addition, it would certainly have involved 'wilful exposure to needless peril'.

In my judgment, the 'wilfulness' has to be directed to the 'exposure to peril'. It is not enough to show an intentional act which results in peril. There must be conscious act of volition, which can include recklessness, directed to the running of the risk. Accordingly, in order to determine where in the spectrum a particular case falls it is necessary to have regard to all the circumstances, including: (a) the likelihood of the insured injury being incurred if the risk is taken; and (b) the opportunity for reflection before the risk if taken.

If one applies the first of these criteria one can draw a clear distinction between Formula 1 motor racing and hang gliding on the one hand and golf and football on the other hand. I regard the second criterion also being of importance.

In addition, it is necessary to take account of the commercial purpose of the policy. It was intended to insure the deceased against the risk of suffering some *serious* injury. It is common ground that the cover includes injuries caused by the insured's own negligence. The insurance company say, however, that the actions of the deceased were not merely negligent but were foolhardy and reckless.

In this case, unusually, this court is in no worse position than the trial judge in making an evaluation of the facts. The judge saw no relevant witnesses. Though we must treat the judge's decision with the utmost respect, we are free in the circumstances to look at the matter afresh.

No one has sought to disturb the judge's conclusion that at the moment when the deceased stepped onto the bumper 'the car was hardly moving'. It seems to me therefore that at that moment there was a risk that the deceased might fall off and cut and bruise himself. He might well have sprained his wrist or twisted his ankle. But the risk at that stage of a fracture of a bone, though a real risk as opposed to a fanciful risk, was to my mind not very great. This modest risk has then to be linked with the opportunity for, and presumed extent of, the appreciation of the risk. I agree with the judge's assessment of what happened as being 'a foolish bit of horseplay which went dramatically wrong'. I respectfully differ from the judge, however, with his description of the horseplay as 'reckless' if, in the context, he equated recklessness with wilful exposure to peril ...

The deceased's action in this case was a momentary act of stupidity. The speed of the vehicle is to be judged by the fact that the judge referred to the deceased as 'stepping onto the bumper'. The peril was clearly 'unnecessary' and the contrary has not been argued. But having given anxious consideration to this case I have come to the clear conclusion that in the circumstances the deceased did not *wilfully* expose himself to unnecessary peril. The exclusion clause should be reserved to deal with cases where either the occurrence of an insured injury is more likely or where the appreciation of the peril can be more clearly demonstrated ...

Beldam LJ: Unless the operation of the exclusion clause is confined in this way, it would in my view unwarrantably diminish the indemnity which it was the purpose of the policy to afford. So I would hold that, on the facts of this case, the respondent did not make good the contention that the deceased wilfully exposed himself to needless peril. Although the bumper bar did not give him a proper foothold and he had no handhold other than steadying himself with his hands on the roof of the car, it was not, in my view, a reasonable inference from such a thoughtless act on the spur of the moment that he appreciated that he was exposing himself to the risk at least of fracture of one of the major bones of the body or that he embarked on that conduct not caring whether he sustained such injury or not.

I would not characterise his impulsive response to a practical joke as wilful exposure to needless peril. In quality and degree, his actions fell short of deliberate risk taking or recklessness of injury of which he was mindful. Accordingly, I would allow the appeal …

APPENDIX 7.8

Amey Properties Ltd v Cornhill Insurance plc [1996] LRLR 259

Tucker J: The plaintiff's argument is that the defence is based on the allegation that the lack of roadworthiness of the tractor was due to negligence, and that there is no allegation of recklessness on the part of the plaintiffs. The plaintiff contends that before defendants can avoid liability they have to show more than negligence – they have to go on to prove that the plaintiffs themselves were reckless – accordingly, casual acts or omissions of the plaintiff's employees are irrelevant.

The defendant's case ... is that although there are cases where it has been held that recklessness has to be established, this is not one of them. There does not appear to be any dispute that the fault, of whatsoever degree, has to be shown to be that of the insured rather than a casual act on the part of an employee. However, this does not mean that the defendants have to show the existence of fault at boardroom level.

The differing contentions have necessitated a detailed review of all the relevant authorities. I shall analyse them in chronological order.

The first significant case is *National Farmers Union Mutual Insurance Society Ltd v Dawson* [1941] 2 KB 424 ... The policy was for car insurance under the Road Traffic Acts. It contained a condition that the insured should keep the car in an efficient state of repair and should use all care and diligence to avoid accidents and prevent loss, and employ only steady and sober drivers. Unfortunately, the insured herself drove the car while under the influence of drink and caused an accident. It was argued that the condition was repugnant to the operative part of the policy which covered liability or negligence, and therefore to the main purpose. The Lord Chief Justice disagreed, since, as he pointed out in his judgment, there might be many ways in which liability might attach under the policy. It was accordingly held that the insurers could recover the amount which they had paid out on insured's behalf. There was no mention in the judgment of any necessity of establishing recklessness.

The next case, and an important one, is *Woolfall and Rimmer Ltd v Moyle* [1942] 1 KB 66. This case concerned an employers' liability policy. It contained a condition that 'The assured shall take reasonable precautions to prevent accidents'. The Court of Appeal held that the condition applied only to the personal acts of the plaintiffs, since the duty which the condition purported to impose was a contractual duty imposed on the plaintiffs towards the underwriters. It was also held that if employers reasonably delegated the performance of a task to a foreman whom they took reasonable precaution to select, then the employers' obligations under the condition was at an end. Lord Justice Goddard made it clear in his judgment that in order to escape liability, the insurers would have to establish that the employers carried on their business in a reckless manner ...

... In my judgment, the cases show that the court have adopted different approaches to the construction of the words of exclusion clauses depending upon the nature of the policies in which they appear and, in particular, whether to give a wide construction would be repugnant to the whole purpose for which the policy was taken out. Thus, in employers' liability policies, the courts have applied the standard of recklessness (see *Woodfall* and *Fraser* [1967] 3 All ER 57). The same test has been applied in property policies (see *Lane, Devco* and *Sofi*). In motor policies, on the other hand, the courts have applied the test of negligence – it has not been held necessary for the insurers to establish that the insured was reckless, before liability could be excluded (see *NFU, Brown, Liverpool Corporation, Conn* and *Lefevre*).

In my view this distinction can be explained and justified by the fact that motor policies impose a positive obligation to maintain the vehicle in good repair, or as in the present case, specific and sensible obligation to impose, and one with which it ought not to be difficult to comply. To hold that if the policyholder, by his negligence, fails to comply with such a condition and thereby loses the protection of the policy is not in my opinion repugnant to the commercial object of the contract. The insurer is not covering and does not intend to cover the insured for liability arising out of negligent maintenance of the vehicle, but there is cover for liability arising out of the negligent uses of a vehicle which is properly maintained. The words of condition II of the present policy are plain. There is no need to put any gloss on them, or to restrict their meaning in order to give proper effect to the terms of the policy …

I think I have made it plain that in my opinion it would not be sufficient to establish a casual act of negligence on the part of the employee. The contract of insurance is made with the employer – the plaintiffs. What has to be shown is that the relevant officer or officers of the plaintiffs was or were negligent in failing to ensure that the tractor was maintained in an efficient and roadworthy condition. This is how the defendants plead their case. It is made plain in para 8 that they do not rely on the failure of the employee himself.

As to the second part of the issue. I hold that it would be sufficient for the defendants to establish that the plaintiffs were negligent. It is not necessary for the defendants to establish that the plaintiffs were reckless.

APPENDIX 7.9

Starfire Diamond Rings Ltd v Angel [1962] 2 Lloyd's Rep 217, CA

Lord Denning MR: I do not think the words 'left unattended' are capable of any precise definition. It is a mistake for a lawyer to attempt a definition of ordinary words and to substitute other words for them. The best way is to take the words in their ordinary sense and apply them to the facts. In this case, the meaning of 'left unattended' is, I think, best found by considering the converse. If a car is 'attended', what does it mean? I think it means that there must be someone able to keep it under observation, that is, in a position to observe any attempt by anyone to interfere with it, and who is so placed as to have a reasonable prospect of preventing any unauthorised interference with it. I must say that it seems to me that this car was 'left unattended'. What impresses me is the distance which Mr Hall went away from the car – 37 yards. As he walked up the track, I cannot think that he could have had his head turned round looking over his shoulder all the time: for a good part of the time he must have been looking ahead. Then he moved round into the bushes ...

At that distance and with those powers of observation, it is quite plain that a thief could come up to the car, crouch down under cover of the car, break the glass – as indeed this thief seems to have done – and extract the suit case – as this thief did – without Mr Hall seeing it or knowing about it at all. Then, as we know, this thief got so far away that he was not seen in suspicious circumstances until after he had passed the other car. It seems to me the distance that Mr Hall went and the obscurity of his view was such that this car was 'left unattended' ...

APPENDIX 7.10

Ingleton of Ilford Ltd v General Accident Fire and Life Assurance Corp Ltd [1967] 2 Lloyd's Rep 179

Phillimore J: What is the position here? Mr Morell went into the shop. He says that thereafter he was keeping the vehicle under observation, but not, of course, absolutely the whole time, but meaning maintaining a regular observation, and he says that in the position he was in in the shop, which he marked on the plan, he could see the whole of the nearside of the vehicle and of course the back. I confess that I find it hard to accept that Mr Morell was really taking even as much in the way of precautions as he says he was, because I think it clear he was in there for a quarter of an hour, I have no doubt he was chatting during that time to the boy, and it seems very doubtful if he was really keeping much observation on his van in the light of the fact that it was removed and the engine presumably started without his ever observing that anything had taken place. The fact is that from where he was of course he could not see the far side of the van, he had no view of the driver's door, he could not see if anybody got into the driver's seat, he was not in a position to keep it under observation, that is to say in a position to observe any attempt by anyone to interfere with it or so placed as to have a reasonable prospect of preventing any unauthorised interference with it.

In my judgment, this is a hopeless claim. This van on the facts was quite clearly unattended, and the best proof of that is that the whole thing was removed with all its contents without its attendant even being aware of what had happened. For those reasons I dismiss this claim …

APPENDIX 7.11

O'Donoghue Ltd v Harding [1988] 2 Lloyd's Rep 281

Otton J: The first defendants denied liability and purported to rely upon a term of the policy in the following terms:

> The policy does not cover ... (7) Theft or disappearance of or from road vehicles of every description owned by or under the control of the Assured and/or their servants or agents or representatives when such vehicles are left unattended ...

Can underwriters avoid their obligation to pay out by reliance upon exclusion cl 7 ...?

The question is: did the loss occur when the vehicle was left unattended ...?

I have ... come to the conclusion that on the particular facts and circumstances of this case that Mr Collins did not leave the vehicle unattended. He acted throughout in a thoroughly responsible manner by driving into a forecourt which was quiet and selecting pump No 1, which was closest to the Kiosk. He locked the car. He filled it with petrol. He left the car locked while he went into the kiosk. He was keeping a proper and reasonable lookout and taking reasonable steps to keep the car under observation. He was not dilatory. He was away for no more than two minutes. During a substantial part of that time, he had most of the car within his vision through the kiosk windows. He was only momentarily distracted by the signing of the American Express slip and picking up the VAT receipt. The time when he had his back to the car, when he was walking from the car to the kiosk, and from the counter back to the door of the kiosk, would only have been a matter of seconds. The purpose of the visit to the petrol station and paying for the petrol was an incident of his driving and employment as a salesman. He was not far away for the purpose or urinating, as in *Starfire* [1962] 2 Lloyd's Rep 217, nor was he away for a substantial period of time chatting, as in *Ingleton* [1967] 2 Lloyd's Rep 179. The circumstances are closer to those in *Langord*'s case [1986] 2 Lloyd's Rep 103. The chance that a sneak thief would come up during such a short period of time and be so skillful as to open the door with a duplicate key, remove the case and relock the car was extremely remote ...

APPENDIX 7.12

Dhak v Insurance Co of North America (UK) Ltd [1996] 1 Lloyd's Rep 632, CA

Neill LJ: This is a tragic case. Indeed no one could read the papers without feeling the greatest sympathy for Mr Kashmir Dhak who lost his wife in such distressing circumstances. At the same time, however, one has to recognise that the case raised important questions of law in the field of personal accident insurance ...

I am quite satisfied that Mrs Dhak's death resulted from bodily injury within the meaning of this policy ...

I turn therefore to the most difficult issue in this case.

It will be remembered that 'bodily injury' was defined in the policy as 'bodily injury caused by accidental means'. It was argued on behalf of Mr Dhak that Mrs Dhak's death was plainly an accident ...

I have come to the conclusion, however, that it has not been established that the bodily injury to Mrs Dhak was 'caused by accidental means' within the meaning of the policy. In reaching this conclusion I have been persuaded that the words 'caused by accidental means' are a clear indication that it is the cause of the injury to which the court must direct its attention.

I can turn at once to the judgment of Lord Justice Mustill in *De Souza* [1995] LRLR 453 ... Lord Justice Mustill adopted as representing his own opinion the summary of the law set out in Welform, *Accident Insurance*, 1923, pp 295–96 and 299 ...

[See Appendix 7.2, above.]

In addition one should consider whether the insured took a calculated risk. I would put the matter as follows.

Where an insured embarks deliberately on a course of conduct which leads to some bodily injury one has to consider these questions: (a) Did the insured intend to inflict some bodily injury to himself? (b) Did the insured take a calculated risk that if he continued with that course of conduct he might sustain some bodily injury? (c) Was some bodily injury the natural and direct consequence of the course of conduct? (d) Did some fortuitous cause intervene?

In this case, there is no suggestion whatever that Mrs Dhak intended any bodily injury to herself. One has, therefore, to examine the other three questions. At the same time one must take account of all the circumstances, including the state of knowledge or presumed state of knowledge of the insured. In considering what could be foreseen one must apply the standard of foresight of the reasonable person with the attributes of the insured.

It was strongly argued, on behalf of Mr Dhak, that the inhalation of vomit was unforeseen and unforeseeable. I have considered this argument with the greatest of care, but I have come to the conclusion that the judge was justified in finding that Mrs Dhak must have been well aware of the consequences and dangers of drinking alcohol to excess and that she must be taken to have foreseen what might happen in the event of someone drinking to excess. She was a ward sister with many years of experience as a nurse. The judge found as a fact that Mrs Dhak must have drunk at least the contents of a bottle of gin over a relatively short period. I am satisfied that there must have been a point at which she would have realised that any further drinking would be dangerous and that vital bodily functions might be impaired or interrupted.

As I said at the outset of this judgment, one feels the greatest sympathy for Mr Dhak at his tragic loss. I feel quite unable to say, however, that Mrs Dhak's injury and death were the result of some fortuitous cause. It was the direct consequence of her drinking to excess. Indeed, I feel bound to say that for someone with her knowledge and experience she must be regarded as having taken a calculated risk of sustaining some bodily injury.

For these reasons I would dismiss this appeal.

APPENDIX 7.13

In re Etherington and Lancashire and Yorkshire Accident Insurance Co [1909] 1 KB 591, CA

Vaughan Williams LJ: We have to construe this policy not merely in reference to this particular case; we must recollect that it is a document in the form which is used for the regular issue of policies by the company to persons who are desirous of insuring with them, and one must consider whither the construction contended for by the company would lead, if we were to adopt it. As far as I can see, if we adopted it, the result would be that it would be very difficult to establish the liability of the insurance company in any case except where the accident resulted in what may be called death on the spot. There is always, in every other case, a possibility of some supervening cause, and it would be very difficult for any one to look forward with any certainty to a sum being receivable on the policy if we were to put such a construction as was suggested upon a policy in this form. I think that some limitation of the terms of the proviso contained in the policy ought to be welcomed by the insurance companies themselves, for otherwise, in my opinion, the number of cases in which the policy could be enforced against the company would be so very much reduced that the practical result would soon be that very few persons would care to insure ...

Farwell LJ: I do not think that anybody, after hearing the arguments on both sides in this case, can have any doubt as to the ambiguity of this policy. I agree that the insurance company which prepares these documents is bound to make their meaning as clear as possible, and, if there is any ambiguity in the document, it does not lie in the mouth of the company, who may have been receiving premiums under it for years, to insist on that construction of an ambiguous clause which is in their favour. It is clear that, apart from the proviso, this case would come within the terms which primarily define the liability of the company under the policy. The words 'within three calendar months from the occurrence of the accident' shew that the company's liability was not intended to be confined to sudden death, or death occurring immediately upon the accident. In cases where a man lingers for two or three months after the accident, I believe that it is never the case that he dies from the accident pure and simple; but in all of such cases there would be some malady supervening upon the accident, such as heart failure, pneumonia, blood poisoning, haemorrhage, or paralysis. In a case like this, where the first onset of the activity of the germs was within an hour and a half of the accident, and pneumonia was fully developed within 29 and a half hours, I think that the case comes within the words which primarily define the liability. It is said that these words are qualified by the proviso, and that this case falls within it. Where there are clear words which *prima facie* import liability on the part of the company, and it is said that their effect is cut down by a subsequent proviso, I think we are bound to see that the terms of the proviso are clear and not repugnant: but, if the company's construction be adopted, the proviso in effect renders the three months period of non-effect, and reduces the company's liability to cases of sudden death. I decline to put such a construction on an ambiguous proviso which it was the duty of the insurance company to make absolutely clear, if they intended it to have such an effect as that for which they contend.

APPENDIX 7.14

English v Western Insurance Co [1940] 2 KB 156, CA

Slesser LJ: I think those words are equivocal. I think they are equally capable of either construction: and in the circumstances I feel that the learned judge should have considered what principles of law he ought to have applied to the construction of this policy, as no doubt he would have done had he come to the conclusion that those words were as equivocal as I think they are. If the words be equivocal or ambiguous, then I find no difficulty for myself in ascertaining what is the true principle to be applied. I think that the doctrine generally known as *contra proferentes* should here be applied. I quote from MacGillivray, *Insurance Law*, 2nd edn, London, Sweet & Maxwell, p 1029, where the authorities are conveniently set out:

> If there is any ambiguity in the language used in a policy, it is to be construed more strongly against the party who prepared it, that is in the majority of cases against the company. A policy ought to be so framed that he who runs can read. A party who proffers an instrument cannot be permitted to use ambiguous words in the hope that the other side will understand them in a particular sense, and that the court which has to construe them will give them a different sense, and therefore, where the words are ambiguous they ought to be construed in that sense in which a prudent and reasonable man on the other side – that is the side to whom the policy is proffered – would understand them.

In my view, if that principle be applied, if those words be ambiguous, one arrives at this result. There is given by the opening words of clause 5A a general indemnity to the assured in respect of passengers; and if the underwriters cannot rely upon these words in the exception as necessarily including the household in the sense which Branson J has indicated, namely, that the assured is one member of the same household which includes his sister, then I think they are not entitled to adopt that favourable construction in order to exclude a construction which is said by the plaintiff to be the proper construction, namely, that this cl 5A (a) and (b) has no relation to his case at all, because he was not at any material time a householder, and had not a household. The exception, therefore, must be ruled out in his case, and the general words of liability apply. That seems to me to state the principles on which the construction of an ambiguous document should be dealt with in favour of the proferee. The result is, I come to the conclusion that Branson J was wrong, that the appeal should be allowed; and that judgment in this case should be entered for the plaintiff.

Clauson LJ: I need scarcely say that it is with the utmost diffidence that, in a matter which involves a question of the construction of a policy of insurance, I find myself differing from the judgment of Branson J. But, as I have formed a reasonably clear opinion that his decision in this case is not correct, I will proceed to explain my reasons for so holding. A man may be related to a household in two ways. He may be a member of the household, or he may be the head of the household. The underwriters, while insuring the assured against his liability to passengers, except in their own favour his liability to a passenger who is a 'member of the assured's "household"'. The question is, accordingly, whether, on the true construction of the policy, the exception covers not only the narrower class of members of a household of which the plaintiff is the head, but the wider class of members of a household of which the plaintiff is a member. Branson J takes the view that the more natural meaning of the phrase covers the wider class, namely, members of the household of which the plaintiff is a member.

The question seems to me to be what is the relationship connoted in this phrase by the possessive pronoun which in the actual clause is concealed beneath the apostrophe 's'. It appears to me that the word 'his' may equally as well connote the one relation that I have stated as the other. In other words, in my judgment, either of the two competing meanings of the phrase 'a member of the assured's household' is possible and natural; and, accordingly, there is in the truest sense an ambiguity in the phrase. There is no doubt that, if the phrase used in the policy is in this sense ambiguous, that meaning must be chosen which is the less favourable to the underwriters who have put forward the policy.

It may well be that one would have expected the underwriters – possibly for very good reasons – to have intended the phrase to carry the wider connotation. But that seems to me to be quite immaterial if one once reaches the conclusion that the phrase is ambiguous. If the underwriters desired the wider meaning to be placed upon it, it was their duty to make that desire clear by using unambiguous language.

For these reasons, I find myself bound to hold that the phrase of exception covers only the narrower class, the member of a household of which the plaintiff is head; and, accordingly, the case is not a case within the exception and the underwriters are liable. It follows if this view is correct, that the appeal succeeds, the judgment below is reversed, and the underwriters declared liable.

Goddard LJ (dissenting): Though I regret that I am unable to share the view expressed by my Lords, I at least have the satisfaction of finding myself in agreement with the view expressed by Branson J, whose judgment in matters of insurance has always been regarded with such respect. I find his judgment so convincing that I should have been content to adopt it as my own: but I propose to add a very few words as to why I have come to a different conclusion from that at which my Lords have arrived in this court. It is true, I agree, that the words 'the assured's household', can be construed in one of two ways. It is also true to say that, where you find a proviso inserted in an insurance policy for the benefit of the underwriters you are, if the words are ambiguous or not clear, to construe those words more strongly against the underwriters than against the assured. But the doctrine generally spoken of as a construction *contra proferentes* is limited in this way. If there is a perfectly good reason for adopting one construction, and no reason, or very little reason, for construing the clause in the other way, the construction which affords good reason for the presence of the proviso should be preferred ...

We are here dealing with an insurance in which the insurers are willing to give the assured an indemnity greater than that which he is obliged by statute to procure for himself – in other words, an indemnity against claims which he may have made against him on the part of passengers in his car who may be injured and say they were injured by the driver's negligence. But the underwriter is not willing to give an unlimited cover. It seems to me that the object of this proviso is to prevent the underwriters being exposed to the risk of claims by people who may be expected to be very frequent passengers in the car. To construe it in the way contended for by the assured, seems to me to lead to the curious result that if the father has a car and the son has a car, and each are insured by separate policies, the son gets a far wider cover than the father would get. I cannot think that that was intended. In my opinion, the words 'the assured's household' in this policy, when one bears in mind the object with which the proviso was put in, are meant to exclude from the benefit of the policy the members of the common establishment in which the assured lives.

For these reasons, I would dismiss the appeal.

Appeal allowed.

APPENDIX 7.15

Rohan Investments Ltd v Cunningham [1999] Lloyd's Rep IR 190, CA

Robert Walker LJ: This is an appeal from the order of His Honour Judge Byrt, QC given on 13 June 1997.

The judge gave judgment for £29,044.82 in favour of the plaintiff against its insurers. The plaintiff's claim was in respect of water damage to the interior of property.

This case involves the construction of insured perils. The judge gave a full judgment.

The house in question has a flat roof. It is the London base of a Nigerian businessman who stays there from time to time. He had made arrangements for it to be looked after in between his visits.

The damage to the property was discovered on 11 February 1995. It actually happened between 21 January and 30 January, a period of heavy rain fall. It was discovered by a Mr Dyer who was a builder working on the adjoining building.

The water was 3–4 inches deep. The Judge had evidence from the meteorological office that there had been heavy rainfall between 15 and 27 January and that half an inch had fallen on 27 January, the day on which the damage occurred. He also found on the balance of probabilities that the damage had been caused by an ingress of water, over the flashings.

The buildings and contents insurance covered insured perils of storm, tempest, flood or the escape of water from fixed water pipes.

The main issue on the appeal is whether the judge was right in concluding that the ingress of water constituted a flood. The question of what is the meaning of the word flood in the context of a household insurance policy was considered in *Young v Sun Alliance and London Insurance Ltd* [1976] 2 Lloyd's Rep 189 at 190; [1976] 3 All ER 561. Shaw LJ at p 563 approved the county court judge who dismissed the appeal in that case who said that, 'A flood is something large, sudden and temporary, not naturally there, such as a river over flowing its banks'.

The policy insured against damage caused by the flood, not the flood itself. Here the damage was severe, the judge referred to the event as catastrophic and said:

> ... it seems apparent that what the policy was intending to cover, whatever may be the colloquial use of the word flood in common parlance, were three forms of natural phenomena which were related not only by the fact that they were natural but also that they were very unusual manifestations of those phenomena: that is to say, storm meant rain accompanied by strong wind; tempest denoted an even more violent storm; and flood was not something which came about by seepage or by trickling or dripping from some natural source, but involved a large movement, an irruption of water ... The slow movement of water, which can often be detected so that the damage

> threatened can be limited, is very different from the sudden onset of water where nothing effective can be done to prevent the damage, for it happens too quickly.

Lawton and Cairns LJJ gave concurring judgments.

Computer and Systems Engineering plc v John Lelliot (Ilford) Ltd and Another (1990) 54 BLR 1 is also a case on the meaning of flood. Here there was an escape of water from a sprinkler system. Beldam LJ at p 10 said that a:

> ... flood, in my view, imports the invasion of the property ... by a large volume of water from an external source, usually but not necessarily confined to the result of a natural phenomenon such as a storm, tempest or downpour.

This appeal has been argued with clarity and brevity by both sides. Miss Egan says that the real cause was the collection of water which found its way into the house through the flashings. Mr Pershad for the respondent/plaintiff submits that it was open to the judge to conclude that the escape of water did constitute a flood.

I accept the importance of keeping a uniformity of words but the definition is not to be construed as statutory. The use of the word external does not exclude the accumulation of water, nor can Beldam LJ have intended to lay down a test that there be a large accumulation. It is a question of degree and the size of the premises must be considered. The judge was entitled to conclude that the accumulation was sufficiently rapid to be abnormal. A sufficient amount found its way in to the building. This was not a slow seepage.

The judge was hampered in his findings by a lack of evidence as to how the ingress occurred, had he had more expert evidence in front of him he might have made more detailed findings.

I consider that the judge did rightly conclude that the damage was caused by a flood therefore despite Miss Egan's excellent submissions I agree that it was a flood.

Auld LJ: A flood as an insured peril in a householder's insurance policy is a straightforward notion, save for any constraints in the document it should be given its normal and ordinary meaning. I don't think that *Young* and *Computer and Systems* intended to confine its meaning to a list of rigid criteria or without thinking of the size and nature of the property or the different circumstances which may give rise to flooding and consequent damage.

No all-purpose list of criteria was set by *Young* which would be described ordinarily and naturally as a flood. All their Lordships appear to have been affected by the lack of drama and scale of flooding of a lavatory, a slow, preventable seepage of water.

In *Computer and Systems* the court drew on that approach to identify two or three characteristics of flood in a JTC contract, namely, first the large volume of water, second, the rapid accumulation of water, and the sudden release from, third a natural phenomenon.

It is important to keep in mind that the flood causes damage, here it is that affecting the contents. Whether or not it was part of larger climactic conditions, regardless of the previous accumulation of water, here was an escape of water from the roof. Looked at it that way it is confusing to require various characteristics appropriate to climactic weather extremes, flooding may result from the slow steady build up of water. It is nevertheless a flood which the insurance is intended to cover.

As to volume, it is the entry and damage to the property that counts, not the depth outside. It is a question of degree. I add that it also depends on the size of the property affected relevant to the amount.

As to natural causes, a flood is no less a flood whatever its original cause. A blocked outlet does not change that. To require some natural phenomenon which the householder can do nothing about is to confuse the insurable event with preconditions.

For the same reasons I reject the second submission that the ingress was not caused by a flood because of contributory factors.

The judge was entitled to find that it was a flood which caused the material damage, however for the reasons given I doubt that he needed to be so restrained. I would dismiss the appeal.

APPENDIX 7.16

Wasik, M, 'Definitions of crime in insurance contracts' [1986] JBL 45

INTRODUCTION

From time to time, cases arise where the question of an insurer's liability under a contract of insurance hinges upon whether, in law, the criminal offence which is the risk insured against has been committed. In a claim on a policy indemnifying the assured against, say, 'theft' or 'burglary', or exempting the insurer in circumstances of 'riot', there may sometimes be genuine doubt whether the constituent elements of the offences of theft, burglary or riot are made out. In the absence of a ruling on the particular matter in hand by a criminal court, the court trying the insurance question has to decide the most appropriate course to take. There are two broadly competing attitudes evident in the decided cases. The first is founded in the principal rule of construction that technical terms in contracts always bear their technical meaning, unless there is some clear evidence to the contrary. This means that if the word 'theft' appears in the insurance contract, all the criminal law learning on that offence must be regarded as crucial. This is a rigorous approach which in one way helps to reduce uncertainty in the interpretation of disputed insurance contracts, but does make highly relevant the perhaps commensurate uncertainties of the modern law of theft. It also opens up the possibility that the expectations of one or both of the parties to the contract will be frustrated by the vagaries of the criminal law. The second approach takes the line that insurance contracts are commercial or business documents, and if it is clear that in using the word 'theft' the parties would, if asked, have expected certain conduct to be included or excluded by that word, then it should be included or excluded by it, whatever the criminal law might say. This view, while allowing the court full use of the principles of construction to determine the intention of the parties, would leave out the additional complexity caused by a detailed analysis of the law of theft. What should matter, on this view, is what the parties *thought* the criminal law was, not what it turns out to be. The merits of these respective approaches are considered in this article, in the light of recent authority.

WHO DEFINES THE CRIME?

The principle that technical terms, such as legal words, bear their technical meanings in contracts, is well established in the law of insurance. A clear example is the observation of Hamilton J in *Debenhams v Excess Insurance Co Ltd* (1912) 28 TLR 505:

> The term 'embezzlement' in this policy meant the same thing as it meant in an indictment. There was no reason for giving it any the less strict meaning in the policy by which the plaintiffs were insured than if a direct charge was being made.

A more grudging acceptance of this view appears in the speech of Viscount Sumner in the House of Lords decision of *Lake v Simmons* [1927] AC 487:

> I dissent from the view that criminal law should be treated as irrelevant merely because a document is commercial. After all, criminal law is still law and so are its definitions and rules.

(i) Riot

The leading authority for what may be referred to as the 'strict' rule is the decision of the House of Lords in *London and Lancashire Fire Insurance Co Ltd v Bolands* [1924] AC 836 ...

It is clear ... that the House of Lords ... got their criminal law right. There is, nevertheless, a common impression that 'riot' must include some element of 'tumult' to be properly so called. This is mistaken, and there may, perhaps, be three reasons for this misunderstanding of the law. The first is the rarity of prosecution, in general, for the offence of riot, and hence the absence of public discussion of the constituent elements of that offence. The second is that in practice prosecutions are only brought for the offence of riot where there *is* also evidence of tumult. The third is the existence of the Riot (Damages) Act 1886, which is a statute designed to provide a civil remedy to persons injured by riots by way of compensation out of the police rate ...

Thus, although there are different definitions of riot in common law and statute, this is not contradictory since different purposes are being pursued – the fixing of criminal liability in the former case and the securing of compensation in the latter. The definition for criminal law purposes is, then, clear though sometimes misunderstood. The House of Lords regarded this matter as crucial, and found for the insurance company. There is much to be said for this point of view. It is doubtful, however, whether many of the parties to insurance contracts containing an exemption from liability in circumstances of riot would appreciate that a robbery involving three of more persons (now 12 or more persons: Public Order Act 1986) without tumult, would not be covered by their theft insurance. It might be that insurance companies, in the interest of good client relations, would tend to refrain from reliance on the exemption in such circumstances. If so, the courts' apparent lack of flexibility should be seen against the discretionary non-reliance on exclusionary terms by the insurance companies themselves. But the existence of the possibility of waiver does not lessen the onus on the court to do justice between the parties.

On the specific question of the interpretation of 'riot', the decision in *Bolands* is certainly the leading authority in English law, but there is an important American case which adopts a far more flexible approach. In *Pan American Airways v Aetna Casualty and Surety Co* [1974] 1 Lloyd's Rep 232 an aeroplane had been hijacked and subsequently destroyed by terrorists. The insurance cover excluded damage by riot. The District Court for the Southern District of New York, in a decision later affirmed by the US Court of Appeals, held that in this case the meaning of 'riot':

> ... was intended by these parties in its popular and usual meaning ... it is the definition of riot that most appeals to common sense. It is unlikely that these parties expected their dealings to be governed by artificial and technical definitions of riot.

The court also observed that if assemblages numbering as few as three ever amounted to 'riots' *for insurance purposes*, they should not do so now, and that the views of the House of Lords to the contrary were 'not impressive'. It was further declared that because of the principle of *contra proferentum* in insurance law, any uncertainty over the meaning of a term will tend to be resolved in favour of the assured, the:

> ... insurers having the burden of showing that their definition is the only reasonable formulation. They have not discharged this burden ... the definitions requiring tumult are at least reasonable.

The first argument, that the term 'riot' does not bear the same meaning for insurance purposes as it does in the criminal law is highly contentious, flying in the face of the principle that legal terms should bear legal meanings, unless the parties have clearly indicated otherwise. The second argument could be more in accord with English law since the *contra proferentum* principle is a well established one, operating in cases of genuine disagreement over the meaning of a term. But the English cases stress that the maxim must be used as a means of resolving a genuine divergence of view and not as a means of creating one which would not otherwise exist. Since, as we have seen, the definition of riot in the criminal law *is* clear, albeit sometimes misunderstood, there seems little scope for the operation of the maxim in this context.

The continuing adherence of the English courts to the 'strict' rule in relation to the meaning of 'riot' is confirmed in the recent case of *Athens Maritime Enterprises v Hellenic War Risks Association (The Andreas Lemos)* [1983] 1 All ER 590. In that case, Staughton J, having expressed 'considerable sympathy ... at least in theory' with the American approach on the interpretation of riot, nevertheless refused to follow that lead. He pointed out that there are numerous terms of art in insurance contracts which are meaningless in popular speech. Further consideration showed that it was not desirable to construe other terms, such as riot, which have both a technical and a popular meaning, in any but the former sense.

(ii) 'Theft' and related offences

The real importance of *Pan Am v Aetna* lies not so much in what it says about the definition of 'riot,' but in its stress upon common sense interpretations of technical words, in preference to grappling with the criminal law definitions. Some English cases *do* support this approach, to some extent. They suggest that criminal law terms in insurance contracts should not be given the 'full significance' of criminal law terms appearing, say, in an indictment ...

The dominance of the 'strict' approach in English law has recently been reasserted by Stuart-Smith J in *Grundy v Fulton* [1981] 2 Lloyd's Rep 661; affirmed [1983] 1 Lloyd's Rep 16, where he concluded that 'theft must be given the same meaning as in the criminal law'. Also, in *The Andreas Lemos*, where a gang of armed men boarded the plaintiff's vessel at night, stole equipment and materials, and used force or the threat to make good their escape, Staughton J had to consider the meaning of the term 'piracy' in order to determine liability under a contract of marine insurance. Seeming to accept that piracy is 'forcible robbery at sea', he applied the wording of s 8(1) of the Theft Act 1968 (definition of 'robbery'), finding that since this was a clandestine theft, no force or threat of force being used until after the appropriation was complete, robbery, and hence no piracy, had taken place. It is fair to add, however, that Staughton J was keen to avoid any 'over elaborate analysis' of the criminal law, and was pleased to find that his conclusion was in 'accord with the commercial sense of the matter'.

REDEFINING THE OFFENCE

Different considerations will apply where the parties to the insurance contract evince an intention to step outside the criminal law definitions and define their risks independently. A clear example is *Re George and the Goldsmiths General Burglary Insurance* (1989) 80 LT 248, where a jeweller had insured his stock against burglary and housebreaking. The policy contained the following explanation of terms:

> ... policy against burglary and housebreaking as hereinafter defined – if at any time after the date thereof and during the continuance of the policy the property above described shall be lost by theft following upon actual forcible and violent entry upon the premises ...

It seems right, in principle, that the parties should be able to confine their cover or to define it as broadly or as narrowly as they wish, not being tied to criminal law definitions, which may be ill suited for the purpose. On the other hand, this assumes a fair degree of consensus, and reasonable equality of bargaining strength between the parties which may not, in fact, be present. Nevertheless, the principal canon of construction, that the document means what it clearly says, should be upheld.

DID THE OFFENCE TAKE PLACE?

In the cases discussed thus far, the question has been whether the parties should be taken to have tied themselves to criminal law definitions, or whether some flexibility of approach is appropriate. A related problem arises where there is some doubt whether the peril insured against, for example, 'theft' or 'burglary', actually took place. Disputes may arise over whether the criminal offence thus defined by the parties actually covers the loss incurred ...

It seems strange that it should be regarded as the function of a judge trying an insurance matter to have to investigate the relative merits of two lines of criminal cases which are undoubtedly in conflict and which, at the time of *Grundy v Fulton*, the criminal courts showed no signs of resolving.

PROSPECTS

What, then, should be the approach of the civil courts in these cases? Surely, a middle course has to be found between the options of rigid adherence to the criminal law where this would greatly detract from the 'commercial reality' of the contract and frustrate the expectations of the parties, and too great a degree of flexibility in a situation where the parties have, after all, defined the risk insured against in terms specific to the criminal law.

The starting point in construing such a document, it is suggested, is that unless they expressly state otherwise, the parties are bound by the technical meanings of the criminal law terms which appear in the insurance contract. The judge, then, should take as his essential starting point the definition of the offence involved, rather than the ordinary man's commercial understanding of the scope of that offence. If, however, there is genuine uncertainty over the criminal law definition, or conflict in the cases over the ambit of a particular offence, then some degree of flexibility must be permitted. The judge's task, of course, is to do justice for both sides but since the insurers drafted the agreement it is submitted that the maxim *contra proferentum* would normally come into play at this stage. It must be stressed, however, that the maximum should be used to resolve a genuine uncertainty in the criminal law, not to create one which would otherwise not exist. There may perhaps be room for a further rule that any flexibility at this point should not involve a departure from what may be termed the 'essential characteristics' of the offence, for example, theft as an offence of 'dishonesty' or as involving the 'intention permanently to deprive'. The task of the judge under this scheme would fall short of deciding between conflicting criminal law authorities. Once it was clear that there was conflict in the cases the policy would be construed against the insurers, unless this involved a substantial departure from the essential characteristics of the offence. In general, this would place on insurers the onus to draft their cover in such a way as to avoid these difficulties. Such drafting would at times be difficult, particularly where offences overlap (for example, theft and obtaining property by deception or theft and criminal damage). It might involve the narrowing of insurance cover in some cases (for example, a clearer demarcation between 'theft' and 'transit' insurance), but it would allow a more informed selection by the assured of appropriate cover, and would secure greater certainty in the interpretation of disputed contracts ...

APPENDIX 7.17

London and Lancashire Fire Insurance Co Ltd v Bolands Ltd [1924] AC 836, HL

> This insurance does not cover loss directly or indirectly caused by or happening through or in consequence of: (a) invasions, hostilities, acts of foreign enemy, riots, strikes, civil commotions, rebellions, insurrections, military or usurped power, or martial law, or the burning of property by order of any public authority; (b) incendiarism directly or indirectly connected with any of the circumstances or causes above mentioned in (a), and, in the event of any claim arising hereunder for loss of the cash as herein described, the assured shall, if so required, and as a condition precedent to any liability of the company hereon, prove that the loss did not in any way arise under or through any of the above excepted circumstances or causes ...

Lord Sumner: It is true that the uninstructed layman probably does not think, in connection with the word 'riot', of such a scene as is described in the case stated. How he would describe it I know not, but he probably thinks of something, if not more picturesque at any rate more noisy. There is, however, no warrant here for saying that, when the proviso uses a word which is emphatically a term of legal art, it is to be confined, in the interpretation of the policy, to circumstances which are only within popular notions on the subject, but are not within the technical meaning of the word. It clearly must be so with regard to martial law; it clearly, I think, must be so with regards to acts of foreign enemies; and I see no reason why the word 'riot' should not include its technical meaning here as clearly as 'burglary' and 'housebreaking' do.

Furthermore, the incidents, out of which this loss occurred, comply in my view with those very tests which were put forward to us as being essential to constitute a riot within the proviso. In broad daylight a gang of armed men, having obtained entrance into the premises by a trick, cow, if not terrorise, a superior number of persons, rushing into the place and shouting to them to hold up their hands and threatening them with death if they fail to do so. If the criminals had had more hardihood and had the courage to fire (which apparently they had not), when a couple of men of considerable nerve resisted them although unarmed, not only the noise but the resulting disturbance generally might have extended very far. It appears to me that if was a scene of tumult, and certainly a scene of disturbance of public peace, which to a layman as well as to a lawyer might well, on consideration of those aspects of it, be called a riot ...

It is suggested further that there is some ambiguity about the proviso, and that, under the various well known authorities, upon the principle of reading words *contra proferentes*, we ought to construe this proviso, which is in favour of the insurance company, adversely to them. That, however, is a principle which depends upon there being some ambiguity – that is to say, some choice of an expression – by those who are responsible for putting forward the clause, which leaves one unable to decide which of two meanings is the right one. In the present case, it is a question only of construction. There may be some difficulty, there may be even some difference of opinion, about the construction, but it is a question quite capable of being solved by the ordinary rules of grammar, and it appears to me that there is no ground for saying that there is such an ambiguity as would warrant us in reading the clause otherwise than in accordance with its express terms ...

APPENDIX 7.18

Dino Services Ltd v Prudential Assurance Co Ltd [1989] 1 All ER 422, CA

Kerr LJ: What happened is that, on a Friday evening, Mr Nash locked up the premises. That involved using quite a number of keys. He then drove away in his car, which I think was also a Ferrari, and which is equipped with every kind of alarm and locking device to prevent theft. He parked the car outside a nearby public house where he often went at the end of the working week. He left the keys to his premises in the glove compartment and later on made his way home, leaving the car parked where it was. In the morning, the car was gone and when he then went to his premises he discovered that during the night they had been entered unlawfully by means of his own keys taken from the car. So, for the purposes of the interpretation of the policy, they were stolen keys which were used to open the various locks of the premises to carry out that theft ...

The word 'violent' is an ordinary English word, which here appears in a common commercial document. It seems to me that there is no reason why its meaning should be in any way different from what any ordinary person would understand. At first sight, I therefore conclude that there should be no need to resort either to a dictionary, or to authorities, to interpret this work; nor to the rule that, this being an insurers' document, it must be construed against them. On that basis, I would take the ordinary meaning of the word 'violent' in this context to be that it is intended to convey that the use of some force to effect entry, which may be minimal, such as the turning of a key in a lock or the turning of a door handle, if accentuated or accompanied by some physical act which can properly be described as violent in its nature or character. An obvious picture that springs to mind is the breaking down of a door or the forcing open of a window, which would be acts of violence directed to the fabric of the premises to effect entry. Or there might be violence to a person, such as knocking down someone who seeks to prevent entry irrespective of whatever may be contained within para (b) of that part of the cover.

Accordingly, on that basis I would not consider for one moment that the ordinary meaning of the phrase 'entry to premises by forcible and violent means' can be applied to the action of moving the lever of a lock into its open position by means of its proper key and then turning a knob or pushing the door open to go inside. That would be 'forcible' in the sense which I have explained, as is conceded on the authorities. But there would be nothing violent about it at all. That would be my impression.

However, counsel for the plaintiff ... does not accept that approach. He obviously cannot. He stresses the fact that the keys were stolen, and he says that 'violent' is a term which characterises the unlawfulness of the act, relying in particular on one short passage in one of the cases to which I shall come. So what he says in effect is that 'forcible and violent' is to be equated with 'forcible and unlawful' in relation to the means of entry.

Unless constrained by authority, which I would be astonished to find, I cannot accept that submission for one moment. I say that for two reasons. First, 'violent' as an ordinary word obviously has a different meaning from 'unlawful' or any similar word such as 'illegal'. Violence is often unlawful, but not always or necessarily so. For instance, if I break down my own door because I have lost my key, I do something violent but nothing unlawful. On the other hand, a forcible entry which is unlawful is not necessarily one which is effected by violent means. There may be unlawfulness in which violence plays a part (that is what is covered by this provision) or there may be unlawfulness without anything which can be described as violence, and in my view that would not be covered.

The second reason why I would not accept the submission of counsel for the plaintiff, even if one dictionary meaning of 'violent' is 'unlawful' as referred to in the judgment to which I come later, is that 'unlawful' cannot have been the intended meaning here, because the phrase 'by forcible and violent means' occurs in a context which assumes a state of unlawfulness, since we are concerned with 'theft or attempted theft' involving entry by the means referred to. Accordingly, I have no doubt that the valiant attempt of counsel for the plaintiff to equate 'violent' with 'unlawfulness' must be rejected, unless astonishingly there were to be any authority binding on this court which compels its acceptance …

But in my view one cannot construe insurance policies in this over analytical way, because they so often contain words which on a strict analysis may be unnecessary but cannot properly be used to distort the ordinary meaning of the main part of the cover …

Counsel for the plaintiff finally says, in my view entirely reasonably, that this is a business document which to the ordinary person would covey that cl 1(a) is intended to cover against burglary, and cl 1(b) against robbery, and that on the facts of this case he was uninsured. I agree and have every sympathy with Mr Nash. Since it is now accepted that he took reasonable precautions and this is an exceptional and novel point, and an important one for insurers generally, I would personally hope that this might be regarded as a deserving case for an *ex gratia* payment. But, having to construe the policy as I must, I have no doubt that it cannot be construed in the way in which the judge construed it, and accordingly I would allow this appeal.

APPENDIX 7.19

Keeton, RE, 'Insurance law rights at variance with policy provisions' (1970) 83 Harv LR 961 and 1281

In any area of law, it is instructive to study simultaneously the doctrinal currents, the decisional patterns by fact types, and the underlying justifications for each. In few areas is it so difficult to reconcile what one sees from these different perspectives as in that area of insurance law concerning rights of policyholders and other claimants at variance with policy provisions. Perhaps as a corollary, judicial opinions in this area are less than ordinarily enlightening about principled bases for decision. Often, too, the favorite generalisation advanced by outside observers to explain a judgment against an insurance company at variance with policy provisions is the ambivalent, suggestive, and wholly unsatisfactory aphorism: 'It's an insurance case.'

Yet one can find in the patterns of decision some compelling currents of principle. Particularly, two broad principles, it is submitted, account for such a high percentage of what might otherwise appear to be deviant decisions that the remainder can be accepted as within the margin the margin of error one should expect in the administration of any set of guidelines. Under these two principles, an insurer will be denied any unconscionable advantage in an insurance transaction, and the reasonable expectations of applicants and intended beneficiaries will be honored. The first of these principles is candidly recognised in some contexts, though less often than it accounts for results. Open acknowledgment of the second began to emerge only in the 1960s. Although the same or closely analogous ideas may be expressed elsewhere in the law, the conditions for their application arise in insurance transactions with distinctive frequency. It is hardly surprising then, that insurance law decisions, viewed apart from these two principles, have so often seemed arbitrary.

Among other principles particularly relevant to rights at a variance with policy provisions, the most significant is the principle of granting redress for detrimental reliance. Doctrines related to the application of this principle have been distorted by the undeclared influence of the two distinctive principles alluded to above. Once these two principles are openly declared, it becomes possible to trace more precisely the influence of this third principle ...

I DISALLOWING UNCONSCIONABLE ADVANTAGE

Some rights against insurers at variance with policy provision can be accounted for as instances of the following principle:

> An insurer will not be permitted an unconscionable advantage in an insurance transaction even though the policyholder or other person whose interests are affected has manifested fully informed consent.

This principle explains much that is called waiver or estoppel in insurance law, in circumstances involving neither voluntary relinquishment nor detrimental reliance – the essence of waiver and estoppel respectively. It also accounts for most of the distinctive controls over defenses based on warranty, representation or concealment.

Typically there is disparity between the bargaining positions of the insurer and the insured. The insurer's opportunity to draft the proposed terms of agreement is an opportunity as well for overreaching. Quite naturally, there have been enough abuses of that opportunity to generate remedial action. In part, the controls developed have been statutory or administrative regulation of policy forms – occasionally by prescription of forms but more often by less rigid regulation. But such explicit regulation of policy forms is only one segment of a more comprehensive pattern of statutory and decisional controls against overreaching.

Opportunities for overreaching in the drafting of policy provisions were confirmed and enhanced by the strict and unyielding law of warranty initially fashioned by Lord Mansfield for marine insurance and extended with perhaps less justification to life and fire insurance. Warranty law opened an expansive and fertile field for insurers to conceive imaginative and sharply restrictive limitations – unconscionable even in bold face and the more so if concealed in the fine print of an obscure passage in a lengthy, bewildering form. In this setting, controls were inevitable. They have been developed not only in statutes and in administrative regulation of the potential effect of warranties, but also in doctrines fashioned by courts. And, as we shall see in part two of this article, controls fashioned in these various ways have been extended to closely similar though perhaps less severe abuses of defenses based on representation or concealment. Many of the legal consequences of these controls are, from another perspective, rights against insurers at variance and policy provisions. Perhaps these two areas – regulation of policy forms and controls over defenses based on warranty, representation or concealment – have accounted for most applications of the principle of disallowing unconscionable advantage …

II HONORING REASONABLE EXPECTATIONS

A Emergence of the principle

At Lloyd's Coffee House in the early days of its history, perhaps insurance contracts were negotiated among persons of relatively equal bargaining power. At the least, it was common for the proposal for insurance to be written by the person desiring insurance, the insurers merely underwriting for designated amounts. It may well be, however, that the nature of the provisions contained in the proposal were very early dictated by the demands of the underwriters. In any event, as the marketing of various kinds of insurance outside the Coffee House developed in magnitude, standardisation of terms for contracting, almost invariably drafted by insurers, became progressively more common.

Insurance contracts continue to be contracts of adhesion, under which the insured is left little choice beyond electing among standardised provisions offered to him, even when the standard forms are prescribed by public officials rather than insurers. Moreover, although statutory and administrative regulations have made increasing inroads on the insurer's autonomy by prescribing some kinds of provisions and proscribing others, most insurance policy provisions are still drafted by insurers. Regulation is relatively weak in most instances, and even the provisions prescribed or approved by legislative or administrative action ordinarily are in essence adoptions, outright or slightly modified, or proposals made by insurers' draftsmen.

Under such circumstances as these, judicial regulation of contracts of adhesion, whether concerning insurance or some other kind of transaction, remains appropriate. Several of the doctrines serving this regulatory purpose – notably the contract law doctrine that ambiguities in contract documents are resolved against the party responsible for its drafting – will be discussed below. Underlying this congeries of doctrines, however, one can discern a principle broader than the separate bodies of doctrine it has sustained. With a focus limited to insurance cases (though surely it applies in other contexts as well), this principle may be stated in the following way:

> The objectively reasonable expectations of applicants and intended beneficiaries regarding the terms of insurance contracts will be honored even though painstaking study of the policy provisions would have negated those expectations.

Although too general to serve as a guide from which particularised decisions can be derived through an exercise of logic, and too broad to be universally true, this principle points in the direction insurance law appears to be moving ...

First, as an ideal this principle incorporates the proposition that policy language will be construed as laymen would understand it and not according to the interpretation of sophisticated underwriters. Arguably, that proposition should be regarded as a corollary of the principle of resolving ambiguities against the insurer. The principle of honoring reasonable expectations should be extended further, protecting the policyholder's expectations as long as they are objectively reasonable from the layman's point of view, in spite of the fact that had he made a painstaking study of the contract, he would have understood the limitation that defeats the expectations at issue. The question whether the policyholder has sufficiently examined the policy is only one part of the overall calculation of the objective reasonableness of his expectations. An objective standard produces an essential degree of certainty and predictability about legal rights, as well as a method of achieving equity not only between insurer and insured but also among different insureds whose contributions through premium create the funds that are tapped to pay judgments against insurers.

An important corollary of the expectations principle is that insurers ought not to be allowed to use qualifications and exceptions from coverage that are inconsistent with the reasonable expectations of a policyholder having an ordinary degree of familiarity with the type of coverage involved. This ought not to be allowed even though the insurer's form is very explicit and unambiguous, because insurers know that ordinarily policyholders will not in fact read their policies. Policy forms are long and complicated and cannot be fully understood without detailed study; few policyholders ever read their policies as carefully as would be required for moderately detailed understanding. Moreover, the normal processes for marketing most kinds of insurance do not ordinarily place the detailed policy terms in the hands of the policyholder until the contract has already been made. In life insurance marketing, for example, the policyholder does not ordinarily see the policy terms until he has signed the application (his offer to contract with the company) and has paid a premium and the company has approved the application and has executed and issued the policy. This often means a delay of weeks, and occasionally even longer, between making an application and having possession of the policy – a factor enhancing the policy holder's disinclination to read his policy carefully or even to read it at all. Thus, not only should a policyholder's reasonable expectations be honored in the face of difficult and technical language but those expectations should prevail as well when the language of an unusual provision is clearly understandable, unless the insurer can show that the policyholder's failure to read such language was unreasonable.

It is important to note, however, that the principle of honoring reasonable expectations does not deny the insurer the opportunity to make an explicit qualification effective by calling it to the attention of a policyholder at the time of contracting, thereby negating surprise to him. The doctrines developed in relation to notice of limitations of liability of an innkeeper provide an analogy to which courts might turn in formulating more precise guidelines on this matter. There are limits, however, on the extent to which full notice to a particular policyholder can be effective; probably it cannot defeat a claim at variance with a clause that is fundamentally unconscionable because it misleads the great majority of policyholders ...

B Individual knowledge of limiting provisions

Are rights at variance that would otherwise be recognised under the expectations principle defeated by a policyholder's specific knowledge of the policy provisions that limit protection in a surprising way? It would seem that knowledge of the limiting provisions should defeat any claim based alone on the principle of honoring reasonable expectations, since such knowledge negates the surprise that would be the basis for departing from ordinary contract principles. But this principle combines with the principle of disallowing unconscionable advantage to support recovery in some cases even in the face of the claimant's unusual knowledge of the surprising provisions. The following generalization is a corollary of the combined principles of honoring reasonable expectations and is allowing unconscionable advantage:

> If the enforcement of a policy provision would defeat the reasonable expectations of the great majority of policyholders to whose claims it is relevant, it will not be enforced even against those who know of its restrictive terms.

Judicial decisions supportable on this ground have imposed controls over not merely form and method but the substantive content of insurance contracts as well – controls that apply even to provisions so central to the contract that they are referred to as coverage clauses. These legal controls are based upon factual assumptions concerning the extent to which substantively complex or otherwise unexpectable policy terms can be effectively brought to the attention of policyholders in a mass marketing process. In such circumstances, no amount of care in drafting and in marketing will avoid the creation of reasonable expectations contrary to the literal terms of policy provisions. It is a sound rule to strike down a surprising policy provision uniformly, sustaining even the claim of that occasional policyholder who can be shown to have known of its restrictive terms. To apply a different rule among various policyholders would produce the result that those who remained ignorant of the terms would receive substantially more protection for their premium dollars than those aware of them. At least when such a knowledgeable policyholder would receive coverage disproportionately small in comparison with his premiums (which ordinarily would be the case if the total premiums received from all policyholders combined were adequate for the coverage afforded), it would be unduly harsh to deprive him of the protection the great majority of policyholders receive at the same price ...

III DETRIMENTAL RELIANCE

A Generally

Many aspects of the law applying to insurance transactions, as to other transactions generally, are founded on a pervasive principle of granting redress for loss resulting from detrimental reliance. To state the principle more precisely one must take a position on issues that are controversial. The following formulation is submitted not as a universally recognised principle but as a principle that is supportable on policy grounds and is fully consistent with the results attained by most relevant modern decisions:

> A policyholder or other person intended to receive benefits under an insurance policy is entitled to redress against the insurer to the extent of detriment he suffers because he or another person justifiably relied upon an agent's representation incidental to his employment for the insurer.

This formulation focuses on rights of policyholders and intended beneficiaries against insurers. The principle applies more broadly, of course. It may apply among insurers, for example, and it may apply to other than insurance transactions. The more particular formulation expresses the sense of the principle in its most common application to insurance transactions.

Most applications of this principle have been referred to as applications of the doctrine of estoppel. But this principle also accounts for much that has loosely been called waiver, and it applies in other contexts as well. An example is the set of decisions imposing liability for negligent delay in processing an application for insurance. The majority of such decisions are reasoned, quite appropriately, as imposing tort liability for negligence, but these cases also illustrate an aspect of the principle of granting redress for detrimental reliance.

B Persons protected

The principle of granting redress for detrimental reliance supports legal relief apart from contract. By nature it may apply even when no contract has been consummated, and it may apply in favor of persons other than the policyholder or intended policyholder.

This is true, for example, when an intended policyholder applies for life insurance, designating intended beneficiaries, and dies before a policy is issued, the insurer having unreasonably delayed in acting on the application. Some courts allowing legal relief in these circumstances have declared that the cause of action belongs to the deceased's estate rather than to the intended beneficiary. Such a decision grants the estate a benefit it would never have received if the contract had been issued. It is also a benefit the estate would not have received if the intended policyholder, not relying upon the insurer to act with reasonable diligence, had instead obtained an identical policy elsewhere. Other courts, consistently with the principle of granting redress for detrimental reliance, have adopted the better rule that the cause of action belongs to the intended beneficiary ...

IV REGULATION OF DEFENSES BASED ON WARRANTY, REPRESENTATION OR CONCEALMENT

A Decisional limitation of warranty

The common law of warranty in insurance cases was extraordinarily rigorous. Though the term itself and many of the phrases commonly used in policies to provide for 'warranties' suggest affirmation, or promise, or both, a warranty was, and is, significant in insurance law primarily as a condition of the insurer's promise to pay, not as an assertion of fact or as a promise of performance by the insured. At common law, noncompliance with a provision construed as a 'warranty' was a complete defense for the insurer regardless of materiality of the 'breach' ...

More often than not, 'warranty' has been defined in writings on insurance law in terms of consequences rather than identifying characteristics. Thus, Vance, expressing the traditional view, defined a warranty as:

> ... a statement or promise set forth in the policy, or by reference incorporated therein, the untruth or non-fulfillment of which in any respect, and without reference to whether the insurer was in fact prejudiced by such untruth or non-fulfillment, renders the policy voidable by the insurer, wholly irrespective of the materiality of such statement or promise.

The common law established a key distinction between warranties and 'representations'. Misrepresentation was ground for avoidance only if material to the risk assumed. Vance, observing that representations are statements made to give information to the insurer, distinguished them from warranties as follows:

(a) warranties are parts of the contract, agreed to be essential; representations are but collateral inducements to it;

(b) warranties are always written on the face of the policy, actually or by reference. Representations may be written in the policy or in a totally disconnected paper, or may be oral;

(c) warranties are conclusively presumed to be material. The burden is on the insurer to prove representations material;

(d) warranties must be strictly complied with, while substantial truth only is required of representations.

Inevitably, pressure developed for amelioration of the law of warranty because its results were often unconscionable, or inconsistent with most policyholders' reasonable expectations, or both. Even before modern statutory developments, judicial decisions had moved far in a remedial direction, and they continue to be the only regulation of warranties in some contexts since in many jurisdictions there still are no warranty statutes generally applicable to all types of insurance.

In addition to developing doctrines of waiver and estoppel rather expansively, as we have seen in part one of this article, courts commonly apply several methods of policy construction to reduce the impact of the harsh law of warranty. First, courts often construe in some other way policy provision that might arguably have been intended as warranties. For example, words describing insured property may be treated as merely identifying property rather than stipulating that it must continue to meet the description in every detail to remain within the coverage. Similarly, phrases specifying such circumstances as the insured's age may be treated as mere representations of present fact, rather than warranties. Also, written provisions may be treated as negating printed warranty clauses.

Second, when treating a policy provision as a warranty, courts tend to construe it so as to minimise its impact. For example, in a leading case the court held that the descriptive warranty 'paper-mill' did not mean that the building must be used as a paper mill but only that it must be ready for use as a paper mill – a state of fact that existed even while the building was being used as a grist mill.

Third, courts favor construing a clause as an 'affirmative warranty' rather than a 'continuing' or 'promissory warranty'. Thus, compliance at the commencement of the contract term is enough to satisfy the warranty, and noncompliance at a later date during the policy term is no defense. Similarly, courts often construe a warranty clause as severable or distributable, so that non-compliance with a clause bearing on one type of risk does not defeat coverage for other types of risks within the policy. Finally, courts tend to construe a warranty clause as suspending liability during the period of noncompliance rather than construing it as terminating all potential liability for loss thereafter and, *a fortiori*, rather than construing it to mean, as suggested in a *dictum* by Lord Mansfield, that there is no liability even as to a loss occurring before the breach ...

[The article continues by describing various statutory enactments in the United States by which warranties are controlled. There is no English equivalent.]

APPENDIX 7.20

Gerhardt v Continental Insurance Cos and Firemen's Insurance Co of Newark [1967] 1 Lloyd's Rep 380

[A decision from the United States.]

Jacobs J: In *Bauman v Royal Indemnity Co* 36 NJ 12 (1961), at p 21, we approved the holding in *Gunther*, pointing out that the company had deliberately described its policy in sweeping terms as a comprehensive personal liability policy, and had sold it as such, and that while it had the legal right to exclude particular types of liability, its responsibility was to do so unequivocally. We noted that fairness to the ordinary layman who is the average insured dictates that exclusions be 'so prominently placed and so clearly phrased should not be subjected to 'technical encumbrances or to hidden pitfalls'. Similarly in *Allen v Metropolitan Life Insurance Co* 44 NJ 294 (1965), where a receipt for the first annual premium, though conditioned, was held to afford interim coverage pending physical examination of the insured, we said:

> While insurance policies and binders are contractual in nature, they are not ordinary contracts but are 'contracts of adhesion' between parties not equally situated ... The company is expert in its field and its varied and complex instruments are prepared by it unilaterally whereas the assured or prospective assured is a layman unversed in insurance provisions and practices. He justifiably places heavy reliance on the knowledge and good faith of the company and its representatives and they, in turn, are under correspondingly heavy responsibility to him. His reasonable expectations in the transaction may not justly be frustrated and courts have properly molded their governing interpretative principles with that uppermost in mind ...

The exclusionary clause in the policy before us was neither conspicuous nor plain and clear. The policy form was prepared unilaterally by the company and was sold on a mass basis as affording broad coverage to homeowners. It was designed to include protection not only against fire and theft but also, as set forth on its face page, 'Comprehensive Personal Liability' to the extent of $10,000 for each occurrence. Also on the face page was the statement that the insured's stated address was her residence and that she employs not more than two full time residence employees, defined on the third page as employees who duties are in connection with the ownership, maintenance or use of the premises. Surely a reasonable homeowner, reading all this on the face page, would assume that she was covered in the event her single domestic was injured while employed at her home. She might not know anything at all about the difference between a common law liability claim and a workmen's compensation claim but would expect coverage in either event. If the company had acted fairly in the effort to exclude coverage of workmen's compensation claims, it would have give the insured clear notice to the effect on the face page of the policy or by a slip attached to the face page; if it had done that, it may readily be assumed that the insured here would have taken suitable steps to obtain broader coverage, available at relatively minor cost ...

While the insured is always supposed to read the policy, only a very hardy soul would have ploughed through all of the fine print here in an effort to understand the many terms and conditions …

As far as the plaintiff here was concerned, nowhere was there any straightforward and unconditional statement that the policy was not intended to protect the insured against a workmen's compensation claim by a residence employee injured at the insured's home. Indeed, her earlier reading of the favoured treatment of residence employees in exclusions (a) and (b) would have tended to confirm her belief to the contrary. And so would her reading of the first exclusion in (d), for if the intent was to have no coverage at all as to such workmen's compensation claims, she might fairly inquire as to why her homeowner's policy contained the broad separate exclusion applicable to instances where the insured carried an independent workmen's compensation policy …

APPENDIX 7.21

Liederman, A, 'Insurance coverage disputes in the United States: a period of uncertainty for the insurer' [1986] LMCLQ 79

American society is commonly viewed as litigious. A significant share of the disputes resolved by the American judicial process has involved disputes between insureds and their insurers. At the source of these disputes is the interpretation and application of the insurance contract, which is dependent solely upon the meaning to be attributed to the contract wording. As expressed by Justice Oliver Wendall Holmes, a 'word is not crystal, transparent and unchanged, it is the skin of a living thought and may vary greatly in color and content according to the circumstances and the time in which it is used'. Thus, inherent in every contract is the potential for varying interpretations and construction of its wording.

Within the last decade, in the face of continued challenges in the courts, insurers have found it increasingly difficult to draft policy wording which offers certainty and stability. Stability and certainty are the key to rating viability in the insurance market. While insurers knowingly accept risks, the insurance contract attempts to draw carefully the boundaries of the assumed risk so that premiums are commensurate with the insurer's known undertaking. Yet, as John H Bretherick, president of the Continental Group of New York recently noted, judicial interpretations broadening policy coverage have 'resulted in insurers being held liable for some aspects of the uninsurable'. Equitable considerations involved in the construction of personal lines insurance have been invoked in the commercial context along with such a doctrine as 'reasonable expectation of the insured', resulting in an inconsistent application and interpretation of law and standard contract wording.

Policy holders and risk management consultants have been encouraged by these legal trends and have actively advocated 'creative interpretation' of policy language as a technique to reduce policy holders' losses. The response of the insurance industry has been a shrinkage in capacity and redoubled efforts at redrafting and restricting coverages. Insureds are now confronting the dilemma of more tightly drawn and limited contracts with little room for interpretation and little more than a Pyrrhic victory gained from past judicial grants of broad coverage for obsolete wording.

The doctrinal seeds of judicial 'redrafting' and regulation of insurance contracts are not of recent design. In 1959, a New York court, in addressing a dispute concerning a provision of the standard comprehensive general liability form, criticised the drafters of the wording by noting:

> ... the language, both in extent and ambiguity, in modern insurance policies is an abomination. Inclusions, exclusions, definitions and coverages set forth in the contracts present the most formidable type of obfuscation which no trained person, let alone a layman, can truthfully say is anything but the cant of insurers. It is, unfortunately, not within the province of this court to order that policies be written briefly and lucidly.

What has magnified the problem of judicial redrafting and regulation, creating a situation of potentially crisis proportions, has been the emergence and proliferation, over the past 10 years, of mass product liability claims including those for latent injuries arising from asbestos exposure as well as toxic exposure to chemicals and hazardous wastes. The sheer magnitude of this litigation has overwhelmed the administrative capacity of the courts and threatened the financial viability of various industries. In turn, the volume of claims, the costs of their defense, and the financial exposure they have created for insurers have caused a crisis in an insurance industry which never anticipated that their insureds would face this kind of liability exposure.

It has generally been recognised that this 'societal problem' demands a societal response. In the absence of legislative action, however, the judiciary has shouldered the burden of addressing the problem. As a first step in fashioning a response we have witnessed an expansive judicial view towards liability and a divorcing of liability from fault. The courts have reasoned that the solution to the societal problem must be premised on the collective social responsibility of all members of the society. Accordingly, the courts have fashioned responses based on a 'deep pocket' theory for spreading losses whenever possible.

William O'Bailey, president of Aetna Life and Casualty Co, recently noted that:

> At the heart of insurers' liability problems is that courts will misinterpret language wilfully as they constantly search for more and more money to deal with societal problems which a decade ago we took care of through the tax mechanism on the part of the government.

Indeed, it has been the willingness of judges to try coverage disputes and the varying court interpretations of policies which have caused the proliferation of coverage lawsuits over the past 10 years. Litigation is no longer a last resort. As noted by Raymond W Stahl, senior vice president of the Travellers Corporation: 'All too often suits are filed precipitously and without much discussion at the top level.'

With each recent catastrophe or wave of new mass claims, the courts have been asked to resolve corresponding coverage issues and in effect help spread the risk of these losses to a 'deeper pocket' the insurer. In November 1984, a national insurance litigation reporter in its premiere issue compiled a list of as many as 145 declaratory judgment actions nationwide involving coverage disputes for a variety of underlying claims. The coverage actions are not only limited to disputes between policyholders and their insurers. There is a ripple effect in the insurance industry and litigation has spread to the reinsurance relationship.

Accompanying this intense judicial scrutiny of the insurance industry has been a willingness on the part of the courts to punish conduct by insurers that the courts describe as malicious or unconscionable, as well as to penalise insurers when they have failed to protect the interests of their insured. The risk of being held in 'bad faith' or being held responsible for extra-contractual damages, including possibly punitive damages, has become a critical element in an insurer's evaluation of a claim and utilised as leverage by the insured to force a settlement providing coverage on the insured's terms. It is reasonable to assume that this threat, together with the judicial tendency to favor an insured's interpretation of wording, has had a chilling effect on insurer readiness to assert what the insurer believes is the coverage afforded within the four corners of its contract.

The American attorney is therefore faced with a difficult task when asked to advise a commercial lines insurer regarding the merits of coverage of a loss. While all insurer attempts at denying coverage are not meritorious, it is not unreasonable to wonder whether a commercial lines insurer will have his fair day in court to challenge coverage for a claim. Result oriented decision making by the courts and misapplication of concern for 'equity' have rendered the resolution of commercial coverage disputes a prisoner of the vagaries of jurists who may strain interpretations of wording to effectuate social goals. The result, at best, is inconsistent application of the law and inconsistent construction of identical wording from jurisdiction to jurisdiction. Rather than being based on an evaluation of the contract as written, the construction and meaning of contract wording and the 'intent' attributed to the contracting parties are controlled by concerns entirely unrelated to that contract.

Traditional contract law requires a court to determine and effectuate the intent of the parties as expressed in the writing. To ascertain this intent, a court will generally look to the contract wording itself and construe the document as whole, attempting to give to the terms their plain and ordinary meaning. It is the objective intent of the parties that the essence of the law, and courts have recognised that it is not their function to redraft the contract when it is clear and unambiguous. Where there is an ambiguity, courts have sought to resolve the ambiguity by effectuating the intention of the parties. However, when there has been no evidence indicating that intent the ambiguity has been construed against the party responsible for the drafting of the contract.

A prime example of the problem confronting the commercial lines insurer has been a tendency by the courts to bypass traditional contract law to resolve coverage disputes in furtherance of equitable considerations arising from a perceived inequality between the contracting parties. The formulation of this principle of insurance contract interpretation, however, has its genesis in litigation focusing on primarily personal lines insurance where the equities are dissimilar to those in the commercial lines context.

Courts have traditionally viewed the insurance policy as a standard form contract which the insurer designs and the insured can either take or leave with little or no option afforded for the altering of its terms. In recognition of an assumed inequality between the parties to the contract, the courts have liberally resolved contract wording disputes against the insurer, utilizing such doctrines as that of adhesion and *contra proferentem* ...

... These rules of construction, however, have presupposed an innocent purchaser of insurance who does not match the more sophisticated insurer who drafted the contract. Does the absence of these equitable considerations in the case of a commercial lines insurance contract dictate the abandonment of these interpretative tools which generally favor the insured?

The most appropriate response to this question was that of the United States Court of Appeals for the Fifth Circuit in *Eagle Leasing Corp v Hartford Fire Insurance Co* 540 F 2d 1257 (1976), wherein the court held that it would not feel compelled to apply the general rule that an insurance policy is to be construed against the insured, based on such doctrines as adhesion, in the commercial insurance field when the insurer is not an innocent but a corporation of immense size, carrying insurance with annual premiums in six figures, managed by sophisticated businessmen, and represented by counsel on the same professional level as the counsel for insurers …

… An even more disconcerting doctrine, again premised upon the purported inequality of bargaining position between the insured and insurer, has evolved which essentially expands judicial inquiry into the realm of determining and effecting the 'reasonable expectations' of the insured. This doctrine contemplates that a court will look towards the insured's objectively reasonable expectations, which will be honored even if a 'painstaking study of the policy provisions would have negated those expectations'. A corollary to this doctrine has been advanced which requires that those policy provisions which are contrary to the expectations of the insured should not be enforced even if the insured knew of the restrictive terms of the provision.

As has been aptly noted, the difficulty with this doctrine is that it is not merely an aid in interpreting contracts of insurance but it has rather become a means of judicial regulation of insurance contracts and more directly a means of avoiding contracts. In fact, the difference between the customary interpretative tools and the doctrine of reasonable expectations is that where the former will seek to resolve ambiguities in favor of the insured, the latter doctrine will assure that the court will find coverage …

… The 1981 decision of the US Court of Appeals for the District of Columbia Circuit in *Keene Corp v Insurance Co of North America* (667 F 2d 1034 (1981), DC Cir) swept away traditional contract interpretation and fashioned a theory of coverage premised solely on maximizing coverage to the insured. The court in *Keene* emphasised the goal of giving effect to the insurance policy's dominant purpose of indemnity insuring an appropriate exchange of an uncertain loss for a certain loss and securing for the insured the certainty the court believed the insured had purchased. In seeking certainty, the court seemed preoccupied with finding the broadest coverage to insure that for each of the claims asserted against Keene coverage would always be available. Courts prior to *Keene* had grappled with medical evidence as to the etiology of the asbestos related injury so as to determine when the injury, as the trigger of coverage, occurred. The *Keene* court virtually ignored such factual evidence and adopted the multi-trigger theory of coverage, utilizing all points in time from first exposure to manifestation of the injury, ensuring that no claims would fall outside of available coverage.

The court enunciated three principles of insurance policy interpretation – to construe the policy's coverage to give effect to a dominant purpose of indemnity; to construe ambiguities in the contract in favor of the insured; and to strive to give effect to the objectively reasonable expectations of the insured. Utilizing these three principles the court avoided a detailed analysis of the claims for which coverage was sought, choosing to formulate the broadest possible approach to coverage since the policies were considered contracts of adhesion, and any reasonable doubts would be construed against the insurer. Accordingly, it was not necessary for the court to scrutinise the policy wording intensely or examine evidence pertaining to when an asbestos-related injury may have actually occurred. The possibility of coverage under each of the points in time from exposure to manifestation was enough for the court to adopt the triple trigger, thereby affording the assured the maximum possible coverage.

In a better reasoned decision, a New York Federal Court in *American Home Products v Liberty Insurance Co* (565 F Supp 1484 (1983); 748 F 2d 760 (1984)) applying similar policy wording, rejected the *Keene* court's blind adoption of a triple trigger in the absence of a specific determination that a coverage-triggering injury had in fact occurred. This determination, the *American Home* court ruled, was clearly required by the policy language.

The court viewed the *Keene* approach as being dictated by result oriented reasoning relying on social policy to justify an expectation of 'complete' coverage for the insured. The court noted that it would be impossible to predict the effect of rules adopted purely on the basis of social considerations on future tort litigants, recognizing that the theory of maximizing coverage for one insured today may be unduly limiting for a different insured tomorrow.

The *American Home* court argued that the application of the reasonable expectations doctrine should be reserved for situations in which the expectations are strongly demonstrated and the policy involved is truly a contract of adhesion, which the commercial lines general liability policy is not. The court in fact held that the insured's expectations were entirely consistent with the policy language and that the manuscript policies at issue were not the usual adhesion contract. Of significance was the court's observation that:

> Once courts deem themselves free to ignore the language and intent of a negotiated contract, they are left with little or no basis upon which to arrive at consistent results in deciding how the contract should be read. Judges in such situations are left to act essentially as legislators and, along with the flexibility they obtain to choose among possible results, they also read the uncertainty that stems from having to rely heavily on personal values and inclinations, as well as upon empirically unsound and potentially disruptive perceptions of fairness.

Despite the concerns expressed in *American Home*, many courts have followed the *Keene* rationale in resolving coverage disputes …

… This article has only touched on the many insurance issues which have been addressed by the courts as a by-product of the proliferation in product liability litigation and the significant increase in the financial exposure associated with the litigation. The courts, in their effort to pass on such exposure to the insurer as a deeper pocket, have eroded the insurance industry's faith in the stability of its product – the insurance contract. The solution must certainly be addressed on two fronts. Clearly, the ever widening scope of insured liability must be controlled to remove the pressures of spreading the financial burdens such liability creates for the insurer as a deeper pocket. Secondly, insurers must act quickly to redraft policy language to exchange certainty for the uncertainty created by judicial construction of wording. Furthermore, insurers must accept the reality of judicial intervention in the insured-insurer contractual relationship unless adequate safeguards, such as arbitration provisions, are grafted onto the contract. Without substantial changes in the environment and pressure under which American courts have acted, the prudent insurer must be wary of any reliance on the judiciary to protect adequately its contracted interest.

APPENDIX 7.22

Clarke, M, 'The reasonable expectations of the insured – in England?' [1989] JBL 389

For many years in the United States courts have interpreted insurance policies against the insurer so as to fulfill the reasonable expectations of the insured. Although any doctrine of that name has been formally rejected in England, this article considers whether a doctrine of that kind has come here in another guise.

REASONABLE EXPECTATIONS IN THE UNITED STATES

> The objectively reasonable expectations of applicants and intended beneficiaries regarding the terms of insurance contracts will be honoured even though painstaking study of the policy provisions would have negated those expectations.

In the United States, this principle has produced some decisions which are unlikely in England – in particular, the disregard of unambiguous exceptions, of which the insured, particularly the consumer, was unaware, because they were, in the view of the court, unconscionable. In *Steven* 337 P 2d 284 (1962), Cal, for example, a person with trip flight insurance, finding his scheduled aircraft grounded, took an unscheduled substitute and was killed. The court refused to apply an exception relating to unscheduled flights, as the insured could reasonably expect to be covered in such circumstances.

Arguments for a rule of reasonable expectation are said to be as follows:

(a) it induces the insurer to give the prospective insured better information about the kind of cover available, and the insured will then make more efficient use of his resources;

(b) it promotes equity, if the insurer has created misleading expectations about cover;

(c) it promotes effective risk spreading.

Arguments against a rule of reasonable expectations are said to be as follows:

(a) it increases uncertainty, particularly by inconsistency between state jurisdictions, and so increases the cost of insurance, as well as leading to delay in settlement of claims;

(b) 'The response of the insurance industry has been a shrinkage of capacity and redoubled efforts at redrafting and restricting coverages. Insureds are now confronting the dilemma of more tightly drawn and limited contracts with little room for interpretation and little more than a Pyrrhic victory gained from past judicial grants of broad coverage for obsolete wording';

(c) it ignores the true intention of the parties in commercial lines insurance, where there has been genuine bargaining.

In the United States, the 'expectations' cases can be divided into two groups. First, those in which an expectation was generated by the particular insurer, usually by creating a misleading impression. Second, cases like *Steven* in which the expectation, if any, was that of the court, which did not expect or wish to see that kind of clause in that kind of (insurance) contract: in short judicial legislation in thin disguise.

REASONABLE EXPECTATIONS IN ENGLAND

Scots lawyers tell me that, while summer reaches England before it gets to Scotland, in legal innovation the position is reversed. Many years ago a legal swallow was flown in Scotland (*Sangster's Trustees* (1896) 24 R 56) that the insurance policy should be construed in accordance with the reasonable expectations of the insured. South of the border the swallow was shot at:

> The weakness of the reasonable expectation principle is its dependence on the notion of reasonableness. Despite many judicial expeditions to find him, the reasonable man has not been reduced to captivity. In truth, as any man on the Clapham omnibus could tell us, the reasonable man does not exist at all.
>
> The law is concerned with legal obligations only and the law of contract only with legal obligations created by mutual obligations between contractors – not with the expectations, however reasonable, of one contractor that the other will do something that he has assumed no legal obligation to do.

The swallow went west, way out west to California, and has since flourished in parts that Lord Diplock could not reach. More recently, however, by s 37(2)(a) of the Insurance Companies Act 1982, the Secretary of State has been given power to protect policyholders 'against the risk that the [insurance] company may be unable to meet its liabilities, or, in the case of long term business, to fulfill the reasonable expectations of policy holders or potential policy holders', notably as to the distribution of profits between policyholders and shareholders. The swallow has returned to Westminster, but has it reached the Strand? In general, courts in England have abjured the rule of revising contracts to make them reasonable: the second group of cases in the United States has no counterpart here. As to the first group in the United States, the question merits a closer look, for there are three lines of cases in England that could converge on the same point to produce law similar to that in the United States. These concern: (a) rectification of the policy in cases of unilateral mistake; (b) cases of misleading interpretation of the policy; and (c) cases of misleading presentation of the cover …

Misleading interpretation

… General contract law contains some support for the proposition, that a contractual document is taken to say what it is represented to say, provided that the representee relies on it and it is reasonable for him to do so. From this base, it can be argued that, if the proposer is led to believe that term X *means* A, when on a proper construction it means B, it will be enforced as if it meant A; and also perhaps, if the insurer or an agent of the insurer leads the proposer to expect that a policy *contains* term X, when the reality is that it contains term Y, it may be enforced as if it contained X rather than Y. The reasonable expectation of the proposer is fulfilled. Before looking at the English cases on this central point, it may be helpful to look sideways at other jurisdictions …

In Canada, in *Baker* 34 DLR (4th) 340 (1987), a group disability policy, arranged by an employer for his employees, provided for its termination 31 days after an employee ceased active full time employment. The insurer issued the insured employee with an insurance certificate, which instructed him to apply to the employer 'for information regarding the benefits', as the employer was the only person at hand with a copy of the policy. When Mr Baker, an employee, did so, he was told by his employer that, if he paid the premiums, cover would continue (indefinitely) while he was laid off. The Supreme Court of Nova Scotia (Appeals Division) held that the insurer was bound by the employer's statement.

By contrast, in Australia in *Gates* (1985–86) 160 CLR 1, a similar representation by an agent of the insurer was without effect ...

... Again, in a case in Victoria, having stressed that the terms of the insurance were there to be read and that, by implication, the insured did not act reasonably in relying on what the insurer said about them ...

The position in Australia has been changed by s 11(1) of the Insurance (Agents and Brokers) Act 1984 (Cth) which provides:

> An insurer is responsible, as between the insurer and an insured or intending insured, for the conduct of his agent or employee, being conduct:
>
> (a) upon which a person in the circumstances of the insured or intending insured could reasonable be expected to rely; and
>
> (b) upon which the insured or intending insured in fact relied in good faith.

The result is that 'misrepresentations by an insurer's agent as to policy benefits ... will be "sheeted home" to the insurer' who faces a statutory liability for damages ...

Misleading interpretation: obstacles to relief

If a contracting party makes a written promise inconsistent with his own standard printed terms, there is little doubt that the former promise prevails, provided that: (a) it was put within the four corners of the written contract; and (b) it was put there by a party to the contract. In the present problem, however: (a) the promise may be outside the policy and hence its enforcement inhibited by the parol evidence rule; (b) the statement is made by an agent, usually an agent not at head office but out in the field whose authority is limited; and (c) in some cases the statement was less about the content of the contract offered than about its meaning or interpretation; interpretation is traditionally seen as a statement of law. These differences suggest obstacles to relief ...

The parol evidence rule

If there is a document, such as an insurance policy, which is of a certain degree of formality and which looks like the whole of the contract, the parol evidence rule excludes evidence to add to, vary or contradict the document ...:

> In England, reference to subsequent conduct has been ruled out, but a similar result has been achieved by the alternative route of estoppel by convention. Moreover evidence, other than subsequent conduct, of the parties' interpretation of their written contract has been admitted, including evidence of pre-contract negotiations. Accordingly, the parol

evidence rule is not an absolute bar to enforcement of an insurance contract as interpreted by the agent. The rule is more difficult to overcome when the agent represents not the interpretation but the contents; but it has been held that a person may be estopped by what he says about the contents of his contract; and the line between interpretation and contents is often hard to draw.

The authority of the agent

In *Joel* [1908] 2 KB 863 and *Kaufmann* (1929) Ll L Rep 315, as well as in *Graves* 489 F 2d 625 (1973), the agent had actual authority to make contracts. But when the insured does not realise that the contract terms were being modified, what counts is not actual or apparent authority to make contracts, but actual or apparent authority to explain the meaning of (apparently unmodified) contracts. If the buyer of goods may rely on the salesman's statements about goods, why not also the buyer of insurance ...

In Indiana the court was more specific:

> It strains credulity to believe that the managers of any insurance company would *actually* (not merely on paper) so limit the authority of the company's soliciting agents as to, in effect, instruct each to say to his prospects, 'Let me take your application for a ... policy, but I cannot tell you what is covers'.

In England, agents less skilled than the agents of insurers have had actual or apparent authority to explain contract terms, and their principals have been bound by the explanation. That is the position of the agent who explains the settlement of an insurance claim, and it is not obvious why the position relating to an insurance contract should be different.

Representations of law

The interpretation of a document has been regarded in England as a question of law and, traditionally, there can be no estoppel on the basis of (mis)statements of law. However, estoppel there can be, if the question is of private rights: that is a question not of law but of fact. Further, a distinction has been drawn between the interpretation of a document (law) and the contents of a document (fact). Obviously, this is a difficult line to draw, for a statement of a document's contents is based on conclusions about its meaning.

However, it is arguable that, provoked by the unreality of the rule against allowing relief or remedy based on misstatements of law, the courts are now most receptive to arguments that the rule does not apply to the case in hand. Arguments include, first, that the true origin of the rule is the premise that the one person had no better knowledge or skill in the matter than the other; in other words, statements of law were on a par with statements of opinion, and the rule against relief assumed that reliance was not reasonable. Secondly, the Privy Council has decided that a mistake of law may be a ground for relief, if the parties are not *in pari delicto*. These arguments head for a point: the rule does not apply when the misstatement is made by a person with significantly greater knowledge of the matter than the other, for that other, we may add, acts reasonably in relying on the statement ...

Misleading presentation

Here, the argument is that the insurer will not be allowed to plead exceptions, if that defeats the expectations of the insured about the general nature of the cover being sold or the main purpose the insurance is patently intended to achieve.

In England, the profferor of contract terms will not be allowed to rely on clauses misleadingly presented by the document itself, or inconspicuously printed in non-contractual written material. This was brought to insurance contracts by Lord Greene MR, saying:

> A policy of this kind is not to be approached with the idea that a large part of the benefit of the insurance which any employers would obviously wish to get, and which is at the outset given in wide terms, is to be eliminated by a 'condition' tucked away at the end of the policy in the context in which this condition is found, for, be it observed, all the other conditions related to matters of comparatively minor importance [*Woodfall and Rimmer v Moyle* [1942] 1 KB 66].

In the same vein, Clauson LJ referred to a 'duty' of the insurer to make clear any term adverse to the insured. More recently, the Insurance Ombudsman has suggested, that 'to convey news of a significant diminution of cover in an obscure note on the back of the renewal notice' is a breach by the insurer of the duty of good faith.

In the United States, if insurance is sold in a context or under a name that suggests cover wider than that actually offered, courts have enforced the insurance to an extent that meets the expectations of the insured. In *Lacks*, flight insurance, excepting cover on charter flights, was offered from a vending machine placed in front of the sales counter of a charter airline. It was held that the insurer's motion, to have the insurance claim for loss on a charter flight dismissed, failed.

In *Kievet* 170 A 2d 22 (1961), 'accident' insurance was sold to a man of 48, who later suffered an accidental blow on the head which triggered latent Parkinson's disease. The insurer pleaded an exception of 'disability or other loss resulting from or contributed to by any disease or ailment'. The court observed that people would expect this kind of accident to be covered; that, if the exception were read literally, 'the policy would be of little value to him since disability or death resulting from accidental injury would in all probability be in some sense contributed to by the infirmities of old age'. It held that the accident was covered by the policy.

The ordinary American is not expected to read the fine print, and the court asks whether the insured was told of an important but obscure provision, and whether it was one known to the public generally. Subject to this, the reasonable expectations of the ordinary man are based on the large print, including titles such as 'Products Liability', 'All Risks', which are then taken to be a statement of general cover, and of purpose. From this perspective, the court in the United States will reject a literal reading of the fine print, if a literal reading defeats the main purpose of the insurance, as perceived by the insured ...

The present argument is that insurance is sold like any other product and should be subject to the same rules and construction. It will be construed so as to fulfill not defeat the main purpose or expectation of the (reasonable) insured ...

In *Port-Rose v Phoenix Assurance plc* (1986) 136 NLJ 333, Hodgson J said:

> An 'all risk' policy means precisely what it says and it is the plainest law that, under such a policy, all that the insured has to do is to prove that there was a loss due to a fortuitous happening of some sort ... In my judgment, you must not construe it in such a way that it means – we cover you against all risks but we do not cover you against all risks.

In this spirit, the judge gave short shrift to a defence based on a policy clause requiring 'reasonable steps to prevent loss'.

CONCLUSION

There is no clear conclusion. The law moves. It remains to be seen whether these cases will be brought together in England to form a rule of reasonable expectations applied to insurance contracts. It is contrary to the common law tradition in England to start from broad principles, or even to extrapolate to them. 'English law has grown in bits according to need and was not laid down in slices by an act of will.' Here, we have some bits. They do not make the kind of picture seen in California, but, nonetheless, leave an impression. A misleading impression?

CLAIMS

INTRODUCTION

A loss has occurred. What steps must now be taken by the insured in order to make a claim on the policy and if he is successful in making the claim how is the value of the loss assessed? A number of distinct topics are dealt with in this chapter: causation, claims procedures, fraud and quantum.

CAUSATION

Although X may have a policy and X has suffered a loss, it may be that the policy does not cover that particular loss. This may be due to the fact that the policy does not extend to that particular loss. In the highly competitive world of insurance, consumers should heed the warning that 'cheapest may not be the best'. Motor insurance premiums vary enormously, but so too does the policy wording. Whether or not the policy extends to the type of loss suffered will largely depend on the construction of the policy wording and this was the subject matter of the last chapter. With regard to the burden of proof, it is for the insured to prove that his loss comes within the policy wording. In appropriate cases, it will then be for the insurer to prove that an exception or exclusion relieves him from liability on the policy (Appendix 8.1).

The leading case is the House of Lords decision in *Leyland Shipping Co v Norwich Union Fire Insurance Society* [1918] AC 35. A ship was insured against perils at sea but the policy excluded 'all consequences of hostilities or warlike operations'. The ship was torpedoed by the enemy, but managed to reach a French port. She was ordered to a particular berth by the harbour authorities. The berth was too shallow and the ship eventually sank. Was the loss due to the attack or due to the consignment to an inadequate berth? If the answer was due to the first reason then the loss was excluded by the policy, if it was caused by the berthing decision then it was a peril at sea and the insurers would be liable. Section 55(1) of the Marine Insurance Act 1906 somewhat unhelpfully states, in part, 'the insurer is liable for any loss proximately caused by a peril insured against, but … he is not liable for any loss which is not proximately caused by a peril insured against'. In *Leyland*, Lord Shaw explained:

> In my opinion, my Lords, too much is made of refinements upon the subject. The doctrine of cause has been … one involving the subtlest of distinctions …

> To treat *proxima causa* as the cause which is nearest in time is out of the question. Causes are spoken of as if they were distinct from one another as beads in a row or links in a chain ... The chain of causation is a handy expression, but the figure is inadequate. Causation is not a chain, but a net ... What does 'proximate' here mean ...? The cause which is truly proximate is that which is proximate in efficiency. That efficiency may have been preserved although other causes may meantime have sprung up which have yet not destroyed it, or truly impaired it, and it may culminate in a result of which it still remains the real efficient cause to which the event can be ascribed.

Thus, applying the 'real efficient cause' test, it was held that the loss was due to the torpedoing and therefore the insurers were not liable on the policy. Reference can also be made to *In re Etherington and Lancashire and Yorkshire Accident Insurance Co* [1909] 1 KB 591 (Appendix 7.13) where the insured fell heavily while hunting, but rode home suffering from shock and exposure. The following day he went to work but developed pneumonia and died a week after the fall. His accident insurance policy stated that it would pay out if his death was directly caused by an accident. The policy also stated that it would not pay out 'where the direct or proximate cause is disease or other intervening cause, even although the disease or other intervening cause may itself have been aggravated by such accident, or have been due to weakness or exhaustion consequent thereon, or the death accelerated thereby'. The Court of Appeal were of the opinion that the phrase was ambiguous and found against the insurer. The pneumonia was considered to be a consequence of the accidental fall. For the insurers to avoid the liability it would have been necessary to show that there had been a new and intervening cause that had led to the insured's death.

It is convenient here to mention two other topics. The first involves the timing or coverage of the policy period. A problem may arise where a policyholder changes insurers, usually at renewal time. This might be done because a more competitive premium has been quoted by another insurer or another insurer's policy coverage is wider than the former insurer's policy. What happens if loss or damage spans the two policy periods? What happens, particularly in professional indemnity insurance, if a negligent act occurred in 1995, but was not discovered until 1997, by which time insurers had changed? A similar difficulty can also arise in a case of injuries that take many years to manifest themselves such as asbestosis or a drug related injury. Insurers greatly dislike uncertainty. They like to be able to calculate annually their profit or loss and recalculate premiums accordingly. Insurers, therefore, prefer what is referred to as a 'claims made' basis of liability, rather then a 'claims occurring basis'. By opting for the 'claims made' formula, the insurer will only be liable for claims notified during the policy period and he will thus avoid the possibility of long tail exposure. One of the major problems of the asbestosis claims was that they were written on a claims occurring basis and thus insurers were forced to meet claims decades later.

In *Irving and Burns v Stone* [1997] CLC 1593, the plaintiffs were a firm of surveyors who obtained professional indemnity insurance from the defendants. During the currency of the policy, a writ was issued alleging negligence against the plaintiffs, but it was not issued or brought to their attention until after that policy had expired. The Court of Appeal found for the insurers. The policy was a claims made policy and there had been no claim communicated to them during the currency of their policy. The judgment makes no reference to the insurers who presumably took over the plaintiff's professional indemnity cover. If there was no claim against the first insurers notified within their policy period, there would, presumably, be a right of action on the subsequent policy, subject to its wording. There is, potentially, great difficulty for the insured, if he knows of a potential claim, but one which is not formally notified and the renewal date comes round. Good faith would require him to notify the insurers on renewal, or new insurers – if he is considering changing insurers. In such circumstances it is difficult to imagine that a renewal or a new policy would be offered. In reality, insurers have responded to this situation in marketing policies that attempt to deal with the problem.

The case of *Kelly v Norwich Union Fire Insurance Society Ltd* [1989] 2 All ER 888 (Appendix 8.2) illustrates how a privately insured can face great difficulties in this area. The plaintiff had an external water pipe break and he had it repaired. He then insured the bungalow. The pipe leaked again. It was later discovered that the bungalow had suffered damage due to water leakage. It was not possible to determine which leak had caused what damage. The Court of Appeal disallowed the insured's claim. No apportionment was possible as between damage caused by the pre-policy leakage and policy leakage, because there was no evidence submitted to distinguish the damage caused by the two leaks.

The second area of difficulty is that relating to mitigation of loss. The requirement in the general law of contract that the innocent party should mitigate his losses is well known. Does this translate to an insurance setting? It is not unusual for the policy to require efforts to be taken by the insured to avert or mitigate potential loss, rather like a motor policy or a buildings policy requiring that the vehicle or building be kept in a good state of repair. The question is, can the costs incurred be passed on to the insurer?

This question arose in *Yorkshire Water Service Ltd v Sun Alliance and London* [1997] 2 Lloyd's Rep 21. The plaintiffs carried out urgent flood alleviation work, at a cost of £4.6 m, to avoid extensive damage to neighbouring landowners. If the surrounding land had been flooded the plaintiffs would have been liable. They sought to recoup the cost from their insurers. The Court of Appeal dismissed their claim. Construing the wording of the policy, sums needed only to be paid when claims had been successfully made against the insured and the court was unwilling to imply a term into the contract to cover mitigation costs. Crucially, the wording of the policy required the insured, at his own expense, to carry out preventative work. The court was not influenced by a number of American decisions which go the other way. Stuart-Smith LJ explained:

> ... the American courts adopt a much more benign attitude towards the insured ... these notions which reflect a substantial element of public policy are not part of the principles of construction or contracts under English law [see Chapter 7, generally, and Appendix 7.19].

After referring to the *Yorkshire Water Services* decision, MacGillivray, *Insurance Law*, 9th edn, 1998, London: Sweet & Maxwell (paras 26–19) states:

> The position under a property damage policy is, perhaps, more debatable. Suppose, for example, a householder insures his house but not his garden against subsidence and the garden subsides to such an extent that the house itself [is] in imminent danger of collapse. If the householder then erects a retaining wall to avert the risk of further subsidence as well as to reduce the risk of insurers becoming liable under the policy, can he recover the cost of erecting the retaining well? We submit that he should be so entitled and that any other result would be manifestly unjust.

This approach would then place English law nearer to that in the United States. (See the Ombudsman's view in Appendix 11.2.)

CLAIMS PROCEDURES

Even where the insured may have suffered a loss within the policy wording, there will be contractual requirements which he must meet in order to present a valid claim. Such requirements are usually to enable the insurer the opportunity to investigate the claim, particularly where a third party is responsible for the loss. A motor collision is an obvious example. Time periods within which notification has to be given are a normal industry practice. Such requirements could be conditions precedent to liability and thus a breach could have dire results for the insured, even though on the facts of the particular case the inconvenience caused to the insurer might be shown to be minimal (see Chapter 5). The court will often be astute, however, in preventing strict use of technicalities by an insurer.

In *Verelst's Administratrix v Motor Union Insurance Co* [1925] 2 KB 137, a motor policy contained a condition precedent that notice should be given 'as soon as possible' following an accident. The insured was killed in India in a motor accident, but it was not until 12 months later that the policy was discovered by her personal representatives. The insurers denied liability for breach of the notification requirement. They argued that knowledge of the accident and not knowledge of the existence of the policy should be the triggering event for the notification period. The court rejected this argument, finding for the personal representatives. A potentially impossible task would have faced the claimants if the language of the policy had used an expression such as, notification must be given within 14 days of the accident. Such set time periods are by no means uncommon. In consumer contracts, the situation is somewhat eased by the Association of British Insurers' Statement of General Insurance Practice (Appendix 4.10) which calls for the use of the phrase, found in *Verelst*'s case 50 years earlier, 'as soon as reasonably possible'.

Another requirement of making a claim is usually to provide particulars of the loss. Such particulars will vary depending on the type of claim being made. In consumer insurance, related to contents insurance, insurers will usually ask, on the claims form, for receipts relating to items destroyed or stolen. Failure to provide such receipts on the grounds that they have not been retained would not be disastrous to the insured's claim, unless there was a condition precedent in the policy that certain receipts must be kept. In consumer policies this would be an unusual step.

Any terms of the policy in a consumer contract would have to meet the requirements of the Unfair Terms in Consumer Contracts Regulations 1999 (Appendix 7.1).

In 2000 the Association of British Insurers (ABI) introduced a Claims Code that their members are expected to abide by in relation to consumers' claims. (See Appendix 8.14.)

As with other ABI Codes/Statements set out in this book this Code espouses high standards of customer care. Only close scrutiny by an independent body will prove whether or not insurer-members achieve the requisite standards.

FRAUDULENT CLAIMS

(See Appendix 11.2 for the Ombudsman's views on fraudulent claims.)

Fraud is more likely to take place because of a decision by the insured. Typical examples would be to bring about the insured event, for example, arson; to claim for items that were never owned and to overestimate the value of the loss.

An important recent case dealing with the content of the duty of good faith at the claims stage is that of the House of Lords in *Manifest Shipping v Uni-Polaris Insurance Co (The Star Sea)* [2001] 1 All ER 743 (Appendix 8.3). The decision involves matters other than good faith, but is here dealt with only on this topic.

The case concerned a claim on a marine policy. The insurers rejected the claim on the grounds that two earlier accident reports relating to other ships owned by the insured had not been disclosed to them at the time of the present claim and this was in breach of the utmost good faith requirement of s 17 of the Marine Insurance Act (MIA) 1906 (see Appendix 4.3). All three courts found for the insured. It was held that the duty of good faith found in s 17, affecting the performance of the contract, was not the same as the duty of good faith required in s 18 which related to pre-contract negotiations. In relation to claims only the finding of fraud against the insured would defeat the claim. Innocent or negligent mistakes would not allow avoidance of the claim under s 17. The policy wording might well cover such situations and if so then the contract rules for breach would come into operation.

Leggatt LJ in the Court of Appeal on three occasions referred to the draconian remedy (avoidance of the policy) being the only remedy that would be available if breach of s 17 was found. Such a remedy should be limited to cases of fraud and not extended to negligent or culpable behaviour on the part of the insured. (See Appendix 8.12.)

If some insurers are unhappy with the interpretation of the House of Lords in *The Star Sea*, then they will find no joy at all in the Court of Appeal decision in *K/S Merc-Scandia v Certain Lloyds Underwriters* [2001] Lloyd's Rep IR 802. (See Appendix 8.13.)

Here, under a liability policy, the insured had written a fraudulent letter during the negotiations leading to a claim. This letter, however, had nothing to do with the substantive claim and its falsity was discovered long before the claim was duly processed. (In fact, it was a claim against the insured that the insurers were seeking to defend after the insured had gone into liquidation and thus it was not a 'claim' by the insured at all.) The insurer sought to avoid on the grounds of fraud arguing that *The Star Sea*, while rejecting a right to avoid merely because there may have been culpable behaviour at the claims stage, had indicated that fraud would be an example of breach of good faith post-contract.

It was held that the insurer was liable.

Longmore LJ explained that it was well recognised that before a contract could be avoided for pre-contract non-disclosure/misrepresentation, the fact not disclosed or misrepresented had, firstly, to be material from the point of view of a prudent insurer when assessing the risk and, second, it must have induced the actual insurer to write that risk. There was no reason why these ingredients should not also be the test where an insurer seeks to avoid liability for lack of good faith or fraud in relation to post-contractual matters. In particular, the requirement of inducement which exists for pre-contractual lack of good faith must exist in an appropriate form before an insurer can avoid the entire contract for post-contract lack of good faith. In this way the requirement of inducement for pre-contract conduct resulting in avoidance is then made to tally with post-contract conduct said to enable the insurer to avoid the contract. The conduct of the assured which is relied on by the insurer must be causally relevant to the insurer's ultimate liability or, at least, to some defence of the insurers before it can be permitted to avoid the policy. 'This is ... the same concept as that insurers must be seriously prejudiced by the fraud complained of before the policy can be avoided.'

Even in a clearly established case of a fraudulent claim, the draconian remedy led to a divided Court of Appeal in *Orakpo v Barclays Insurance Services and Another* [1995] LRLR 443 (Appendix 8.4). The insured had obtained buildings insurance based on a material misrepresentation as to the state of repair of the building. He also made a grossly exaggerated claim as to loss of income that followed from damage to the building. It is the latter point with which we are concerned. The majority of the court were clear that any fraud in the making of the claim goes to the root of the contract and entitles the insurer to be discharged. Staughton LJ thought the claim was grossly exaggerated and that it was a breach of good faith, but he had doubts as to the punishment, particularly as the policy itself did not provide for a specific penalty. He expressed the opinion that he did not know of any other branch of the law that disentitled a claimant to that to which he was entitled, on the grounds that he was to forfeit other claims on the basis of fraud. This is an interesting view but one clearly without support from the insurance cases. It found no supporters with the Court of Appeal in *Diggens v Sun Alliance and London* [1994] CLC 1146. The facts of *Diggens* are interesting and probably reflect a not uncommon situation. The insured made a legitimate claim on his policy but the builders also carried out non-insurance work on the building and the value of that work was merged with the insurance claim. The Court of Appeal allowed the plaintiff claim for the insurance repair and dismissed the insurer's argument that it was a fraudulent claim. There was no evidence that the insured was party to or had instructed the builders to make the additional claim. There was no evidence that he had fraudulently suppressed an earlier and lower tender for the work.

If the court is of the opinion that a contract is tainted by fraud and that contract would lead to an insurance claim, then it will not only refuse to enforce any insurance claim but also the primary contract. Thus in *Taylor v Bhail* [1996] CLC 377 a builder claimed a sum for work done for the defendant which was overpriced so that the defendant could ultimately claim that sum from his insurers and in turn the defendant promised the plaintiff that he would be awarded the job. In effect the overpricing was £1,000 on a £12,000 job. The Court of Appeal held that the builder was not entitled to the price for the job, the defendant would not be entitled to any insurance claim and if any had been paid then the insurer would be entitled to reclaim such sum. In the words of Millett LJ: 'Let it be clearly understood if a builder or a garage or other supplier agrees to provide a false estimate for work in order to enable its customer to obtain payment from his insurers to which he is not entitled, then it will be unable to recover payment from its customer and the customer will be unable to claim on his insurers even if he has paid for the work.' Here both parties are 'guilty' of fraud but English law has no method of allocating responsibility thus the 'guilty' defendant has his repairs done without making full payment.

Merely to exaggerate a claim may not amount to fraud. It would depend largely on the scale of the exaggeration. The courts in a number of cases have accepted that the size of the claim is seen as a bargaining position. Insurers will often attempt to reduce the claim. The insured, wary of the approach, may therefore increase the claim with a view to it being reduced and thus arrive at a figure near to the true value. The annual reports of the Insurance Ombudsman (see Chapter 11) refer, on several occasions, to the value insurers put on vehicles that are written off. Such values are often below what the Insurance Ombudsman Bureau regards as the fair value and thus lead to a higher figure being suggested by the Insurance Ombudsman. Is offering a figure held to be too low by the insurer a sign of breach of good faith by the insurer? Probably not, as long as a slightly exaggerated claim is not seen as fraud by the insured.

In *Sofi v Prudential Assurance Co Ltd* [1993] 2 Lloyd's Rep 559 (Appendix 7.6), while the Court of Appeal found for the insured for the theft of his jewellery, the trial judge had disallowed unfair parts of the insured's claim in relation to the contents of suitcases on the grounds that it was exaggerated. Thus, in that case, the over valued loss was not equated to fraud. (See s 56 of the (Australian) Insurance Contracts Act 1984 (Cth) (Appendix 8.10), for its approach to fraudulent claims.)

MEASURE OF INDEMNITY

The guiding principle of insurance is that the insured should be indemnified against his loss whether the loss is total or partial. He should not be under compensated nor should he receive a windfall. The chances, however, of reaching a figure that accurately reflects each side's view of what is true compensation are probably rare. It is possible to have a valued policy wherein both sides agree at the outset the value of the object and that figure is paid if there is a total loss. Such policies are rare outside marine insurance, but a vintage car might attract such a policy. House contents policies are usually written on a 'new for old' basis whereby the 10 year old television, stolen or destroyed in a fire, will be replaced by a new set equivalent to the model lost or destroyed. In that sense it can be said that the insured receives more than a true indemnity. Premiums will, of course, reflect this approach. Insurers usually reserve for themselves a choice between payment or repairing or reinstating (see below). Obviously they will choose whichever remedy most suits them. Payment is normally the chosen option, the main reason being it is administratively the simplest method – claim, pay, close file, increase premiums(!?).

How is the loss or damage to be calculated? First, it should be said that it is calculated at the time of loss or damage and not when the policy was taken out. Thus, in motor insurance, you value the car at £5,000 on 1 January (and, even then, this may not be a figure which, if the car was stolen on that day, you would receive) and the car was written off on 1 November. It is the value on 1 November that will be paid. Choosing the correct figure at that date is clearly an area ripe for disagreement and a fertile ground for the Insurance Ombudsman (see Chapter 11).

A useful illustration of the above points is found in *Leppard v Excess Insurance Co Ltd* [1979] 2 All ER 668 (Appendix 8.5). See also comments on this case in Appendix 8.6 and Appendix 8.7. The insured bought a remote country cottage for £1,500 in 1972. In 1994, he insured it for £10,000, declaring this to be the value that it would cost to replace it should it be totally destroyed. The policy reserved for the insurer the option of payment, reinstatement or repair. In 1975, the plaintiff increased the value to £14,000. The cottage was destroyed by fire that year. The agreed cost of reinstatement was £8,694 taking into account betterment (see *Reynolds*, below). However, the insurers discovered that the cottage was for sale at the time of the fire. Due to difficulties the insured was having with his neighbour, he admitted that he would have accepted £4,500 for the cottage. Obviously, the insurers chose not to repair or reinstate and they successfully argued that the market value of the cottage to the insured was the figure that he would have accepted on a sale the day before the fire. Was that £4,500? No, it was £3,000. Why? Because the land or the site was worth £1,500 and he still had that to sell even after the fire. This last point is important. Are most of those who live in the south east of England over-insuring their houses? Do most people insure at the price they paid for the property? If so, they have included the value of the land as part of the price. What should be insured are the *rebuilding* costs of that property: do insurers warn customers not to over-insure? The rebuilding costs formula is probably to be found somewhere in the policy, but who reads that far? In the property slump of the late 1980s and early 1990s, did insurers advise customers to recalculate their figures? If the buildings cost formula had been correctly used, then those costs remained roughly similar to before the slump, but, if the land value had been incorrectly included, then there was massive over insurance.

While 'new for old' may apply to house contents, it does not apply to property. That brings us to the question of betterment. This is a phrase which reflects the fact that repair or reinstatement provides the insured with a building superior to the original. A deduction is usually made to reflect this. This was a technique used by the trial judge in *Leppard*, but the Court of Appeal tackled the problem in the way described above.

Betterment is illustrated in *Reynolds and Anderson v Phoenix Assurance Co Ltd and Others* [1978] 2 Lloyd's Rep 440 (Appendix 8.8 and also on another issue, see Appendix 4.11). The plaintiffs insured the premises in 1973 for £550,000. The policy contained a pay, reinstate or replace clause. Following a fire, which destroyed seven 10ths of the building, the insured claimed a sum for reinstatement. The insurers argued that the true method of compensation was the modern replacement value, about one 10th of the figure claimed, and that no commercial man would consider spending in excess of £1 m in rebuilding an obsolete building. The court found for the insured. He had convinced the court that his desire to rebuild was no eccentricity, and equally he had convinced the court that he genuinely intended to reconstruct the building if he was awarded an adequate sum as compensation. In that case, the sum claimed by the insured was the true method of indemnification. Betterment should be taken into account but as the insured intended to use a great deal of second hand material and to use a certain amount of inferior material the betterment figure should not be too great.

In *Exchange Theatre Ltd v Iron Trades Mutual Insurance Co* [1983] 1 Lloyd's Rep 674, however, the court did not consider that a Victorian hall used for bingo merited rebuilding to its original splendour and awarded the costs of a modern equivalent.

Is it possible for an insurer to be held liable for losses that the handling of the claim has caused to the insured? While it is obviously the right of the insurer to defend a claim there are times when that defence could be shown to be one of incompetence, negligence or even a sign of bad faith on the part of the insurer. The effect of late payment of the claim, either as a result of the insured's successful litigation or a change of position by the insurer, will attract interest on the award. The actual loss suffered by the insured may be shown to be far greater than mere interest added to the insured sum.

The answer is that no additional sum is possible and this is a situation on which the Court of Appeal has, on two recent occasions, had cause to comment adversely.

The unease was clearly reflected by the judges in *Sprung v Royal Insurance (UK) Ltd* [1999] Lloyd's Rep IR 111.

The claimant insured a factory which was seriously damaged by vandals in April 1986. The defendant insurers visited the premises, made a small payment but refused the major claim arguing that it was not covered by the policy. Without insurance monies the claimant could not afford to carry out the repairs, a possible sale of the premises that existed before the insured event occurred fell through and the claimant had to close the works.

A writ was issued in 1988; in 1990 a consent order for £30,000 interim payment was made; in 1994 the question arose as to whether claimant was entitled to further sums.

Even though the court decided that the insurers had no good defence, in fact Evans LJ was of the opinion that the insurer's stance was unattractive both from a commercial and moral point of view, nevertheless English law does not recognise a cause of action in damages for the late payment of what might be due as damages. All that was possible was the interest on those damages. This, of course, was no help to the claimant whose business had been wound up because of the failure of the insurers to accept liability.

Lord Justice Beldam said:

> There will be many who share Mr Sprung's view that in cases such as this such an award is inadequate to compensate him or any other assured who may have had to abandon his business as a result of insurers' failure to pay, and that early consideration should be given to reform of the law in similar cases.

In *Pride Valley Foods Ltd v Independent Insurance Co Ltd* [1999] Lloyd's Rep IR 120 the Court of Appeal granted leave to appeal to them on a similar point of law so that the matter could be further considered by them or ultimately the House of Lords. (See [1998] LMCLQ 154.)

It is not difficult to find a contrary approach to the present English position. Australia and New Zealand recognise the award of damages in a situation similar to *Sprung* and some of the United States go a lot further with their tort of bad faith doctrine in awarding damages as multiples of the original insured loss in the form of punitive damages. (See Appendix 4.22.)

Selecting the appropriate value of goods or property at the time of insuring, or renewing, is not always an easy matter. That requires discussion of the possibility of over valuing or under valuing by the insured and the effect that this might have on the claim.

Over valuing might be a sign of fraud on the part of the insured. If it is a genuine mistake, then the insured will only receive the true market value at the time of the loss and he will have paid too high a premium.

Under valuing is more common. As the premium is largely linked to the declared value, some insureds may under value to keep down the premium. They may have house contents worth £30,000 but believe that not everything could be stolen, or even in the case of a fire, the chances are that not everything will be lost before the fire brigade arrives. They may simply think they cannot afford the full premiums. Wary of this technique, insurers countered with their own technique of 'subject to average clauses' or the rateable proportion clause. A typical clause reads:

> Whenever a sum insured is declared to be subject to average, if the property, shall at the breaking out of any fire, be collectively of greater value than such sum insured, then the insured shall be considered as being his own insurer for the difference, and shall bear a rateable share of the loss accordingly.

If there is total loss then the insured will receive up to the insured sum, which of course will be less than the true value. If there is partial loss, however, he will not receive the loss he had suffered but only a percentage of that, assessed as follows:

> The policy value over the true value, times the amount of loss.

To use simple figures: if X insures his house for £50,000 whereas the true value is £100,000 and the fire damage is assessed at £10,000 then he will receive 50,000/100,000 multiplied by £10,000 = £5,000.

Insurers may decide to offer a settlement figure rather than use the average clause. If the undervaluing is due to negligent advice from an intermediary it may be possible to sue the intermediary: see *Bollom v Byas Mosley* [1999] Lloyd's Rep PN.

The average condition can apply to any type of insurance, other than life, but usually it is applied to fire insurance and buildings. It is commonly stated, in the major texts, that it does not apply to domestic contents insurance. But that may lead an insured into a false sense of security. One needs to go back to Chapter 4 ('Misrepresentation and Non-Disclosure'). If the value required by the policy is falsely stated, then there is the possibility of the insured losing everything, or having to accept an *ex gratia* (that is, lesser) sum, whereas the use of the average clause would have given him a percentage of the loss.

The recent Court of Appeal decision in *Economides v Commercial Union Assurance Co plc* [1997] 3 All ER 636 (Appendix 8.9) is of considerable importance in this area, Peter Gibson LJ stating that the case raised 'issues of significance to all who have household insurance policies as well as to all insurers under such policies'.

The plaintiff insured the contents of his flat with the defendant in 1988 stating their value to be '£12,000 (including property of members of your family permanently residing with you. The figure must represent the full cost of replacing all your contents as new ...)'. That figure was increased to £16,000 in 1990. The policy also covered valuables but only up to one third of sum insured. The policy was index linked, a commonly used technique to save the insured from making a fresh calculation on each renewal. In 1990, the plaintiff's parents came to live permanently in England and stayed with him. They brought with them their family valuables. The flat was burgled and property worth £31,000 was stolen. Most of the value consisted of valuables belonging to the parents. There was no subject to average clause and the insurers argued that there had been a misrepresentation, which if successful would have led to no payment. The court held that there was no misrepresentation because the insured's statement as to value was one of opinion and s 20(5) of the Marine Insurance Act 1906 states: 'A representation as to a matter of expectation or belief is true if it be made in good faith ...' The insured had been honest (but certainly forgetful). Based on the discussion above as to indemnity, to what sum was the insured entitled? He could not have more than the sum insured and he could not, on the policy wording, have more than one third for the valuables of the sum insured. Therefore, the answer was that he was awarded £7,815, representing the fact that, as most of items stolen were classed as 'valuables', the claim was subject to the one third of £16,000 formula.

This decision will have come as something of a shock to insurers generally and only time will tell whether it will lead to subject to average clauses being used more regularly in domestic contents insurance.

Section 44 of the (Australian) Insurance Contracts Act 1984 (Cth) (Appendix 8.10) deals with the question of average in a different way. The intention is to relieve, to a certain extent, the insured from the dangers of under valuation. This is achieved by allowing an under valuation of 20% before it is actionable under valuation and, if it is in excess of the 20% margin, using the 80% valuation as the criterion for assessing the damages. The section does, however, unlike present English law, apply this approach to all types of general insurance. This decision was based on a majority view of the Australian Law Reform Commission Report (ALRC 20, para 271), which revised its earlier discussion paper view (ALRC DP 7, para 71) in the light of the insurance industry's response.

English law does in fact have a 'special condition of average' which is based on a 75% variation but appears to be limited to special types of insurance cover. Agricultural produce is one example where it would be difficult at the start of the policy to fix on a specific valuation.

The possibility of reinstatement as an option available for an insurer has been referred to in several cases used in this chapter, for example, *Leppard* and *Reynolds*. To insist on reinstatement, the insurers must have reserved for themselves the option in the policy. Even when they have done so they will still choose to adopt the least costly method available to them. *Reynolds* illustrates that the court may insist on reinstatement as the correct method of indemnification.

Brief reference should be made here to a statutory form of reinstatement found in the Fires Prevention (Metropolis) Act 1774 (Appendix 8.11 and Appendix 8.8).

Assume a worst case scenario. The insured is heavily in debt; he has an interest in an insured building; desirous to obtain the cash value of the insurance he deliberately sets fire to it; arson cannot be proven. The purpose of the 1774 Act is to prevent insureds from obtaining the cash proceeds and allows the insurer to insist on reinstatement. Others with an interest in the building can also so insist. Despite its title, the Act has been held to apply to the whole of England, but it does not apply to Lloyd's underwriters because the Act is directed to 'governors or directors' of insurance companies, words considered inappropriate to describe the Lloyd's market. However, with changes to the financial basis on which Lloyd's now functions, that is, the growth of corporate membership in the 1990s, and recent suggestions to 'buy-out' the remaining names, perhaps the Act could be applied to fire business at Lloyd's.

CLAIMS

APPENDIX 8.1

Clarke, M, 'Insurance: the proximate cause in English law' (1981) 40 CLJ 284

The proximate cause, whether an event covered by a policy ('peril') or an event excluded from a policy ('exception'), 'is the dominant or effective or operative cause'. So says MacGillivray and Parkington. So say the courts. It is hard to disagree. It is also hard to understand what it means and hence hard to apply it. The result is that most judges are reluctant to commit themselves to greater precision and that those lawyers who press further, judges or writers, do not agree.

Professor Ivamy contends that:

> ... where there is no break in the sequence of causes from the peril insured against to the last cause, each cause in the sequence being the reasonable and probable consequence, directly or naturally resulting in the ordinary course of events from the cause which precedes it, the peril insured against is the cause of the loss within the meaning of the policy.

This is true of case in which the insurer is liable, but does not provide a rule to separate the cases in which the peril was held too remote; in other words, it is submitted than an event which 'is the reasonable and probable consequence' may not be close enough in its connection to what went before for the latter to be its proximate cause.

Lord Denning is not the only judge to claim that the proximate cause can be identified by the application of common sense. But Professors Hart and Honoré comment:

> Textbook writers often echo this, but sometimes with the warning that it is impossible to characterise any principles on which common sense proceeds. This seems a counsel of despair ... We must not think of a common sense notion as necessarily a matter of mere impression, or so intuitive that it cannot further be elucidated, at least in its application to standard cases, however vague a penumbra may surround it. Common sense is not a matter of inexplicable or arbitrary assertions, and the casual notions which it employs ... can be shown to rest, at least in part, on stateable principles.

The learned editors of MacGillivray and Parkington state that:

> ... if the loss or damage is the necessary consequence of the peril insured against under the existing physical conditions, there is, *prima facie*, damage by that particular peril. Similarly, if the peril is one of the causes in a chain of events following in inevitable sequence, all the causes in the chain are *prima facie* proximate causes of the ultimate change.

This emphasis on what follows 'inevitably' or 'necessarily' underlines a causal connection tighter than that observed by Professor Ivamy. However, it is submitted to be imprecise without more – more by way of qualification and development. It is the purpose of this paper to pursue the line marked by MacGillivray and Parkington, to map the contours of any qualifications that appear and to see if that line can be reconciled with the view of Professor Ivamy.

THE PROBLEM

The problem of the proximate cause is old; but modern English law dates largely from 1918 when it took a new direction with the decision of the House of Lords in *Leyland Shipping Co Ltd v Norwich Union Fire Insurance Society Ltd* [1918] AC 35 ...

... During the First World War a ship off Le Havre was torpedoed by an enemy submarine. She was towed to a quay in the outer harbour at Le Havre but, being low in the head, she could not be brought to the inner harbour or to the dry dock. It was the end of January and the weather, already rough, deteriorated and caused the ship to bump the quay. The port authorities, fearful that she would sink there and obstruct a quay needed for Red Cross embarkation, ordered the ship out of the harbour. She was taken out to a breakwater where the master hoped to continue to take off cargo but, buffeted by the heavy seas, she soon sank. The shipowners contended that this was a loss through perils of the sea, a peril covered by the respondents' policy. The respondents argued that this loss was a consequence of hostilities, an exception under their policy. The House of Lords, like the courts below, held that the proximate cause was the torpedo and, therefore, that the action on the policy failed.

Their Lordships rejected previous judicial emphasis on the last cause in point of time and earlier cases must be viewed with caution and in the light of this shift of opinion: 'The cause which is truly proximate is that which is proximate in *efficiency*.' Their Lordships declined to elaborate about the 'efficient' or 'dominant' cause. However, the question had come before a number of distinguished judges and it seems profitable to seek the implications of the decision.

It was clearly not decisive that any one cause was the last in point of time. Their Lordships said so; moreover this would be an impracticable test, at loggerheads with the apparent intention of the parties. As Lord Shaw pointed out: 'How could there be any exception in the case of a vessel lost in harbour or at sea to a loss by perils of the sea if the proximate cause in the sense of nearness in time to the result were the thing to be looked to?' Entry of seawater is usually the last thing that happens.

A second possible test is a test of inevitability; that given the event, whether peril or exception, the loss should follow inevitably from that event. But at the time when the torpedo struck, it was not at all inevitable that the ship would sink. The master might have decided to beach her, though nobody doubted that, on the information available to him, he decided wisely in not doing so. Lord Shaw said of the ship that 'from the time of her being torpedoes everything was done to save her from the fatal effects'. Further, the weather might not have deteriorated: even in late January or early February bad weather in the Channel is not inevitable. There was general agreement that, if the ship had been allowed to remain at the quay in the outer harbour, she would probably have been saved, though still damaged by the explosion of the torpedo.

A third test looks much like the test of remoteness of damage in tort: given the event, the firing of the torpedo (at the particular time, place and manner), was the total loss of the ship reasonably foreseeable? In view of the vagueness inherent in this test, it is not surprising that it does fit the decision. Storms from the sea and congestion from the war were both eminently foreseeable.

The same can be said of a fourth possible test approximating to the test of remoteness of damage in the law of contract: was the loss not unlikely to occur? Some trace of this view is found in these words of Lord Haldane:

> The fact that attempts were made to obviate the *natural consequences* of the injury inflicted by the torpedo does not introduce any break in the direct relation between the cause and its effect which culminated in the damage sustained ...

A fifth and final test is one which mixes features of the second with those of the fourth: loss of the *kind* covered must be inevitable, but the *extent* of the loss need only be such as would have been within reasonable contemplation or not unlikely to occur. This fits, given the torpedo, loss by seawater and explosion was inevitable. What was not inevitable was that the ship would sink: but given the time of year and the wartime conditions this was surely not unlikely to occur. Some trace of this view is found in these words of Lord Haldane:

> The fact that attempts were made to obviate the *natural consequences* of the injury inflicted by the torpedo does not introduce any break in the direct relation between the cause and its effect which culminated in the damage sustained ...

[Note: This article extends over a further 18 pages dealing with the problem of proximate cause in English Law.]

APPENDIX 8.2

Kelly v Norwich Union Fire Insurance Society Ltd [1989] 2 All ER 888, CA; [1989] 1 Lloyd's Rep 333

Bingham LJ: An insurance policy of the kind here under consideration is a contract of indemnity. By it the insurer undertakes to indemnify the insured against loss or damage to the subject property caused by certain perils specified in the policy.

The leakage of water which took place in 1978 was quickly remedied and was held to be of no significance. That finding has not been challenged.

The leakage of water during 1980 is accepted as a peril specified in the policy then current, and occurred during the policy term. But the insured cannot show that his house suffered any quantifiable loss or damage as a result of that leakage alone. It is accordingly accepted on his behalf that he must, to make good his claim against these insurers, show that they agreed to indemnify him against loss or damage suffered by his house during the four policy years when the insurer was on risk as a result of the water leakage in 1977. It is accepted that that leakage was a peril specified in the policies, and, despite Mr Samuels' argument to the contrary, I am satisfied that the judge found the resulting damage to have occurred during the cumulative term of the policies. The insured's problem is that the 1977 leakage admittedly began and ended before the term of the first policy began.

The insured argues that under the policies he is entitled to be indemnified if damage caused by a specified peril occurs during the cumulative term of the policies, even though the peril occurred before that term began.

The insurers argue that the insured is under the policies entitled to be indemnified if the insured peril occurs during the term of one or other policy and causes damage, even though the damage may occur, or become evident after expiry of the term of any policy or the cumulative term of all the policies.

Neither party contends that the right to indemnity is dependent on the occurrence of both the specified peril and the resulting damage during the term of one or all of the policies, and neither party contends that there can be alright to indemnity if neither the specified peril nor the resulting damage occurs during the term of one or all of the policies.

In agreement with my Lord, I am of the clear opinion that under these policies the insured's right to indemnity is dependent upon his showing that the specified peril in question occurred during the term of one or other policy. I give five reasons for that conclusion:

(1) the reference to 'events occurring during the period of insurance' in the insurers' crucial contractual undertaking most aptly applies to the occurrence of specific perils and not to the occurrence of damage resulting therefrom;

(2) subsidence is specified as an insured peril. Heave is not. Heave is not a phenomenon of which I was formerly aware, but one should not assume that the insurers were similarly ignorant. It is noticeable that whereas the insured warranted in his initial proposal that the house had not been damaged by

subsidence, the insurers are not similarly protected in the case of heave. The two cases are not the same, since even on the insured's argument he can recover for damage caused by heave only where that is caused by a specified peril, whereas subsidence of itself founds a claim unless its cause is one of those specifically excluded. But, if this policy had intended to cover an insured against loss or damage to the house caused by heave caused by a specified peril occurring before the policy began, I think it overwhelmingly likely that an appropriate warranty would have been exacted from the insured at the outset;

(3) I think it contrary to common understanding that an event may qualify as an insured peril if occurring before the policy term. This common understanding is reflected in the traditional language of the Lloyd's ship and goods voyage policy annexed to the Marine Insurance Act 1906:

> Touching the adventures and perils which we the assurers are contented to bear and do take upon us in this voyage: they are of the seas ... etc.

It would be somewhat startling if a claim would lie for damage suffered during a voyage as a result of perils which had occurred before the insurers came on risk, or if (in the non-marine field) an insurer were liable for dry or wet rot which became apparent during his policy term although caused by an escape of water years earlier when another insurer, or no insurer, had been on risk;

(4) if asked what he had insured against during the policy year, an insured under a policy such as these (if he knew the policy terms) would in my view reply 'fire, explosion, lightning, earthquake, storm, flood', etc, not 'loss or damage caused by fire, explosion, lightning, earthquake, storm, flood', etc. This is in my view a case where the colloquial response accurately reflects the legal reality;

(5) the researches of counsel unearthed no reported case in which an insurer had been held liable to indemnify the insured although the specified peril occurred before the insurer came on risk. While ultimately all must turn on the wording of the policy in question, it would in my view need compelling language of a kind not found here to lead to so unusual a result.

The insurers may well be right to accept that if the specified peril occurs during the policy term it makes no difference that the resulting damage occurs after, perhaps well after, its expiry. But the point does not arise for decision here and I think it is best not to decide it until it does.

My conclusion is, in all essentials, the same as that of the learned judge, as also of my Lord. I, too, would dismiss the appeal ...

APPENDIX 8.3

Manifest Shipping Co Ltd v Uni-Polaris Shipping Co Ltd (The Star Sea) [2001] 1 All ER 743, HL

Lord Hobhouse:

Section 17: the legal problems

[41] Section 17 raises many questions. But only two of them are critical to the decision of the present appeal the fraudulent claim question and the litigation question. It is, however, necessary to discuss them in the context of a consideration of the problematic character of s 17 which is overlaid by the historical and pragmatic development of the relevant concept both before and since 1906.

[42] The history of the concept of good faith in relation to the law of insurance is reviewed in the speech of Lord Mustill in *Pan Atlantic Insurance Co Ltd v Pine Top Insurance Co Ltd* [1994] 3 All ER 581; [1995] 1 AC 501 and in a valuable and well researched article (also containing a penetrating discussion of the conceptual difficulties) by Mr Howard N Bennett, 'Mapping the doctrine of utmost good faith in insurance contract law' [1999I Lloyd's MCLQ 165. The acknowledged origin is Lord Mansfield CJ's judgment in *Carter v Boehm* (1766) 3 Burr 1905; (1558–1774) All ER Rep 183. As Lord Mustill points out, Lord Mansfield was at the time attempting to introduce into English commercial law a general principle of good faith, an attempt which was ultimately unsuccessful and only survived for limited classes of transactions, one of which was insurance. His judgment in *Carter v Boehm* was an application of his general principle to the making of a contract of insurance. It was based upon the inequality of information as between the proposer and the underwriter and the character of insurance as a contract upon a 'speculation'. He equated non-disclosure to fraud. He said ((1766) 3 Burr 1905 at 1909; (1558–1774) 1 All ER Rep 183 at 184):

> The keeping back [in] such circumstances is a fraud, and therefore the policy is void. Although the suppression should happen through mistake, without any fraudulent intention; yet still the under-writer is deceived, and the policy is void ...

It thus was not actual fraud as known to the common law but a form of mistake of which the other party was not allowed to take advantage. Twelve years later in *Pawson v Watson* (1778) 2 Cowp 785 at 788; [1778] 98 ER 1361 at 1362 he emphasised that the avoidance of the contract was as the result of a rule of law:

> But as, by the law of merchants, all dealings must be fair and honest, fraud infects and vitiates every mercantile contract. Therefore, if there is fraud in a representation, it will avoid the policy, as a fraud, but not as a part of the agreement.

[43] Echoes of his more universal approach could still be found nearly a century later in a judgment of Lord Cockburn CJ in *Bates v Hewett* (1867) LR 2 QB 595 at 606–07:

> If we were to sanction such [non-disclosure], especially in these days, when parties frequently forget the old rules of mercantile faith and honour which used to distinguish this country from any other, we should be lending ourselves to innovations of a dangerous and monstrous character, which I think we ought not to do.

[44] It was probably the need to distinguish those transactions to which Lord Mansfield's principle still applied which led to the coining of the phrases 'utmost' good faith and '*uberrimae fidei*', phrases not used by Lord Mansfield and which only seem to have become current in the 19th century. Storey used the expression 'greatest good faith', Wharton 'the most abundant good faith'; a Scottish law dictionary (Traynor) used 'the most full and copious' good faith; some English judges referred to 'perfect' good faith (see *Britton v Royal Insurance Co* (1866) 4 F & F 905; 176 ER 843 *per* Willes J) and to 'full and perfect faith' (see *Bates v Hewitt* (1867) LR 2 QB 595 at 607 *per* Cockburn CJ). But 'utmost' became the most commonly used epithet and its place was assured by its use in the 1906 Act. The connotation appears to be the most extensive, rather than the greatest, good faith. The Latin phrase was likewise a later introduction. It has been suggested that its use may have been inspired by the use of similar language in Book IV of the Codex of Justinian (4 37.3) in relation to the contract of partnership. The best view seems to be that it had been unknown to Roman law and had no equivalent in Roman law (see *Mutual and Federal Insurance Co Ltd v Oudtshoorn Municipality* 1985 (1) SA 419 at 432 *per* Joubert JA). The first recorded use of the phrase in the law reports was by Lord Commissioner Rolfe (later Lord Cranworth LC) in *Dalglish v Jarvie* (1850) 2 Mac & G 231 at 243; [1850] 42 ER 89 at 94 in connection with the duty of disclosure to the court which arises when an *ex parte* application is made for an injunction; the phrase was, however, already current by that date as the judgment shows.

[45] Lord Mansfield's universal proposition did not survive. The commercial and mercantile law of England developed in a different direction preferring the benefits of simplicity and certainty which flow from requiring those engaging in commerce to look after their own interests:

> Ordinarily the failure to disclose a material fact which might influence the mind of a prudent contractor does not give the right to avoid the contract. The principle of *caveat emptor* applies outside contracts of sale. There are certain contracts expressed by the law to be contracts of the utmost good faith, where material facts must be disclosed; if not, the contract is voidable. Apart from special fiduciary relationships, contracts for partnership and contracts of insurance are the leading instances. In such cases the duty does not arise out of contract; the duty of a person proposing an insurance arises before a contract is made, so of an intending partner. (See *Bell v Lever Bros Ltd* [1932] AC 161 at 227; [1931] All ER Rep 1 at 32 *per* Lord Atkin.)

[46] In relation to insurance Lord Mansfield was specifically addressing 'concealments which avoid a policy'. This concept of avoidance most obviously applies to the making of the contract and derives, as he said in *Pawson v Watson* and as confirmed by Lord Atkin, from the application of a rule of law not from the parties' agreement. Later developments have applied the requirement of disclosure to matters occurring after the making of the contract of insurance, namely the affidavit of ship's papers and the making of fraudulent claims; I will have to discuss these further. But, apart from some

dicta, this has still been as a matter of the application of a principle of law and not through an implied contractual term. Nor was there any case prior to the Act where the principle was used otherwise than as providing a basis for resisting liability; no case was cited where the principle gave a remedy in damages, as would the tort of deceit or the breach of a contractual term. Whether there was a remedy in damages for a failure to observe good faith was finally and authoritatively considered by the Court of Appeal in *Banque Financière de la Cité SA v Westgate Insurance Co Ltd* [1989] 2 All ER 952; [1990] 1 QB 665, affirmed by your Lordships' House (see [1990] 2 All ER 947 at 959; [1991] 2 AC 249 at 280). In order to answer the question, both Steyn J at first instance (see [1987] 2 All ER 923 at 942 ff; [1990] 1 QB 665 at 699 ff) and the Court of Appeal (see [1989] 2 All ER 952 at 990; [1990] 1 QB 665 at 773 ff) examined the basis of the requirement that good faith be observed. Having concluded on the authorities that the correct view was that the requirement arose from a principle of law, having the character I have described, the Court of Appeal held that there was no right to damages.

[47] The arguments of counsel in the present case disclosed a certain amount of common ground between them. The principle of utmost good faith is not confined to marine insurance; it is applicable to all forms of insurance (see *London Assurance v Mansel* (1879) 11 Ch D 363; *Cantiere Meccanico Brindisino v Janson* [1912] 3 KB 452) and is mutual as s 17 itself affirms by using the phrase 'if the utmost good faith be not observed by either party' and as was expressly stated by Lord Mansfield in *Carter v Boehm*.

[48] Secondly, both counsel submitted that the utmost good faith is a principle of fair dealing which does not come to an end when the contract has been made. A different inference might have been drawn both from the language of s 17 and from its place in the Act – beneath the heading 'Disclosure and Representations' and above ss 18–21 which expressly relate to matters arising before the making of the contract. But there is a weight of *dicta* that the principle has a continuing relevance to the parties' conduct after the contract has been made. Why indeed, it may be asked, should not the parties continue to deal with one another on the basis of good faith after as well as before the making of the contract? In his book The Marine Insurance Act 1906 (1st edn, 1907), Sir MacKenzie Chalmers added this note to s 17: 'Note: The general principle is stated in this section because the special sections which follow are not exhaustive.' There are many judicial statements that the duty of good faith can continue after the contract has been entered into. The citations which I make during the course of this speech will demonstrate this. To take just one example for the moment, in *Overseas Commodities v Style* [1958] 1 Lloyd's Rep 546 at 559, McNair J referred to the obligation of good faith towards underwriters being an obligation which rests upon the assured 'throughout the currency of the policy'. However, as will also become apparent from the citation, the content of the obligation to observe good faith has a different application and content in different situations. The duty of disclosure as defined by ss 18–20 only applies until the contract is made.

[49] Thirdly, both counsel accept and assert that the conclusion of the Court of Appeal in the *Banque Financière* case is good law and that there is no remedy in damages for any want of good faith. Counsel also drew this conclusion from the second half of s 17 – 'may be avoided by the other party'. The sole remedy, they submitted, was avoidance. It follows from this that the principle relied upon by the defendants is not

an implied term but is a principle of law which is sufficient to support a right to avoid the contract of insurance retrospectively ...

[51] The right to avoid referred to in s 17 is different. It applies retrospectively. It enables the aggrieved party to rescind the contract *ab initio*. Thus, he totally nullifies the contract. Everything done under the contract is liable to be undone. If any adjustment of the parties' financial positions is to take place, it is done under the law of restitution not under the law of contract. This is appropriate where the cause, the want of good faith, has preceded and been material to the making of the contract. But, where the want of good faith first occurs later, it becomes anomalous and disproportionate that it should be so categorised and entitle the aggrieved party to such an outcome. But this will be the effect of accepting the defendants' argument. The result is effectively penal. Where a fully enforceable contract has been entered into insuring the assured, say, for a period of a year, the premium has been paid, a claim for a loss covered by the insurance has arisen and been paid, but later, towards the end of the period, the assured fails in some respect fully to discharge his duty of complete good faith, the insurer is able not only to treat himself as discharged from further liability but can also undo all that has perfectly properly gone before. This cannot be reconciled with principle. No principle of this breadth is supported by any authority whether before or after the Act. It would be possible to draft a contractual term which would have such an effect but it would be an improbable term for the parties to agree to and difficult if not impossible to justify as an implied term. The failure may well be wholly immaterial to anything that has gone before or will happen subsequently.

[52] A coherent scheme can be achieved by distinguishing a lack of good faith which is material to the making of the contract itself (or some variation of it) and a lack of good faith during the performance of the contract which may prejudice the other party or cause him loss or destroy the continuing contractual relationship. The former derives from requirements of the law which pre-exist the contract and are not created by it although they only become material because a contract has been entered into. The remedy is the right to elect to avoid the contract. The latter can derive from express or implied terms of the contract; it would be a contractual obligation arising from the contract and the remedies are the contractual remedies provided by the law of contract. This is no doubt why judges have on a number of occasions been led to attribute the post-contract application of the principle of good faith to an implied term.

[53] The principle relied on by the defendants is a duty of good faith requiring the disclosure of information to the insurer. They submit that the obligation as stated in s 17 continues throughout the relationship with the same content and consequences. Thus, they argue that any non-disclosure at any stage should be treated as a breach of the duty of good faith: it has the same essential content and gives rise to the same remedy – the right to avoid.

[54] In the pre-contract situation it is possible to provide criteria for deciding what information should be disclosed and what need not be. The criterion is materiality to the acceptance of the risk proposed and the assessment of the premium. This is spelled out in the 1906 Act and was the subject of the *Pine Top* case. But when it comes to post-contract disclosure the criterion becomes more elusive: to what does the information have to be material? Some instructive responses have been given. Where the contract is being varied, facts must be disclosed which are material to the additional risk being

accepted by the variation. It is not necessary to disclose facts occurring, or discovered, since the original risk was accepted material to the acceptance and rating of that risk. Logic would suggest that such new information might be valuable to the underwriter. It might affect how hard a bargain he would drive in exchange for agreeing to the variation; it might be relevant to his reinsurance decisions. But it need not be disclosed. In *Lishman v Northern Maritime Insurance Co* (1875) LR 10 CP 179 at 182 Blackburn J said:

> ... concealment of material facts known to the assured before effecting the insurance will avoid the policy, the principle being that with regard to insurance the utmost good faith must be observed. Suppose the policy were actually executed, and the parties agreed to add a memorandum afterwards, altering the terms: if the alteration were such as to make the contract more burdensome to the underwriters, and a fact known at that time to the assured were concealed which was material to the alteration, I should say the policy would be vitiated. But if the fact were quite immaterial to the alteration, and only material to the underwriter as being a fact which shewed 'that he had made a bad bargain originally, and such as might tempt him, if it were possible, to get out of it, I should say that there would be no obligation to disclose it.

...

[57] These authorities show that there is a clear distinction to be made between the pre-contract duty of disclosure and any duty of disclosure which may exist after the contract has been made. It is not right to reason, as the defendants submitted that your Lordships should, from the existence of an extensive duty pre-contract positively to disclose all material facts to the conclusion that post-contract there is a similarly extensive obligation to disclose all facts which the insurer has an interest in knowing and which might affect his conduct. The courts have consistently set their face against allowing the assured's duty of good faith to be used by the insurer as an instrument for enabling the insurer himself to act in bad faith. An inevitable consequence in the post-contract situation is that the remedy of avoidance of the contract is in practical terms wholly one-sided. It is a remedy of value to the insurer and, if the defendants' argument is accepted, of disproportionate benefit to him; it enables him to escape retrospectively the liability to indemnify which he has previously and (on this hypothesis) validly undertaken. Save possibly for some types of reinsurance treaty, it is hard to think of circumstances where an assured will stand to benefit from the avoidance of the policy for something that has occurred after the contract has been entered into; the hypothesis of continuing dealings with each other will normally postulate some claim having been made by the assured under the policy ...

Fraudulent claims

[61] This question arises upon policies which up to the time of the making of the claim are to be assumed to be valid and enforceable. No right to avoid the contract had arisen. On ordinary contractual principles it would be expected that any question as to what are the parties' rights in relation to anything which has occurred since the contract was made would be answered by construing the contract in accordance with its terms, both express and implied by law. Indeed, it is commonplace for insurance contracts to include a clause making express provision for when a fraudulent claim has been made. But it is also possible for principles drawn from the general law to apply to

an existing contract – on the better view, frustration is an example of this, as is the principle that a party shall not be allowed to take advantage of his own unlawful act. It is such a principle upon which the defendants rely in the present case. As I have previously stated there are contractual remedies for breach of contract and repudiation which act prospectively and upon which the defendants do not rely. The potential is also there for the parties, if they so choose, to provide by their contract for remedies or consequences which would act retrospectively. All this shows that the courts should be cautious before extending to contractual relations principles of law which the parties could themselves have incorporated into their contract if they had so chosen. The courts should likewise be prepared to examine the application of any such principle to the particular class of situation to see to what extent its application would reflect principles of public policy or the overriding needs of justice. Where the application of the proposed principle would simply serve the interests of one party and do so in a disproportionate fashion, it is right to question whether the principle has been correctly formulated or is being correctly applied and it is right to question whether the codifying statute from which the right contended for is said to be drawn is being correctly construed.

[62] Where an insured is found to have made a fraudulent claim upon the insurers, the insurer is obviously not liable for the fraudulent claim. But often there will have been a lesser claim which could properly have been made and which the insured, when found out, seeks to recover. The law is that the insured who has made a fraudulent claim may not recover the claim which could have been honestly made ... The logic is simple. The fraudulent insured must not be allowed to think: if the fraud is successful, then I will gain; if it is unsuccessful, I will lose nothing ...

[72] For the defendants to succeed in their defence under this part of the case the defendants have to show that the claim was made fraudulently. They have failed to obtain a finding of fraud. It is not enough that until part of the way through the trial the owners (without fraudulent intent) failed to disclose to the defendants all the documents and information which the defendants would have wished to see in order to provide them with some, albeit inadequate, evidential support for their alleged defence under s 39(5). The defence under s 17 fails. It must be added that, on the facts found, had the defendants' defence succeeded it would have produced a wholly disproportionate result. The defence under s 39(5) failed after a full disclosure and investigation of all the material evidence. The claim was in fact a good one which the owners were, subject to quantum, entitled to recover under the policy. The defendants were liable to pay it. The policy was valid and enforceable. For the defendants successfully to invoke s 17 so as to avoid the policy *ab initio* and wholly defeat the claim would be totally out a of proportion to the failure of which they were complaining. Fraud has a fundamental impact upon the parties' relationship and raises serious public policy considerations. Remediable mistakes do not have the same character ...

Conclusion

[79] I have in the course of this speech referred to some cases from other jurisdictions. It is a striking feature of this branch of the law that other legal systems are increasingly discarding the more extreme features of the English law which allow an insurer to avoid liability on grounds which do not relate to the occurrence of the loss. The most

outspoken criticism of the English law of non-disclosure is to be found in the judgment in the South African case to which I have already referred, *Mutual and Federal Insurance Co Ltd v Oudtshoorn Municipality* 1985 (1) SA 419. There is also evidence that it does not always command complete confidence even in this country (see *Container Transport International Inc v Oceanus Mutual Underwriting Association (Bermuda) Ltd* [1984] 1 Lloyd's Rep 476; *Pan-Atlantic Insurance Co Ltd v Pine Top Insurance Co Ltd* [1994] 3 All ER 581; [1995] 1 AC 501). Such authorities show that suitable caution should be exercised in making any extensions to the existing law of non-disclosure and that the courts should be on their guard against the use of the principle of good faith to achieve results which are only questionably capable of being reconciled with the mutual character of the obligation to observe good faith.

[Note: Now read Appendix 8.12.]

APPENDIX 8.4

Orakpo v Barclays Insurance Services and Another [1995] LRLR 443, CA

Staughton LJ (dissenting in part):

FRAUDULENT CLAIM

The case put by Mr Phillips in this court was that the claim we are concerned with is that made in the statement of claim for the various sums totalling £265,000. He submits that, as the judge found, it was grossly exaggerated. The judge dealt with this aspect of the case quite briefly since he had already concluded that Mr Orakpo's claim failed. He did not make any specific findings as to the details of that gross exaggeration pleaded in the defence.

It is, I think, clear that the part of the claim based on loss of rent was indeed grossly exaggerated. It assumed that all 13 bedrooms would have been fully occupied for the ensuing two years and nine months after the first casualty, notwithstanding that there were only three occupants when that casualty occurred.

Other aspects of the claim, such as the items of dry rot and damage to furniture were so implausible as to cast doubt on their integrity. Of course, some people put forward inflated claims for the purpose of negotiation, knowing that they will be cut down by an adjuster. If one examined a sample of insurance claims on household contents, I doubt if one would find many which stated the loss with absolute truth. From time to time, claims are patently exaggerated; for example, by claiming the replacement cost of chattels, when only the depreciated value is insured. In such a case, it may perhaps be said that there is in truth no false representation, since the falsity of what is stated is readily apparent. I would not condone falsehood of any kind in an insurance claim. But in any event I consider that the gross exaggeration in this case went beyond what can be condoned or overlooked. Nor was it so obviously false on its face as not to amount to a misrepresentation ...

There is ... one aspect of this second defence which gives me pause. For a long time it has been very common for insurance policies to state expressly that, if any claim is made which is false or fraudulent, all benefit under the policy will be forfeited. There is no such provision in the insurance contract in this case. What is more, the contract bears all the signs of having recently been rewritten in plain English, a commendable manoeuvre as I should be the first to say. Why did the draftsman omit the provision which had previously been so common? Can he have done so by accident? Or was he afraid to spell it out in words that all would understand? I do not know of any other corner of the law where the plaintiff who has made a fraudulent claim is deprived even of that which he is lawfully entitled to, be it a large or small amount. I certainly would not imply such a term in order to give business efficacy to the contract, or because it is so obvious that it goes without saying. But Mr Phillips says that it is to be implied as a matter of law; in other words, it is a term which the law imposes unless the parties contract out of it.

The argument is that a contract of insurance is one of the utmost good faith. So it is in the formation of the contract. The customer must disclose every material circumstances in his knowledge, even if, or that especially if it increases the risk. If he does not do so the insurer may avoid the contract. It is said that the same duty of good faith applies in making claims, and that the same consequence follows if it is not observed. I can readily accept that there is a duty not to make fraudulent claims; but I have doubts about the suggested punishment for breach of that duty. True, there is distinguished support for such a doctrine. Mr Justice Willes told the jury, in *Britton v Royal Insurance Co* (1866) 4 F & F 905, at p 909, that an express condition to that effect was:

> ... only in accordance with legal principle and sound policy.

And in *Black King Shipping Corp v Massie (The Litsion Pride)* [1985] 1 Lloyd's Rep 437 the point was essential to the decision and was decided by Mr Justice Hirst in favour of the insurers. There are also textbooks, both highly regarded and others, which state that view. But we were not told of any authority which binds us to reach that conclusion. I would hesitate to do so, so I am not convinced that a claim which is knowingly exaggerated in some degree should, as a matter of law, disqualify the insured from any recovery. If the contract says so, well and good – subject always to the Unfair Contract Terms Act. But I would not lend the authority of this court to the doctrine that such a term is imposed by law. Consequently, I would dismiss the appeal on the ground of misrepresentation in the proposal form, but not on any other ground.

Hoffmann LJ: In principle, insurance is a contract of good faith. I do not see why the duty of good faith on the part of the assured should expire when the contract has been made. The reasons for requiring good faith continue to exist. Just as the nature of the risk will usually be within the peculiar knowledge of the insured, so will the circumstances of the casualty; it will rarely be within the knowledge of the insurance company. I think that the insurance company should be able to trust the assured to put forward a claim in good faith. Any fraud in making the claim goes to the root of the contract and entitles the insurer to be discharged. One should naturally not readily infer fraud from the fact that the insured has made a doubtful or even exaggerated claim. In cases where nothing is misrepresented or concealed, and the loss adjuster is in as good a position to form a view of the validity of value of the claim as the insured, it will be a legitimate reason that the assured was merely putting forward a startling figure for negotiation. But, in cases in which fraud in the making of the claim has been averred and proved, I think it should discharge the insurer from all liability. It is true that an express term to this effect is commonly inserted into insurance policies and that there is no such term in this one. But, in my view, the direction to the jury by Mr Justice Willes in *Britton v Royal Insurance Co* (1866) F & F 905, to which my Lord has referred, is sufficient authority for holding that such a term is implied by law as one which, in the absence of contrary agreement, it would be reasonable to regard as forming part of a contract of insurance ...

Sir Roger Parker: The appellant submits that the law, in the absence of a specific clause, is that an insured may present a claim which is to his knowledge fraudulent to a very substantial extent, but may yet recover in respect of the part of the claim which cannot be so categorised. To accept this proposition involves holding that, although an insurance contract is one of utmost good faith, an assured may present a positively and substantially fraudulent claim without penalty, save that his claim will to that extent be defeated on the facts. He may yet, it is said, recover on the honest part of the claim. I would be unable to accept such a proposition without compelling authority and there is none. To do so would, in my view, require me to hold that utmost good faith applies only to inception or renewal and not to matters subsequent thereto, or, in the alternative, that, whilst the law provides for avoidance of mere representation or non-disclosure on inception or renewal, given only that it is material, it provides no similar remedy for the most heinous fraud in the making of a claim on the policy. I can see no ground for so holding.

On what basis can an assured who asserts, for example, that he has been robbed of five fur coats and some valuable silver, when he has only been robbed of one fur and no silver, be allowed, when found out, to say, 'You must still pay me for the one of which I was truly robbed'?; I can see none and every reason why he should not recover at all. Just as on inception, the insurer has to a large extent to rely on what the assured tells him, so also is it so when a claim is made. In both cases, there is therefore an incentive to honesty, if the assured knows that, if he is fraudulent, at least to a substantial extent, he will recover nothing, even if his claim is in part good. In my view, the law so provides ...

APPENDIX 8.5

Leppard v Excess Insurance Co Ltd [1979] 2 All ER 668; [1979] 2 Lloyd's Rep 91, CA

Megaw LJ: The first question which arises is whether, on the true construction of the insurance policy, the plaintiff is entitled to require the defendants to pay him the cost of reinstatement of the cottage, even, assuming – and, to answer the first question, one makes this assumption – that the loss actually suffered by the plaintiff was less than the cost of reinstatement. If the answer to that be 'no', then the second question falls to be answered: on the facts of this case, was the amount of the loss actually suffered by the plaintiff the cost of reinstatement (agreed at £8,694) or was it the figure of £3,000 for which the defendants contend ...?

Ever since the decision of this court in *Castellain v Preston* (1883) 11 QBD 380, the general principle has been beyond dispute. Indeed I think it was beyond dispute long before *Castellain v Preston*. The insured may recover his actual loss, subject of course, to any provision in the policy as to the maximum amount recoverable. The insured may not recover more than his actual loss ...

What the insurers have agreed to do is to indemnify the insured in respect of loss or damage caused by the fire. The 'full value' is the cost of replacement. That defines the maximum amount recoverable under the policy. The amount recoverable cannot exceed the cost of replacement. But it does not say that that maximum is recoverable if it exceeds the actual loss. There is nothing in the wording of the policy, including the declaration which is incorporated therein, which expressly or by any legitimate inference provides that the loss which is to be indemnified is agreed to be, or is to be deemed to be, the cost of reinstatement, the 'full value', even though the cost of reinstatement is greater than the actual loss. The plaintiff is entitled to recover his real loss, his actual loss, not exceeding the cost of replacement.

There remains the second question. Was the plaintiff's actual loss the cost of the reinstatement of the cottage? Or was it, as the defendants contend, the market value of the property as it was at the time of the fire? The defendants do not rely upon any general principle in support of their submission. They say, rightly in my judgment, that this is a question of fact, and that one must look at all the relevant facts of the particular case to ascertain the actual value of the loss at the relevant date. Of course, one is entitled to look to the future so as to bring in relevant factors which would have been foreseen in the relevant factors which would have been foreseen at the relevant date as being likely to affect the value of the thing insured in one way or the other, if the loss of it had not occurred on that date. But, on the evidence in this case, and the judge's statement of the relevant facts in the passages from his judgment which I have read earlier, it is beyond dispute that the plaintiff himself, at the relevant date, wished to sell the house, and was ready and willing to sell it for £4,500 – indeed, on his own evidence, for less. Mr Millett submits that he was not bound to sell it. Of course not. He might thereafter, if the loss had not occurred, have changed his mind. The value of the property might have increased or it might have decreased. But there is no getting away from the reality of the case: 'It was (I am quoting again from the judgment) 'an empty cottage that he had for the purpose of sale.' The judge says:

> I do not think that this man, the plaintiff, would be put in the same position as he was before this fire merely by being paid the sum of £3,000, the difference between the price that he was prepared to accept for the property at the time of its loss and its site value.

With very great respect, I am unable to see why not. If the plaintiff himself was ready and willing, as he plainly was, to sell the property for £4,500, or less, on 25 October 1978, just before the fire, how can it be said that that was not its actual value at that time: unless, indeed, some reason could be shown why the plaintiff himself should have made a mistake about, or under estimated, its real value. No basis is shown for any suggestion. The amount of the loss here, in my judgment, is shown by the facts to have been the figure agreed, hypothetically, on this basis, as £3,000 ...

[Read on.]

APPENDIX 8.6

Birds, J, 'The measure of indemnity in property insurance' (1980) 43 MLR 456

Until recently, there was a dearth of conclusive authority on the question of the measure of indemnity the insured who suffers a loss is legally entitled to under his property insurance policy. Perhaps authority was unnecessary; in the case of a total loss, the market value of the destroyed property would generally provide adequate compensation, whereas the cost of repairing partially lost property was generally assumed to be the proper measure, subject, if relevant, to an allowance for 'betterment'. In both cases, of course, the 'sum insured' set the maximum recoverable. Two recent decisions have confirmed that partial losses generally attract the cost of repair, though there may be problems in working that out precisely. More interestingly, the relevance of market value as against reinstatement cost in the case of a total loss has been raised in the recent Court of Appeal decision in *Leppard v Excess Insurance Co Ltd* [1979] 2 Lloyd's Rep 91.

Increased rates of inflation have dramatically affected the insurance of buildings because, quite simply, it is now likely to cost more to reinstate a destroyed building than is represented by the market value of the property. Insurers have taken to exhorting people to insure for the cost of replacement and they almost invariably link sums insured to the rate of inflation, so that the insured has no option but to increase his cover each year. All this is fair enough; the dangers of being under insured are serious. But what is the legal position as to the entitlement of the insured who has made sure that he is properly covered. Clearly, if the policy expressly undertakes to pay reinstatement value, as do 'new for old' policies on personal property, he is quite secure. But standard fire policies on buildings do not commit themselves in the same way, as Mr Leppard discovered ...

... The first issue, raised for the first time in the Court of Appeal, was whether the plaintiff was contractually entitled to the cost of reinstatement. To show this he had to prove that the policy was not a normal 'indemnity' policy, whatever indemnity might mean. There was evidence at the trial that he intended to cover himself against reinstatement when he effected the insurance through brokers, though this clearly could not affect the contractual position between insured and insurer. In support of his argument on the contract, he could point to several references in the proposal form and the policy, in particular, the declaration in the proposal whereby he warranted that 'the sums to be insured represent not less than the full value (the full value is the amount which it would cost to replace the property in its existing form should it be totally destroyed)' and that in the policy – 'The sum insured is declared by the insured to represent and will as all times be maintained at not less than the full value of the buildings'. However, in the view of the Court of Appeal, these references were merely to the maximum sum recoverable. Otherwise, the policy was in standard form and undertook merely to indemnify the insured:

> There is nothing in the wording of the policy, including the declaration which is incorporated therein, which expressly or by any legitimate inference provides that the loss which is to be indemnified is agreed to be, or is deemed to be the cost of reinstatement …

It is difficult to argue with that conclusion. On its face, the policy was a straightforward indemnity policy and the declarations did not clearly amount to a binding undertaking to pay reinstatement cost. On the other hand, the plaintiff might quite reasonably have assumed that, because he had to warrant that the sum insured covered reinstatement and pay a premium calculated on that basis, and because he intended to cover the cost of reinstatement, that was the cover he was getting. The vast majority of policyholders are quite probably unaware of the intricacies of insurance and insurance law and the meaning of concepts like indemnity, or if they have gained some awareness by virtue of the publicity in recent years regarding the effect of inflation on insured values, consider that they are covered for reinstatement if they have properly taken account of that in estimating the sum insured. There seems a clear case for a change in the standard wording of fire policies so that if insureds are obliged to cover the cost of reinstatement on pain of the policy being voidable for breach of warranty, they are beyond dispute entitled to that measure of recovery. This is no doubt a pious hope as there is no body which is likely to be willing to bring pressure for such a change …

[Read on.]

APPENDIX 8.7

Lewis, A, 'A fundamental principle of insurance law' [1979] LMCLQ 275

An insurance policy is a contract of indemnity. That bids fair to be the most fundamental principle in our law of insurance. The insured is entitled to recoup his loss, but nothing more. Before an award can be made, his loss has first to be identified and then quantified. One has to keep the two steps of identification and quantification distinct, or confusion arises. Upon any claim for damages, it is necessary to identify the heads of loss first and then to put a value on each. It is them open to the other party to contend either that the scheme of heads of loss is improperly collated, or that a particular head of loss is misconceived, or that it is wrongly quantified, or – and this is particularly important in the context of insurance law – that, even if the heads of loss are in themselves unimpugnable, they or some of them do not fall within the range of the defendant's liability (for example, are not covered by the terms of the relevant policy).

Thus, if a factory burns down the owner may identify his loss as the destruction of a building and contents and also loss of production. He may quantify the first head by reference to the market value of the building (not including the site value) or by the cost of reinstatement, which may or may not be the same, and the second by reference to actual or estimated profits lost. If his policy is framed to cover consequential loss, the head of lost profits will be acceptable (identification) but its quantification may be the subject of argument. Similarly, as will be seen when we look at the recent decision that prompted this article, the building loss quantification may be challenged. What if the cost of reinstatement far exceeds the market value? Is the excess to be disallowed as betterment? In the case, for example, of motor vehicles, an agreed value operates in the insurer's interest to disallow a claim for repair when it exceeds the market value. But, in the absence of an agreed value, are we to say that where the cost of reinstatement exceeds the market value the destruction may not be quantified by reference to the cost of reinstatement? We may perhaps say this where similar property can be purchased by the insured for that market value, but where that consideration is inappropriate, as with land and buildings, it is at least arguable that, if the policy does not in terms deal with the point, the loss is not to be quantified, even for the purposes merely of indemnity, by reference only to market value. That, we shall see, was the issue considered by the Court of Appeal in *Leppard v Excess Insurance Co* [1979] 2 Lloyd's Rep 91 ...

The *locus classicus* for the indemnity principle is *Castellain v Preston* (1883) 11 QBD 380 ...

The judge at first instance awarded the sum of £8,694, but the Court of Appeal disagreed. Megaw LJ said that the fundamental principle of insurance required that the plaintiff could only recover his loss. If the cost of reinstatement was greater than his loss, he could not recover that cost. One had therefore to identify and quantify his loss (my phrase) to see if it was as much as the cost of reinstatement. The learned judge said that the case was to be decided on its facts; the plaintiff had on his hands an empty cottage for the purposes of sale. The agreed market value of the cottage, not including the site, at the time of the fire was £3,000 and this was the *quantum* of the plaintiff's loss. The cost of reinstatement could not, therefore, be recovered as it exceeded the loss sustained. Geoffrey Lane LJ, agreeing that the proper award was £3,000, said that the real question was: 'What did the plaintiff lose as a result of the fire? Was it the market value of the cottage at that time, or was it the reinstatement cost?' He said that, if the plaintiff recovered the cost of reinstatement, he would not only be indemnified against his loss but would also recover a bonus, for, as he had been willing to sell the property for £3,000 (not including the site value), why should he recover more upon its destruction?

The result, therefore, of this decision is that a houseowner who insures for reinstatement – and this is surely what this plaintiff had done – cannot recover the cost of reinstatement (even allowing for betterment) if the market is less. This is not good news for the average houseowner.

If it be objected that this plaintiff was in a peculiar position because he wanted to sell, one must reply that market value is market value whether the owner is intending to sell or not. Otherwise, one will have an inquiry into whether the owner really wishes to stay in the house, or at least retain it. Perhaps the real question should be phrased thus: on what has he lost, an asset to be equated with its value, or a facility, viz, the use or occupation of the house? If the loss is first *identified* in this way, it then becomes easy to quantify, either by the cost of replacing the asset with its money equivalent, or by the cost of restoring the facility, that is, the cost of reinstatement. If viewed in this light, it becomes possible to distinguish this case from the usual circumstance or a home destroyed by fire in that the plaintiff's interest on his own evidence lay in the money equivalent – not in the use or occupation of the property.

APPENDIX 8.8

Reynolds and Anderson v Phoenix Assurance Co Ltd and Others [1978] 2 Lloyd's Rep 440

Forbes J:

EXTENT OF INDEMNITY

The material provision of the policy under which the plaintiffs claim is as follows:

> The insurers severally agreed that if the property insured described in the said schedule or any part of such property be destroyed or damaged by fire the insurers will pay to the insured the value of the property at the time of the happening of its destruction or the amount of such damage or the insurers at their option will reinstate or replace such property or any part thereof, provided that the liability of the insurers shall in no case exceed in respect of each item the sum expressed in the said schedule to be insured thereon.

The schedule expressed the sum of £450,000 to be insured on that part of the premises damaged by fire ...

Three possible ways of evaluating the loss have been canvassed. They may perhaps be referred to as: (1) market value; (2) equivalent modern replacement; and (3) reinstatement.

Market value

This is the value which the premises would have fetched if sold in the open market immediately before the fire. I have had a considerable body of evidence about other maltings in East Anglia designed to show that such buildings would be extremely difficult to sell because alternative uses for obsolete floor maltings were difficult to find ...

In truth, the market value of premises such as the maltings in Stonham Parva may be very difficult to determine because there was no ready market for buildings of this type. If the willing seller instructs his estate agent to dispose of a property such as this quickly and at any price I would not be at all surprised to find the appropriate figure one approaching that which Mr Parker put forward. If, on the other hand, the willing seller was in no hurry for his money and was able to wait until a suitable purchaser came along (and he might have to wait some time), then a figure nearer to, but not, I think, going as far as that put forward by Mr Rankin might be achieved. As I stated earlier, I found none of this evidence satisfactory and I am left in considerable difficulty in arriving at an appropriate point between Mr Parker and Mr Rankin, neither of whose values I feel able entirely to accept.

Equivalent modern replacement

This is a method of arriving at a valuation of premises which is sometimes used in difficult cases involving old buildings where no other suitable method of valuation is available. The rationale behind its use is that, at any rate in cases of commercial interests, a building does not exist merely as a collection of bricks and mortar; it exists to be used for a purpose and, in commercial cases, for a commercial purpose. In such cases therefore, so runs the argument, if one can find the purpose for which the building is to be used, one can then find what type of building could be erected to fulfill that purpose. The value of the old building could therefore in no case exceed the cost of erecting such a new building because, given a choice, no sensible commercial concern would choose an old and inefficient building which was costly to maintain when they could have a modern purpose built construction which could be efficiently operated and cheaply maintained …

Although, frequently during the argument, this method of arriving at a value seemed to be regarded as a wholly separate possibility, I do not think this is the right way of looking at it. It must be seen as a mere valuer's device – an alternative way of arriving at the market value of the old maltings. The question of whether it is an appropriate alternative I shall leave under later.

Reinstatement

Again, I have heard a very great deal of evidence on this question. I can shortly describe the various estimates which have been put before me during the course of the trial …

… you are not to enrich or impoverish: the difficulty lies in deciding whether the award of a particular sum amounts to enrichment or impoverishment. This question cannot depend in my view on an automatic or inevitable assumption that market value is the appropriate measure of the loss. Indeed, in many, perhaps most cases, market value seems singularly inept, as its choice subsumes the proposition that the assured can be forced to go into the market (if there is one) and buy a replacement. But buildings are not like tons of coffee or bales of cloth or other commodities unless perhaps the owner is one who deals in real property. To force an owner who is not a property dealer to accept market value if he has no desire to go market seems to me a conclusion to which one should not easily arrive. There must be many circumstances in which an assured should be entitled to say that he does not wish to go elsewhere and hence that his indemnity is not complete unless he is paid the reasonable cost of rebuilding the premises *in situ*. At the same time the cost of reinstatement cannot be taken as inevitably the proper measure of indemnity. There must be cases where no one in his right mind would contemplate rebuilding if he could re-establish himself elsewhere. The question of the proper measure of indemnity thus becomes a matter of fact and degree to be decided on the circumstances of each case …

The upshot is that I am satisfied that the plaintiffs do have the genuine intention to reinstate if given the insurance moneys; that this is not a mere eccentricity but arises from the fact, as I find, that they will not be properly indemnified unless they are given the means to reinstate the building substantially as it was before the fire but with appropriate economies in the use of materials. I am fortified in this conclusion by the fact that throughout the considerable correspondence and negotiations which preceded this action (to some of which I have already referred) everyone on the defendants' side appears to have been ready to accept that, so long as the plaintiffs intended to reinstate, the true measure of indemnity was the cost of reinstatement. No one suggested that this was a mark of eccentricity; it appears top have been accepted that it was not an unreasonable course to pursue. On the basis of reinstatement, therefore, I consider that the plaintiffs are entitled to £246,883 ...

FIRES PREVENTION (METROPOLIS) ACT 1774

It seems quite clear to me that s 83 of the 1774 Act was intended to deal with a situation which arises in this way. An insurance company giving fire cover is bound under the contract to pay the insurance moneys to the assured. If it does so, the assured is quite entitled simply to put the money into his pocket without in any way reinstating the building. Two possible dangers arise from this. One is that it may be a temptation to an ill minded owner to set fire to the building in order to pocket the insurance money. The insurance company is accordingly entitled under the section, upon suspicion that this is the case, of its own volition to use the money to reinstate the building instead of paying to the assured. The other danger is that there may be other persons interested in the building who would be damnified if the money were not so used. In such a case, they are authorised to serve a notice on the insurance company requiring the money to be used for reinstatement, that is, not to be paid to the assured. That the assured and the person serving the notice should ever be one and the same person I am quite sure never entered the heads of the draftsmen of the Act or of the Parliament who passed it. This is shown by the final provisions. These allow for the assured to give a sufficient security to the insurance company that he will himself spend the insurance money on reinstatement, or to arrange for the insurance money to be divided appropriately between himself and the other persons interested in the building. Neither of these provisions would be at all appropriate to a case where it was the assured who had made the request. The whole scheme of the section is to prevent the insurance money being paid to an assured who might make away with it. It was not intended for the purpose for which the plaintiffs purported to use it and in my view their claim for a declaration fails.

The result of all the above is that in my view the proper figure to provide an indemnity under the policy was £346,883, but this, of course, was the sum for which Haymills would have done the work had they been instructed to do so in July 1974. Since then increases in building tender prices have occurred and the cost of the work today would be greater. How it seems quite clear that:

> ... a policy of insurance is only a promise of indemnity giving a right to action for unliquidated damages in case of non-payment ... *per* Hamilton J in *Williams Pickersgill and Sons Ltd v London and Provincial Marine and General Assurance Co* [1912] 3 KB 614.

The damage which the plaintiffs have suffered is measured by the failure of the defendants to indemnify them against their loss, that is, the cost of reinstating the building.

APPENDIX 8.9

Economides v Commercial Union Assurance Co plc [1997] 3 All ER 636, CA

Simon Brown LJ: On 7 January 1988, the appellant completed and signed a proposal form entitled 'Priority Application Form', which reads in part as follows:

> Yes I wish to insure the contents of my home and I understand that I will be covered on acceptance of my application and payment of my first premium.
>
> Please send my personal policy documents to study at home without obligation for a full 15 days.
>
> Please read carefully before completing this form.
>
> The questions on this application form generally provide sufficient information for the insurers to assess the risk. However there may be some special feature concerning you or your family or your property, its location or use that is not covered by the questions but which might, nevertheless, affect their judgment. If you can think of anything which might influence the likelihood or severity of a loss, please give full details. If you are in any doubt whether a fact may affect their judgment, you should give details as failure to do so could invalidate the insurance ...
>
> **Home contents**
>
> ... Sum to be insured £12,000 (including property of members of your family permanently residing with you. The figure must represent the full cost of replacing all your contents as new ...).
>
> **Contents questions**
>
> (4) Does the total value of precious metals or stones, jewellery, furs, curios, works of art, watches, exceed one third of the sum insured ...?
>
> [To the latter question the Plaintiff answered 'no'.]
>
> **Declaration**
>
> I/We declare that the statements and particulars given above and overleaf are to the best of my/our knowledge and belief, true and complete, that the sums insured under this Plan will be maintained on an up to date basis and that this proposal shall form the basis of the contract between me/us and the insurers.

That proposal was accepted by the respondent and a copy of its policy wording was sent to the appellant. The only parts I need read are these:

> **Sum insured**
>
> The amount shown in your current Schedule or latest renewal invitation, being the maximum amount insurers will normally pay in respect of a claim.

> **Contents**
>
> *Valuables* up to 33 1/3% of *Sum insured* ...
>
> all owned by or the responsibility of you or members of your *Household* ... while contained within your *Home*.
>
> [I need not set out the definition of *Valuables*.]
>
> Insurers will pay the cost of ... replacement as new following total loss ...
>
> If at the time of any loss or damage the cost of replacing all the *Contents* as new is greater than the *Sum insured* then any payment under the *Home contents* section will be made after a deduction for any wear or depreciation ...

It would seem that towards the end of 1990 the appellant must have telephoned the respondent and told it to increase the sum insured to £16,000. The single document evidencing the January 1991 renewal is a renewal notice dated 6 December 1990 referring to the sum insured as £16,000 and reminding the appellant that his policy was renewable on 14 January 1991. The notice contains a paragraph headed 'IMPORTANT NEWS', reading:

> It is important to remember that when you proposed for this insurance you gave information which enable [*sic*] the insurer to assess the risk and arrive at the premium terms and conditions of your present insurance. You should advise us of any facts not already passed on to us, and of any circumstances which may have changed since the proposal was made, so that the insurer can reassess the risk if necessary. FAILURE TO DO SO MAY MEAN THAT THE POLICY MAY NOT OPERATE FULLY OR EVEN AT ALL.

As stated, the loss occurred on 22 October 1991 and it was only then – when the appellant and others (in particular his sister) obtained from his mother a description of the items stolen, researched their appropriate retail prices, and thereby calculated their replacement cost – that the total value of the loss was established, fairly and in good faith as the judge below accepted, at £30,970 (the total value of the contents being found to be some £40,000 ...)

The claim on the policy was made ... the respondents ... asserted an entitlement to avoid liability on grounds of misrepresentation and non-disclosure ...

So much for the facts. I shall now consider each defence in turn.

MISREPRESENTATION

The appellant has conceded throughout that at the time of the 1991 renewal he represented that to the best of his knowledge and belief (hereafter 'he believed that') the full cost of replacing all the contents of his flat as new (hereafter 'the full contents value') was £16,000 ...

Mr Bartlett submits that the approach adopted by the judge below and urged afresh by Ms Kinsler on appeal is fundamentally flawed. His starting point is s 20 of the Marine Insurance Act 1906 – one of a group of sections which it is now established apply equally to non-marine as to marine insurance ... The relevant sub-sections of s 20 are:

> (3) A representation may be either a representation as to a matter of fact, or as to a matter of expectation or belief.

> (4) A representation as to a matter of fact is true, if it be substantially correct, that is to say, if the difference between what is represented and what is actually correct would not be considered material by a prudent insurer.
>
> (5) A representation as to a matte of expectation or belief is true if it be made in good faith ...

Mr Bartlett relies in particular on sub-s (5) ...

I accept, of course, that ... what may at first blush appear to be a representation merely of expectation or belief can on analysis by seen in certain cases to be an assertion of a specific fact. In that event, the case is governed by sub-ss (3) and (4), rather than sub-s (5) or s 20. And I accept too, as already indicated, that there must be *some* basis for a representation of belief before it can be said to be made in good faith ...

In my judgment, the requirement is rather, as s 20(5) states, solely one of honesty.

There are practical and policy considerations too. What, would amount to reasonable grounds for belief in this sort of situation? What must a householder seeking contents insurance do? Must he obtain professional valuations of all his goods and chattels? The judge below held:

> ... it would have been necessary for him to make substantially more inquiries than he did make before he could be said to have reasonable grounds for his belief. It is not necessary to specify what those inquiries might have involved.

The problem with not specifying them, however, is that householders are left entirely uncertain of the obligations put on them and at risk of having insurers seek to avoid liability under the policies. There would be endless scope for dispute. In my judgment, if insurers wish to place on their assured an obligation to carry out specific inquiries or otherwise take steps to provide objective justification for their valuations, they must spell out these requirements in the proposal form.

I would hold, therefore, that the sole obligation on the appellant when he represented to the respondent on renewal that he believed the full contents value to be £16,000 was that of honesty ...

NON-DISCLOSURE

... In short, I have not the least doubt that the sole obligation on an assured in the position of this appellant is one of honesty. Honesty, of course, requires, as Lord Macnaghten said in the *Blackburn Low* case (1887) 12 App Cas 531, that the assured does not wilfully shut his eyes to the truth. But that, sometimes called Nelsonian blindness – the deliberate putting of the telescope to the blind eye – is equivalent to knowledge, a very different thing from imputing knowledge of a fact to someone who is in truth ignorant of it.

The test, accordingly, for non-disclosure was, in my judgment, precisely the same as that for misrepresentation, that of honesty. And by the same token that the appellant was under no obligation to make further inquiries to establish reasonable grounds for his belief in the accuracy of his valuations, so too was not required to inquire further into the facts so as to discharge his obligation to disclose all material facts known to him. Indeed, the appellant's case on non-disclosure seems to me a fortiori to his case on misrepresentation. The Association of British Insurers' Statement of General Insurance Practice states with regard to proposal forms: '... (d) Those matters which insurers have found generally to be material will be the subject of clear questions in proposal forms.' Where, as here, material facts duly are dealt with by specific questions in the proposal form and no sustainable case of misrepresentation arises, it would be remarkable indeed if the policy could then be avoided on grounds of non-disclosure.

By way of footnote, I wish to add this. The issue of non-disclosure has throughout been dealt with, as stated, on the appellant's concession as to materiality. Certain aspects of this concession have, however, made me uneasy. In the first place, I note these paragraphs in MacGillivray and Parkington, *Insurance Law*, 8th edn, 1988, London: Sweet & Maxwell, p 1731:

> *1730 Under insurance.* Under a non-marine policy of insurance, the insured can recover the whole amount of his loss up to the limit of the sum insured. He may, therefore, obtain insurance at a small premium by understating the value of the subject matter insured, but nevertheless make recovery in a sum up to the amount insured; where there is a partial loss he may even be able to recover the full amount of his loss and suffer no penalty for being under insured.
>
> *1731.* It has therefore become the almost invariable practice for insurers to declare that the policy is 'subject to average' or 'subject to the under mentioned condition of average' which means that, if the sum insured does not represent the value of the property insured at the time of the loss or damage, the insured is to be his own insurer for the requisite proportion of the insurance and must therefore bear a part of the loss accordingly. In *Carreras Ltd v Cunard Steamship Co* [1918] 1 KB 118, where the plaintiff company warehoused goods with the defendant company at a fixed rental to include insurance against loss or damage by fire, Bailhache J held that the so called *pro rata* condition of average was so common in fire insurances on merchandise that it must be implied as a term of the warehouse agreement. The average clause now occurs in almost all policies, except those relating to private dwelling houses and household goods, and to buildings (and their contents) use wholly or mainly for religious worship.

Ordinarily, therefore, it appears, under insurance, so far from being regarded as material non-disclosure justifying the avoidance of the policy, results instead in averaging, or indeed in full recovery without penalty. Why then should the position be so very different in the present case, not least given that the policy itself expressly envisages at least some degree of under insurance:

> If, at the time of any loss or damage, the cost of replacing all the *Contents* as new is greater than the *Sum insured* then any payment under the *Home contents* section will be made after a deduction for any wear or depreciation.

And that leads me to the second point. Just how substantial must be the extent of under insurance (or the excess beyond one third in the proportion of valuables to the total) before it is said, assuming always that the assured had knowledge of these facts, that the policy can be avoided on grounds of non-disclosure?

None of these questions were addressed before us, nor indeed having regard to my conclusions on the central issues, did they need to be. I raise them, however, because in other circumstances it seems to me that they are likely to have considerable importance and accordingly should not be lost sight of.

For the reasons earlier, however, I would allow this appeal and enter judgment for the appellant against the respondent in the sum of £7,815.38, together with interest.

Peter Gibson LJ: This case raises issues of significance to all who have household insurance policies as well as to all insurers under such policies. If the recorder's decision is correct, such a policy is liable to be avoided at the option of the insurers if the insured, in giving the insurers (whether in the proposal form or on renewal) a value for what is to be insured, gives too low a value, even though the insured in giving that value was purporting to do so to the best of his knowledge and belief and was acting honestly and – subjectively – reasonably. So surprising a result prompts a close scrutiny of the facts and the applicable law …

APPENDIX 8.10

(Australian) Insurance Contracts Act 1984 (Cth) (as amended)

AVERAGE PROVISIONS

44 (1) An insurer may not rely on an average provision included in a contract of general insurance unless, before the contract was entered into, the insurer clearly informed the insured in writing of the nature and effect of the provision.

(2) Where the sum insured in respect of property that is the subject matter of a contract of general insurance that provides insurance cover in respect of loss of or damage to a building used primarily and principally as a residence for the insured, for persons with whom the insured has a family or personal relationship, or for both the insured and such persons, or loss of or damage to the contents of such a building, or both, is not less that 80% of the value of the property, the liability of the insurer in respect of loss of or damage to the property is not reduced by reason only of the operation of an average provision included in the contract.

(3) Where:

(a) the sum insured in respect of property that is the subject matter of such a contract is less than 80% of the value of the property; and

(b) but for this subsection, an average provision included in the contract would have the effect of reducing the liability of the insurer in respect of loss of or damage to the property to an amount that is less than the amount ascertained in accordance with the formula AS/P, where:

A is the number of dollars equal to the amount of the loss or damage;

S is the amount of the sum insured under the contract in respect of the property; and

P is 80% of the number of dollars equal to the value of the property,

the average provision has the effect of reducing the liability of the insurer to the amount so ascertained.

(4) A reference in this section to the value of property is a reference to the value of that property at the time when the relevant contract was entered into ...

ENTITLEMENT OF NAMED PERSONS TO CLAIM

48 (1) Where a person who is not a party to a contract of general insurance is specified or referred to in the contract, whether by name or otherwise, as a person to whom the insurance cover provided by the contract extends, that person has a right to recover the amount of his loss from the insurer in accordance with the contract notwithstanding that he is not a party to the contract.

(2) Subject to the contract, a person who has such a right:

(a) has, in relation to his claim, the same obligation to the insurer as he would have if he were the insured; and

(b) may discharge the insured's obligations in relation to the loss.

(3) The insurer has the same defences to an action under this section as he would have in an action by the insured.

LIFE POLICY FOR THE BENEFIT OF ANOTHER PERSON

48A (1) This section applies to a contract of life insurance effected on the life of a person but expressed to be for the benefit of another person specified in the contract ('the third party').

(2) The following provisions have effect in relation to a contract to which this section applies:

(a) any money that becomes payable under the contract is payable to the third party, even though he or she is not a party to the contract;

(b) money paid under the contract does not form part of the estate of the person whose life is insured.

(3) Nothing in this section restricts the capacity of a person to exercise any right or power under a contract of life insurance to which the person is a party. In particular, nothing in this section restricts the capacity of a person:

(a) to surrender a contract of life insurance to which the person is a party; or

(b) to borrow money on the security of a contract of life insurance; or

(c) to obtain a variation of a contract of life insurance, including a variation having the result that the contract ceases to be a contract.

RIGHT OF THIRD PARTY TO RECOVER AGAINST INSURER

51 (1) Where:

(a) the insured under a contract of liability insurance is liable in damages to a person (in this section called the 'third party');

(b) the insured has died or cannot, after reasonable enquiry, be found; and

(c) the contract provided insurance cover in respect of the liability,

the third party may recover from the insurer an amount equal to the insurer's liability under the contract in respect of the insured's liability in damages.

(2) A payment under subsection (1) is a discharge, to the extent of the payment, in respect of:

(a) the insurer's liability under the contract; and

(b) the liability of the insured or of his legal personal representative to the third party ...

PART VI: CLAIMS

FRAUDULENT CLAIMS

56 (1) Where a claim under a contract of insurance, or a claim made under this Act against an insurer by a person who is not the insured under a contract of insurance, is made fraudulently, the insurer may not avoid the contract but may refuse payment of the claim.

(2) In any proceedings in relation to such a claim, the court may, if only a minimal or insignificant part of the claim is made fraudulently and non-payment of the remainder of the claim would be harsh and unfair, order the insurer to pay, in relation to the claim, such amount (if any) as is just and equitable in the circumstances.

(3) In exercising the power conferred by subsection (2), the court shall have regard to the need to deter fraudulent conduct in relation to insurance but may also have regard to any other relevant matter.

APPENDIX 8.11

Fires Prevention (Metropolis) Act 1774 (14 Geo 3, c 78)

An Act … for the more effectually preventing Mischiefs by Fire within the Cities of London and Westminster and the Liberties thereof; and other the Parishes, Precincts, and Places within the Weekly Bills of Mortality, the Parishes of Saint Mary-le-bon, Paddington, Saint Pancras and Saint Luke at Chelsea in the County of Middlesex … [1774] …

[Whole Act, except ss 83 and 86, repealed by s 34 of the Metropolitan Fire Brigade Act 1865.]

83 MONEY INSURED ON HOUSES BURNT HOW TO BE APPLIED

And in order to deter and hinder ill minded persons from wilfully setting their house or houses or other buildings on fire with a view of gaining to themselves the insurance money, whereby the lives and fortunes of many families may be lost or endangered: Be it further enacted by the authority aforesaid, that it shall and may be lawful to and for the respective governors or directors of the several insurance offices for insuring houses or other buildings against loss by fire, and they are hereby authorised and required, upon the request of any person or persons interested in or entitled unto any house or houses or other buildings which may hereafter be burnt down, demolished or damaged by fire, or upon any grounds of suspicion that the owner or owners, occupier or occupiers, or other person or persons who shall have insured such house or houses or other buildings have been guilty of fraud, or of wilfully setting their house or houses or other buildings on fire, to cause the insurance money to be laid out and expended, as far as the same will go, towards rebuilding, reinstating or repairing such house or houses or other buildings so burnt down, demolished or damaged by fire, unless the party or parties claiming such insurance money shall, within sixty days next after his, her or their claim is adjusted, give a sufficient security to the governors or directors of the insurance office where such house or houses or other buildings are insured, that the same insurance money shall be laid out and expended as aforesaid, or unless the said insurance money shall be in that time settled and disposed of to and amongst all the contending parties, to the satisfaction and approbation of such governors or directors of such insurance office respectively.

86 NO ACTION TO LIE AGAINST A PERSON
WHERE THE FIRE ACCIDENTALLY BEGINS

And … no action, suit or process whatever shall be had, maintained or prosecuted against any person in whose house, chamber, stable, barn or other building, or on whose estate any fire shall … accidentally begin, nor shall any recompence be made by such person for any damage suffered thereby, any law, usage or custom to the contrary notwithstanding …: provided that no contract or agreement made between landlord and tenant shall be hereby defeated or made void.

APPENDIX 8.12

Soyer, B, '*The Star Sea* – a lode star?' (2001) LMCLQ 428

[Note: *The Star Sea*, Appendix 8.3.]

In *The Star Sea*, all statements and reports, alleged to be fraudulently or recklessly non-disclosed or misrepresented were produced after the litigation had begun. There were allegations that anything awkward had been done by the assured or their legal advisers before the writ was issued at least in respect of the presentation of the claims. Therefore, the first point, which was in need of clarification, was whether the duty of utmost good faith continued after the commencement of the litigation. The first instance judge, Tuckey J, and the Court of Appeal both held that the duty of utmost good faith came to an end once the writ was issued. However, there was a divergence between the judgments of these two courts. Tuckey J, held that the continuing duty came to an end at the latest when proceedings were issued, at which point the court's own procedures governed disclosure, or possibly at the earlier stage at which the insurers had rejected the claim. The Court of Appeal refused to accept that the insurers' rejection of a claim brings the duty to an end. According to the Court of Appeal, only the commencement of proceedings has that effect. The House of Lords seems to adopt the Court of Appeal's view ...

The judgment of the House of Lords on this point seems to be in accordance with general principles of law. The nature of the relationship between the assured and insurer is very different before and after the commencement of litigation. Before the litigation the parties' relationship is contractual, so it is natural to expect the contractual principles, including remedies, to govern the relationship. However, after the commencement of litigation, the nature of the relationship changes and it is the procedural rules which determine the relationship between the parties.

To restrict the duty of good faith to the procedural rules after the rejection of claim, as suggested by Tuckey J, would be against the realities of insurance law. In practice, when an insurer receives notice of claim, his first task is to have the loss investigated. Even if the loss is accepted as valid as a result of this investigation, in many cases further negotiations take place and this process might include the rejection of the initial claim for bargaining purposes. The occurrence of such rejection does not make parties rivals automatically. There is still a community of interest and the contractual principles should govern this relationship.

Even though the House of Lords held that utmost good faith existed and s 17 had a role to play during the litigation process, this would not have helped the insurers in *The Star Sea*. This is because the House of Lords decided that s 17 does not extend the duty of utmost good faith, as stated by Hirst J, in *The Litsion Pride*, to the avoidance of culpable non-disclosure or misrepresentation during the claims process. The House clearly expressed that only fraud in the claims process would amount to breach of a duty of good faith and no fraud was found on the part of anyone relevant, namely the assured and their advisers.

When restricting the scope of utmost good faith to a duty of precluding fraudulent claims, their Lordships took a number of points into account. First, there seemed to be a problem in identifying what would have been a material fact that had to be disclosed or not misrepresented in the context of making a claim, if the duty was wider than one not; to present a fraudulent claim. It is generally accepted that the facts in which the insurer will be interested at the claims stage can be regarded as material as they will affect his consideration of the claim. However, even the disclosure of facts which are related to a claim would put the assured under a massive duty at this stage. In such a case, the assured would be required to disclose not only information contained in documents, but also information imparted orally. Lord Scott of Foscote regarded such a situation as 'lacking any commercial justification or sense'. Furthermore, the harshness of the remedy afforded for breach of s 17, namely avoidance *ab initio*, played a crucial role in the House of Lords decision not to expand the utmost good faith duty in the claims context. In *The Star Sea* the assured, presumably culpably, failed to disclose material facts while submitting his response to a s 39(5) defence. Had this defence been successful, it would have deprived the assured from recovery only for that claim. Lord Hobhouse was of the opinion that extending the duty to culpable non-disclosures and enabling the application of s 17 in this context would produce a wholly disproportionate result. Finally, their Lordships, by considering the previous authorities on this point, came to the conclusion that the content of the duty owed by an assured post-contract is not the same as the duty owed in the pre-contractual stage. Taking this point into account, they decided that making further extensions to the post-contractual duty of good faith would harm the balance between the parties. The remedy of avoidance of the contract, which would be available in such a case, is in practical terms wholly one-sided. Save possibly for some types of reinsurance treaty, it is hard to think of circumstances where an assured will stand to benefit from avoidance of the policy for something which has occurred after the contract has been entered into.

Another point clarified by their Lordships in *The Star Sea* is the legal basis of the post-contractual duty of utmost good faith. Two theories had been developed by courts to explain the legal basis of this duty. The first theory is that the duty arises at common law as embodied in the MIA 1906, s 17. The alternative theory is that the duty of good faith arises from an implied term of the insurance contract. Identifying the nature of the duty is not simply an academic issue, as this might have a significant role in the remedies available. Logic suggests that a distinction should be made between the post-contractual duty of good faith arising during variation of the contract and the one in the claims context. Since variation of contract extends the scope of the cover, the duty of good faith for the extension might be considered as similar to the pre-contractual duty. This is the case because in both instances the insurer is required to undertake a new risk and in this respect the assured's conduct becomes crucial. Accordingly, s 17 could be regarded as the legal basis of the duty of utmost good faith arising during variation of the contract. However, the same could not be said for the utmost good faith duty which arises in the claims context. Here the insurer does not undertake a new risk, so the situation is not similar to the pre-contractual stage. Therefore, only an implied term could be the basis of such a duty ...

Since it has been confirmed that the basis of the post-contractual duty of good faith arising at the variation stage is that under s 17, the assured is expected to disclose all material facts and not to make a material misrepresentation. However, Lord Hobhouse made clear that materiality in this context is going to be assessed in a restricted manner, as discussed earlier. Accordingly, where the contract is being varied, facts must be disclosed which are material to the additional risk being accepted by the variation. It is not necessary to disclose facts occurring, or discovered, since the original risk was accepted, material to the acceptance and rating of that risk. Whether the remedy available, avoidance *ab initio*, is also going to be assessed in a similar manner and only the variation is going to be affected from such a breach, has not been considered by Lord Hobhouse. In such a case only the avoidance of the amendment should be permitted and Lord Hobhouse's flexible approach to the issue strengthens this argument.

Lord Hobhouse's analysis as to the existence of an implied term, which requires the assured to observe utmost good faith in the claims process, could lead to dramatic changes in law. One would expect some clarification in the judgment of the House of Lords as to the implications of such finding. Unfortunately, this was not the case. The grey areas are going to be evaluated in the final part of this article.

c Elusive points and the future of post-contractual duty of utmost good faith in the claims process

Tracing the legal basis of the post-contractual duty of good faith in the claims context to an implied term brings two serious questions to mind. Is it appropriate to apply s 17 in this context from a legal point of view? Is the remedy proportionate to the breach committed? No seems to be the answer to both questions.

It has been established that there is a contractual obligation requiring the assured not to submit fraudulent claims. In that case, it will be illogical if the common law imposes the same obligation on the assured by virtue of s 17. Enabling the application of s 17 in this context would mean that 'avoidance *ab initio*' will be regarded as one of the remedies available. This remedy is not a contractual remedy, in the sense that it is imposed by common law. Lord Hobhouse, on the other hand, is of the opinion that only contractual remedies provided by the law of contract should have application in this context. Therefore, applying s 17 in the claims context is inconsistent with the existence of an implied term ...

Therefore, despite the indications made by Lords Hobhouse and Scott, it has not been expressly stated that s 17 has no application in the claims context. This is a point which needed to be clarified. In my opinion, s 17 has no application in this context anymore due to the reasons illustrated above. There is an obligation on the assured not to make fraudulent claims and this obligation is imposed by a contractual term. In case of breach of this contractual term, the legal consequences should be determined by considering the contract law principles. Bearing the significance of this implied term for the insurance contract, it is possible to classify it as a 'condition'. That would be consistent with the analysis of the majority of the Court of Appeal in *Orakpo v Barclays Ins Services*, which analysed the duty of dealing with the claim as a contractual obligation and characterized the breach (by presenting a fraudulent claim) as going to the root of the contract and entitling the insurer to be discharged from further liability under the contract. If this analysis is accurate, in case of submission of a fraudulent claim, the insurer has a right to be discharged from all liability under the policy prospectively.

Classifying this implied term as a 'condition' brings us to another significant issue. In contract law, in case of breach of a term classified as a condition the aggrieved party is entitled not only to be discharged from the contract but also to damages. In this respect, is the insurer entitled to the costs of investigating a fraudulent claim? As examined earlier, the Court of Appeal has confirmed in *Banque Keyser Ullmann SA v Skandia (UK) Ins Co Ltd* that breach of the pre-contractual duty of disclosure only gives rise to a right to avoid the insurance contract and does not entitle the innocent party to damages. Similarly, the Court of Appeal in *The Good Luck*, tracing the basis of post-contractual duty of good faith to a principle of law, namely s 17, held that breach of such obligation could not support a claim in damages. In *The Star Sea*, both counsel accepted and asserted that the conclusion of the Court of Appeal in *Banque Keyser Ullmann* was good law, and there was no remedy for damages for any want of good faith. However, these submissions were made on the understanding that the legal basis for the post-contractual duty of utmost good faith was a legal principle. The House of Lords seems to be of the opinion that the duty not to make fraudulent claims is an implied term of the contract. Therefore, there is nothing preventing the courts from awarding damages to the aggrieved party in case of breach of this 'implied condition'. The House of Lords should have clarified the state of law as far as concerns damages, particularly after tracing the origins of the duty to an implied term of the contract.

If the damages are available in case of breach of the utmost good faith duty in the claims context, then could insurers be liable in damages for a breach of the post-contractual duty of good faith? For instance, the insurer decides that he will deliberately delay in paying a claim, if necessary by going to court and fighting the case. He knows that in fact there is no defence to the claim but he manufactures enough doubts to get past a claim for summary judgment on the claim. Why should the underwriter be immune from a claim for damages for breach of the duty of utmost good faith by deliberately delaying payment of the claim, provided that the assured can show what loss he suffered in consequence? In some other jurisdictions, particularly in the United States, the insurer owes a duty of good faith and fair dealing to the assured. Accordingly, the insurer is under a duty of good faith to investigate and settle a claim in a timely manner. Without a doubt, deliberate delay in paying a claim would be a breach of this obligation. In most States, there are statutory rules enabling the assured to claim damages in case of breach of this obligation. So why should things be different in England? I believe that, just like s 17, the duty imposed in the claims context is a reciprocal duty. There is an implied term imposing on the insurer a duty of utmost good faith during the presentation of a claim that he should not fraudulently delay a settlement and mislead (by conduct or statements) the assured as to the state of affairs in relation to the claim or its consideration by him. If this analysis is accurate, in the future the English courts may reverse their current rule that insurers are not liable for the late payment of claims. Unfortunately, the House of Lords failed to clarify this point as well.

A final point which is left in the shade by the House of Lords is the destiny of a claim which starts honestly but continues fraudulently. I think the answer to this question varies depending on the stage at which the fraud arises. If the assured submits an honest claim for loss of his goods and while the insurer is considering the claim he learns that the goods are in fact not lost, he is expected to withdraw his claim. If he does not, he is in the process of making a fraudulent claim. This conclusion could be drawn from the judgment of the Court of Appeal in *Piermay Shipping Co SA and*

Brandt's Ltd v Chester (The Michael) [[1978] 1 WLR 411; [1978] 1 All ER 1233; [1979] 1 Lloyd's Rep 55]. In that case the assured submitted a claim for total loss, alleging that the vessel was lost by perils of the sea. The insurer denied the claim. Before the writ was issued, the assured learned that the second engineer had deliberately sunk the vessel. Accordingly, the perils of the sea claim was abandoned and a new claim brought for actual total loss by barratry. The insurer denied liability on the ground that a fraudulent claim for a loss by perils of the sea was maintained. The Court of Appeal held that no fraudulent claim was maintained. The court based its decision on the fact that it is not possible to maintain a fraudulent claim merely because during interlocutory proceedings the assured or his solicitors become aware of evidence which might militate against the correctness of the assured's case and its likelihood of ultimate success. Therefore, had there been evidence suggesting that the assured acted fraudulently after the submission of the claim for a loss by perils of the sea, this would have amounted to a fraudulent claim.

On the other hand, if a claim starts honestly and a fraud is committed after the commencement of litigation, the solution seems to be straightforward. Bearing in mind the judgment of the House of Lords in *The Star Sea* about the duty of utmost good faith in the litigation process, it is probably safe to say that the issue is going to be regulated by the procedural rules. What is not clear is the position in cases where a claim starts honestly and after it is settled the assured finds out that the claim is not in fact a good one. This problem may be illustrated by modification of the facts of *The Michael*. Let it be supposed that the vessel suffers a partial loss and the assured makes a claim for a loss by perils of the sea. After this claim is settled and while the policy is still in force, the vessel becomes an actual loss due to a storm. Just before the assured submits his claim for actual loss, he finds out that the partial loss is caused deliberately by the second engineer. Will the assured be in breach of the duty of utmost good faith if he does not disclose this to the insurer? There is no definite answer to this question. My own view is that, once the claim is settled, the assured is not under a duty of good faith in relation to that claim. There is also recent authority suggesting that not all the fraudulent conduct of the assured would amount to breach of the utmost good faith duty.

4 CONCLUSION

It is settled by the highest judicial authority that there is a difference in the scope of the post-contractual duty of utmost good faith which arises during variation of contract and that in the claims context. Also their Lordships, in a decisive way, restricted the possibility of extending the scope of the post-contractual duty of utmost good faith any further ....

However, the House of Lord's decision in *The Star Sea* has been disappointing for many people who expected the clarification of all elusive points. This was a great opportunity to determine the nature and scope of the post-contractual duty of good faith. However, the general feeling is that this opportunity is rather wasted. The highest judicial authority should not have the privilege to suggest, in such a significant matter, that certain points are best left for another case. One conclusion which the insurance world should draw from this decision is probably the necessity to regulate fraudulent conduct of the assured with a contractual provision. In this way, most of the potential problems highlighted above could be avoided.

[Postscript: See the Court of Appeal judgment in *Agapitos v Agnew* 6/3/2002.]

APPENDIX 8.13

K/S Merc-Scandia v Certain Lloyd's Underwriters [2001] Lloyd's Rep IR 802

Longmore LJ:

20 It thus becomes necessary to consider section 17 of the Marine Insurance Act 1906, how it came to be enacted and how it has subsequently been interpreted.

21 The Marine Insurance Act 1906 was and is a codification of the law of marine insurance. The law as there stated is, in general, no different from that for other forms of insurance in so far as the duties in relation to good faith, disclosure and representations are concerned. Generally speaking again, the duties to disclose material matters and not to make material misrepresentations apply before the contract is concluded and do not continue after the contract is concluded. An insurer is not able to require disclosure of matters which show he has made a bad bargain. One question that has arisen is whether there is a continuing duty to disclose material matters, if the insurer is entitled to cancel the policy by serving a notice of cancellation. This court held in *New Hampshire Insurance v MGM Ltd* [1997] LRLR 24 that there was not. Staughton LJ gave the judgment of the court, he set out section 17 of the Act and the requirement in section 18(1) that the assured must disclose, before the contract is concluded, every material circumstance known to the assured. He then proceeded:

> A novice could be forgiven for thinking that the only duty of disclosure is by the insured and that it only applies before the contract is concluded (which would no doubt include the new contract which is made upon renewal). But the maxim that mention of one of two things excludes the other must be applied with caution when considering the draftsmanship of Sir Mackenzie Chalmers. His method of codification was, at any rate at times, to state the effect of rules decided by the Courts and not to pronounce upon points which had not been decided.

Staughton LJ then recorded a submission that section 18(1) was merely one example of the general duty that was placed upon both parties at all times by section 17 and said:

> We can see force in that argument. But it is questionable whether in practice the law has been treated in that way.

I would respectfully echo that sentiment. In the light of this remark and the judge's conclusion that the duty of good faith only applies post-contract if the insurer is invited to renew or vary his speculation or risk or if the insured is pursuing a claim under the policy, it is necessary to trace the development of this area of the law in a little detail. I do not intend a comprehensive survey and use the phrase 'pre-contract good faith' in its usual sense and 'post-contract good faith' to indicate the requirement of good faith (as and when it exists) once the contract has been made and while it lasts.

Development of the law of post-contract good faith

22 (1) *Fraudulent claims*

The law about the making of fraudulent claims originally developed in fire insurance cases, see *Levy v Baillie* (1831) 7 Bing 349; *Goulstone v Royal Insurance Co* (1858) 1 F & F 276; *Britton v Royal Insurance Co* (1866) 4 F & F 905. The inclusion of some such clause as is now in Lloyd's J Form has always been common; the same principle will apply as a matter of law, even in the absence of an express term. I have already observed that there is some debate whether the relevant principle of law is an example of the application of the good faith principle giving rise only to a right of avoidance or a separate development of law. There is no evidence that Sir Mackenzie Chalmers had this line of authority in fire insurance cases in mind when he drafted section 17 of his marine insurance code. The concept would, in any event, be alien in a field such as marine insurance, where most, if not all, policies, were 'valued' policies. One of the important conclusions of *The Star Sea* was that when it came to making a claim, the duty of the insured was one of honesty only. In any event the present case is not a case where the insured has made a claim at all, let alone a fraudulent claim.

(2) *Variations to the risk*

A duty of good faith arises when the assured (or indeed the insurer) seeks to vary the contractual risk. The right of avoidance only applies to the variation not to the original risk, *Lishman v Northern Maritime Insurance Co* (1875) LR 10 CP 179; and *Iron Trades Mutual v Cie de Seguros* [1991] 1 Re LR 213, 224; and *The Star Sea* paragraph 54 page 188D–F. There is no authority for a proposition that a fraudulent misrepresentation leading to a variation will avoid the original contract as well as the variation.

(3) *Renewals*

A duty of good faith exists when the insured seeks to renew the contract of insurance. That is a prospective right and if it is not observed by each party, the other party can avoid the contract. It is never suggested that, although the breach takes place during the currency of the earlier contract, the earlier contract is avoided as well as the renewal.

(4) *'Held covered' cases*

The requirement that an insurer hold the insured covered in certain circumstances has been held to require the exercise of good faith by the insured. To the extent that the result is a variation of the contract, eg, because an additional premium has to be assessed, these cases are examples of (2) above; to the extent that they are only an exercise by the insured of rights which he has under the original contract they are somewhat puzzling; but, although it is settled that good faith must be observed, it is never suggested that lack of good faith in relation to a matter held covered by the policy avoids the whole contract of insurance.

(5) *Insurer having right of cancellation*

I have already said that the existence of such a right has been held not to give rise to the duty of good faith, *New Hampshire v MGM* [1997] LRLR 24, 58–62 ...

(6) *Insurer asking for information during the policy*

If the insurer has a right to information by virtue of an express or an implied term, there may be a duty of good faith in the giving of such information. Typically such requirements will be in liability policies and reinsurance contracts (which are, of course, only one form of liability insurance), see, eg, *Phoenix General Insurance Co v Halvanon Insurance Co Ltd* [1985] 2 Lloyd's Rep 599. It is not usually suggested that breach of any such term gives rise to a right to avoid the contract rather than a claim to damages. To the extent that *Alfred McAlpine v BAI Insurance* [2000] 1 Lloyd's Rep 437 accepts that giving of information attracts obligations of good faith, it does not support any concept of avoidance in the absence of prejudice to underwriters in connection with their ultimate liability for the claim. If there is no right in the insurer to be given information but he asks for information, no duty of good faith arises as such. The only duty of the insured will be not materially to misrepresent the facts in anything he does say to insurers. If he does make any such misrepresentation, the insurer will have ordinary common law remedies for any loss he has suffered, *Iron Trades Mutual v Cie de Seguros* [1991] 1 Re LR 213, 224.

(7) *Other situations where good faith may be implied*

Such other situations may arise under liability policies, particularly if the insurers decide to take over the insured's defence to a claim. Interests of the insured and the insurers may not be the same but they will be required to act in good faith towards each other. If for example the limit of indemnity includes sums awarded by way of damages, interest and costs, insurers may be tempted to run up costs and exceed the policy limit to the detriment of the insured. The insured's protection lies in the duty which the law imposes on the insurer to exercise his power to conduct the defence in good faith. In such circumstances Sir Thomas Bingham MR could not 'for one instant accept ... [the] suggestion that a breach of this duty, by an insurer, once a policy is in force, gives the assured no right other than rescission', see *Cox v Bankside* [1995] 2 Lloyd's Rep 437, 462.

(8) *Litigation*

An important matter decided by *The Star Sea* is that the duty of good faith (whatever its precise context) is superseded, once the parties become engaged in litigation, by the rules of court contained in the Civil Procedure Rules. There had over the years arisen a view that the ancient rights of a marine insurer to obtain pre-defence discovery stemmed from the post-contract obligation of good faith, but failure to comply with an order for ship's papers never gave rise to a right to avoid the policy; so as Lord Hobhouse observed, in paragraph 60 of his speech, in relation to an insured's obligation to submit to an order for ship's papers:

> ... whatever it was, it was not the obligation referred to in section 17.

There is a certain irony about this conclusion. When Sir Mackenzie Chalmers published the second and last edition of his Digest of the Law of the Marine Insurance (1903), on which the Act as ultimately passed was to be based, he included what is now section 17 without any explanation of how (if at all) he envisaged any post-contract requirement of good faith would work in practice. When he published the first edition of his book *The Marine Insurance Act 1906* (1907) he added a note in relation to post-contract good faith, instancing the order of the court for ship's papers as the example of the operation of post-contract good faith. Thus does the whirligig of time exercise its reversals.

23 It appears from this account of the development of post-contract good faith principles that it is by no means in every case of non-observance of good faith by the insured that the insurer can avoid the contract. It is necessary to find some principle by which it is possible to decide whether, in the event of good faith not being observed by either party, the result is that the contract can be avoided ...

35 Section 17 states that the remedy is the remedy of avoidance but does not lay down the situations in which avoidance is appropriate. It is, in my judgment, only appropriate to invoke the remedy of avoidance in a post-contractual context in situations analogous to situations where the insurer has a right to terminate for breach. For this purpose (A) the fraud must be material in the sense that the fraud would have an effect on underwriters' ultimate liability as Rix J held in *Royal Boskalis* and (B) the gravity of the fraud or its consequences must be such as would enable the underwriters, if they wished to do so, to terminate for breach of contract. Often these considerations will amount to the same thing; a materially fraudulent breach of good faith, once the contract has been made, will usually entitle the insurers to terminate the contract. Conversely fraudulent conduct entitling insurers to bring the contract to an end could only be material fraud. It is in this way that the law of post-contract good faith can be aligned with the insurers' contractual remedies. The right to avoid the contract with retrospective effect is, therefore, only exercisable in circumstances where the innocent party would, in any event, be entitled to terminate the contract for breach.

36 The desirability of aligning the right to avoid with the right to terminate the contract for breach is self-evident. It is often observed that the right of avoidance is disproportionate (see the speech of Lord Hobhouse, paragraphs 61 and 72 at pages 191E and 196B). If the right to avoid in a post-contract context is exercisable only when the right to terminate for breach has arisen, the disproportionate effect of the remedy will be considerably less and the extra advantages given to insurers when they exercise a right of avoidance (eg, non-liability for earlier claims) will be less offensive than they otherwise would be ...

37 The requirement of materiality has, of course, always been required for avoidance for lack of pre-contract good faith. More significantly, it is also a requirement for the operation of the rule about fraudulent claims. The case of *Goulstone v Royal Insurance Co* (1858) I F & F 276 is instructive. The insured made a claim under a fire policy in the amount of £660 in respect of furniture, linen and china. It emerged in evidence: (1) that on the insured's marriage in 1846 there was a settlement of a quantity of furniture; (2) that in 1854 he had become insolvent and declared to his creditors that he had no furniture except that which belonged to his wife under the settlement and which was valued at £50; and (3) that the linen and china (which were not included in the

settlement) had been furtively removed at the time of the insolvency. This concealment from the creditors was, of course, fraudulent; Chief Baron Pollock said to the jury that the plaintiff's interest was nevertheless legally insurable, whether or not the creditors ought to have the benefit of the insurance. He continued:

> But the question is whether the claim [viz the claim on insurers] was fraudulent, ie, whether it was wilfully false in any substantial respect; for instance, as to private furniture which was sworn to be worth only £50 in 1854 and has not since been added to.

The Chief Baron is there drawing a distinction between the material and substantial fraud in the claim on underwriters in respect of the over-valuation of the furniture and the immaterial fraud of concealing the linen and china from the creditors ...

38 In the context of deliberate and culpable (but not fraudulent) post-contract conduct, Rix J in *Royal Boskalis* said that a fact would only be material if it had ultimate legal relevance to a defence under the policy [1997] LRLR 523, 589 column 2 and Aikens J has adopted that as the appropriate test of materiality where fraud has been proved, see paragraph 76.

39 Aikens J expressed his conclusion as to the law in that and the following paragraph of his judgment. His view was that there was a continuing duty on the assured to refrain from a deliberate act or omission intended to deceive the insurer through either positive misrepresentation or concealment of material facts and facts would only be material for the purpose if they had ultimate legal relevance to a defence under the policy. I agree with the Judge's conclusion summarised in this way save that I would also add (even if it is usually or invariably to state the same conclusion in different words) that the insurer cannot avoid the contract of insurance for such fraudulent conduct unless the conduct was such as to justify their terminating the contract in any event. If and in so far as Aikens J was intending to go further than this and say that the insurers' defence of bad faith was inapplicable because no 'good faith occasion' had arisen (and Professor Clarke thinks that this was the judge's preferred view) I would not agree, since it seems to me that the duty not to be materially fraudulent does continue at all times after the contract has been made ...

Application to the facts of the case

...

42 In my view the fraud was not relevant, ultimately or at all, to insurers' liability. The fraud was in relation to the jurisdiction in which and the law by which the claim against the insurers was to be tried, In the event, it turned out that the law of England and the law of Trinidad were the same so it made no difference to insurers' liability under the policy that it fell to be determined by English law. It is impossible to imagine that the place of trial of the claim against the insured ship repairers would have made any difference to insurers' liability. I have already given reasons for saying that I am not persuaded that fraud by either or both of the Baboolal brothers would have made the evidence of their employees on the matter of responsibility for tightening the bolts of the engine

to the correct tension any more or less believable than it would otherwise have been. It is also the fact that the fraud was never directed at the insurers; the deception was aimed at the shipowners; it was incidental that the assured had also to deceive their own solicitors who had been appointed by and were being paid for by the insurers. All that can be said is that these solicitors maintained their summons opposing English jurisdiction somewhat longer than they might otherwise have done.

43 None of these conclusions is, in any way, intended to condone or belittle the fraud perpetrated by the assured. The fact that it was a fraud which was never likely to work and was exposed within about six months of being committed does not make it any the less reprehensible. The assured were, to coin a phrase playing with fire, as these proceedings (now culminating 13 years after the original engine explosion) have shown. Nevertheless it would, in my judgment, be absurdly disproportionate that insurers should be entitled to avoid the insurance policy and thus be able to avoid a liability to their assured which they always had and to which there could never have been any defence, if the insured had not been so over-enthusiastic in trying to assist the insurers to defeat the shipowners' claim.

44 For these reasons, the defence based on section 17 of the 1906 Act fails and I would dismiss the appeal.

[Postscript: For further discussion of fraud and s 17 of the MIA 1906, see the Court of Appeal decision in *Agapitos v Agnew* (2002) unreported, 6 March, CA.]

APPENDIX 8.14

Association of British Insurers, *General Insurance Claims Code*

What this code does

This code sets out the standards of service you can expect when you make a claim.

It applies if you, as a private individual, make a claim on a general insurance policy that was issued by an insurance company which is a member of the Association of British Insurers. For example, this includes claims on household, motor, travel, payment protection and private medical insurance policies.

You can make claims in different ways. This code covers the following types of claims:

- Claims you make on insurance policies you have taken out, for example, your own motor or household policy.
- Claims on group policies, for example, a private medical insurance policy a company has taken out for its employees.
- Claims you make against someone else which are dealt with under an insurance policy they have taken out, for example, a motor accident caused by another driver.

These types of claims are very different from each other. They are often processed and settled in different ways, which are all covered by the code, so some parts of the code may not apply to your claim.

If you are claiming against someone else and their insurance company, the company should tell you that they need the other person to agree to the company handling your claim. They should also tell you that if the other person does not agree to the company handling your claim, you may need to take legal action against the other person and you want to go further.

You should be aware that for some claims, especially if you are injured and claim against someone else, the law and the courts set different requirements which insurance companies must follow. The insurance company you claim against will explain this to you.

General principles

At all stages, you can expect that insurance companies will:

- respond promptly, explain how they will handle your claim and tell you what you need to do;
- give you reasonable guidance to help you make a claim under the policy;
- consider and handle your claim fairly and promptly and tell you how your claim is progressing;

- tell you if they cannot deal with all or any part of your claim, and explain why;
- settle your claim promptly, once they have agreed to do so; and
- handle complaints fairly and promptly.

When you first make a claim

You can expect:

- a response, on the phone or in writing, to your claim, and action within five working days;
- an explanation of whether your type of claim is normally covered by the policy;
- an explanation of what should happen and when; and
- if you are claiming against someone else's insurance company, to be told, within 10 working days, what information and evidence they need to consider your claim.

Processing your claim

You can expect:

- replies to your letters within 10 working days;
- explanations of why other people (for example, loss adjusters, solicitors, surveyors, doctors or consultants) will be involved in your claim and what their role will be; and
- your insurance company to contact any other insurance company that is involved in your claim within 10 working days of finding out who they are.

Settling your claim

You can expect:

- an explanation of how your type of claim is usually settled, for example:
- by paying you;
- by paying someone else, such as the garage repairing your car, your loan or mortgage company or your doctor if your claim is on a private medical insurance policy; or
- by repairing or replacing something;
- payments to be made to you within 10 working days of you agreeing to it;
- the insurance company to arrange repairs to, or a replacement of, whatever was damaged, within 10 working days of you agreeing to it; and
- an explanation of why the amount the insurance company offers, or plans to pay, is different from the amount you claimed, or why your claim has been rejected.

Complaints

If you make a complaint, you can expect insurance companies to:

- acknowledge it promptly, explain how they will handle your complaint and tell you what you need to do;
- consider and handle your complaint fairly and promptly, and tell you how your complaint is progressing;
- send you a copy of their complaints procedure;
- acknowledge complaints made in writing within five working days;
- investigate complaints made in writing independently at a senior level within the insurance company;
- give a final response to complaints made in writing within 40 working days; and
- tell you, if you are a policyholder, that if you are not satisfied with the final response, you can refer your complaint to an independent disputes settlement organisation that will sort out the problem.

All insurance companies that follow this code belong to independent disputes settlement organisations which provide a free service for policyholders who are private individuals.

If you are not a policyholder and you have a complaint about someone else's insurance company, these disputes settlement organisations will not be able to help. You may have to consider taking legal action.

CHAPTER 9

SUBROGATION AND CONTRIBUTION

It is convenient to discuss the topics of subrogation and contribution in the same chapter. They are often interrelated, but it must be stressed that their functions in insurance law are different.

The equitable doctrine of subrogation is a 'doctrine adopted solely for the purpose of preventing the insured from recovering more than a full indemnity by placing the insurers in the position of the insured'.

Contribution is a:

> ... term used in both marine and non-marine insurance to describe the right of an insurer, when he has discharged their liability to the assured, to call on another insurer to bear his share of the loss and pay his proportion of the amount already paid under the first policy [Ivamy, *Dictionary of Insurance Law*, 1981, London: Butterworths].

In a case of subrogation, the plaintiff insured appears to be suing the defendant, who is also usually insured. In reality, it is the plaintiff's insurer who is formulating the action, which is being defended by the defendant's insurer. This is what Hasson calls the 'fictitious plaintiffs v fictitious defendants' (see Appendix 9.1).

In a case of contribution, the case is brought in the name of the insurance company who is seeking to obtain a contribution from another insurer or insurers.

SUBROGATION

(See Derham, *Subrogation in Insurance Law*, 1985, Sydney: Lawbook Co; Mitchell, *Law of Subrogation*, 1994, Oxford: Clarendon.)

Introduction

It has been stressed throughout the preceding chapters that insurance is a contract of indemnity (save for the major exception of life assurance). Thus, the insured must not be permitted to make a profit from his insurance contract. Again, there is a possible exception to this statement, in that the great majority of home contents policies provide for a replacement of 'new for old' as the basis of the indemnity. In that sense, it could be said that the insured 'profits' from the theft or destruction of the old television when it is replaced by a new one.

Subrogation comes into operation when the insured has a legally enforceable right against another party who caused the loss. The phrase 'legally enforceable right' covers the widest possible rights. One of the classic statements on the operation of subrogation was given by Brett LJ in *Castellain v Preston and Others* (1883) 11 QBD 380 (Appendix 9.2). He said:

> ... as between the underwriter and the assured, the underwriter is entitled to the advantage of every right of the assured, whether such right consists in contract, fulfilled or unfulfilled, or in remedy for tort capable of being insisted on or already insisted on, or in any other right, whether by way of condition or otherwise, legal or equitable, which can be, or has been exercised or has accrued and whether such right could or could not be enforced by the insurer in the name of the assured by the exercise or acquiring of which right or condition the loss against which the assured is insured, can be, or has been diminished.

Most subrogation cases follow the pattern of the insurer compensating their insured and then enforcing their insured's rights against the other party. The facts of *Castellain* were, however, different. The insured vendor of property contracted to sell the property. Before completion the property was destroyed by fire. The insurers paid the full value of the property. Subsequently, the purchaser completed the sale and the purchaser was paid the full price. The insurer successfully recouped the insurance monies from the insured.

Another foundation case in subrogation is the House of Lords decision in *Burnand v Rodocanachi Sons and Co* (1882) 7 App Cas 333 (Appendix 9.3). Lord Blackburn explained the application of subrogation in these words:

> The general rule of law and its obvious justice is that where there is a contract of indemnity (it matters not whether it is a marine policy, or a policy against fire on land, or any other contract of indemnity) and a loss happens, anything which reduces or diminishes that loss reduces or diminishes the amount which the indemnifier is bound to pay; and if the indemnifier has already paid it, then, if anything which diminishes the loss comes into the hands of the person to whom he has paid it, it becomes an equity that the person who has already paid the full indemnity is entitled to be recouped by having that amount back.

The facts of the case were, however, unusual and provide an exception to the principle set out in the above quotation. The insured insured a cargo, which was lost due to attack by a Confederate cruiser at the time of the American Civil War. The insurers paid out on the valued policy, that is, a policy for an agreed sum, even though this may not reflect the true value at the date of the loss.

After the war an Act of Congress granted compensation for any losses that had not been covered by any insurance policy and therefore the insured recouped the balance of their losses. The legislation also prohibited any subrogation rights. The insurer sought to recover and their claim was rejected. The Act was intended to cover, and did cover, only those losses which the insurance did not cover. The sum received by the insured was a 'pure gift' from the American Government. This is, admittedly, an unusual situation. Where an *ex gratia* gift is made to the insured then the insurer is probably allowed to recoup such sum from the insured.

Situations in which subrogation commonly arises

Tort situations

The simplest example of the application of subrogation arises in tort situations. The simplistic example within tort is probably a road traffic accident. Thus, X's car is damaged due to Y's negligent driving. X's insurers, under comprehensive cover, reimburse X for his losses. X's insurers may now subrogate to X's rights against Y, who will normally be compensated by his own insurers. Before subrogation rights impinge it is, of course, necessary that the insurer has first paid on the policy: see *Page v Scottish Insurance Corp Ltd* (1929) 33 Ll L Rep 134 (Appendix 9.4).

What of the situation where X is injured due to the negligence of employee Y? X will be compensated by the employer's insurers. Can the insurer then subrogate, standing in the employer's shoes, against the employee? This question arose in *Lister v Romford Ice and Cold Storage Co Ltd* [1957] 1 All ER 125, and was answered in the affirmative. Such a decision, correct though it may be on subrogation principles, would clearly have an adverse effect on labour relations within a company. To counteract such developments the British Insurers' Association (now the Association of British Insurers) drew up a 'gentleman's agreement'. This states:

> Employers liability insurers agree that they will not institute a claim against the employee of an insured employer in respect of the death of or injury to a fellow employee unless the weight of evidence clearly indicates: (i) collusion; or (ii) wilful misconduct on the part of the employee against whom a claim is made.

While such a 'gentleman's agreement' is not legally binding, it did have an influence on the Court of Appeal decision in *Morris v Ford Motor Co Ltd* [1973] 2 All ER 1084 (Appendix 9.5).

Section 66 of the (Australian) Insurance Contracts Act 1984 (Cth) puts the 'gentleman's agreement' into statutory form, omitting the reference to 'collusion' (see Appendix 9.6). The Act also, in s 65, goes further and limits the right of subrogation in situations where the insured would not personally have chosen to exercise any rights against the wrongdoer, because of a family or personal relationship with such a person. The section goes further still, and prohibits the right of subrogation against any third party who is not insured in respect of the alleged liability, or, where he is insured, the subrogation is limited to the financial limit of any such insurance.

The National Consumer Council Report, *Report on Insurance Law Reform*, 1997, also recommends changes in this area, clearly influenced by the Australian changes (Appendix 9.7).

Contractual situations

Where an innocent party suffers due to breach of contract by the other party and the innocent party is insured against such loss then the insurer, once he has paid out on the policy, may subrogate to the innocent party's claim in contract.

Statutory rights

If a statute gives an insured rights of compensation then the insurer, once he had paid his insured, can subrogate to such statutory rights, unless the statute forbids such subrogation. Such a right can be seen in s 2(2) of the Riots (Damages) Act 1886.

Salvage

Where there has been a total loss but the damaged item still has some value, for example, where a car is written off by the insurer, because the repair costs, as a percentage of the value of the vehicle, do not make it financially viable to repair, the damaged goods become the property of the insurer. It often happens that the insurer will then give the insured the option of purchasing such goods if he wishes to repair them himself.

Special problems relating to subrogation

The insurer's rights can be no greater than the insured's rights

We have seen that subrogation means that the insurer steps into the shoes of his insured. What if the insured has relinquished his right against a wrongdoer and thus extinguished any hope of reimbursement that the insurer might have expected?

In *West of England Fire Insurance Co v Isaacs* [1897] 1 QB 226, the insured was paid for fire damage that he had suffered. The insured had a right of action against the lessee for breach of covenant, but the insured chose to relinquish such rights, thus preventing the insurer from exercising those rights. The Court of Appeal held that the insured was liable to repay the insured sum to the insurers.

A similar result would follow if the insured agreed to accept a lesser sum than that to which he was entitled from the wrongdoer. The insurer would be able to recoup the difference from the insured.

A difficult area for motor insureds is where they institute proceedings to recover any uninsured losses. In order to receive a discount on a motor policy, an insured may choose (and sometimes it is compulsory) to accept that he will carry the first, say, £200 of any loss. In such a situation, the insured may commence an action against the other party to recoup the £200. By so doing, he thus abandons any further rights against that party and thus relinquishes any subrogation rights for the greater amount that the insurer has already paid to him.

The Court of Appeal dealt with such a situation in *Hayler v Chapman* [1989] 1 Lloyd's Rep 490. The insurers paid the write off value of the insured's car. The insured then commenced a county court action for his uninsured loss, car hire, phone calls and taxi fares from the third party's insurers and was duly successful. The court refused to set aside this judgment and, therefore, the insurers attempted subrogation claim against the third party's insurers failed. The danger of such eagerness by the insured is that he would then be liable to his insurers for frustrating the subrogation proceedings.

Who is entitled to any payment produced by subrogation which is in excess of the indemnity originally paid?

The situation has arisen in cases where the subrogated claim has produced judgment in a foreign currency and, due to currency fluctuations, the final amount exceeds the original indemnity that had been paid to the insured.

Thus, in *Yorkshire Insurance Co Ltd v Nisbet Shipping Co Ltd* [1961] 2 WLR 1043 (Appendix 9.8), the insured's vessel was insured for £72,000. Due to the third party's negligence, the vessel was a total loss and the insurer paid. The following year, the insurer subrogated to the insured's claim in Canadian proceedings and the loss was quantified in Canadian dollars. The pound was subsequently devalued and the converted dollars produced an excess of £72,000 over £55,000. Diplock J held that the insured was entitled to the excess on the grounds that subrogation cannot produce for the insurer more than the sum he has paid out.

Any doubts as to who should take the excess could be clearly set out in the original policy documentation if the parties are in agreement (see *Lucas v EGCD* [1974] 2 Lloyd's Rep 69).

Co-insurance

Co-insurance is a phrase open to more than one meaning. Crucially, it should not be confused with double insurance or contribution, which will be covered below.

It is used here to describe a situation where two parties' interests are covered in one policy, even though only one of the parties took out the insurance. If one of the parties is responsible for a loss, can the insurer subrogate against the other party? Two cases illustrate the problem.

In *Petrofina (UK) Ltd and Others v Magnaload Ltd and Another* [1983] 2 Lloyd's Rep 91 (Appendix 2.19) the main contractor took out a contractor's all risks policy which indemnified the contractor against loss or damage caused to property. Those insured under the policy were stated to include the main contractor and sub-contractors. Sub-contractors were employed defendants to carry out certain aspects of the work. Due to their negligence, damage was caused to the property and the insurers paid. The insurers then sought to subrogate against the defendants, who argued that they were insured under the same policy. The court held that there should be no subrogation rights because the defendants were covered by the policy wording. The judge based his answer partly on what he considered to be commercial convenience. Mr Justice Lloyd explained:

> I would hold that a head contractor ought to be able to insure the entire contract works in his own name and the name of all of his sub-contractors ...

What then is the 'commercial convenience' of this approach? The judge explained:

> In the case of a building or engineering contract, where numerous different sub-contractors may be engaged, there can be no doubt about the convenience from everybody's point of view, including, I would think the insurers, of allowing the lead contractor to take out a single policy covering the whole risk, that is to say covering all contractors and sub-contractors in respect of loss of or damage to the entire contract works. Otherwise, each sub-contractor would be compelled to take out his own separate policy. This would mean, at the very least, extra paperwork; at worst it could lead to overlapping claims and cross claims in the event of an accident ... the cost of insuring his liability might, in the case of a small sub-contractor, be uneconomic. The premium might be out of all proportion to the value of the sub-contract. If the sub-contractor had to insure his liability in respect of the entire works he might well have to decline the contract.

The wording of the policy and its construction will, of course, be crucial, as we have seen in Chapter 7. Such a problem arose in *National Oilwell (UK) Ltd v Davy Offshore Ltd* [1993] 2 Lloyd's Rep 582 (Appendix 9.9). Suppliers had contracted to supply the defendants with equipment for their oil production facility. The equipment was faulty and caused damage to the defendants' property which was covered by their insurance policy. Their insurers sought to subrogate against the suppliers, who in turn claimed that they were co-insureds under the defendant's policy. This was true, but the question for the court was to interpret the scope of the insurance cover available to the suppliers. It was decided that the suppliers' insurance protection was narrower than that which they claimed. The loss caused by the suppliers was not covered by the policy wording and therefore there could be a subrogated claim against them. The case illustrates that it is crucial for the co-insured not to be lulled into a false sense of security merely because a policy exists which provides him with some protection. It is essential for him to satisfy himself that the protection extends to his entire potential liability. Because of the difficulties in policy interpretation this may not be an easy task. This difficulty is also illustrated in the Court of Appeal decision in *Stone Vickers Ltd v Appledore Ferguson Ship Builders Ltd* [1992] 2 Lloyd's Rep 578.

Thus, it is common practice when several parties are involved in a joint project for one party to obtain insurance cover intending that it should provide cover for the other parties. Problems can arise, however, as to whether the wording in the policy achieves what the parties intended or expected. The above recent cases have revolved around the question whether or not the insurer can subrogate against one of the parties having paid out under the policy and also whether contribution is possible. The Court of Appeal had to deal with these problems, and to assess several of the earlier decisions, in *Co-operative Retail Services Ltd v Taylor Young Partnership Ltd and Others* [2001] Lloyd's Rep IR 122. The claimant appointed the first and second defendants, under separate contracts, as architects and engineers for the construction of a new building. The claimants also contracted with W to be the main contractors. W sub-contracted electrical work to H. W obtained a policy with CGU which named the claimants, W and H, as joint insureds.

A fire occurred for which the claimants held the two defendants responsible. The three heads of damages for which the claimants claimed were covered under the CGU policy and another policy that the claimants held. The two defendants in turn argued that the fire had been caused by breaches of contract by W and H and therefore the defendants claimed contribution under the Civil Liability (Contribution) Act 1978. W and H argued that the CGU policy should be construed whereby it was not possible for a subrogated claim to be brought against them for damage caused to the claimants. At this preliminary stage it was assumed that W, H and the two defendants were all responsible for the fire damage. The crucial question was whether W and/or H were liable to make contribution to the two defendants.

The Court of Appeal held that they were not liable.

Although the defendants accepted that the CGU policy prevented CGU from subrogating against W and H because they were protected in that policy, it was argued that this did not prevent the defendants from claiming a contribution under the 1978 Act. This was rejected by the court on an interpretation of the wording of the Act and a consideration of the decisions based on the Act. The crucial words of the Act are that there can be contribution from another party 'whose liability in respect of the same damage has been or could be established in an action brought by or on behalf of the person who suffered the damage'. But the time for determining such liability is the time when the contribution is sought not when the damage occurred. However, there was no liability to be faced by W or H because the CGU policy protected them from such liability and thus no contribution was possible.

Landlord and tenant situations

Where a landlord leases property he can obviously require the tenant to insure such property. For financial security and peace of mind, however, the landlord will often choose to insure the property himself and usually expect the premiums to be paid to be reflected in the rent.

If damage is caused to the property by the tenant's negligence, can the landlords insurers subrogate against the tenant? The answer will depend on the words used in the policy and in the lease. The point is illustrated in *Mark Rowlands Ltd v Berni Inns Ltd* [1985] 3 All ER 473 (Appendix 2.3), a case which raised 'an issue of far reaching importance in relation to fire insurance' (*per* Kerr LJ). The question was whether the landlord's insurers could subrogate against the tenant, who had negligently caused a fire at the premises, in a situation where the lease provided that the tenant was to contribute to the cost of the insurance; the tenant was to be relieved from repairing obligations should there be damage by fire and the landlord would expend any insurance moneys to repair the building. The answer was that the tenant was protected by such provisions and therefore no subrogation rights were enforceable against him.

Again, it is essential that the wording of the lease or of the policy leads to such an interpretation. In the Scottish case of *Barras v Hamilton* 1994 SLT 949, it was decided that the tenant's immunity from a subrogated claim did not extend to those parts of the building not covered by the agreement between landlord and tenant.

The House of Lords decision in Napier v Kershaw

(See Appendix 9.10.) This House of Lords decision came as a result of the Lloyd's litigation cases that took up so many pages of the law reports, in addition to the unreported decisions. The matter is beyond the scope of this book. The present case is, however, concerned with subrogation and the leading judgment by Lord Templeman should be studied.

A critique

(See Derham, *Subrogation in Insurance Law*, 1985, Sydney: Lawbook Co, Chapter 14; Mitchell, *Law of Subrogation*, 1994, Oxford: Clarendon.)

Insurers are, of course, great supporters of the doctrine of subrogation. They raise arguments in support of it, not least of which is, that by recouping payments, they have helped reduce their losses and thus prevented premiums from increasing. This and other reasons for supporting the doctrine are criticised by Hasson (Appendix 9.1).

The obvious fallacy in the argument that premiums will not increase is that subrogated claims are only worth pursuing if the defendant is also insured. The fact that insurer A recoups at the expense of insurer B does not bode well, in terms of premium increases, for others who are insured with B and it will not be long before insurer A is on the receiving end of a subrogated claim. In *Berni Inns* (above), if the decision had gone the other way, it would have been the tenant's public liability insurer who would have have had to pay out. Subrogation cases clearly lead to legal costs being added to the loser's bill and such costs will be passed on to the policyholders.

As Young in *Insurance: Cases and Materials*, 1971, New York: Foundation Press, explains:

> Insurance subrogation would have more friends than it does if it could be shown that recoveries enter into premium rate calculations in an equitable way.

For more extensive criticisms of the doctrine, see Fleming, 'The collateral source rule and loss allocation in tort' (1966) 54 Calif L Rev 1478, p 1526 ff.

DOUBLE INSURANCE AND CONTRIBUTION

Introduction

The foundation principle of insurance is that of indemnity and, therefore, an insured must not be allowed to receive more than the financial loss which he has suffered. Subrogation seeks to put that principle into operation.

Double insurance and contribution have the same aim. If X is covered under different policies for the same loss, he should not be permitted to recover more than his loss. How could such a situation arise?

At one end of the spectrum X might be a cheat who insures the same goods with a number of different insurers, with the intention of receiving far in excess of his losses. Hopefully, as the Claims Underwriting Exchange becomes more effective, such crimes will be more readily detectable (Appendix 4.17).

More realistic, however, is the situation where the insured is covered under more than one policy because of overlapping cover. A simple example is seen in holiday insurance, which covers loss of valuables, when in fact the insured also has an all risks policy on his home-contents policy covering the same items. A claims form will invariably ask if the loss is covered elsewhere. Answered correctly this will lead the insurer against whom the claim is made to seek a contribution from the other insurer(s).

History of double insurance

The possibility of double insurance was recognised as early as the 18th century and rules were created to deal with its possible encroachment on the principle of indemnity. The insured might decide to demand his entire loss from only one insurance policy, assuming that it is sufficient to cover his losses; or he might decide to make his claim against all of the companies who had covered the perils. If he chose the former procedure, then the question arose as to whether the company paying could then seek some reimbursement from the other company or companies. If he chose the latter procedure, then the question arose as to how his claim would be handled by the various companies.

In the early case of *Newby v Reed* (1763) 1 Wm Bl 416, the insured took out a policy with company A to cover a voyage of his ship from Newfoundland to Barbados. He later insured the same ship on the same voyage but from Newfoundland to Dominica, with company B. He made his claim against the second company only and the court (Lord Mansfield) allowed that company's claim for some reimbursement from the first company. The short judgment makes no mention of the peril, the value of the claim, or the method of allocating the loss between company A and B.

More information can be found in an earlier judgment of Lord Mansfield in *Godin v London Assurance Co* (1758) 1 Burr 489 and some of the present rules governing the principle of contribution between companies can be seen emerging at this early date. Merchants in London insured a ship for £500 on a voyage from London to St Peterburg and back and insured goods onboard for £600, both with X & Co The merchants then took out a second policy valued at £800 on the goods with Y & Co from St Peterburg to London. The merchants then took out a third policy valued at £900 on the goods from the Sound to London, with Z & Co This third policy was taken out at the request of the sellers in St Peterburg and they stated the account to which the premium was to be debited. The sellers in St Peterburg then endorsed the bill of lading to the plaintiffs in Moscow. The plaintiffs instructed A in London to insure the goods and this was done with the defendant insurance company. Full disclosure of the other policies was made to the defendants, and they issued a policy valued at £2,316 on the goods from the Sound to London. The goods were lost on the voyage. The defendants argued that they were liable for half of the insured value and that X, Y, and Z & Co were liable for the other half.

Lord Mansfield held that the defendants were liable for the whole loss. He said:

> Where a man makes a double insurance of the same thing, in such a manner that he can clearly recover against several insurers in distinct policies, a double satisfaction, 'the law certainly says that he ought not to recover doubly for the same loss, but be content with one single satisfaction for it'. And if the same man really, or for his own proper account, insures the same goods doubly, though both insurances be not made in his own name, but one or both of them in the name of another person, yet that is just the same thing: for the same person is to have the benefit of both policies. And if the whole should be recovered from one, he ought to stand in the place of the insured, to receive contribution from the other who was equally liable to pay the whole ... but if the plaintiff was not to have the benefit of both policies *in all events*, then it can never be considered as a double policy.

The reason against it being a matter of double insurance was the fact that the interests of the parties were not the same. Here several parties were insuring their own interests in the same thing, but that does not amount to double insurance. As Lord Mansfield explained, double insurance is where:

> ... the same man is to receive two sums instead of one, or the same sum twice over, for the same loss, by reason of his having made two insurances upon the same goods or the same ship.

Conditions relating to double insurance

Godin's case illustrates that there can be difficulties in establishing whether or not double insurance exists. In particular, what is meant by the word 'same' in the phrases 'same loss' and 'same goods'? Do the various policies have to cover identical subject matter?

Same subject matter

There appears to be no English case illustrating whether it is necessary that the subject matter, for example, goods or property, be identical to the various policies. There is disagreement in the United States as to whether this is an essential requirement. A leading English legal textbook considers that exact duplication is not necessary and the authors suggest that there will be double insurance:

> ... where item A is insured by one insurer and items A and B are insured for a single undivided premium by another insurer and also where goods are covered by a floating policy and part of the goods so covered is also insured specifically.

The nearest English case authority in point is *American Surety Co of New York v Wrightson* (1910) 103 LT 663 (Appendix 9.11). The plaintiff American insurance company agreed to reimburse an American bank for loss or damage caused by the dishonesty of any of the bank's employees, but only up to a limit which was set out against every employee's name. K's name had $2,500 set against it and the total cover value of the policy was $595,000. The bank also insured at Lloyd's for £40,000, covering a far wider range of losses than the first policy, but including the perils listed in that first policy. K committed defalcations to the extent of $2,680. The bank claimed $2,500 from the plaintiff insurer and $180 from Lloyd's. The plaintiff insurer then claimed from the defendant Lloyd's underwriter for contribution – and the case becomes an important one on how such a contribution should be assessed. This point will be dealt with later. Unfortunately, with regard to the present problem of determining the 'same property' definition, the defendants *admitted* that they were liable to contribute something. Clearly, the two policies covered widely differing perils. As Hamilton J said:

> The two instruments ... differ very considerably in scope, both as regards the hazards covered and the persons or things bringing those hazards into operation. ... what I have to say (that is, regarding the contribution ratios) is intended to be entirely without prejudice to the discussion or the decision of the contention, should it ever arise, that in a case similar to this the principle of contribution does not, in the case of double insurance, apply at all.

A comparison of the two policies showed very considerable differences and clearly this fact worried Hamilton J. What we do not know is how great the divergence between the two, or more, policies would need to be in order to justify a rejection on the grounds that there was a double insurance. If the court allows the argument that there is double insurance, even though there is not identical subject matter the further difficulty of ascertaining the ratio of liability then needs to be decided (below).

Same interest

If the opinion of the authors referred to above is correct, and identical subject matter is not a prerequisite for double insurance, it is certainly agreed the policies must cover a common risk. Again, this does not mean that the policies must be identical in which risk they cover, but the loss for which a claim is made must be common to both policies.

In *North British and Mercantile Insurance Co v London, Liverpool and Globe Insurance Co* (1877) 5 Ch D 569 (Appendix 9.12), X & Co were wharfingers and they held floating policies on seed and grain, which either they owned or held on commission, in circumstances whereby they would be liable to the owners if the goods were lost or damaged. Some grain was destroyed and it was also insured by Y & Co as owners. X & Co were paid by their several insurers and an action was commenced to determine the contribution, if any, that might be due from Y & Co's insurers. The court held that Y & Co's insurers were not liable to contribute because double insurance, and, therefore, rights to contribution, could only exist where the same risk was covered. As James LJ explained:

> Contribution exists where the thing is done by the same person against the same loss, and to prevent a man first of all from recovering more than the

> whole loss, or if he recovers the whole loss from one which he could have recovered from the other, then to make the parties contribute rateably. But that only applies where there is the same interest with more than one office.

In this case, the facts showed that X & Co were liable to Y & Co for the loss of their goods by fire. What then would happen if Y & Co had claimed from their insurers? The answer is that subrogation would apply and not contribution. Y & Co have contractual rights against X & Co on these facts and therefore if Y & Co's insurers had compensated Y & Co, then they would have been subrogated to Y & Co's legal rights and could have sued X & Co, who in turn would have turned to their insurers for compensation. The fact that the policies contained rateable proportion clauses, to become operative when there was in force more than one policy, could not be interpreted in a way that would ignore the basic requirement of contribution, namely that the same interest must be doubly insured. It should be noted, however, that insurance market agreements may often choose to ignore these requirements. Formulas exist that deal with divisions of financial contribution. Such agreements may provide for contribution on the same property, even if the interests are not the same. These agreements do not affect the rights of insured under the policy (see Lewis, 'Insurers' agreements not to enforce strict legal rights: bargaining with government and in the shadow of the law' (1985) 48 MLR 275. See also MacGillivray, *Insurance Law*, 9th edn, 1998, London: Sweet & Maxwell, paras 23-36–23-47, for examples of the complex formulations used by the Fire Loss Association).

Even when there is an overlapping of risk, it may not be considered sufficient to be called double insurance if the overlap is only for a brief period. In *Australian Agricultural Co v Saunders* (1874–75) 10 LRCP 668 (Appendix 9.13), the plaintiff took out first a policy with the defendant company for fire cover up to £3,000 'on wool ... in any shed, store or station or in transit to Sydney by land only or any shed store or wharf in Sydney, until placed on a ship'. This policy contained a clause stating that no property was insured if previously or subsequently insured elsewhere, unless particulars of such other insurance was notified to the company in writing. A second policy was then taken out for £16,500 on wool at and from the river Hunter to Sydney per ships and steamers and thence per ship or ships to London, including the risk of crafts from the time that the wools were first waterborne and of transshipment or landing and reshipment at Sydney. The practice at Sydney was to put wool into stores for pressing prior to loading on board. The wool was destroyed by fire while in store. The plaintiff claimed under the first policy and the defendant argued that the second policy had not been brought to their knowledge as required by their policy. The court allowed the plaintiff's claim on the grounds that the policy requirement relating to information need only be applied if the subsequent policies covered substantially the same risk, and here they did not. Bramwell B explained:

> ... it seems to me this is not a case of double insurance ... inasmuch as the plaintiffs could not have recovered this loss on the marine policy ... I doubt

> whether a mere possibility that some portion of the risk covered by both policies might accidentally coincide constitutes such a double insurance as was meant.

Another example of the requirement that the same risk must be covered by the policies can be seen in *Boag v Economic Insurance Co Ltd* [1954] 2 Lloyd's Rep 581 (Appendix 9.14). A & Co insured their tobacco and cigarettes under a Lloyd's all risk policy to cover losses while in transit in the UK, including loading and unloading from the time of taking delivery to delivery of the goods. This was also to cover temporary off loading in the course of transit. The goods were to go from A & Co's warehouse in Luton to London Docks. They were taken to another of A & Co's warehouses in Luton and to remain there for the first night. They were destroyed by fire. Lloyd's paid A & Co but then sought contribution from A & Co's fire insurers of the second warehouse. The policies on this warehouse were to cover 'stock in trade' of these premises. Lloyd's claim failed because the goods could not be described as 'stock in trade' of that warehouse. Lord McNair MR explained that for the defendants to be liable to contribute the plaintiff would have to show:

(a) that he was liable under his own policy;

(b) that he had paid under his policy;

(c) that the defendants were liable under their policy; and

(d) that the defendants had not paid under their policy.

The policy issued by the defendants clearly showed that they were insuring only goods (and equipment) that were entered in the books relating to the second warehouse.

All policies must be in force at the time of the loss

Therefore, if one policy has lapsed or if it has not yet attached, at the time of the loss, then no contribution is possible. But contribution is possible if the repudiation only takes place after the loss.

No policy may exclude the rules of contribution

Interconnected with sub-heading (c) is the rule that no policy may exclude the rules of contribution. But it is common to find in the proposal form a question asking for information relating to other insurances on the risk. The answers on a proposal form are usually made the basis of the contract and therefore failure to divulge such information will allow the insurance company to avoid their liability. It is normal also for companies to ask for information regarding the issue of later policies. Occasionally, a company will state that it will be a breach of the policy for the insured to take out a subsequent policy on the same risk.

There have been examples where policies state that where another policy covers the same risk, then their policy will no longer be operative. If the insured has two policies, both of which use this device, it might seem that he has then lost all of his insurance cover. The courts, however, will not permit this interpretation and they avoid such a situation by stating that the effect of such provisions is that each cancels out the other.

In *Weddell and Another v Road Transport and General Insurance Co Ltd* [1931] All ER Rep 609 (Appendix 9.15), a motor policy taken out by X stated that it:

> ... would treat as though he were the insured, any relative or friend of the insured while driving the insured's car ... provided that such person was not entitled to an indemnity under any other policy.

Y, who was the brother of X, injured Z when driving X's car. Y also owned a car and his policy covered his liability to Z. But his policy also contained a condition avoiding liability if Y was covered for the same risk by any other policy. Y also failed to inform his company of the accident and was thus in breach of one of his policy conditions. X therefore asked his company to indemnify Y's liability to Z. X's company then attempted to avoid liability on the grounds of the double insurance condition. The court held that in the first place they would not allow each company to avoid its liability by the use of such clauses. Both were liable to contribute equally. But, as Y's company were able to avoid their liability, because of Y's failure to notify them of the accident, X's company were liable for 50% of the damages.

Whether or not the notice condition is enforceable depends on the court's construction of the policy wording. Thus, in *Equitable Fire and Accident Office Ltd v Ching Wo Hong* [1907] AC 96 (Appendix 9.16), the requirement for notification of additional insurance was not breached where the insured had never in fact paid the second premium and thus the second policy had not been activated.

Contribution and apportionment

Assuming that the legal rules leading to double insurance are met, then the practical rules of contribution need to be explained.

It must be stressed at this point that there is no universally accepted formula. Insurance company agreements tend to dominate market practices rather than legal rules.

There are good reasons why inter-office agreements dominate, particularly where the insured finds himself over insured by no wish of his own. A simple example of such over insurance would be where the insured has an all risks policy on his household goods, personal possessions and at the same time his motor insurance or holiday insurance also covers, perhaps with a low financial limit, the same personal effects. If a coat is stolen from the car, both insurers could be asked to pay. The insured is more likely to turn to his all risks insurer. This may be due to the fact that he believes it is the obvious company to turn to and also he has no wish to prejudice his no claims bonus on his motor insurance. From the companies' point of view, they have two problems. It is not good public relations to appear to pay an insured only part of his (small) loss and then tell him to claim the remainder from his other insurers. It is administratively costly, having paid in full, to seek (a small) contribution from other insurers.

The following formula is adopted by those companies subscribing to an agreement. If the claim for the coat is made from the all risks insurer, it is settled by that insurer without seeking contribution from the motor insurer. If the claim is made against the motor insurer, he will settle it up to the limit of indemnity in his policy, without seeking a contribution from the all risks insurer. If the claim exceeds the limit of indemnity in the motor policy, then contribution will be sought from the other insurer. The formula used for this calculation is based on the independent liability basis.

Where an item is specifically listed on an all risks policy as opposed to its inclusion in a global sum, then that insurer will meet the claim, unless there are other similar all risks policies, in which case a contribution will be applied.

In the case of other claims for loss or damage to personal effects, the insurer to whom the claim is made will settle it. If the claim is below a stated sum, no contribution is possible. If it is above that sum, then other insurers will be asked to contribute. The independent liability formula can be seen thus:

Example

(a) Policy A has a limit of £2,000.

Policy B has a limit of £4,000.

Item lost is valued at £1,000.

A claim from A or B would be paid in full. Therefore, each will contribute equally, that is, £500:£500.

(b) Policy A has a limit of £1,000.

Policy B has a limit of £4,000.

Item lost is valued at £1,500.

A claim from A alone would produce only £1,000.

A claim from B alone would produce £1,500.

The total limits are therefore £2,500.

Policy A will therefore pay 10/25 of the loss = £600.

Policy B will therefore pay 15/25 of the loss = £900.

It is now necessary to look in greater detail at the basic principles that appear to dominate the general application of apportionment. As Ivamy comments (*General Principles of Insurance Law*, 6th edn, London: Butterworths, p 523): 'Such rules are not entirely satisfactory, and it is difficult to see precisely upon what principles they are based.'

It is necessary to divide the discussion between policies that are: (a) not subject to average; and those that (b) are subject to average.

Policies not subject to average

Unfortunately, this topic must again be subdivided, reflecting the fact that the policies concerned, may be 'concurrent' or 'non-concurrent'.

Concurrent policies

This means that the insured items are covered by both, or all, policies, for the same risk and interest. This provides the easiest calculation and follows the principles set out in the Marine Insurance Act 1906, which is followed in non-marine insurance, s 32 states:

(1) Where two or more policies are effected by or on behalf of the assured on the same adventure and interest or any part thereof, and the sums insured exceed the indemnity allowed by this Act, the assured is said to be over insured by double insurance.

(2) Where the assured is over insured by double insurance:

(a) the assured, unless the policy otherwise provides, may claim payment from the insurers in such order as he may think fit, provided that he is not entitled to receive any sum in excess of the indemnity allowed by this act;

(b) where the policy under which the assured claims is a valued policy, the assured must give credit as against the valuation for any sum received by him under any other policy without regard to the actual value of the subject matter insured;

(c) where the policy under which the assured claims is an unvalued policy he must give credit, as against the full insurable value, for any sum received by him under any other policy;

(d) where the assured receives any sum in excess of the indemnity allowed by this act, he is deemed to hold such sum in trust for the insurers, according to their rights of contribution among themselves.

By s 80:

(1) Where the assured is over insured by double insurance, each insurer is bound, as between himself and the other insurers, to contribute rateably to the loss in proportion to the amount for which he is liable under his contract.

(2) If any insurer pays more than his proportion of the loss, he is entitled to maintain an action for contribution against the other insurers, and is entitled to the like remedies as a surety who has paid more than his proportion of the debt.

See, however, the conflicting decision of the Court of Appeal and the Privy Council, in motor insurance settings, in *Legal and General Assurance Society Ltd v Drake Insurance Co Ltd* [1992] 1 All ER 283 (Appendix 9.17); and *Eagle Star Insurance Co Ltd v Provincial Insurance plc* [1993] 3 All ER 1 (Appendix 9.18).

Section 80(1), however, appears to advocate a division of liability that is not one of independent liabilities, so that if Policy A insures for £4,000 and Policy B for £2,000 and the loss is £1,000, s 80(1) would lead to the calculation of £1,000 = £666 as A's liability; and of £1,000 = £333 as B's liability. Under the independent liability, used elsewhere as the basic method of calculation, the loss would be divided £500:£500.

Non-concurrent policies

This poses great difficulties for non-concurrent policies and may bring into contribution two or more widely differing policies. As we have seen above, contribution may not be appropriate at all if the divergence is too great, but there is great difficulty in making that decision. Assuming there is just sufficient similarity to produce double insurance, the divergence may still be substantial when it comes to making an equitable distribution of liability, cf *American Surety Co of New York v Wrightson* (1910) 103 LT 663 (above).

The difficulties under this heading are so great, and can be caused by such a number of different reasons, that no basic principles of general application can, therefore, be put forward with any certainty. An example of such difficulty is where the same subject matter is covered by both policies, but in one it is one of two objects covered, while in the other policy it is one of many and no specific values are attached to each item.

It may well be that the independent liability rule that now appears to be favoured by the courts in general would be best applied in all cases. It can be said, however, that insurers have always attempted to see that the insured's position should not be jeopardised by the insurers' calculations.

Historically, the courts have had little to say on the method of calculating contribution. The Court of Appeal has helped to fill that gap. In *Commercial Union Assurance Co Ltd v Hayden* [1977] 1 All ER 441 (Appendix 9.19), X & Co took out two policies to cover their public liability for injuries caused by negligence. Insurer A had a limit of £10,000 and Insurer B a limit of £100,000 (interestingly the premium difference was £1). A claim was made against X & Co for £4,425 and Insurer B paid. The problem then arose as to how much Insurer A should contribute to Insurer B. The Court of Appeal, overruling the Commercial Court, held that the contribution should be of equal amounts and thus approved of the 'independent liability' formula, at least for liability policies. If the claim had been for (example) £11,000, then treated separately:

Insurer A would pay £10,000 (that is, his limit).

Insurer B would pay £11,000 (that is, within his limit).

Therefore, if contribution applied there would be 10 + 11 = 21 units.

Therefore, A would pay 10/21 of £11,000 = £5,240.

B would pay 11/21 of £11,000 = £ 5,760.

X & Co would receive £11,000.

Lord Justice Cairns explained the problem:

> ... [referring to the leading textbooks] all that can be extracted from these passages of any possible relevance to the present appeal is that in property insurance the usual basis of contribution is the maximum liability basis except where the policies contain pro rata average clauses (which are now almost universal except in domestic policies). I am not persuaded that the same basis should apply to liability insurance as to property insurance ... In liability insurance, there is no corresponding 'value' (as there is in property insurance) to which the limit (if any) of the insurer's liability is related. Premiums for the two types of insurance are quite differently assessed. For the purposes of the present case, the parties agreed to the following propositions:
>
> (i) premiums on property insurance are calculated on a percentage of the sum or value insured;
>
> (ii) liability insurance premiums are not calculated on this basis and do not increase pro rata as the limit increases. The insurer who increases his limit does not receive a premium greater by an amount proportionate to the increased limit;
>
> (iii) different insurers may charge different percentages in property insurance and in liability insurance;
>
> (iv) the bulk of claims in liability insurance fall within a low limit and claims over £10,000 are relatively rare. [This refers to 1970s figures.]

In arriving at his answer, Cairns LJ admitted that he was dealing with a novel point in the law of insurance. He attempted to reach an answer which he thought a businessman would expect.

Policies subject to average

Many policies contained 'subject to average' clauses. This means that the insured must bear proportion of his loss on his own shoulders, if he has under valued his policy (see Chapter 8). The problem then arises as to the combination of this rule with the rules of contribution. There are two conditions of average.

First condition of average

This is also known as the pro rata condition of average and is usually found in policies on property and goods. When there is partial damage and the property is under insured by say, one third, then the insured will only receive two thirds of the value. Where the property is a total loss he will, however, receive the full figure for which he insured. If there is no pro rata clause, which today is unlikely, then the insured is entitled to claim up to the policy limit.

Second condition of average

It is usual to find this second condition where there is the first condition. This normally states:

> But if any of the property included in such average shall at the breaking out of any fire be also covered by any other more specific insurance that is, by an insurance which at the time of such fire applies to part only of the property actually at risk and protected by this insurance and to no other property whatsoever, then the policy shall not insure the same except only as regards any excess of value beyond the amount of such more specific insurance or insurances, which said excess is declared to be under the protection of this policy as subject to average as aforesaid.

This second condition of average is regarded as nothing more than a limiting contribution clause. It also raises again the problem of whether or not two policies can be said to cover any right of contribution between them. Ivamy (*General Principles of Insurance Law*, 6th edn, London: Butterworths, p 534) describes the condition as 'badly worded, and is in consequence somewhat difficult to understand or to apply'.

If both policies are similar in cover then the second condition does not apply and the normal rules of contribution apply. If, however, they are dissimilar but capable of some comparison and one can be regarded as more specific in its cover than the other, then the second condition comes into operation to limit the amount of contribution that the less specific insurer will have to pay. In fact, the less specific insurer will only have to contribute if the specific insurer has paid his contractual price in full (or less if subject to average). The less specific insurer in reality 'tops up'.

Section 76 of the (Australian) Insurance Contracts Act 1984 (Cth) (Appendix 9.6) also fails to provide much help in this difficult area of insurance law. The Australian Law Reform Commission Report, *Insurance Contracts*, ALRC 201, stated (para 292):

> Difficulties have occurred in determining and in applying the principles upon which the loss should be apportioned between various insurers ... The Commission recommends that, in the absence of contrary agreement between affected insurers, losses should be apportioned on the basis of equal independent liabilities.

This would be in keeping with the decision in *Commercial Union Assurance Ltd v Hayden* (Appendix 9.19).

SUBROGATION AND CONTRIBUTION

APPENDIX 9.1

Hasson, R, 'Subrogation in insurance law – a critical evaluation' (1985) 5 OJLS 416

... When a loss occurs, it is open to the legal system to adopt one of three alternatives: (i) to allow the insured party to keep *both* the insurance proceeds and to allow full recovery against the tortfeasor (or other party against whom the insured could enforce contractual rights); (ii) to allow the insured party to recover his/her own loss while the insurer is denied the right to proceed against the tortfeasor or contract breaker; or (iii) to allow the insured to recover from his/her own insurer but also to allow the insurer to use the insured's name to recover such payout from the tortfeasor or contract breaker.

It is the third option that the legal system has chosen to deal with most insured losses and which is called subrogation. This doctrine operates throughout the field of property and liability insurance – to all so called contracts of indemnity.

This principle does not hold sway throughout the law of insurance. In the field of personal injury because life insurance and accident insurance are (strangely) not thought to be contracts of indemnity, the insured person is allowed to accumulate recoveries ...

FICTITIOUS PLAINTIFFS v FICTITIOUS DEFENDANTS

We tend today to look upon legal fictions as the product of a primitive age and 20th century lawyers are normally quick to attack fictions as being a blotch on the legal system.

Yet, in the field of subrogation, the presence of fictions seems to escape notice as well as criticism. In subrogation, not only do we invariably have a fictitious plaintiff who is suing in the name of the insured but very often – perhaps in the vast majority of cases – a fictitious defendant. Sometimes, the courts are aware that the contest is between two insurance companies. In other cases, judges speculate that the contest is between two insurance companies.

Insurance companies use the device of the fictitious plaintiff because they think it will increase their chances of success in litigation. Whether they do, in fact, increase their chances of recovery is not something that can be proved.

It may be that in at least some cases, insurers gain an advantage by suing as the XYZ company instead of suing as the XYZ insurance company. A court may be more likely to find for private uninsured individuals than for an insurer ...

... So long as we have a doctrine of subrogation, there can be no justification for concealing the true identity of parties in litigation. The idea of letting insurance companies use disguises so as to influence the outcome of a case is an obscenity which should not be tolerated in a civilised legal system.

Unfortunately, there is no sign that legal scholars in the Commonwealth have begun to address this problem.

THE ALLEGED GOALS OF SUBROGATION

It is difficult to write about the goals of subrogation since to most commentators the doctrine appears to be so just as not to need any justification. However, various rationales have been advanced by insurance company representatives, academics and judges.

(a) Subrogation is necessary for the survival of the insurance industry

According to one insurance executive: 'Effective subrogation practices by insurers can mean the difference between an underwriting profit or a loss.' There is no description what is meant by 'effective'. Does it mean the same as aggressive? The statistics that are provided make it *extremely* unlikely that the amounts recovered through subrogation are likely to prove the difference between a profit and loss.

Thus, in 1972 fire insurance companies in the United States paid out $973,636,000. Subrogation recoveries amounted to $6,621,000 a net recovery of 0.68% of paid losses. Again, consider the figures for homeowners' insurance provided by the same author. In 1972, homeowners' claims paid by the insurance industry came to $1,636,147,000. Subrogation recoveries totalled $13,089,000 a net recovery of 0.80% of paid loss. These sums appear to be too trivial to make much difference to anything. In the absence of more compelling evidence it is impossible to argue that subrogation is necessary to keep insurance companies solvent.

(b) Subrogation is a cost saver

The notion that insurance companies might after taking 'net subrogation recoveries' into account be able to offer their customers lower premiums has been advanced ...

PROPERTY INSURANCE

The difficulty with this theory is that it flies in the face of the information we have about the workings of subrogation ...

The reason why subrogation recoveries cannot play an important part in fixing insurance premiums is because most subrogated claims are, in effect, contests between two insurers. In this state of affairs, it will not be enough to compute subrogation recoveries. One would also have to take into account subrogation liabilities. Since one would expect subrogation recoveries and subrogation liabilities to cancel each other out on a 'swings and roundabouts basis', it is difficult to see how subrogation could help lower rates.

In sum, it seems most unlikely that subrogation can have any appreciable effect on the cost of premiums. On the other hand, by requiring overlapping premiums and especially the occasional expensive lawsuit, it would seem that subrogation might well have the effect of making insurance more expensive.

(c) Subrogation is a deterrent against negligent behaviour

It is clear that subrogation is justified by some as a deterrent against negligent behaviour ...

... The real deterrent against negligent behaviour on the part of corporations is not the possibility of subrogated claims, against which they are insured, in any event. The real deterrent against negligent behaviour in the case of a corporation is the fear of the loss of business which may follow an accident ...

... It is perhaps significant that no representative of the insurance industry has, to the best of my knowledge, made the claim that subrogated claims deter negligent behaviour. It would appear that judges accept the efficacy of fault notions much more readily than do representatives of the insurance industry.

III THE REAL FUNCTIONS OF SUBROGATION

(a) Subrogation and overlapping coverage

The main function of the subrogation doctrine is that it requires overlapping insurance coverage. Thus, in a sale both the vendor and the purchaser will have to insure the same piece of property, unless the purchaser wishes to pay a substantial sum of money for 'a charred ruin'. Again, in the mortgagee-mortgagor relationship, it will be prudent for the mortgagor to protect his/her interest by taking out insurance. In both these cases, two policies are being taken out to cover one risk. This is the real attraction of subrogation for insurers.

The situation becomes even more promising for insurers if we consider the situation of a landlord and a commercial tenant. In this case, both the landlord and tenant will carry insurance on the same building. In addition, the tenant's employees would be well advised to carry liability insurance. Similarly, people who supply the tenant with goods would be well advised to take out liability insurance, as would people who come to effect repairs. Thus, in this situation five groups of people may well be paying insurance premiums in respect of one risk ...

V THE SHAPE OF A REFORMING STATUTE

Although some courts have been chipping away at the doctrine of subrogation, it must be clear to even the passionate devotees of the common law method of reform, that the doctrine will not be abolished by attrition. In fact, the only thing likely to be achieved by common law sniping is to reduce this branch of the law to a state of complete confusion.

I shall not attempt to draft a model statute, but I shall outline a proposed statute.

First, two general problems must be faced.

The need for comprehensive reform

If a statute is to be passed reforming subrogation, it seems clear that the reforms must be comprehensive. If this is not done, then arbitrary distinctions will remain ...

... It seems preferable to limit subrogation to a few cases of intentional wrongdoing. Thus, in a case where a bank has insured against losses by forgery, there would be no objection to a bank bringing a subrogated claim against the forger. Again, in a fidelity insurance policy, there would seem to be little objection to allowing the insurer to proceed against an employee who had been convicted of dishonesty. These claims would not usually be worth pursuing but there can be no objection to them. In the first place, the difficulty of overlapping coverage does not arise since the wrongdoer cannot obtain liability insurance against wrongdoing of this kind. Secondly, losses of this kind are difficult to distinguish from the theft from an insurer.

I have great difficulty in deciding whether to allow subrogated claims against arsonists. My hesitation derives from the fact that in many cases it is either someone who is mentally disturbed or else is a child who sets fire to someone else's property. An enquiry into the arsonist's sanity or an infant's ability to understand his/her act does not appear to be an edifying prospect.

The following changes in the law of subrogation seem to be desirable:

(1) It should be made clear whether disability insurance benefits fall within the definition of indemnity or not …

(2) Both the assignment of claims, as well as subrogated claims are to be abolished with the very minor exceptions for forgery insurance and fidelity insurance.

(3) It is important to make sure that after the action for subrogation has been abolished, the insured cannot bring an action to recover the deductible. The deductible may be large in which case the problem of overlapping coverage remains. Even where the deductible is small, the waste caused by these actions is indefensible.

(4) It is essential that those people who have underinsured should have to bear their own losses. Unless this is done, everyone who presently carries liability insurance will continue to do so.

(5) The problem of those who cannot obtain insurance either because of poverty or because of 'redlining' will have to be tackled. To allow these groups to sue in tort for damage to their property is undesirable. First, many of the people who would wish to sue could not afford to do so. Second, and more important, once a certain group is allowed to sue, the advantages of abolishing subrogation would be lost. The question then becomes whether one assigns uninsurable risks to private insurers or to the government. It seems clear that there are great difficulties in devising and operating an assigned risk scheme. Moreover, a government run scheme can be more cheaply run than a private insurance scheme.

(6) There is a very good case for dealing with the vendor-purchaser problem separately. The sections should be drafted so as to cover real and personal property. They should provide that whether it is the vendor or purchaser who insures, that person holds the insurance proceeds to protect his/her own interests. Any surplus will be held in trust for the vendor or purchaser, as the case may be …

VI CONCLUSION

It is tempting, when one is permitted to find out so little about the workings of the insurance industry, to leave things unchanged. But the defects of some parts of the law of insurance such as subrogation are so striking that it would be the height of irresponsibility not to point them out and to advocate radical change.

APPENDIX 9.2

Castellain v Preston and Others (1883) 11 QBD 380, CA

Brett LJ: In order to give my opinion upon this case, I feel obliged to revert to the very foundation of every rule which has been promulgated and acted on by the courts with regard to insurance law. The very foundation, in my opinion, of every rule which has been applied to insurance law is this, namely, that the contract of insurance contained in a marine or fire policy is a contract of indemnity only, and that this contract means that the assured, in case of a loss against which the policy has been made, shall be fully indemnified, but shall never be more than fully indemnified. That is the fundamental principle of insurance, and if ever a proposition is brought forward which is at variance with it, that is to say, which either will prevent the assured from obtaining a full indemnity, or which will give to the assured more than a full indemnity, that proposition must certainly be wrong ...

In order to apply the doctrine of subrogation, it seems to me that the full and absolute meaning of the word must be used, that is to say, the insurer must be placed in the position of the assured. Now it seems to me that in order to carry out the fundamental rule of insurance law, this doctrine of subrogation must be carried to the extent which I am now about to endeavour to express, namely, that as between the underwriter and the assured the underwriter is entitled to the advantage of every right of the assured, whether such right consists in contract, fulfilled or unfulfilled, or in remedy for tort capable of being insisted on or already insisted on, or in any other right, whether by way of condition or otherwise, legal of equitable, which can be, or has been exercised or has accrued, and whether such right could or could not be enforced by the insurer in the name of the assured by the exercise or acquiring of which right or condition the loss against which the assured is insured, can be, or has been diminished.

APPENDIX 9.3

Burnand v Rodocanachi Sons and Co (1882) 7 App Cas 333, HL

Lord Blackburn: The general rule of law (and it is obvious justice) is that where there is a contract of indemnity (it matters not whether it is a marine policy, or a policy against fire on land, or any other contract of indemnity) and a loss happens, anything which reduces or diminishes that loss reduces or diminishes the amount which the indemnifier is bound to pay; and if the indemnifier has already paid it, then, if anything which diminishes the loss comes into the hands of the person to whom he has paid it, it becomes an equity that the person who has already paid the full indemnity is entitled to be recouped by having that amount back.

The first question is this. There had been a policy of insurance and a total loss by capture and destruction of the property insured and a payment of the full value insured – a payment of the total loss under that policy. Subsequently to that payment there came the Treaty of Washington; and afterwards, in consequence of an Act of Congress, a sum of money was paid to the persons who had received payment under the policy; and the question, I apprehend, comes to be, Was that sum or was it not paid so as to be a reduction of diminution of their loss ...?

In the present case, the Government of the United States did not pay it with the intention of rescuing the loss ... when Congress in express terms say, 'We do not pay the money for the purpose of repaying or reducing the loss against which the insurance company have indemnified, but for another and a different purpose', it effectually prevents the right arising ...

Lord Watson: In this case, the Act of Congress declares in very express terms, when you take the whole of s 12 together, in the first place that no compensation is to be given by the commissioners on account of loss which has been insured against or covered by insurance, and secondly that underwriters are not to receive any benefit from the funds distributed under the Act, and that the compensation given to any claimant must be given to compensate him for any loss either from want of insurance or from being under-insured. In the present case, it is perfectly obvious from the statements made by the parties, upon which they agreed, that compensation was awarded to the respondents upon the second of these grounds, namely, in respect that the insurance which they effected fell short of protection against the whole loss which they sustained. It is conceded that the compensation might be given to the respondents in these very terms and upon this footing by any benevolent individual, who being under no obligation to give it, chose to indemnify the respondents; and it is conceded that in the event of his doing so no claim would lie to that money at the instance of the underwriters.

APPENDIX 9.4

Page v Scottish Insurance Corp Ltd, Forster and Page (1929) 33 Ll L Rep 134, CA

Scrutton LJ: The action by the company against Page was brought in the name of Forster. The statement of claim is curious; it began as a claim by Forster himself for damages for negligence and finished as a claim by the company for a set off. At the time when the company issued their writ against Page in the name of Forster they had not paid either the cost of repairing Forster's car or the sum for which Forster was liable to the owner of the Rolls Royce car; but while the action was pending they went to arbitration with regard to the latter sum and the arbitrator awarded in favour of Forster, and the company then paid Forster the amount which was due. They then continued their action in Forster's name against Page for negligence, contending that they had a right to do so by subrogation. Now, the rights which arise by subrogation differ from those which arise by abandonment. In the latter case, an underwriter may obtain far more than he has paid; but in subrogation the underwriter is using the right of his assured and he cannot make use of it until he has fully indemnified the assured under his policy. And as he can only make use of the right of the assured, if the assured himself has done the damage there is no right to which the underwriter can be subrogated.

This case shows that there are still some points with regard to the law as to subrogation which are not clear. If an underwriter has paid all that is due from him personally under the policy but the assured has not received all that he has lost can the underwriter claim to be subrogated? Or if an underwriter has paid all that is due under a particular head of claim has he a right to be subrogated although there are other claims under the same policy which he has not paid? In my view, where there is a single policy and a single premium covering different risks the right to subrogation only arises when the underwriter has paid all the assured's liabilities arising out of the same accident. In this case when one looks at the dates one sees that at the time when the company issued their writ in the name of Forster against Page they had not paid Forster all claims due under the policy in connection with the accident. It is true that later on, after an arbitration had taken place, they did discharge Forster's liability to the owner of the Rolls Royce car, but they could not by doing so redeem their mistake in bringing their action too soon. When they issued their writ against Page they had no right to sue in the name of Forster. They cannot set off a claim by Forster for unliquidated damages against Page against a claim by Page to recover the price of the repairs from the insurance company. The two claims do not arise in the same right. The appeal must be allowed, and judgment must be entered for Page against the company for £117 2s 6d in the first action, and judgment must be entered for Page against Forster in the second action.

Greer and Sankey LJJ delivered judgments to the same effect.

APPENDIX 9.5

Morris v Ford Motor Co Ltd [1973] 2 All ER 1084, HL

Lord Denning MR: Now, this firm of cleaners had obviously no claim on their own account against Roberts. Roberts by his negligence had done no damage to the property or person of the cleaners themselves. He had only done damage to their servant Morris. Roberts was, therefore, liable to Morris. So also were Fords liable to Morris because they were the employers of Roberts. Roberts and Fords were joint tortfeasors. Morris could, if he had wished, have sued them together and got judgment against both of them. As it was, he sued Fords only. He got damages against them. Thereupon Fords could themselves have sued their own servant Roberts on the ground that Roberts owed Fords a duty to drive the truck carefully: and that his negligence had involved Fords in liability to Morris. If Fords had sued Roberts, they would no doubt have got judgment against him for the full amount which they had had to pay to Morris. That is clear from the decision of the House of Lords in *Lister v Romford Ice and Cold Storage Co Ltd* [1957] AC 555 ...

But, in point of fact, Fords would never, for a moment, have dreamt of suing their own servant Roberts. If they did so, all the men would have come out on strike. The men would say, with great force: 'This sum should be paid by the insurance company, and not by Roberts himself.' To make him pay personally for an accident at the works would be most unfair.

But, although Fords would not themselves sue their own servant Roberts, the firm of cleaners seek to sue him. The cleaners cannot, of course, sue Roberts in their own name. But they assert that they are entitled to use Fords' name to sue Roberts. Using the lawyer's words, the cleaners say that they are entitled to use Fords' name to sue Roberts. Using the lawyer's words, the cleaners say that they are entitled 'to be subrogated' to the rights of Fords against Roberts. Using the layman's words, the cleaners say that they are entitled to 'stand in the shoes of Fords' and to exercise against Roberts all the rights which Fords have against him.

If the cleaners are right in this contention – if they can thus force Roberts to pay the damages personally – it would imperil good industrial relations. When a man such as Roberts makes a mistake – like not keeping a good lookout – and someone is injured, no one expects the man himself to have to pay the damages, personally. It is rather like the driver of a car on the road. The damages are expected to be borne by the insurers. The courts themselves recognise this every day. They would not find negligence so readily – or award sums of such increasing magnitude – except on the footing that the damages are to be borne, not by the man himself, but by an insurance company. If the man himself is made to pay, he will feel much aggrieved. He will say to his employers: 'Surely this liability is covered by insurance.' He is employed to do his master's work, to drive his master's trucks, and to cope with situations presented to him by his master. The risks attendant on that work – including liability for negligence – should be borne by the master. The master takes the benefit and should bear the burden. The wages are fixed on that basis. If the servant is to bear the risk, his wages ought to be increased to cover it.

It was such considerations as these which prompted the Minister of Labour in 1957 to appoint an interdepartmental committee to study the implications of *Lister v Romford Ice and Cold Storage Co Ltd* [1957] AC 555. The committee made its report in 1959 … It did not recommend legislation to reverse that decision it felt that insurers would not abuse it. It said:

> The decision in the *Lister* case shows that employers and their insurers have rights against employees which, if exploited unreasonably, would endanger good industrial relations. We think that employers and insurers, if only in their own interests, will not so exploit their rights …

In consequence of that report, the members of the British Insurance Association adhered to this 'gentleman's agreement':

> Employers' liability insurers agree that they will not institute a claim against the employee of an insured employer in respect of the death of or injury to a fellow employee unless the weight of evidence clearly indicates: (i) collusion; or (ii) wilful misconduct on the part of the employee against whom a claim is made.

According to that agreement, if Roberts, the driver of the fork-lift truck, had injured one of Fords' own employees, the injured employee would have his remedy against Fords' insurers, but those insurers would not seek to recover the amount from Roberts, the driver.

The present case does not come within the 'gentleman's agreement'; because the injured man, Morris, was not an employee of Fords but was an employee of the firm of cleaners. So the cleaners claim to make Mr Roberts, Fords' driver, personally liable. Fords object to this. In their view it would produce serious industrial repercussions. But, despite Fords' objection, the cleaners are determined to press their claim to be subrogated to the rights of Fords …

THE DOCTRINE OF SUBROGATION

This is a contract which contains an indemnity. As such, it gives rise to a right in the indemnifier to be subrogated to the rights of the indemnified. But it is necessary to analyse this right. In particular, to see whether it gives the indemnifier a right to sue in the name of the indemnified …

Now I turn to contracts of indemnity. Where an insurer – or any other person who enters into a contract to indemnify another – pays the amount of the loss or damages to the insured, he is entitled to the advantages of every right of action of the assured, wether in contract or in tort, which may go in diminution of the loss …

WHAT IS THE EQUITY IN THIS CASE?

In my opinion, therefore this case is to be tested according to the principles of equity …

It is not just and equitable. In the contract with the cleaners, Fords advised the cleaners to arrange with their insurance company to cover their liability under the indemnity. I expect they did so. Their insurance company has received the premiums, and should bear the loss. It should not seek to make Roberts personally liable. Everyone knows that risks such as these are covered by insurance. So they should be, when a man is doing his employer's work, with his employer's plant and equipment, and happens to make a mistake. To make the servant personally liable would not only lead to a strike. It would be positively unjust. *Lister v Romford Ice and Cold Storage Co Ltd* ... was an unfortunate decision. Its ill effects have been avoided only by an agreement between insurers not to enforce it. It would not be extended to this case. I would apply this simple principle: where the risk of a servant's negligence is covered by insurance, his employer should not seek to make that servant liable for it. At any rate, the courts should not compel him to allow his name to be used to do it ...

CONCLUSION

In my opinion the doctrine of subrogation cannot be used here so as to entitle the cleaners or their insurers to sue Roberts and make him personally liable. No matter whether it arises in equity or in contract, the doctrine cannot be carried so far. I would, therefore, allow the appeal and dismiss the claim for subrogation.

APPENDIX 9.6

(Australian) Insurance Contracts Act 1984 (Cth) (as amended)

SUBROGATION TO RIGHTS AGAINST FAMILY, ETC

65 (1) Subject to subsection (1A), this section applies where:

(a) an insurer is liable under a contract of general insurance in respect of a loss;

(b) but for this section, the insurer would be entitled to be subrogated to the rights of the insured against some other person (in this section called the 'third party'); and

(c) the insured has not exercised those rights and might reasonably be expected not to exercise those rights by reason of:

(i) a family or other personal relationship between the insured and the third party; or

(ii) the insured having expressly or impliedly consented to the use, by the third party, of a road motor vehicle that is the subject matter of the contract.

(2) This section does not apply where the conduct of the third party that gave rise to the loss:

(a) occurred in the course of or arose out of his employment by the insured; or

(b) was serious or wilful misconduct.

(3) Where the third party is not insured in respect of his liability to the insured, the insurer does not have the right to be subrogated to the rights of the insured against the third party in respect of the loss.

(4) Where the third party is so insured, the insurer may not, in the exercise of his rights of subrogation, recover from the third party an amount that exceeds the amount that the third party may recover under his contract of insurance in respect of the loss.

(5) An insured need not comply with a condition requiring him to assign those rights to the insurer in order to be entitled to payment in respect of the loss and an insurer shall not purport to impose such a condition on the making of such a payment or, before making such a payment, invite the insured so to assign those rights, or suggest that he so assign them.

Penalty ...:

(6) An assignment made in compliance with such a condition or in pursuance of such an invitation or suggestion is void ...

SUBROGATION TO RIGHTS AGAINST EMPLOYEES

66 Where:

(a) the rights of an insured under a contract of general insurance in respect of a loss are exercisable against a person who is his employee; and

(b) the conduct of the employee that gave rise to the loss occurred in the course of or arose out of the employment and was not serious or wilful misconduct,

the insurer does not have the right to be subrogated to the rights of the insured against the employee.

RIGHTS WITH RESPECT TO MONEYS RECOVERED UNDER SUBROGATION

67 (1) Where an insurer, in exercising a right of subrogation in respect of a loss, recovers an amount, the insured may recover that amount from the insurer.

(2) Unless the contract expressly provides otherwise, the insured may not recover under subsection (1):

(a) an amount greater than the amount (if any) by which the amount recovered by the insurer exceeds the amount paid to the insured by the insurer in relation to the loss; or

(b) an amount that, together with the amount paid to the insured under the contract, is greater than the amount of the insured's loss.

(3) The rights of an insured and insurer under the preceding provisions of this section are subject to any agreement made between them after the loss occurred.

(4) A reference in this section to an amount recovered by an insurer shall be construed as a reference to the amount so recovered less the administrative and legal costs incurred in connection with the recovery of the amount …

PART X – MISCELLANEOUS

CONTRIBUTION BETWEEN INSURERS

76 (1) When 2 or more insurers are liable under separate contracts of general insurance to the same insured in respect of the same loss, the insured is, subject to subsection (2), entitled immediately to recover from any one or more of those insurers such amount as will, or such amounts as will in the aggregate, indemnify him fully in respect of the loss.

(2) Nothing in subsection (1) entitles an insured:

(a) to recover from an insurer an amount that exceeds the sum insured under the contract between the insured and that insurer; or

(b) to recover an amount that exceeds, or amounts that in the aggregate exceed, the amount of the loss.

(3) Nothing in this section prejudices the rights of an insurer or insurers from whom the insured recovers an amount or amounts in accordance with this section to contribution from any other insurer liable in respect of the same loss.

APPENDIX 9.7

National Consumer Council, *Report on Insurance Law Reform*, 1997, London: NCC

TERMS AND CONDITIONS: SUBROGATION

Recommendation 10

We recommend law reform to restrict the insurer's subrogation rights in the following circumstances:

(a) where there is an implied benefit to the person providing payment of a premium, as with mortgage indemnity guarantees, unless the effects were fully explained to the consumer who is the object of the insurer's subrogation rights when payment was made and she/he did not have the opportunity to insure the risk herself/himself;

(b) where the subrogation rights are against members of the insured's family or against employees by their employer's insurer.

Recommendation 11

We recommend law reform to entitle the insured person, where the insurer has successfully pursued a right of subrogation, to recover from the insurer enough money to cover his loss. The loss pursued under the subrogation right should be the insured person's loss and the insurer should be accountable to the insured person for money recovered, notwithstanding excess, under-insurance or average clauses affecting cover within 20% of a valuation ...

APPENDIX 9.8

Yorkshire Insurance Co Ltd v Nisbet Shipping Co Ltd [1961] 2 WLR 1043

Diplock J: This action raises the neat point as to who is entitled to this windfall. The assured has accounted to the insurer for the sums received on the basis that it is entitled to retain all moneys in excess of the £72,000 in fact paid to the assured under the policies by the insurer. The insurer claims to be entitled to the full amount received by the assured …

I therefore will deal with the matter on the basis that the assured, in 1958, received from the Canadian government, the tortfeasor responsible for the loss of the Blairnevis, the net sum of £126,971 14s 11d, and repaid to the insurer the sum of £72,000, which was paid to the assured by the insurer for the total loss of the vessel in 1945.

The question of principle involved can, I think, be stated thus: Where an insurer pays for a total loss of the subject matter insured and the assured, in the exercise of his remedies in respect of that subject matter, recovers from a third party an amount which exceeds the sum so paid by the insurer, can the insurer recover from the assured the amount of such excess …?

In my view this case turns on what is meant by the word 'subrogated' in this context. The doctrine of subrogation is not restricted to the law of insurance. Although often referred to as an 'equity' it is not an exclusively equitable doctrine. It was applied by the common law courts in insurance cases long before the fusion of law and equity, although the powers of the common law courts might in some cases require to be supplemented by those of a court of equity in order to give full effect to the doctrine; for example, by compelling an assured to allow his name to be used by the insurer for the purpose of enforcing the assured's remedies against third parties in respect of the subject matter of the loss …

It seems to me to follow that the only terms to be implied to give business efficacy to the contract between the parties are those necessary to secure that the assured shall not recover from the insurer an amount greater than the loss which he has actually sustained. The insurer has contracted to pay to the assured the amount of his actual loss. If, before the insurer has paid under the policy, the assured recovers from some third party a sum in excess of the actual amount of the loss he can recover nothing from the insurer because he has sustained no loss, but it has never been suggested that the insurer can recover from the assured the amount of the excess. It is difficult to see why a term should be implied in a contract of insurance which would involve a fundamentally different result merely because the insurer had already paid for the loss under the policy before the assured had recovered any sum from the third party …

In my opinion, the words (in s 79(1) of the Marine Insurance Act 1906):

> … he is thereby subrogated to all the rights and remedies of the assured in and in respect of that subject matter as from the time of the casualty causing the loss,

mean that he is entitled, as against the assured, to the benefit of the assured's rights and remedies against third parties to the extent which I have indicated above as constituting the rights of the insurer under those implied terms of the contract of insurance which are connoted by the expression 'subrogation' in the law applicable to policies of insurance. This seems to me to be natural meaning of the words. If it be right, the insurer's rights under the second part of s 79(1) with which I am alone concerned are limited to recovering any sum which he has overpaid. He cannot recover more than he has in fact paid …

I am fortified in this view by the fact that the law apparently is, and has for many years been, the same in the United States; see *The St Johns* [(1900) 101 Fed Rep 469, at p 474] … where Brown J says:

> If the amount recoverable from the wrongdoer, after payment of the damage claims of third parties, were in excess of the amount paid by the underwriters to the assured, no doubt that excess would belong to the latter; since the insurer's right of subrogation in equity could not extend beyond recoupment or indemnity for the actual payments to the assured …

APPENDIX 9.9

National Oilwell (UK) Ltd v Davy Offshore Ltd [1993] 2 Lloyd's Rep 582

Colman J: In determining whether and, if so, to what extent, the benefit of the waiver clause is available to NOW, it is important to bear in mind the nature of the contractor of insurance to which, having regard to the issue which I have already decided NOW was a party. That contractor insured NOW in respect of all risks for loss and damage to the equipment to be delivered under the agreement up to the time of delivery to DOL and the period of the policy extended to the moment of time when the last item of equipment was indeed delivered. The scope of the risk insured was, however, loss of or damage to such equipment up to delivery. Thus the underwriters were off risk in respect of any item of equipment once it had been delivered to DOL, albeit the policy continued to protect NOW in respect of items of equipment not yet delivered. If there were no waiver clause and, subsequent to delivery of item X, DOL sustained loss and damage caused by that item of equipment, there would be nothing to stop DOL's insurers by way of subrogation claiming from NOW the amount in which they had indemnified DOL. It would be nothing to the point that not all the equipment had yet been delivered under the contract. NOW would simply not have been insured by the policy in respect of that loss.

It follows that if the effect of the waiver clause would be to preclude DOL's insurers from pursuing by subrogation post delivery claims which but for the waiver clause would not arise out of losses insured for the benefit of NOW under the policy, this would place NOW in exactly the same position vis à vis insurers as regards such claims as if those losses had been fully insured under the policy. In effect the waiver clause would extend the scope which were never actually insured for the benefit of NOW. This gives rise to the question whether, as a matter of construction of the policy, if the provisions to the contrary clause limit the cover available to a sub-contractor to a scope less than the full scope provided by the policy to DOL, the waiver clause has the effect of protecting the sub-contractor against subrogated claims for loses which, so far as that sub-contractor is concerned, were uninsured by that policy. Such a consequence would indeed be remarkable. The policy would limit the cover with one hand and indirectly by waiver of subrogation remove the limit by another hand.

In my judgment the waiver of subrogation clause by the words:

> ... against any Assured and any person, company or corporation whose interests are covered by this policy ...,

confines the effect of the waiver to claims for losses which are insured for the benefit of the party claimed against under the policy. In other words, one does not qualify for the benefit of the waiver clause merely by being a party to the contract of insurance. The benefit is only available for insured losses. Thus, where the 'provisions to the contrary' clause limits the interests insured, it is only in respect of losses that fall within that party's insured interest that the waiver clause operates. It may be objected that if that is the only effect of the clause it is doing no more than giving effect to what has been held in *Petrofina (UK) Ltd v Magnaload Ltd* [1983] 2 Lloyd's Rep 91; and *Stone Vickers Ltd v Appledore Ferguson Shipbuilders Ltd* [1992] 2 Lloyds Rep 578, be the automatic consequence of the sub-contractor being co-assured in respect of losses on the basis of which underwriters attempt a subrogated claim, namely to preclude the bringing by underwriters of such a claim by reason of circuity of action or of an implied term to that effect. Such an argument is not compelling. I adhere to the view which I expressed in my judgment in the *Stone Vickers* case where I sought to explain the basis of a subrogation defence in the following way:

> Where a policy is effected on a vessel to be constructed and it is expressed to be for the benefit of sub-contractors as co-assured, if a particular sub-contractor negligently causes loss of or damage to the whole or part of the vessel which has been insured under the policy and the sub-contractor has an insurable interest in the vessel, it is not open to underwriters who have settled in the insured shipbuilders' claim to exercise rights of subrogation in respect of the same loss and damage against the co-assured sub-contractor. To do so would be completely inconsistent with the insurer's obligation to the co-assured under the policy. The insurer would in effect be causing the assured with whom he had settled to pursue proceedings which if successful would at once cause the co-assured to sustain a loss arising from loss or damage to the very subject matter of the insurance in which that co-assured has an insurable interest and a right of indemnity under the policy. In my judgment so inconsistent with the insurer's obligation to the co-assured would be the exercise of rights of subrogation in such a case that there must be implied into the contract of insurance a term to give it business efficacy that an insurer will not in such circumstances use right of subrogation in order to recoup from a co-assured the indemnity which he has paid to the assured. To exercise such rights would be in breach of such a term. In such a case the law recognises the rights of the co-assured by enabling him to rely on his rights under the policy by way of defence in the proceedings which the insurers have caused to be commenced in breach of their implied obligation under the policy. This is an effective means of enforcing the co-assured's rights and makes it unnecessary for him to join the insurers as third parties in the action.

Given that, if the parties had not inserted an express waiver of subrogation, such a term would have been implied and such a term would have had the effect of a waiver of subrogation only in respect of losses insured for the benefit of the sub-contractor, it is, in my view, entirely unsurprising that the parties should have inserted a waiver clause in their policy and that its proper construction should give it an effect exactly equivalent to the term which business efficacy would otherwise require to be implied ...

The meaning of the waiver of subrogation clause cannot therefore be stretched to accommodate a commercial purpose which this particular contract on its proper construction simply does not have. The waiver clause operates consistently with the commercial purpose of the contract if its meaning is confined to the waiver of claims based on losses insured for the benefit of NOW, that is to say, pre-delivery losses, and that is how, in my judgment, it must be construed.

It follows that in as much as the subrogated claims advanced against NOW are based on losses arising in relation to particular items of equipment after delivery to DOL of that equipment, the waiver clause does not preclude or provide a defence in respect of such claims ... In my view, no such waiver was included in the policy for the benefit of NOW. Once the scope of cover procured for NOW was limited by the authority given to DOL or by the provisions to the contrary clause, the effect of the waiver clause in the contract between NOW and the underwriters was as a matter of construction limited in the manner I have described.

THE *MARK ROWLANDS* POINT

The next point advanced on behalf of NOW is that even if it is, as I have held, not a co-assured in respect of the post delivery losses claimed against it, the fact that it is a co-assured under the policy to a limited extent and that the policy was taken out in part for its benefit amongst others gives rise to an implied term in the agreement between DOL and NOW or a principle of law on some other basis to the effect DOL must give credit to NOW for any insurance monies which DOL has received or is entitled to receive from the underwriters of the policy in question. This submission rests primarily upon the decision of the Court of Appeal in *Mark Rowlands Ltd v Berni Inns Ltd* [1985] 3 All ER 473 ...

In order to ascertain whether NOW, not being a co-assured, can rely by way of defence on reasoning analogous to that in the *Mark Rowlands* case the analysis which has to be pursued is to ask whether on the proper construction of the agreement there was an obligation on DOL to insure against post delivery loss and damage and to apply the proceeds of such insurance to making good the loss for the benefit of NOW and whether the presence of such obligation leads to the conclusion that rights of subrogation could not be exercised by the insurers through DOL against NOW. I have already held that on the proper construction of the agreement the obligation of DOL to procure all risk property insurance for the benefit of NOW was confined to the period terminating at the time of delivery of each item of equipment to DOL. The consequence of that conclusion is that most of the features of the lease essential to the reasoning of the Court of Appeal in that case are missing from the agreement between DOL and NOW. Thus there was no obligation on DOL to expend what it recovered from the insurers in respect of post delivery losses or indeed to apply such moneys in any particular way. Nor was there undertaken by NOW any obligation to pay or contribute an amount referable to the cost of insurance to be procured by DOL analogous to the 'insurance rent' in the *Mark Rowlands* case. Whereas Mr Falconer contents that NOW, as well as DOL, had an insurable interest in the equipment after the time when it was delivered to DOL under the agreement, and he relies in support of this submission on *Petrofina (UK) Ltd v Magnaload* and on *Stone Vickers v Appledore Ferguson Shipbuilders*, and submits that to this extent NOW is in a similar position to the tenant in *Mark Rowlands*, nonetheless his argument cannot succeed in the absence of provisions in the agreement similar to the other features of the lease regarded by the Court of Appeal as the basis of its conclusion in that case. The mere coincidence of an insurable interest in the same property at the post delivery stage could not of itself provide the basis for a submission that NOW had a defence to the subrogated claim. Accordingly, the argument that there is available to NOW a defence to the claim by DOL in so far as it extends to post delivery losses which is founded on the reasoning of the Court of Appeal in the *Mark Rowlands* case cannot be sustained. The fact that DOL had already recovered its losses under the policy would be irrelevant by application of the well established principle confirmed by the House of Lords in *Parry v Cleaver* [1970] AC 1. This case could not on that basis be brought within Lord Reid's exception to the general principle required by considerations of 'justice, reasonableness and public policy'.

I therefore reach the conclusion that in respect of loss or of damage to property or expense caused by events occurring after delivery of the equipment in question by NOW to DOL the fact that NOW was insured under or entitled to the benefit of the policy effected by DOL, in so far as it provided all risks property insurance, affords NOW no defence to the claims in respect of such loss and damage advanced by way of subrogation or otherwise in DOL's counterclaim.

APPENDIX 9.10

Napier and Ettrick v Kershaw Ltd [1993] 1 Lloyd's Rep 197, HL

Lord Templeman: My Lords, when an insured person suffers a loss he will be entitled to the insurance money and may also be entitled to sue for damages anyone responsible for the loss. For example, if a house is insured for £100,000 against fire and is damaged by fire to an extent exceeding £100,000, the insurance company will pay £100,000. If the fire has been caused by a negligent builder or some other contractual or tortious wrongdoer, the insured person will sue the wrongdoer for damages. If the house has been damaged to the extent of £160,000, the insured person will receive damages from the wrongdoer of £160,000. At that stage the insured person will have made a profit since he will have only suffered a loss of £160,000 but will have collected a total of £260,000 from the insurance company and the wrongdoer. A policy of insurance is however a contract of indemnity and by the doctrine of subrogation the insured person must pay back to the insurer the sum of £100,000. The insured person will then have made neither a loss nor a profit. This appeal requires consideration of the principles and application of the doctrine of subrogation ...

When the hypothetical Name suffered a loss of £160,000 as a result of the negligence of Outhwaite the stop loss insurers were bound to pay and did pay £100,000 under the policy. The stop loss insurers immediately became entitled to be subrogated to the right of the Name to sue and recover damages in an action against Outhwaite, albeit that the amount payable to the stop loss insurers by way of subrogation could not be quantified until the action had been concluded and the damages paid. Nevertheless, in my opinion, the stop loss insurers had an interest in the right of action possessed by the Name against Outhwaite. That action, if brought by the Name, would be an action for the benefit of the Name and for the benefit of the stop loss insurers. Where an insurer has paid on the policy, the courts have recognised the interests of the insurer in any right of action possessed by the insured person which will enable the insurer to claim back the whole or part of the sum which he has paid under the policy. The courts recognise the interests of the insurer by allowing him to sue in the name of the insured person against the wrongdoer if the insured person refuses to pursue the action.

In *Randal v Cockran* (1748) 1 Ves Sen 98, a vessel was insured against loss and the insurance company paid the amount of the insurance when the vessel was captured by the Spaniards. The owner of the vessel became entitled to share in the prize money from the sale of captured Spanish vessels in accordance with a Royal Proclamation. The commission for the distribution of the prize money refused to entertain a claim from the insurer. Lord Hardwicke LC:

> ... was of opinion, that the plaintiffs had the plainest equity that could be. The person originally sustaining the loss was the owner; but after satisfaction made to him, the insurer. No doubt, but from that time, as to the goods themselves, if restored *in specie*, or compensation made for them, the assured stands as a trustee for the insurer, in proportion for what he paid ...

In *Blaauwpot v Da Costa* (1758) 1 Eden 130, a ship insured for £1,635 was seized by the Spaniards and the insurance company paid the sum insured. Subsequently prize money amounting to £2,050 18s 6d was paid to the executors of one of the former owners of the vessel. The executors were ordered to pay the sum £1,636 7s 3d to the insurers in accordance with the following judgment of the Lord Keeper, Lord Northington:

> I am of opinion that upon the policy and the peril happening, and the payment of the money by the underwriters, the whole rights of the assured vested in them. The assured had this right of restitution vested in them against the Spanish Captors, which was afterwards prosecuted by the Crown by reprisals. Satisfaction having been made in consequence of that capture, I think the plaintiffs are entitled to that benefit; and that it was received by the executors ... in trust for them.

In *Mason v Sainsbury* (1782) 3 Dougl 61, a house had been insured against damage and the insurance company paid under the policy when damages was caused by the riots of 1780. The insurance company brought an action under the Riot Act 1714 against the local authority. The insurance company sued in the plaintiff's name and with his consent and for the benefit of the insurance company. Lord Mansfield said that the contract of insurance was an indemnity and that 'every day the insurer is put in the place of the insured'.

In *Yates v White* (1838) 1 Arnold 85, the owner of a vessel sued the defendant for damaging his ship by collision. The defendant claimed to deduct from the amount of damages the sum which the plaintiff had received from his insurers in respect of such damage. The claim was rejected.

In *White v Dobinson* (1844) 116 LTOS 233, the ship *Diana* was insured against damage. After a collision the insurers paid £205 in respect of the damage. The owner of the vessel, Hicks, was awarded damages of £800 against a defendant who was held liable for the collision. Sir Lancelot Shadwell VC granted an injunction restraining the insured person Hicks from receiving and the wrongdoer Dobinson from paying the sum of £800 in respect of damages without first paying or providing for the sum of £205 in respect of which the insurers were entitled to be subrogated. On appeal, Lord Lyndhurst LC said:

> What is an insurance but a contract of indemnity? Then Hicks having received a full satisfaction under the award, what right has he to retain money received from the insurance office as an indemnity for damage ...? If Hicks had received an indemnity before the payment of the money by the company, it would clearly have been contrary to equity that he should retain that money. *Parke on Marine Assurances* says, that a contract to insure is one of indemnity only, and that the insured shall not receive double compensation for a loss; but in case the loss has been paid, and the insured afterwards recovers from another source, the insurer shall stand in his place to the extent of the sum they have paid.

Hicks then argued that the plaintiff had no remedy in equity and that his only course was an action in a court of law for money had and received. This argument was rejected and the Lord Chancellor said:

> Here the company have paid for a loss, for which the insured afterwards obtains full satisfaction, and it is contrary to equity that he should retain the money. The underwriters have a claim upon the fund awarded, and they are entitled in some shape or other to recover back the money they have paid.

The injunctions were accordingly upheld.

This is authority for the proposition that if application is made to the court before the wrongdoer has paid damages in respect of which an insurer is entitled to subrogation, the court will not allow the damages to be paid over without satisfying the claims of the insurer ...

It may be that the common law invented and implied in the contracts of insurance a promise by the insured person to take proceedings to reduce his loss, a promise by the insured person to account to the insurer for moneys recovered from a third party in respect of the insured loss and a promise by the insured person to allow the insurer to exercise in the name of the insured person rights of action vested in the insured person against third parties for the recovery of the insured loss if the insured person refuses or neglects to enforce those rights of action. There must also be implied a promise by the insured person that in exercising his rights of action against third parties he will act in good faith for the benefit of the insured person so far as he has borne the loss and for the benefit of the insurer so far as he has indemnified the insured person against the insured loss. My Lords, contractual promises may create equitable interests. An express promise by a vendor to convey land on payment of the purchase price confers on the purchaser an equitable interest in the land. In my opinion promises implied in a contract of insurance with regard to rights of action vested in the insured person for the recovery of an insured loss from a third party responsible for the loss confer on the insurer an equitable interest in those rights of action to the extent necessary to recoup the insurer who has indemnified the insured person against the insured loss ...

APPENDIX 9.11

American Surety Co of New York v Wrightson (1910) 103 LT 663

Hamilton J: First of all, with regard to the authorities, it was agreed upon both sides that there is no authority in the strict sense of the word directly in point. There are analogies in marine insurance and fire insurance, and I do not think it can be disputed that this form of insurance is one to which the analogy of both marine and fire insurance may legitimately be applied where the analogy is a true one, but beyond the general propositions that contribution is based upon principles of equity; that equality is sometimes equity; and that there should be a rateable proportion amongst those who have to contribute, I do not think the English cases advance the matter any further, because the whole difficulty in this case is upon what ratio the conceded contribution ought to be made ...

The result, therefore, is that the case comes before me as one of first impression. I am told it depends upon natural justice and upon principles of equity, and therefore I am driven to do the best with it I can. I think the key to the plaintiffs' whole argument is that the policy which the underwriters have subscribed must for this purpose be treated as though it were a separate policy on Kohler's honesty. I think, however the argument is put, it always come back to that. Under the Lloyd's policy the underwriters may have been liable for £40,000, if Kohler stole so much, or for any sum less than £40,000, according to the amount Kohler got away with, and therefore the point is that whereas the plaintiffs were running a line of £500 on Kohler and no more, the defendants were running a line of £40,000 on Kohler. Therefore, it is identical with the ordinary case of double insurance, where there is an insurance on the same adventure against the same risk for the protection of the same interest, and the insurances, two or more, differ only in the amounts insured ...

If it is once assumed that merely because the underwriters might have been liable for £40,000 in respect of Kohler, therefore that sum is to be deemed to be the amount of their insurance upon Kohler, irrespective of the other features in the policy, it may be that it follows that the proportions in which the plaintiffs and the underwriters ought to bear the loss are as £500 is to £40,000. But it appears to me that these two factors are not really commensurate, and that they are not having regard to the intention of the transaction, the two factors which ought to be compared. I am convinced that this view is the proper view by reason of the self renewing clause in the Lloyd's policy, the object of which is to re-adjust the insurance not only from time to time by annual periods, but at irregular intervals, according as losses occur, so that there may always be a total liability of £40,000 on the underwriters and a total insurance applicable, as occasion may arise, of £40,000 in favour of the assured. It appears to me that the problem of discovering some terms which can be rateably compared with one another between two policies so widely different as these is one that differentiates it so much from the simple rule of double insurance – namely, same interest, same assured, same adventure, same risk and different amounts – as to make any consideration drawn from those hardly applicable at all, and make it desirable to leave open the question whether anything that can be called contribution in the nature of double insurance arises in such a case as this ...

If the dishonesty had resulted in a loss less than the plaintiffs' line, then I think the plaintiffs' loss would have been that lesser sum. That sum would have been also insured by the defendants, and they would have contributed equally. In the event which has happened, there has been an insurance applicable to the protection of the assured in excess of the amount of the loss. The amount of the loss has also been in excess of the plaintiffs' insurance. It appears to me, therefore, that the figure comparable with the plaintiffs' risk of $2,500 is the figure which actually is the risk that has fallen upon the underwriters of $2,680, and that the total amount of the defalcations must be apportioned between the plaintiffs and the underwriters in the proportion of 2,500 to 2,680. An equal division of the two does not appear to me to be the principle which ought to be adopted in the event that has happened, because that disregards the fact altogether that in the case of the plaintiffs' policy there was a specific limitation upon the risk in respect of Kohler, whereas in regard to the defendants' policy there was not. This conclusion, which bases the ratio upon actual liability and not upon contingent obligations, seems to me to be more in accordance with the nature of the transaction, because it is clear that, were the principle as contended for by the plaintiffs, there would be an end, as a matter of business, of insurance in the form in which the defendants have subscribed, because on such a policy as theirs it would be impracticable to proceed by the method of a schedule of employees with a limit opposite each name, and they would be obliged to refuse any omnibus insurance such as they have granted, and be compelled to do the fidelity part of the risk in the form in which the American company does it, so that they might be protected against the happening of the event which the plaintiffs say determines the liability, namely, the whole £40,000 being treated as comparable with the smaller sum of $2,500. I think the £40,000 is comparable with the sum of £595,000, the aggregate of the limits taken on each one of the employees mentioned in the schedule, and in that form the business can proceed as it has been done in the present case, no doubt with great convenience to the parties ...

APPENDIX 9.12

North British and Mercantile Insurance Co v London, Liverpool and Globe Insurance Co (1877) 5 Ch D 569, CA

Mellish LJ: There are two questions to be considered. The first is whether, independently of the 9th clause, Rodocanachi's insurers were entitled merely to a contribution as against Barnett and Barnett's insurers, or whether they were entitled to be subrogated into Rodocanachi's rights, so as to be fully indemnified by Barnett.

Now, I do not know of any English cases on the subject of contribution as applied to fire policies; but I can see no reason why the principle in respect of contribution should not be exactly the same in respect of fire policies as they are in respect of marine policies, and think if the same person in respect of the same right insures in two offices, there is no reason why they should not contribute in equal proportions in respect of a fire policy as they would in the case of a marine policy. The rule is perfectly established in the case of a marine policy that contribution only applies where it is an insurance by the same person having the same rights, and does not apply where different persons insure in respect of different rights. The reason for that is obvious enough. Where different persons insure the same property in respect of their different rights they may be divided into two classes. It may be that the interest of the two between them makes up the whole property, as in the case of a tenant for life and remainderman. Then if each insures, although they may use words apparently insuring the whole property, yet they would recover from their respective insurance companies the value of their own interests, and of course those values added together would make up the value of the whole property. Therefore, it would not be a case either of subrogation or contribution, because the loss would be divided between the two companies in proportion to the interests which the respective persons assured had in the property. But then there may be cases where, although two different persons insured in respect of different rights, each of them can recover the whole, as in the case of a mortgagor and mortgagee. But, whenever that is the case, it will necessarily follow that one of these two has a remedy over against the other, because the same property cannot in value belong at the same time to two different persons. Each of them may have an interest which entitles him to insure for the full value, because in certain events, for instance, if the other person became insolvent, it may be he would lose the full value of the property, and therefore would have in law an insurance interest; but yet it must be that if each recover the full value of the property from their respective offices with whom they insure, one office must have a remedy against the other. I think whenever that is the case the company which has insured the person who has the remedy over succeeds to his right of remedy over, and then it is a case of subrogation.

Now, this is really a case of bailment of goods upon particular terms. If there were no special terms at all, but the goods were simply bailed on terms that they were to be taken reasonable care of, and the bailee insured the goods for the purpose of protecting himself against any liability he might sustain, and then they were lost by fire by the carelessness of the bailee, there would not be the least doubt that that would be a right of subrogation in the ordinary case of an action for negligence ... it makes no difference that here the bailment, instead of being in the mere ordinary terms that the bailee should be liable to take due care, is upon the terms that he should be absolutely liable in the case of loss by fire. That is not a contract of insurance so as to make the bailee himself an insurer, but it is really the terms of a contract of bailment by which he says: 'If the property is lost by fire I will not put you to proof whether it is lost by carelessness or not, it is part of the contract of bailment that I am absolutely liable in the case of a fire.' That is merely part of the terms of the contract of bailment …

APPENDIX 9.13

Australian Agricultural Co v Saunders (1874–75) 10 LRCP 668

Bramwell B: I am of the opinion that the judgment should be affirmed. I think no action could have been maintained against the underwriters on the marine policy in respect of the loss. It seems to me clear that the words of that policy did not cover any loss by fire during the time when the goods were stored on land, as described in the case. The time when they were so on land formed no part of any act of transshipment or landing and reshipment. The suggestion is that there was a virtual reshipment when they were delivered to the stevedore. But, in point of fact, they were not on board ship, and we must deal with words, in the absence of any usage, according to their natural ordinary signification. In point of fact, these goods were not in the course of landing and re-shipment. Inasmuch as the loss would not have been recoverable from the underwriters of the marine policy, I think the plaintiffs are not brought within the words of the 5th clause of the fire policy. It is true that there was a subsequent insurance of the goods, but the words must be read with some limitation, or the result would be absurd. The insurance elsewhere must, to be within the clause, be an insurance as to a portion of the risks covered by the policy sued on. If that is so, it seems to me this is not a case of double insurance such as was intended, inasmuch as the plaintiffs could not have recovered this loss on the marine policy. It was argued on the defendant's behalf that a possibility that the same risk might be covered by both the policies was sufficient under cl 5 to defeat the fire policy. I doubt very much whether that is so. I doubt whether a mere possibility that some portion of the risk covered by both policies might accidentally coincide constitutes such a double insurance as was meant. But whether this be so or not, there seems to be no evidence here of any such overlapping of the two policies as referred to; that is, of the possibility of any case in which both policies would have covered the same loss ... though the marine policy should attach to a loss by fire on a wharf while the goods were in the process of landing and reshipment, such a loss would not be within the fire policy. The latter, it seems to me, applies not to a loss by fire while the goods are on a wharf in the course of a landing and reshipment, but while they are in a place of storage. For these reasons I think there was not such a double insurance as to vitiate the fire policy, and consequently that our judgment must be for the plaintiffs.

APPENDIX 9.14

Boag v Economic Insurance Co Ltd [1954] 2 Lloyd's Rep 581

McNair J: In this case the plaintiff, Mr Graham Cochran Boag, a Lloyd's underwriter who subscribed to a Lloyd's All Risks Transit Policy, claims to recover from the defendants, Economic Insurance Company, Ltd, a contribution on the basis that the loss for which he, Mr Boag, has paid was also covered by the defendant company ...

Under that policy Mr Boag paid his proportion, seeing that the risks covered by it were all risks, which included, of course, loss by fire. He seeks to recover his proportion of the contribution from the defendants. In order to do that it seems to me that he has to establish: (a) that he was liable under his own policy; (b) that he has paid under his policy; (c) that the defendants were liable under their policy; and (d) that the defendants have not paid under their policy. (a), (b) and (d) of those requirements he has proved, or rather admitted: the main issue here is whether the defendant company were ever liable under their policy ...

On behalf of the defendant company, the primary argument is, as I understand it, that it is not sufficient to prove that the cigarettes were stock in trade of the company and were the stock in trade of the company in relation to their Hitchin Road premises: in other words, that in that in the definition of the subject matter insured which is found in item 1 one can find words of description which define the stock and materials in trade, and not merely words which limit the locality in which the stock in trade must be in order to be covered.

It seems to me that considerable assistance can be found in support of the defendants' contention in two phrases in the specification. First, I think the fact that the phrase 'Offices, cigarette making work-rooms, packing department and stock rooms' follows under a column headed 'Description', indicates that those are words of description rather than words defining any locality. Secondly, I think that the fact that in a further memorandum called 'Memo 2' it is provided that:

> For the purpose of determining where necessary the column heading under which any property is insured, the insurers agree to accept the designation under which such property has been entered in the insured's books,

also points to the fact that what the parties have in mind is that one will find in the books of Hitchin Road some reference to the subject matter insured. Furthermore, seeing that, according to the agreed statement of facts, there were other fire policies covering the Melson Street factory in addition to this policy covering the Hitchin Road factory, I think it is reasonable to assume that what the parties had in mind was that this policy should cover in effect under column 3 the stock and materials of the Hitchin Road Factory just as it quite clearly covers under column 1 the buildings of the Hitchin Road factory, and under column 2 the machinery and plant of the Hitchin Road factory. Unless there is some limitations to the description of the stock in trade which is covered under this policy, and seeing that the policy covers not only the Amalgamated Tobacco Corporation, but all their associated and subsidiary companies, if on any occasion as a matter of convenience any goods belonging to one of their subsidiary companies came and stayed overnight in a lorry in the Hitchin Road yard, although other wise they had no connection at all with the Hitchin Road factory, they would be covered.

That seems to me to be an unreasonable result. The conclusion which I have reached in that these particular cigarettes, never having formed any part of the stock and materials in trade of the Hitchin Road factory, never came under this policy at all. They never became part of 'the property' referred to in Memo 1, and therefore the extension granted by Memo 1 to cover 'the property whilst in the open yards' never attached. Accordingly, the plaintiff has failed to establish the third requisite, which I stated earlier, of his entitlement ...

APPENDIX 9.15

Weddell and Another v Road Transport and General Insurance Co Ltd [1931] All ER Rep 609

Rowlatt J: In this case, the claimant, Justin R Weddell, held a motor car policy issued by the respondent, the Road Transport and General Insurance Company, of which the following provisions are material. By s II(A):

> The company will at the request of the insured treat as though he were the insured any relative or friend of the insured whilst driving such motor car for social, domestic or pleasure purposes with the insured's general knowledge and consent, provided (a) that such relative or friend is not entitled to indemnity under any other policy.

By condition 4:

> If at the time any claim arises under this policy there is any other existing insurance covering the same loss, damage or liability the company shall not be liable ... to pay or contribute more than its rateable proportion of any loss, damage, compensation, costs or expense. Provided always that nothing in this condition shall impose on the company any liability from which but for this condition it would have been relieved under the provisions of s II of this policy.

The claimant's brother, Laurens W Weddell, had an accident while driving the claimant's car with the claimant's consent, and the claimant made the request to the company referred to in s II, that they should treat his brother as though he were the insured. Laurens W Weddell also owned a car, in respect of which he held a policy of the Cornhill Insurance Company, which contained the following clause:

> Section L: driving other cars. The indemnity granted under s A herein is hereby extended to cover the insured whilst driving any private motor car not belonging to him for pleasure or professional purposes if no indemnity is afforded the insured by any other insurance.

This policy contained no rateable proportion clause.

The question is, what is the position between the claimant, Justin R Weddell, and the respondents, the Road Transport Company. Laurens W Weddell cannot recover against the Cornhill Company, because he omitted to give them notice of the accident within three days, which by the Cornhill policy is a condition precedent to liability. The arbitrator has held that the Road Transport Company is liable, but by reason of condition 4 liable only for a rateable proportion, treating the Cornhill policy as being an 'other existing insurance' within condition 4.

For the claimant it was argued before me that he was entitled to recover in full; and the first point made was the Cornhill policy was not an 'other existing insurance' because, owing to the omission to give notice of the accident, liability under it could not be enforced. This, in my view, is too obviously unsound to require further notice. The position is to be regarded as at before the time for giving the notice expired.

The second point made, as I understood it, was that the Road Transport Company were liable notwithstanding proviso (a) to s II(A) relating to collateral insurance, but only on the footing that, according to the decision of Roche J in *Gale v Motor Union Insurance Co* [1928] 1 KB 359 ... that proviso was cut down by the operation of the rateable proportion clause; and that the Cornhill company were not liable, because in their case there was no rateable proportion clause. Therefore, the argument concluded, the Road Transport Company being alone liable, there was no other existing insurance, and they were liable in full. It was pointed out by Mr Jardine for the defendants that on this basis, if neither policy contained a rateable proportion clause, they would destroy each other entirely, and further, that such might be the position in this case, seeing that the proviso to the rateable proportion clause in condition 4 of the Road Transport company's policy seems to negative its use to cut down the proviso as to collateral insurance in the case of a friend or relative. However, he did not contend for this result, his clients being content to accept the decision of the arbitrator.

It is to be borne in mind that the risk covered by the clause as to a relative or friend is an extension of the scope of the policy. It gives protection to a person other than the assured. So, too, the clause in the Cornhill Company's policy covering the assured when driving a car not belonging to him is an extension of the primary purpose of the policy, which is to cover risks to and in connection with a particular car or cars of the assured mentioned in the schedule. The general purpose of the proviso seems to be to make such extensions operate only as secondary cover, available only in the absence of other insurance regarded as primary, not including, one would suppose, other insurance also of a secondary character. In my judgment, it is unreasonable to suppose that it was intended that clauses such as these should cancel each other (by neglecting in each case the proviso in the other policy) with the result that, on the ground in each case that the loss is covered elsewhere, it is covered nowhere. On the contrary, the reasonable construction is to exclude from the category of co-existing cover any cover which is expressed to be itself cancelled by such co-existence, and to hold in such cases that both companies are liable, subject of course in both cases to any rateable proportion clause which there may be. In other words, it is true to say that the relative or friend is not 'entitled to indemnity under any other policy' within the meaning of the Road Transport policy, and not 'afforded' indemnity 'by any other insurance' within the meaning of the Cornhill policy, when the other policy, negatives liability where there are two policies. At that point the process must cease. If one proceeds to apply the same argument to the other policy and lets that react upon the policy under construction, one would reach the absurd result that whichever policy one looks at it is always the other one which is effective.

In these circumstances, I come to the conclusion that the Cornhill Company (apart from the omission to give the notice) were liable notwithstanding that their policy contained no rateable proportion clause, and I confirm the decision of the arbitrator. It does not escape me that in the result the Cornhill policy is disregarded for the purpose of s II, but not for the purpose of condition 4. The considerations applicable are, however, different.

Rowlatt J: In my judgment, it is unreasonable to suppose that it was intended that clauses such as these should cancel each other (by neglecting in each case the proviso in the other policy) with the result that, on the ground in each case that the loss is covered elsewhere, it is covered nowhere. On the contrary, the reasonable construction is to exclude from the category of co-existing cover any cover which is expressed to be itself cancelled by such coexistence, and to hold in such cases that both companies are liable, subject of course in both cases to any rateable proportion clause which there may be. In other words, it is true to say that the relative or friend is not 'entitled to indemnity under any other policy' within the meaning of the Road Transport policy, and not 'afforded' indemnity 'by any other insurance' within the meaning of the Cornhill policy, when the other policy, negatives liability where there are two policies. At that point the process must cease. If one proceeds to apply the same argument to the other policy and lets that react upon the policy under construction, one would reach the absurd result that whichever policy one looks at it is always the other one which is effective ...

APPENDIX 9.16

Equitable Fire and Accident Office Ltd v Ching Wo Hong [1907] AC 96, PC

Lord Davey: The policies sued on were in the same form. They both contained a clause ... immediately following the operative part of the policy in these words:

> No additional insurance on the property hereby covered is allowed except by the consent of this company indorsed hereon. Breech of this condition will render this policy null and void.

And one of the conditions indorsed on the policies was as follows:

> 12 ... The insured must, at the time of effecting the insurance, give notice to the company of any insurance or insurances already made elsewhere on the property hereby insured, or any part thereof, and on effecting any insurance or insurances during the currency of this policy elsewhere on the property hereby insured, or any part thereof, the insured must also forthwith give notice to the company thereof so that the particulars thereof may be indorsed on the policy, and unless such notice be given, the insured will not be entitled to any benefit under this policy, and on the happening of any loss or damage, the insured shall forthwith declare in writing, to the company, all other insurances effected by him, or by any other person, on any of the property, and the giving of such notices at the respective times aforesaid shall be a condition precedent to the recovery of any claim under this policy ...

The question is, therefore, whether, the premium not having been paid either wholly or partially, the policy executed by the Western Assurance Company ever became effective, and this must be decided in the same way as if an action had been brought by the respondents on that policy. The Western company, it should be said, always repudiated any liability, and the respondents, of course, did not seek to enforce it.

It is plain from the language of the condition that it applies as well to the first premium as to any renewal premium, or indeed it may be said that it applies primarily to the first premium. The instrument must be read as a whole for the purpose of ascertaining the intention of the parties, and effect, so far as possible, must be given to every part of it. Their Lordships are of the opinion that the 11th condition qualifies and restricts the engagement of the company and converts what would otherwise be an absolute engagement into a conditional one, and that the words 'having paid' to the company are common form words or words of style for expressing the consideration for the company's engagement which would become accurate when that engagement became effective ...

The only meaning which can be given to the words is that the consideration must be not only expressed to be paid, but actually paid. Their Lordships cannot treat the fact of the executed policy having been handed to the respondents as a waiver of the condition or attach any importance to the circumstance. What was handed to the respondents was the instrument with this clause in it, and that was notice to them, and made it part of the contract that there would be no liability until the premium was paid. It is not a question of conditional execution, but of the construction of what was executed …

APPENDIX 9.17

Legal and General Assurance Society Ltd v Drake Insurance Co Ltd [1992] 1 All ER 283, CA

Lloyd LJ: In this case we are concerned with the right of contribution between co-insurers. The principles on which one insurer is entitled to recover from another in a case of double insurance have been settled since Lord Mansfield's day. Yet the particular problem which has arisen in the present case seems never to have been considered save for a decision in the Mayor's and City of London Court (see *Monksfield v Vehicle and General Insurance Co Ltd* [1971] 1 Lloyd's Rep 139). The question is whether that case was correctly decided.

The problem can be stated very simply on assumed facts. Suppose there are two insurances in the same interest on the same subject matter, each policy covering the same risks, so that each would be liable to the assured for the whole of the loss which has occurred. The conditions giving rise to a claim for contribution are thus satisfied. If the assured recovers 100% from Insurer A, Insurer A can recover 50% from Insurer B. Why? Not, clearly, because there is any contract between then, whether express or implied. There is no such contract. The insurers may be complete strangers. Each may have entered into the insurance in ignorance of the other. No: the right of contribution is based not in contract, but on what has been said to be the plainest equality, that burdens should be shared equally. For well over two centuries the right of contribution has been enforced, and the same principles applied, not only between co-insurers, but also between co-obligators in various other branches of the law, notably in the case of co-sureties ...

Now suppose that each of the policies contains a provision that claims must be notified within 14 days. Since the assured is entitled to go against A for the whole of his loss, he gives notice of claim to A within 14 days, and in due course recovers. No commercial purpose is served by the assured giving notice to B, since he does not intend to claim against B. Does the failure of the assured to give notice to B within 14 days deprive A of his right of contribution?

My answer to that question is No. Since the assured could have gone against B, had he chosen to do so, in which case B would have been liable for the whole of the loss, the burden as between A and B should be shared equally. It would be inequitable for either of the insurers to receive the benefit of the premium without being liable for their share of the loss.

A more difficult question arises, at any rate in theory, when the giving of notice is a condition precedent to liability. In such a case, B is not liable to indemnify the assured until after he has been given notice. So it could be argued that A cannot claim contribution, since B has never been liable to the assured.

The answer to this difficulty lies in a correct appreciation of the conditions which have to be satisfied for a claim in contribution. It is said that B must be 'liable' to the assured. Obviously, this cannot mean held liable. Nor does it mean presently liable. It is enough that B is potentially liable. In other words it is enough if the assured could have made B liable, instead of A, by giving notice in time, and taking whatever other steps might be required to enforce his claim.

But, when I say potentially liable, there is a sharp distinction between steps required to enforce a valid claim under a policy in force at the time of the loss, and a claim which never was valid, and never could be enforced. Thus, if B has a good defence to the assured's claim on the basis of misrepresentation or non-disclosure, there is no double insurance. Since the effect of the defence is that the contract is avoided *ab initio*, it is as if B had never been on risk at all. So also where the assured is in breach of condition, or has repudiated the contract, *prior* to the loss, even if (though this is not so clear) the repudiation is only accepted thereafter. It may be said that the distinction between breach of condition prior to the loss and breach of condition subsequent to the loss is a narrow one. So it may be. But the difference is crucial. For it is at the date of the loss that the co-insurer's right to contribution, if any, accrues ...

The fact that a co-obligator has no 'say in the handling of the claim' has never been an answer to a claim for contribution, whether in the field of insurance or in any of the other fields in which the equitable doctrine prevails. As to the right to repudiate, this would, as I have said, have been a good defence to a claim for contribution if the assured had been in breach of condition *prior* to the loss. The failure to distinguish between breaches of condition prior to the loss and a breach of condition subsequent to the loss by failing to give notice in time vitiates, if I may respectfully say so, the learned judge's conclusion. So I would hold that *Monksfield*'s case was wrongly decided.

Should it be overruled? When a case has stood for a long time, and may therefore be assumed to have been the basis on which commercial men have conducted their business, and settled their disputes, the courts are always reluctant to upset it. I do not regard *Monksfield*'s case as coming within that class ...

I conclude that the course of business would not be greatly disturbed if we now overrule *Monksfield*'s case. In taking this view, I bear in mind the widespread use of the rateable proportion clause ...

Nourse LJ: In other circumstances, I would have been content to adopt the reasoning of Lloyd LJ, but the division of opinion in this court makes it desirable that I should briefly express myself in my own words.

In the simple case, where one of two insurers, who are independently and unconditionally liable to the same assured for the whole of his loss, accepts sole liability for settling the claim, he has an undoubted right to contribution from the other insurer for half the coast of the settlement. There being no contract between the two insurers, the right of contribution depends, and can only depend, on an equity which requires someone who has taken the benefit of a premium to share the burden of meeting the claim.

Why should that equity be displaced simply because the assured has failed to give the notice which is necessary to make the other insurer liable to *him*? At the moment of the accident either insurer could have been made liable for the whole of the loss. Why should he who accepts sole liability for settling the claim be deprived of his right to contribution by an omission on the part of the assured over which he has no control? As between the two insurers the basis of the equality is unimpaired. He who has received a benefit ought to bear his due proportion of the burden.

While accepting that a line must be drawn somewhere, I am of the opinion that a denial of the right to contribution in circumstances such as these would be unduly restrictive and indeed inequitable. An attempt to state in general terms where the line ought to be drawn is neither necessary nor desirable. For present purposes it is enough to say that it ought not to be drawn so as to exclude the right to contribution in a case where, at the moment of the accident, each insurer is potentially liable for the whole of the loss.

As to the second question, there is little which I wish to add to the judgment of Lloyd LJ. The plaintiffs' right to recover the excess over 50% from Mr Arora himself under s 149(4) of the Road Traffic Act 1972 (re-enacted in s 15(7) of the Road Traffic Act 1988) seems to be a conclusive objection to their having a right to contribution against the defendants. I agree that the appeal must be allowed on that ground.

APPENDIX 9.18

Eagle Star Insurance Co Ltd v Provincial Insurance plc [1993] 3 All ER 1, PC

Lord Woolf: This appeal is from a decision of the Court of Appeal of the Bahamas. It concerns the rights to contribution between two insurance companies where both companies, having issued a certificate of insurance, are under a statutory liability to meet an injured person's claim when the driver responsible fails to do so ...

In his dissenting judgment, Melville JA followed the decision of the majority of the Court of Appeal in England in *Legal and General Assurance Society Ltd v Drake Insurance Co Ltd* [1992] 1 All ER 283 and concluded that Eagle Star was entitled to be indemnified by Provincial because Eagle Star had cancelled the policy prior to the occurrence of the collision ...

Approaching the issue as a matter of principle, in a case such as the present, where both insurers are required to indemnify a third party by statute, there can only from a practical point of view be two solutions to the question of contribution: either the insurers should contribute in accordance with their respective statutory liabilities so that, if they are statutorily equally liable, they will so share the loss; or contribution is determined in accordance with the extent of their respective liabilities to the person insured under the separate contracts of insurance. Of these two alternatives, the contractual approach is the more appropriate since the extent of their respective liabilities to the person insured will indicate the scale of the double insurance.

If the contractual approach is adopted, then there can be no justification for departing from the contractual position by creating for the purposes of contribution between the co-insurers a special cut off point which requires the position to be judged at the date of the loss. Having such a cut off point could produce results which do not reflect the contractual situation so far as liability to the insured is concerned. Looking at the issue from the insurer's and the insured's standpoint, it makes no difference if an insurer defeats a claim by relying on action taken before or after the loss has occurred. If both insurers would be under no liability to the person who would be insured, then they should share the statutory liability for loss equally irrespective of the date upon which they repudiated liability. If both insurers are liable at least in part to the person insured, then they should contribute to their statutory liability in accordance with their respective liability to the person insured for the loss. While this could have the result that the action of a person insured in relation to one insurer can affect the rights of contribution of the other insurer, this is an inevitable consequence of one insurer being able to take advantage of any limitation of his contractual liabilities on the question of contribution. However, before suggesting this could be unfair it has to be remembered that it is unlikely that the existence of the other insurer would have been known at the time that the contract of insurance was made ...

The only case which had a direct bearing on the issue now being considered is the decision of Judge Rogers in the Mayor's and City of London Court in *Monksfield v Vehicle and General Insurance Co Ltd* [1971] 1 Lloyd's Rep 139 ... That case was disapproved of by the majority in the Court of Appeal because it did not accord with their conclusion that the date of the loss was the cut-off point at which contribution had to be decided. However, far from that decision being wrong, it is correctly decided and properly regarded in *Halsbury's Laws of England*, 4th edn, London: Butterworths, Vol 25, para 539, as being support for the third of the conditions which *Halsbury* accurately states must be satisfied before a right of contribution can arise. That condition is that:

> Each policy must be in force at the time of the loss. There is no contribution if one of the policies has already become void or the risk under it has not yet attached; the insurer from whom contribution is claimed can repudiate liability under his policy on the ground that the assured has broken a condition.

In this case, therefore, both insurers are in the same position. They were both under a statutory liability in relation to the claim of the third party but they both would have been entitled to repudiate liability to the insured person. No distinction should be made in relation to their respective positions and accordingly they should each contribute equally to the amount payable to Mr Simms …

APPENDIX 9.19

Commercial Union Assurance Co Ltd v Hayden [1977] 1 All ER 441, CA

Lawton LJ: For over 200 years the British insurance market has had to cope with the problem of double insurance. By 1763, insurers had evolved a practice for dealing with it. In that year, Lord Mansfield CJ in *Newby v Reed* 1 Wm Bl 416, had to rule whether it reflected the rights in law of the assured and the two or more insurers. He decided that it did. The only report of his judgment is a short note made by Sir William Blackstone:

> It was ruled by Lord Mansfield CJ, and agreed to be the course of practice, that upon a double insurance, though the insured is not entitled to two satisfactions; yet, upon the first action, he may recover the whole sum insured, and may leave the defendant therein to recover a rateable satisfaction from the other insurers ...

From Lord Mansfield CJ's time until the present, counsel's researches have revealed few cases in British courts dealing with contribution between insurers when there has been double insurance and only one *American Surety Co of New York v Wrightson* (1910) 103 LT 663 ... which dealt with double insurance under indemnity liability policies with which this appeal is concerned. The facts of that case and the way it was argued make it a somewhat special one, from which it is difficult to extract principles of general application.

Despite the lack of guidance from the courts in the two centuries since Lord Mansfield CJ's time, the insurance market has coped with double insurance problems. According to the textbooks on insurance and insurance law, practices have evolved for the settlement of contributions; but the plaintiffs in this case did not plead or call any evidence to prove that such practices as there are amount to usages. It follows, in my judgment, that my task is to decide without reference to any existing practices what consequences follow in law from the fact that the plaintiffs paid out in full the assured who was also insured against the same risk with the defendant. That some consequences follow is not in dispute. Identifying them when there are so few judicial signposts presents the difficulty ...

I am not satisfied that comparing contribution between sureties and between insurers under indemnity liability policies is helpful. I prefer to look behind the application of principles to sureties to the principles themselves. The underlying principle is my judgment, that 'burdens' should be shared. I infer that this is what the phrase 'rateable satisfaction' in *Newby v Reed* 1 Wm Bl 416, means.

What is the burden under an indemnity liability policy? It is the claim which is made, not the claim which could be made. This kind of policy may be unlimited as to the amount of the indemnity, as it always is under motor car policies and often is under employers' liability policies, or limited as it almost always is under professional negligence policies. Even when a policy limits the amount of the indemnity, it is a matter of judicial experience that most claims are well below the limit. To ascertain the proportions of contribution by reference to the limits of indemnity would, in my judgment, be an odd way of sharing the burden in equity between insurers; and in cases where there was a limit under one policy but none under another, it would be a difficulty judicial task, probably an impossible one, to assess …

Further, using the limits as the basis for apportionment of contributions would be unfair to the insurer who gave a much higher limit for a small increase in premium. This case provides an example. The plaintiffs gave the assured a limit of £100,000; the defendant a limit of £10,000. The difference in premium was £1.

It is a matter of my experience both as a judge and a practitioner that the assessment of premiums under liability policies is based on underwriting experience backed up by statistical information and actuarial projections. The risk underwritten is at its greatest with small claims and at its least with large claims. It follows that the upper limits for claims can be increased with only a small increase in premiums. When there are two insurers with differing upper limits for claims, the inference I would draw is that they were both accepting the same level of risk up to the lower of the limits. If this be so, in my judgment, 'a rateable satisfaction', to use Lord Mansfield CJ's phrase, would be an equal division of liability up to the lower limit the burden of meeting that part of the claim above the lower limit would fall upon the insurer who had accepted the higher limit …

Under property policies, the insurer's task in assessing the premium to be charged is different from that of assessing premiums under liability policies. What may be a 'rateable satisfaction' under liability policies may not be so under property policies. My judgment is concerned solely with contribution under liability policies. The specific clauses providing for contribution in the two policies under consideration in this appeal, in my judgment, did not more than reflect the law as to contribution under liability policies. We were told that nowadays property insurance policies usually contain pro rata average clauses which have the effect of applying the same rules as to contribution to such policies as apply to liability policies. This may be so; but we were not required to construe such clauses.

APPENDIX 9.20

Mitchell, C, 'Defences to an insurer's subrogated action' [1996] LMCLQ 343

1 DEFENCES GOING TO THE INSURERS' ENTITLEMENT TO SUBROGATION

Even after he has been indemnified by his insurer, an insured can refuse to allow his name to be used in a subrogated action against a third party. If he does so, the insurer must bring an action in its own name, joining the insured and third party as co-defendants, and seeking a court order that the insured allow his name to be used. In these circumstances, the insured can obviously raise in his defence matters relevant to the insurer's entitlement to the order.

Less straightforward is the question whether a third party defending a subrogated action can ever raise in his defence matters relevant to the insurer's entitlement to subrogation. As a general rule, when dealing with a subrogated action the courts ignore the insurer's interest in the outcome of the action, and treat it as though it were brought by the insured for his own benefit. This approach is reflected in various procedural rules: a subrogated action must be brought in the insured's name, and the insurer does not appear on the record as a party to the action; any judgment against the third party must be entered in the insured's name, with the result that to obtain discharge the third party must pay the insured; the law applicable to the insured's cause of action governs the subrogated action, irrespective of the law applicable to the insurance contract; the insured is liable to make discovery in the action but the insurer is not; in the event that the action is successful, costs are awardable to the insured even though they have been incurred at the insurer's direction; in the event that it is unsuccessful, the burden of paying for the costs falls on the insured in the first instance; the fact that an insurer and its insured have previously agreed the amount of the insured's losses between themselves is irrelevant to the calculation of damages payable by a third party in a subrogated action; an agreement to refer the disputed matter of a subrogated claim to arbitration will be effective only if it has been made with the insured; an insurer sued in his own name by a third party cannot counter-claim for damages to which it is only entitled via subrogation to the insured's position. A third party cannot raise the insurer's contributory negligence as a defence to a subrogated action brought in the insured's name. A third party wishing to raise matters going to the insurer's entitlement to subrogation is therefore faced with the problem that the courts are liable to refuse to go behind the form of the action in order to consider matters which are strictly irrelevant to the only question it is constituted to address: viz, the question of the third party's liability to the insured. The cases discussed in this section suggest that a third party is only likely to succeed in persuading the courts to do this where he himself has a contractual relationship with the insurer, as a co-insured under the policy on which the insurer has paid, and possibly also as an insured under a separate policy ...

2 DEFENCES GOING TO THE THIRD PARTY'S LIABILITY TO THE INSURED

An insurer which has been subrogated to its insured's right of action against a third party can occupy no better position than that occupied by the insured, with the result that its subrogated action will be subject to whatever defences the third party is entitled to raise against the insured. Various defences of this kind will be discussed in turn.

(a) Insurer's payment to the insured

The courts have consistently rejected the argument that an insurer's payment should be taken to have discharged or diminished a third party's liability to the insured (and through him, to the subrogated insurer). More often than not, the courts' negative response to this argument is conditioned by the fact that the third party is a wrongdoer whom they wish to make primarily liable for the insured's loss. But the assumptions underlying this approach, particularly with regard to the efficient distribution of risk and to the punishment and deterrence of negligent wrongdoing, have been forcefully criticised by academic commentators. And where the third party is neither a tortfeasor nor a contract breaker but, for example, a tenant contractually liable to repair damage to property under the terms of a lease, with the result that his liability cannot be described as fault based, it is particularly hard to accept that in principle he should be made to bear the whole burden of a loss which the insurer has also agreed (and been paid) to bear.

It is sometimes asserted that subrogated recoveries constitute a windfall for insurers because they are not taken into account when premium levels are set. However, the writer's own research into actuarial practice in the British insurance industry does not bear this out; in 1994, the writer carried out a postal survey of the 12 largest motor insurers in Great Britain, and of the seven who replied to the writer's questionnaire, all seven stated that amounts recovered via subrogated actions are included in their records of recoveries of claims payments, with the result that they find their way into bottom line claims costs, and so influence premium rates.

(b) Factual defences

A third party will be liable neither to the insured, nor to the insurer bringing a subrogated action, if he can show, for example, that as a matter of fact an insured loss did not result from his negligence.

(c) Contributory negligence

If a third party tortfeasor is entitled to raise the defence of contributory negligence to an insured's claim, then he is entitled to raise the same defence to the insurer's subrogated action.

(d) Delay

If an insured's action against a third party in respect of an insured loss has become time-barred, his insurer's subrogated claim against the third party must also fail for that reason, and it is not open to the insurer to argue, for example, that the limitation period for its subrogated action should start to run from the time that it paid the insured, rather than from the time when the insured's right of action accrued ...

(e) Set off

A third party is entitled to raise in defence to a subrogated action any right of set off he may enjoy against the insured.

(f) Exclusion clauses

An insurer will be unable to recover in a subrogated action against a third party whose liability to the insured is excluded by an effective term of pre-existing contract between the insured and the third party, or by trade usage. The existence of such a term of trade usage may be a material fact which the insured should disclose to the insurer at the time of taking out the policy, and if its existence is not disclosed the insurer may therefore be entitled to avoid liability. However, if the insurer knows of its existence and pays the insured on the policy nonetheless, the insurer will be taken to have reaffirmed the validity of the policy, and presumably will be estopped from denying thereafter that it was liable to pay. An exclusion clause in a contract between an insured and a third party will be ineffective against the insured (and so against his subrogated insurer), if the third party commits a breach of contract of a kind which on proper construction of the contract disentitles him from relying on the clause.

(g) Benefit of insurance clauses

Where the relationship between an insured and a third party is such that it is possible to infer an agreement between them that they intend the insurance to enure to the benefit of the third party, the insured will lose his right to sue the third party in respect of insured losses, and his insurer will therefore be prevented from recovering via a subrogated action. Many of the cases in this area are concerned with subrogated actions by landlords' insurers against tenants, and the courts usually look to the terms of the lease for evidence of the parties' intentions. The case law suggests that they are most likely to hold that a tenant is intended to have the benefit of insurance on the property where the lease contains a covenant by the landlord to insure on his behalf and/or a covenant by the tenant to pay insurance premiums; certainly the absence of either covenant is likely to be fatal to a tenant's claim.

Some insurers insert an express term into their policies, that the coverage provided is not intended to ensure to the benefit of third parties. The question arises, whether such terms are effective to prevent a third party from relying on a benefit of insurance term in his contract with the insured? Support for the view that they are can be drawn from *Court Line Ltd v Canadian Transport Co Ltd* [1940] AC 934, where the House of Lords held that a benefit of insurance clause in a charterparty between an insured owner and a time charterer could take effect only as far as the rules of the owner's P & I club allowed and that, since the rules preserved the club's subrogation rights and prohibited the assignment of cover, it followed that the time charterer could not rely on the clause against the insured's subrogated action ...

It must be doubted, though, whether the more recent line of authority noted above, preventing insurers from bringing subrogated actions, is in line with this approach. More recent cases have tended to focus not on the terms of the insured's relationship with the insurer, but on the terms of his relationship with the third party, and to hold that, where he has agreed that the third party should not bear the burden of any insured loss, this effectively disqualified him from suing the third party, regardless of the terms of his relationship with the insurer.

The dissenting minorities of the Court of Appeal and the House of Lords in *Lister v Romford Ice and Cold Storage Co Ltd* [1957] 1 All ER 125 would have withheld subrogation from the insurer in the case on the ground that there was an implied term in the third party's contract of employment with the insured, that the third party should have the benefit of the insurance effected by his employer. It is submitted that this argument is more convincing than both the reasoning adopted by the majority of both courts in *Lister* (who allowed the insurer's subrogated action against the employee) and the reasoning of Lord Denning MR, in *Morris v Ford Motor Co* [1973] 2 All ER 1084 (who withheld the remedy from an indemnifier in an analogous position on equitable grounds).

(h) Settlements and releases

If an insured agrees to settle or relinquish his claim against a third party, the third party may well be able to raise this agreement in defence to any subrogated action subsequently brought against him by the insurer, even though the insured entered the agreement without his insurer's authority. If the settlement reached between the insured and the third party is clearly intended to refer only to the insured's uninsured losses, the insurer's subrogated action in respect of insured losses will not be affected by the agreement. There is also some authority that a subrogated action will not be affected by an agreement releasing the third party if the insurer has paid the insured before the agreement is entered into, and the third party is aware of this fact. Otherwise, the third party should be able to raise the agreement in his defence.

The insurer is not left without a remedy in this situation. If it has not already paid the insured when the agreement is made, and the policy contains a clause forbidding the insured from entering such an agreement without the insurer's consent, the insurer can repudiate its liability on the policy for breach of this express term. And, even in the absence of such a clause, the insurer will be entitled to set off against the amount payable on the policy damages for the insured's breach of his duty at law not to prejudice the insurer's right to recover from the third party via a subrogated action. And if the insurer pays the insured after the agreement has been made, it can recover damages from the insured for breach of this duty. But the insurer will not be entitled to recover damages from the insured if it fails to establish that the insured would have recovered anything from the third party.

(i) Unilateral discontinuances

If an insured commences an action against a third party independently of his insurer, and then unilaterally discontinues his action (that is, without having agreed with the third party that he should do so), the question arises whether the insurer can subsequently bring a second subrogated action against the third party on the same set of facts? It was held in *The Milwall* [1905] P 155 that a claimant could not be subrogated to a right of appeal that had been lost as a result of a discontinuance. But a discontinuance will not normally render an action *res judicata*, and the insurer should therefore usually be able to bring a subrogated action. If the insured is required as a condition of the discontinuance to pay the third party's costs in the first action, he (and hence the insurer claiming through him) will be barred from bringing a second action until these costs are paid. And if the court exercises its discretion to order as a condition of the discontinuance that no further action be brought, this too will prejudice the insurer's position. Otherwise, it should be no bar to the insurer's second, subrogated action that the insured's previous action has been discontinued.

(j) Judgments and stays

It sometimes happens that an insurer pays its insured in respect of a loss and, independently of the insurer, the insured then sues a third party for his uninsured losses only. If the insured recovers judgment against the third party, or accepts a payment into court with the result that further pursuit of the action is stayed, the insurer will not be permitted to bring a second action in the insured's name against the third party with a view to recouping its payments, as this would constitute an abuse of court process. In some circumstances, it can have the judgment reopened, or the stay lifted with a view to pursuing its subrogated claim, but it should be stressed that the courts will only exercise their discretion to do this if the insurer can bring forward some definite evidence of wrongful behaviour by the third party (for example, submission to the insured's claim in a deliberate attempt to disadvantage the insurer) – the fact that the insurer's position has been prejudiced is not enough in itself.

(k) Statute

Where a third party's liability to an insured is limited by statute, the insurer's subrogated rights against him will be similarly limited.

(l) Illegality

Where a third party is entitled to rely upon an *ex turpi causa* defence against an insured he can raise the same defence against the insurer's subrogated action.

CHAPTER 10

THIRD PARTIES (RIGHTS AGAINST INSURERS) ACT 1930

INTRODUCTION

This short chapter is concerned with the application of the Third Parties (Rights Against Insurers) Act 1930, alterations to which are now the subject of a Law Commission Report in 2001 (Law Com No 272; Scot Law Com No 184).

The title of the Act is misleading to anyone who is not a lawyer or an insurance practitioner. The application of the Act is not without its problems to those who *are* lawyers or insurance practitioners.

The reader might be forgiven for assuming that third parties, for example, victims of a negligent insured, can bring actions directly against the insurer of the negligent person. This is not so. Lack of privity of contract between victim and insurer prohibits such an action (Appendix 10.2) and no decision has recognised a duty of care to be owed by an insurer to a victim in these circumstances. In practice, however, it would seem that some insurers do choose to act in relation to a complaint made directly to them by a victim. Presumably, this may occur where the victim appears to have a 'cast iron' case against the insured. It may lead to an *ex gratia* settlement, which will often be less than the true value of the claim. When this does occur a fiduciary relationship between victim and insurer comes into existence. In *Horry v Tate and Lyle Refineries Ltd* [1982] 2 Lloyd's Rep 416, the victim was negligently injured at work. An offer of compensation was made by the insurers, intended to be in full settlement and satisfaction of the claim. The court rejected the effectiveness of the settlement, which was held to be financially inadequate. The insurer's dealings with the victim had created a fiduciary relationship, and the insurer was in breach of the duty in offering a lesser sum without informing the victim of his true legal rights in the matters.

Mr Justice Peter Pain explained:

> I take the view that they should have advised the plaintiff to think the matter over and to delay until he had had the opportunity of testing himself back at work and had had a proper opportunity of considering the offer. I held that the defendants were in breach of their duty of fiduciary care, in that they did none of these things ...

THIRD PARTIES (RIGHTS AGAINST INSURERS) ACT 1930

When does the Act apply? There are two requirements that trigger the application of the 1930 Act. One is that the insured has become bankrupt or has made a composition or arrangement with his creditor, if an individual; or the creditor, if a company, has been wound up. The other requirement is that the insured, either before or after that event, incurs a liability to the third party, in which case the insured's rights against his insurer are transferred and vested in the third party.

THE *POST OFFICE* CASE

It can be seen from the two requirements above that the Act is really only concerned with situations where insolvency of the insured arises. The reasons for the introduction of the Act are explained by Lord Denning, in *Post Office v Norwich Union Fire Insurance Society Ltd* [1967] 1 All ER 577 (Appendix 10.3). The plaintiffs claimed that contractors had negligently damaged their property. Before proceedings began the contractors went into compulsory liquidation. The plaintiffs issued a writ against the contractor's insurers. The plaintiff's argument was that every year they had about a dozen cases pending against bankrupt tortfeasors and, if the Act was to be construed whereby they first had to obtain judgment against the tortfeasor, followed by an action to enforce judgment against the insurer, then the cost and delay of two legal actions would be incurred, rather than one action against the insurer. Whilst the argument was successful before the trial judge, it was rejected by the Court of Appeal and the plaintiff's claim failed.

Lord Denning explained that the prime purpose of the Act was to reverse the pre-1930 situation whereby insurance payments owed to an insured went into the pool to the benefit of the general body of creditors. The Act's intention was to alter this unfair situation and to see that the insurance moneys reached the hands of the victim. The crucial legal question for the court was the meaning of the phrase 'liability ... incurred'. This was interpreted as meaning that there must be a legal liability, which has been established. At that point, the Act assigns to the victim the insured's right to be compensated by the insurer in the event of the insured's insolvency. It cannot be said that the accident or damage is the same as liability incurred.

THE *BRADLEY* CASE

It is necessary to obtain judgment, but that can create problems for the third party. What if the defendant company is no longer in existence, a not uncommon situation, particularly at times of economic malaise. Such a problem was faced by the House of Lords in *Bradley v Eagle Star Insurance Co Ltd* [1989] 1 Lloyd's Rep 465 (Appendix 10.4), wherein the House had to decide if the *Post Office* case had been correctly decided. The plaintiff had worked in a cotton spinning mill at various periods dating back to 1933. She developed byssinosis – a lung ailment associated with such a working environment. The mill was wound up in 1976. The defendants had been the insurers of the mill. The plaintiff sought disclosure of the terms of the policies issued by them to the mill. Her application was denied. The *Post Office* decision was approved: there could be no claim under the 1930 Act until liability against the defendant mill had been established by action, arbitration or agreement.

While the construction of the 1930 Act in the *Post Office* and *Bradley* cases is correct, the great hardship that *Bradley* causes, particularly in relation to actions for industrial diseases, is obvious. Within a short space of time, Parliament acted to alleviate the situation. Prior to *Bradley*, it was possible to resurrect a company and therefore obtain judgment against it, but only within two years of its dissolution. That period has now been greatly extended by s 141 of the Companies Act 1989 which alters s 651 of the Companies Act 1981. The new procedure is that, for actions founded on the 1930 Act, a dissolved company can be restored to the register at any time and the alteration has retroactive effect for 20 years prior to 1989.

There still remains, however, another difficult hurdle for the victim. Even if the company is restored to the register, perhaps many years after it was wound up, will it always be possible to discover which insurance company was on risk at the time of the accident? In 1990, the government, together with other relevant parties such as the Association of British Insurers (ABI) and Lloyd's, published a Code of Practice for Tracing Employers' Liability Insurance Policies in an effort to overcome this problem.

DUTY TO GIVE NECESSARY INFORMATION TO THIRD PARTIES

This is the title heading for s 2 of the Act and looks promising for third parties. Assume the third party considers that he has a strong case against the defendant. He is concerned however that the defendant's insurance cover may not be sufficient to meet the extent of such liability. He may also be concerned that the policy wording may in some way provide the insurers with a defence against the insured. Before embarking on costly litigation it would be a sensible precaution to try to discover the answers to these questions. Section 2 has been interpreted as not permitting such a voyage of discovery: see *Nigel Upchurch Associates v Aldridge Estates Investment Co Ltd* [1993] 1 Lloyd's Rep 535 (Appendix 10.5). The reason is that the 'rights' under s 2 are those 'rights' which are given under s 1 and, as we have seen above, those 'rights' have been interpreted as covering liability which has been incurred, and not contingent rights.

If, despite the potentially financially ruinous hurdles that confront the third party, he *does* decide to pursue his claim and does so successfully, there remains yet another possible danger. What if the insurance policy limits are insufficient to meet all the potential claims? This question arose in one of the Lloyd's litigation cases. In *Cox v Bankside Members Agency Ltd* [1995] 2 Lloyd's Rep 437 (Appendix 10.6), the total of successful Lloyd's Names claims exceeded the total cover held by the defendant members agents. Should payments be made on a 'first past the post', 'first come first served' basis, or should the court hold back and introduce some kind of rateable distribution? The 1930 Act is silent on this point and the Court of Appeal decided on 'first past the post'. These Names had taken the cost and risk of litigation and therefore it was fair that they should be compensated as and when they fulfilled the requirements of the 1930 Act.

THIRD PARTY TO HAVE NO GREATER RIGHTS THAN THE INSURED

The effect of the 1930 Act is to give to the third party a statutory assignment of the insured's rights against his insurer. If the insurer has defences available to him as against his insured, for example, non-disclosure, then the third party has no hope of enforcing the judgment against the insurer.

An example of such limited rights can be seen in the House of Lords decisions in *The Fanti v The Padre Island* [1990] 2 Lloyd's Rep 191 (Appendix 10.7). Shipowners who are members of P & I clubs can insure themselves in what is a shipowners' protection and indemnity mutual insurance society. It is usual for such policies to contain a 'pay to be paid' condition precedent to liability. This means that the insurer does not need to pay out on the policy until the insured has himself paid out to any third party. In the present joint appeals the insureds had been wound up before they discharged their liabilities to the third party. Section 1(3) of the 1930 Act states that any attempts between insurer and insured to avoid the liability of the insurer under the Act is prohibited. The third party unsuccessfully argued that the pay to be paid provision contravened sub-s (3). The reason for the decision was that until the insured paid out, he had no enforceable right against his insurer and, if he had no such right, then the 1930 Act fails to give the third party any greater right. This sequence of events did not come about on insolvency, but were part of the policy conditions, and therefore did not fall foul of s 1(3).

ROAD TRAFFIC ACT 1988

The 1930 Act covers motor vehicle claims by third parties but, more importantly, the Road Traffic Act 1988 allows claims by third parties against the insured motorist and, for certain uninsured losses, even without that motorist being declared bankrupt. Crucially, as with the 1930 Act, there must first be a judgment obtained against the insured. There is no direct right of action unsupported by a judgment against the insurer, no matter how blatant the insured's negligence is. A brief summary of the relevant sections will suffice.

Section 151

Where judgment has been obtained in respect of compulsory insurance liability, that is, death, personal injury and property damage below £250,000, such judgment must be met by the insurer irrespective of the fact that that insurer could avoid or cancel the policy (but see s 152, below). This last point is in stark contrast to the operation of the 1930 Act. The insurer is also liable to meet any judgment against an authorised driver who permits someone to drive who is not covered in the policy. The insurer is also liable in the case of a thief or joy rider. However, there is no liability where the victim at the time of the accident knew or had reason to believe that he was being carried in a vehicle that had been stolen or unlawfully taken.

Section 152

There are, however, occasions when the insurer will not be liable under s 151. There will be no liability to pay:

(a) if formal notice of the bringing of proceedings was not given to the insurer within seven days after commencement;

(b) where execution of judgment is stayed pending an appeal;

(c) if, before the event which gives rise to liability, the policy had been cancelled; and

(d) if the policy was obtained by misrepresentation or non-disclosure of a material fact and within three months after the commencement of the proceedings the insurer has obtained a declaration from the court to this effect.

It is also a requirement that the third party receives notice within seven days of the commencement of the action for the above declaration. The third party is also entitled to receive information relating to all those alleged non-disclosures or misrepresentations on which the insurer intends to rely.

These defences available to an insurer when faced with a claim by the third party are more apparent than real. This is because of the role played by the Motor Insurers' Bureau (MIB), under its various agreements with motor insurers. It will be sufficient here merely to quote part of the Uninsured Drivers' Agreement to illustrate the purpose behind the establishment of the

MIB. Paragraph 2(1), in part, reads:

> If judgment in respect of any relevant liability is obtained against any person or persons in any court in Great Britain whether or not such a person or persons be in fact carried by a contract of insurance and any such judgment is not satisfied in full within seven days ... then the MIB will ... pay or satisfy ... any sum payable in respect of the relevant liability ...

Section 153

This section largely duplicates the requirements of the 1930 Act but, as seen above, the Road Traffic Act 1988 does not require the bankruptcy of the insured as a prerequisite for enforcing a judgment directly against the insurer.

BANKRUPTCY OF INSURER

This chapter is concerned with the bankruptcy of the insured. In the event of a third party obtaining judgment, but the insurer concerned faces solvency problems, then the provisions of the Policyholders Protection Acts 1975 and 1997 will come into play (see Chapter 1).

REFORM

This chapter has been concerned mainly with the Third Parties (Rights Against Insurers) Act 1930, which is concerned only with the problems caused by the insolvency of the insured. For problems and suggested reform of the privity rule and insurance contracts, see Appendix 10.2. A most important article, which deserves to be read in its entirety is that of Mance (see Appendix 10.8). As the author states: 'It is time for the legislature to revisit the area covered by the Third Parties (Rights Against Insurers) Act 1930.'

The first important step has been taken along that road with the publication by the Law Commission and the Scottish Law Commission in their joint report, *Third Parties – Rights Against Insurers*, Law Com No 272; Scot Law Com No 184.

The Consultation Paper No 152 sets out a number of criticisms of the 1930 Act:

- third parties may have to establish the liability of the insured in separate proceedings before they can proceed against the insurer under the Act or obtain policy information;
- where the insured is a dissolved company which has been struck off the Register of Companies, third parties may have to restore the company to the register and establish its liability before they can proceed against the insurer;

- third parties may find their claims defeated because insurers can rely on defences which they would have had against the insured;
- the scope of the provisions in s 2 relating to who owes a duty of disclosure and as to what information should be disclosed is narrow;
- third parties potential claims under the Act may be defeated by the insurer and the insured settling the insured's claims under the policy before the happening of one of the insolvency situations set out in the Act;
- an insurance fund which is inadequate to meet the claims of all third parties is distributed to those who establish their claims first rather than rateably to all claimants;
- the territorial scope of the Act is unclear;
- it is unclear under English Law when limitation periods governing claims under the Act start to run and whether third parties can substitute themselves in arbitrations started by the insured against the insurer;
- the current operation of the Act may cause unnecessary costs to third parties, insurers and officeholders.

Several of the above criticisms have been referred to in the above text and the cases illustrating these points appear in the appendices to this chapter. The Law Commissions' proposals in relation to some of the above problem areas include the following:

- it should not be necessary for the third party first to establish the insured's legal liability;
- two events should be required to trigger the third party's rights: that the incident gave rise to the liability and the happening of one of the procedures or events set out in the draft Bill. Once these two events have occurred, the third party should then acquire the insured's rights under the policy. In this way the liability of the insured and the liability of the insurer would be dealt with in one set of proceedings leading to a saving of costs and time;
- an insurer should not be permitted to insist that policy conditions be met by the insured if the third party could meet those conditions. The most obvious example would be where the policy contains a notification provision;
- while there is no condemnation of other defences available to insurers, there is the tentative suggestion that there should be a causal connection between the breach and the loss. Reference is made to the Association of British Insurers' Statement of General Insurance Practice (see Chapter 4 and Appendix 4.10);
- it is suggested that disclosure of policy information should also be triggered at the time of the incident that gives rise to the liability, followed by one of the insolvency events. A list of information requirements is set out in the paper;

- legal expenses and health insurance would be included in any new legislation.

Appendix F to the consultation paper sets out briefly the position adopted in several countries in relation to the present problem. Many have adopted an approach similar to the 1930 Act, in requiring the two trigger responses of proven liability followed by the insolvency of the insured. Others have chosen a position that is more favourable to the third party. The consultation paper has provisionally suggested a midway position. As we have seen, it has suggested dropping the requirement for establishing liability and has replaced that with the trigger of the incident giving rise to liability. What has not been advocated is the French and Belgian approach of direct action. This approach, which is much the most favourable to third parties, has been explained by Tournois, 'Direct actions by victims against insurers of wrongdoers in France' (1996) 1 JIL 194, p 196:

> In order to protect the victim further, the case law and Acts have produced more autonomy for the *action directe*, with the result that the victim's rights are stronger than those of the insured. For instance, the insurer may not allege that the insured failed to perform his or her obligations specified in the insurance contract after the occurrence of the damage as a defence for compensation of the victim. This is a special case, however. As a general rule, the aim of French case law has been to join *action directe* and the victim against the insured in the same procedure, so that all issues concerning the liability of the insured and the insurance contract are decided at the same time.

This approach dispenses with the need of an insolvency event, which the consultation paper suggests be retained, as part of English and Scots law. Belgian law allows a direct action against the insurer, and policy defences are not permitted against a third party, where the insurance is compulsory in nature, although the insurer can seek to recover any sums paid for the third party from the insured.

THIRD PARTIES (RIGHTS AGAINST INSURERS) ACT 1930

APPENDIX 10.1

Third Parties (Rights Against Insurers) Act 1930

An Act to confer on third parties rights against insurers of third party risk in the event of the insured becoming insolvent, and in certain other events.

(1) RIGHTS OF THIRD PARTIES AGAINST INSURERS ON BANKRUPTCY, ETC, OF THE INSURED

(1) Where under any contract of insurance a person (hereinafter referred to as the insured) is insured against liabilities to third parties which he may incur, then:

(a) in the event of the insured becoming bankrupt or making a composition or arrangement with his creditors; or

(b) in the case of the insured being a company, in the event of a winding up order [or an administration order] being made, or a resolution for a voluntary winding up being passed, with respect to the company, or of a receiver or manager of the company's business or undertaking being duly appointed, or of possession being taken, by or on behalf of the holders of any debentures secured by a floating charge, of any property comprised in or subject to the charge [or of [a voluntary arrangement proposed for the purposes of Pt I of the Insolvency Act 1986 being approved under that part]],

if, either before or after that event, any such liability as aforesaid is incurred by the insured, his rights against the insurer under the contract in respect of the liability shall, notwithstanding anything in any Act or rule of law to the contrary, be transferred to and vest in the third party to whom the liability was so incurred.

(2) Where [the estate of any person falls to be administered in accordance with an order under s [421 of the Insolvency Act 1986]], then, if any debt provable in bankruptcy [(in Scotland, any claim accepted in the sequestration)] is owing by the deceased in respect of a liability against which he was insured under a contract of insurance as being a liability to a third party, the deceased debtor's rights against the insurer under the contract in respect of that liability shall, notwithstanding anything in [any such order], be transferred to and vest in the person to whom the debt is owing.

(3) In so far as any contract of insurance made after the commencement of this Act in respect of any liability of the insured to third parties purports, whether directly or indirectly, to avoid the contract or to alter the rights of the parties

thereunder upon the happening to the insured of any of the events specified in para (a) or para (b) of sub-s (1) of this section or upon the [estate of any person falling to be administered in accordance with an order under s [421 of the Insolvency Act 1986]], the contract shall be of no effect.

(4) Upon a transfer under sub-s (1) or sub-s (2) of this section, the insurer shall, subject to the provisions of s 3 of this Act, be under the same liability to the third party as he would have been under to the insured, but:

(a) if the liability of the insurer to the insured exceeds the liability of the insured to the third party, nothing in this Act shall affect the rights of the insured against the insurer in respect of the excess; and

(b) if the liability of the insurer to the insured is less than the liability of the insured to the third party, nothing in this Act shall affect the rights of the third party against the insured in respect of the balance.

(5) For the purposes of this Act, the expression 'liabilities to third parties, in relation to a person insured under any contract of insurance', shall not include any liability of that person in the capacity of insurer under some other contract of insurance.

(6) This Act shall not apply:

(a) where a company is wound up voluntarily merely for the purposes of reconstruction or of amalgamation with another company; or

(b) to any case to which sub-ss (1) and (2) of s 7 of the Workmen's Compensation Act 1925 applies.

(2) DUTY TO GIVE NECESSARY INFORMATION TO THIRD PARTIES

(1) In the event of any person becoming bankrupt or making a composition or arrangement with his creditors, or in the event of [the estate of any person falling to be administered in accordance with an order under s [421 of the Insolvency Act 1986]], or in the event of a winding up order [or an administration order] being made, or a resolution for a voluntary winding up being passed, with respect to any company or of a receiver or manager of the company's business or undertaking being duly appointed or of possession being taken by or on behalf of the holders of any debentures secured by a floating charge of any property comprised in or subject to the charge it shall be the duty of the bankrupt, debtor, personal representative of the deceased debtor or company, and, as the case may be, of the trustee in bankruptcy, trustee, liquidator, [administrator] receiver, or manager, or person in possession of the property to give at the request of any person claiming that the bankrupt, debtor, deceased debtor, or company is under a liability to him such information as may reasonably be required by him for the purpose of ascertaining whether any rights have been transferred to and vested in him by this Act and for the purpose of enforcing such rights, if any, and any contract of insurance, in so far as it purports, whether directly or indirectly, to avoid the contract or to alter the rights of the parties thereunder upon the giving of any such information in the events aforesaid or otherwise to prohibit or prevent the giving thereof in the said events shall be of no effect.

[(1A) The reference in sub-s (1) of this section to a trustee includes a reference to the supervisor of a [voluntary arrangement proposed for the purposes of, and approved under, Pt I or Pt VIII of the Insolvency Act 1986].]

(2) If the information given to any person in pursuance of sub-s (1) of this section discloses reasonable grounds for supposing that there have or may have been transferred to him under this Act rights against any particular insurer, that insurer shall be subject to the same duty as is imposed by the said sub-section on the persons therein mentioned.

(3) The duty to give information imposed by this section shall include a duty to allow all contracts of insurance, receipts for premiums, and other relevant documents in the possession of power of the person on whom the duty is so imposed to be inspected and copies thereof to be taken.

(3) SETTLEMENT BETWEEN INSURERS AND INSURED PERSONS

Where the insured has become bankrupt or where in the case of the insured being a company, a winding up order [or an administration order] has been made or a resolution for a voluntary winding up has been passed, with respect to the company, no agreement made between the insurer and the insured after liability has been incurred to a third party and after the commencement of the bankruptcy or winding up [or the day of the making of the administration order], as the case may be, nor any waiver, assignment, or other disposition made by, or payment made to the insured after the commencement [or day] aforesaid shall be effective to defeat or affect the rights transferred to the third party under this Act, but those rights shall be the same as if no such agreement, waiver, assignment, disposition or payment had been made.

APPENDIX 10.2

Hanson, J and Flynn, V, 'Cutting through confusion? The rights of third parties under insurance and reinsurance contracts' (1997) IJIL 50

INTRODUCTION

In English law, because of the privity rule only the parties to a contract can be legally bound by it and take rights under it. The rule has two basic aspects. The first is the 'burdens' aspect, which prevents contracting parties from agreeing to subject a third person to legal obligations without that third person's consent. The second aspect of the rule is the 'benefits' aspect. This aspect, which is referred to in this article as the 'privity rule' or 'third party rule', prevents A and B from conferring a benefit on C by their contract and giving C the right to enforce that benefit directly in his own name.

The privity rule has been regarded as an anachronism for years and has been under attack from academic lawyers, judges and ingenious practitioners. Many would say that it has been so thoroughly hedged around with exceptions that it causes little difficulty in practice and can, in any event, be avoided by altering the structure of any transaction. But this ignores two important considerations. First, the validity of any device used, based on the exceptions, to avoid the rule in factual situations not identical to those of a decided case will always be open to attack. Secondly, the cost of the legal advice and transactional restructuring necessary to avoid the rule in business dealings may run to millions of pounds each year.

Lawyers coming from a civil law system no doubt find the continued strict application of the privity rule in England anachronistic. It is, of course, still applied in many common law jurisdictions, or, where it has been relaxed, this is a result of relatively recent law reform activity. The difficulties which result from it are felt in all areas of commercial activity but are at their must acute in industries where the contractual structure is complex. This article will focus on the difficulties caused by the present third party rule for lawyers drafting insurance and reinsurance contracts. It will also examine the effect of the Law Commission's recent report recommending reform of the rule ... [*Privity of Contract: Contracts for the Benefit of Third Parties*, Law Comm No 242, 1996].

There are obvious situations where it makes commercial sense to relax the third party rule to permit an individual to claim benefits under an insurance policy taken out by someone else. An employer may take out group health insure or personal accident insurance on behalf of a group of employees. A building contractor may take out a construction all risks policy protecting itself, its sub-contractors, agents and employees against public liability and its and their property and works in progress during the construction process. A trading company with a captive may wish to be able to claim reinsurance proceeds directly from the reinsurers if the captive becomes insolvent, rather than proving its claim in the captive's liquidation.

(1) Exceptions

The exceptions to the third party rule recognise the commercial necessity, in certain cases, of permitting enforcement by third party beneficiaries. Some exceptions apply to all types of contracts, while some are specific to insurance contracts, the majority having been introduced by statute to address particular perceived evils. The following exceptions are directly relevant to insurance and reinsurance contracts:

(a) Using an agent: the doctrines of agency are often thought to constitute a general exception to the privity rule. In insurance and reinsurance contracts, it is well established that an agent can insure on behalf of all persons interested, whether he has authority to do so or not, and that those persons, provided they fall within a sufficiently identifiable generic class, may later ratify and thus become direct contracting parties. The doctrine of agency may also be the basis of composite insurances, whereby a single policy covers the different interests of a number of persons. In some common clauses, the underwriter agrees, if there is more than one named assured, that the policy is to take effect as if a separate policy is issued, and contract made, with each of them. The principal assured who is in direct contract with the underwriter thus makes a series of contracts on behalf of other assureds, supported by the consideration which it is deemed to provide on behalf of all of them.

(b) 'Commercial trusts': it is possible for a person to contract insurance on property in his own name for the benefit of a third party and to hold the loss payable under the policy (to the extent that it exceeds his own loss) on trust for those whose loss it is. This commercially useful doctrine, often described as a 'commercial trust', whereby a person with an insurable but limited interest in goods may insure them and in the event of loss recover the full amount of the loss or damage holding the balance over his own loss for others with an interest in the goods, is not in fact a trust at all. And it is not clear on what basis its enforcement rests. The exception is however commonly used. A jewellers' block policy will cover 'stock and merchandise used in the conduct of the assured's business ... whether the same be the property of the assured or entrusted to him or them for any purpose whatsoever'. If property left for repairs with a jeweller assured under such a policy was stolen, the indemnity payable to the assured would be held by him on trust as to the balance over his own interest for the owners.

(c) Creating a trust: a trust permits a beneficiary, C, to enjoy a legally enforceable right to property held by B on his behalf. This property may be a contractual promise made by A to B for C's benefit. It is safest to assume that a trust will only operate in insurance and reinsurance contracts to defeat the operation of the privity rule where this falls within well established pre-existing categories. There are trusts created in some types of policy by operation of statute. Otherwise, trust can either be express, implied or resulting and may either be a trust of the promise of the insurer or reinsurer to pay, or a trust of the policy proceeds once these have actually been paid. Finding a trust under English law where one has not been created expressly is not straightforward. Even where technical language is not used an implied trust may be found, but in the commercial context the courts are generally very reluctant to do so because of the serious consequences which creating a trust entails. Trusts have however been implied in group insurance where trustees take out group life, health or personal accident policies on behalf of a particular class of employees, but the cases depend heavily on their particular facts: where the policy provides for payment to be made to the employer on behalf of the employee and there is no other legal obligation requiring the employer to pass the payment on, it is unlikely that a trust will be found.

(d) Establishing a collateral contract ...:

The courts have been willing in certain circumstances to imply separate contracts between a contractual promisor, A, and the third party, C, but this approach necessarily depends on the facts of each case ...

(e) Assigning the benefit of the policy or the proceeds of it: where the benefit of a contractual obligation is legally assigned, this will permit the contractual assignee to sue to enforce the promise in his own name. Assignment of insurance policies is difficult and technical, because of the multiplicity of statutory provisions which govern assignment, together with the possibility of equitable assignments which exist alongside statutory or legal assignments.

(f) Promisee assisting the third party: where A and B contract for the benefit of C, B will always be able to enforce A's obligations, if he chooses to do so, and pass the benefit thus received on to C. This will however, be subject to the rules on insurable interest and B will find it impossible to enforce the policy unless he had sufficient interest to support it in the first place, and may find it impossible to enforce it for more than his interest.

(g) Direct statutory rights of action for third parties: the provisions of certain statutes make it possible for third parties benefited by or intended to be benefited by certain types of insurance policies to enforce those policies directly. At present the relevant provisions are s 83 of the Fire Prevention (Metropolis) Act 1774, s 151 of the Road Traffic Act 1981, s 11 of the Married Women's Property Act 1882 and the Third Parties (Rights against Insurers) Act 1930. The 1882 and 1930 Acts deserve some comment. Section 11 of the 1882 Act creates a statutory trust for certain types of life policy entered into by one spouse for the benefit of the other spouse or for the benefit of children of the marriage. Consequently, insureds under such policies become subject to onerous obligations as trustees and this may be highly inconvenient. It is arguable that the provisions of the Third Parties (Rights Against Insurers) Act 1930 do not constitute an exception to the privity rule at all. This is because the provisions of the Act give claimants against persons with liability insurance cover the right, in the event that they obtain a final quantified judgment against that person who has in the meantime become insolvent, to bring a direct action against the liability insurer for payment under the policy. It is difficult to construe a liability insurance policy as a contract for the benefit of an identified third party at all – it is in fact a contract which is taken out for the benefit of the person assured to protect him or her against possible liability to unspecified third parties.

(2) Problems remaining for third party beneficiaries

Despite (and perhaps because of) this web of exceptions to the third party rule, genuine difficulties remain in permitting any person who is not a party to an insurance or reinsurance contract from taking a directly enforceable benefit under it. The sheer complexity of the existing law means that it is virtually impossible to advise a third party confidently as to his rights. Additionally, problems involving third party beneficiaries can arise frequently. A loss payee clause, which directs that the insurance money is to be paid to a named third party in the event of loss, gives no rights to the loss payee unless it also constitutes or evidences an assignment of the assured's rights under the policy or evidences the fact that the designated person is an original assured. It is, however, beyond doubt that a loss payee clause which is not sufficient to constitute an assignment of the policy proceeds would nevertheless be a clause purporting to benefit a third party, and with a relaxation of the privity rule would be enforceable by that third party ...

The Law Commission's proposals

The Law Commission published a report in July 1996 examining the present English law and considering the practical difficulties caused by it in certain industries, one of which is the insurance industry. The purpose of the report was to produce a general reform scheme which could be employed throughout English contract law. In its report the Commission defined the circumstances in which it believes that third party beneficiaries should be able to enforce contracts.

The draft Bill which is annexed to the Commission's report provides as follows:

(1) ... a person who is not a party to a contract (in this Act referred to as a third party) may in his own right enforce the contract if:

 (a) the contract contains an express term to that effect; or

 (b) subject to sub-s (2) below, the contract purports to confer a benefit on the third party.

(2) Sub-section (1)(b) above does not apply if on a proper construction of the contract it appears that the parties did not intend the contract to be enforceable by the third party ...

The Commission's proposals also set out a second test which if satisfied permits a third party to enforce a contractual provision (cll 1(1)(b) and 1(2), above). This is where the provision purports to confer a benefit on that person; but such a provision will only create a rebuttable presumption where 'on a proper construction of the contract' it appears that the parties did not intend the third party to have the right to enforce the provision in question. The uncertainty which could be generated by this second test is obvious. It will, in the final analysis, be up to the courts to decide whether a contract, properly construed, indicates an intention by the contracting parties that the third party should have the right to enforce a particular provision.

In addition to satisfying one or other of the proposed tests of enforceability, the third party must be expressly identified in the contract by name, as a member of a class or as answering a particular description in order to have a right of enforcement. This will cause no difficulty under the first limb where the contract must contain an express term granting the third party the right of enforcement – in order to do this, the contract must at least refer to him by description. However under the second limb, it will not be possible for a person to argue that a particular provision of a contract purports to confer benefits on him unless he is at least referred to by description in the contract itself. Thus, for example, an agreement between a reinsurer and a reinsured to pay the proceeds of particular claims to a parent company could not be enforced by a subsidiary who stood to benefit because funds would have become available for the parent to invest in the subsidiary. The contract would be likely to contain no reference to the subsidiary, whether expressly, as a member of a class or by description. However, the contract might contain other obligations on the part of the reinsurer to benefit the subsidiary, such as, for example, notifying the subsidiary of direct payments. The subsidiary would then be able to enforce these obligations if it was either expressly given that right or if the reinsurer could not, on a construction of the contract, rebut the presumption that the reinsurer and reinsured intended it to have the right to enforce them.

Finally, the Commission's proposals seek to define when a third party benefit is to crystallise or become fixed. It is at this point that the law would prevent the contracting parties from exercising their normal rights to vary or cancel any contractual provision. The Commission recommends that the parties should be free to lay down detailed rules in their contract providing for the circumstances in which the third party's benefit may be varied. In the absence of specific provision, the default rule, in general terms, is that once the third party has either assented to the benefit or relied on it, it cannot then be varied or cancelled ...

APPENDIX 10.3

Post Office v Norwich Union Fire Insurance Society Ltd [1967] 1 All ER 577, CA

Lord Denning MR: In the days before the Act of 1930, when an injured person got judgment against a wrongdoer then went bankrupt, the injured person had no direct claim against the insurance moneys. He could only prove in the bankruptcy. The insurance moneys went into the pool for benefit of the general body of creditors: see *In re Harrington Motor Co Ltd ex p Chaplin* [1928] 1 Ch 105, applied in *Hood's Trustees v Southern Union General Insurance Co of Australasia* [1928] 1 Ch 793. That was so obviously unjust that Parliament intervened. In the Act of 1930, the injured person was given a right against the insurance company. Section 1 says that: 'Where under any contract of insurance a person ... is insured against liabilities to third parties which he may incur,' then in the event of the insured becoming bankrupt if he is an individual, or, in the case of the insured being a company, in the event of a winding up:

> ... if, either before or after that event, any such liability as aforesaid is incurred by the insured, his rights against the insurer under the contract in respect of the liability shall, notwithstanding anything in any Act or rule of law to the contrary, be transferred to and vest in the third party to whom the liability was so incurred.

Under that section, the injured person steps into the shoes of the wrongdoer. There are transferred to him the wrongdoer's 'rights against the insurers under the contract'. What are those rights? When do they arise? So far as the 'liability' of the insured is concerned there is no doubt that his liability to the injured person arises at the time of the accident, when negligence and damage coincide. But the 'rights' of the insured person against the insurers do not arise at that time.

The policy says that the company will indemnify the insured against all sums which the insured shall become legally liable to pay as compensation in respect of loss of or damage to property. It seems to me that the insured only acquires a right to sue for the money when his liability to the injured person has been established so as to give rise to a right of indemnity. His liability to the injured person must be ascertained and determined to exist, either by judgment of the court or by an award in arbitration or by agreement. Until that is done, the right to an indemnity does not arise. I agree with the statement by Devlin J in *West Wake Price and Co v Ching* [1957] 1 WLR 45 ... 'The assured cannot recover anything under the main indemnity clause or make any claim against the underwriters until they have been found liable and so sustained a loss'.

Under the section it is clear to me that the injured person cannot sue the insurance company except in such circumstances as the insured himself could have sued the insurance company. The insured could only have sued for an indemnity when his liability to the third person was established and the amount of the loss ascertained. In some circumstances the insured might sue earlier for a declaration, for example, if the insured company were repudiating the policy for some reason. But where the policy is admittedly good, the insured cannot sue for an indemnity until his own liability to the third person is ascertained ...

When the rights of the insured are transferred to the injured person, they are transferred on the ordinary understanding, that is, subject to such conditions as the contract provides. Under condition 3 of this policy, it is stipulated that:

> No admission offer promise payment or indemnity shall be made or given by or on behalf of the insured without the written consent of the company which shall be entitled if it so desires to take over and conduct in the name of the insured the defence or settlement of any claim.

In the face of that condition, I do not see how the insured could sue the insurance company before his liability is ascertained. He is not a liberty to say: 'I *admit* I am liable and therefore I ought to recover an indemnity.' He cannot make that admission: and therefore cannot sue.

In these circumstances, I think the right to sue for these moneys does not arise until the liability of the wrongdoer is established and the amount ascertained. How is this to be done? If there is an unascertained claim for damages in tort, it cannot be proved in the bankruptcy; nor in the liquidation of the company. But, nevertheless, the injured person can bring an action against the wrongdoer. In the case of a company, he must get the leave of the court. No doubt leave would automatically be given. The insurance company can fight that action in the name of the wrongdoer. In that way liability can be established and the loss ascertained. Then the injured person can go against the insurance company.

In confirmation of this view, I would remark that at the time when the Act of 1930 was passed, the practice in these courts was to keep secret the fact that the defendant was insured. It was misconduct on the part of counsel to indicate to the jury that the defendant was insured. If this Act had enabled the injured person to sue the insurance company direct, before liability was ascertained, it would have cut right across that practice. I am sure that at that date the legislature never contemplated any such thing. Of course, it is different now. We assume that the defendant in an action of tort is insured unless the contrary appears. Nevertheless, casting one's mind back to 1930, I am sure the legislature did not contemplate an action in tort against an insurance company direct.

There is a further point. If a third person, who suffered personal injury, could sue the insurance company direct, there would be a strange anomaly about the period of limitation. The action of the injured person against the wrongdoer (for the tort) would be barred after three years from the accident, but his action against the insurance company (as a transferee of the rights under the contract) would not be barred until six years from the accident.

This is simply a matter of procedure. I think the right procedure is for the injured person to sue the wrongdoer, and having got judgment against the wrongdoer, then make his claim against the insurance company. This attempt to sue the insurance company direct (before liability is established) is not correct.

I would, therefore, allow the appeal.

APPENDIX 10.4

Bradley v Eagle Star Insurance Co Ltd [1989] 1 Lloyd's Rep 465, HL

Lord Brandon of Oakbrook: In 1984, the appellant's solicitor decided to bring an action on her behalf against the respondents under s 1(1) of the Third Parties (Rights against Insurers) Act 1930. In order to enable him to have the necessary material on which to found the action, the appellant's solicitor required to have prior discovery of the relevant insurance policies issued by the respondents to Dart Mill Ltd ...

The Court of Appeal, rightly in my view, considered themselves bound to reach the conclusion which they did by an earlier decision of that court in *Post Office v Norwich Union Fire Insurance Society Ltd* [1967] 1 All ER 577 ... It follows that this appeal requires your Lordships to consider whether that earlier case was rightly decided ...

In my opinion the reasoning of Lord Denning MR and Lord Justice Salmon ... in the *Post Office* case, set out above, on the basis of which they concluded that, under a policy of insurance against liability to third parties, the insured person cannot sue for an indemnity from the insurers unless and until the existence and amount of his liability to a third party has been established by action, arbitration or agreement, is unassailably correct. I would, therefore, hold that the *Post Office* case was rightly decided, and that the principle laid down in it is applicable to the present case.

There is, however, a vital difference between the *Post Office* case and the present case. In the *Post Office* case, the wrongdoing company, although in compulsory liquidation, was still in existence. It was, therefore, still open to the Post Office, as Lord Denning MR explained, to bring an action, with the leave of the Companies Court, against that company, in order to establish the existence and amount of the liability in issue. By contrast, in the present case, because Dart Mill Ltd no longer exists and can no longer be resurrected, the same solution to the problem is not available, with the result arrived at by the Court of Appeal ...

The complaint may be made, and has been forcefully made on behalf of the appellant in this appeal, that the decision reached by the Court of Appeal, with which it is apparent that I fully agree, depends really on procedural technicalities and produces a result which is unfair to the appellant and gives an unmerited bonus to the respondents. In answer to that complaint, I think that it is right to draw attention to two matters: first, the historical reason for the passing of the 1930 Act; and, secondly, the inference to be drawn from the terms of s 1(2) of that Act with s 1(1) ...

It was not passed to remedy any injustice which might arise as a result of the dissolution of a company making it impossible to establish the existence and amount of the liability of such company to a third party. That kind of situation was not, in my view, contemplated by the legislature at all.

The significance of s 1(2) of the 1930 Act is this. In that sub-section, the legislature dealt expressly with the situation where a deceased's estate was ordered to be administered in bankruptcy, and provided that, if any debt provable in bankruptcy was owing to the deceased in respect of a liability against which he was insured as being a liability to a third party, the deceased debtor's rights against the insurer should be transferred to and vest in the person to whom the debt was owing. While the legislature dealt expressly in this way with the case of a deceased debtor's estate being administered in bankruptcy, it made no provision of any kind with regard to the case of a company dissolved after being wound up. This again leads to the inference that the legislature, in enacting the 1930 Act, did not have a situation of that kind in contemplation at all.

My Lords, for the reasons which I have given, and despite the natural sympathy which one is bound to feel for the difficulty in which the appellant finds herself, I would dismiss this appeal …

APPENDIX 10.5

Nigel Upchurch Associates v Aldridge Estates Investment Co Ltd [1993] 1 Lloyd's Rep 535

Barbara Dohmann QC, Official Referee: The plaintiff is an architect who sues for fees, damages, and a quantum meruit, his claim is included as a trade debt in an individual voluntary arrangement ('IVA') for the benefit of his creditors.

The defendants deny liability and counterclaim damages which very greatly exceed the claim. The trial is fixed for October, 1993 and is estimated to last 12–20 weeks.

The defendant counterclaimants are anxious to discover, before fully launching themselves into such a lengthy and expensive action, whether the plaintiff has appropriate insurance cover and what the limits of any cover are. Their requests for this information, made by letters dated 18 and 21 May 1992, have been refused on the grounds that they were premature: liability of the plaintiff to the defendants is not yet established. The plaintiff resists the present application on the same grounds.

The defendants make this application under s 2 of the Third Parties (Rights Against Insurers) Act 1930 as amended ...

Section 2 imposes a statutory duty to give information for specified purposes: namely of ascertaining whether any rights have been transferred and vested by the Act, and of enforcing such rights, if any. The question is what rights have been transferred in the present case.

It is clear from the language of s 1(1), and common ground between the parties, that the rights to be transferred must be 'in respect of the liability', not the insured's general rights under the contract of insurance. A contractual right to obtain the insurer's support for the defence of the third party's claim could evidently not be transferred: but is this (as counsel submits) because such is not 'in respect of the liability', or is this because there is no transfer of any right in respect of the liability until liability has been established? For while liability is incurred when a cause of action is complete, that is only the case *if* legal liability is in due course established. If it is not, no liability has been incurred.

Both parties rely on the decision of the Court of Appeal in *Post Office v Norwich Union Fire Insurance Society Ltd* [1967] 1 All ER 577 ... which was approved by the House of Lords in *Bradley and Eagle Staff Insurance Co Ltd* [1989] 1 Lloyd's Rep 465 ... It is clear that under a policy of insurance against liability to third parties the insured person cannot sue for an indemnity from the insurer unless and until the existence and amount of his liability to a third party have been established by a judgment of a court in an action, or by an award in an arbitration, or by an agreement between the insured and the third party, and the third party can be in no better position than the insured and can claim no greater rights. Accordingly, no right to claim an indemnity from the insurer can as yet have been transferred to the defendants in the present case.

But, says Mr Powell, the insured, though he cannot sue for an indemnity before his liability to a third party has been established, might sue earlier for a declaration, for example if the insurance company were repudiating the policy for some reason, see the observation by Lord Denning MR in the *Post Office* case ... However, what the Act transfers to the third party is the insured's right 'in respect of the liability', that is the right to be indemnified for his monetary loss in having to meet his liability to the third party. I do not find that s 1 transfers to the third party some contractual right to seek declaratory relief before a specific liability has been established.

Nor do I find that s 1 transfers to the third party a right to be indemnified contingent upon liability being established ...

Bradley was not decided by reference to s 2 of the 1930 Act, nor, apparently, is there any reported case deciding the meaning of that section. Mr Powell relies greatly on the phrase in s 2: '... any person *claiming* that the insured is under a liability to him.' If liability has to be established before there is a duty to give information, why have language which refers to claim? However, the word 'claiming' is in my opinion apt to cover the concept of someone asserting that he has established liability by one or other of the means listed in the *Post Office* case and in *Bradley*. I must, in any case, construe the Act as a whole, and must construe s 2 in the light of s 1. I am therefore unable to say that the duty to give information arises where liability is only claimed to have been incurred.

Mr Powell also sought to stress the phrases 'whether *any* rights have been transferred', and 'enforcing such rights, if *any*', so that his clients should be entitled to the information, and in particular to a copy of the policy, even if the answer is negative. I do not accept that submission. The phrases 'whether any' and 'if any', simply deal with the possibility that there were no rights against insurers to be transferred or enforced. The defendants, and other third parties in the like position, do not reasonably require to be told that they have not yet established liability and that hence no rights to any indemnity have yet been transferred.

Mr Powell urges that commercial common sense requires early information as to insurance cover, so that time and money are not wasted on what may turn out to be a fruitless effort. But the Act was not designed to deal with such mischief, it was designed to remedy the injustice that a creditor had no right to the proceeds as such of any third party insurance effected by an insolvent person when the insurance monies became payable to meet his claim. The monies payable by way of indemnity under any policy of insurance were available for distribution *pari passu* among all the unsecured creditors. The 1930 Act was passed to remedy that injustice, see Lord Brandon's speech in *Bradley* ... Other perceived injustices remain. I would add, however, that there is no great difference in practice between the insolvent defendant to a very large and expensive third party claim and the solvent defendant to such a claim: plaintiffs in fact rely heavily upon third party liability insurance, without any right to pre-judgment discovery of contracts of insurance or any other particulars relating to cover.

The application under s 2 of the 1930 Act is dismissed.

Note: The Law Commission proposals would allow the third party to require information relating to the insurance policy once the event has occurred and the insured is insolvent and not on liability being established.

APPENDIX 10.6

Cox v Bankside Members Agency Ltd [1995] 2 Lloyd's Rep 437, CA

Sir Thomas Bingham MR: The huge losses suffered by some Names at Lloyd's in recent years are common knowledge. Many of these Names blame their losses on the negligence of their members and managing agents. Numerous actions have been started. Some of these actions have run their course, leading to judgments for the plaintiff Names. Some actions are still proceeding to trial. In other cases claims have been intimated but actions have not yet been brought.

The agents so sued have the benefit of errors and omissions ('E & O') insurance cover, obtained either by individual agents or groups of agents. The extent of such cover is not known, but it is generally accepted that it will not be adequate to indemnify all the agents against claims which have been and may yet be established. Some agents are already in liquidation. Others will become insolvent if the claims made against them are made good. Thus the plaintiff Names' best hope of effective compensation in large measure depends on their exercise, under the Third Parties (Rights Against Insurers) Act 1930, of the agents' right to be indemnified by E & O underwriters. But because the E & O cover is accepted to be inadequate to meet all the claims which have been and may be established, it is of acute practical importance to the Names to establish the basis upon which the funds payable by E & O underwriters should be allocated.

One view is that Names are entitled to enforce claims, against agents when they are solvent or directly against E & O underwriters when they are not, as and when their claims are fully proved. This view, colloquially known as 'first past the post' or 'first come, first served', rests on a simple principle of chronological priority.

The competing view is that funds available from underwriters to meet claims by Names against insured agents should be rateably distributed among Names who have established or hereafter establish claims against each agent or (in the case of a group policy) those agents. The underlying rationale of this view is that chronological priority, particularly where this is not under the sole control of the litigant, should not determine the right to substantial recovery ...

Although the liability of the insured party arises at the time when he is negligent and damage results, the insured party only acquires a right to sue the insurer when the liability of the insured party to the injured party has been established so as to give rise to a right of indemnity ...

Nothing in the Act of 1930 in any case decided under it, in my view, provides a shred of support for any scheme of rateable allocation. The Act was addressed to a specific problem, which it effectively solved. It is not suggested that Parliament could have had in mind or sought to make provision in any way for a problem such as the present. Mr Martin argued that Parliament cannot have intended latecoming plaintiffs to be worse off than under the old law, which would at least have given them a rateable share in an insolvency fund swollen by the insurance proceeds. I agree that Parliament cannot so have intended; but that is because Parliament never considered such a situation at all ...

To my mind the most difficult problem of all is to be sure what fairness demands in this extremely complex situation. The ordinary rule of chronological priority involves obvious hardship for plaintiff Names who are not at the from of the queue. But there is obvious hardship for plaintiff Names if, having obtained favourable judgments at very great expense, they are denied the fruits of their judgments, perhaps facing bankruptcy before the judgments can be effectively enforced. It is said that the plaintiffs in the leading actions went ahead knowing that no ruling had been given on the basis of recovery, and that accordingly they took the risk that immediate recovery would be denied. That is true. But it was not unreasonable for the plaintiffs in the leading actions to judge that the rule of chronological priority would prevail in the absence of any contrary ruling, and these plaintiffs also took the financial risk of funding these expensive actions ...

One is of course sympathetic to all those who have suffered heavy losses in the Lloyd's insurance market, but I am not on balance persuaded that greater fairness would be achieved by a scheme of rateable allocation along the lines proposed by Mr Martin, even if this were feasible, than by application of the ordinary rule of chronological priority. I am not even persuaded that the court has a sufficiently comprehensive view of the whole complex scene to be able to determine with confidence where the balance of fairness lies ...

Note: The Law Commission proposals are that the *Cox* decision should not be changed.

APPENDIX 10.7

Firma C-Trade SA v Newcastle Protection and Indemnity Association (The Fanti) Socony Mobil Co Inc v West of England Ship Owners Mutual Insurance Association (London) Ltd (The Padre Island) [1990] 2 Lloyd's Rep 191, HL

Lord Brandon of Oakbrook: My Lords, these two appeals which have been heard together, raise the same important question of law in the field of marine insurance. It is a question which has been long debated but never until now come before the courts for decision.

The question arises in this way. It is the long established practice of shipowners to enter their ships in protection and indemnity associations (P & I clubs) for the purpose of insuring themselves against a wide range of risks not covered by an ordinary policy of marine insurance. By so entering one of more of their ships in a P & I club, shipowners become members of that club. P & I clubs operate on a system of mutual insurance under which the successful claim of one member is paid out of the contributions of, and the calls made on, all the members including himself. Each member is accordingly both an insurer and an insured. Among the wide range of risks covered by P & I clubs is liability incurred by members to cargo owners for loss of our damage to cargo carried in an entered ship.

P & I clubs have bodies of rules governing the relationships between the club and its members and between one member and all the other members. When shipowners enter one of their ships in a P & I club there comes into being a policy of marine insurance relating to that ship on the terms of the club's rules.

The rules of most, if not all P & I clubs contain what is commonly called a 'pay to be paid' provision. That is a provision, capable of being expressed in a variety of different terms, which stipulates that a member, in order to be entitled to an indemnity in respect of liabilities or expenses incurred by him, must first himself have discharged the liabilities or expenses concerned. It may happen, however, that after a member of a P & I club has incurred an insured liability, for example, a liability for loss of or damage to cargo carried in an entered ship, he is disabled by insolvency from discharging it. The question then arises whether the owners of the cargo lost or damaged are entitled, under the Third Parties (Rights Against Insurers) Act 1930, to recover an indemnity directly from the P & I club in which the ship concerned is entered. That is the question which arises for decision by your Lordships in each of these two appeals ...

The reasoning on which the judgments in the Court of Appeal proceeded can be summarised as follows. First, no cause of action against either club was transferred under s 1 of the 1930 Act, because neither member at the time of winding up had a cause of action. Such contingent rights, however, as the members had in respect of the third party claims concerned were so transferred; those contingent rights would only grow into effective rights of immediate indemnity on payment by the members of those claims ...

Secondly, under the rules of the two clubs it was the members who were subject to the burden of making payment and entitled to the benefit of the right to be indemnified. On the statutory transfer taking place it was more natural to treat both burden and benefit as being transferred to the third parties. The bundle of rights and duties which were transferred included the right or duty to arbitrate, the right of payment and the condition of prior payment. However, the condition of prior payment was impossible to perform once the statutory transfer had taken place and was therefore ineffective, leaving the third parties with immediate rights against the clubs for an indemnity ...

Thirdly, so far as s 1(3) of the 1930 Act was concerned, the condition of prior payment expressed in the two insurance contracts did not have the substantial effect of avoiding the contracts on the winding up of the members. Nor could it be said that this condition had the substantial effect of altering the rights of the parties on the members being ordered to be wound up. What was affected or altered by the members being ordered to be wound up was the ability of the members to enjoy their rights, and not the rights themselves. Those rights remained the same before and after the event save that, on the order for winding up being made, they were transferred to the third parties ...

Both clubs now appeal to your Lordships' House against the decisions of the Court of Appeal with the leave of that court.

My Lords, it is not in dispute that the 'pay to be paid' provisions in the rules of the two clubs which I set out earlier were terms of the contracts of insurance made between the members and the clubs. That being so, it seems to me that it is necessary, in order to determine these appeals, to pose and answer three questions. First, immediately before the members were ordered to be wound up, what rights, if any, did the members have against the clubs under contracts of insurance in respect of the liabilities which the members had previously incurred to the third parties? Second, did the 'pay to be paid' provisions, being terms of the contracts of insurance made between the members and the clubs, purport, whether directly or indirectly, to avoid those contracts, or to alter the rights of the parties under them on the members being ordered to be wound up, so as to render those provisions to that extent of no effect under s 1(3) of the 1930 Act? Third, having regard to the answers to the first and second questions, what rights against the clubs, if any, were transferred from the members to the third parties on the members being ordered to be wound up?

With regard to the first question, on the ordinary and natural construction of those rules of the clubs which contained the 'pay to be paid' provisions, the members were not entitled to be indemnified by the clubs in respect of liabilities to third parties which they had incurred unless and until the members had first discharged those liabilities themselves. In other words, payment by the members to the third parties was a condition precedent to payment by the clubs to the members. That interpretation of the relevant rules appears to have been accepted before Staughton and Saville JJ. In the Court of Appeal, however, it was argued for the first time on behalf of the third parties that under equitable principles the members were entitled to be indemnified by the clubs as soon as the existence and amounts of the liabilities had been established and without any need for them to discharge such liabilities first themselves ...

In the result, I would answer the first question by saying that immediately before the members were ordered to be wound up they had only contingent rights against the clubs in respect of the liabilities to third parties incurred by them. The rights were contingent in that it was a condition precedent to the members being indemnified by the clubs in respect of those liabilities that they should first have been discharged by the members themselves.

With regard to the second question, it was contended for the third parties that s 1(3) of the 1930 Act rendered the 'pay to be paid' provisions in the clubs' rules of no effect, on the ground that they purported, directly or indirectly, to alter the rights of the parties under their contracts of insurance on the members being ordered to be wound up.

There are, in my view, substantial difficulties in the way of this contention. The 'pay to be paid' provisions applied throughout the lives of the contracts of insurance made between the members and the clubs, imposing a condition necessary to be fulfilled before any liability of the clubs to indemnify the members could arise. There were not provisions which only applied on the happening of a specified event, such as an order for the winding up of a member. They applied equally before and after such an event. It is no doubt true that, on any member being ordered to be wound up because of insolvency, that member would be likely to be prevented from discharging any liability to a third party which he had incurred and so be unable to obtain an indemnity from his club in respect of it. This situation, however, does not result, directly or indirectly, from any alteration of the members' rights under his contract of insurance. It results rather from the member's inability, by reason of insolvency, to exercise those rights.

Both Saville J and the Court of Appeal rejected the argument for the third parties based on s 1(3) of the 1930 Act, and in my opinion they were right to do so. I would, therefore answer the second question by saying that the 'pay to be paid' provisions, being terms of the contracts of insurance made between the members and the clubs, did not purport, either directly or indirectly, to avoid those contracts, or to alter the rights of the parties under them, on the members being ordered to be wound up, so as to render those provisions to that extent of no effect under s 1(3) of the 1930 Act.

With regard to the third question, there are two views as to what rights against the clubs, if any, were transferred from the members to the third parties on the members being ordered to be wound up ...

It is abundantly clear from the express terms of the 1930 Act that the legislature never intended, except as provided in s 1(3), which I have held not to apply to the 'pay to be paid' provisions in the clubs' rules, to put a third party in any better position as against an insurer than that of the insured himself. Section 1(1) expressly provides that on the happening of any of the specified events 'his [that is, the insured's] rights against the insurer under the contract in respect of the liability shall ... be transferred to and vest in the third party ...'. Section 1(4) expressly provides that 'Upon a transfer under sub-s (1) ... of this section, the insurer shall ... be under the same liability to the third party as he would have been under to the insured ...'. The effect of these provisions is that, in a case where the insurer would have had a good defence to a claim made by the insured before the statutory transfer of his rights to the third party, the insurer will have precisely the same good defence to a claim made by the third party after such transfer. In the two present cases, it is not in doubt that the clubs would have had good defences to any claims to an indemnity made by the members before they were ordered to be wound up, on the ground that the condition precedent to their rights to such indemnity, namely the prior discharge by the members of their liabilities to the third parties, had not been satisfied. It must follow that the clubs had the same good defences to claims for an indemnity made by the third parties after the members were ordered to be wound up.

My Lords, having regard to the answers which I have given to the three questions discussed above, I am of opinion that the clubs' appeals against the decisions adverse to them made by the Court of Appeal should, in both cases, be allowed ...

[Note: The effect of the Law Commission proposals would be to reverse the decision in this case. Thus Clause 4(3) reads:

Where–

(a) rights of an insured under a contract of insurance have been transferred to a third party under section 1 or 2; and

(b) under the contract, the rights are subject to a condition requiring the prior discharge by the insured of his liability to a third party,

the transferred rights are not subject to the condition.

This change does not apply to marine insurance unless there is liability in respect to death or personal injury.]

APPENDIX 10.8

Mance, J, 'Insolvency at sea' [1995] LMCLQ 34

SCOPE

The trigger to the operation of the Act is insolvency, defined as bankruptcy, winding up and certain other allied events which can for the most part be ignored in what follows. Section 1(1) and (2) provide that, if either before or after the bankruptcy or winding up, a person who is insured against third party liability incurs any such liability, his rights against the insurer under the insurance contract in respect of the liability 'shall be transferred to and vest in the third party to whom the liability is incurred'. Section 1(5) excludes from the scope of the Act reinsurances, that is, insurances of another insurer's liability under his insurances.

INFORMATION

Section 2(1) says that a bankrupt or liquidator shall give at the request of any person claiming that the bankrupt ... or company is under a liability to him such information as may reasonably be required by him for the purpose of ascertaining whether any rights have been transferred to and vested in him by this Act and for the purpose of enforcing such rights, if any ...

Section 2(2) extends this duty to insurers: if any information given under s 2(1) discloses reasonable ground for supposing that there have or may have been transferred to him under this Act rights against any particular insurer, that insurer shall be subject to the same duty ...

ANTI-AVOIDANCE

The general structure of the Act takes care – possibly even too much – to respect the existing insurance relationship in all its aspects. But there are three provisions under this head. First, so far as any provision of any contract of insurance in respect of third party liability 'purports, whether directly or indirectly, to avoid the contract or to alter the rights of the parties thereunder' upon the bankruptcy or winding up of insured, 'the contract shall be of no effect'. Secondly, any provision purporting to prohibit the giving of information about the insurance under s 2 or to avoid or alter the insurance upon the giving of such information is also of no effect. Thirdly, by s 3, 'no agreement between insurer and insured after liability has been incurred to a third party and after the commencement of the bankruptcy or winding up and no waiver, assignment or other disposition or payment made after such commencement shall be effective to defeat or affect the rights transferred to the third party under the Act'.

It is well known that the 1930 Act was passed in the exhaust of the motoring revolution, to remedy a palpable anomaly displayed by two cases: *Re Harrington Motor Co Ltd* [1928] 1 Ch 105 and *Hood's Trustees v Southern Union General Insurance Co of Australasia Ltd* [1928] 1 Ch 793. This anomaly was that the proceeds of a third party liability insurance held by a bankrupt or company in winding up went into the bankruptcy or winding up 'pot'; the third party was remitted to any dividend to which he might (along with other creditors) be entitled out of the 'pot'. In the case of a tort claim not established until after the bankruptcy, the subject of *Hood's* case, he would not even receive a dividend. Atkin LJ commented in *Re Harrington* that, so long as this remained the law:

> ... it would appear as though a person who is insured against risks and who has general creditors whom he is unable to satisfy, has only to go out in the street and to find the most expensive motor car or the most wealthy man he can to run down, and he will at once be provided with assets, which will enable him to pay his general creditors quite a substantial dividend!

ESTABLISHING THE INSURED'S LIABILITY

The greatest problem now faced by the 1930 Act is that its draftsmen had not the advantage of the judgments of the Court of Appeal in *Post Office v Norwich Union Fire Insurance Society* [1967] 1 All ER 577 and of the House of Lords in *Bradley v Eagle Star Insurance Co Ltd* [1989] 1 Lloyd's Rep 465. Those cases decide that the cause of action under an ordinary liability insurance does not arise until the insured's liability to the injured third party has been established. This includes its quantum – or one would suppose (though this remains unclear) the existence of at least part of its quantum, since otherwise the enforcement of rights under the Act would, for example, have to wait final taxation of costs. Liability may be established by the third party obtaining a judgment or arbitration award against the assured, or by agreement between the third party and the assured. Until then, the third party has no completed cause of action under which he can sue on the insurance ...

The immediate consequence of *Bradley* was an amendment to the law – but only for the purposes of personal injuries and Fatal Accident Act 1976 claims. A clause was added to the Companies Bill 1989 which amended the Companies Act 1985 to allow the restoration to the register of a company for up to 20 years. Initially this was not to apply to companies dissolved more than two years previously. But ultimately the Government was persuaded that the result in *Bradley* was a windfall for insurers which justified retrospection. The two year limitation was removed. When the Bill was debated in the House of Lords, the flexibility of our constitution was displayed. Lord Templeman, who had dissented judicially, spoke twice legislatively to ensure the clause's survival, in the form of what is now s 651(5) of the Companies Act 1985 ...

The right to information from the insured and insurers about any liability insurance is on its face of great value to an injured third party. With information a third party can assess and pursue his claim knowing whether this is likely to be worthwhile. Any such expectation has however been largely nullified by an after shock of the *Post Office* and *Bradley* cases. In *Nigel Upchurch Associate v Aldridge Estates Investment Co Ltd* [1993] 1 Lloyd's Rep 535, it was held that before liability was established *nothing* was transferred to the third party, and that, since nothing had been transferred, there was in effect nothing about which a third party could reasonably require information ...

There is an alternative view. Third party liability either exists or not from the moment it is incurred. Any citizen is free to advise himself, with the aid of lawyers and others, as to his legal position. Why should it be regarded as unreasonable for a third party, if he has a reasonable basis for considering that third party liability exists, to ask for any relevant insurance policy to ascertain whether, if he be right about liability, there will be third party insurance making it worth his while establishing this through the courts?

At root the issue is one of policy ... To find the true policy in the context of insolvency, it is permissible, in this forum at least, to delve more explicitly into *Hansard*. On the third reading of the Bill, Mr RA Taylor MP proposed that the obligation to give information should extend to insurers. He was not it appears himself a lawyer, but he explained his case thus:

> I am concerned with the poor person, the ordinary pedestrian who is knocked down by a motor car and injured. In the majority of cases, this person would not be likely to be insured. He would, therefore, not have the assistance of expert legal advice unless he was in a position to pay for it. It is entirely with that type of person that I am concerned in the amendment.

He then made his proposal that there should be an obligation of disclosure, not merely on the persons stated in cl 2(1), but also on the insurer, continuing:

> I regard it as of great importance that the injured poor person should have the right to demand from the insurance company, before they resort to the expensive and uncertain processes of the law, all the relative facts disclosed to them, in order to enable them to make up their minds as to whether they have a substantial claim or not.

In response, the Solicitor General proposed what became cl 2(2), saying:

> I quite agree with the Hon Member that we might have gone a step further in Committee and imposed a similar duty on the insurance company themselves. I have drafted an amendment which I think will meet his desires.

So s 2(2) came into existence. Its purpose was to enable injured third party claimants to obtain pre-action discovery so that they might know whether it was worthwhile 'before they resort to the expensive and uncertain processes of the law' at all. It is the hindsight of *Post Office* and *Bradley* that gives rise to the suggestion that the right to pre-action discovery was only intended to be available *after* the third party had laboriously and expensively established liability.

In the circumstances, the material deriving from the Bill's third reading must, on the principle in *Pepper v Hart*, be a candidate for admission in any future litigation under s 2 of the Act ...

In summary, if, following *Bradley*, the Act falls to be interpreted in the manner decided by the *Nigel Upchurch* and *Woolwich* cases, this is a matter which the legislature could usefully reconsider. True, a plaintiff must normally take his defendant as he finds him. But the key to the 1930 Act is to recognise the fundamental difference between an insolvent defendant and other defendants. First, the insolvent defendant is and is known to be unable to pay. Secondly, despite his own insolvency, his insurers can and will often make the task of establishing liability against him extremely onerous, a problem which all the inventiveness of Lord Woolf's enquiry into access to justice will be hard put entirely to eliminate.

Sometimes even the amount of insurers' costs of defending the claim will come off the policy limit. In other cases insurers may defend under reservation of a right to repudiate the policy or policy liability. Of course, there are, in some modern schemes, provisions precluding or restricting the right to avoid or deny liability. Even then, the third party needs to know of their precise wording, and their protection may depend on the insured satisfying the insurer of matters such as his innocence of fraud. Once a company is in liquidation, its liquidator may not undertake this task with either the means or the motivation possessed by the injured third party. There can be little doubt that s 2 embraces information going to the status and validity of an insurance. There seems every reason for a third party to have such information immediately after the winding up. It could actually enable him to ensure that the anticipated benefits do arise …

The cases also demonstrate that the Act has failed to give effective protection after insolvency. The most basic problem is illustrated by *Farrell v Federated Employers Insurance Association Ltd* and *Pioneer Concrete (UK) Ltd v National Employers Mutual General Insurance Association Ltd*. In each case the insured company failed after its insolvency to pass on to its insurers a writ in accordance with a condition precedent to liability contained within the policy. In each case this meant the failure of the third party's subsequent claim to enforce the judgment against insurers under the Act. The reasoning was that the insured's obligations under the policy remain unchanged by the insolvency. There is no relevant anti-avoidance provision. The insured's failure to comply with them could not be regarded as a 'waiver … or other disposition' within s 3. The contingent or inchoate rights transferred to the third party on the insolvency never therefore mature into an actual right to indemnity.

I do not suggest that is unfair in any case where the insurer has not received notice of the action against its insured, and has not had the opportunity to take over its defence. I do, however, suggest that there is a strong case why a re-enactment of the 1930 Act should:

(a) make clear that a third party claimant has the right to information about any liability insurance immediately on the insured's insolvency, irrespective of whether the insured's liability has yet been established; and also

(b) make clear that he has the right to be treated as standing in the shoes of the insured for the purpose of satisfying any policy preconditions or other provisions triggering insurer's liability and of taking any steps necessary under the policy to preserve the policy cover and bring to fruition any contingent or inchoate rights to indemnity …

CONCLUSION

The Third Party (Rights Against Insurers) Act 1930 has served us quite well for most of its life. The recent exposure of weaknesses in the protection which it offers has resulted from a variety of factors: development or, as some might have it, clarification of the principles governing liability insurance; the increased prevalence of schemes of liability insurance, often compulsory for members of certain professions or groups; the increased practical importance of the Act in times of recession; the willingness of insurers over the last 15 years to fight points, which in former times they might have conceded or compromised; and perhaps a certain forgetfulness of the climate in which the Act was originally passed and the strength of the desire to protect 'the injured poor person' which so strongly motivated its passage.

Unattainable perfection is a problem for legislators as for judges and lecturers …

[Note: Additional articles include:

'What is left of the Third Parties (Rights Against Insurers) Act 1930' [1993] JBL 590;

'Liability Insurance – the rights of third parties' [1997] P & I 178;

'Claims against insolvent insureds' [1998] CFILR 98.]

CHAPTER 11

THE FINANCIAL OMBUDSMAN SERVICE: THE INSURANCE OMBUDSMAN

INTRODUCTION

When a policyholder's initial claim for compensation is rejected by his insurer, he is understandably aggrieved. The next decision will be whether or not to continue his claim with outside help. Until recently, the only viable option was to seek legal advice. Unfortunately, legal advice is expensive and as the majority of general insurance claims are relatively small in amount, the legal costs, together with the chance of an unsuccessful claim as the outcome, probably acted as a disincentive to the insured in seeking to take the matter further.

Legal aid is always a possibility, but for many years the justifiable criticism has been that the financial limits, whereby a person is eligible for assistance, have been far too low and thus unavailable to the vast majority of people. It is doubtful that conditional contingency fee arrangements will make any difference in insurance contract law.

Although insurers would argue that they are always prepared to give the insured a full and fair hearing, there is almost no way in which a party can be judge, in its own cause, and at the same time convince the other party that it has received an impartial hearing. Insurance complaints are newsworthy items, usually because the subject matter of the complaint may cut across the area of general public interest. There is little point in insurers spending vast sums in media advertising, only to see the work undone with one television programme or newspaper story highlighting an unfortunate confrontation in which the insured failed to gain compensation.

In order to defuse this type of adverse publicity, and to give the private policyholder access to impartial and, above all else, a free complaints body, several leading insurers set up, in 1981, the Insurance Ombudsman Bureau (IOB). It was heralded by many sources to be a great success.

Ombudsman schemes have proliferated over the last two decades. Such schemes cover central and local government matters, health, police, prisons and probation services. There is even a funeral Ombudsman! There were also several schemes dealing with complaints concerned with financial matters. Thus, there were Banking, Building Societies, Estate Agents, Investment, Pensions and Insurance Ombudsmen.

In relation to some of these latter schemes the Financial Services and Markets Act 2000 (FSMA) has made major administrative changes. (See Part XVI of the Act and Schedule 17.) The aim has been to create one statutory body, the Financial Ombudsman Service (FOS), to deal as informally and as cost-effectively as possible with the range of matters previously covered by eight schemes: the Banking, Building Societies, Insurance, the Personal Insurance Arbitration, the Personal Investment Authority, Investment (IMRO), SFA Complaints Bureau and Arbitration Service and the FSA Independent Investigator. The concept is to provide a 'one-stop shop' or a 'single port-of-call' for complaints. In its first full year of operations the FOS dealt with 259,848 telephone enquiries and 154,874 written enquiries which together resulted in 31,347 'cases' being transferred to the relevant division of the FOS. The intention is to seek to close 70% of cases within six months and 95% within a year. The cost of the service in its first full year of operation was over £20 m which represented a unit cost (that is, administrative cost per case) of £753. When considering these statistics it should be remembered that the FOS remit extends beyond insurance based problems.

In his first annual report the chief ombudsman of the FOS set out (see www.financial-ombudsman.org.uk) the main aims of the FOS as being:

- to provide consumers with a free one-stop service for dealing with disputes about financial services;
- to resolve disputes quickly and with minium formality;
- to offer user-friendly information as well as adjudication; and promote avoidance of disputes as well as resolution;
- to take decisions which are consistent, fair and reasonable;
- to be cost-effective and efficient; and be seen as good value;
- to be accessible to disadvantaged and vulnerable people;
- to be forward-looking, adaptable and flexible, making effective use of technology;
- to be trusted and respected by consumers and the financial service industry.

There are a number of basic rules set out in the FSA Handbook with regard to the FOS. The following summary concentrates on insurance based problems. (See: Appendix 11.1 for more details of the FOS procedures.)

An immunity from liability is extended to FOS Ltd, any member of its governing body, any member of its staff, or any Ombudsman. However such immunity will not apply if it can be shown that the act or omission has been in bad faith or in granting an immunity there would be a contravention of s 6(1) of the Human Rights Act 1998 (right to a fair trial). The award of the Ombudsman may be a 'money award' and/or an order requiring the member to take such steps as is deemed appropriate even if those steps would not be within a court's jurisdiction. The financial limit remains at a maximum of £100,000 as under the former IOB but recommendations can be made above the limit and the participant can choose whether or not to pay the excess figure. Any determination, if accepted by the complainant, is binding and final on the participant and may be enforced by the complainant in the courts. Decisions by the FOS would be subject to judicial review.

In order to seek the assistance of the FOS the complainant must be either a private individual who is, was or wanted to be a potential customer of the participating firm; a business with a turnover of less than £1 m; a charity with an annual income of less than £1 m or a trustee of a trust which has a net value of less than £1 m. Under the former IOB only private policyholders had a right to seek assistance.

It is possible to be an eligible complainant where a person was intended to be the beneficial recipient of an insurance policy or on whom legal rights to the benefits of a policy have devolved, for example, employees covered by a group health policy taken out for their benefit.

The territorial scope of the FOS extends to policies carried on from an establishment in the United Kingdom; however there are no limits on where the complainant resides.

To a large extent the previous ombudsmen schemes have been left to continue their work according to their original working practices. The advantages of the new statutory arrangements are that there will now be a streamlining of incoming complaints and the best of each scheme can be absorbed into the other schemes where appropriate.

There can be little doubt that the original Insurance Ombudsman Scheme established in 1981 has proven to be a great success both from the point of view of the consumer and for enhancing the (somewhat tarnished) reputation of the insurance industry. This success has played a major role in the growth of similar schemes and the creation of the present FOS. The IOB has also provided a role model for numerous other countries to follow.

A brief survey of the working of the original IOB will provide a greater insight.

In exercising any of his functions, the Ombudsman must pay due regard to the terms of the contract and act in conformity with any applicable rule of law or relevant judicial authority, with general principles of good insurance practice, with his terms of reference and with the Statements of Insurance Practice and Codes of Practice issued by the Association of British Insurers (ABI) (see Appendices 4.10 and 6.5). Most importantly, the Ombudsman is to be guided by the Statements when they conflict with any rule of law, if the Statements are more beneficial to the complainant. He is not, however, bound by his or his predecessor's own previous decisions, although he is to have regard to them. In order to determine the principles of good insurance practice he should, where he considers it appropriate, consult within the industry.

This last point exposes him to the possible criticism that he will become the spokesman of the insurance industry: but that would destroy his position as an independent adjudicator. Presumably, he will interpret this term of reference as providing him with the opportunity of obtaining a range of advice about insurance matters in order to gauge what response should be given to the complaint before him on a particular occasion. Even then, he should be free to criticise any firmly held industry practice as being unfair or out of touch.

The award making powers are considerable. Member companies must accept the decision, whereas insureds can reject it and proceed to exercise their legal rights in court.

Where the subject matter concerns a policy of permanent health insurance, he has jurisdiction where the benefits are up to £20,000 per annum. In other areas of insurance he has authority to deal with claims up to £100,000. If the above limits are exceeded, the Ombudsman's decision becomes a recommendation which does not then bind the member, but presents the basis of a possible equitable solution which the member might adopt. In situations where he has awarded a figure in excess of the above, the particular insurer has often agreed to abide by it.

In order to carry out his task, the Ombudsman has the power to request any information relevant to the subject matter of the complaint from the member.

Before the Ombudsman carries out any of his duties he must be satisfied that the subject matter for reference has been duly considered by the senior management of the company and that their answer has proved to be unacceptable to the complainant. Thus, the insured cannot set in motion a complaint merely because a branch office has not met his demands, he must exhaust the member company's 'appeals' procedure.

If the complainant has instituted legal proceedings, these must first be discontinued. If reference to arbitration has been made, this must be withdrawn.

The time limit within which he may receive a reference is six months from the date of the member company's final decision. It is possible for this rule to be relaxed.

Every year, the Ombudsman publishes his annual report and more recently he has issued case summaries as guidance. It is the annual reports that provide the real insight into the work and thinking of the scheme.

Policyholders should realise that an appeal to the Bureau more often than not results in a rejection of the complaint. The Ombudsman is bound by the rules of insurance law, subject as mentioned above, to the Statements of the ABI.

The number of references dealt with has grown steadily each year. In 1982, the first year of full operation, 179 adjudications took place and 1,053 enquiries relating to member companies were received. In addition, a further

1,272 enquiries relating to non-member companies were noted over which the Bureau had no jurisdiction. Of the cases adjudicated, the Ombudsman confirmed the members' decision in 141 cases (79%) and revised 38 (21%).

The 1997 Annual Report shows that the number of adjudications had grown to 5,000 and the Ombudsman revised 35%. The average award was £3,000.

The Bureau has varied the presentation in its annual reports and therefore it is not always easy to appreciate the branches of insurance that cause the most problems for the policyholder. If this could be done it would provide members with important information about points of conflict, which they might be able to remedy in-house.

Although the method of presentation of the workload has changed over the years, the general contents of the reports are similar. Troublesome areas arising from the preceding year are highlighted and the Ombudsman explains how he approached his decision making. The newly created FOS has continued with this approach.

If there is to be reform in general insurance law, either by legislation or by more self-regulation, the growing institutional wisdom of the Bureau must be seen as an important repository of information. A survey of some of the more troublesome areas gives some idea of where changes may be needed.

Lloyd's: The history of Lloyd's generally very much reflected a system of self-regulation and thus with little statutory intervention. However, it was decided that the FSMA should be extended to Lloyd's and therefore the dealings at Lloyd's are now subject to the overall supervision of the FSA.

Lloyd's has its own internal complaints department to which policyholders can turn. Ultimately, however, a complainant had a right to apply to the IOB. It was decided under the FSMA that the existing internal complaints arrangements should stay and that the FOS, replacing the IOB, should provide the additional avenue of complaint but only after the internal procedures have terminated or until eight weeks have passed since the complaint was lodged with Lloyd's.

European Economic Area (EU and EFTA)

Reference has been made in Chapter 1 to the single market in insurance. A follow-up is an intended single market in the broader area of financial services. The two markets will inevitably lead to cross-border consumer problems that will require solving. The FOS is working with similar organisations in other States. The declared intention is that the home State will establish a central point for advising consumers as to the availability of complaints-handling schemes in other States. (See Commission Working Document on the creation of an Extra-Judicial Network (EEJ-Net) SEC (2000) 405.)

The following is a summary of several Member States' systems which show a common core approach although there are areas of difference.

France: There are several voluntary schemes in France although a common post-box for all insurance companies has been established. But only where an insurer has joined one of the schemes can the consumer look for help. The leading scheme is the Ombudsman of the French Federation of Insurance Companies (FFSA) and, as in England, is funded by the insurance company members. Complaints can be made in French or English but decisions are given in French and, unlike the FOS jurisdiction, there is no financial limit to the award that may be made. Although, as in England, the process is free of charge, the decision, unlike England, is not binding on the insurer. An alternative scheme is the Ombudsman of the Association of Mutual Insurers (GEMA). It works in the same way as the FFSA, the only difference being that its decisions are binding on the insurer in the same way as the FOS.

Germany: The German scheme is voluntary and is run by the German Insurer's Association (GDV) and is available only where the insurer is a member of the GDV. It is a free service, it has no financial ceiling but its decisions are not binding on either party.

Sweden: The Swedish scheme is on a different footing to both France and Germany and closer to the FOS in nature. The National Board for Consumer Complaints is a statutory scheme that covers all financial institutions, products and brokers. It is publically funded and run by an independent body. There is no financial ceiling but the matter must be worth approximately £80. However the decisions are not legally binding on either side.

Netherlands. The Institute for the Treatment of Complaints in Insurance is a voluntary scheme open to all insurers and brokers but compulsory for insurers who are members of the Dutch Insurance Association. There are two Ombudsmen, life and non-life, it is funded by the industry. There is no financial ceiling, it is free to the consumer and, while its decisions are not binding, it seems that they are always followed (similar sentiment is to be seen in the Swedish scheme).

Belgium. The Belgian Ombudsman scheme is voluntary and funded by the insurer members. It is free of charge to consumers, it has no financial ceiling but its recommendations are not binding.

With various EU States establishing systems to cope with complaints from consumers it will come as no surprise that the EU has published its own views on the matter. Commission Recommendation on the principles applicable to bodies responsible for out-of-court settlement of consumer disputes (98/257/EC. See also Commission Recommendation 2001/310/EC, the aim of which is to provide a similar regime for matters not covered by 98/257/EC) recognised the need for a consumer user-friendly method of resolving such disputes, in part in furtherance of the declared aim of the single market, and called for such national bodies to respect certain minimum principles:

- the independence of the decision making body;
- to ensure the transparency of the procedure. Thus there should be an available explanation of the rules by which the body operates, the cost, the enforceability of its decisions, whether it is subject to legal, equitable rules or codes of conduct. There should be provision for an annual report sufficient for others to assess its results;
- adversarial procedures should exist whereby each side may set out its views;
- effectiveness should be measured by low or free access for the consumer and a short adjudication period.

Examples of the Bureau at work

Below is a synopsis of some of the more problematic areas that come to the Bureau. At the end of this chapter (Appendix 11.2), there are gathered together extracts from various years' reports dealing with individual topics. These should be read in conjunction with, in particular, Chapter 4 (Misrepresentation and Non-Disclosure) and Chapter 7 (Construction of the Policy).

Motor insurance

One of the continual problems under motor cover is the loss of a no claims discount when a company pays out in circumstances in which one driver considers himself to be innocent. Policyholders are obliged by their policies to notify insurers of an accident. They are not obliged, however, to make a claim. It is important that insurers make it absolutely clear to policyholders that they have this option when no damage to the other party has occurred. The Ombudsman declared his intentions (1982) to explore the feasibility of seeing if insurers could make it clear to policyholders that the option was theirs. Once the insured has put the claim into the insurer's hands, he cannot then dictate how the third party claim should be handled.

Another area of concern involves third parties who agree to pay the damages themselves but renege when presented with the bill. The Ombudsman suggested that a partial cure would be to adopt what exists in some countries, namely, a register of insurance cover that would assist the claimant in locating the other parties' insurers. To date, no such central register exists in this country.

Where two drivers are insured with the same company, the apportionment of blame and the resulting effect on no claims discount is often an area of contention. The claims manager may decide that both are to blame and thus both parties may lose their discounts. The problem was described by the Ombudsman as 'a most undesirable state of affairs'. It is difficult to see a solution. In one particular case, counsel's opinion was sought which had the effect of contradicting the claims manager's assessment of liability. It would clearly become a drain on the Bureau's resources if counsel's opinion was sought on too many occasions. What is important, is that insurers are aware of the conflict in such cases, and give the matter special consideration rather than treat it as purely an internal claims matter.

'Knock for knock' agreements are the cause of numerous complaints by motorists. These are intended largely as accounting procedures between insurers in an effort to keep down administrative costs. Unfortunately, it would appear that such insurers will often accept at face value the counter accusations of blame made by each policyholder, and thus deduct from the no claims discount. The Ombudsman accepted that this often happened, and called upon insurers to guard against the unfair implementation of these arrangements in cases where one party could show that he was blameless. Insurers should remember that they should defend the insured's rights, not simply accepting blame because it might be administratively easier for them to do so. There is little point in asking for witnesses if their views are not to be taken seriously. In recent years, knock for knock agreements between insurers have been abolished on the grounds that they did not lead to administrative cost savings as they once did.

Motor policies usually require that vehicles be kept in a roadworthy condition. A problem may then arise when the insured chooses to do his own repairs. If a subsequent crash can be traced to faulty home servicing, then insurers are right to reject the claim. The Ombudsman suggested that where an expensive or special car is insured, it might be worth considering a 'special' policy endorsement calling for professional servicing to be undertaken.

The value of a 'write-off' is often another area of contention. The Ombudsman appreciated that offers, rejections and new offers might occur when the claim was against a third party insurer because, as he explained, this is the realm of contentious business. Where, however, it was a claim of one's own insurer, the offer should not be one intended for further negotiation. It should be a genuine offer based on the best evidence available. That evidence has now been declared by the Ombudsman to be the cost to the insured of purchasing a car of similar quality on the open market.

An area of great misunderstanding in motor insurance is the scope of the cover to drive. Two specific problems arise. When other named drivers appear on the certificate of insurance, this does not give them cover to drive other vehicles, unless that other vehicle is insured for that driver. The misunderstanding arises because the certificate does give the policyholder, but not the other driver, the cover to drive another vehicle. But that leads to the second problem. The extension to drive another vehicle does not usually give comprehensive cover to the second vehicle, but only the basic requirements of the Road Traffic Act 1988, namely, cover against third party liability. The Ombudsman makes no criticism against insurers for this, it is merely a part of motor insurance law. He does suggest, however, that it might be worthwhile for certificates to reflect this all important point in clearly expressed language.

Repair costs and valuation of vehicles is another problem area. The Ombudsman's advice is clear. The principle of indemnity which runs through all insurance demands that either the repairs are paid for up to the policy limit or the pre-accident value of the car is paid in return for the salvage which then becomes the property of the insurer. The problem is often exacerbated by the wide difference between the two parties' views of the pre-accident value. That can only be worked out by negotiation. It should also be remembered that if the market value of the repaired car is less than its pre-accident pristine value, that financial difference is not one which insurers are bound to cover.

House buildings cover

One of the crucial misunderstandings in this area is the extent of the cover. Normally, policies make it quite clear that inevitable wear and tear, which ultimately will result in repair work, is not part of household buildings cover. There is little that insurers can do in educating the public to this fact other than by making it explicit in the insurance proposal form and introductory documentation and policy wording. In particular, insurers should be certain that their advertising does not mislead prospective policyholders.

A particular source of confusion for policyholders is the difference between standard cover and 'all risks' cover. The policy tends to list what is not covered under the latter. The public tend to think that everything is covered unless specifically excluded. What is needed is a more explicit policy document. Many companies have, in recent years, attempted to spell out more clearly the cover offered in their accompanying literature. One might be allowed the pessimistic view that policyholders only read the insurance documentation when a claim arises. At that date, it is too late to discover that the policy is more limited than originally presumed.

Insureds should be wary of accepting advice on insurance claims from those who stand to benefit from such advice. The example given by the Ombudsman concerns builders. They may give the impression that more extensive repairs are covered by the policy than is in fact the case. When the insurers point out that such repairs are not covered by the policy, the insured will be left to pay the bill. The answer is not to instruct builders until authorisation has been given by the insurer.

The policyholder should also remember that when he has presented an estimate to his insurer which has been accepted, he is not at liberty to give the work to another builder who will undertake the repair work for a lesser sum. The insurer could authorise the change of builder, but, if this is done, then the insurer would be liable only for the lesser sum. There is nothing to stop an insured from carrying out his own repairs, if competent to do so, and then charging the insurer a fair rate for the job. If the work is incompetently done, he would, however, have no further recourse to his insurer for further repairs.

The Ombudsman is frequently faced with problems relating to subsidence claims. It is necessary to distinguish subsidence from settlement. The latter occurs in new buildings, usually resulting in minor cracks and is often excluded from policies. But, where the damage is greater, it might then be described as subsidence and it is not always easy to decide if it is covered by the policy. The fact that damage may occur over a period of time raises the problem of liability where the house has had a change of owners. The Ombudsman's view is that so long as a substantial amount of damage has taken place during the new ownership, then his company should pay for the repairs within the policy wording. But, if it can be shown that there must have been considerable damage prior to the change of ownership, then the new insurer and insured should apportion the costs between them. If the new owner is aware at the time he takes out the policy that there has been some subsidence, then failure to declare this on the proposal form will amount to non-disclosure and the company will be able to avoid the policy. Even then, the Ombudsman prefers very specific questions to be asked relating to subsidence and not questions of a general nature.

Another source of friction between the insurer and insured relates to claims for decoration repairs resulting from a leaky roof. Policies normally cover only storm damage. They would not cover faulty roofs. The problem then is to define 'storm' or 'tempest'. Each case must depend on its facts, but what the Ombudsman looks for is usually a 'disturbance of the atmosphere which has to be present when any violent meteorological phenomenon' arises. The insured must be able to point to a particular storm on a particular day. What the insured cannot do is to point to an accumulation of bad weather over a given period, because this would lead to a claim which might hinge on a lack of maintenance rather than a storm.

A Court of Appeal decision in 1999, *Rohan Investments Ltd v Cunningham* [1999] Lloyd's Rep IR 190 (Appendix 7.15), has given the Ombudsman the opportunity to look at flood claims with a more sympathetic eye (see the case studies below under House Buildings Cover). In an earlier decision, *Young v Sun Alliance* [1976] 3 All ER 561, the word flood had been construed by looking at the context in which it is normally found in policies. That context is usually in conjunction with the words 'storm and tempest' and thus 'flood' was considered to reflect a sudden and large influx of water and therefore did not cover the damage caused by the seepage of water from a natural underground source. However Auld LJ in *Rohan* did not consider that *Young* had set down a rigid criteria and a flood was a flood whatever its original cause.

The Ombudsman fully supports the use of 'average' in indemnity insurance. Where insureds have negligently or fraudulently under estimated the value of buildings or contents, then they deprive insurers of a full premium. It is understandable that in such a situation full indemnification should not take place. If the correct figure is chosen at the outset, the use of index linking usually takes care of the increasing value of the goods or building (see Chapter 8).

There could be a problem in deciding on the correct figure at the outset. Where a building society or bank provides the mortgage advance and advises on the value of the building, they owe it to the borrower to select an accurate figure. The Ombudsman has been faced with cases where the figure only represents the value of the advance and not the value of the building. This will lead to under insurance and, if the insurer refuses to pay in full, the borrower should be able to sue the lender, unless it is made quite clear to him that the value of the advance should not be used as the insurance figure.

House contents cover

An elementary rule of insurance law is that contents insurance applies to the address given on the proposal form. The type of building and the geographic location are usually important indicators for setting the premium. Where an insured, therefore, changes his address he should inform the insurer of this. The change may involve a lower or higher premium. When moving from one place to another it is wise to take out transit insurance to cover such a move.

Multiple occupancy also presents problems. The incidence of theft is higher where several people share accommodation. Insurers prefer to insure single occupancy situations and, therefore, full disclosure should be made to the insurers where such occupancy is not the case. This would affect young people sharing a house or flat and even couples who live together but are not married could find themselves faced with difficulties in the event of a claim.

Another area of conflict is cover for accidental loss and damage. Claims for such loss have been high, and it is now the normal thing that a policy will not cover such losses unless an 'all risks' extension is added to the policy. The wording of such an extension is often itself narrowly worded. Only by asking for and paying for a wide inclusion of such losses will the insured obtain such cover. This is a topic which reflects the constant, underlying problem in insurance, that the insured believes that he has far wider cover than in fact he has. Such cover is usually available, but at a much higher premium.

A related 'all risks' problem is where goods are lost or stolen outside the building. Policies will not normally cover such losses unless the 'all risks' section has been purchased. Loss from a vehicle is a typical example. The motor policy will often not cover such items, or if it does, then only up to a certain (low) financial limit.

Most policies under this heading, and also travel insurance, require the policyholder to take reasonable steps to safeguard his property. The Ombudsman appears to interpret this strictly against the insured. Leaving valuable objects in view on the back seat of a car is not taking reasonable steps. Leaving valuables on the beach while you go swimming is a sign of not taking reasonable care.

In the first example, there is an obvious alternative, namely, lock the object in the boot of the car. In the second example, it is not easy to see what the insured is expected to do. The Ombudsman's advice is simply stated, 'exercise towards the goods the same care as if they were not insured'. One would have some sympathy with the insured who responded that the whole point of taking out the insurance was to cover the occasions when he failed to heed that warning. The problem is not easy to answer because there is a grey area between doing what is obviously reckless and doing what is obviously ideally cautious.

The Ombudsman has clearly been faced with numerous problems under this heading. In his 1985 report, he explained the questions he posed himself in deciding on a claim:

> What was the value of the goods? What was the reason for having them in the place from which they were stolen? What precautions were actually taken to safeguard them? Were there any alternatives open to the policyholder?

The decision in *Port-Rose v Phoenix Assurance* (1986) 136 NLJ 333, clearly posed problems for him. Although, in his 1986 report, he said that he had not been influenced by the decision, it should be remembered that he is bound by case precedents. While repeating the guidelines quoted above he also said that there was a 'fundamental difference between failing to take the care appropriate to the value of the property at risk, and taking such care and yet losing the property due to momentary inadvertence when one's attention is distracted'. This presumably would then cover the facts of the *Port-Rose* case.

Claims relating to jewellery often cause concern for the Ombudsman. The problem usually revolves around valuations. Where the insured had jewellery valued it may turn out that an over valuation has taken place. If this is so, then only the true value will be the level of indemnity required. If the over valuation is not the fault of the insured, the Ombudsman has directed that the extra premium paid should be refunded. This, of course, is no great consolation to the insured. He has gone to the trouble of paying for a valuation and understandably, believes that it is a correct valuation. He has paid his premium based on that valuation. The fact that valuations are sometimes inflated, perhaps to increase the fee payable, is not something which the average insured appreciates, nor should he.

Policies often reserve for the insurer the right to choose to replace the jewellery or to pay a cash indemnity. It is for the insurer to choose which option he will follow. If he does intend to replace the item, then he is obliged to match the lost piece with something that is almost identical and acceptable to a reasonable insured.

The Ombudsman has been critical of insurers' practices that have grown up in the wake of the decision in *Geismar v Sun Alliance and London Insurance Ltd and Another* [1978] QB 383 (Appendix 3.16. In that case, the plaintiff had imported goods which he had not declared at customs. He later insured them and a loss occurred. The company was not liable to indemnify the insured because to do so would allow him to profit from his illegal behaviour. It appears that some claims investigators began to ask the insured if duty had been paid on imported goods. If it had not been paid, the claim was often rejected. But it must be remembered that the obligation is to declare goods. It may be that they were within the permitted import limits. Thus, failure to pay is not the same as failure to declare.

Damage by fire claims also caused problems. The Ombudsman has set out his approach in dealing with such claims. There must first of all be combustion generating heat and light. Thus damage caused by an electric fire, iron or radiator is not damage due to combustion. Damage due to a cigarette or damage due to an open fire would, however, qualify because both came into being by a process that can be described as 'combustion'. It may be that a company will pay for scorching due to exposure to an iron or electric fire, but they are not bound to do so under the fire section of the policy.

In the first year of the FOS jurisdiction 'buildings and contents' claims provided just over a quarter of the Insurance Ombudsman's workload.

Travel insurance

Travel insurance problems have risen in recent years. Often sold through travel agencies by people untrained in the intricacies of insurance, such increase is perhaps inevitable. The Ombudsman goes as far as stating (2001 Annual Report) that 'it is perhaps the most complex financial product they purchase during the year'.

The intention is there should be greater training in insurance sales and advice generally but it may be a far away day before the industry can meet the declared intentions of the General Insurance Standards Council (GISC) Code requirement that 'all the important details of cover and benefits (and) any significant or unusual restrictions' are explained to the customer (see Chapter 6 generally and Appendix 6.1).

The greatest problem is that such policies usually contain various exceptions and limitations rather than providing the customer with financial security. In particular the Ombudsman does not feel that customers are normally capable of fully understanding the provisions without guidance. In particular he lists the areas of cancellation, curtailment, baggage and medical expenses as the areas of greatest concern (in other words just about the whole policy!). A selection of 2001/2002 case studies under this subject can be seen in Appendix 11.2(D).

Insurers, intermediaries and the ombudsman service

(Taken from the FOS Annual Report 2001.)

'The GISC (General Insurance Standards Council) Code for private customers (Appendix 6.1) is starting to have a significant role in our casework. This new Code builds on the position established under the ABI (Association of British Insurers) Code of Practice. Our initial assessment is that – so long as the GISC Code is widely adopted and complied with by intermediaries and insurers – it should enhance the protection available to customers. As a matter of good industry practice, we would expect all firms that are covered by the Financial Ombudsman Service to observe the Code and to take reasonable steps to ensure that other firms involved in selling their policies do so as well.

Customers often contact us with complaints that turn out to be about an intermediary or other company that is not covered by our jurisdiction. At present, few intermediaries are covered by the Ombudsman Service and matters are made more confusing for customers by the recent growth in insurance products branded with the names of intermediaries or other firms, where the name of the actual insurer is all but invisible to the policyholder.

In many of the cases referred to us, further enquiry shows that the complaint is actually about payment of a claim by the insurer, and hence something with which we can deal. We have been looking at other circumstances where we believe it appropriate for us to investigate complaints about intermediaries or other companies that we do not cover. In essence, this will be when the company complained about acts with the authority of the insurer, or as its agent.

During many transactions, an intermediary will be acting both for the insurer and for the customer (albeit at different stages of what customers may consider a seamless single process). The position is complicated further by the fact that the precise position will depend on any agreements made between the insurer and intermediary to allow the intermediary to act on the insurer's behalf. These agreements are not usually evident to the customer or indeed always immediately apparent to us when we first look at a case.

Normally, an intermediary will be acting for its customer when it is seeking out the best quote to meet the customer's requirements. However, if it has an arrangement to generally recommend a particular insurer, then the advice it gives may be a matter for us to consider in relation to that insurer.

Similarly, an intermediary is usually acting for its customer when it receives customer policy documentation from the insurer and forwards it to the customer. But intermediaries often write motor cover notes on behalf of the insurer and some may have wider authority to prepare and issue policy documents. In these cases, we may be able to consider any resulting complaints.

Sometimes, the insurer may delegate authority to the intermediary to accept proposals and even to decide some terms. The intermediary may also have a role on behalf of the insurer in the claims process. In these cases the actions the intermediary takes on behalf of the insurer fall within our jurisdiction. These are not the only examples where we are able to settle disputes which, initially, may appear to be directed against intermediaries not covered by the Financial Ombudsman Service. It is by no means straightforward to identify which cases we can deal with. We are therefore working closely with the GISC and its disputes resolution service to ensure cases are handled by which ever of us is best placed to deal with the matter. In the longer term, the objective must remain to bring complaints about intermediaries into the jurisdiction of the Financial Ombudsman Service.' [FOS, 2001.]

(Note: See also Chapter 6.) In late 2001 it was announced that the FSA will absorb the work of the GISC. This should mean that all complaints concerning insurance (sales, service and coverage) will then be dealt with by one supervisory body.

Miscellaneous problems

Apart from these illustrations of the Ombudsman's approach to problems in certain areas of insurance, he has also expressed views on the wider problems of proposal forms, advertising, claims, intermediaries and other matters of general importance.

Previous rejection of applications for insurance causes difficulties for the proposer. Freedom of contract clearly permits an insurer to reject any proposal it wishes, as long as it is not done in breach of the race or sex discrimination laws. But, when a disappointed proposer applies elsewhere, he will usually be asked if previous proposals have been declined. Before long, he may be left with the feeling that he is uninsurable. It is difficult to see a solution without infringing the basic rule of freedom of contract. The Ombudsman asked members for suggestions to remedy the problem. The insurer should, whenever possible, give the reasons for the refusal and the reasons given to a broker should be the same as those given to the proposer.

It is to be hoped that a company will not reject an application merely because an earlier application to another insurer has been rejected. A company should make an assessment in accordance with its own underwriting practices.

Answers given to questions on proposal forms usually form the basis of the contract of insurance, subject to the refinements in the Association of British Insurers' Statement of General Insurance Practice (see Chapter 4, Appendix 4.10). Great care must be taken to see that the answers are truthful. The matter can be complicated by the form of words used. The Ombudsman has asked companies to check their wording to see that it is clear and unambiguous. Usually, one word answers are wanted, but sometimes questions are so inelegant that a simple 'yes' or 'no' makes no real sense. The Ombudsman's advice is that the question section should be prominent, well laid out and close to the proposer's signature. Questions should be made as simple as possible and contain only one subject in each. Only in the most obvious of cases should a 'tick "yes" or "no" box' be used. With regard to renewal forms, it is suggested that specific questions should be asked and the common usage, of general warnings of a duty to disclose changes, are considered to be an inadequate technique. Copies of completed proposal forms should be given to the insured. This is particularly important, not only from the point of view of verifying at the time of renewal what answers had originally been given, often many years earlier, but also because of the use of the basis of the contract clause found on many proposal forms.

The use of the phrase, 'basis of the contract', was criticised by the Law Commission Report of 1980, but is still used. It has the effect of promoting all answers on the proposal form into conditions of the contract. No matter how immaterial to the risk the answer might be, it is transformed by the 'basis' clause into an all important matter. Thus, any inaccuracy in the answer will adversely affect any claim under the policy. However, if the ABI's Statement (above) is followed by members, then the problem should be ameliorated.

The Ombudsman set out his views on the duty of disclosure in his 1984 Annual Report. He considered that there was a place for utmost good faith in insurance law. This would even include situations where no specific question had been asked if a reasonable proposer would have been aware that the information withheld would adversely affect the insurer's decision making. But the emphasis should be on the insurer to ask questions which relate to matters he considers important in evaluating a proposal. It should not be left to proposers to estimate what is required of them.

There are examples, however, where the Ombudsman has little sympathy with the insured when giving misleading answers in the proposal form. A common situation can be taken from motor cover. When more than one driver wishes to be covered on a policy, common sense dictates that the best rate will apply to the 'best' driver. But, if that person is not the usual driver, then the policy has been obtained by a misrepresentation. Thus, it is wrong for a father to use his good driving record to obtain insurance, when in fact his young son will normally drive the vehicle. Such problems appear to be regular items on the Ombudsman's agenda. Again, very specific warnings on the proposal and the accompanying literature would help to bring home the message to the parties.

Insurers spend vast sums on advertising. Various codes of conduct govern such advertising. But this does not always protect the general public from being misled. An advertisement, for maximum impact, needs to be put across as a simple message. It would be odd if it was full of exclusions and limitations. The policy will indeed contain such drawbacks. The proposer, however, pays more attention to the advertisements than he does to the dull wording of the policy. It is often the advertising slogans which the insured quotes in support of his claim rather than the policy wording. All that the Ombudsman can do is to advise insurers to take care that their advertising does not create false impressions or where it does raise false expectations, then the insurer should attempt to meet those claims.

Delay in dealing with claims is an inevitable area of conflict between the parties. Where an insurer intends not to meet a claim, they should notify the insured as soon as possible, so that he can set in motion his appeal. It must be understood, however, that some claims are complicated and will take longer to process than the insured thinks necessary. Where quantum is the problem, it would be wise for insurers to pay some money early, so that essential repairs can be carried out. If avoidable delays do occur, the Ombudsman can award interest on sums paid out to the insured.

THE FINANCIAL OMBUDSMAN SERVICE: THE INSURANCE OMBUDSMAN

APPENDIX 11.1

FSA, *Financial Services Authority Handbook: Complaint Handling Procedures of the FOS* (extracts only)

Rule 3.2.1 On receipt of a complaint (and subsequently if necessary) the Ombudsman must have regard to the following matters:

(1) whether or not the complaint meets the criteria in DISP 2.2

(Which complaints can be dealt with under the Financial Ombudsman Service?);

(2) whether or not the complaint is within the time limits in DISP 2.3

(Time limits for referral of complaints to the Financial Ombudsman Service);

(3) whether or not the complainant is an eligible complainant; and

(4) whether or not the complaint is one which should be dismissed without consideration of its merits under DISP 3.3 (Dismissal of complaints without consideration of the merits).

R 3.2.3 Where the firm has not had the eight weeks provided for under DISP 1.4.5R to consider the complaint, the Ombudsman will refer the complaint to the firm, unless the firm has already issued a final response.

R 3.2.4 Where a firm fails to send a complainant a final response by the end of eight weeks, the Ombudsman may consider the complaint.

R 3.2.5 Where the Ombudsman considers that the complaint or the complainant may be ineligible under the jurisdiction rules (see DISP 2 (Jurisdiction of the Financial Ombudsman Service)) he must give the complainant an opportunity to make representations before he reaches his decision and he must give reasons to the complainant for that decision and inform the firm of his decision.

R 3.2.7 Where the firm disputes the eligibility of the complaint or the complainant, the Ombudsman must give the parties an opportunity to make representations before he reaches his decision and he must give reasons to the parties for that decision.

R 3.2.8 Where the Ombudsman considers that the complaint may be one which should be dismissed without consideration of its merits, under DISP 3.3 (Dismissal of complaints without consideration of the merits), he must give the complainant an opportunity to make representations before he makes his decision. If he then decides that the complaint should be dismissed, he must give reasons to the complainant for that decision and inform the firm of that decision.

R 3.2.9 Where the Ombudsman considers that both the complaint and the complainant are eligible and that there is a reasonable prospect of resolving the complaint by mediation, he may attempt to negotiate a settlement between the parties.

R 3.2.11 If the Ombudsman decides that an investigation is necessary, he will:

(1) during the investigation, give both parties an opportunity of making representations;

(2) send to the parties a provisional assessment, setting out his reasons and a time limit within which either party must respond; and

(3) if either party indicates disagreement with the provisional assessment within the time limit prescribed in DISP 3.2.11R(2), proceed to determination (see DISP 3.8 (Determination by the Ombudsman)).

R 3.2.12 The parties will be informed of their right to make representations before the Ombudsman makes a determination. If he considers that the complaint can be fairly determined without convening a hearing, he will determine the complaint. If not, he will invite the parties to attend a hearing. No hearing will be held after the Ombudsman has determined the complaint.

R 3.2.13 A party who wishes to request a hearing must do so in writing, setting out the issues he wishes to raise and (if appropriate) any reasons why he considers the hearing should be in private, so that the Ombudsman may consider whether the issues are material, whether a hearing should take place and, if so, whether it should be held in public or private.

3.3 Dismissal of complaints without consideration of the merits

R 3.3.1 The Ombudsman may dismiss a complaint without considering its merits if he:

(1) is satisfied that the complainant has not suffered, or is unlikely to suffer, financial loss, material distress or material inconvenience; or

(2) considers the complaint to be frivolous or vexatious; or

(3) considers that the complaint clearly does not have any reasonable prospect of success; or

(4) is satisfied that the firm has already made an offer of compensation which is fair and reasonable in relation to the circumstances alleged by the complainant and which is still open for acceptance; or

(5) is satisfied that the complaint relates to a transaction which the firm in question has reviewed in accordance with the regulatory standards for the review of such transactions prevailing at the time of the review, or in accordance with the terms of a scheme order under section 404 of the Act (Schemes for reviewing past business),

including, if appropriate, making an offer of redress to the complainant, unless he is of the opinion that the standards or terms of the scheme order did not address the particular circumstances of the case; or

(6) is satisfied that the matter has previously been considered or excluded under the Financial Ombudsman Service, or a former scheme (unless material new evidence likely to affect the outcome has subsequently become available); or

(7) is satisfied that the matter has been dealt with, or is being dealt with, by a comparable independent complaints scheme or dispute resolution process; or

(8) is satisfied that the subject matter of the complaint has been the subject of court proceedings where there has been a decision on the merits; or

(9) is satisfied that the subject matter of the complaint is the subject of current court proceedings unless proceedings are stayed or sisted (by agreement of all parties or order of the court) in order that the matter may be considered under the Financial Ombudsman Service; or

(10) considers that it would be more suitable for the matter to be dealt with by a court, arbitration or another complaints scheme; or

(11) is satisfied that it is a complaint about the legitimate exercise of a firm's commercial judgment; or

(12) is satisfied that it is a complaint about employment matters from an employee or employees of a firm; or

(13) is satisfied that it is a complaint about investment performance; or

(14) is satisfied that it is a complaint about a firm's decision when exercising a discretion under a will or private trust; or

(15) is satisfied that it is a complaint about a firm's failure to consult beneficiaries before exercising a discretion under a will or private trust, where there is no legal obligation to consult; or

(16) is satisfied that a complaint which involves or might involve more than one eligible complainant has been referred without the consent of the other complainant or complainants and the Ombudsman considers that it would be inappropriate to deal with the complaint without that consent; or

(17) is satisfied that there are other compelling reasons why it is inappropriate for the complaint to be dealt with under the Financial Ombudsman Service.

3.4 Referral of a complaint to another complaints scheme for determination

R 3.4.1 The Ombudsman may refer a complaint to another complaints scheme where he considers that it would be more suitable for the matter to be determined by that scheme and the complainant consents to the referral.

3.5 Evidence

R 3.5.1 The Ombudsman may, in relation to the evidence which may be required or admitted when he considers and determines a complaint, give directions as to:

(1) the issues on which evidence is required;

(2) the extent to which the evidence required to decide those issues should be oral or written; and

(3) the way in which the evidence should be presented to the Ombudsman.

R 3.5.2 The Ombudsman may:

(1) exclude evidence that would otherwise be admissible in a court of law or include evidence that would not be admissible in such a court;

(2) where he considers it necessary or appropriate, accept information in confidence, so that only an edited version or (where this is not practicable) a summary or description is disclosed to the other party;

(3) reach a decision on the basis of what has been supplied and take account of the failure by a complainant or a firm to provide information that an Ombudsman has requested; and

(4) dismiss a complaint if a complainant fails to supply required information.

3.6 Time limits

R 3.6.1 The Ombudsman may fix time limits and extend fixed time limits for any aspect of the consideration of a complaint by the Financial Ombudsman Service.

R 3.6.2 If a firm fails to comply with a time limit, the Ombudsman may proceed to the next stage of consideration of the complaint and may, if appropriate, make provision for any material distress or material inconvenience caused by that failure in any award which he decides to make.

R 3.6.3 If a complainant fails to comply with a time limit, the Ombudsman may either proceed to the next stage or dismiss the complaint.

...

3.8 Determination by the Ombudsman

R.3.8.1 Opinion as to fairness and reasonableness

(1) The Ombudsman will determine a complaint by reference to what is, in his opinion, fair and reasonable in all the circumstances of the case.

(2) In considering what is fair and reasonable in all the circumstances of the case, the Ombudsman will take into account the relevant law, regulations, regulators' rules and guidance and standards,

relevant codes of practice and, where appropriate, what he considers to have been good industry practice at the relevant time.

R 3.8.3 The Ombudsman's determination

The Ombudsman's determination will include the following stages:

(1) When a complaint has been determined, the Ombudsman will give both the complainant and the firm a signed written statement of the determination, stating the reasons for it.

(2) The statement will invite the complainant to notify the Ombudsman in writing before the date specified in the statement whether he accepts or rejects the determination.

(3) If the complainant notifies the Ombudsman that he accepts the determination within the time limit set, it is final and binding on both the complainant and the firm.

(4) If the complainant either rejects the determination or does not notify the Ombudsman by the specified date that he accepts the determination, the complainant will be treated as having rejected the determination, and the firm will not be bound by it.

(5) The Ombudsman must notify the firm of the complainant's response (or lack of response).

3.9 Awards by the Ombudsman

...

R 3.9.2 Where the Ombudsman decides to make a money award, in addition to (or instead of) awarding compensation for financial loss, he may award compensation for the following kinds of loss or damage, whether or not a court would award compensation:

(1) pain and suffering; or

(2) damage to reputation; or

(3) distress or inconvenience.

...

Limits on money awards

R 3.9.5 The maximum money award which the Ombudsman may make is £100,000.

Costs

R 3.9.10 When the Ombudsman finds in a complainant's favour, he may also award an amount which covers some or all of the costs which were reasonably incurred by the complainant in respect of the complaint.

...

R 3.9.12 The amount payable under the award of costs may, if the Ombudsman orders, bear interest at a reasonable rate specified in the order and from a date specified in the order.

...

Complying with awards and settlements

R 3.9.14 A firm must comply promptly with:

(1) any money award or direction made by the Ombudsman; and

(2) any settlement which it agrees at an earlier stage of the procedures.

R 3.9.15 The Ombudsman must maintain a register of each money award and direction made.

APPENDIX 11.2

Insurance Ombudsman, *Annual Reports 1982–2001*

[Full citations of cases have been added to the extracts and cross-referencing to earlier chapters for ease of reference. There are many references to the Association of British Insurers' Statement of General Insurance Practice. These can be found above, in Appendix 4.10.]

(A) APPROACH TO ADJUDICATION

Reaching a 'fair and reasonable' result in the circumstances of particular cases as now expressed by my Terms of Reference calls, of course, for fairness and reasonableness to be shown towards both sides. Since so much must turn upon balancing the perceived merits of individual complainants and their insurers, a fair and reasonable outcome might be though not susceptible to prediction. Nevertheless, in an attempt to reduce the uncertainties, I have formulated general rules for guiding our case handlers in their approach to particular cases. It might prove instructive, even reassuring, for those dealing with us to be aware of our actual approach:

(i) The onus is always on the complainant at the outset to show *prima facie* sufficient grounds for his complaint.

(ii) Any disputes about material facts must then be determined on a balance of probabilities (that is, civil standard of proof not criminal of beyond reasonable doubt). This is to be done after consideration of all available information, documentary or oral (that is, informal hearings/meetings can be held), about the relevant circumstances tested by appropriate questioning, investigations and other enquiries. Although the balance may sometimes seem fine and the outcome of the balancing exercise open to argument in the less clear cases, especially to the losing side but also to non-parties who have not seen or heard all the evidence, this basic fact finding must not involve giving either side the benefit of the doubt. The onus is still on the complainant to establish the complaint by tipping the balance in his or her favour (although it will be on the insurer if seeking to rely on an exclusion).

(iii) There is no assumption that complainants are fraudulent; in the absence of rebuttals supported by something more persuasive than simply assertion (for example, significant discrepancies in statements, patently suspicious circumstances, complainant's past record or indeed anything more cogent than claim manager's 'nose') the complainant's own account of the facts cannot properly be disbelieved and disregarded. But the truth of what he or she says may be tested at an informal hearing or otherwise as appropriate.

(iv) Having found the facts, if the law (which includes applying contractual terms of the policy) is clear, that often concludes the case. However, the principles of good insurance, investment or marketing practices coupled with the Statements and Codes of Practice and Conduct issued by the Association of British Insurers … may mitigate the strict application of the law to the facts so as to benefit the complainant. This mitigation must be adopted and applied so as not to let the law prevail.

(v) Further, the complainant must be given the benefit of genuine doubt not only where there is uncertainty and ambiguity in the construction of policy wording but also where his or her uncertainty or confusion as to cover can properly be regarded as the responsibility of the insurer (for example, because of unsatisfactory marketing, brochures, proposal forms or sales presentations or interviews, misleading advice from insurers' agents or loss adjusters, etc).

(vi) Beyond this, whenever the existence or not of liability calls for lengthy or complicated technical explanations or arguments, whether legal, scientific or semantic, the inclination must be to decide against the party (mostly but by no means always the insurer) attempting to rely on that explanation or argument.

(vii)Overall the basic merits of each case will be viewed throughout in the light of all the circumstances to see whether the man (or woman) on the Clapham omnibus, not being a party to the particular complaint and neither a consumerist nor an insurer, would consider the outcome fair and reasonable. This not infrequently benefits insurers (although more likely complainants) and also leads to equitable developments as outlined and explained in 1989 and subsequent Annual Reports.

(viii)Finally, the decision reached following this approach and after considering all reasoned arguments must not be influenced by objections however forthright and/or threatening from complainants or insurers.

The object of the exercise is achievement of the Bureau's Mission Statement which is 'to resolve disputes between members and consumers in an independent, efficient, user friendly and fair way'. Or, to put it another way, not rough but smooth justice. [IOB, 1992.]

(B) MOTOR INSURANCE

(i) Theft of motor vehicle

A young driver insured his car against fire, theft and third party risks only. He lent the car keys to a 17 year old friend, who was not licensed to drive. His friend told him that he only wished to entertain a girl on the backseat.

Unfortunately, the driver had been deceived by his friend, who drove off in the car. It was written off in an accident. His friend was convicted of 'aggravated vehicle taking', contrary to s 12 of the Theft Act 1968.

The driver claimed for loss of his car. The insurer refused payment, explaining that the conviction was not for 'theft' and thus it had no liability. The driver argued that he had not given permission for his friend to take the car and that it was lost by theft.

Complaint rejected

The crime of 'theft' was only committed if there was an intention to take it away from the owner permanently. Driving away in someone's car, even without permission, was not 'theft' unless the joyrider planned to keep the car or transfer it to another person. There was no such evidence in this case.

'Joyriding' damage will normally be covered if the insurance is comprehensive, but not if 'theft' is the only appropriate peril.

In any event, the policy specifically excluded loss 'by deception'. As the friend had only obtained the car keys by deception, there would have been no cover under the policy even if the friend had intended to keep the car permanently [IOB, 1996] ...

(ii) Valuation

The policyholder insured his car, a 1990 H-registration Subaru 1.6 DL four wheel drive estate model. In February 1996, it was stolen and the insurer assessed its market value at £2,700. The policyholder was dissatisfied and the insurer increased its valuation to £3,065, conceding that its original offer had been on the low side. The policyholder remained aggrieved and submitted advertisements to prove that his car was worth over £4,000.

Complaint rejected

The true construction of 'market value' was the amount which it would cost the policyholder to replace his vehicle with a similar model, bearing in mind its age, condition and mileage. We regarded the trade guides as offering the proper yardstick, since they were assessed on the returns submitted by garages for the prices actually achieved on sale. Advertisements from papers would reflect only the asking prices, which might not be realised by the vendors.

The money spent by the policyholder on maintaining his car in good condition and on buying a new stereo system had not actually increased the value of the car. Taking full account of all the evidence, we considered that the insurer's revised offer was fair [IOB, 1996] ...

(iii) Motor vehicle valuations [again!]

Disputes over the value of motor vehicles that have been stolen or written off continue to be referred to the Bureau with almost monotonous regularity. The analysis of cases in para 1.2 indicates there were 274 of these during 1994. It surprises me that most insurers in the UK continue to be resistant to a practice which I understand is widely adopted by their counterparts in South Africa: policies specify that the value of a vehicle in a total loss claim will be determined by reference to a standard trade guide. The publishers of the guide selected need to satisfy all concerned that it is free from bias in favour of insurer, motorist or motor dealer, and insurers need to make sure that policyholders are aware that this objective yardstick is included in their policies. Subject to that, such a practice ought to reduce considerably the scope for disputes of this kind, and I was pleased to hear from one member of the Bureau recently that it is planning to give it a try here.

Meanwhile, in those cases referred to us, we do the best we can. Usually the policy provides for payment of the 'market value' of the vehicle (or words to that effect). How do we establish that? So far as the Bureau is concerned, two points are now clear. First, following both my predecessors in this connection, I consider that market value is not the secondhand value of the car (unless the policyholder was in fact intending to sell it before it was stolen or written off) but what a replacement of similar age, condition and so on would cost. Second, as my immediate predecessor observed in his 1993 Annual Report (para 6.77) there are different markets. The appropriate one is not, as insurers often assume, the market for private sale and purchase of vehicles, through newspaper ads and the like, unless there is evidence to suggest that that is the market in which the policyholder intends to buy a replacement. As a general rule, the appropriate market will be the public one, so the policyholder gets what it would cost to replace the vehicle through a motor dealer. How do I find out what that would be? All relevant evidence has to be considered, but in particular I have to rely on … standard trade guides!

(iv) Profiteering policyholders and reticent insurers

In most vehicle valuation disputes, a decision on the market value of the vehicle is the end of the problem. In one case, it was only the beginning. The unfortunate policyholder's car was stolen. When recovered, it was in such a terrible state that the insurer agreed it should be considered a total loss. The car had been a considerable bargain. It had been bought at auction only three months prior to the loss, for £2,800. The insurer's engineer had valued the vehicle at £4,250. The insurer did not disclose this to the policyholder, but said that as the vehicle had been purchased in an auction, it would offer £2,700, subject to the policy excess of £350. It subsequently increased this offer to £3,500, but the policyholder was still not satisfied that that would enable him to obtain a comparable vehicle, whether at auction or elsewhere, so the matter came to me. The insurer's main argument was that to pay the policyholder anything substantially more than he had paid for the vehicle would enable him to profit from his loss. This was a logic which I could not accept. The policyholder had made a good buy. It was not something he could necessarily repeat, even at auction, and in any case he was not obliged to replace the vehicle in that way. He was entitled to be indemnified on the basis of the actual value of the car, not what he had paid.

I concluded (with the help of a standard trade guide) that the value of the car was in the region of £4,575. This was not so different from the engineer's valuation. I had to point out to the insurer my considerable concern over its failure to tell the policyholder that the actual value of the vehicle, as assessed by its engineer, was so much greater than the amount it was offering. For it to tell the policyholder that its offer took into account the fact that the vehicle had been purchased at auction was not enough. I am sorry to say this is not the only case in recent months in which I have seen insurers being economical with the truth in this way. Insurers depend on their policyholders acting in good faith when pursuing claims. They must accept that the obligation is mutual. If the insurer has had the benefit of a professional valuation for the vehicle in one of these valuation disputes, it should normally tell the policyholder what that is. If the insurer does not accept the valuation, the policyholder should be told why. Then everyone is on a more or less level playing field when it comes to agreeing on a figure that is fair. [IOB, 1994.]

(v) Defective repairs

A policyholder submitted a claim in respect of damage to his car. His insurer accepted the claim, but insisted on his using a particular garage to effect the repairs. When a question arose as to whether the repairs were defective, the insurer disclaimed responsibility, on the basis that the contract was between the policyholder and the garage making the repairs. I was unable to agree. In a case of this nature, where the insurer nominates the repairer, the latter becomes the agent of the insurer for the purpose of effecting the repairs. The contract of insurance is superseded by a contract for services to be provided by the insurer, or by the garage on its behalf, the service in question being the repair of the vehicle. Insurers surprised by this reasoning will find judicial authority for it in the Scottish appellate decision of *Davidson v Guardian Royal Exchange Assurance* [1979] 1 Lloyd's Rep 406. In that case an insurer was held responsible for the unreasonable delay of its nominated repairer in repairing a car. An exclusion in the policy in respect of loss of use was held ineffective by the court, as that related to claims under the policy, and the claim had become one under the insurer's repair contract with the policyholder ...

It is different if the insurer has allowed the policyholder to obtain quotes and choose between those which are relatively competitive. Then it may well be reasonable for the insurer to say that it has not accepted responsibility for the quality of the repairs, it has simply undertaken to the policyholder to pay the bill. In such cases, the contract for repairs will indeed be between the policyholder and the repairer, and it is the policyholder who will have to sort out with the repairer any problems that arise. That is not a licence to policyholders to hold insurers to the highest quote, if there is reason to doubt whether it is genuinely competitive. Neither is it a licence to insurers, however, to walk away when a simple phone call or letter, lending muscle to the policyholder's arguments with the repairer, could make all the difference. [IOB, 1994.]

(vi) Unattended vehicles and hidden items

Increasingly, policies are being amended in an attempt, not always successful, to clarify the position and remove the more subjective element involved in considering whether or not there has been breach of a reasonable care condition. For instance, many policies now exclude theft from unattended vehicles completely. This may still, of course, allow some discussion over whether or not a vehicle was unattended. The well established test propounded by Lord Denning in *Starfire Diamond Rings Ltd v Angel* [1962] 2 Lloyd's Rep 217 [see Chapter 7, Appendix 7.9] ... that, in order not to be 'unattended', the vehicle must have been kept under observation so that there was someone able to observe any attempt to interfere with it and to prevent any unauthorised interference, continues to be of assistance.

Other policies may, in an attempt to be more generous to policyholders, exclude loss from unattended vehicles unless the property is locked in the boot or glove compartment or is otherwise 'hidden from view'. This then leads to discussion about whether an item is sufficiently concealed. Insurers argue that they intend that the presence of the property should be hidden from view but that is not what the words say. Policyholders argue, in cases such as that which went to the Deputy District Judge on the reasonable care issue, that money or valuables in a handbag or wallet are hidden even if the handbag or wallet itself is not. Some balance has to be found between extreme arguments either way that takes into account both the literal sense of the wording used and the fact that it is for the policyholder to show he is entitled to the benefit of such an 'exclusion to an exclusion'. The approach we take is to say that where something unhidden is taken from an unattended vehicle, anything in the thing taken or attached to it or 'going with it' (for example, underlying items in a pile of clothing) cannot be regarded as hidden from view even though itself not visible. On the other hand, the exclusion may not catch items not 'going with' a stolen thing and hidden from view notwithstanding the fact that their presence in the vehicle was not effectively concealed. Nevertheless, the nature of an item may be so evident despite the fact that it is covered over, either because of its distinctive shape or other features, that it cannot sensibly be said that it is hidden from view.

These unattended vehicle exclusions, with or without the 'hidden from view' addendum, will almost always be accompanied by a reasonable care condition, and the interplay between them also has to be considered. Thus, it could well be reckless within the *Sofi* test [*Sofi v Prudential Assurance Co Ltd* [1993] 2 Lloyd's Rep 559, Appendix 7.6] to leave valuables under an attractive item such as a mink coat on the back seat even if those items could be regarded as hidden from view. On the other hand, items left exposed on the back seat in a locked car which were not in themselves so attractive that a breach of the reasonable care condition could be assumed would nevertheless not be hidden from view.

Lastly, in this connection, I must refer to the Association of British Insurers' Code of Practice for selling general insurance [see Appendix 6.5]. I have referred ... to the fact that this contains a requirement that the basic provisions of a policy should be explained to a policyholder and exclusions drawn to his or her attention. I tend to consider that reasonable care conditions should come as no surprise to a policyholder, but an unattended vehicle exclusion can amount to a trap for the unwary, so even if such an exclusion is otherwise applicable insurers may find I regard it as unreasonable for them to rely on it if the Code has not been complied with. [IOB, 1993.]

(vii) Clean hands

The policyholder's car was stolen from near his home. The insurer requested the policyholder to forward to it the car's MOT certificate before settling the claim. Before making payment the insurer noticed that the certificate was not a genuine certificate issued by an approved MOT testing station but was a forgery. When challenged the policyholder admitted that he had bought it from a supplier of false documents as he did not want to endure the inconvenience of being without a car for one day whilst it was undergoing an MOT test. The insurer repudiated liability on the basis that: (i) lack of a genuine MOT certificate suggested that the car may be unroadworthy; and (ii) submission of a spurious MOT certificate is a breach of utmost good faith. We rejected the former argument as it was not a condition precedent to liability that the policyholder forward an MOT certificate in order to substantiate a claim and also because a mere *assumption* as to unroadworthiness is insufficient reason to repudiate liability. However, we upheld the insurer's repudiation on the second ground as we cannot condone the use of fraudulent documentation in order to substantiate a claim and it would be inequitable to do so. [IOB, 1992.]

(viii) Loss through theft

A car had been stolen and ended up in the possession of an innocent purchaser. The claim for 'loss' by theft was rejected by the insurer on the grounds that as the whereabouts of the car were known to the policyholder, and as *NEM v Jones* [1988] 2 All ER 425 effectively confirmed her as still having good title to it, she could and should take steps to recover the car. As she had already had her solicitor write to the person in possession of the car requiring its return, to no avail, and since the insurer had also written in these terms with no result, this position meant that the policyholder must sue the possessor. However, her solicitor had told her that despite *NEM v Jones* legal action might not be straightforward. We regarded this as inequitable; in the *Webster v General Accident* [1953] 1 All ER 663 case it was said of 'loss' that:

> ... it is never necessary for a claimant to prove that in all circumstances the chattel is irrecoverable ... An assured is not entitled to sit by and do nothing. Equally, he is not bound to launch into legal proceedings ... the test is whether he has taken all reasonable steps, and he having taken all reasonable steps, whether recovery is uncertain.

Loss was, therefore, found to have been established and the insurer would have to meet the claim and pursue the recovery of the car for its own benefit. [IOB, 1992.]

(ix) Accessories and spare parts

Two contrasting cases highlight the misunderstandings which can arise with regard to motor vehicle accessories and spare parts. A motorist in Scotland purchased a spare set of wheels and snow tyres for his BMW, which cost £1,500. They were stolen from his garage. His policy covered accessories and spare parts which were in the insured's locked garage but the insurer declined the claim on the grounds that what it meant by accessories were 'wing mirrors, seat covers and the like'. There was no monetary limit with regard to accessories and so the policyholder's complaint was upheld. On the other hand a policyholder paid for a new engine for his Metro, using his Amex card. The car was stolen the day after the new engine had been fitted. The motor insurer paid the market value for the car which was less than the policyholder thought it should be. He therefore claimed on the insurance which covered purchases by means of Amex on the grounds that the engine, bought with an Amex card, had been stolen. However, the policy specifically excluded loss of or from motor vehicles and the policyholder's claim failed. [IOB, 1992.]

(x) Tale of two policies

The case concerned the theft of two car radios which were specifically designed to be removed from the vehicles when they were unattended. The radios had been placed in the policyholders' flat whilst they were on holiday – the flat was broken into and the radios and other items stolen. A claim under a house contents policy failed as it excluded motor vehicles and their accessories. A claim under the motor policies also failed as the radios were not in or on the vehicles or their garages at the time of theft. An application was made in respect of the contents policy only. The insurer was asked to agree to a recommendation that it meet 50% of the claim. It did so on an *ex gratia* basis. [IOB, 1992.]

Unattended

A policyholder had his suitcase stolen from his car whilst on holiday, and the insurer declined his claim on the ground that his travel policy excluded liability for 'loss' or damage to property left unattended whilst away from the person insured's personal accommodation. The suitcase was stolen when the policyholder decided to go for a drink with his girlfriend whilst waiting for his brother to return to his flat (the policyholder did not have keys to the flat). In the decision, we stated that the exclusion clause was not unreasonable in the circumstances, and that the policyholder and his girlfriend could either have stayed with the suitcase while waiting for the policyholder's brother to return to the flat, or 'if you had wanted a drink, one of you could have remained in the car with the suitcase whilst the other purchased drinks to bring back to the car'. The policyholder replied that he was 'shocked' that the Ombudsman would even suggest drinking alcohol in a motor vehicle and said that 'we as the public do not expect letters from a person of your position in society to encourage the breaking of laws'. [IOB, 1992]!

(C) DIRECT SELLING – MARKETING ISSUES

Direct telephone selling of motor and other general insurance has become increasingly common. Usually the prospective policyholder telephones for a quotation. A member of the insurer's staff then poses a series of questions to which the policyholder provides answers. If these answers are acceptable to the insurer it quotes a premium figure. In the event of the applicant agreeing to this figure, the applicant's answers to the questions posed are either printed out on a proposal form, or marshalled as the terms of the insurance contract. The document is usually sent to the applicant for signature.

We have been receiving a number of complaints where insurers have rejected claims on the ground that the answers given to questions posed over the telephone were incorrect. The complainant maintains either that the question in point was not asked or that the question asked was different from that recorded on the acceptance form. Direct telesales staff have computer generated question scripts but it is not normally possible to check whether or not the script was gone through in full.

A number of disputes has arisen over who said what. In one recent case a telephone based insurer assured us that anyone who had not held a full driving licence for 12 months would be informed on telephoning for a quotation that their policy would not cover them for 'driving other cars'. The complainant denied having been told this and to prove his point he arranged for a friend to telephone for a quotation and to pretend that he had passed his test only five months earlier. Another similar case involved an assertion by the complainant that he had not been asked whether his car had been modified in any way; while another complainant maintained that he had not been asked about his No Claims Discount entitlement. No doubt the telesales staff concerned had spotted that they could clinch more sales (and most are rewarded on the basis of sale targets) if they ignored answers which would mean that a sale would have to be declined.

Such disputes can really only be avoided by the introduction of call recording, and I am keen to encourage the industry to move in this direction. I recognise that if insurers made the heavy investment in call recording systems to maintain evidence of the contract, they would expect to drop the process of requiring the applicant to sign and return a printed proposal, in favour of merely sending the policyholder a print out of key statements relied on. This is a procedure adopted by one insurer, and I have confirmed to representatives of those operating in the direct market that I would accept such tape recordings as evidence of the basis of the contract. Tape recording should help to ensure that instructions are properly followed by staff. Human nature being what it is however, if companies place too great a reliance on commissions and sales bonuses to remunerate their staff, some employees will always be tempted to find ways to bend the rules. This has been the greatest single cause of the problems faced by the financial services industry [IOB, 1996] ...

(D) TRAVEL INSURANCE

(i) Cancellation – ill health

In May 1995, a son booked a fortnight's holiday, including insurance against cancellation. He planned to leave on 27 June, but his 89 year old mother died on 26 June. He claimed for the cost of cancelling the holiday, but the insurer argued that it did not have to pay anything because the policy excluded: 'Any claim arising from a chronic pre-existing medical condition or a physical infirmity of a close relative.'

The son appealed, explaining that he would not have planned a holiday if his mother's condition had been as serious as the insurer believed.

Complaint upheld

It was clear that no one had anticipated the mother's demise. Her general practitioner had stated that he did not expect her death at the time or warn the son that it was approaching. One of the purposes of the policy was to protect against unexpected death and illness. If the claim were rejected, the commercial purpose of the policy would be defeated.

Furthermore, we were not satisfied that this exclusion had been drawn to the son's attention. In view of the mother's health, it was a particularly onerous condition which the son should have been made aware of.

The insurer did not agree, but was willing to meet the claim [IOB, 1996] …

(ii) Cancellation

In *travel policies*, it is common to find a provision that the premium is not refundable. Once the policyholder has gone on holiday that would usually be fair enough. If the policyholder never goes on holiday but claims successfully under the cancellation cover, no premium refund could still seem fair enough. If the cancellation is through no fault of the policyholder, but in circumstances not covered by the policy, what then? Our usual approach is to accept that the cancellation cover has nevertheless been operative, but the travel cover, which only comes into effect when the holiday starts, has not been. Legally, both form part of the same contract, for which a single premium is quoted. But, in substance they may be regarded as two distinct covers, one ending where the other begins. If the holiday is cancelled in the circumstances I have described, we usually ask the insurer to refund 50% of the premium. This is an estimate of the proportion of the premium applying to the risks arising during the holiday itself, which never began to run. The figure may be adjusted if the insurer produces more specific calculations.

(iii) Personal money

Travel policies illustrate other issues of substance. I have seen some which provide cover for loss of 'Personal money'. But, when the definition section of the policy is referred to, 'Personal money' is defined there as:

> … bank and currency notes, cash, cheques, postal and money orders, current postage stamps, travellers' cheques, coupons or vouchers which have a monetary value and travel tickets, all held for your private purposes while away from your Home (as defined) … and while in your personal custody at all times unless deposited in a hotel safe.

I have held that despite the fact that this is a definition, and therefore appears to relate to the scope of the cover, it contains what is substantially a warranty or condition, and an onerous one at that: if the policyholder wants the benefit of his insurance cover, he must never let his money out of his custody, or he must put it in an hotel safe. Such a provision cannot take effect unless it has been properly brought to the attention of the policyholder in accordance with the *Interfoto* case [1989] QB 433 and the requirements of the ABI Code of Practice for the Sale of General Insurance. Secreting it in the definition section of the policy will not make it easy for the insurer to pass this test. I am pleased to note that more recent travel policies are making the position clearer [IOB, 1995] …

Mr H took out an annual travel policy for his two adult sons before they went to America in May 1999. The insurer took approximately three weeks to issue the policy and then sent it to Mr H. As he was away at the time, the sons were unable to check – before they set out on their trip – whether the policy was suitable for their needs. In fact, it was not. It restricted cover for individual trips to 30 days, whereas they planned to be away for 74 days, and it did not cover claims arising from hazardous activities, including riding motorcycles over 125cc.

The following April, one of Mr H's sons went out to Australia. Whilst there, he had a fatal accident riding a 600cc motorcycle. Mr and Mrs H put in a claim for repatriation and funeral expenses and for the accidental death benefit of £30,000.

The insurer explained that, because of the motorcycle exclusion, the policy did not provide any cover. However, it accepted that it had not sold, issued or explained the policy correctly. It therefore met the repatriation and funeral expenses as a gesture of goodwill. Mr and Mrs H did not accept that the motorcycle exclusion was valid, since it had not been drawn to their attention, and they felt they were entitled to the full death benefit.

Complaint rejected

Mr H bought the policy specifically for the trip to America and had decided to buy an annual policy because of the length of the trip. The insurer had accepted that the policy had not been properly sold and it confirmed that it would not have relied on the exclusions or restrictions to repudiate any claims arising during the trip to America.

However, by the time of the second trip, the family was aware that the policy did not cover all hazardous activities and the policyholders had had ample opportunity to check whether the policy was appropriate for their needs and to request an amendment if necessary. The policy was, in any event, due to lapse shortly after the son's departure to Australia yet they had not checked that it would cover the trip or the activities he planned. In these circumstances, we took the view that the insurer's offer to pay the repatriation and funeral costs was reasonable and that it had no liability for the death claim. [FOS, 2001.]

…

Miss H went on holiday with her partner to Crete. They left a beach bag containing a camera, two mobile phones, a tape player and some cash, in the locked boot of their hire car. The car was broken into and Miss H claimed for theft of the bag. The insurer rejected the claim on the ground that all the items were within the policy definition of 'valuables' and therefore excluded from cover in unattended motor vehicles.

The policy defined 'valuables' as *'photographic and video equipment, camcorders, radios and personal stereo equipment, computers, computer games and associated equipment, hearing aids, mobile telephones, telescopes and binoculars, antiques, jewellery, watches, furs, precious stones and articles made of or containing gold, silver or other precious metals or animal skins or hides'*.

Miss H argued that the policy was self-contradictory, in that another exclusion stated that the insurer would not be liable for *'any theft from motor vehicles left unattended at any time between 10 pm and 8 am'*.

Complaint upheld in part

We did not agree that there was a contradiction between the two exclusions; the more onerous exclusion applied only to valuables and meant that they were not covered at any time in an unattended car.

However, that exclusion was unusually onerous and required Miss H to take specific action in order to maintain cover under the policy. The insurer should therefore have drawn it to her attention at the time she bought the insurance. There was no evidence that the insurer had done so.

The fact that she had been given time to read the policy and the option to cancel it was not sufficient for the insurer to comply with its duty to draw such exclusions to the attention of anyone purchasing the policy. We required the insurer to deal with the claim. However, the policy contained a limit of £200 for all valuables and an excess of £45 for cash. These meant that Miss H and her partner would not be reimbursed for the majority of their losses. [FOS, 2001.]

...

In January 2000, Mr W and Mrs G arranged to go on a holiday in July. Mrs G's son was admitted to hospital in April and underwent a series of tests. Mr W and Mrs G paid the balance of the holiday costs on 5 May. The son was discharged in the middle of that month but was referred back to a consultant on 24 May, readmitted to hospital a few days later, and died on 13 June, one day after his illness had been diagnosed.

Mr W and Mrs G claimed reimbursement of the cost of cancelling their holiday, but the insurer refused to make any payment beyond the £200 deposit. It relied on a condition in the policy which required policyholders to notify the insurer's helpline if an immediate relative was 'receiving, recovering from, or on a waiting list for, in-patient treatment in a hospital' or 'waiting for the results of tests or investigations or referral for an existing medical condition'.

Complaint upheld

We interpreted the requirement as applying only at the time the policy was issued in January 2000, as is usual with this type of wording. If the insurer had intended this requirement to cover the whole period until the date of departure, that would be an onerous obligation and the insurer would have had to have made it much clearer in its documentation, as well as drawing it to the attention of potential policyholders.

Moreover, even if we considered it reasonable to treat the condition as if it applied when the balance of the money was paid, the claim would still be valid. Although Mr G was in hospital when the payment was made on 5 May, the insurer accepted that it would have provided full cover after his discharge from hospital in mid-May. He would therefore not have come within the terms of the condition when he saw the consultant on 24 May or was readmitted to hospital on 28 May. The insurer agreed to pay the balance of the holiday cost, which the couple had forfeited when they cancelled. [FOS, 2001.]

...

Mr N was on holiday in New York. While he was sitting on a subway platform bench waiting for a train, another traveller started a conversation with him. When Mr N looked around a minute or two later, he found his rucksack had been taken from the seat beside him. He claimed for theft of £2,000 of personal belongings and about £400 cash. The insurer rejected the claim on the ground that the rucksack was 'unattended' and therefore specifically excluded from cover.

Complaint upheld

It could not be said that the bag was unattended when Mr N was in reasonable proximity at the time. Indeed, this was borne out by the circumstances of the theft. There would have been no need for one of the thieves to distract Mr N by engaging him in conversation if the bag had been unattended: the thieves could just have taken it.

The mere fact that a theft had occurred did not prove that property was 'unattended'. If there had been any indication that Mr N had walked away from his bag and returned to find it stolen, it would have been different. The insurer accepted our view that it should meet the claim, subject to the policy limits of £1,500 per bag and £400 total cash, less the policy excess. [FOS, 2001.]

(E) REASONABLE CARE CONDITIONS

(i) Reasonable care

Most property protection policies include a condition requiring the policyholder to take reasonable care of the property. The purpose of this (according to the courts) is to ensure that the policyholder will not, because he is covered against loss by the policy, refrain from taking precautions which he knows ought to be taken. Applying this condition requires a consideration of what was passing through the mind of the policyholder at the relevant time. The courts require that the attitude of the insured should amount to recklessness, rather than mere negligence.

Even the most understanding insurer will be unable to do this where inadequate information is available about the details of the insured's circumstances at the time. And yet what may be substantial claims will succeed or fail in their entirety on the strength of such artificial and elusive considerations.

This arises frequently (but not exclusively) in disputes involving theft of vehicles where keys have been left in the ignition. Which of us can honestly say we have never done this? Were we acting recklessly when we did so? Not always.

This may be an issue which will stand comparison with developments in the practice of insurers over recent years in relation to precautions against loss in the sphere of household contents insurance. Not too long ago it was a universal practice that the penalty for failing to comply with a security measures condition would be repudiation of the claim if the security requirements were not in force and this was connected to the loss. More recently, however, a number of insurers have been adopting an alternative practice, where instead of losing all cover for the loss if specified precautions are not taken, an increased excess applies.

If policyholders were properly made aware of a specific effect on claim settlement of keys being left in the ignition, by which an identifiable and certain financial loss would be suffered (perhaps a proportion of the value) in the event of a claim for theft of the car, this could have as much of a salutary effect on their behaviour as reasonable care conditions. The element of uncertainty would be removed from the assessment of the claim, and, from the insurers' point of view, investigation costs should be lower. Of course, insurers could exercise their discretion to pay claims in full in appropriate cases. [IOB, 1996.]

(ii) Reasonable care reviewed

During the course of the year there was a discernible increase in cases referred to the Bureau where the policyholder's claim for loss had been declined on the ground that he or she was in breach of a 'reasonable care' condition. Although this increase spread across the range of property insurance it was particularly marked in the field of travel insurance. Some travel insurers have argued that there has over the last few years been an overwhelming increase in theft abroad whether it be from unattended vehicles, unattended bags or indeed from policyholders in person, and no one should have been unaware of it. Well known danger exists not only in notorious places like Florida but across Europe generally. On the basis that these risks attract considerable publicity, it was suggested that the principles had somehow shifted away from the position expressed by the Court of Appeal in *Sofi v Prudential Insurance Co Ltd* [1993] 2 Lloyd's Rep 559 [Appendix 7.6]. One insurer went so far as to suggest that this was 'old law' with no application in today's lawless world.

However, also during the course of the year, a decision issued by us in May 1992 in favour of the insurer concerned was rejected by the policyholder who then instituted proceedings in the county court. The Deputy District Judge found in the policyholder's favour. We had taken the view that it was reckless to leave a handbag containing a ring valued at £2,950 in full view on the passenger seat of a car while the policyholder visited her dressmaker. Our conclusion was that the policyholder was aware of the danger in leaving the car unattended but left the handbag because she had a load of dress making material to carry. Although she maintained she had not intended to leave the car long it was actually left unattended for about half an hour. The car was locked but no attempt had been made to hide the bag. The Deputy District Judge accepted that the policyholder had not intended to enter the dressmaker's house but had been invited in unexpectedly and he found that she had not been inside for more than 10 minutes. He considered this to be a momentary lapse and accordingly not a failure to have regard to the safety of her property.

The decision of a Deputy District Judge under the Small Claims procedure of the county court has no weight as a precedent and in this case appears in any event to have been based on different arguments from those addressed to the Bureau by the policyholder's solicitor husband. Nevertheless, in the light of it, and of the increase of 'reasonable care' cases, I undertook a review of the Bureau's approach to cases of this nature. Insurers and the public alike may find it of assistance for the position to be restated ...

It is well to remember that the *Sofi* case was significant because it applied to property insurance an approach which had already been held by the courts to apply to liability insurance. Effectively, *Sofi* was saying nothing new in terms of what constitutes 'reasonable care'. Given its ordinary meaning lack of 'reasonable care' could mean simple negligence. However, the courts have consistently held that a provision that a policyholder would not be covered if he were negligent would be contrary to the commercial purpose of the policy and so the words 'reasonable care' cannot be taken at face value. The breach requires something much more than mere negligence. It is also worth remembering that there is no implied term or 'common law duty' requiring a policyholder to take reasonable care. If there is anything, it must be a contractual term and the burden of proving breach is on the insurer.

Negligence may not amount to breach of such a condition but recklessness does. In his judgment in *Sofi*, Lord Justice Lloyd quoted Lord Justice Diplock in the leading case of *Fraser v BN Furman (Productions) Ltd* [1967] 1 WLR 898, at p 906 [Appendix 6.19], as explaining:

> What, in my judgment, is reasonable as between the insured and the insurer, without being repugnant to the commercial purpose of the contract, is that the insured where he does recognise a danger should not deliberately court it by taking measures which he himself knows are inadequate to avert it. In other words, it is not enough that the employer's omission to take any particular precautions to avoid accidents should be negligent; it must be at least reckless, that is to say, made with actual recognition by the insured himself that a danger exists and not caring whether or not it is averted. The purpose of the condition is to ensure that the insured will not, because he is covered against loss by the policy, refrain from taking precautions which he knows ought to be taken.

In brief, therefore, the legal position is that the insured who is to deprive himself of benefit under his policy through 'lack of reasonable care' or the like must 'court' a danger the existence of which he recognises. He courts danger by taking measures which he knows are inadequate to avert it or indeed no measures at all. Recognition of the risk is subjective as is knowledge of the adequacy (or lack) of the steps taken to avert that risk. The fact that others might have taken different steps or that the policyholder himself would with the benefit of hindsight is irrelevant. The policyholder does not have to satisfy any basic test of reasonable prudence in order to make a successful claim. The test is recklessness. There must also, of course, be a causal connection between the recklessness and the loss. The Deputy District Judge's recent decision very well illustrates this approach. Indeed, there are very few instances in which the courts themselves actually have found against a policyholder and in those cases where they have there has been extreme or blatant or gross negligence which has obviously amounted to recklessness.

This leaves us with the strict test of recklessness which has had to be applied by us since *Sofi* in 1989. There is no judicial authority or other justification for this test to be relaxed in an insurer's favour. By way of comfort to insurers, I can only emphasise that there are a number of factors which we can and do properly take into consideration in assessing whether or not a policyholder should be treated as having been reckless. One of them is the value of the property: the greater the value, the greater the risk and the easier it will be for an insurer to establish it was deliberately courted – in particular valuable property should not be left temptingly exposed to view. Other factors are the length of time that the property has been left and the vulnerability of the place in which it is left. The issue of a safer alternative can only be relevant if what might have been done is so obvious and comparatively so safe and easy that by failing to do it the policyholder must be taken to have deliberately courted the risk.

Essentially, the Bureau cannot properly and to the disadvantage of policyholders apply standards stricter than those applied by judges: to do so would be contrary to my Terms of Reference. Until such time as the current legal position is successfully challenged in the courts the principles set out above must prevail. [IOB, 1993.]

(F) NOTICES OF RENEWAL – NON-DISCLOSURE

(i) General

Direct insurers all rely on computer generated schedules, and most of the industry maintains key data on computers, so generating an updated schedule to be sent to a policyholder inviting renewal should not be too difficult. My predecessors have drawn attention to the need at renewal stage to remind policyholders of the key data on which the insurer is relying, when offering renewal, and to ask whether the facts remain unchanged or indeed whether there have been changes. Yet few insurers do this.

In my view it is insufficient if the insurer asks policyholders to send a renewal cheque (or extracts continuing direct debits) with a general invitation to mention any relevant changes in circumstances. In a recent case an applicant for household insurance was asked whether any member of the family had convictions or pending prosecutions and answered truthfully 'no'. By the time of renewal his son had been convicted of offences, but no clear question was asked of the policyholder. I decided that the insurer could not repudiate the policy on the ground of non-disclosure and required it to meet a claim when the house burned down. [IOB, 1996.]

(ii) Renewals

There are other situations in which I look to the spirit of insurance codes or regulations. This was the case recently, when I was considering the way in which insurers invite renewal of general insurances, and the obligation of the policyholder at that time to declare any material changes in the nature of the risk being insured.

A policyholder with *motor insurance* took out her policy at a time when her husband had the use of a company van for work. She was not allowed to drive his van. Subsequently, after the insurance was taken out, her husband lost the use of the company van, and bought his own car in order to be able to get to and from work. When the policyholder put in a claim for the cost of repairing her vehicle after an accident, the insurer wanted to avoid the policy. It is said the policyholder had failed to disclose at the time of proposal that her husband had the use of a company vehicle, and she had failed to disclose at a subsequent renewal of the policy that her husband had by then bought a vehicle for his private use.

The policyholder explained that she had not disclosed that her husband had the use of another vehicle when she took out the policy because he was only allowed to drive it in company time. His employer confirmed this. Bearing in mind that the husband no longer had the use of the company van anyhow, I did not consider this point worth pursuing.

The real point in issue was the policyholder's failure to disclose at renewal the fact that her husband now had a car of his own. There was no dispute that this information was material from the insurer's point of view. Statistics show that, with a second vehicle in the family, the risk of young drivers having more frequent use of one of the vehicles is higher. That normally means a higher premium is payable, as statistics also show that younger driver have more accidents.

The problem for the policyholder was that she had not realised that this kind of information was required. The renewal notice asked her to notify the insurer of any changes affecting the policy which had occurred since the policy commenced, or since the previous renewal date. The renewal notice specifically referred to: '... motor convictions, disqualifications or impending prosecutions and any physical or mental disability or infirmity of any person likely to drive.' It did not refer to any change in the situation regarding access by the policyholder or her spouse to any other vehicle. She said that, at the time of renewal, she did not remember the question about this on the proposal form. I did not consider that she could be reasonably expected to remember this, particularly in the case of a proposal some years before.

The ABI's Statement of General Insurance Practice specifically requires insurers to ask clear questions on all matters commonly found to be material, at the time of proposal (para 1(d)). Looking to the spirit of the Statement, I expect insurers to be equally clear at renewal. Where an insurer fails to be sufficiency clear in this connection, it must be taken to have waived the requirements of disclosure, as much at renewal as at proposal.

I suggested to the insurer concerned that the simplest answer would be for insurers to remind policyholders at renewal of the material facts which were disclosed at the time of proposal. Policyholders could then confirm whether or not there had been any changes. The insurer said that was not practicable. I was not persuaded by its arguments, but I did not need to be. If my suggestion could not work, it was up to the insurer to find some other way to deal with the matter. The principle remains: it may not be fair and reasonable for the insurer to allege non-disclosure at renewal if it has not made clear what information it requires. Accordingly, in the case before me, the insurer had to meet the policyholder's claim [IOB, 1995] ...

(iii) ... my Terms of Reference require me to reach a decision which I consider in all the circumstances would be a fair and reasonable resolution of the dispute. Inherent in that formula is the type of discretion referred to and, as I explained in my 1990 report, if the circumstances are such that I could conclude, on a balance of probabilities, that any non-disclosure was innocent I would not allow the insurer to avoid the policy but would require it to adopt the proportionality principle.

Some insurers regard this as allowing those they perceive as wrongdoers to get away with deceit, and others point out that it is bad underwriting practice to set a premium, in effect, at the time of a claim. However, I will not apply the principle where there is sufficient evidence of fraud, and the underwriting point only differs in degree from insurers wishing to decline cover altogether at claim time.

In this respect, some insurers appear to be all too willing to underwrite at the claims stage. Two examples serve to illustrate this. The first case concerned a non-disclosure in a proposal for life assurance. The question asked was: 'Have you ever had or been advised to seek medical advice, treatment or investigation (including blood tests) from a medical specialist, hospital or clinic?'

The answer was negative but in fact some months prior to completion of the proposal the applicant's husband had been treated for depression and three years earlier was treated by an ophthalmologist for an eye problem. He died in 1991, the cause of death being certified as 'alcohol poisoning – misadventure'. The applicant said that her husband believed himself to be in good health both mentally and physically, and the specialist who had visited some months previously had said that the depression could be rectified. Furthermore, he had completed his medication at the time of proposal. It was noted that the doctor's name and address were included on the proposal form, along with the proposer's consent for the assurer to obtain a medical report. I concluded that the assurer had failed to provide sufficient evidence that the non-disclosure was deliberate. Equally there was no evidence that the deceased had not appreciated that the facts should be disclosed. Of course, even where the non-disclosure is innocent, as assurer is entitled to avoid the policy and reject the claim. However, according to the expert's report there was no causal link between the non-disclosed facts and the cause of death which is pertinent. Moreover, the reasonable expectation of the ordinary policyholder for life assurance would surely be that, where the details of a doctor are asked for, he would be approached by the assurer and would supply all relevant details before the proposal could be accepted.

It seems to me that insurers should not, in effect, try to underwrite at the time of a claim by saying what they would have done if the relevant information had been acquired. The fact is that in this case it could have obtained the information by writing to the doctor. Indeed, many people wonder why assurers ask for such details if they only intend to use them if a claim is made. By underwriting the risk without carrying out full enquiries at the underwriting stage, the assurer lulls the policyholder into a false sense of security that he has cover when the reality is that he has none because as soon as a claim is made, the assurer will write to his doctor and discover the information then said to be material. If it is that material, it should have been investigated earlier and the risk declined or a higher premium charged, or cover restricted. In cases such as this it is the dependents, rather than the person who non-disclosed, who suffer when thorough pre-inception enquiries could have resulted in a policy which was properly and reliably underwritten. In all the circumstances of the case I concluded that the fair and reasonable result would be to apportion liability equally and ask the assurer to meet 50% of the £40,000 claim, plus interest.

(iv) On the general side, a similar issue arises in subsidence cases. The proposal often asks whether the property to be insured is free of any signs of subsidence. In accordance with the Statements of General Insurance Practice, the insured is only required to answer such a question in accordance with his knowledge and belief which is not expected to be expert knowledge. When a claim for subsidence is made, the insurer as a rule asks to see any surveys which have been carried out at the time of purchase and proceeds to highlight parts of the survey which they suggest should have put the policyholder on notice that there were early signs of subsidence present. Sometimes the survey refers only to settlement, which is a different matter. Unless there is evidence that the applicant must have known because, for example, he had bought the property at a gross under value because it was defective, and could be said to have deliberately misled the insurer, I will ask the insurer to meet the claim. The fact is that the insurer had the means of knowledge prior to commencement of the policy. All it needed to do was to request a copy of any survey obtained and decide for itself, on technical advice if necessary, whether it was a good risk.

The Statements of General Insurance Practice proclaim that insurers will not repudiate liability on grounds of: (i) non-disclosure of a material fact which a policyholder could not reasonably be expected to have disclosed; or (ii) misrepresentation unless it is a deliberate or negligent misrepresentation of a material fact. It is these questions of reasonableness and of guilt or innocence that can be difficult to determine. [IOB, 1993.]

(v) Summary of *Pan Atlantic*

[See Appendix 4.24.]

Summarising the effect of this so far as the Bureau is concerned, when there is an allegation of non-disclosure/misrepresentation on the part of the policyholder, I have to consider the following issues:

- **Has the insurer asked clear questions on the matters alleged to be material?**

  If not, it has waived the right to avoid the policy in that connection. If so, it is entitled to correct answers.

- **Did the misrepresentation induce the insurer to enter into the contract?**

  There is a presumption that inducement follows materiality, so normally answers to questions specifically asked will be regarded as relevant so far as the insurer in concerned. However, if the insurer paid no attention to representations being made, or if they were irrelevant for its underwriting purposes, then it is difficult to accept that there was inducement. If there is no inducement, there is no right to avoid and the claim succeeds in full.

- **Was the misrepresentation inadvertent or deliberate?**

  Deciding this is not easy, particularly if the policyholder has been negligent. Mere carelessness, in my view, counts as inadvertence. On the other hand, a total failure to give completion of the proposal form the care and attention it obviously requires is effectively recklessness as to whether the answers are not true or false and should have the same consequences as deliberate misrepresentation. If the misrepresentation is regarded as deliberate, the policyholder may have a hard time rebutting the presumption that the false answer to the insurer's questions induced the insurer to enter into the contract.

- **Has the insurer waived the requirement for disclosure of the information in question?**

  If so, there is no right to avoid the policy for misleading answers to questions concerning that information (provided the policyholder made a fair presentation) and the claim succeeds in full.

- **Is proportionality applicable?**

  Where both the materiality test and the inducement test have been satisfied, and waiver is not applicable, proportionality may be applicable if I am satisfied that it would be too harsh an outcome for the policyholder to be deprived of all benefit under the policy. To reach this conclusion, I normally need to be satisfied that the misrepresentation was inadvertent. Provided that is the case, then I will not rely solely on what the insurer says it would have done if it had known the facts, although that is highly relevant. I may also need to look at what prudent underwriters elsewhere have done in similar circumstances, to determine what the fair and reasonable result would be.

Mutuality

The Law Lords confirmed that the obligation of utmost good faith is reciprocal, applying to the insurer as much as to the policyholder. Lord Lloyd added:

> Nor is the obligation of good faith limited to one of disclosure. As Lord Mansfield warned in *Carter v Boehm* (1766) 3 Burr 1905, there may be circumstances in which an insurer, by asserting a right to avoid for non-disclosure, would himself be guilty of want of utmost good faith.

Lord Lloyd did not elaborate on the sanction which the courts might apply for such a default. It would have to be something more than the refund of premiums which the insurer would normally be offering anyhow as a consequence of the avoidance. In the Bureau at least, manifestly unjustified attempts by the insurer to avoid a policy for misrepresentation might merit a maladministration award, in addition to the normal consequences of my affirming that the policy stands and claims under it must be met.

(vi) Proportionality

Insurance policies tend to be printed in black and white. Even if colours are introduced on the printed page for added emphasis, the objective of those who draft the policies tends to remain the same: the application of the policy in any particular situation should still be on a black and white basis. Either the claim will succeed, and the policyholder will be paid in full: or the claim will fail and the policyholder will receive nothing.

In the Bureau, we sometimes have to ask whether such an approach leads to a fair and reasonable solution. My predecessor reported the introduction of a principle of proportionality to deal with cases of *unintentional non-disclosure and misrepresentation* in his Annual Report 1989 (paras 2.16–2.17). In my Annual Report 1994 (para 2.10), I illustrated how I had been applying a principle of proportionality to deal with the interplay of pre-existing medical conditions and accidental injuries in the case of *personal accident policies* covering permanent and temporary total disability. In the Summer 1995 edition of the IOB Bulletin I reported a similar line I was taking over the interplay of latent defects and storm damage in connection with claims under *household buildings policies*, where the storm in question was required to be the *'sole cause'* of the loss or damage suffered. Looking at issues of form and substance in para 2.5.1, above, I have shown how we may decide on a proportionate *refund of premium.*

The original 'judgment of Solomon' was, of course, a proposal for a proportionate solution, although in his case the proposal was only a gambit, to enable that most famous judge to flush out the truth of the matter. He knew that the real mother of the infant being claimed by the two women before him would not be able to bear seeing her child shared between them in the manner he was proposing. Fortunately, my Terms of Reference do not require me to consider maternity claims for children. I am restricted to considering complaints '*in connection with or arising out of a policy of insurance*'. I therefore do not need to have ulterior motives when proposing proportionate settlements. On the contrary, a readiness by policyholder and insurer to agree to a reasonable compromise may demonstrate to me that all concerned are acting in good faith ...

Limits of proportionality

'Splitting it down the middle' works well in some insurance disputes, but I have to ensure that it does not become a cop-out from making a difficult decision in others. Solomon's baby may be involved, after all. Something less than all will be quite unfair if the policyholder is entitled to his claim in full, or if the insurer has reasonable grounds for declining to make any payment whatsoever. Adopting a proportionate solution must involve no less an exercise of judgment than deciding one way or the other.

In a claim under a *travel policy*, raising this issue, the balance went in favour of the insurer. A provision in the policy entitled the policyholder to payment of £30,000 in the event of an accident resulting in total permanent disability. I decided that this did not entitle the policyholder to payment of 50% in the event of an accident resulting in partial total disability. Similarly, in such policies, the provision that a delay in departure of more than 12 hours will entitle the policyholder to a payment of £20 does not mean that in the event of a delay of only 6 hours the policyholder will be entitled to £10.

A case involving *permanent health insurance* shows the balance going in favour of the policyholder. The policy defined incapacity as:

> ... the total inability of the Insured, by reason of sickness or injury, to follow his Occupation.

The policyholder had suffered from crippling anxiety and depression. Initially, the insurer was willing to meet his claim, and for two years it continued to do so. In 1994, the policyholder's condition began to improve, and the insurer stopped payments on the basis that the policyholder was now fit to go back to work. His doctors did not agree.

The problem was the nature of the work. The policyholder had been an 'Insurance Inspector' or, less euphemistically, a salesman. His employer said that he was: '... too much of a perfectionist, which hampers him in the demanding occupation of selling life insurance.' The PHI insurer said that this showed that the policyholder was not disabled by unreasonable standards. It suggested that a salesman in the policyholder's condition, but with a more realistic approach, would be quite well enough to sell life insurance. As we deal in the Bureau with continual complaints about life insurance salesmen whose standards are too low, rather than too high, we could not help noting this unusual turnaround.

The case itself, of course, had to be determined on objective grounds. In the end, the medical evidence was conclusive. A consultant psychiatrist confirmed that the policyholder was not totally incapacitated. He could do some work. But he was not fit to resume his former occupation as an insurance salesman: '... because it is probably a very stressful job which requires robust ability to cope with the world's demands and rebuffs.'

If the policyholder could do some work, why not give him a proportion of the benefit? This would not have been fair to him. He was insured against incapacity to do his job. The medical evidence showed that he was not fit to cope with the essential demands of the job. That was the substance of the matter.

After further consideration, and some straight talking from the Bureau, the insurer agreed to go on paying full benefit under the policy until it was due to terminate in 1998 [IOB, 1995] ...

(vii) Where the insurer's underwriting guide or other evidence satisfies me that the facts withheld or misrepresented would have had a bearing on the premium or acceptance of risk, I may apply the principle of proportionality. This involves my requiring the same proportion of the claim to be met as the premium paid ... Thus, if the premium would have been loaded by 50%, my award will be two thirds of the amount otherwise payable. The House of Lords confirmed that so far as the common law is concerned the principle of proportionality has no application in these cases, but *dicta* suggest that it may not be inappropriate in the field of consumer insurance. The observations on this point of Sir Donald Nicholls VC in the Court of Appeal in *Pan Atlantic* [1993] 1 Lloyd's Rep 496 were not disapproved of in the House of Lords. He made a strong indictment of the harshness of the 'all or nothing' result of the English common law rules, and provided an affirmation of the essential fairness of the principle of proportionality in appropriate cases. [IOB 1994.]

(G) FRAUD

(i) Dodgy claims

As my predecessor emphasised in his 1992 Annual Report ... fraud is a serious business. The insurer relying on it as grounds for refusing to meet a claim has a heavy burden of proof to establish that this is justified. Mere exaggeration of a claim does not amount to fraud. It has to be clear that the policyholder is trying to get substantially more than he or she is entitled to. When fraud of this kind is established, then the consequences are no less serious for the policyholder. The whole claim is tainted, and the insurer will have no obligation to pay even for those items which could legitimately have been claimed for. That this is the legal position was affirmed by the Court of Appeal in the case of *Orakpo v Barclays Insurance Services and Another* [1995] LRLR 443 [Appendix 8.4] ... As Sir Roger Parker put it:

> Just as on inception the insurer has to a large extent to rely on what the assured tells him, so also it is when a claim is made. In both cases there is therefore an incentive to honesty, if the assured knows that, if he is fraudulent, at least to a substantial extent, he will recover nothing, even if his claim is in part good.

A harsh reality which we sometimes have to explain to policyholders.

(ii) Is fraud an issue?

In a greater number of cases, however, the Bureau is asked to determine the initial question of whether such fraud is established. The contribution I can make in such circumstances is limited. Where fraud is alleged by the insurer, but denied by the policyholder, it is rare that the evidence is so compelling against the policyholder that I can uphold the insurer's allegations without reservation. Satisfactory resolution of the issues raised in such circumstances normally requires the formal procedures of a court of law, where the relevant evidence can be given under oath and subjected to cross examination. This is not within the scope of the Bureau's informal procedures. My contribution, therefore, is to consider whether the existing evidence is sufficient at least to raise the issue. If it is, then I normally feel obliged to exercise the discretion conferred on me by my Terms of Reference ... to decline to deal with the matter. So far as the Bureau is concerned, the issue is 'non-proven'. The consequence is that the loss lies where it falls, and the insurer is not obliged to meet the claim until its liability has been established in court. It is up to the policyholder to decide whether to pursue the matter in that way.

Gut feelings/hard evidence

Insurers have to accept that in deciding whether to take this relatively drastic step I cannot rely on the 'gut feeling' of their Claims Managers, however reliable they may consider the sensitivities of that particular organ to be. I need something more tangible in the form of hard evidence if allegations of fraud are to be taken seriously. One colourful case concerned a substantial claim for a total of £13,000 for loss due to theft. I am afraid to say my decision may have caused the Claims Manager in question some indigestion. He regarded the claim as fraudulent, because the insurer had been told, and so had the police, that the policyholder had been overheard in a pub planning with a third party how the theft should be perpetrated. This was a scenario which, if true, justified total repudiation of the claim and the instigation of criminal proceedings. The difficulty was that the individuals providing the information had either declined to identify themselves or had made it clear they would refuse to go on the record. Meanwhile, the policyholder was stoutly maintaining that there were people in the neighbourhood who were conducting a vendetta against him, and deliberately trying to spike his claim. This was a scenario which, if true, could have explained the shadowy accusations being made against him. I had to point out to the insurer that the police had said that they did not have enough evidence to charge the insured, and the evidence which the insurer had was not likely to stand up in court. The claim had to be met, and the insurer's suspicions did not justify it in taking an unreasonably harsh attitude so far as requiring the policyholder to substantiate each item of his claim was concerned. Even so, there were arguments on that score too, and I was unable to uphold the claim in full. A final assessment of £3,220 was considered appropriate against the original claim of £13,000. This was reluctantly accepted by the policyholder.

(iii) Cards on the table

Where there is sufficient evidence to cast doubt on the validity of the policyholder's claim, and to justify my concluding that as things stand I cannot reasonably require the insurer to meet it, I need to be satisfied that the policyholder is at least aware of what this evidence is. The insurer needs to put enough cards on the table for the policyholder to see why the outcome of the trick is in doubt. A problem can then arise, particularly in connection with disability claims, when the insurer is unwilling for us to provide policyholders with details of the evidence against them, or even to tell policyholders of its existence, on the grounds that this may prejudice the insurer's case in the event of proceedings in court. Such an approach raises worrying questions of natural justice. I am grateful to a Bureau member for drawing my attention to the Court of Appeal's ruling in *McGuinness v Kellog Co of Great Britain Ltd* [1988] 2 All ER 902, which has helped me to resolve some of those difficulties. The plaintiff had brought proceedings against the defendants alleging that an injury suffered in the course of his work was caused by the defendant's negligence and breach of statutory duty, and had resulted in disability. The defendants were contending that the plaintiff was exaggerating the affect of is injuries and the extent of his continuing disability. They maintained they had evidence in the form of a cine film demonstrating this. The issue for the court was whether the defendants were entitled to produce the film as evidence at the trial without affording the plaintiff or his solicitors the opportunity of inspecting the film before the hearing. It was held that although such an order should be comparatively rare, it was justified in the circumstances of the case. The leading judgment was given by Neill LJ. Applying his reasoning and the authorities he relies on to our situation in the Bureau, it is clear that the basic rule must always be that either party is entitled to have particulars of the evidence against him or her on which the other party relies if we are to take it into account when making a decision. This is a requirement of natural justice, and it is also consistent with the currently accepted principle of alternative dispute resolution, that the sooner a party is in a position to realise the weight of the other side's evidence, the sooner he or she may be persuaded to drop unreasonable arguments and agree to a reasonable conclusion. In some cases, showing video evidence to a policyholder on Bureau premises, in the present of an insurer's representative, has led to the policyholder's conceding that he had no claim, and thus saved the insurer the possible costs of litigation to arrive at the same result. 'One of my good days', said an allegedly totally disabled policyholder at the sight of himself clambering over his roof, but it was the end of the argument.

Departures from the basic rule therefore need to be clearly justified. Such justification may exist when there is an issue about the primary facts, for example if the insurer has available to it evidence which tends to show that the policyholder is either faking or grossly exaggerating the symptoms of the condition of which he complains. That was the position in the *McGuinness* case. To bring a case into this category:

- the insurer will need to establish to my satisfaction that there are grounds for suspecting the initial good faith of the policyholder or that the revelation of the evidence would lead to the policyholder's trimming his or her evidence. I do not have to determine whether such suspicions are justified, only that there are reasonable grounds for them;
- the insurer must have already indicated to the policyholder that it has such suspicions, or agree to our advising the policyholder that such suspicions exist. In other words, the insurer cannot relay on the Bureau to cover for it or to take responsibility for raising such allegations itself;
- some indication of the grounds on which such suspicions are based will also have to be given to the policyholder. Normally, when I write to the policyholder, I will identify discrepancies in his or her version of events, and

explain why I do not consider the Bureau's informal procedures provides a satisfactory method for resolving them;

- the insurer must clearly identify for me the evidence it wishes to withhold. Some indication of the nature of this evidence will normally also have to be provided to the policyholder, particularly if the insurer is relying on this evidence as part of its grounds for suspicion. By way of illustration, this was done in a recent decision in the following terms:

  > You ask for clarification concerning the surveillance evidence to which my Assistant referred. In addition to the medical reports the insurer's file includes video evidence filmed on two occasions. This evidence has also been seen by Mr X, Consultant Orthopaedic Surgeon, and it shows that your client is apparently able to carry shopping, walk at a reasonable pace, drive a car and stand unaided for prolonged periods, and undertake other physical activity around and away from the home.

  This is not entirely consistent with the account which your client gave to Mr X, for example, that he always needed a stick when going outdoors;

- the practice followed by some insurers of providing me with stills from video evidence to pass on to the policyholder can help to avoid any question as to the identity of the person filmed, and can also help to indicate the nature of the activities observed;

- the manner in which the policyholder is pursuing the case may also be relevant. If policyholders swear loudly at the insurer and at me and my Assistants that they will go to court if their claims are not met, it may be easier for me to tell them (politely) that I agree they should do just that. [IOB, 1994.]

(iv) Dealing with fraudsters

The most notorious and significant fraudsters featuring in recent cases have been insurance salesmen preferring to be rewarded by embezzlement instead of commission. Nevertheless, nobody would seriously deny that the insurance industry, in common with tax collectors, suffers from some people's apparent inability to recognise that a fraud against it is a fraud against the premium paying population at large. The Association of British Insurers has recently launched a campaign against insurance fraud, but actions speak louder than words and insurers seem not always to help themselves or their honest policyholders. They may make a commercial decision to pay out, rather than challenge the insured and suffer a difficult and costly lawsuit. Although this is understandable in the light of the practical problems of proving fraud, it does seem that insurers may carry a measure of responsibility for encouraging fraudsters to believe that insurance fraud is easy to get away with.

The dilemma between wishing to deter and reluctance to take action which will deter is not easy. Some insurers may believe that the prosecuting authorities will not treat insurance fraud with the same seriousness as other frauds because it is not the State which is being defrauded, and seemingly lenient sentences may not be much incentive to private prosecutions. Yet if something positive is not done, and simply repudiating a claim is merely negative, a fraudster may just move on to the next unsuspecting insurer.

Although the Bureau has always taken a serious view of fraud, the suggestion has been made that our attitude appears ambivalent. The observation was offered that the Bureau:

> ... presents the fraudulent proposer with an each way winner. If the non-disclosure is not discovered the fraud will succeed and payment will be made. If it is, all that will happen is that payment will be made, subject to a relatively small deduction for extra premiums. Who said that crime does not pay?

However, the fact is that I certainly accept that a deliberate non-disclosure for the purpose of obtaining a policy of insurance or of getting it on more favourable terms is fraudulent and I will not in such a case require any payment to be made even with a deduction. Nevertheless, it always has to be shown as a fact that the non-disclosure was deliberate, that is, fraudulent and not innocent. I do not accept the suggestion that the Bureau facilitates the commission of crime, in particular in the case of claims, by turning attempted fraud into the completed offence through requiring insurers to meet claims despite dishonesty being shown. But before I can dismiss an application on the grounds of fraud, I do need cogent evidence that that is what has been perpetrated.

There may be differences of perception as to when the circumstances indicate fraud. However, I have ... experienced Assistants, from legal and insurance backgrounds, who handle the cases. I rely upon them as well as insurers to provide me with the fruits of their investigations before it can be asserted and accepted by me that a case is fraudulent within the legal meaning of that term. A claim will be treated as fraudulent whenever it can be shown that there was an intention to defraud the insurer. However, the burden of proof is on the insurer and it is a high one. In the case of *S and M Carpets v Cornhill Insurance* [1882] 1 Lloyd's Rep 423, Lord Justice Watkins said that although the standard of proof in a civil case was on a balance of probabilities, in deciding a case in which such a serious allegation had been made, a very high degree of probability within that general standard had to be applied. In *Broughton Park Textiles v Commercial Union* [1987] 1 Lloyd's Rep 194, Mr Justice Simon Brown, in applying that standard and finding for the insurer, said that had he been presiding at a criminal trial he would not have reached the same conclusion. Thus the standard is lower than the criminal standard but higher than the civil. We cannot properly apply a different standard from the courts for the basic reason that the insured should not be worse of by applying to the Bureau than if he had chosen to sue the insurer. That said, it is not our role to assist people to defraud insurers, but this does not mean that we can be expected to support unsubstantial accusations against policyholders.

In my view, it is fundamental that complainants to the Bureau seeking the benefit of equitable principles should come with 'clean hands'. We are wholly unwilling to help where there is sufficient evidence of fraud. Nevertheless, I am not prepared to 'read between the lines', as some insurers have put it, in order to conject or conjure a case against a policyholder. Against this, where there are good enough grounds for suspecting a fraud but the evidence does not meet the judicial standard of proof, I may well fall back on my inherent power to refuse to make a decision one way or the other. Instead I will simply conclude that the matter would be more appropriately dealt with in a court of law.

I have no judicial powers of calling witnesses and administering oaths for the purpose of cross-examination, nor do I enjoy any immunities and am not protected from defamation proceedings and the like to any greater extent than are insurers. This being so, insurers should not 'pass the buck' to me, as it sometimes seems that they do. It would be in the best interests of insurers to investigate cases properly before allowing them to come to me. It cannot be consistent with the *principles* of good insurance practice for a suspect claim to be repudiated on some spurious ground which may deprive the policyholder of an opportunity to be heard on the real issue. A very frequent example of this is reliance upon lack of reasonable care or an unconnected non-disclosure where what the insurer really means is that it does not believe the loss occurred. If that reliance proves to be misplaced then I will be unable to uphold the repudiation on that ground with the result that payment might have to be made to a person who has not in reality suffered any loss. I am not prepared to distort legal tests (for example, as to what constitutes reasonable care) or industry practice (for example, as to questions in proposal forms) in order to justify an insurer's repudiation which should have been made on grounds of fraud.

As it is, I find it surprising how often patent discrepancies go unchallenged. It is never clear whether these have been missed or merely ignored because the insurer is avoiding confrontation with an insured, who may be a difficult individual to deal with. Some insurers appear to think that we are better left to deal with the matter, presumably because any adverse publicity from our crying fraud will do us no harm in terms of sales. Whilst equitable principles may cause us to investigate issues which have not been addressed in order to assess the merits, particularly because our procedure is inquisitorial, there is no good reason why insurers who conduct thorough investigations should subsidise those who do not. Also, although we are not restricted by pleadings, I am anxious that insurers should not assume that we will automatically raise issues which they have overlooked or chosen not to pursue.

Genuine claimants ought to be able to explain apparent improbabilities or discrepancies and insurers should give them an opportunity so to do. Natural justice requires no less. On the basis that we will put a policyholder's case to the insurer notwithstanding that he has not raised the right grounds to support it, we are prepared to adopt the same approach on behalf of the insurer and allow allegations of fraud to be fallen back on even at the eleventh hour. However, there is a fine line between seeking to arrive at an equitable result and being used, or abused, by certain insurers as an adjunct to their claims department. [IOB, 1992.]

Miss F submitted a claim after her car was damaged by thieves. The insurer's engineer decided the car was beyond economical repair and the insurer would not settle the claim without proof of the amount Miss F had paid for the car. In fact, Miss F's boyfriend had given the car to her, but she produced a receipt showing she had paid £3,800.

The investigator appointed by the insurer discovered that it was the boyfriend who had purchased the car and that he had only paid £2,700. The insurer advised Miss F that it would not make any payment because she had presented false evidence in support of her claim. It explained that the policy terms justified its rejecting a claim entirely if a claimant submitted any forged or false document. Miss F argued that her boyfriend had given her the receipt and that she had no reason to believe it was not genuine.

Complaint upheld

The insurer's liability under the policy terms was limited to settling the claim by paying the car's market value. The insurer's aim in asking to see the receipt was not to establish the car's value but to obtain proof that Miss F had owned the car and to confirm its make, model and age. There was independent proof both of the car's existence and of Miss F's ownership of it. Clearly, we would not support any customer who produced fictitious evidence to gain more than their just entitlement, but that was not the situation here. The insurer's liability would have been the same even if Miss F had told the truth and said the car was a present from her boyfriend.

In the circumstances, we were satisfied that Miss F had suffered a genuine loss and that she had not attempted to claim more than her proper entitlement under the policy terms. We concluded that the insurer should pay Miss F the car's market value, plus interest. [FOS, 2001.]

(H) HOME CONTENTS

(i) Home security

A policyholder with *household contents insurance* was the sole resident of her home. She went out one evening, and returned early the following morning to find that her house had been burgled. The thieves had entered the house through a double glazed casement window beside the kitchen. The window was fitted with two catches, one of which incorporated a key lock. The lock, however, had not been in operation.

The insurer repudiated her claim, saying there had been a breach of the condition in the policy which required the policyholder to maintain and operate suitable locks on doors and ground floor windows. At first sight, the breach was materially connected with the loss, as contemplated by the ABI's Statement of General Insurance Practice, because the thieves had come through one of the unlocked windows. However, in this particular case, the police, the glazier, and even the loss adjuster, agreed that even if the window lock had been set, it would not have impeded the thieves to any significant degree. They would still have been able to force the window open without much difficulty. The insurer had not actually specified that the locks in question should comply with a particular British Standard.

All in all, the evidence pointed to the conclusion that the loss would have occurred in any event. In such circumstances I could not see that the breach of condition had may any difference, and I required the insurer to meet the claim. This decision was complied with by the insurer, but that did not prevent it from arguing strenuously with me over the correctness of the decision at a public meeting a few months later.

Another case, also concerning *household contents insurance*, raised a slightly different issue on similar facts. Once again, an unfortunate policyholder suffered a theft. On this occasion, the thieves had broken in through her bedroom window. The insurer attempted, not merely to repudiate the claim, but to avoid the whole policy. On the proposal form, the policyholder had confirmed that the final exit door of her home was fitted with a mortice deadlock conforming to British Standard BS3621, and that all other external doors were either secured in the same way, or alternatively fitted with a deadlock and certain types of bolt. The loss adjuster had noted that the rear door of the policyholder's home had a deadlock which did not conform to the relevant British

Standard, and did not have any of the specified types of bolt. The policyholder's explanation was that she had answered the question in the proposal form under the mistaken impression that she had the required protection.

The insurer supplied documentary evidence to the Bureau confirming that it would not have accepted the policyholder's business if it had known the true position about the existing security locks. Strictly speaking, therefore, the insurer was entitled to avoid the policy on the grounds of misrepresentation. However, I considered that the policyholder's insistence that she had not deliberately intended to mislead the insurer should be taken into account. There were questions of form and substance.

The insurer was quite reasonably requiring certain security precautions to be maintained by the policyholder. Some insurers deal with this by imposing a warranty that such precautions will be maintained, others do it by asking questions of the kind that had been asked in this case. Is it fair that technically different approaches to the same situation should produce radically different results? The difference in this case was that if the security precautions had been the subject of a warranty, then the fact that the break in had occurred through a window, rather than through one of the inadequately secured doors, would have meant that the loss was not materially connected with the breach, so that the claim could still succeed. Was it fair that the result should be different in the case before me?

I did not accept that it was. I was satisfied that the policyholder had not intended deliberately to mislead the insurer. For the insurer to avoid the whole policy on the grounds that there had been an inadequately protected door which had no bearing at all on the theft seemed excessive. In the circumstances, I required the insurer to meet the claim [IOB, 1995] ...

(ii) Legal responsibility

A household contents policy covered property belonging to the policyholder himself and other members of his family living in the house and those items for which he was legally responsible. Amongst items stolen from his home were pieces of jewellery belonging to his mother who was not resident in the United Kingdom at the time. The insurer argued that there was no legal liability on the policyholder for these items of jewellery and accordingly a claim for items not belonging to him or a member of his family living with him could not succeed. Legal responsibility and legal liability are not the same. Other insurers already concede this as indeed did the insurer in question following consideration of the arguments. A policyholder may well be responsible for goods without being liable for them. He will become *liable* if he is, for instance, negligent in the way he looks after someone's possessions but is *responsible* simply because they are in his care. [IOB, 1992.]

(iii) Computing game

A home contents policy was not extended to cover accidental damage. However it had a section headed Additional Cover that provided insurance against accidental damage to televisions, videos and computers. The policyholder claimed under this section when a Nintendo Gameboy was accidentally dropped and damaged beyond repair. The insurer stated that it was not a computer. The *Concise Oxford Dictionary* defined computer as: '... automatic electronic apparatus for making calculations or controlling operations that are expressible in numerical or logical terms.' We therefore queried the rejection.

The insurer replied:

> I have taken soundings from various people within the office and, in particular, from individuals working in the computer department. There would appear to be a difference of views between those people who say it is not a computer because it cannot be programmed and those who say that it is a computer in that it does fit in with the definition contained in the Concise Oxford Dictionary. In the circumstances, we are prepared to go quietly on this one and arrange settlement of the loss. [IOB, 1992.]

(I) CONSTRUCTION

[See Chapter 7.]

(i) What is the ordinary meaning of the words?

Previous convictions

If the policy does not clearly say otherwise, words must be given their ordinary meaning. In commercial contracts, it may be reasonable for insurers to rely on the fact that particular words have legally defined meanings, but personal policyholders cannot be expected to be equally acquainted with the law. This was a point made by the first Insurance Ombudsman (Annual Report 1988, para 2.5).

The principle applies to all relevant documents, not just the insurance policy itself. A motorist proposing for *motor insurance* was asked if he had any previous convictions for motoring offenses. He answered no. He was subsequently involved in an accident and submitted a claim. At that stage, he was asked whether he had any penalty points endorsed on his licence. He confirmed that he did have an endorsement, for a fixed penalty offence. The insurer tried to avoid the policy for non-disclosure. The policyholder said that he had not regarded the fine paid in respect of a fixed penalty offence as a 'conviction'.

It seemed to me that, under the Road Traffic Offenders Act (1988), a motorist paying a fine for a fine for a fixed penalty offence is, for all practical purposes, treated as having been convicted of the offence. But I could understand the policyholder's confusion. A standard dictionary gave the principal meaning of conviction as: '1. proving or finding guilty', and the meaning of convict as: '... prove guilty (of offence); declare guilty by verdict of jury or decision of judge; cause (person) to admit he is guilty (of sin, etc).' The policyholder in question had not been required formally to admit his guilt or to attend proceedings in court. His fine had been determined by reference to a fixed tariff, not judicially. When the penalty points had been endorsed on his licence, the column headed 'date of conviction' had been left blank.

All in all, I considered the policyholder could reasonably have concluded that he did not have any previous convictions in the ordinary sense of the word. The insurer was, in my view, at fault for not having updated its wording to take into account more clearly this new category of offence without conviction.

I have seen other proposal forms in which insurers have asked clear questions about previous convictions and penalty offences. Then there can be no doubt. In the circumstances, I considered that the insurers, in the case before me, was not entitled to avoid the policy. It was required to meet the claim in full.

Relations

The ordinary meaning of words changes as time goes by, and insurers need to make sure that their policies reflect this. In a case concerning a claim for theft, under a *household contents policy*, there was an exclusion for loss or damage caused by the policyholder or his household. The policyholder's household was defined in the policy as: (a) the policyholder; (b) *'other relations'* who normally lived with the policyholder; (c) *'resident domestic servants'*.

Relatively few people would come into category (c) nowadays, or at least there would be few in households in the United Kingdom with standard contents cover. What intrigued me was that para (b) did not cater at all for the kind of household, increasingly common nowadays, where people may be living together without being *'relations'*. The word 'relationship' has acquired a new and more extended meaning.

These considerations were relevant in the case in question, because commission of the theft itself had been assisted by the daughter of the policyholder's common law wife, who had allowed the thief to stay in the property while the adults were away. Was the daughter a *'relation'* for the purpose of the exclusion?

The conclusion, reached in a consultation between the Assistant dealing with the case, the Deputy Ombudsman and myself, was that neither the common law wife nor the daughter were *'relations'*. The exclusion therefore did not apply. However, the insurer was liable to compensate for the loss of the common law wife's property as well as that of the policyholder, because the policy definition of contents included property for which the policyholder or his household were responsible. He was responsible for his common law wife's property, even if he was not legally liable for the loss by theft, in the absence of negligence. An exclusion based on a more up to date definition of what constitutes a household might have relieved the insurer of any obligation to meet the claim.

(ii) Holistic approaches

As I indicated at the beginning of this section, my Terms of Reference require me to have regard to a number of different criteria when assessing the fair and reasonable solution in each case. They require me, in other words, to take a holistic approach. In the Spring 1995 issue of the IOB Bulletin, I elaborated on a case in which I had done this. It was a question of whether death resulting from a totally unexpected and horrific reaction to drugs administered during the course of an operation could be regarded as accidental. A combination of three facts led me to believe that, in the particular circumstances of that case, it could:

- my interpretation of a leading decision by the Court of Appeal, *De Souza v Home and Overseas Insurance Co Ltd* [1995] LRLR 453 [Appendix 7.2]. This was an interpretation which the insurer concerned did not accept;
- comparative practice and law in other countries, particularly a New Zealand case, and certain American authorities on which the judge in that case had relied. He had also reviewed the English authorities in a situation remarkably close to the one I was considering;
- the application of the relevant law was by no means clear. A court might well reach a decision either way. A decision giving the benefit of the doubt to the unfortunate policyholder could therefore be justified by my overriding

mandate to come to the conclusion on the facts of the case which I considered to be fair and reasonable.

Taking all these factors into account, I made a holistic decision. The policyholder's estate got £61,000, plus interest, as a result.

(iii) Accidents and bodily injuries

Personal accident and sickness policies, in particular, can raise difficult questions from a holistic point of view. Has there been an accident? Has there been an injury? Is the accident the sole cause of the injury? Is the injury 'bodily'? Has the injury resulted in death or disability? Is the disability permanent? Is the disability total? Adding the answers to these questions together, do we have a case in which a policyholder has died or become disabled solely and directly as a result of accidental bodily injury?

Just how difficult it can be to answer these questions is illustrated by a case in which my Assistant and I reached different conclusions, and had to acknowledge this to the policyholder. She was a nurse who suffered the misfortune of being subjected to a complaint of unprofessional conduct by a fellow employee. The complaint concerned a routine procedure involving the giving of an injection to an elderly patient, which she had carried out in the course of her duties and with proper authority. This led to a disciplinary hearing, and her complete exoneration. Unfortunately, she was so affected by the episode that she went into a deep depression, as a result of which she was no longer able to work. The DSS awarded her benefit for an industrial accident, on the basis that she had suffered an injury to the mind.

My Assistant's view was that there had been an accident, in the sense of an unlooked for mishap, but he did not consider that there had been bodily injury. On the other hand, I considered that there may have been bodily injury, because I would not restrict that to visible physical harm, but I did not consider that there had been an accident. The action taken by the policyholder's colleague might have been unexpected for her, but there was nothing particularly abnormal about a query being raised about professional judgment, even if it proved groundless. Subsequent events followed naturally from that. The severe effect on her of these events might not have been foreseen as likely, but itself followed in a natural way from the obvious strain of the charges, the suspension from duty and the hearing.

It was rather like the unfortunate consequences for the man in *De Souza*, who died as a result of sunstroke. The Court of Appeal did not consider that amounted to an accident. My Assistant and I did not actually have to resolve these differences between us, because one thing was clear: neither of us accepted that there had been an accidental bodily injury if the matter was looked at as a whole. Accordingly, we did not question further whether the disability the policyholder had suffered was permanent and total.

Post-traumatic stress disorder

The same issue has been raised in cases concerning post-traumatic stress disorder (PTSD). Does this amount to bodily injury? In one case, the policyholder had the benefit of a *personal accident and sickness policy* taken out through his employer, a chemical company. He had an accident at work, when he fell into a chemical reactor. His airline became blocked and he subsequently experienced respiratory difficulties.

He was in hospital for four days. The crisis was resolved but he never returned to full health. Eventually he was diagnosed as being disabled due to PTSD. I had to consider two questions: can PTSD amount to bodily injury, and did it amount to bodily injury in the particular circumstances of the case before me, having regard to the particular policy wording and the fact that physical injury had anyhow been involved.

The insurer cited a number of legal authorities to support its contention that PTSD could not amount to bodily injury. My concern was over the extent to which a distinction between injuries to the body and conditions affecting the mind can be maintained, where an injury to the body has been involved. In the recent case of *Page v Smith* [1995] 2 All ER 736, the House of Lords was split on this very issue. The House of Lords was concerned there with damages for personal injury, not merely bodily injury. Nevertheless, Lord Lloyd, giving the majority judgment, said:

> In an age when medical knowledge is expanding fast, and psychiatric knowledge with it, it would not be sensible to commit the law to a distinction between physical and psychiatric injury, which might already seem somewhat artificial, and might soon be altogether outmoded ...

Turning then to the facts of the particular case, the policyholder had suffered physical injury at the time of the accident, so I considered that his PTSD could be regarded as part of the bodily injury. The insurer was reluctant to accept this conclusion. It eventually confirmed that it would treat the disability as solely due to the physical injury and long term effects of inhaling noxious fumes. This was contrary to the expert evidence that the disability was due to PTSD, but the important point was, the insurer agreed to meet the claim. The policyholder received £60,000, plus interest, as a result.

In the line of duty

In a different case concerning post traumatic stress disorder and a claim under a *personal accident and sickness policy*, I was unable to help the policyholder. He was a fireman, suffering from PTSD as a result of two horrific experiences. The first was where he had been called out to help deal with the awful consequences of a road traffic accident. The second was where he had been called out to deal with a domestic fire, in which some of the occupants of the house had been burnt alive.

That anyone would suffer as a result of such experiences was more than understandable. I had little difficulty in accepting that the policyholder's PTSD amounted to bodily injury, as he had been physically involved on both occasions. However, I could not accept that the PTSD was due to an accident.

On both occasions the policyholder attended the incidents in question in his professional capacity. He had been responding to an emergency call, and would have had some idea of what he was going to find, even if he was not aware in advance that there would necessarily be fatalities. That is the nature of his job: it is extremely stressful, and rightly commands in the eyes of the rest of the public immense respect for the courage and endurance and strength of character which is required. But it was difficult for me to accept that if one particular member of the fire services finds himself more adversely affected than his colleagues by the stress the situation has placed upon him, that is accidental ...

I was unable to conclude that his particular situation was covered by his policy. It could have been different, for example, if his cover had been for permanent health insurance, rather than personal accident.

If sympathy alone could decide a case, then the fireman would have had it all. But my discretionary power to determine what is 'fair and reasonable' does not enable me to compel insurers to meet the claims of all policyholders who have suffered a misfortune, regardless of the scope of their cover. [IOB, 1995.]

Severance

A holiday maker watching a fiesta in Spain had a leg severed when a cannon misfired. Fortunately, due to early surgical intervention, the leg was reattached and, therefore, saved but several operations and extensive treatment were required for broken bones and other injuries to the leg. The Personal Accident section of his travel insurance included:

> ... total loss by physical severance ... of one or both feet.

We took the view that as the insurer had not specified that loss of a foot by severance had to be a permanent loss, the capital sum for severance became payable even thought the leg was later sewn back on. [IOB, 1992.]!

(J) 'FIRE' DAMAGE

In one case this year, damage had been caused to an accordion when it was left in front of an electric fire although the instrument probably never actually ignited. The question arose as to whether heat damage of this nature should be treated as 'fire' damage for the purposes of a household contents insurance policy.

In his 1984 Annual Report, the first Insurance Ombudsman said that for there to be fire damage there had to be combustion either as the course of heat (that is, a coal fire but not an electric fire) or of the damaged item itself. Subsequently it became apparent that rigid application of this principle could lead to unfair results in the light of the development of flame retardant materials. We therefore asked insurers to treat damage as being within the 'fire' peril if, but for these materials, the item would have ignited, and we understand that the general practice of insurers is to do so.

There has remained some confusion about the extent to which insurers should take an equally lenient approach when flame retardant materials were not involved. Inquiries within the industry as to the general practice in this connection have established that some insurers will meet claims for heat rather than fire damage if there has been major distortion of or real damage to the item and not just cosmetic damage, but the basis on which such payment is made may vary. We have concluded from our inquiries that with regard to heat damage caused by electric fires is good practice for insurers to treat these claims in the same way as if the damage was caused by a coal fire. Such a conclusion recognises that whilst calling what is technically an electric heating appliance a 'fire' may be a misnomer, it is one sanctioned by common usage in a way that makes it difficult to justify not extending cover for fire damage to such situations, at least in the absence of a clearly worded exclusion to that effect. On the other hand claims for heat damage resulting from an iron or radiator would strictly not be counted as fire damage. They might still be met by an *ex gratia* payment, but that would not be something we could insist on. There might, of course, be cover for them elsewhere under the policy, for example, as accidental damage.

In the light of this it was decided that the insurer should meet the claim for the accordion damaged by an electric fire. [IOB, 1993.]

(K) PERSONAL ACCIDENT AND SUICIDE

This year we have had two particularly unfortunate but significant personal accident cases involving the suicide exclusion. Both policies covered accidental death as a result of bodily injury provided none of the exclusions applied. An exclusion in each case read 'suicide, or attempted suicide or intentional self injury'. In both cases the issue was whether the death was 'accidental'.

In one case, a man jumped from a bridge into the path of a lorry. The cause of death was certified as multiple injuries and acute paranoia. There was a suggestion that he thought he was being followed, and jumped to escape. He had marital difficulties and was depressed. The verdict of the Coroner's court was 'accidental death'. We were asked by the insurer to disregard the verdict – Coroner's courts are apparently always reluctant to bring in a verdict of suicide. We were not prepared to do this. There seemed no element of doubt at all that the balance of the man's mind was affected at the time to such an extent that he could not appreciate the nature and likely consequence of his actions. The required mental element necessary to bring the death within the exclusion clause and outside the scope of cover was not therefore, in our view, sufficiently established by the insurer and so his wife's case succeeded.

So, too, did the second case for similar reasons. This involved a woman who some ten years before had suffered a psychotic episode and after her recovery she wrote an article which helped us to understand what was going on in her mind. Following the birth of her child, she again became psychotic and was admitted to a psychiatric hospital. She believed that she was virtually immortal – that she could only die by decapitation. Her psychotic state had saved her from a previous suicide attempt – she had refrained at the last minute from throwing herself off Beachy Head because she would not die, that drowning would not kill her. She was much distressed by the fact that no one would believe her. She was not considered a danger and one day she went for a walk. She threw herself from the third floor of a multi-storey car park, in her family's view, in order to prove that she would not die. Indeed, she did not immediately die but suffered a broken back, two broken legs and other injuries and, according to witnesses at the scene, appeared to be in no particular pain or distress, was able to give her name and address and kept trying to get up. The cause of death was said to be multiple injuries and the Coroner returned a verdict of misadventure, apparently accepting that far from trying to kill herself, she was trying to prove that she could not. The insurer agreed that this was not suicide although argued intentional self injury. We agreed with the solicitor for the estate that the evidence supported the contention that she did not intend to injure herself. The insurer's primary argument was that this was not accidental death and so it was not necessary to go further to see whether the exclusion applied. In our view the same principle applied as in the earlier case: the state of mind was such that she did not appreciate what she was doing. Although she deliberately jumped she did not deliberately die. [IOB, 1993.]

Drowned in bed

A claim was submitted under a Personal Accident policy, which covered death from accidental bodily injury. The policyholder had died in his sleep. The insurer expressed its sympathy, but took the view that this was not an accident claim. The case was referred to the Bureau, and enquiries made of medical experts. Surprisingly, the doctors seemed to find nothing unusual about a fit young man apparently dying in his sleep. In fact it seems that such deaths are not at all uncommon.

The full story was as follows. The policyholder, a young labourer, returned to his home around 9 pm, having worked overtime. He opened a can of lager while his wife heated a prepared lasagna in the microwave. After a light meal, he watched television for a short while, and drank another lager. He then went to bed, complaining of tiredness. Around an hour later, his wife noticed that he was 'tossing and turning', but she drifted off to sleep. She then became aware that her husband seemed to be catching his breath. In fact, the man was dying. He choked to death on his own vomit. Although he had not been drunk, the alcohol and his exhaustion had combined to such an extent that his natural defences failed to function. When the contents of his stomach began to move upwards, his brain would normally have detected the problem and produced a cough. His fatigue was such that his body's alarm systems were effectively switched off, however, and the stomach contents were simply inhaled into the lungs. In layman's terms, he drowned. There had been a fatal combination of factors, one which the doctors had seen before.

We took the view that an injury or death is accidental provided that it is fortuitous, unexpected, and unforeseen. This man did not deliberately drink himself to death. He could not realistically have expected the combination of lager and lasagna which was his downfall to have the result it did. A person who drowns whilst bathing is a similar example. The case of *Commercial Insurance Co of Newark New Jersey v Orr* 379 F 2d 865 (1967) (8 Cir, PA) seemed similar. That concerned the death of an alcoholic who choked on his own vomit. The court said that death was caused by an accident. Although this was in the USA, it did go to appeal, and we thought we could properly take it into account as a persuasive precedent.

We had to consider whether or not there was actually an injury. We were certain that to have one's lungs suffocatingly full of lager and lasagna does indeed constitute an injury. The person who died was in good health – like a swimmer who gets into trouble and drowns. After a full discussion with the insurer, it agreed to accept the claim. [IOB, 1993.]

(L) INDEMNITY, DAMAGE AND MEASUREMENT OF LOSS

Repair, replace or cash?

Most household policies now provide 'new-for-old' cover but leave it to the insurer (not the policyholder) to decide whether the claim should be settled by repair, replacement, reinstatement or cash settlement. We take the view that the insurer must exercise this power reasonably, in the circumstances of the individual case. This has a number of implications for both parties.

Where insurers opt for repair, we consider they have a duty to explain the implications of any choices made by either party. If the repairer is chosen by the insurer - or its agents (such as loss adjusters) – then it is normally the insurer who will be liable to make good any deficiencies in the repair.

Where a policyholder insists on a particular repairer carrying out the work, then it is the policyholder who will generally be responsible for the quality of the work. This does not mean that every repairer who has provided a claimant with an estimate will be regarded as the claimant's chosen contractor. We have considered complaints where the insurer told the policyholder to obtain estimates and the policyholder sought the loss adjuster's assistance in doing so. In these circumstances, we have concluded that the insurer, rather than the policyholder, was liable for the repairer's shortcomings.

Even if the policyholder chose the repairer entirely independently, the insurer will be responsible for rectifying deficiencies in the work if it or its agents 'controlled' the repairer, for example by requiring the repairer to cut his costs or to use certain materials or parts. In those circumstances, the repairer can no longer be regarded as the policyholder's agent.

Opting for 'replacement' is only a reasonable option on the insurer's part if the object claimed for can be replaced. If the object is antique jewellery, for example, then it is not open to the insurer to insist the claimant buys a modern replacement from a chain shop. Similar issues arise whenever the replacement options are limited. It may, for example, be unreasonable to limit a policyholder's choice of replacement to a particular retailer.

Policyholders should be allowed to choose where they purchase a replacement and they are entitled to a cash settlement if they cannot find an acceptable alternative. In such circumstances, we would not regard it as reasonable for the insurer to make a deduction from the cash settlement to represent any discount it would have got if the policyholder had bought a replacement from one of the insurer's nominated suppliers. Nor would it necessarily be appropriate for the insurer to offer vouchers to the policyholder. If the option of replacement is not available, then the only way in which the insurer can indemnify a claimant is by a cash settlement.

In some cases, policyholders may not wish to purchase a replacement for the damaged or stolen goods. This may be, for example, because their circumstances have changed, or the object had sentimental value. Where this is the case, we will normally ask the insurer to agree a cash settlement. [FOS, 2001.]

A policyholder, himself a loss adjuster, suffered damage to his property as a result of work carried out by contractors working on the demolition of the neighbouring property. In the course of their work the contractors had excavated below the foundation of his building. Precautions taken by them had proved insufficient to prevent cracking in the front of the policyholder's property. A structural engineer's report confirmed the cause of the damage and estimated the cost of the repair to be £1,664.64. Accordingly, the policyholder submitted a claim to his insurer for that amount.

At the time the damage occurred, the policyholder had already agreed in principle to sell the property. He had first been approached several months before the damage occurred, but had rejected the original offer. He received increased offers of £150,000, £175,000 and £200,000 before eventually accepting an offer of £225,000 some nine months after the damage occurred. The building was not repaired before completion, and had in fact been purchased with a view to demolition and redevelopment of the site.

The insurer declined to make any payment in respect of the estimated costs of the repair, because the work was never done, and because it maintained that the policyholder had not suffered any financial loss on account of the damage. The policyholder maintained that he was entitled to the estimated costs of repair regardless.

The law is clear that where a policyholder is intending to sell his property before the damage occurs, the measure of indemnity is not the cost of repairing the damage, but the diminution in value reflected in any reduction in the sale price on account of the damage (*Leppard v Excess Insurance Co Ltd* [1979] 2 Lloyd's Rep 91) [Appendix 8.5]. There was no convincing evidence in the case before me that the sale price had been affected by the damage. It was difficult to accept that it could have been, since the purchaser wished to use the site for development purposes rather than to inhabit the property. Nor could I see that applying the principle in *Leppard* would produce an unfair result. I was therefore unable to support the policyholder's claim.

Some months later, the policyholder informed me that he had taken the contractors to the Small Claims court where a district judge had awarded him £1,000 (the court maximum) in respect of the damage they caused. The contractor's defence had been that the policyholder had not suffered any loss, just as the insurer had alleged. The District Judge upheld the policyholder's claim against the contractor. The policyholder regarded this as confirmation that my decision was wrong in law. He demanded that I should require the insurer to pay the balance of the costs of the repair, plus interest, and he also demanded that I should record his case in my Annual Report as one in which I got the decision wrong.

I am happy to oblige the policyholder by specifically noting the implications of his case, but not because I consider my decision was wrong. What I have endeavoured to explain to the policyholder is that the basis on which the contractors' liability for damages in negligence is assessed and the basis on which the insurer's liability to indemnify for loss is assessed are not the same. The district judge did not give reasons for his decision, but I can well understand how he might have concluded that the policyholder was entitled to the cost of the repairs so far as the contractors were concerned. I am not satisfied that he would have taken a different line from me if he had been considering a claim against the insurer rather than the contractors. Were he to do so, I would certainly be interested to know his reasons for holding that the principle confirmed by the Court of Appeal in *Leppard* should not apply to the policyholder. [IOB, 1994.]

(M) HOUSE BUILDINGS COVER

During heavy rainfall, Mr B's cellar filled with around four inches of water. He claimed under his household buildings insurance, which included cover for accidental damage. The insurer concluded that the damage was due to a rise in the water table and informed Mr B that this was not covered by the policy.

Mr B argued that the damage was clearly due to a 'flood' and that therefore it was covered under his policy. Complaint upheld. Although in the past we had held that such claims were not covered, the 1998 decision by the Court of Appeal referred to above (*Rohan Investments Ltd v Cunningham* [1999] Ll Rep IR 190 [Appendix 7.15]) indicated that they might be valid.

We considered that, as a result of this decision, the complaint should succeed. This was partly because the wider interpretation of 'flood' was closer to the ordinary expectations of householders. The decision in this court case was contrary to a previous Court of Appeal ruling (*Young v Sun Alliance* [1977] 3 All ER 561 in 1977), but we considered Mr B was entitled to the benefit of the more favourable case.

A lot of rot

Do exclusions for wet rot and dry rot in household policies apply even when the rot is the direct result of an insured event (such as escape of water from a bath)? Much depends on how the exclusion is worded.

Although, increasingly, insurers include a general provision that excludes dry/wet rot however it has arisen, a few of these insurers do not apply the exclusion where the rot was caused directly by an insured event. From the policyholder's perspective, this is clearly a better position for insurers to adopt and we may need to consider whether it should be taken to represent good insurance practice generally. It certainly reflects a general theme of providing cover for the unexpected. For the time being, however, if the exclusion is worded and positioned in a way that makes reasonably clear the insurer's intention to exclude damage by rot – however it arises – we consider the insurer is entitled to disclaim liability for rot, even if it was caused by an escape of water or other insured event.

Of course, separate considerations apply where the rot developed as a result of an incomplete or inadequate repair of water damage caused by an insured event, where the repair was carried out on behalf of the insurer. In such cases the insurer would be responsible for the consequences of inadequate repair, regardless of the exclusion.

...

Mr N's household buildings insurer agreed to repair his property when it was affected by subsidence. The property was underpinned and superstructure repairs were undertaken. However, the repairer then found rising damp and stopped work until it had been rectified. While installing a damp-proof course, workmen found widespread woodworm and dry rot.

Mr N accepted that his policy did not cover the cost of eradicating either woodworm or dry rot and he arranged for the additional work to be carried out. However, his contractor discovered that the bearer wall supporting the infected timbers along the flank side of the house had collapsed in several places.

The insurer accepted this was further subsidence damage and it paid for rebuilding the wall. But it refused to meet the cost of removing and replacing the timbers and joists, maintaining that it was not liable, even though this work was required in order to carry out the subsidence repairs. This was because the timbers and joists were affected by dry rot, which was excluded from cover.

Mr N argued that the insurer should at least pay the proportion of the costs which related to the damaged part of the wall.

Complaint upheld in part

The insurer was responsible for repairing property damaged as a result of an insured peril. Had the insurer noticed the damage to the bearer wall at a different time, it would have had to remove and replace the floor in order to complete the repairs. We concluded that the fact the damage was only noticed in the course of other repairs did not affect the insurer's liability.

However, that liability was limited to the section of the floor affected by the insured damage. The insurer accepted our view that it was liable for the cost of removing and refitting the timbers adjacent to the damaged part of the bearer wall.

Mr N argued that the insurer should reimburse the full cost of removing the floor. We did not agree. It was clear that the timbers were rotten and could not be replaced. The cost of putting in new boards and joists was not covered by the policy and the insurer was not liable. Moreover, the replacement wood meant that Mr N was in a better position after the repairs than before. [FOS, 2001.]

A bit of damage in time ...

Occasionally we see cases where, although policyholders have acted sensibly to protect their property, their preventative action has caused some damage. Insurance is obviously not there to cover deliberate damage by policyholders and policyholders must take reasonable precautions to safeguard their property. However, it seems strange that there are circumstances where policyholders may sometimes be better off allowing serious damage to take place, rather than taking steps to prevent it and ending up with an unrecoverable loss.

The following case is an example of just these circumstances. We concluded that the policyholder had acted reasonably and that, in all probability, his actions saved the insurer from a far larger claim. It was therefore reasonable to require the insurer to meet the costs of the damage.

When a blocked pipe caused water to flow back up into Mr J's kitchen, he quickly called out a plumber. The plumber broke the pipe and diverted the water before it caused any damage. However, when Mr J put in a claim for reimbursement of the plumber's charges (£70.50), the insurer rejected the claim on the grounds that the policy did not include any cover for accidental damage. Damage due to escape of water was covered under the policy, but Mr J had not claimed for any damage to his property other than the broken pipe. He argued that it was only the plumber's prompt action that prevented damage from occurring.

Complaint upheld.

We agreed with Mr J that the plumber's actions were a direct and necessary consequence of the escape of water and were consistent with his duty under the policy to take all reasonable steps to prevent loss. The insurer did not dispute that the plumber's action had prevented considerable damage to the cupboards and floors. This damage would have been covered under the policy and could well have exceeded the cost of fracturing and repairing the pipe.

In such cases we would not consider it reasonable to require an insurer to reimburse the cost of deliberately-caused damage unless the claimant satisfied us that:

- he had acted reasonably and in order to prevent damage which was covered under the insurance policy; and
- the damage he was acting to prevent would cost significantly more than the damage deliberately caused.

Mr J satisfied both elements of this test and we therefore required the insurer to reimburse him for the plumber's bill. [FOS, 2001.]

INDEX